THE JOY OF
INTERNATIONAL
COOKING

THE JOY OF INTERNATIONAL COOKING

With over 1,000 illustrations in color

Translated and adapted by
Marie-Christine Conte
with an introduction by Gill Edden

GREENWICH HOUSE
Distributed by Crown Publishers, Inc.
New York

© Istituto Geografico de Agostini, Novara 1969, 1970

English edition © Orbis Publishing Limited, London 1974, 1979, 1983

This 1983 edition is published by Greenwich House, a
division of Arlington House, Inc., distributed by
Crown Publishers, Inc.

Recipes adapted from l'Unil-IL. SpA
Much of the material in this book was previously published
in the U.S.A. under the title *The Cook's Book*.

ISBN 0-517-414740

h g f e d c b a

Printed in Czechoslovakia

Library of Congress Catalog Card Number: 83-81047

Contents

Kitchen Equipment 6
Introduction 8

Hors d'oeuvre and Sauces 9
Hors d'oeuvre Recipes 10
Sauce Recipes 82
Herb and Spice Chart 105
Catering Quantities 106
Garnishes 107

Rice, Pasta and Soups 108
Rice 109
Pasta 110
Soups 111
Rice, Pasta and Soup Recipes 113
Successful Sauces 209

Eggs and Fish 211
All about Eggs 212
All about Fish 213
Egg and Fish Recipes 217

Meat, Poultry and Game 313
Beef 314
Veal 315

Lamb 316
Pork 317
Variety Meats 317
Poultry 318
Game 320
Meat, Poultry and Game
   Recipes 321
Nuts 417

Vegetables and Cheese 418
Glossary of Vegetables 419
Cheeses of the World 422
Preserving Vegetables 424
Vegetable, Salad and Preserving
   Recipes 425

Desserts 521
Guide to Pastry Making 522
Glossary of Fruit 523
Preserving Fruit 526
Menu Planning 527
Liqueurs 528
Cake and Dessert Recipes 529
Index 625

Kitchen Equipment

Every cook needs a set of good basic kitchen equipment in order to produce good meals efficiently. There are several modern electrical appliances that are particularly labor saving, and are a delight to own and use. The most important of these is probably the blender, which will purée and chop all kinds of food very fast indeed; it is invaluable for making soups, pâtés and purées of all sorts, it will also make breadcrumbs very quickly, chop nuts and some will grind coffee. Other electrical aids include the mixer, for cake making, whipping cream, kneading dough etc., the juicer for extracting juice from raw fruit and vegetables, the citrus press for extracting juice from oranges and lemons, knife sharpeners and can openers, toasters and mini-ovens.

Very few traditional kitchen utensils have been completely superseded, though, and every cook should try to collect the following kitchen equipment.

Kitchen Cutlery

A set of different sized cooks' knives; carbon steel are best because they sharpen well, though they need more care than stainless steel.

Carving knife, and fork with a finger guard.

Serrated bread knife.

Serrated fruit knife; this must be stainless steel because carbon steel will discolor some fruits.

Curved, serrated grapefruit knife.

Steel, or knife sharpener.

Palette knife, 8–9 inch blade.

Potato peeler and apple corer.

2 or 3 wooden spoons and spatulas of different sizes.

Soup ladle; basting spoon.

Slotted draining spoon.

Slotted spatula.

Stainless steel kitchen scissors.

Pans

3 or 4 good quality saucepans of varying sizes, with lids and heatproof handles; 2–4 pint capacity are probably the most useful size, plus 1 big one of, say, 7–8 pint capacity.

10–12 inch pan for general frying (preferably with lid) and 6–7 inch pan for omelets and pancakes. These should be heavy based to give a good even heat.

Milk saucepan, 1–1½ pint capacity, without a lid but with pouring lip.

Pressure cooker.

Preserving pan.

Deep frying pan and wire basket, or a folding wire basket that fits your large saucepan.

2 sizes of roasting tin.

Baking Tins

1 springform pan, 8–9 inch diameter.

2 identical sandwich tins, 7–9 inch diameter.

1 or 2 sheets of muffin tins.

2 loaf tins, 1 lb and 2 lb capacity.

Plain and fluted flan tins.

Ring mold and flan rings.

Wire cooling rack for cakes.

Decorative jelly molds.

2 baking sheets.

Oven Dishes

3 casseroles; a 2 pint capacity casserole for general family use; an oval one that will take a whole chicken; a 7–8 pint capacity casserole for party cooking.

Ovenproof pie dishes, 8–9 inches diameter.

Ovenproof soufflé dish.

2 oval gratin ovenproof dishes, 9–12 inches long.

Individual soufflé dishes or ramekins.

Sieves

Wire sieve, 8–9 inch diameter.

2 nylon sieves (these are finer than wire), 1 about 8 inch and the other 2–3 inch diameter.

Conical sieve for sauces.

Mouli sieve.

Colander.

Flour sifter.

Beating and Mixing

Large mixing bowl.

3 or 4 mixing bowls ($\frac{1}{2}$–3 pint).

Balloon whip.

Egg beater (you may not need this if you have a hand-held electric mixer).

Small flat whip.

Miscellaneous

Chopping board.

Rolling pin.

Pastry brush.

Pastry cutters.

Pie funnel.

Pastry bag and decorating pipes.

Poultry pins and skewers.

Can opener.

Bottle opener.

Corkscrew.

Grater for cheese, vegetables and nutmeg.

Garlic press.

Lemon squeezer.

Kitchen scales/standard measuring cup.

Set of measuring spoons.

Note: All quantities given are for 4 servings unless otherwise stated.

Storage

Airtight storage jars for flour, sugar etc.

Airtight tins for storing cakes and biscuits.

Polythene bags, large and small.

Various polythene boxes and bowls with lids, for refrigerator and freezer storage.

Greaseproof and waxed paper.

Kitchen foil; absorbent paper.

Introduction

This collection of almost 1200 recipes and variations has just one object in mind – to help you be a success in whatever you cook. Concentrating mainly on traditional Italian and French cooking, the book nevertheless covers an enormous range of recipes from all over the world; giving you plenty of choice in all the courses.

The hors d'oeuvre recipes in *The Joy of International Cooking* vary from tiny canapés, to serve with the aperitif before a grand dinner party – little mouthfuls that will not impair your guests' appetite for the tempting, rich food to follow – to meat and fish dishes that will add substance to a light luncheon, as well as sauces and savory butters to accompany them.

The preparation of all the dishes included in this book is carefully explained and two thirds of the recipes have full color illustrations, showing you clearly the steps to success. There are comprehensive glossaries and other detailed information, so you can check on terms and equipment, calorie requirements and food values (helpful to the weight conscious) as well as suggestions on how to make the best of different foods. Preserving is well covered so that you can take advantage of cheap fruit and vegetables throughout the year. There are also sections on menu planning and catering (for family gatherings as well as parties) plus many interesting ideas for drinks including ones without alcohol.

You will find few shortcuts in *The Joy of International Cooking* but if you follow the methods given you will earn the reputation of keeping a good and varied table both for your family and for your friends.

Hors d'Oeuvre
and Sauce Recipes

Cold Hors d'Oeuvre

Avocados with Shrimps

Ingredients: *2 avocados · 1 tablespoon vinegar, preferably tarragon vinegar · ¼ cup olive oil · ¼ cup lemon juice · 1 teaspoon Worcestershire · salt · pepper · cayenne pepper · ½ cup heavy cream · about 30 shrimps, cooked, shelled and deveined · homemade (see p.104) or commercial aspic*

Halve the avocados lengthwise, discard the seeds and scoop out the pulp, keeping shells intact (steps 1, 2 and 3). Work the pulp through a sieve (always use silver, stainless steel or nylon utensils or the avocado pulp will turn black). Add the vinegar and oil, Worcestershire, salt, pepper and cayenne pepper to taste. Add the cream, whipped until it holds its shape, and mix gently. Fill the avocado shells with the mixture, place them on a serving platter and garnish each shell with shrimps brushed with cold but still liquid aspic. Decorate the platter to taste and chill.

Stuffed Avocados

Halve 2 avocados lengthwise, discard the seeds and sprinkle the halves with lemon juice and salt. Mix 1 can tuna fish and its oil with 3–4 celery stalks and 1 cucumber, both chopped, 2–3 tablespoons mayonnaise, lemon juice to taste and salt. Fill the avocado shells with the mixture and place them on a serving platter.

Avocado Dip

Halve 1 or more avocados lengthwise, scoop out the pulp, keeping 1 shell for each avocado used, and mash it with a fork. Mix with 1 small onion, finely chopped, lemon juice to taste, a few drops Worcestershire, mayonnaise and salt. Pile the mixture into the shell, chill and serve on a platter surrounded by potato chips.

11

Kaleidoscope of Appetizers

Ingredients: *1 cauliflower · sliced white bread · salami · cheese · shrimps · artichokes in olive oil · frankfurters · gherkins · hard-boiled eggs · olives*

Clean the cauliflower, place it on a serving platter and garnish it with appetizers (step 1) prepared with the above foods (step 2), sliced and arranged on cocktail picks (step 3). Garnish the platter with sliced hard-boiled egg. Grapefruit and watermelon are equally decorative and can be substituted for the cauliflower when in season.

Cheese Appetizers

Cut an assortment of cheeses, such as Gruyère, Emmenthal, Bel Paese, Cheddar and cacciotta, into cubes and arrange them on cocktail picks. Set the picks on a serving platter and surround them with an assortment of crackers.

Shrimp Appetizers

Shell and devein 2 lb cooked shrimps and chill them. Pierce the shrimps with cocktail picks and place them on a serving platter around a small bowl of mayonnaise (see p.98).

Salami Rolls

Put 3 cups chicken broth or stock into a saucepan with 2 teaspoons wine vinegar, 1 tablespoon dry sherry and a pinch of sugar. Bring to a boil, then strain through cheesecloth or a very fine sieve and leave to cool.

Dissolve 2 tablespoons gelatin in a little of the broth mixture, then stir into the remaining broth mixture. Chill until set.

Mix $\frac{1}{2}$ lb cream cheese with 1 tablespoon sour cream, 2 tablespoons grated Parmesan cheese and $\frac{1}{2}$ cup finely chopped bottled cocktail onions. Spread over 12 large salami slices. Pull each slice together at the top and secure with a toothpick.

Chop the jellied broth and spread out on a serving platter. Arrange the salami rolls on top and garnish with piped mayonnaise, parsley sprigs and chopped parsley.

Italian Hors d'Oeuvre

Ingredients: ½ lb Italian prosciutto · ¼ lb each of ham, Italian salami, mortadella and smoked tongue · butter · ¼ cup green olives · canned artichoke hearts

Place a ring or decorative mold upside down in the center of a serving platter (step 1), cover it with aluminum foil (step 2) and with the prosciutto slices, putting one slice in the form of a flower in the middle (step 3). Place the other cold meats around the mold and garnish them with butter curls, olives and artichoke hearts. The last two ingredients can also be served separately, with olives, mushrooms and onions in olive oil, and gherkins.

To make a more complete hors d'oeuvre, add sardines, anchovies in olive oil and chopped parsley, tuna fish in olive oil, eggplant slices, white bean salad with onion slices, grated carrots with mayonnaise and cream dressing, stuffed hard-boiled eggs, frankfurter (or beef sausage) salad dressed with mayonnaise, beet and endive salad, all on different platters.

Do not add cold meats to hors d'oeuvres until the last minute, to keep them fresh.

Eggplant Slices

Peel 1 large eggplant and cut it into ½-inch slices. Put the slices in an oven-proof dish and cover them with olive oil and 1 clove of garlic, thinly sliced. Marinate the eggplant slices for about 1 hour, drain them and discard the garlic. Broil the slices until golden brown. Let them cool and sprinkle them with chopped parsley.

Ligurian Anchovies

Soak anchovy fillets in an equal mixture of water and vinegar for about 3 hours, or until desalted. Drain and rinse the fillets. Place them on a serving platter, surrounded by sliced ripe tomatoes, and sprinkle them with olive oil, finely chopped garlic and oregano to taste.

Celery Hors d'Oeuvre

Clean 3 or 4 celery stalks and marinate them in white wine vinegar for at least 12 hours. Drain them and cut them thinly lengthwise. Dress the celery with home-made or commercial mayonnaise and chill in refrigerator before serving.

Broiled Peppers

Cook 1 yellow pepper and 1 red pepper, or 2 green peppers, under the broiler or directly on the flame (using a long-handled fork in the latter case), and peel and seed them. Cut each pepper in eighths and place them in a deep platter. Add olive oil, salt and chopped parsley, and, to make the dish more appetizing, pressed garlic to taste. The peppers can be cooked days in advance as they keep very well as long as they are covered with olive oil. They go well with anchovies in olive oil.

Shrimp Cocktail

Ingredients: *1¼ lb small fresh or frozen
shrimps · mayonnaise made with 2 eggs (see
p.98) · 2 or 3 tablespoons ketchup · 1 teaspoon
Worcestershire · 2 teaspoons brandy · salt.
paprika · 2 or 3 tablespoons heavy cream ·
1 lettuce heart*

To serve: *lemon wedges*

Wash the shrimps, cook them in boiling salted
water for 5 minutes, drain, shell and devein
them. Mix the mayonnaise together with the
ketchup, Worcestershire, brandy, salt, paprika
and heavy cream. Put lettuce leaves, sliced
lengthwise, in the bottom of 4 crystal goblets
or sherbet glasses (step 1), add the shrimps,
putting 24 aside to use as decoration. Pour
the mixture over the shrimps (step 2), and
garnish each goblet with shrimps set around
the rim of the crystal and one whole lettuce
leaf on one side (step 3). The goblets can be
served as they are or set in crushed ice on a
silver platter.

Canadian Herring Salad

Broil smoked herring directly on the flame, skin, remove bones and cut flesh in cubes. Add an equal quantity of potatoes, boiled and peeled, and cored green apples, both cut in cubes, minced chives and parsley, and fennel seed to taste. Dress the salad with oil, vinegar, salt and pepper.

Mussels in Piquant Sauce

Clean thoroughly $3\frac{1}{4}$ lb mussels in cold running water, drain and dry them. Cook 1 clove of garlic in 2 tablespoons olive oil until golden and discard garlic. Add the mussels to the pan with 2 anchovies, desalted and mashed to a paste, and 1 cup each of vinegar and dry white wine. Cover the pan and cook the mixture over high heat until mussels open. Remove mussels and continue cooking the stock over high heat until it is reduced by half. Shell the mussels, put them in a covered earthenware dish, sprinkle with chopped parsley and pepper and add the stock. Chill 2–3 days before serving.

Grapefruit and Crab Cocktail

Peel 2 ripe grapefruit, chilled, and cut them in pieces. Combine together with 1 can crabmeat, drained and cleaned, and 1 cup mayonnaise mixed with 1 teaspoon each of lemon juice and vinegar and a few drops Tabasco. Spoon into 4 sherbet glasses. Chill.

German Kippers

Place 4 kipper fillets upright in a pitcher, pour in enough boiling water to cover and leave for 5 minutes. Drain the kippers, dry on paper towels and cut into thin strips. Divide between 4 serving glasses.

Mix $1\frac{1}{4}$ cups plain yogurt with 2 sieved hard-cooked eggs, and hot pepper sauce, dry mustard and salt and pepper to taste. Fold in 2 tomatoes, peeled and finely chopped. Spoon this sauce over the kippers and sprinkle with chopped parsley.

How to Serve Caviar and Smoked Salmon

Ingredients: *1 small can caviar or salmon roe ·
¾ lb smoked salmon, very thinly sliced · lemons ·
butter · pepper · parsley, preferably Italian
parsley · black bread · white bread*

Keep the caviar in the refrigerator until serving
time. Serve it in its can or in a small crystal
dish, set in a bigger dish on crushed ice, with
lemon quarters, sliced black bread and butter
curls. In Russia it is traditional for caviar to
be served with hot blini, melted butter, sour
cream and vodka.

Put the smoked salmon on a serving platter,
garnished with black olives, parsley or lettuce
leaves. Serve it with toasted white bread slices
covered with a napkin (to keep them warm),
butter curls and lemon halves on separate
platters. Add a pepper mill so that everyone can
grind their own pepper at the last moment.

Russian Blini

Ingredients: *1 cup flour · 1 teaspoon each of
sugar and double-acting baking powder ·
1½ cups milk · 2 eggs · 1 cup sour cream*

Sift the flour into a bowl and add the sugar
and baking powder. Make a well in the center
and pour in the milk. Blend with the fingers
until all ingredients are incorporated. Break
the eggs in a separate bowl, beat them hard
and blend them into the dough with 3
tablespoons sour cream. Beat the batter lightly
but thoroughly and add milk and sour cream
until it is the consistency of thick cream. Cover
and let stand at room temperature for 20
minutes. Heat a little butter in a very small
frying pan, add a small amount of batter and
fry quickly until golden on both sides. Repeat
with remaining batter, keeping blini in a hot
oven. Serve very hot.

Caviar Canapés

Trim the crusts off slices of white bread and
cut bread into quarters. Spread with butter.
Put caviar on one half of each bread quarter
so that it is diagonally covered and spread the
other corner with white and yolk of hard-
boiled eggs, mashed separately. Garnish the
platter with lemon quarters and sprigs of
parsley, if liked.

Taramasalata

Remove the crusts from 6 thick slices of white
bread, then crumble into a bowl. Pour over ¾ cup
milk and soak for 10 minutes.

Meanwhile, remove any skin from 3 oz poached, parboiled or smoked cod roe. Pound the roe
in a mortar or put into a blender. Squeeze the
bread crumbs dry and add to the roe. Pound or
blend to a smooth paste.

Peel and grate 1 small onion. Add to the paste
with 1 crushed garlic clove and 4 tablespoons
lemon juice. Gradually add 4 tablespoons olive
oil, a drop at a time, pounding or blending
between each addition. The taramasalata
should be firm, not runny. Cover and leave in a
cool place overnight.

Serve garnished with ripe olives and accompanied by lemon wedges and pitta bread.

Crudités

Crudités, or raw vegetables, make a very healthy hors d'oeuvre. Various raw vegetables are cleaned and cut into fairly large pieces to be dipped into a vinaigrette sauce, made of oil, vinegar, salt and pepper. As guests may like to season their own crudités, it is best to serve the vinaigrette separately.

Artichokes: discard the stems and hard outer leaves; cut the softer leaves to $\frac{3}{4}$ of their height, quarter the artichokes and discard the chokes; sprinkle them with lemon juice (step 1) and keep them in cold water to prevent discoloration until serving time.

Carrots: scrape and wash young carrots (step 2) and slice them lengthwise in 4 or more pieces.

Celery: use only the hearts of the celery. Wash well and remove the bigger leaves.

Fennel: discard the outer leaves and each end of the fennel bulbs (step 3). Quarter bulbs and wash them very carefully.

Peppers: wash them and discard the stems. Quarter peppers and discard the seeds and white membranes.

Radishes: wash them, trim the ends and scrape them lightly.

Carrot Salad

Scrape young carrots and grate them. Season with oil, lemon, salt and pepper, or with salt, pepper, mayonnaise and whipped cream. Chill before serving.

Mushroom Salad

Slice mushrooms very thinly and mix with an equal proportion of fresh Parmesan or Gruyère cheese, cut in thin strips. Add a few paper-thin slices of white truffle if available, oil, lemon juice, salt and white pepper.

Creamed Cucumbers

Peel 4 cucumbers and slice them thinly. Add salt, pepper and 4 or more tablespoons vinegar. Whip 1 cup heavy cream until slightly thickened and mix it gently with the cucumbers. Chill.

Artichoke Salad

Discard the stems and hard outer leaves of 3–4 tender artichokes. Starting from the bottom and using a very sharp knife, slice the artichokes very thinly and discard the chokes. Put the slices in cold water seasoned with lemon juice to prevent discoloration. Drain and dry them and season with 3 tablespoons oil, salt, pepper and lemon juice.

Celeriac Rémoulade

Peel and trim 1 celeriac, cut it in thin strips and sprinkle with the juice of 1 lemon. In a small bowl whip 1 egg yolk with a dash each of mustard, salt and white pepper, and olive oil, added drop by drop. Add the celeriac.

Gorgonzola Mousse

Ingredients: *¼ lb Gorgonzola or other blue cheese · 2 cups heavy cream · walnut halves (optional)*

Work the cheese through a sieve and mix it with 1 cup heavy cream in small amounts. Heat the mixture in a bain-marie (step 1), or in the top of a double-boiler, stirring constantly, until it is smooth. Let the mixture stand until it is cool and whip and add the remaining cream (step 2). Pour the mousse in a 1½–2 pint rectangular mold or bread pan (step 3) and freeze for at least 4 hours. Unmold the mousse on a serving platter and serve with triangles of toasted bread. Garnish the top and the sides with rows of walnut halves, if desired. Serves 4–6.

This dish is very good served with stalks of raw celery.

Stuffed Celery

Wash and trim 1 bunch of celery, discarding the strings. Cut each stalk into 5-inch pieces and fill the centers with the following creams.

Lemon cream: mix together $\frac{1}{4}$ cup softened butter with $\frac{1}{4}$ cup cottage or cream cheese, 2 tablespoons lemon juice, 1 teaspoon grated lemon peel and salt to taste.

Olive cream: mix together $\frac{1}{4}$ cup softened butter with $\frac{1}{4}$ cup cottage or cream cheese, $\frac{1}{4}$ cup green olives, pitted and chopped, and salt. Chill.

Cheese Balls

In a bowl blend 1 cup cottage or cream cheese with about $\frac{1}{2}$ cup black or green olives, pitted and chopped, and 1 tablespoon softened butter. Shape the mixture into small balls, roll in chopped walnuts and chill for a few hours or until they have hardened. Serve on cocktail picks.

Cheese Balls with Curry

Blend 1 cup cottage or cream cheese with 1 tablespoon softened butter and 1 teaspoon curry powder. Shape the mixture into small balls, roll in freshly grated coconut and chill for 2 hours, or until they have hardened.

Fromage Mystère

Mash $\frac{1}{4}$ lb Roqufort cheese with 3 petits suisses cheeses in a bowl with a fork. Add 1 cup shredded Gruyère or Swiss cheese and 2 tablespoons chopped mixed fresh herbs. Mix well together.

Shape the mixture into flat cakes or cylinders and coat in dried bread crumbs. Chill for 3 hours before serving.

Oysters

Ingredients: *32 oysters · lemons · sauce made with minced shallots, vinegar, salt and ground pepper; or sauce made with 2 tablespoons tomato ketchup, 1 teaspoon each of chilli sauce, mayonnaise and horseradish, and salt and pepper · freshly ground pepper · buttered rye or white bread slices*

Open the oysters just before serving as shown in step 1. They may also be opened 2 hours before and kept in the refrigerator until serving time. Fill each plate with crushed ice and place 8 oysters on each; decorate with lemon quarters. A small container of the chosen sauce can be placed in the center or served separately. Ground pepper, extra lemon quarters and slices of bread are served separately. Clams and mussels can also be served in this manner (steps 2 and 3).

Mussels

Scrub and wash fresh mussels thoroughly, discarding the beards. Just before serving, insert the point of a small knife between the two shells and move it round, being careful not to go in too deeply. Serve the mussels on crushed ice with lemon quarters and freshly ground pepper.

Sea Urchins

Hold the sea urchin in the left hand in a heavy folded cloth. Insert the tip of scissors in the soft part of the shell (about $\frac{3}{4}$ of the way up) and cut all around, discarding the liquid and digestive tube. To eat scoop out the fleshy part with a teaspoon or with bread, as with a boiled egg. Season with lemon juice.

24

Shellfish Salad

Clean $\frac{3}{4}$ cup fresh or frozen small cuttlefish, wash and drain them and cook in boiling salted water for 10 minutes. Add $\frac{3}{4}$ cup shelled shrimps and continue cooking for 10 minutes. Drain the shellfish and let cool. Scrub and wash $1\frac{1}{4}$ lb mussels thoroughly, discarding the beards. Heat 1 tablespoon oil in a pan, add the mussels and cook them over high heat, stirring occasionally, until all the shells are open. Let cool and discard the shells. Combine with cuttlefish and shrimps on a serving platter and season the salad with oil, salt, pepper and a generous amount of chopped parsley.

Mussel and Potato Salad

Peel $1\frac{1}{2}$ lb potatoes and cut into neat dice. Cook in boiling salted water until just tender. Drain well and put into a bowl.

Scrub 1 quart of fresh mussels and put into a saucepan with 1 tablespoon olive oil and 1 garlic clove. Cover and cook over high heat, shaking the pan frequently, until the mussels open (discard any that remain closed). Remove the mussels from their shells and add to the potatoes.

Strain the mussel cooking liquid through a cheesecloth-lined sieve into a clean saucepan. Add $\frac{3}{4}$ cup dry white wine and 1 tablespoon vinegar and boil until reduced by half. Remove from the heat and stir in 3 tablespoons olive oil and seasoning to taste. Pour over the potato and mussel mixture and fold together gently. Serve warm or cold.

Stuffed Tomato Platter

Tomatoes with Shrimps

Ingredients: *4 large tomatoes, firm and not too ripe · salt · mayonnaise made with 1 egg (see p.98) or commercial mayonnaise · ¾ lb fresh or frozen shrimps · parsley*

Wash and dry the tomatoes, cut tops off each and discard (step 1), vandyke the edges (step 2) and gently scoop out the pulp (step 3), being careful not to break the tomato shells. Salt them and turn upside down to drain. Mix the mayonnaise with most of the shrimps (reserving a few to use as garnish), and pile the mixture into the tomato shells. Place the reserved shrimps around the top of each tomato, as shown in the top picture.

Tomatoes with Russian Salad

Prepare 4 large tomatoes as for Tomatoes with Shrimps. Mix ¾ cup Russian salad (see p.44) with ⅓ cup chicken meat, cooked and cut in thin strips. Fill tomato shells with the mixture and garnish with anchovy fillets.

Tomatoes with Tuna Fish

Prepare 4 large tomatoes as for Tomatoes with Shrimps. Drain the oil from about ¼ cup tuna fish, crumble the tuna fish and mix with enough mayonnaise to make a smooth mixture. Add a few capers and fill tomato shells with the mixture. Garnish with extra capers and chill.

Tomatoes with Potatoes

Prepare 4 large tomatoes as for Tomatoes with Shrimps. Combine 2 large potatoes, cooked and diced, with ¼ lb Swiss cheese, diced, 1 small onion, finely chopped, and 1 teaspoon minced dill. Season the mixture with oil, vinegar, salt and pepper. Sliced frankfurters may be used if liked as well as potatoes. Fill the tomato shells with the mixture and garnish the tops.

Salad Marylène

Halve tomatoes and gently scoop out most of the pulp with a teaspoon. Fill each half with sliced gherkins and celery, cubed cold roast veal and a little thinly sliced carrot, all previously seasoned with oil, vinegar, salt and pepper. Garnish with mustard mayonnaise to taste (see p.98).

Cheese Tomatoes

Sieve $\frac{3}{4}$ lb ricotta cheese into a bowl and beat in 4 tablespoons grated Parmesan cheese, 1 crushed garlic clove, 1 tablespoon olive oil and seasoning. Prepare 4 large tomatoes as left, fill with the cheese mixture and chill for 30 minutes. Serve sprinkled with chopped fresh basil.

Melon with Prosciutto

Ingredients: *1 large or 2 medium ripe
cantaloups or other melons · salt · pepper ·
8 thin slices of Italian prosciutto · butter*

Chill the melon(s) and cut into eight slices.
Remove and discard the skin and seeds (steps
1 and 2). Sprinkle lightly with salt and pepper
and wrap each slice with 1 slice of prosciutto
(step 3). Place the melon slices wheel-fashion
on the serving platter. Garnish with butter
curls. The most classic way of serving this
dish is to cut the skin from the melon only
partially and to serve the melon and prosciutto
separately.

Prosciutto Surprise

In a bowl mix boiled chicken meat and Emmenthal cheese, both minced, with sliced celery, a
few tablespoons mayonnaise, chopped capers,
a little mustard, salt and lemon juice. Divide
the mixture between slices of Italian prosciutto
and roll up the slices. Pour a thin layer of cool
but still liquid aspic in a deep serving dish, add
the prosciutto rolls and cover with a thin layer of
aspic. Refrigerate the dish for a few hours or
until the aspic is set. Garnish with gherkins, cut
in fan shapes, or with little artichoke hearts in
olive oil.

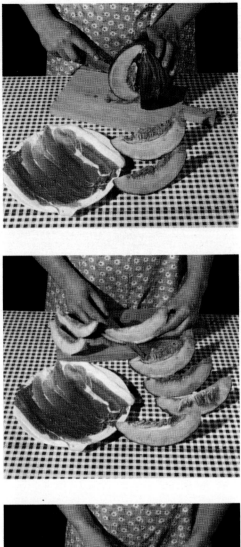

Prosciutto Roll

In a skillet melt a knob of butter or margarine, add 1 chicken liver, sprinkle with brandy and flame. Add salt and cook for a few minutes. Put $\frac{3}{4}$ cup boiled chicken meat, $\frac{1}{3}$ cup smoked tongue and the cooked chicken liver through the finest blade of a food chopper then work the mixture through a sieve, alternating with $\frac{3}{4}$ cup softened butter. Whip the mixture with a wooden spoon until it is light and fluffy and add a few slices of truffle if liked. Place 6 thick slices of Italian prosciutto, trimmed of their fat, so as to form a rectangle on wax paper, and add the chicken mixture. Roll up the prosciutto, cover the roll with wax paper or aluminum foil and refrigerate for a few hours. Pour a little cool but still liquid aspic on a serving platter and refrigerate it until it is almost set. Cut the roll in thick slices, place the slices on the aspic and cover them with more aspic. Garnish with a border of canned artichoke hearts in oil and slices of red pepper. Chill before serving. Serves 6.

Figs with Prosciutto

Place slices of Italian prosciutto on a serving platter. Chill figs, peel them and serve separately.

If desired, the figs can be peeled by each individual diner. This dish is a classic Italian hors d'oeuvre.

Ham and Horseradish Rolls

Whip $\frac{3}{4}$ cup heavy cream with $\frac{3}{4}$ cup mayonnaise (see p. 98) until thick. Fold in 1 tablespoon grated horseradish and 1 tablespoon lemon juice. Season to taste with salt.

Roll up 8 cooked ham slices to form tubes about 1 inch thick and pipe the horseradish mixture into each end. Serve garnished with gherkin fans, sliced stuffed olives and wedges of tomato.

Marinated Fish Fillets

Ingredients: *1 lb fresh sardines, sole or white fish fillets · salt · $\frac{1}{2}$ lb onions · 1 carrot · 1 celery heart · flour · 1 glass or more white wine vinegar mixed with white wine or water · oil · bay leaves*

Clean, wash and dry the fish, roll it lightly in flour (step 1) and fry it in deep hot fat until golden on both sides (step 2). Drain the fish on absorbent paper and salt it. In about $\frac{1}{2}$ glass oil sauté the sliced onions with the chopped carrot and celery heart until golden. Add 2 bay leaves, the vinegar and a pinch of salt, and boil the mixture for a few minutes. Put the fish in layers in a deep serving platter, putting a little vinegar mixture (step 3), some onion slices and 1 bay leaf on each layer. Top with onion slices and add enough vinegar mixture to cover the fish. Let stand for 24–48 hours. Before serving remove onion and bay leaf from top and garnish with fresh ones. This makes a very appetizing hors-d'oeuvre and can be enriched with 2 tablespoons each of seedless raisins and pine nuts to be added to the vinegar mixture.

Anchovy Fillets with Olives

Desalt anchovy fillets by letting them soak in equal measures of water and vinegar for a few hours. Wind each fillet around 1 olive, pitted and stuffed with anchovy butter (see p.100) or with 1 hard-boiled egg yolk blended with butter, chopped parsley and salt. Serve the fillets with curls of butter. They can also be used on canapés.

Marinated Eel

Wash, clean thoroughly and skin a 2-lb fresh eel and cut it into 4–5 pieces, discarding the head and tail. Put the pieces in an oven-proof casserole with a little oil, 1 bay leaf, salt and pepper, and cook in the oven for about 2 hours. Drain the eel pieces and put them close together in a dish. Bring to a boil 4 cups vinegar, salt, a few peppercorns, 2 cloves of garlic, 2 bay leaves, 1 pinch of rosemary and 3 cloves, and pour the mixture on the eel pieces.

Cover and let stand for 3 or 4 days, stirring occasionally.

Anchovies with Green Sauce

Desalt anchovy fillets by letting them soak in equal measures of water and vinegar for a few hours. Wind each fillet around a pitted olive and put them in a deep serving platter. Prepare a green sauce with parsley, minced with $\frac{1}{2}$ clove of garlic, hard-boiled egg yolk, salt and pepper. Thin the mixture with oil and vinegar, work it through a sieve and pour on the fillets.

Let the fillets marinate for a while and serve with hard-boiled sliced eggs.

Liver Mousse

Ingredients: *¾ cup veal or goose liver · 1 slice onion · ¾ cup butter or margarine · ¾ lb veal · 1 bay leaf · salt · 2 tablespoons Marsala · 2 tablespoons grated Parmesan cheese · pepper · mixed herbs · thyme · slices of truffle to taste · 4 cups homemade (see p.104) or commercial aspic*

In a skillet sauté the onion in a little butter. Discard the onion and add the veal, diced, bay leaf and salt, and cook the mixture without letting it brown on very low heat for 1 hour and 15 minutes. Soak the liver in lukewarm water, slice it finely, add it to the skillet, and continue cooking for 15 minutes. Put the mixture through the finest blade of a meat chopper twice, add the Marsala, a little more of the butter, Parmesan cheese, salt, pepper, herbs and thyme, and heat the mixture slowly. Work the mixture through a sieve a little at a time, alternating with the remaining butter in pieces. Using a wooden spoon, whip the mixture until it is light and fluffy. Add sliced

truffle if liked. Line a long rectangular mold with aluminum foil and pour in the mousse, tightening the foil around it so that there is a 1-inch space between it and all sides of the mold. Refrigerate the mousse until it is set. Remove the mousse from its mold, put a little cool but still liquid aspic in the bottom of the mold and refrigerate until almost set. Cut the truffle into slices with a knife, or shape with cutters and place on the aspic (step 1), add the mousse (step 2), and pour the remaining aspic around it (step 3). Refrigerate until set. To unmold the mousse dip the mold quickly into boiling water, dry it and immediately turn it over on the serving platter. Garnish with diced aspic. Serve with olives, if liked. Serves 6–8.

Ham Mousse

Chop and pound in a mortar $1\frac{1}{4}$ cups ham with $\frac{1}{4}$ cup butter. Stirring constantly, add 2 tablespoons cold béchamel sauce, made with $\frac{1}{2}$ tablespoon each of butter and flour and 3 tablespoons milk. Put the mixture through the finest blade of a food chopper and add 2 tablespoons diced ham, salt and cayenne pepper. Fold in 1 cup whipped cream. Pour the mixture in a mold lined with a damp cheesecloth and cover with wax paper and a lid so it is airtight. Refrigerate for a few hours.

Unmold the mousse on the serving platter, remove the cheesecloth and garnish with diced aspic. Serves 4–6.

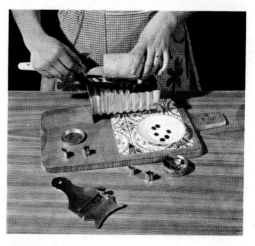

Tuna Fish Mousse

In a bowl blend $\frac{1}{2}$ cup softened butter or margarine with $\frac{1}{2}$ cup tuna fish in olive oil, 4 desalted anchovy fillets and a few capers, forced through a sieve. Whip the mixture until it is light and fluffy. Add the juice of $\frac{1}{2}$ lemon and pour the mixture into a small fish mold, lined with a damp cheesecloth. Refrigerate for a few hours. Unmold the mousse on the serving platter, remove the cheesecloth and garnish with mayonnaise. Decorate the platter with lemon and green pepper slices, hard-boiled egg and tomato slices, or very simply with diced aspic.

Canapés

Ingredients: *sliced white bread · butter · maître d'hôtel butter (see p.101) · smoked salmon · caviar · shrimps · liver mousse (see p.32) · truffles · gherkins · 1 hard-boiled egg · olives · mayonnaise (see p.98) · peeled almonds · home-made (see p.104) or commercial aspic*

Trim the crusts from the bread slices and cut them into squares and triangles (step 1). Spread the squares with butter and the triangles with maître d'hôtel butter. Spread the canapés with smoked salmon slices, caviar, shrimps and liver mousse, and garnish them with stars of truffles (step 2), gherkins, hard-boiled egg slices, olives, mayonnaise and peeled almonds (step 3). Set the canapés on a serving platter in a decorative way, as seen in the picture, brush them with cool but still liquid aspic and chill before serving.

34

Canapé Variations

Trim the crusts from white or rye bread slices and cut them into squares, triangles, circles and flower shapes. Spread them with softened butter mixed with salt or with mustard, anchovy paste or chopped herbs. Spread the canapés with the following mixtures:

Hard-boiled eggs and anchovies: blend 2 hard-boiled eggs with 6 desalted anchovy fillets, mashed, and 2 tablespoons mayonnaise.

Artichokes: in the center of each bread circle spread with butter and anchovy paste, place 1 small canned artichoke heart, spread it open as a flower and garnish the edges of the canapé with mayonnaise.

Russian salad: spread the bread with butter and with Russian salad (see p.44). In the center put 1 tomato slice, 1 dollop of mayonnaise and 1 cooked shrimp.

Mushroom and egg: spread bread circles with butter. Add hard-boiled egg, mashed with a little mayonnaise and parsley. Garnish with slices of raw mushroom and slices of hard-boiled egg.

Radish Canapés

Toast 4 slices of white or rye bread and spread them with mayonnaise. Add radishes and gherkins, both sliced.

Smoked Eel Canapés

Spread 4 slices of black bread with mayonnaise, sprinkle with dill and add smoked eel pieces.

Egg Flowers

Ingredients: *4 eggs · 1 tablespoon softened butter · 1½ tablespoons anchovy paste · 1 tablespoon mayonnaise · salt · pepper · capers*

Cook the eggs in boiling salted water for 9 minutes, pass them under cold running water and shell them (step 1). Using a small sharp knife, cut off the top of each egg, without touching the yolk (step 2). Whip the butter with the anchovy paste, mayonnaise, salt and pepper to taste until the mixture is fluffy. Using a pastry bag fitted with a star tube, pipe the mixture on each egg (step 3) and garnish with 1 caper. Chill before serving.

Eggs with Shrimps

Halve hard-boiled eggs lengthwise. Blend the yolks with enough mayonnaise, ketchup and Worcestershire to make a smooth mixture. Fill the whites with the mixture and garnish each half with 1 big shrimp (cooked in boiling salted water for a few minutes, shelled and deveined), a few slices of black olive and sprigs of parsley. Chill before serving.

Spring Eggs

Halve hard-boiled eggs lengthwise, work the yolks through a sieve and blend them with enough mayonnaise to make a smooth mixture. Add salt and pile the mixture in the whites. Garnish as shown in the picture by using pieces of red pepper or tomato and parsley.

Eggs with Radishes

Halve hard-boiled eggs lengthwise, work the yolks through a sieve and blend with a little cottage or cream cheese, 1 or 2 tablespoons mayonnaise, a few drops of Worcestershire sauce, salt and pepper. Pile the mixture in the whites and garnish with slices of radishes, as shown in the picture. Chill before serving.

Eggs with Tuna Fish

Halve hard-boiled eggs lengthwise and work the yolks through a sieve with 2 tablespoons tuna fish in olive oil and 1 teaspoon capers. Add 2 tablespoons softened butter and whip the mixture until it is fluffy. Using a pastry bag fitted with a small tube, pipe the mixture in the whites and garnish with petals of green peppers or carrots and 1 caper in the center.

Eggs with Lobster

Halve hard-cooked eggs lengthwise, work the yolks through a sieve and mix with diced cooked lobster and finely chopped truffle. Pile the mixture in the whites and garnish with finely chopped mushrooms.

Eggs with Artichokes

Halve hard-cooked eggs lengthwise, work the yolks through a sieve and mix with finely chopped cooked artichoke hearts and salt and pepper to taste. Pile the mixture in the whites and garnish with parsley sprigs.

Vegetables à la Grecque

Ingredients: *4 small artichokes · 2 celery hearts · ¼ cauliflower · 2 carrots · 2 zucchini · 1 eggplant · 8 asparagus · 4 mushroom caps · 4–8 small white onions · 4 tablespoons olive oil · 2 tablespoons white wine vinegar or the juice of 1 lemon · 1 clove of garlic · 6 peppercorns · salt · bouquet garni made of parsley, 1 bay leaf, and thyme*

Wash and clean thoroughly all vegetables. Discard the hard outer leaves of the artichokes, halve them and discard the chokes; halve the celery hearts, separate the cauliflower in flowerets, scrape and slice the carrots (step 1), and dice the zucchini and eggplant. Put the vegetables in a saucepan with the oil, vinegar or lemon juice, garlic, pepper, salt and the bouquet garni, and add enough boiling water to just cover. Bring to a boil and cook over moderate heat until the vegetables are *al dente* (step 2). Strain the cooking liquid into a pan (keeping the vegetables on one side) and cook over low heat until reduced by half. Put the vegetables in an earthenware casserole, add the cooking liquid (step 3) and let stand until cool. Chill for a few hours before you serve the vegetables.

Marinated Mushrooms

Clean and wash 8 large mushroom caps and slice them finely. Very small mushroom caps may also be used but kept whole (the tails can be kept for use in soups, stews or casseroles). Put the mushrooms in a deep serving platter with the juice of 1–2 lemons, 2 tablespoons olive oil, salt and freshly ground pepper. Let the mushrooms marinate for 2½ hours before serving.

Olives with Garlic

Pound ¾ cup green olives lightly so as to be able to pit them without breaking them too much. Put the olives in a sterilized jar with 2 cloves of crushed garlic, 1 piece of pimiento and olive oil to cover. Seal immediately and let stand for 2–3 days.

Salad Niçoise

Ingredients: *potatoes · green beans · oil ·
vinegar · salt · pepper · tomatoes · parsley ·
anchovy fillets · black olives · capers*

Cook the potatoes and green beans separately
in boiling salted water until tender, drain
them and let cool. Cut the potatoes in cubes
and slice the beans (step 1). Season them with
oil, vinegar, salt and pepper, and pile them in
a salad bowl (step 2). Add tomatoes, quartered
and sprinkled with chopped parsley, and
decorate with desalted anchovy fillets, olives
and capers (step 3). Serve with lemon wedges.
This salad is good with grilled meats.

Fish and Potato Salad

Mix gently 2 cups cooked white fish, cleaned
and flaked, with 2 cups cooked potatoes, cubed,
½ cup thinly sliced celery, 1 tablespoon chopped
onion, salt, pepper, oil and lemon. Put the
salad on a serving platter and garnish with
mayonnaise. Chill. Sprinkle with chopped
parsley just before serving.

Spring Salad

Cook separately 1 cup each of asparagus tips,
green beans and small peas, and 3 artichoke
hearts (optional) in boiling salted water until
tender. Cook 2 eggs in boiling salted water
for 9 minutes. Mix a dash of pepper with ½
teaspoon each of salt and English powdered
mustard, 5–6 tablespoons olive oil and about
2 tablespoons vinegar in a salad bowl. Add
the cooked vegetables, the hard-boiled eggs,
coarsely chopped, 5–6 thinly sliced radishes
and chopped parsley, basil and chives to taste.
Mix lightly and chill for about 1 hour. Add
4 or more tablespoons homemade mayonnaise
(see p.98), mix gently and serve.

Rice salad

Ingredients: *1¼ cups rice · ⅓ cup each of fresh or frozen peas and tuna fish in olive oil · 4 anchovy fillets · ¼ cup black olives · 1½ oz Gruyère cheese · 4–5 canned artichoke hearts · 1 tomato, peeled · 2 hard-boiled eggs · capers · oil · salt · pepper · lemon juice*

Cook the rice in boiling salted water until it is *al dente*, pass it under cold running water and drain. Cook the peas in boiling salted water, flake the tuna fish, mash the desalted anchovies, pit and slice the olives, cube the Gruyère and tomato and quarter drained artichoke hearts and eggs. Put all ingredients except eggs in a salad bowl, add capers and season gently with oil, salt, pepper and lemon juice to taste (steps 1 and 2). Garnish with egg (step 3).

Meat and Rice Salad

In a salad bowl combine 1¼ cups rice, cooked *al dente*, passed under cold running water and drained, with ¾ cup boiled or roast meat, cut into strips, a few pitted and sliced olives and 1 celery heart, thinly sliced. Season with oil, lemon juice, salt and pepper, and sprinkle with chopped parsley.

Rice Salad Flamenco

To 1¼ cups rice, cooked *al dente*, passed under cold running water and drained, add garlic sausage, thinly sliced, 2 eggs, cooked as an omelet, chilled and cut into strips, 2 tomatoes, quartered, and a little sliced onion. Season the salad with oil, lemon juice or vinegar, salt and pepper to taste.

Rice and Asparagus Salad

Cook 1¼ cups rice in boiling salted water until it is *al dente*, pass it under cold running water and drain. Add fresh or frozen asparagus tips to taste, cooked in boiling salted water, 2 or 3 raw mushrooms, wiped, trimmed and sliced very thinly, and ¾ cup thinly sliced celery. Season with 3 generous tablespoons mayonnaise mixed with the juice of 1 lemon, 2 teaspoons Worcestershire or mustard and chopped parsley. Mix the salad very gently and let it stand for about ½ hour before you serve it.

Stuffed Tomatoes

Ingredients: *¾ cup rice · ¼ cup mushrooms · juice of 1 lemon · 4 tomatoes · 1 tablespoon tomato paste · 3–4 tablespoons mayonnaise · tarragon · salt · white pepper*

Cook the rice in boiling salted water. Wipe and trim the mushrooms, slice thinly and sprinkle with lemon juice to prevent discoloration. Wash the tomatoes, cut a thick slice from the top of each and reserve. Press the tomatoes gently to extract the water and seeds and salt them lightly. Mix the rice with the mushrooms, tomato paste and mayonnaise. Fill the tomatoes with the mixture, sprinkle with tarragon, season and replace the tops.

Stuffed Peppers

Cook 4 peppers on the broiler or directly over the flame (using a long-handled fork in the latter case) and peel them. Using a sharp knife, cut off a cover from the stem end of each pepper and gently scrape out the seeds. Cook 1 cup rice in boiling salted water until it is *al dente*. Crush garlic in a bowl and blend it with saffron, cayenne pepper and paprika, vinegar and oil. Add chopped gherkins and the rice. Pile the mixture into the peppers.

43

Russian Salad with Ham Rolls

Ingredients: *1¼ cups potatoes · ½ cup each of carrots, green beans and fresh or frozen peas · 2 tablespoons pickled vegetables · 1 cup homemade (see p.104) or commercial aspic · oil · vinegar · salt · pepper · mayonnaise made with 1 egg (see p.98), 1 teaspoon mustard, juice of 1 lemon · 6 slices ham · ¾ cup homemade (see p.32) or bought liver mousse*

To garnish: *1 hard-boiled egg · 1 tomato (optional)*

Wash, prepare and cook the raw vegetables separately in boiling salted water. Drain them, let them cool, and cut potatoes, carrots and green beans into cubes. Put the vegetables in a bowl, add the pickled vegetables and season with a little oil, vinegar, salt and pepper. Add the cool but still liquid aspic in small amounts to the mayonnaise, reserving 2–3 tablespoons. Add the seasoned vegetables, mustard and lemon juice, and pour the mixture in a lightly

44

oiled ring mold (step 1). Chill for about 2 hours. Make a roll of each ham slice and, using a pastry bag fitted with a large star tube, fill them with liver mousse. Unmold the Russian salad on a serving platter (step 2), place the ham rolls sunburst-fashion and brush them with the reserved liquid aspic. Put the hard-boiled egg, topped with liver mousse, or a small stuffed tomato in the center. Chill before serving. Serves 6.

Red Cabbage Salad

Trim and wash 1 small red cabbage and slice it finely. Put it in a bowl, sprinkle generously with vinegar and sugar and marinate for 4 hours. Add 1 minced onion, and season the salad with mustard, oil, vinegar, salt and pepper. Garnish with 12 black olives, chopped parsley and chervil, and other herbs, if liked. Serves 6.

Salad Marly

In a salad bowl combine $\frac{3}{4}$ cup cold roast beef, cut in thin strips, with 2 potatoes, boiled and cubed, $\frac{1}{2}$ cup cooked green beans, cut in pieces, 3 or 4 radishes, sliced, and 1 small onion, thinly sliced. Mix 2 tablespoons mayonnaise with oil, vinegar, a few drops of Worcestershire, salt and pepper. Pour the dressing on the salad and mix gently. Sprinkle with finely chopped parsley and basil, and other herbs, if liked, just before you serve the salad.

Fruity Celeriac Salad

Peel $\frac{1}{2}$ lb celeriac and grate into a bowl. Peel, core and grate 2 apples. Peel 1 orange and roughly chop the flesh. Add the apples and orange to the celeriac and sprinkle with 2 tablespoons lemon juice. Make a dressing with 3 tablespoons light cream, 5 tablespoons plain yogurt, $\frac{1}{2}$ teaspoon prepared mustard, a pinch of sugar and salt and pepper to taste. Add to the salad, toss well and chill for 30 minutes before serving.

Shellfish in Aspic

Ingredients: *4 cups homemade (see p.104) or commercial aspic · 10 oz scampi or shrimps · 1 black olive · 1 hard-boiled egg · 1½ cups Russian salad (see p.44) · ½ cup stuffed olives · gherkins*

Prepare the aspic and let it cool. Cook the scampi or shrimps in boiling salted water for about 10 minutes, drain, shell and devein them. Place black olive in center of a ring or decorative mold, of the type illustrated. Pour into the mold some cool but still liquid aspic (step 1) and refrigerate until set. Add the sliced hard-boiled egg (step 2), cover it with a layer of Russian salad and surround it with a border of scampi or shrimps (step 3). Add a little aspic and refrigerate until set. Add some Russian salad in the center, surround it with stuffed olives, pour a little aspic over it and refrigerate until set. Add a border of scampi or shrimps set vertically, fill the center with the remaining Russian salad, add the rest of the aspic and return to the refrigerator until set.

To serve dip the mold in hot water and unmold onto a serving platter. Serves 4–6.

Multicolored Aspic

Prepare 6 cups homemade (see p.104) or commercial aspic and let it cool. Put ½ cup tuna fish in olive oil, 4 anchovy fillets and 1 teaspoon capers through the fine blade of a food chopper or blender, add 3 tablespoons butter at room temperature and whip the mixture until it is light and foamy. Pour a thin layer of cool but still liquid aspic into a rectangular mold with high sides and refrigerate until almost set. Put 1 slice hard-boiled egg in the center and surround it with a crown made of the remaining slices of the egg, sliced gherkins, ¼ cup stuffed green olives and strips of red pimiento. Add a little aspic and return the mold to the refrigerator until almost set. Cover with a layer of 5 oz ham, trimmed of its fat, and a layer of aspic and return the mold to the refrigerator. Using a pastry bag fitted with a large tube, add a layer of tuna fish mixture, being careful to leave a space all around sides. Pour in the remaining aspic and return to the refrigerator until set.

To serve, dip the mold quickly in boiling water and unmold quickly onto a serving platter. Garnish the platter with sliced gherkins, carrots and red peppers. Serves 8.

Stuffed Leeks

Trim 4 big leeks, discarding the green parts. Remove the hearts, keeping long cylinders. Marinate the cylinders in oil, vinegar, salt and pepper. Cook the hearts in boiling salted water for 20 minutes and drain them. Chop them very finely with 2 hard-boiled eggs and ¼ cup ham, and bind the mixture with mayonnaise. Stuff the drained cylinders with the mixture and decorate with mayonnaise.

Galantine of Chicken

Ingredients: *a 3-lb chicken · $\frac{1}{4}$ lb each of mortadella and Italian prosciutto in one piece · bacon to taste · $\frac{1}{4}$ cup pistachios · black truffle to taste (optional) · Marsala · 1 lb chopped veal · 1 handful of white bread soaked in milk and squeezed dry · salt · pepper · cinnamon · nutmeg · 1 egg · 1 egg yolk*

For the stock: *1 veal knuckle · 1 stick celery · 1 carrot · 1 onion*

To garnish: *chaud-froid sauce (see p.95) · home-made (see p.104) or commercial aspic*

Place the chicken, breast side down, on a wooden board. Using a very sharp knife, make an incision from the neck down the middle and remove and reserve the bones, being careful not to cut the skin. Gently remove the meat from the skin (step 1). Put the chicken skin, diced breast, prosciutto, trimmed of its fat, mortadella and bacon, all cut into strips, pistachios, soaked in boiling water for a few minutes and peeled, and black truffle, if using, to marinate in Marsala for a few hours. Mix the chopped veal with the remaining chicken meat, chopped with the prosciutto fat and white bread. Mix in seasonings and bind together with egg and egg yolk. Remove the ingredients from the marinade, dry the chicken skin with absorbent paper towels and place it

48

on the board. Cover it with a layer of the chopped mixture and a layer of prosciutto, mortadella and bacon strips, diced chicken, pistachios and diced truffle (step 2). With slightly damp hands, shape the filling into a roll, cover it with the chicken skin and sew the edges together with thread. Tie the roll with string, cover it tightly with a cloth and tie again securely with string (step 3). In a large pan put the reserved chicken bones, veal knuckle, celery, carrot and onion. Add the galantine and water to cover, and cook, covered, over low heat for about $1\frac{1}{2}$ hours. Remove the galantine from the stock and let cool for 15 minutes. Remove the cloth, rinse it well and again cover the galantine with the cloth. Put the galantine between two dishes and put a weight on top. Let it stand until completely cool. Remove the cloth, put the galantine on a serving platter and brush it generously with chaud-froid sauce. Garnish with slices of truffle and aspic. Serves 8–10.

Sweet Peppers with Anchovies

Wash $2\frac{1}{2}$ lb red and yellow sweet peppers, halve, remove the seeds, pith and tops, and cut into wedges. In $\frac{1}{4}$ cup hot oil soften on low heat $\frac{1}{4}$ cup anchovy fillets, desalted by soaking in a little milk and mashed. Add the peppers, a little salt, and cover. Cook slowly for about $1\frac{1}{2}$ hours, stirring occasionally, and adding a few spoonfuls of stock if the peppers become dry. Serve hot or cold.

Pepper Salad

Halve 4 large sweet red and yellow peppers and broil, rounded sides up, until the skins are charred. Peel and remove the seeds and pith. Cut the halves in half.

Heat $\frac{1}{2}$ cup olive oil in a frying pan and fry the peppers gently for 7 minutes on each side. Arrange the pepper pieces in a serving dish, alternating colors to give a spoked effect. Sprinkle over $\frac{1}{4}$ cup grated Parmesan cheese, 1 tablespoon dried bread crumbs, 2 tablespoons capers, a pinch of dried marjoram and salt to taste. Leave to cool slightly, then sprinkle over 1 tablespoon vinegar. Serve warm or chilled.

Médaillons of Ham

Ingredients: *10 oz ham, sliced · 4 tablespoons butter or margarine · 1 slice onion · $\frac{1}{4}$ lb veal liver · $\frac{1}{2}$ bay leaf · pinch of thyme and mixed herbs · salt · 1 tablespoon Marsala · 1 tablespoon grated Parmesan · black truffles (optional) · 3 cups homemade (see p. 104) or commercial aspic*

To garnish: *sprigs of parsley · liver mousse (see p. 32), optional*

In a skillet, melt $\frac{1}{3}$ of the butter, add the onion, sauté it for a few minutes and discard it. Add the thinly sliced liver, bay leaf, thyme, mixed herbs and salt and cook the mixture for a few minutes. Discard the bay leaf and put the mixture through the finest blade of a food chopper or blender. Return the mixture to the skillet, add 1 knob of butter, the Marsala and Parmesan and cook it on a very low heat for a few minutes. Work the mixture through a sieve with the remaining butter and whip it with a wooden spoon until it is light and fluffy. Add slices of black truffle to taste. Put the mixture on a piece of wax paper or aluminum foil, making a roll 3 inches in diameter, cover it with the paper and refrigerate it for a few hours or until it has hardened. Slice the roll with a knife dipped in boiling water. Using a cookie cutter, cut the ham slices into 3-inch rounds

50

(step 1). Make each médaillon with 1 round of ham, 1 slice of liver roll and another round of ham (step 2). Pour a thin layer of cool but still liquid aspic in a deep platter and let it stand until almost set. Add the médaillons, brush them with aspic (step 3), put a slice of truffle or black olive in the center of each and let stand until the aspic is set. The remaining ham trimmings can be chopped and mixed with butter, mustard, chopped gherkins etc., and piped onto a serving platter using a pastry bag fitted with a star tube, or used for canapés or appetizers.

Garnish serving platter with sprigs of parsley and piped liver mousse, if liked.

Médaillons of Tongue

Using a cookie cutter, cut ½ lb sliced tongue into 3-inch rounds. Chop the tongue trimmings with 1 hard-boiled egg and a few gherkins. Add softened butter or magarine and 1 table-spoon mayonnaise to make a paste. Brush half the rounds with the paste and cover them with the rest of the rounds. Prepare the médaillons as described in the basic recipe left, decorating each with 3 slices of stuffed olive.

Médaillons with Russian Salad

Prepare 2 cups homemade (see p.104) or commercial aspic, pour a thin layer in a deep platter and let it set. Cover 8 slices of Italian prosciutto or other ham with Russian salad and roll them up. Using a cookie cutter, cut 4 slices of Italian prosciutto or other ham into 16 rounds and join them in pairs with remaining Russian salad.

Place them on the aspic, alternating with the ham rolls, and decorate them with mayonnaise, gherkins cut in fan shapes, and ½ red pepper cut in triangles or strips. Cover with the remaining aspic and chill in the refrigerator before serving.

Garnish with parsley, if liked.

51

Veal, Ham and Pork Pie

Ingredients: for the pastry, *2 cups flour ·
1 teaspoon salt · ¼ cup butter or margarine ·
2 eggs, whipped with 2 tablespoons cold
water*

For the filling: *½ lb lean veal · ¾ lb ham in
one piece · 1 glass brandy · ¼ lb chopped veal ·
2 oz salt pork · salt · thyme · 1 black truffle
(optional) · ¼ lb chopped pork · 1 egg · pepper ·
mixed herbs · 3 hard boiled eggs · bay leaves ·
1 egg yolk · 2 cups homemade (see p. 104) or
commercial aspic*

To garnish: *diced aspic*

Sift the flour with the salt into a bowl. Using
two knives or a pastry blender, cut in the
butter or margarine until the mixture is
mealy. Add the eggs and water, beating with a
fork. Knead the dough quickly for a few
moments, form a ball, cover with wax paper
and refrigerate for a few hours. Cut the lean
veal and ham in 1-inch strips, add half the
brandy, cover and marinate for a few hours.
In a bowl mix the chopped veal and salt pork
with a good pinch each of salt and thyme and
remaining brandy. Remove a little of the
mixture, add diced truffle if liked and reserve.
To the bowl add the chopped pork, 1 egg,

pepper and mixed herbs. Roll out ⅔ of the
dough on a floured board into a rectangle,
reserving remaining dough for cover. Lightly
oil a 9-inch loaf pan and line it with the
dough, leaving an extra inch all around (step
1). Add ¾ of the veal and pork mixture, a layer
of veal strips and a layer of ham strips (⅓ of
the two ingredients). Add the hard-boiled eggs,
the veal and truffle mixture (step 2), and the
remaining veal and ham strips with the
remaining marinade. Cover with the remaining
veal and pork mixture and a few bay leaves.
Fold the extra dough toward the center, brush
with beaten egg yolk and cover with reserved
dough rolled out into a rectangle. Roll out any
remaining dough to make a border and leaves
or other decoration to put on top of the pie.
Brush top with beaten egg. Make a hole in the
center and put in a double roll of aluminum
foil to make a funnel (step 3) so that the
steam can escape during cooking. Bake the
pie in a moderate oven (350°F) for about
2 hours. Remove the pie from the oven and,
using the roll of aluminum foil, pour in, a
little at a time, enough cool but still liquid aspic
to fill the mold (step 4).

When pie is cool, refrigerate for a few
hours until cold and then turn out on a
serving platter. Serves 8.

Garnish with diced aspic if liked.

Individual Pies

Prepare flaky pastry as for Barquettes (p.60) or
use frozen puff pastry. In a mortar pound
6 drained and desalted anchovy fillets with
1 piece of onion and 1 clove of garlic, both
minced, and 3–4 peppercorns. Add 2 teaspoons
oil (the oil from the anchovy fillets will do very
well) and 1 tablespoon brandy. Let the mixture
stand for ½ hour. Add 1 egg yolk, 1 knob
softened butter and about ¾ cup finely chopped
ham.

Roll out the dough on a floured board and cut
it into 4-inch rounds. Put 1 tablespoon of the
mixture in the center of each round, dampen
the edges and fold over the dough, pressing
the edges tightly together. Brush the pies with
beaten egg white and cook them in a moderate
oven (350°F) for 35–40 minutes.

Serve immediately while still hot. Garnish
with a little chopped parsley, if liked.

Tartlets with Ham Mousse

Ingredients: for the flaky pastry, *6 tablespoons sifted flour · 2¼ tablespoons butter or margarine · 1 tablespoon cold water · 1 pinch of salt*

For the filling: *¼ cup chopped ham · 1 tablespoon each of mayonnaise and mustard · 1 pinch of paprika · ½ cup heavy cream · Worcestershire · chopped parsley*

Using two knives or a pastry blender, blend the flour with the butter or margarine, water and salt until it is mealy. Knead the dough for a few minutes, shape it into a ball, wrap in wax paper and let stand in the refrigerator for ½ hour. Roll out the dough on a floured board and cut out 8 rounds to fit tartlet molds. Fill the shells with wax paper and rice or dried beans and bake 'blind' in a hot oven (400°F) for about 15 minutes. Remove the tartlets from their molds, discard the wax paper and rice and allow to cool. Blend the ham with the mayonnaise, mustard and paprika. Fold in the cream, whipped until stiff (step 1), and a few drops of Worcestershire. Fill the tartlets with ham mixture and sprinkle with chopped parsley and paprika (step 2).

Tartlets with Cream Cheese

Mash 6 green olives, pitted and chopped, with ½ chopped celery stalk, 3 small packets cream cheese, 1 or more tablespoons mayonnaise and salt. Using a pastry bag fitted with a large tube, pipe the mixture into 8 tartlets.

Tartlets with Baby Octopus

Make mayonnaise with 1 egg (see p.98) or use commercial mayonnaise, and blend it with Worcestershire and 2 baby octopuses, cooked in boiling salted water and chopped. Fill into 8 tartlets. Garnish each tartlet with 1 baby octopus (step 3).

Tartlets with Liver Mousse

Prepare about ¾ cup liver mousse (see p.32). Using a pastry bag fitted with a star shape, pipe the mousse into 8 tartlets.

Club Sandwich

Ingredients for each sandwich: *3 slices of fresh bread · lettuce · ham · mayonnaise · sliced cheese, either Gruyère or Emmenthal · tomato · chicken meat · butter · oil · vinegar · salt*

To garnish: *tomato · 1 black olive*

Toast and butter each slice of bread (step 1). Put some lettuce, dressed with oil, vinegar and salt, on the first slice of bread, add a slice of ham, brushed with mayonnaise, and a slice of cheese (step 2). Add the second slice of bread, some more lettuce and tomato slices, also dressed, and the chicken meat, cubed and mixed with mayonnaise. Add the last slice of bread (step 3), brush it with mayonnaise and add a slice of cheese, a tomato quarter and a black olive. Decorate by piping mayonnaise in a border on top.

These sandwiches also make an ideal light lunch or snack.

Ham and Egg Sandwiches

Butter 8 slices of whole-wheat or rye bread. On 4 slices put gherkins and 2 hard-boiled eggs, both sliced, and 4 slices of ham. Add 2 hard-boiled eggs and gherkins, both sliced, and close the sandwiches with the remaining slices of buttered bread.

Sardine and Egg Sandwiches

Butter 8 slices of whole-wheat or rye bread. On 4 slices put sardines, drained, and 3 sliced hard-boiled eggs, and brush generously with mustard. Close the sandwiches with the remaining slices of bread.

Provencal Sandwiches

Halve 4 crusty rolls and rub the cut surfaces with a cut garlic clove. Place a large lettuce leaf on the bottom half of each roll, then cover with sliced tomatoes and sliced hard-cooked eggs. Add pickled vegetables or gherkins, ripe olives, cooked green beans, desalted anchovy fillets and sweet green or red pepper strips according to taste. Sprinkle with olive oil and vinegar, then put the tops on the rolls. Press each sandwich together gently before serving.

Tuna Rolls

Halve 4 long rolls, not cutting all the way through. Butter the cut surfaces and spread a thick layer of mayonnaise over the bottom half of each roll. Drain a 7-oz can of tuna fish and flake it. Divide between the rolls and sprinkle with chopped parsley. Top with sliced hard-cooked eggs and press the sandwiches together gently before serving.

Hot Hors d'Oeuvre

Rice Croquettes

Ingredients: for the risotto, 1½ cups rice ·
¼ chopped onion · 2 tablespoons butter or
margarine · 4 cups stock · 1 egg · 2 tablespoons
grated Parmesan cheese

For the filling: ¼ chopped onion · 2 tablespoons
butter or margarine · 2 tablespoons diced ham ·
1 tablespoon dried mushrooms, softened in water
and sliced · 4 tablespoons chopped veal ·
2 tablespoons chopped chicken giblets · ¼ glass
dry white wine · flour · salt · pepper ·
4 tablespoons diced mozzarella or Bel Paese
cheese (optional) · 1 egg · breadcrumbs · oil

To prepare the risotto sauté the onion in the
butter or margarine until golden, add the rice
and pour in the stock slowly (reserving a little
for the filling). Cook the rice until it is *al dente*
and has absorbed the stock, remove it from
the heat, add the beaten egg and grated cheese,
transfer the mixture to a working surface,
spreading it out, and let cool (step 1).

To prepare the filling sauté the onion in
butter until it is golden, add the ham, mushrooms, veal and giblets and cook the mixture
for a few minutes. Add the wine and continue
cooking until it has evaporated. Sprinkle with
flour, salt and pepper, add some stock and
cook over low heat until the sauce has thickened. Remove from the heat. Put a generous
tablespoon of rice in the palm of the left hand,
make a depression in the center (step 2), and
fill it with some filling and a few pieces of
mozzarella cheese if liked (step 3). Close the
croquette with more rice and pat it into a ball.
Dip the croquettes in flour, in egg beaten with
salt and in breadcrumbs. Fry a few at a time.
Drain and serve immediately garnished with
parsley.

Chicken Croquettes

Chop about 1½ cups cooked and boned chicken
and add diced ham or salami. Prepare
a béchamel sauce (see p.84) and add it to
the meat mixture with 2 tablespoons grated
Parmesan cheese, chopped parsley and 1 egg
yolk. Prepare and cook as above.

Barquettes of Mussels

Ingredients: for the flaky pastry, 6 *tablespoons sifted flour* · *2¼ tablespoons butter or margarine* · *1 tablespoon cold water* · *1 dash of salt (or use frozen puff pastry)*

For the filling: *1 lb mussels* · *¼ glass dry white wine* · *1 slice of onion* · *1 tablespoon butter mixed with ½ tablespoon flour (beurre manié)* · *1 teaspoon chopped parsley* · *1 tablespoon dried mushrooms, softened in water and sliced* · *pepper* · *breadcrumbs* · *butter*

Using two knives or a pastry blender, blend the flour with the butter or margarine, water and salt until it is mealy. Knead the dough for a few moments, shape it into a ball, wrap it in wax paper and let it stand in the refrigerator for ½ hour. Roll out the dough on a floured board and cut out 8 boat-shaped pieces to fit barquette molds. Fill the shells with wax paper and rice or dried beans and bake 'blind' in a hot oven (400°F) for 15 minutes. Meanwhile, wash and scrub the mussels, put them in a deep pan with the wine and chopped onion and cook them on high heat until all the shells have opened. Strain the cooking liquid through a cheesecloth into a pan (step 1), cook over high heat until reduced by ⅔; remove from heat, add beurre manié (step 2) and return to high heat until mixture boils and is thick. Remove from heat, add the parsley, mushrooms, mussels, with shells removed, and pepper. Remove the barquettes from their molds, discard the wax paper and rice and fill them with the mussel mixture (step 3). Sprinkle them with breadcrumbs and melted butter and brown them in a hot oven (400°F) for a few minutes. Serve immediately garnished with sprigs of parsley.

Barquettes of Shrimps

Prepare 8 barquettes as in the basic recipe left. Cook about 24 shrimps in boiling salted water, drain, shell and devein them. Put 3 shrimps in each barquette, cover them with Mornay sauce (see p.85), sprinkle with grated Parmesan cheese and cook in a very hot oven (425°F) for a few minutes or until golden. Serve immediately, garnished with sprigs of parsley.

Barquettes of Mushrooms

Prepare 8 barquettes (see left). Heat a little butter and oil, add a little chopped onion and $\frac{3}{4}$ cup mushrooms and cook them. Add $\frac{1}{2}$ tablespoon flour, stir in $\frac{1}{2}$ glass chicken stock and cook for 10 minutes. Add $\frac{1}{2}$ cup heavy cream, salt and pepper, and bring to a boil. Fill barquettes and cook in a moderate oven (350°F) for 10 minutes.

Chicken Liver Appetizers

Ingredients: for the puff pastry, $\frac{3}{4}$ cup flour · $\frac{1}{4}$ cup water · salt · $3\frac{3}{4}$ tablespoons butter or margarine · 1 egg yolk

For the filling: 2 tablespoons butter or margarine · $1\frac{1}{4}$ cups chicken livers · Marsala · salt · $\frac{1}{2}$ cup heavy cream

Sift the flour onto a pastry board and make a well in the center. Put the water and salt in the well and work the flour quickly into the liquid. Knead the dough for 2–3 minutes, form into a ball, cover with wax paper and refrigerate for a few moments. This first part of the puff pastry is called the *détrempe*. With the fist flatten the ball and place the butter, which must be of the same consistency as the dough, in the middle of it. Fold all sides of the dough over the butter and seal by pressing the edges firmly. Lightly roll out the dough into a long rectangle $\frac{1}{2}$ inch thick. Do not press too hard on the rolling pin and use flour sparingly. Fold the top third of the rectangle over the center and the bottom third over the top. This is known as giving it a 'turn'. Turn the folded dough around, roll it out lightly in a long rectangle and fold in three again. Cover the dough with wax paper, refrigerate for 15 minutes and give it 2 more turns. Cover the dough with wax paper, refrigerate for 30 minutes and give it another 2 turns. Roll out the pastry and cut into 14–16 3-inch rounds with a cookie cutter or glass. Remove the centers from half the rounds so as to have rings. Brush the edges of the rounds with water and place 1 ring on each round. Prick the rounds with a fork and brush with egg yolk. Cook the snacks in a hot oven (400°F) for 15–20 minutes. (The oven temperature must be 400°F. If the oven is too hot or too cold, the puff pastry will not rise.) Meanwhile, melt the butter in a skillet, add the chopped chicken livers (step 1), sprinkle with Marsala and salt and cook for a few minutes. Add the cream (step 2) and continue cooking until the sauce has thickened. If the mixture is not thick enough, add a little beurre manié (see p.100) off the heat, then return to heat and boil 1–2 minutes until thick. Fill the cooked pastries with the mixture (step 3) and serve.

Mushroom Bouchées

Make the pastry as left, then roll out and cut into 2-inch rounds. Press a 1-inch cutter into the center of each round, cutting only about half-way through. Prick, brush with egg yolk and bake as above, allowing about 15 minutes.

For the filling, thinly slice 1 cup button mushrooms and fry in $\frac{1}{4}$ cup butter until golden. Stir in 3 tablespoons flour and cook for 1 minute, then gradually stir in $1\frac{1}{4}$ cups hot milk. Bring to a boil, stirring, and cook until thickened. Stir in 4 tablespoons light cream and salt and pepper to taste. Keep hot.

Cut out the centers from the pastry cases and fill with the mushroom mixture. Serve hot.

Stuffed Croissants

Ingredients: *1 cup sifted flour · 4 tablespoons butter or margarine · 4 tablespoons ricotta or cottage cheese · 2 eggs · salt · 4 tablespoons chopped ham or frankfurters*

In a bowl blend together the flour, butter in little pieces, cheese, 1 egg and salt. Roll out the dough and cut into 4-inch squares (step 1). Put chopped ham or frankfurter on one corner of each square and roll up dough in the shape of a croissant (step 2). Place the croissants on an oiled cookie sheet, brush with 1 beaten egg (step 3) and cook in a hot oven (400°F) for 20 minutes or until golden and crisp; serve immediately.

Allumettes au Paprika

Cook 1 large potato (6 oz) in boiling salted water, peel and work it through a potato ricer. Blend with 4 tablespoons butter, 1 cup sifted flour, $2\frac{1}{2}$ tablespoons grated Parmesan cheese, 1 egg yolk, $\frac{1}{2}$ teaspoon yeast, salt and pepper. Roll out the dough finely and cut in strips. Cover half with strips of Emmenthal; cover these with the remaining strips of dough, sealing edges. Place allumettes on an oiled and floured cookie sheet, brush with the white of 1 egg and sprinkle with paprika. Cook in a hot oven (400°F) for 30 minutes. Serve immediately.

Welsh Rarebit

In a bowl mix 1 tablespoon mustard powder, 1 pinch each of salt and cayenne pepper, $1\frac{1}{2}$ teaspoons Worcestershire, and 1 tablespoon beer. Put in a double boiler 1 lb grated Cheddar-type cheese and 1 tablespoon butter. Stir with a wooden spoon while the cheese begins to melt, and add gradually $\frac{3}{4}$ cup beer opened a few hours before. Add the Worcestershire mixture, and finally 1 whole egg, beating vigorously until all the ingredients are well blended. Serve on hot buttered toast.

Croque-Monsieur

Butter 4 slices of white bread. Place on each slice 1 thin slice of Gruyère cheese, ½ slice cooked ham, another slice Gruyère cheese, and 1 slice of bread. Butter the outsides of the bread. Place on a metal plate or cookie sheet, sprinkle with grated Gruyère cheese, and put in a moderate oven (350°F) until the bread is golden on both sides and the cheese begins to melt. You can also fry the croque-monsieur in butter in a skillet. Serve as an entrée, or, cut in four, as a cocktail appetizer.

Croque-Madame

Proceed exactly as for the croque-monsieur, using cooked white chicken meat, cut into strips, instead of ham.

Golden Rolls

Ingredients: *1 cup sifted flour · 2 eggs ·
1 tablespoon oil · salt*

For the béchamel sauce: *1⅓ tablespoons
butter · 3 tablespoons flour · 1 cup milk · salt ·
nutmeg · 3 oz Gruyère cheese · 1 egg ·
2 tablespoons milk · breadcrumbs ·
oil*

Blend the flour with the eggs, oil and a pinch
of salt and let the mixture stand for a few
moments. Roll out the dough very finely on a
floured board and cut it into about 12 rectangles 4 inches wide by 7 inches long. Make
a béchamel sauce (see p.84) with the butter,
flour, milk, salt and grated nutmeg. Let it cool
and add the Gruyère cheese cut into small
cubes. Shape the cool béchamel sauce into as
many fingers as there are rectangles, and put 1
finger on each rectangle (steps 1 and 2). Roll
up each rectangle, dip it in the egg, beaten
with the milk and a pinch of salt, and in
breadcrumbs. Let the rolls stand for ½ hour,
then fry them in hot deep fat until golden
(step 3).

Drain and serve very hot. Garnish serving
platter with olives.

Artichoke Beignets

Clean and cook artichokes in boiling salted water until they are *al dente*. Quarter them and discard the chokes. Mix olive oil with lemon juice, salt and pepper, and let the artichokes marinate for 35–40 minutes, turning them occasionally. In a bowl whip 2 egg yolks until fluffy, add 10 tablespoons milk, and 1 tablespoon each of melted butter and lemon juice. Sift $\frac{1}{2}$ cup presifted flour with $\frac{1}{2}$ teaspoon salt and add it to the egg mixture. Let it stand for 2 hours and fold in 2 egg whites whipped until stiff. Drain the artichokes and dip them, a few at a time, in the mixture and fry them in hot deep fat until golden. Drain on absorbent paper towels, salt and serve on a heated serving platter.

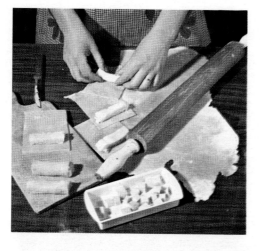

Ham Beignets

In a bowl beat 1 egg yolk with 1 tablespoon melted butter and add $\frac{1}{2}$ cup presifted flour, sifted with a pinch of salt. Add $\frac{2}{3}$ cup beer, opened 1 hour in advance, and blend without beating. Let the mixture stand for about 1 hour or until it has risen, and add 1 egg white, whipped until stiff. Add $\frac{3}{4}$ cup chopped ham, 1 generous tablespoon chopped parsley, a few drops Worcestershire, salt and freshly ground pepper to taste. Drop the mixture by spoonfuls in hot deep fat and fry the beignets until they are golden.

Drain and serve very hot with parsley and lemon quarters.

Cheesy Tapioca Fritters

Peel and finely chop 1 onion. Put into a pan with $\frac{2}{3}$ cup tapioca, 3 cups milk and 1 bay leaf and bring to a boil, stirring. Simmer for about 30 minutes, stirring occasionally, until thick and creamy. Cool slightly, then remove the bay leaf.

Separate 3 eggs and beat the yolks into the tapioca mixture. Stir in $1\frac{1}{2}$ cups shredded cheese, $\frac{1}{2}$ teaspoon dry mustard and salt and pepper to taste. Beat the egg whites until stiff and fold into the mixture. Drop the mixture by spoonfuls into hot deep fat and fry until crisp and golden. Drain and serve hot, garnished with parsley sprigs.

67

Artichoke Hearts

Ingredients: *4 artichoke hearts (fresh or canned) · 4 round bread rolls · butter · 5 slices Emmenthal cheese · 1 egg · 2 tablespoons milk · salt · pepper*

Cook fresh artichokes in boiling salted water and lightly sauté them in butter. Cut the top part from the rolls (step 1), empty them and brush with melted butter. In each cavity place 1 cooked or canned heart (step 2). Mix the Emmenthal, chopped, with the egg, milk, salt and pepper, and spoon the mixture on the artichoke hearts (step 3). Brush with butter and cook in a hot oven (400°F) for about 20 minutes or until golden and crisp. Serve immediately, garnished with sprigs of parsley and slices of frankfurter sausage if liked.

Egg in a Roll

Prepare 4 bread rolls as described in the basic recipe left. Brush them with butter, add 1 slice bacon, cooked, drained and chopped, 1 egg, salt and pepper. Cook the rolls in a hot oven (400°F) until they are crisp and the eggs are cooked. Serve immediately.

Gougère

Bring to a boil 1 cup water with 1 pinch of salt and 1 knob of butter, stirring constantly with a wooden spoon. Add $\frac{5}{8}$ cup sifted flour all at once and continue stirring vigorously until the dough leaves the sides of the pan. Remove from the heat, allow to cool a little then add 3 eggs one by one, mixing well after each addition until paste looks shiny. Add $\frac{1}{3}$ cup grated Gruyère cheese and mix well. Oil a cookie sheet and pour the mixture onto it, shaping in the form of a ring. Sprinkle with 1 tablespoon grated Gruyère cheese, and cook in a very hot oven (450°F) for 20–25 minutes. Serve immediately. Serves 6.

Anchovy Brochettes

Cut 8 slices of white bread and $\frac{1}{2}$ lb Mozzarella or Gouda cheese into small squares of about the same size. Thread alternately on to 4 or 8 skewers and arrange in an ovenproof dish so that each end of each skewer is supported on the rim of the dish. Brush with melted butter and sprinkle with salt and pepper. Cook in a hot oven (400°F) for 15–20 minutes, basting occasionally with melted butter, until golden brown.

Meanwhile, melt 6 tablespoons butter in a saucepan. Mash 16 anchovy fillets and add to the butter with $\frac{1}{2}$ cup milk. Bring to a boil, stirring.

Pour the hot anchovy sauce over the brochettes and serve.

Piedmontese Fondue

Ingredients: *10 oz Italian fontina or Gruyère cheese · 1 cup milk · 3 egg yolks · 1 tablespoon butter · salt · truffle (optional)*

Slice the cheese into a bowl, add $\frac{3}{4}$ of the milk (step 1) and let it stand for 2–3 hours. Pour the mixture in a fondue dish (step 2) or in the top of a double boiler and cook, stirring constantly and always in the same direction, until the cheese is completely melted. Add the egg yolks mixed with remaining milk, warmed, and the butter a little at a time and continue cooking, stirring constantly, until the fondue is smooth and creamy (step 3). Add salt to taste and a few slices of truffle, if liked.

Swiss Fondue

Cut $\frac{1}{2}$ lb each of Swiss Emmenthal and Gruyère cheese into cubes and put the cheese in a fondue dish or in the top of a double boiler, previously rubbed with a cut clove of garlic, with $\frac{1}{2}$ cup Neuchâtel or other dry white wine. Melt the cheese over low heat, stirring constantly and adding another $\frac{1}{2}$ cup white wine a little at a time. As soon as the mixture starts to boil, add 3–4 teaspoons potato flour mixed with 3 tablespoons kirsch (cherry brandy) or brandy. Continue cooking, stirring constantly, until the mixture is smooth, and add salt, pepper and grated nutmeg to taste. Remove the fondue from the heat and put it on a fondue burner or heater in the middle of the dining-room table, adjusting the heat so that it is kept simmering very gently. A little more kirsch can be added if the fondue thickens too much.

Fondue is served with bread cubes or with bread croûtons fried in butter. Each diner impales a bread cube with a long-handled fork, dips it in the fondue, coating the bread completely, lifts it and twists it until it stops dripping, and quickly brings it to his plate. Black tea and a small glass of kirsch or dry white wine are the traditional drinks to serve with the fondue.

Moussaka

Ingredients: *6 large, long eggplants · oil · 4 teaspoons lemon juice · 10 tablespoons hot water · flour · 2 tablespoons butter · ½ lb fresh mushrooms, chopped, or 1 tablespoon dried mushrooms, softened in water · 1 clove of garlic · 3 tablespoons chopped onion · 2 tablespoons chopped parsley · 2 medium tomatoes, peeled, seeded and chopped · ¾ lb cold roast lamb or veal, chopped · 2 or 3 lightly beaten eggs · salt · freshly ground pepper*

For the tomato sauce: 1 clove of garlic · ½ glass olive oil · 1 lb canned peeled tomatoes · basil · salt · pepper

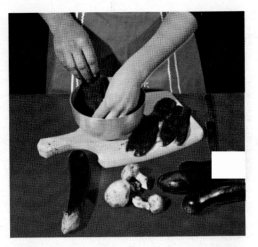

Wash the eggplants and halve 4 of them lengthwise. Using a sharp knife, make incisions in the pulp, being careful not to cut the skin. Heat a little oil in a large saucepan, add the eggplants and cook for 1 minute. Add the lemon juice mixed with the hot water, cover and cook over low heat for 10 minutes. Drain the eggplants, let them cool and remove the pulp with a spoon into a bowl, reserving the skins. Peel and slice the 2 remaining eggplants. Salt the slices, dip them in flour, sauté in a little oil until golden, drain and reserve. Sauté the mushrooms in butter together with the onion and 1 clove of garlic until golden. Discard the garlic and add the mushrooms to the eggplant pulp. Add the parsley, the 2 tomatoes, chopped meat, eggs, salt and pepper, blending all the ingredients well. Oil a large cake mold and line it completely with the eggplant skins, purple side toward the mold, allowing the skins to overlap the sides (step 1). Fill the mold with alternate layers of filling and eggplant slices, beginning and ending with a layer of filling (step 2). Fold the excess skins over the filling, adding aluminum foil to cover the filling completely if the skins are not long enough (step 3). Put the mold in a bain-marie in a moderate (350°F) oven for 65–70 minutes or until cooked through.

Prepare the tomato sauce: sauté 1 clove of garlic in the oil, discard it and add the tomatoes, basil, salt and pepper. Cook the sauce for about 20 minutes, work through a sieve and reheat for a few minutes. Remove the moussaka from the oven, let it stand for 10 minutes and unmold on a warmed serving platter. Serve surrounded by the hot tomato sauce.

Pissaladiera

Ingredients: for the pastry, $\frac{3}{4}$ cup sifted flour ·
$3\frac{1}{2}$ tablespoons butter or margarine · salt ·
$\frac{1}{2}$ glass water

For the filling: $\frac{1}{2}$ lb onions · $2\frac{1}{4}$ tablespoons
butter or margarine · 1 tablespoon cold water ·
salt · pepper · finely chopped garlic and rosemary
to taste · 2 tomatoes · 5 black olives ·
2 cans anchovy fillets

Sauté the sliced onions in the butter or margarine, add the water, salt and pepper, cover and cook over very low heat for 15 minutes. Meanwhile, sift the flour on a board, make a well in the center and add the butter or margarine and salt. Work ingredients with the fingers, add the water and knead the dough with the palm of hand. Form a ball, flatten it out with the palm of the hand and form again. Repeat this 3 times and roll out the pastry very thinly on a floured board. Line a 10-inch pie pan with the dough, crimping the edges (step 1). Add the cooked onions (step 2), and sprinkle with chopped garlic and rosemary. Place 1 tomato slice in the center and surround it with 7 tomato slices (step 3). Place 1 desalted anchovy fillet between each tomato slice and garnish with olives wrapped in desalted anchovy fillets. Dot with remaining butter and sprinkle with salt and pepper. Cook in a hot oven (400°F) for 20–25 minutes or until golden and crisp. Serve immediately.

Pizza with Shellfish

Sift 1 cup presifted flour onto a pastry board and make a well in the center. Dissolve $\frac{1}{3}$ oz yeast and 1 pinch of salt in a little lukewarm water and pour it into the well. Work the flour gradually into the liquid and knead the dough, adding a few more tablespoons water, until it is smooth and light. Shape the dough into a ball, put it in a floured dish, cover with a cloth and let it rise in a warm place for about 3 hours. Scrub and wash 3 lb mussels or clams, and cook over high heat until all the shells have opened. Discard the shells. (The cooking liquid, strained through a cheesecloth, can be used to make a tomato sauce for spaghetti, with the addition of a little minced garlic and parsley.) When the dough has risen, knead for a few minutes on a floured board and roll it out to form a large circle. Lay the dough in a lightly oiled 12-inch pie pan and brush with melted butter. Add $\frac{1}{2}$ lb tomatoes and the shellfish. Season and cook as above.

Pizza with Mozzarella

Sift 2 cups presifted flour onto a pastry board and make a well in the center. Dissolve $\frac{2}{3}$ oz yeast in 1 small glass lukewarm milk and pour it into the well with 2 eggs, 4 tablespoons melted butter and salt. Work the flour gradually into the liquid ingredients and work the dough as above. In a skillet cook 1 onion, thinly sliced, in 2 tablespoons butter until it is transparent but not browned, add 2 lb canned peeled tomatoes, and salt and pepper. Cook the mixture until the liquid has reduced and the sauce has thickened. Slice 2 mozzarella cheeses and chop 2 tablespoons drained, desalted anchovy fillets. When the dough has risen, knead it for a few minutes on a floured board and roll it out to form a large circle, slightly thicker at the edges than in the middle. Lay the dough in a lightly oiled pie pan and cover with the anchovy fillets, sliced mozzarella and tomato sauce. Season and cook as above.

Easter Torte

Ingredients: for the pastry, *3 cups sifted flour ·
2 tablespoons olive oil · 1 cup water · salt*

For the filling: *8 artichokes · juice of 1 lemon ·
¾ cup spinach · salt · 1 clove of garlic ·
2¼ tablespoons butter · chopped parsley · ¾ lb
ricotta or cottage cheese · 2¼ tablespoons grated
Parmesan cheese · 11 eggs · 2 tablespoons
flour · pepper · ⅝ cup butter*

Discard the hard outer leaves of the artichokes,
halve them lengthwise and discard the chokes.
Slice them lengthwise thinly and let the slices
soak in water with lemon juice to prevent
discoloration. Sift the flour on a pastry board
and make a well in the center. Put the oil,
water and salt in the well. Work the flour
gradually into the liquid and knead the dough
for 15 minutes. Cover the dough with a dry
cloth and a wet cloth and let it stand. Wash
the spinach leaves and cook them in a little
water and salt until tender. Drain and chop
them. In a skillet sauté the garlic in the butter,
add the drained artichoke slices and cook over
low heat until they are tender, adding a little
chopped parsley in the last 5 minutes. Remove
the artichokes and leave to cool, add the
spinach leaves to the skillet and cook for a
few minutes. Remove and leave to cool. In a
bowl mix the ricotta cheese with the Parmesan

cheese, 4 eggs, flour, salt and pepper. Add the
cooled spinach and artichokes, discarding the
clove of garlic, and blend all ingredients well.
Divide the dough into 10 equal pieces. Roll out
1 piece as thinly as possible on a floured board,
keeping the other pieces covered so that they
do not dry. Repeat this 3 times and line the
bottom and sides of a cake mold with the
pastry leaves, leaving a generous ½ inch over
the edges (step 1) and brushing each leaf
except the fourth with oil. Add the filling (step
2) and make 7 depressions in it with the bowl
of a spoon. In each depression break 1 egg
(step 3) and season it with 1 teaspoon each of
melted butter and grated Parmesan cheese,
salt and pepper. Roll out the remaining pieces
of dough and cover the filling with pastry
leaves, brushing each one with oil. Cut off
the excess pastry and use it to make a border.
Prick the last leaf with a fork, being careful not
to break the eggs. Cook in a moderate oven
(350°F) for 1 hour or until it is golden. Serve
immediately. Serves 6.

76

Fantasia Torte

Ingredients: *6 eggs · 1 tablespoon flour · a few tablespoons milk · 2 tablespoons grated Parmesan cheese · salt · pepper · ¼ cup fresh or frozen peas · ¼ cup carrots · 1 onion · 2 tablespoons butter or margarine*

Beat the eggs in a bowl with the flour, milk, Parmesan cheese, salt and pepper. Parboil the peas and diced carrots in salted water. Sauté the onion, sliced thinly (step 1), in a little butter until it is golden, add the peas and carrots and cook for a few minutes. Add the vegetable mixture to the beaten eggs (step 2). Melt a knob of butter in a pie dish, add the mixture and cook for about 20 minutes or until the bottom is set (step 3). Bake in a hot oven (400°F) until the torte is golden and completely cooked. Turn out on to a serving platter and serve cold garnished with a little fried onion, if liked.

Artichoke Frittata

Parboil 4–6 artichoke hearts, dice them and sauté in a little butter. Beat 6 eggs in a bowl with salt, pepper and chopped parsley, and add the artichokes. Melt a little butter or margarine in an omelet or frying pan, add the egg mixture and cook on both sides until set.

Onion Frittata

Melt 2 tablespoons butter or margarine in a cast-iron frying pan, add 1½ cups thinly sliced onions and cook over low heat for about 20 minutes. Beat 6 eggs in a bowl with salt and pepper and add the onions. Melt a little butter in the frying pan, add the egg mixture and cook on both sides until set. Turn out on a serving platter and serve immediately.

Spinach Frittata

Beat 8 eggs in a bowl with ¾ cup fresh cooked spinach, chopped, 3 tablespoons grated Parmesan, chopped parsley and salt. Sauté ½ onion in butter in a frying pan until golden, discard onion. Pour the egg mixture in the frying pan and cook over low heat for 8–10 minutes. Turn out onto a serving platter and serve immediately.

Vol-au-vent with Giblets

Ingredients: *12 oz puff pastry (see p.62), or frozen puff pastry · 1 egg yolk · 2¼ tablespoons butter · ¾ cup chicken giblets · ¾ cup sweetbreads · ⅓ cup mushrooms · Marsala · salt · pepper · stock · ½ cup heavy cream · a few spoonfuls béchamel sauce (see p.84)*

Roll out the dough on a floured board and cut out two 10-inch circles (step 1). Remove the center from one circle so as to make a 1-inch wide border. Prick the second circle with a fork (step 2), dampen the edges with water and place the border on them (step 3). Brush the border and the center taken out of the

circle (which will be used as a cover) with egg yolk, and stand both on a dampened cookie sheet. Cook in a hot oven (400°F) for about 20 minutes or until golden. Melt the butter in a pan and add the giblets, sweetbreads and sliced mushrooms. Sauté the mixture for a few minutes, sprinkle with Marsala, salt and pepper and cook for about 20 minutes, adding a little stock if necessary. Add the cream and thicken the mixture with a few spoonfuls of béchamel sauce. Pour the mixture in the vol-au-vent, top with pastry, cover and serve immediately.

Vol-au-vent with Fondue

Prepare the vol-au-vent as in the basic recipe left. Fill it with Piedmontese Fondue (see p.70) and thinly sliced truffles, or with Swiss Fondue (see p.70). Serve very hot

Vol-au-vent with Game

Prepare a vol-au-vent as in the basic recipe left. Work about 1¼ cups roast breast of pheasant or partridge through a sieve, add ¾ cup Maderia sauce (see p.92), ½ small glass Cognac and fill the vol-au-vent.

Crusty Mushroom Bread

Slice the top off a round loaf of bread and scoop out most of the crumb, leaving a shell about ½ inch thick. Spread the inside of the bread shell with softened butter, then bake in a moderate oven (350°F) for 10 minutes.

Meanwhile, finely chop 1 lb mushrooms and fry in ¼ cup butter for 5 minutes. Stir in 3 tablespoons lemon juice, then add to 1 cup béchamel sauce (see p. 84). Separate 2 eggs and beat the yolks into the mushroom sauce. Beat the egg whites until stiff and fold into the mixture.

Pour the mushroom mixture into the bread shell and bake for a further 30 minutes or until well risen and crisp. Serve hot.

Hot Sauces

Bagna Cauda

Ingredients: $\frac{7}{8}$ *cup very fresh butter* · $\frac{3}{4}$ *cup olive oil* · *5–6 cloves of garlic* · *8 anchovy fillets* · *salt* · *white truffle to taste*

Put the butter, cut in little pieces, oil and pressed garlic in a flameproof earthenware casserole. Cook the mixture over low heat, being careful not to let the garlic brown. Add the anchovies, drained, desalted and mashed with a fork (step 1), and continue cooking the mixture, stirring constantly with a wooden spoon. Add salt and sliced truffle to taste, and keep the sauce warm on a burner or heater in the middle of the table (step 2).

Raw vegetables should be dipped in the sauce at table. Vegetables to use are celery hearts cut in pieces (previously washed and trimmed, and kept in cold water mixed with lemon juice), quartered green peppers, sliced Jerusalem artichokes, radishes, cabbage leaves, etc. (step 3).

Anchovy Sauce

For pasta: in a skillet cook 4 tablespoons oil, 1 large clove of garlic, pressed, a little hot red pepper and 2 tablespoons anchovy fillets, desalted and mashed with a fork, over moderate heat. Add $\frac{3}{4}$ lb fresh or canned peeled tomatoes, drained and worked through a food chopper, or 2 tablespoons tomato paste diluted in a little lukewarm water if preferred. Cook the sauce over low heat for about 10 minutes, stirring occasionally, add chopped parsley and pour it over $\frac{3}{4}$ lb spaghetti, cooked in boiling salted water until it is *al dente* and drained.

Salsa Amatriciana

For pasta: sauté $\frac{1}{3}$ cup thick smoked bacon, diced, and a little chopped onion in 2 tablespoons olive oil, until the bacon is transparent. Add $\frac{1}{2}$ lb canned peeled tomatoes, drained and cubed, and salt and pepper, and cook the mixture over high heat for a few minutes, being careful not to let the tomatoes become mushy. Pour the sauce over $\frac{3}{4}$ lb spaghetti, cooked in boiling salted water until it is *al dente* and drained. Sprinkle with grated cheese.

Béchamel Sauce

Ingredients: *2 ¼ tablespoons butter · ¼ cup flour · 2 cups milk · salt · pepper · nutmeg*

Melt the butter over low heat (step 1), blend in the flour (step 2) and cook the mixture for 1 minute. Add the lukewarm milk all at once (step 3), salt, pepper and grated nutmeg, and cook the mixture, stirring constantly, with a wooden spoon or a wire whisk, over low heat for 10 minutes or until the béchamel has thickened. Yield: 2 cups sauce.

Maître d'Hôtel Sauce

For eggs and boiled, fried or grilled fish: blend 4 tablespoons hot water with 1 cup hot béchamel sauce. Add 3–4 tablespoons butter, one at a time, the juice of ½ lemon and 1 tablespoon chopped parsley.

Aurore Sauce

For eggs, vegetables and poultry: add 2 tablespoons tomato sauce and 1 tablespoon butter to 2 cups hot béchamel sauce.

Caper Sauce

For boiled fish: add 3–4 tablespoons capers, coarsely chopped, 1 teaspoon lemon juice and 2 tablespoons fresh butter to 2 cups hot béchamel sauce.

Curry Sauce

For meat, hard-boiled eggs and asparagus: melt 1 teaspoon butter over low heat, add 1 garlic clove, pressed, and 1 teaspoon each of minced shallots, chives or onion and curry powder.

Cook the mixture for 3 minutes, add 1 cup béchamel sauce and bring to a boil.

Mornay Sauce

For pasta, egg, vegetable, fish and poultry gratins: add 1 or 2 egg yolks, beaten with 1 cup cream, to 1 cup béchamel sauce. Bring the mixture to a boil and remove from the heat. Add 2 tablespoons butter and 3 tablespoons grated Gruyère cheese.

Cream Sauce

For eggs, vegetables, fish and poultry: add 1 cup cream and 2 tablespoons fresh butter, a little at a time, to 1 cup hot béchamel sauce.

Soubise Sauce

For eggs, fish, meat, poultry and vegetables: cook $\frac{3}{4}$ cup chopped onion in boiling water for 2–3 minutes, drain and sauté in 1 tablespoon butter until soft but not browned. Add the onion to 2 cups hot béchamel sauce and continue cooking the mixture for 10–12 minutes. Pass the sauce through a sieve, return to the heat and add $\frac{7}{8}$ cup cream, a little at a time, and salt to taste.

White Wine Sauce

For eggs and boiled, fried and grilled fish: add 2–3 egg yolks, one at a time, and 1 tablespoon grated Parmesan cheese alternately with 5 tablespoons dry white wine to 1 cup hot béchamel sauce. Cook over low heat.

Mushroom Sauce

For fish: thinly slice 1 cup button mushrooms and fry in 2 tablespoons butter until golden. Add to 1 cup hot béchamel sauce with 4 tablespoons light cream and 1 teaspoon chopped parsley.

Mustard Sauce

For fish and hard-cooked eggs: add 2 teaspoons prepared mustard and 1 teaspoon vinegar to 1 cup hot béchamel sauce.

Hollandaise Sauce

Ingredients: *⅝ cup butter · 3 egg yolks ·*
1½ tablespoons lemon juice · salt · pepper

Cut the butter in little pieces. Put 1 piece of
butter in the top of a double boiler or in a
bain-marie with the egg yolks and lemon juice.
Stirring constantly with a wire whisk, cook
the mixture over low heat until the butter has
melted. Add the remaining butter, one piece at
a time (step 1), and continue cooking, stirring
constantly, until each piece of butter is
incorporated into the sauce (step 2). The
water of the bain-marie must not boil and the
stirring must be constant. When the sauce
has the consistency of a mayonnaise, add salt

and pepper and strain it through a sieve (step
3). If the sauce does not thicken, add 1 or 2
tablespoons cold water. Keep the sauce in the
bain-marie until serving time without stirring
it again. Hollandaise sauce is used for eggs,
vegetables, fish and shellfish. Yield: 1 cup.

Béarnaise Sauce

For grilled meat and fish: add 1 teaspoon
onion sauce, 1 pinch of tarragon and minced
parsley and 1 tablespoon vinegar (preferably
tarragon vinegar) to 1 cup hot Hollandaise
sauce.

Choron Sauce

For tournedos and grilled steak: add 2 tablespoons tomato sauce to 1 cup hot Béarnaise sauce.

Foyot Sauce

For tournedos and grilled steak: mix 1 tablespoon meat extract with 1 tablespoon stock, and add the mixture, a little at a time, to 1 cup hot Béarnaise sauce. Mix very gently and serve the sauce immediately.

Tomato Hollandaise

For cold pork, fish and game: stirring constantly, add 2 tablespoons tomato purée or 1 tablespoon tomato paste to 1 cup hot Hollandaise sauce. Blend in 1 teaspoon finely chopped parsley and cayenne pepper to taste.

Mustard Hollandaise

For eggs, fish, shellfish, chicken and vegetables: add ½ tablespoon English powdered mustard, mixed with 1 tablespoon water, to 1 cup hot Hollandaise sauce just before serving.

Maltese Sauce

For boiled asparagus and grilled fish: add 2–3 tablespoons orange juice and a little grated orange peel to 1 cup Hollandaise sauce. A little Curaçao may be added.

Mousseline Sauce

For fish: add 2 tablespoons whipped cream to 1 cup Hollandaise sauce just before serving.

Hollandaise Noisette

For fish and steaks: heat the butter for Hollandaise sauce till golden, then cool before stirring into the egg yolk and lemon juice mixture.

Tomato Sauce

Ingredients: *2 lb fresh tomatoes or 1 lb canned peeled tomatoes · 2 tablespoons butter or margarine · ¼ cup diced Italian prosciutto or bacon (optional) · 1 celery stalk · 1 carrot · ½ onion · basil leaves · salt · pepper*

Dip the tomatoes in boiling water, drain them, peel them and remove the seeds. Melt the butter over moderate heat, add the prosciutto, celery, carrot and chopped onion (steps 1 and 2), and cook the mixture for a few minutes. Add the tomatoes, cut into chunks (step 3), basil, salt and pepper, and cook the mixture over a moderate heat for 35–45 minutes (a little less if using canned tomatoes), stirring occasionally. The sauce can be served like this for pasta, gnocchi or rice or it may be sieved.

Bolognese Sauce

For pasta: in a skillet lightly sauté 2 tablespoons diced bacon in 2 tablespoons butter or margarine, add 1 carrot, ½ onion and 1 celery stick, all chopped, and cook the mixture until it starts to turn golden. Add ¾ cup chopped beef and some dried mushrooms, softened in water and chopped, and stir the mixture until the meat has whitened. Add ½ glass dry red or white wine and let it evaporate. Stir in 2–3 tablespoons tomato sauce, thinned with a little warm water, salt, pepper and grated nutmeg. Cook the sauce, covered, over low heat for 2–3 hours, adding a little hot water occasionally.

A little milk may be added during the last 15 minutes if liked.

Tomato Mushroom Sauce

For rice and pasta: in a heavy pan heat $2\frac{1}{2}$ tablespoons butter or margarine, add 1 clove of garlic, sauté it for a few minutes and discard it. Add $\frac{1}{4}$ cup diced ham, 1 tablespoon dried mushrooms, softened in lukewarm water, drained and sliced, 2 tablespoons tomato sauce, thinned with a little stock, or $\frac{3}{4}$ lb canned peeled tomatoes, worked through a sieve, and salt and pepper. Cook the sauce over low heat for 30–35 minutes or until it has thickened.

Tomato Clam Sauce

For spaghetti: cook $1\frac{1}{2}$ lb clams in 1 tablespoon oil over high heat until the shells open. Drain, shell and reserve them. Strain the cooking liquid through a fine cloth and reserve. Sauté 1 clove of garlic, pressed, in 4 tablespoons olive oil and discard it. Add $\frac{3}{4}$ lb canned peeled tomatoes, drained and coarsely chopped, salt and a generous amount of freshly ground pepper. Cook the mixture over high heat for about 15 minutes, add the clams and a little of the cooking liquid, and continue cooking the sauce for 5 minutes. Pour over $\frac{3}{4}$ lb spaghetti, cooked in boiling salted water until it is *al dente* and drained, and sprinkle with parsley.

Fresh Tomato Sauce

Dip $1\frac{1}{4}$ lb Italian plum tomatoes in boiling water, then drain them, peel and remove the seeds. Put the tomatoes in a blender with 1 garlic clove, 12 fresh basil leaves or $\frac{1}{2}$ teaspoon dried basil and salt and pepper to taste. Process until smooth. Leave for at least 10 minutes, then stir in 5 tablespoons olive oil.

Espagnole Sauce

Ingredients: *¼ cup chopped salt pork ·
1 carrot · 1 onion · 2−3 slices dried mushroom
(optional) · 3½ tablespoons flour · 8 cups
meat stock · 1 celery stalk · parsley ·
½ bay leaf · thyme leaves · garlic · ½ clove*

Heat the salt pork in a large pan, add the
carrot and onion, both coarsely chopped (steps
1 and 2), and the mushroom slices if using,
softened in water and drained, and sauté the
mixture for a few minutes. Add the flour (step
3), and cook the mixture, stirring constantly,
until it is golden and the vegetables have
thickened. Add 3 cups stock, the celery, parsley,
bay leaf, thyme, clove of garlic and cook the
sauce, stirring occasionally, until it has
thickened. Add another 3 cups stock and cook
the sauce over very low heat, stirring occasionally, for 1−1½ hours or until reduced to 3
cups.

If necessary, skim the sauce. Strain (step 4),
add the rest of the stock and cook until reduced
to 4 cups.

If the sauce is not to be used right away, let
it cool, stirring occasionally, pour it in a
sterilized jar and seal immediately. Keep the
jar in the refrigerator. If the sauce is to be kept
for more than 1 week, reheat and pour in a
newly sterilized jar. Seal immediately.

Genevoise Sauce

For salmon and trout: cook $\frac{1}{4}$ cup chopped onion, $\frac{1}{4}$ cup chopped carrot, $\frac{1}{2}$ bay leaf, a dash of thyme and 3 parsley sprigs in 1 tablespoon butter over low heat for 15 minutes. Add about $\frac{3}{4}$ lb fish heads and bones and cook the mixture over very low heat for 10–15 minutes. Add 2 cups good red wine and reduce it, over medium heat, by half. Stir in 1 cup Espagnole sauce and continue cooking the mixture over low heat for 45 minutes, adding a little fish stock if necessary. Strain the sauce through a fine sieve and blend in 1 teaspoon anchovy paste and $2\frac{1}{4}$ tablespoons butter. If little time is available, the Espagnole sauce may be substituted by 1 tablespoon flour blended with 1 tablespoon softened butter, to be added to the sauce before the wine.

Pepper Sauce

For marinated meat and game: sauté $\frac{1}{4}$ cup each of carrot and onion, both chopped with a little parsley, bay leaf and thyme, in 4 tablespoons oil for a few minutes. Drain the oil and add 6 tablespoons each of vinegar and dry white wine and cook the mixture, stirring constantly, over high heat until it has reduced by $\frac{1}{2}$. Add 2 cups Espagnole sauce and continue cooking the sauce over low heat for 30–35 minutes. Add 6 peppercorns, pounded in a mortar, and continue cooking the sauce for 10 minutes. Strain and reheat.

Neapolitan Sauce

For fish: add 1 tablespoon each of grated horseradish and diced lean cooked ham to 1 cup Espagnole sauce. Stir in 4 tablespoons each Madeira and beef broth and add a bouquet garni. Bring to a boil and simmer for 30 minutes. Strain and add 2 tablespoons currant jelly.

Demi-glace Sauce

Ingredients: *2 cups Espagnole sauce (see p.90)*
1 teaspoon meat extract · 2 tablespoons dry
Madeira or other similar wine

Reduce the Espagnole sauce by half over
moderate heat (step 1) and add the meat
extract. Remove the sauce from the heat and
stir in the wine (step 2). To make more sauce,
add ½ cup wine for every 4 cups sauce.

Madeira Sauce

For beef, veal and chicken: cook 2 cups demi-
glace sauce over low heat until reduced by ½.
Add 3–4 tablespoons Madeira and reheat the
sauce slowly without letting it boil.

To make Périgueux sauce, remove the sauce
from the heat, add a little thinly sliced truffle
and 1 tablespoon butter, and serve with game
or guinea-fowl.

Devil Sauce

For roast poultry and pigeon: cook 2 chopped shallots (or 1 tablespoon chopped onion) and 6 peppercorns, pounded in a mortar, in 9 tablespoons dry white wine until reduced by $\frac{2}{3}$. Add 1 cup demi-glace sauce and boil the mixture for a few minutes. Work the sauce through a sieve. Add 1 teaspoon each of Worcestershire and chopped parsley, reheat the sauce, if necessary, and remove it from the heat. Blend in 1 tablespoon butter before serving.

Bordelaise Sauce

For grilled meat: cook 1 shallot, $\frac{1}{2}$ bay leaf, 2 thyme leaves and 1 cup good red wine until it is reduced by $\frac{3}{4}$. Add 1 cup demi-glace sauce and continue cooking the mixture over low heat, stirring occasionally, for 8–10 minutes. Slice or cube $\frac{1}{4}$ cup beef marrow, cook it in boiling water for 1–2 minutes and drain it. Pass the sauce through a sieve, add the beef marrow and $\frac{1}{2}$ teaspoon chopped parsley.

Chasseur Sauce

For game, meat and chicken: sauté $\frac{1}{3}$ cup fresh mushrooms in 1 tablespoon butter, add 1 teaspoon finely minced onion and cook the mixture for a few minutes. Add 8 tablespoons dry white wine and cook it until it is reduced by half. Add 1 tablespoon tomato sauce and 1 cup demi-glace sauce and boil the mixture for 2 minutes. Remove from the heat and blend in 1 tablespoon butter and parsley.

Port Sauce

For roast game, duck or beef: add $\frac{3}{4}$ cup port and the juice of $\frac{1}{2}$ orange to 1 cup demi-glace sauce. Simmer for 10 minutes, then strain and stir in 3 tablespoons light cream.

Robert Sauce

For broiled meats: peel and finely chop 1 onion and cook in $\frac{1}{4}$ cup butter until transparent. Add 6 tablespoons dry white wine and 1 cup demi-glace sauce and boil until reduced by $\frac{1}{3}$. Stir in 2 teaspoons prepared mustard. Strain and serve hot.

Charcutière Sauce

For fried or broiled pork: peel and finely chop 1 onion and cook in 2 tablespoons butter until transparent. Add 1 tablespoon wine vinegar and 1 cup demi-glace sauce with 2 tablespoons shredded gherkins.

Velouté Sauce

Ingredients: *1½ tablespoons butter · 2 table-spoons flour · 2 cups veal stock · a few sprigs of parsley (optional) · salt · pepper · nutmeg · 1 tablespoon butter*

Melt the butter in a saucepan, add the flour and cook it for a few minutes. Stir in the stock and bring the mixture to a boil, stirring constantly. Add the parsley, salt, pepper and nutmeg and cook the sauce over low heat for 20 minutes, stirring occasionally. Discard the parsley, strain the sauce through a sieve into a bowl and pour 1 tablespoon melted butter on top to prevent a skin forming. Chicken or fish stock can also be used. Yield: 2 cups.

Parisian Sauce

In a heavy saucepan mix 1 egg yolk with ¼ cup mushroom water (1 tablespoon dried mushrooms softened in water, cooked in 1 cup water and reduced to ¼ cup) and ½ cup cold chicken stock. Stir in 1 cup velouté sauce, a dash of nutmeg and a dash of freshly ground pepper. Cook the mixture, stirring occasionally, over high heat for 25–30 minutes or until it coats a wooden spoon. Strain the sauce through a fine sieve into a bowl and float 1 tablespoon melted butter. Keep the sauce in a bain-marie until serving time and add 2 tablespoons cream or 1 tablespoon fresh butter and a few drops of lemon juice just before serving. Yield: 1 cup.

Suprême Sauce

Cook 2 cups chicken stock with 3 slices dried mushrooms, softened in water and drained, over high heat until reduced by $\frac{2}{3}$. Discard the mushrooms, add 1 cup velouté sauce and bring the mixture to a boil. Cook the sauce, adding $\frac{1}{2}$ cup cream, a little at a time, for 45–50 minutes or until it is reduced to 1 cup and coats a wooden spoon. Strain the sauce through a sieve and add 1 tablespoon butter just before serving. Yield: 1 cup.

White Chaud-Froid Sauce

For eggs, chicken and galantines: prepare $\frac{1}{4}$ oz gelatin according to the instructions (step 1). Bring 1 cup velouté sauce to a boil and cook for a few minutes. Add the cool but still liquid gelatin (step 2) and $\frac{1}{2}$ cup cream (step 3), a little at a time, and continue cooking the mixture, stirring occasionally, for 45 minutes or until it coats a wooden spoon. Strain the sauce through a cheesecloth and let it cool, stirring occasionally. Yield: 1 cup.

Thin Chaud-Froid Sauce

For fish and shellfish: prepare chaud-froid sauce with velouté sauce made with fish stock.

Andalouse Sauce

For eggs, fish and poultry: add 2 tablespoons tomato paste, 1 teaspoon sugar, 1 tablespoon chopped parsley and 1 diced canned pimiento to 1 cup velouté sauce.

Royale Sauce

For eggs and poultry: add 4 tablespoons light cream, $\frac{1}{4}$ cup butter, 1 tablespoon chopped truffle and 2 tablespoons sherry to 1 cup velouté sauce.

Cold Sauces

Pesto alla Genovese

Ingredients: *2 big handfuls fresh basil leaves · 2 cloves of garlic (or less if desired) · 1–2 tablespoons pine nuts · 1 tablespoon each of grated Parmesan and pecorino cheese, or 2 tablespoons grated Parmesan cheese · butter · oil · salt*

Wash and dry the basil leaves and pound them in a mortar with the garlic and pine nuts (step 1). Add the cheese and continue pounding until all the ingredients are mixed. Add a little butter and enough oil, a little at a time (step 2), to make a thick sauce. Before pouring it on pasta, add salt and a little cooking water from the pasta (step 3).

Italian Green Sauce

For boiled meat and fish and eggs: wash, dry and chop 1 big bunch of parsley. Pound it in a mortar with the yolk of 1 hard-boiled egg, 2 drained and desalted anchovy fillets, a few capers, 2 gherkins, $\frac{1}{2}$ clove of garlic, and 1 slice of onion. Transfer the mixture to a large bowl and thin it with a few tablespoons oil and vinegar. Add salt and pepper to taste. The egg yolk may be substituted by white bread, soaked in vinegar and squeezed dry, or a small potato, boiled and cooled. This sauce may also be prepared in an electric blender.

Green Pepper Sauce

For boiled meat and fish and eggs: wash 2 lb green peppers, remove the stems, seeds and white membranes. Chop them finely with 1 big bunch washed and dried parsley. Put the mixture in an enamel or stainless steel pan with 1 cup wine vinegar and 2 tablespoons tomato sauce and cook over moderate heat for 45 minutes or until all the ingredients are well mixed. Remove the sauce from the heat, let it cool and thin with olive oil. To keep the sauce for a few days, pour it into a jar, float a layer of oil on top and seal the jar tightly.

Mint Sauce

For hot and cold roast lamb and boiled zucchini: in a bowl blend together about 2 tablespoons chopped mint leaves, 1–2 tablespoons sugar, a pinch each of salt and pepper and 1 cup good vinegar, boiling hot. Mix well and let cool. Chill before serving.

Mayonnaise

Ingredients: *2 egg yolks at room temperature ·*
½ teaspoon salt · dash of pepper · the juice of 1
lemon, or 2–3 tablespoons vinegar · 1½ cups
oil

Put the egg yolks, salt, pepper and a few drops
of lemon juice or vinegar in a bowl (step 1).
Stirring slowly with a wooden spoon and then
faster, add the oil drop by drop and then in a
thin stream as the mayonnaise thickens,
alternating with the remaining lemon juice
(steps 2 and 3). If the mayonnaise turns or
curdles, put 1 egg yolk in a clean bowl and
add, stirring constantly, the turned mayonnaise
drop by drop at first and then in small
amounts. Yield: 1 cup.

Mayonnaise can also be made in an electric
blender or bought commercially.

To make a successful mayonnaise all
ingredients must be at room temperature, the
oil must be added very slowly at first and
stirring must be done in the same direction.

Aïoli Mayonnaise

For snails, cod, and vegetables: pound 4 garlic
cloves in a mortar. Put the garlic, 1 egg yolk, a
little salt and a small boiled potato in a bowl.
Stirring constantly with a wooden spoon, add
¾ cup oil drop by drop and then in a thin
stream until the mayonnaise has thickened.

Tuna Mayonnaise

For boiled meat, poultry, and eggs: work ¾ cup
tuna fish in olive oil, 2 anchovy fillets, desalted,

98

and a few capers through a sieve. Blend the
mixture into 1 cup mayonnaise. If the sauce
is too thick, thin it with a few tablespoons
cold stock and add a few drops of lemon juice
to taste.

Rémoulade Sauce

For boiled and grilled meat and fish: add 2–3
gherkins and 2 tablespoons capers, both
chopped and dried with a clean cloth, 1
tablespoon mustard and 1 tablespoon chervil,
tarragon and parsley, all chopped together, to
1 cup mayonnaise. If the sauce is too thick,
thin with lemon juice.

Tartare Mayonnaise

For eggs, fish and meat: add 1 tablespoon each
of chopped green olives, gherkins, parsley,
shallots or chives and tarragon, 1 teaspoon
mustard, a dash each of salt and freshly
ground pepper to 1 cup mayonnaise and mix
well.

Aspic Mayonnaise

For salads and to cover a variety of dishes:
prepare a mayonnaise following the basic
recipe left. Soften about $\frac{1}{4}$ oz gelatin in a little
warm water or in meat or fish stock and
let it cool. Blend the cool but still liquid
gelatin into the mayonnaise, a little at a time.
Use the aspic mayonnaise immediately (before
it sets) to cover hard- or soft-boiled eggs, fish,
boiled chicken, etc. If a firmer mayonnaise is
desired, add more gelatin.

Chantilly Mayonnaise

For asparagus and other cold boiled vegetables:
fold 3–4 tablespoons whipped cream into
1 cup mayonnaise. If a lighter sauce is preferred,
add the white of 1 egg, beaten until stiff.

Cocktail Sauce

For shellfish cocktail: add 3 tablespoons
tomato ketchup, 1 teaspoon Worcestershire,
1 teaspoon brandy or gin, 2–3 tablespoons
heavy or whipped cream, salt and paprika to
1 cup mayonnaise.

Hot and Cold Savory Butters

Very fresh butter, kept at room temperature, must be used to make these various butters, particularly the cold ones. Margarine also gives very good results.

Shrimp Butter

For various dishes: work 4 tablespoons salted butter in a bowl until it is creamy. Pound 15 shrimps, cooked in boiling salted water for a few minutes, drained, shelled and deveined, in a mortar and add them to the butter. Work the mixture through a very fine sieve (steps 1, 2 and 3).

Anchovy Butter

In a bowl beat 4 tablespoons butter with 2 tablespoons anchovy paste or 3–4 anchovy fillets, drained, desalted and mashed to a paste, until it is light and foamy. Work the mixture through a fine sieve.

Garlic Butter

For steak and other dishes: peel 5 cloves of garlic, scald them in boiling water for a few minutes, dry them and pound them in a mortar. Add them to 4 tablespoons butter, beat until light and foamy and sieve.

Beurre Manié

To bind sauces: make a paste of equal amounts of butter and flour and add it a little at a time to bind the sauce.

Clarified Butter

For sauces and fine pastry: melt the necessary quantity of butter in a bowl in a bain-marie. Carefully pour the clear fat through a cheesecloth placed in a fine sieve, (leaving the milky sediment caught in the cloth).

Maître d'Hôtel Butter

For grilled fish, poultry, and meat: beat 4 tablespoons butter in a bowl with $\frac{1}{2}$ tablespoon chopped parsley, 1 tablespoon lemon juice, and salt and pepper until light and foamy.

Beurre Meunière

For fish: melt 4 tablespoons butter and add a little lemon juice, chopped parsley, salt and pepper.

Paprika Butter

For cold hors d'oeuvres, canapés, grilled fish and poultry: blend 4 tablespoons butter with 2 teaspoons paprika. Or cook 1 tablespoon butter with 2 teaspoons paprika and 2 teaspoons finely chopped onion over low heat for a few minutes. Strain the butter through a fine sieve, let it cool and blend it well with $2\frac{1}{2}$ tablespoons salted butter.

Horseradish Butter

For various dishes: pound 5 teaspoons fresh grated horseradish in a mortar and blend it with 4 tablespoons butter. Sieve.

Green Butter

For garnish and for fish: in a small saucepan put 12 spinach leaves, chopped, 2 tablespoons chopped parsley and 2 teaspoons chopped tarragon, add water just to cover and cook the mixture over high heat for 5 minutes. Drain, dry, sieve. Blend with 4 tablespoons butter and sieve again.

Marinades

Uncooked Marinade

Ingredients for about 2 lb red or white meat, poultry or game: *1 onion · 1 shallot · 1 carrot · 1 celery stalk · 1 clove of garlic · 4 sprigs of parsley · thyme · 1 bay leaf · 3 juniper berries · 2 cloves · 6 peppercorns · salt · ½ cup vinegar · 3 cups dry white wine · ¾ cup olive oil*

Slice the onion, shallot, carrot and celery finely, press the garlic, chop the parsley and thyme and crush the bay leaf, juniper berries, cloves and peppercorns (step 1). Put half the ingredients in a high-sided bowl, add the meat (step 2), and cover with remaining dry ingredients. Add salt, pour in the vinegar (step 3), the wine and finally the oil, which must always be added to prevent the meat from darkening.

Keep the bowl in a cool place for 2–3 days, or less if the piece of meat is small, turning the meat occasionally. Drain the meat and dry with a clean cloth. The marinade should then be used in the cooking and to make a sauce to go with the meal.

There are three kinds of marinades: uncooked marinades, cooked marinades and quick marinades. The marinade is used first to soften the meat and then to impregnate it with flavor. It is then always used in the accompanying sauce.

Meats should usually be marinated for about 48 hours.

Cooked Marinade

For about 2 lb red or white meat, poultry or game: in a heavy pan sauté 1 onion, 1 shallot, 1 carrot, and 1 celery stalk, all finely sliced, and 1 pressed clove of garlic in 1 cup olive oil for a few minutes, and stir in 4 cups dry white wine and 1 cup vinegar. Add chopped parsley and thyme, 1 crushed bay leaf, salt and 6 crushed peppercorns, bring the mixture to a boil and cook over low heat for 30–35 minutes.

Let the marinade cool, pour it over the meat and let it stand in a cool place for 24–36 hours, turning the meat occasionally. If you have only a very little time, cube the meat, add the boiling marinade to it, and let it stand for about 5 hours.

Uncooked Marinade for Fish

For about 1 lb fish: pour 1 cup dry white or red wine (depending upon the recipe to be followed) in a deep platter. Blend in 1 tablespoon each of olive oil and vinegar, 1 carrot and 1 lemon, both finely sliced, 2 sprigs of parsley a few thyme leaves, 1 bay leaf, 2 cloves, 8 crushed peppercorns and salt. Add the fish and let it stand in a cool place for a few hours, turning it occasionally.

Drain the fish and dry with a clean cloth before cooking.

Quick Marinade

For pâtés: this mixture is used to marinate the game or other meats that go into the making of a pâté.

It is made of Cognac, pepper, bay leaf, nutmeg and thyme.

Savory Jellies

Jellied Stock or Aspic

Ingredients: 2 calves' feet, cracked (about 4 lb ·
1 lb veal knuckle, cracked · ¼ lb fresh or salt
pork rind · ¼ cup onion · ¼ cup carrot ·
1 tablespoon celery · bouquet garni made of
parsley, bay leaves and thyme · salt · pepper ·
12 cups cold water · ¼ cup chopped beef ·
2 egg whites

Put the feet, knuckles, salt pork, onion, carrot,
celery, bouquet garni, salt, pepper and water
in a large pan (step 1). Bring the mixture
slowly to a boil, skim for about 5 minutes
or until there is no scum left and cook for
about 3½ hours or until the stock has reduced
to 6 cups. Strain the stock into a bowl, let
it cool and remove the fat completely (step 2).
A perfect jellied stock must be transparent,
brilliant and light amber in colour. To achieve
this the stock must be clarified in the following
manner: transfer the stock into a pan, add
the chopped beef and the egg whites and
whip the mixture gently with a wire whisk
(step 3). Bring the mixture to a boil and cook
it over moderate heat, stirring with a wooden
spoon, for 15 minutes. As the egg whites cook,
they will come up to the surface taking with
them all the particles in the stock. Strain the
stock through a fine sieve covered with a thin
cloth dipped in lukewarm water and wrung
out . The stock is now ready for use.
Yield: 4 cups.

Jellied Fish Stock

Put 1 lb fish, cut into cubes (including the
heads, mashed bones, etc.), ¼ cup sliced onion,
1 sprig of parsley and 1 bay leaf, salt and a
few peppercorns in a large pan. Add 8 cups
water, bring to a boil and cook for about 40
minutes. Proceed as for the basic recipe. To
clarify the stock, add ½ cup cod or other white
fish, chopped, and 1 egg white. In this case, add
¼ oz powdered gelatin, softened in cold water.
Yield: 4 cups.

Herb and Spice Chart

HERBS AND SPICES	Meat	Fish	Poultry and Game	Soup	Vegetables	Salads and Dressings	Cheese	Eggs	Sauces	Preserves	Cakes and Pies
ALLSPICE	•	•		•	•				•	•	•
BASIL	••	•		••	•	•		•	•		
BAY	••	••	•	•••					••		
CAYENNE	•	•	•	•					•		
CHERVIL	•	•	•	•	•	••	•	•	•		
CHILLI	•		•		•				•	•	
CHIVES	•	•	•	•	•	•••	•	•	•		
CINNAMON	•				•			•		•	••
CLOVES	•		•	•	•				•	•	•
DILL	•	••	•	•	•	••		•	•	•	•
GARLIC	••	•	•	••	•	•	•		••		
JUNIPER			•		•						
MACE	•	•		•	•		•		•	•	•
MARJORAM	•	•	•	•	•	•	•	•	•	•	
MINT	•		•		•	•			•		
MUSTARD	•	•	•	•	•	••	•	•	•	•	
NUTMEG	•	•			•			•	•		
OREGANO	•	••	•	•	••	•	•	•	•		
PAPRIKA	•	•	•	•	•	•	•	•	•		
PARSLEY	••	••	••	•••	•	••	•	••	••		
PEPPER	••	••	••	•	••	••	•	•	••	••	
ROSEMARY	•	•	•	•	•		•			•	
SAFFRON	•	•	•	•	•	•	•	•		•	
SAGE	•		•	•			•				
TARRAGON	•	••	••		–				•	•	
THYME	•	•	•		•	•	•	•			
TURMERIC	•	•			•			•	•	•	•

* Indicates type of food with which herb or spice is best used.

Catering Quantities

Family Catering

(Approximate quantities per person per meal)

Meat

with bone	4–6 oz
boneless	3–4 oz
for made-up dishes	2–3 oz

Poultry and game

Chicken:

spring, broiler or poussin	1 bird for 2 portions
roaster or boiler	½ lb (250 g) per portion drawn weight (250 g)
Duck and duckling	¾ lb drawn weight for birds under 3½ lb (2 kg)
	½ lb (250 g) per portion birds over 3½ lb (2–3 kg)
Turkey	½ lb (250 g) drawn weight
Pheasant	1 bird for 2–4 portions;

Fish

with a lot of bone	6–7 oz
filleted	3–4 oz
for made-up dishes	2–3 oz

Vegetables (weight unprepared)

Broad beans	8–12 oz
Butter beans	2 oz
Haricot beans	2 oz
Runnerbeans	6 oz
Beet (beetroot)	4–6 oz
Brussels sprouts	6 oz
Cabbage	8 oz
Carrots	4–6 oz
Celeriac	4–6 oz
Celery	¼ of a large head
Curly kale	6–8 oz
Greens (spring)	8 oz
Onions (served alone)	6 oz
Parsnips	6 oz
Peas	8 oz
Potatoes	6–8 oz
Rutabaga	8 oz
Sea kale	4 oz
Spinach	8–12 oz
Turnips	8 oz

Cereals

Rice or pasta	1–1½ oz

Soup	½–¾ cup

Sauces and Gravies	¼ cup

Party Catering

Sandwiches

2 lb loaf gives 20–24 slices, using ¼ lb butter. Allow 1 round of sandwiches (4 quarters) per person.

Sandwich fillings

For a 2 lb loaf allow one of the following: 1 lb tomatoes, 1 cucumber, 12 oz cooked and sliced ham, 3 cans sardines, or 3 scrambled eggs.

Cold meat, poultry, etc.

Sliced and without bone – 2 oz per person.

Turkey

14 lb turkey will serve about 25 people (cold with salads).

Lobster

A good sized lobster gives 3–5 portions (cold with salads).

Sausage rolls

1½ lb pastry (i.e. made with 1½ lb flour, etc.), and 2 lb sausages give about 50 small rolls.

Vol-au-vents

1½ lb puff pastry makes about 75 small vol-au-vent cases.

Lettuce

1 large lettuce serves 6–8 people.

Tea

For 100 people allow about 5 gallons of tea, using 3 oz tea per gallon of water. Allow 6–8 pints milk, 2 lb sugar.

Coffee

For 100 people allow about 4 gallons. Use 3 gallons water and 1 gallon milk. The quantity of coffee depends very much on variety, but if using instant coffee 2–3 oz per gallon should be about right.

Wine

1 bottle gives 6 glasses (3¾ fl oz).

Champagne

1 bottle gives 5 glasses.

Sherry

1 bottle gives 16 glasses (2½ fl oz).

Spirits

1 quart or liter bottle gives from 20–32 single measures according to desired amount.

Garnishes

A garnish improves both the look and the flavor of a dish. It must always be edible and may either be very simple, such as chopped herbs scattered over before serving, or something more elaborate such as the following:

Croûtons Small fancy shapes of bread (toasted or fried) or potato (fried). The most common shape is a simple cube, about $\frac{1}{4}$–$\frac{1}{2}$ inch thick, but the croûtons may be triangles, crescents or more elaborate shapes cut with a cookie cutter. Scatter on top of soup, or use slightly larger croûtons with meat dishes.

Cheese croûtes Slightly larger croûtons of bread may be scattered with grated cheese and baked in a moderate oven. Float on top of a thick vegetable soup, or overlap round the edge of a savory dish.

Fleurons Puff pastry makes an attractive garnish for meat and poultry dishes if rolled out to about $\frac{1}{4}$ inch thick and cut into small fancy shapes, a crescent being the traditional one. Place the pastry shapes on a baking sheet, brush the tops lightly with beaten egg to glaze them and bake in a hot oven for about 10 minutes, until risen and golden brown.

Crumbs Breadcrumbs are used in several forms as garnishes. They can be freshly grated, in which case they give a lightly colored, softish topping or coating. Dried crumbs give a darker, drier finish.

To make dried crumbs, spread the fresh crumbs on baking sheets and dry in a very low oven or some other warm place; work them in the blender or rub them through a sieve to make them an even size and store when cool in an airtight jar.

To make buttered crumbs, melt 1 tablespoon butter and add 2 cups fresh white crumbs. Allow the crumbs to absorb the fat, turning the mixture occasionally with a fork, then spread them out on baking sheets (as for dried crumbs) and dry them in a low oven. These can be stored as for dried crumbs and used for gratin dishes.

Vegetable Shapes

Most root vegetables can be sliced and cut into fancy shapes with a cookie cutter. Beetroot and carrot make the most colorful garnishes. Potato, parsnip etc should be sautéed.

Julienne strips Cut thin strips of raw vegetable, about $1\frac{1}{4}$–$1\frac{1}{2}$ inches long, by about $\frac{1}{8}$ inch thick. Cook lightly if required, or use raw.

Turned mushrooms Cut tiny triangular fillets from the edges of the caps of button mushrooms to notch them all the way round, and then sauté the caps in butter.

Crimped cucumber Cucumber and other vegetables with a dark skin and light flesh can be prepared this way. Run the prongs of a fork down the whole vegetable, to remove strips of skin. Repeat all the way round. Then cut the cucumber into slices a little thicker than normal, so that the remaining strips of dark skin show.

Gherkin fans These make an ideal garnish for a mixed hors d'oeuvre tray. Slice the gherkin lengthwise almost to the base but without cutting through, then open out the slices into a fan.

Radish roses Cut a narrow slice from the root end of each radish, then cut thin petals from stem to root. Drop the radishes into ice water until the petals open out.

Celery curls Cut strips of celery about $\frac{1}{2}$ inch wide and 2 inches long. Slit both ends in narrow strips almost to the centre, but do not join the slits. Leave the celery in ice water until the ends curl.

Scallions Slit down the stems in fine strips and leave in ice water until the ends curl.

Carrot curls Scrape raw carrots and slice them lengthwise using a potato peeler, so that the slices are paper thin. Roll up the strips and fasten them with a cocktail pick. Drop them in ice water and they will adopt the curl and the pick can be taken out.

Introduction to Rice, Pasta and Soups

Rice and pasta are two of the world's basic foods. Apart from being staple in the diets of their countries of origin, they are gradually becoming more and more popular in places all around the globe. They add bulk to a meal and help to make it go further but they can also be used imaginatively in many ways, as the recipes in this section show.

Soups, by virtue of how they are made, are filled with nutrients. They can quite easily be main meals (as they have been for centuries to the people of Middle Europe) or the first course of an elegant dinner.

You need to take the trouble to cook all of them – rice, pasta and soups – well, and when you do you will have the makings of many a fine repast.

Rice

The staple food of about half the human race, rice thrives in hot moist climates such as in India, China, Japan, Indonesia and parts of the USA. Until recently it was somewhat despised in European cooking, particularly in France, but this was chiefly due to a lack of understanding of how best to cook it – there is nothing worse than soggy rice, with all the grains stuck together and broken; the pleasures of eating well-cooked rice, all the grains whole and separate, are now more appreciated and rice is taking its place alongside potatoes as one of our main starch foods.

The peoples who rely on rice for their principal nourishment always use it unpolished because most of its vitamin B content (rice's chief nutritive value) lies just under the husk. Polished rice has almost all its nutritive value removed. If these peoples were to substitute polished rice in their diet they would start to contract beriberi; it was the study of this disease which first led scientists to the theory of vitamins, which now plays a large part in nutritional sciences.

Types of Rice

There are three main types of white rice used in the West: the long, medium and round grain rice. The shorter grained Carolina rice is used chiefly for desserts and long grained Patna rice for boiling and serving with savory dishes. Remember that 'Carolina' and 'Patna' are used to identify types of rice, not necessarily to indicate the place of origin. As the round grain variety absorbs most liquid – and medium grain only slightly less – these types are good to use for pilaffs and puddings where the liquid adds to the general flavor of the dish.

Brown rice, which is the unpolished white grain, is richer in vitamins, and needs to be well cooked – for about 35 minutes in boiling water.

Wild rice, being the seeds of a grass, is a different plant altogether. It has a distinctive nutty flavor and firm texture, and takes longer to cook than white rice.

Ground rice and rice flour are also used for making puddings, molds and cakes. For use with cakes, however, rice flour has to be mixed with wheat flour as alone it does not give a sufficiently elastic dough to produce a good textured cake.

Most of us associate rice pudding with the nursery, but this is simply because a rice and milk baked pudding is the easiest way of using the grain to produce a palatable and nourishing dish. But there are several classic dessert dishes based on rice that are worthy of any dinner table. The chief of these is Riz à l'Impératrice, and there are many variations.

Rice for savory dishes demands quite a different treatment. More often than not this is served as plain boiled rice to accompany spicy meat dishes such as curry, where its bland, neutral flavor makes an ideal background for hot spices. A pilaff, however, can be a dish in itself, including a variety of ingredients, or be highly flavored to accompany other dishes.

Risottos are best made with unwashed round grain rice (pick this over well to remove any grains with the husks left on), and a really strong veal or chicken stock. Whereas the rice in a cooked pilaff is traditionally fluffy and dry, that of an Italian-style risotto should be firm yet creamy.

The Iranians like their rice very dry, even with a brown undercrust, while most Orientals prefer it moist so as to pick it up easily with chopsticks.

How to Cook Rice

The way the Indians cook their rice is the best from the nutritional point of view. The rice is poured lightly into a pan containing just enough boiling salted water to last the duration of the cooking. When cooking is complete all the water should have been absorbed by the rice, leaving it tender, dry and fluffy. The difficulty with this method is of course judging the exact amount of water required, though some brands of rice carry instructions for this method on the package, indicating just the amount of water needed. The advantage is that none of the valuable vitamins are thrown away with the cooking water.

The second method demands less precision. A large quantity of water is brought to a boil, the rice is poured in and cooked until *al dente*, just tender (not more than 12 minutes); the water is then drained off and if necessary the rice may be rinsed of the excess starch with a cup of hot water. The rice must be drained thoroughly in a colander, preferably over a low heat. To reheat rice cooked in this way, spoon it into a buttered ovenproof dish, cover the rice with foil and reheat in a moderate oven for about 30 minutes. The chief points to remember with either of these methods are the same:

1   The water must be boiling when the rice is added.
2   The rice should be 'rained' lightly into the water so that the water never stops boiling.
3   The rice should never be stirred.
4   The water must be kept boiling throughout cooking, as this keeps the grains moving, preventing them sticking to each other and the pan.
5   Never overcook rice; there is no way of recovering it once it becomes too soft. It should be cooked until it is just *al dente* and no more.

An alternative method of cooking rice, favored with Chinese food, is by frying. The rice is boiled first, or sometimes steamed, then fried quickly in hot oil, with savory additions.

Pasta

Chiefly an Italian product, pasta is made from a hard wheat grain called durum wheat, mixed with water and flavored with oil and salt. It may be flavored additionally with eggs and spices such as turmeric or dyed with vegetable coloring. There are a number of traditional variations on the basic product but few people outside Italy now make their own pasta as it is readily available in grocery stores, and is relatively cheap. As far as food value is concerned, about ½ cup pasta is the equivalent of about 5 oz bread.

Apart from the variations in consistency, color and flavoring, there are traditional variations in shape and it is by these that the different pasta products are known. The most common varieties are:
Spaghetti Made as long, round strands which when cooked expand to about ⅛ inch diameter. Sold in lengths of 12–18 inches. Serve as a starter or main dish.
Macaroni Similar to spaghetti but tubular. The diameter of the tube is slightly larger than that of spaghetti. This is traditionally sold in long strands, but can also be bought cut into short lengths of 1–2 inches. Serve as spaghetti.
Noodles This egg pasta comes in fine, long strands, fine strands cut into short lengths, or small decorative shapes such as shells, alphabet shapes, stars etc. It is often used as a garnish for soups.
Ravioli Small envelopes of pasta containing a stuffing of meat or vegetable. Serve as starter or main dish.
Cannelloni Large tubes of pasta about 1 inch in diameter, served with a meat filling and a rich sauce as a starter or main dish.
Lasagne Squares of pasta, usually measuring about 4–5 inches. Green spinach coloring is common in this type. Lasagne is served in a large baking dish, layered with meat and cheese sauces.
Other pasta comes in long flat strands and all sorts of shapes and sizes. Some of the better known names not already mentioned are vermicelli, crescioni, ditalini, strichetti, tagliatelli, tortellini.

Gnocchi are also classed as pasta, but are slightly different from the other types in that they are nearly always made at home. French gnocchi are made like a choux paste, with water or milk, flour, butter and eggs, but poached instead of baked (though they may be baked after poaching, to give them a good color). Italian gnocchi, or gnocchi alla Romana, are made of polenta or maize meal, or if this is not available a coarse semolina may be substituted. The meal is mixed with milk, flavored with cheese and either baked or boiled. For frying, Italian gnocchi are sometimes coated with egg and breadcrumbs. The third type of gnocchi is potato gnocchi, made from freshly boiled and mashed potato mixed with flour; this is shaped into rolls or triangles and poached.

Potato gnocchi vary considerably in quality because different types of potato require the addition of different quantities of flour, and this is a matter of experience. Small gnocchi are sometimes called 'gnocchetti'.

How to Cook Pasta

The basic method is the same for all types, though the cooking time will vary according to the thickness of the pasta. As with rice, the pasta goes into a large pan of fast boiling, salted water. The longer shapes such as spaghetti are gently coiled round the pan as they soften, never broken up. The water is then brought back to a boil and allowed to simmer (*not* fast boil this time) until the pasta is *al dente*. The following is a rough guide to cooking times:

Macaroni   15 minutes
Spaghetti, ravioli, noodles   12 minutes
Vermicelli   7–10 minutes

When it is cooked, turn the pasta into a colander, drain it and rinse with a cup of hot water. Rinse out the cooking pan, put in it a large knob of butter and return the pasta to the pan. Season it well with freshly ground black pepper and toss it until it is well coated and glistening with the butter or serve it according to whatever recipe you are following.

Most pasta recipes take their names from the sauce that accompanies them, and many sauces can be used with the various types of pasta. The most common ingredients for the sauces are tomatoes, onions, mushrooms and Parmesan cheese. Chicken livers and other meats also make their appearance, but in lesser quantities.

How to Serve Pasta

All pasta is served either as a hot hors d'oeuvre or as a main dish, depending on the quantity served. Remember that if you serve pasta as a starter, it should be in small quantities and be followed by something quite light. The success of a pasta dish depends not only on how well the pasta itself is cooked, but also on the sauce served with it. In Italy, pasta is often served simply tossed in butter and sprinkled with grated Parmesan cheese; this tends to be rather dull for unaccustomed palates, though, and outside Italy a more interesting sauce is appreciated. Alternatively, of course, pasta may accompany any meat dish (not a roast) instead of potatoes.

Whenever you serve it, remember that pasta is very filling and will not need a starchy vegetable to accompany it – tomatoes are the most obvious choice.

Soups

There are still many parts of the world where soup, perhaps alongside a loaf of bread and a jug of wine, is synonymous with the word food. In Germany and Austria and other mid-European countries there are still many families whose main meal of the day goes under the simple name of soup. In Vienna, one of the traditional centers of good cooking, any first class hotel will serve a three or four course meal starting with soup. In less civilized parts of the world, where packages and cans predominate in the kitchen cupboard, the ability and willingness to make a good homemade soup is perhaps the one single item that divides the real cooks from the rest.

Soup making is really not difficult or time consuming, as many people seem to imagine. True, the stock bones must cook for a long while, but that does not mean the cook has to be watching them, and the final process of adding vegetables or other ingredients takes no time at all. Finally, if you have a blender, that friend of all modern cooks, purée and cream soups come within your reach with only the slightest exertion on your part.

Hot tasty soups can make an appetizing starter to a meal, or a meal on their own. Made in large quantities, they will keep in the refrigerator for 3–4 days provided they do not contain cream, and they are ideal subjects for home freezing. In fact it pays always to make large quantities of soup. Serve it either with bread and cheese for a quick and nourishing lunch, or as a starter to the main meal for all the family.

A blender isn't essential for soup making, but it is the ideal accessory for making smooth, creamy purées. If you don't have a blender, buy a Mouli sieve; this will give you a little more work but the results will be good just the same. Even if you do have a blender, a sieve will still be necessary for some soups to remove tiny hard lumps such as tomato

seeds. If you sieve after blending it will be that much easier.

The basis of all good soups is a stock. Once in a while, of course, we all use a stock cube, but beware of doing this too often; cube stock has a distinctive flavor all of its own and is instantly recognizable. It is very salty and also lacks the characteristic jellied quality of the real bone stock.

Criteria for a good soup

A well-prepared soup should be free from any greasiness, so use a fat-free stock, skim during cooking, remove any fat from meat, and carefully sweat any vegetables to absorb all the fat used. The consistency of a thick soup should be like cream – not like porridge, nor as thin as milk, and it should be smooth and without lumps. The flavor should be full and good and well-blended with sufficient seasoning so that it does not need seasoning after being sent to the table. The colour should be appropriate to the soup, that is a white soup should be white and not cream and a brown soup a good rich color and not insipid.

Serving

Soups are first courses, intended to stimulate the appetite and set the gastric juices flowing to aid the digestion. Therefore it is important that the soup should be served at the correct temperature. Hot soups should be served piping hot, so use well-warmed tureens with lids, lidded bowls or cups, or deep soup plates. Cold soups should be served very well chilled, in chilled dishes, particularly jellied soups which tend to break down fairly rapidly once they are removed from the refrigerator as they contain a low proportion of gelatine. There are some soups, such as Vichyssoise, that can be eaten either hot or cold.

111

Bisques

A bisque is a cream soup prepared from shellfish such as lobster, shrimp or crayfish. The shellfish are sautéd in butter with a vegetable mirepoix, flambéed with brandy and white wine, moistened with fish stock, seasoned with tomato purée and a bouquet garni and thickened with rice. The bisque, before serving, is crushed with a mortar or liquidized, finished with butter and cream and garnished with some of the flesh.

Chowders

These are thick, heavy soups, similar to bisques but the main ingredients can be lentils, potatoes, sweet corn, tuna fish, clams and milk or cream. The word chowder means a 'cooking kettle'.

Fruit soups

Fruit soups served either hot or cold are popular in Scandinavia and middle European countries such as Poland. They can be made from apple, plum, cherry, blueberry, raspberry, strawberry and blackberry. The basis is a fruit purée thickened with potato flour and sharpened with sour cream or served lightly sweetened.

Consommé

There are two basic types of soup — clear and thick. A clear soup is known as a consommé. It consists of a good stock enriched still further with meat, poultry or game. The meat is not served with the soup, but may be served separately if you wish. The best consommés are clarified through a filter of egg white before serving; the white of an egg is whipped into the boiling liquid then allowed to set into a crust, the egg white collects into its mass many of the tiny particles of meat and herbs that have remained in the liquid after ordinary straining. As a final clarification the filter is tipped gently on to a scalded cloth and the consommé is strained right through the filter and cloth into a bowl. By this time the liquid should be positively sparkling — if not the process can be repeated.

Garnishes for Consommé

There are literally hundreds of possible garnishes for a consommé, many of them very specific and traditional. In the ordinary way a consommé may be served with a little vermicelli or shell pasta in it, with a handful of rice in each serving, or with julienne strips of vegetables — the latter garnish is particularly attractive since it adds color to the soup. Alternatively you can add some of the meat used to make the soup, cut into julienne strips. Another common way to serve a consommé, known as Stracciatella, and one that enriches it as a family dish is to whip a little beaten egg into the boiling soup; the heat will cook the egg in strands.

Apart from these substantial garnishes, there are many that simply add a little color to the consommé — croûtons of fried bread or potato for instance, a sprinkling of chopped parsley or fresh tarragon or chervil. Some consommés, especially those garnished with pasta, are served with grated Parmesan cheese to sprinkle on top.

Thick Soups

These may be a simple purée of vegetables in stock. If the vegetable contains a certain amount of starch, no extra thickening will be necessary; if a vegetable is used that contains little starch, another one is often added to provide the thickening — leek and potato is a common mixture that illustrates this principle. Alternatively, cream soups may be based on a béchamel sauce, to which the flavoring ingredient and extra stock are added, or they may be thickened with a liaison. The most common liaison is a mixture of egg yolks and cream.

Liaisons

The yolks and cream are worked together, a little of the hot soup is blended in and then the liaison is stirred gradually into the main bulk of the soup. Reheat after adding the liaison, stirring continually, but take care not to boil it or it will curdle. This gives a particularly rich soup, but remember, it does not keep like other soups so do not try to store and reheat it. If you have made a large quantity of soup that you want to thicken this way, thicken only that portion that you intend to use each time, and store the rest unthickened. Simpler but less rich liaisons are arrowroot and beurre manié.

To thicken a soup with arrowroot, simply blend a teaspoon of arrowroot with a couple of tablespoons of water and stir the mixture slowly into the hot soup, off the heat. Bring the soup back to a boil, stirring all the time, to cook the arrowroot, then it is ready to serve. This soup can be stored and reheated for several days.

For beurre manié, work together a mixture of flour and butter, using twice as much butter as flour. Add the beurre manié to the soup in small pieces, stirring it in until the soup is sufficiently thick. This can also be stored and reheated without problems arising.

Other Types of Soup

Some vegetable soups fall mid-way between thick and clear. These are the soups like minestrone, where there are so many vegetables in the soup that the basic stock can hardly be seen, but the vegetables are not puréed and there is no liaison added. To make a more substantial soup it is also common to add small meatballs or dumplings.

Rice,
Pasta and Soup
Recipes

Rice

Paella

Ingredients: *1 quart mussels · 3½ tablespoons oil · a 2-lb chicken · ¼ cup veal · ¼ cup beef · 2 onions, chopped · 3 cups shrimps · 2 green peppers, deseeded and quartered · salt · pepper · 1–2 zucchini, peeled and diced · ¾ cup tomatoes, peeled and diced · 4 tablespoons sausage, peeled and sliced · 2 cloves of garlic, peeled and crushed · 1 cup rice · 2 teaspoons saffron · 1 cup peas · 4 artichoke hearts, sliced · a few olives, pitted*

Wash and scrub the mussels thoroughly and cook in a little oil over high heat until the shells have opened. Drain and shell, reserving a few in their shells for garnish. Strain the cooking liquid through a fine cloth and reserve. Cut the chicken into 8 pieces and cube the meats. Sauté the meat in a frying pan, preferably an iron one, in remaining hot oil (step 1). Add the onions, raw shrimps, green peppers, salt and pepper (step 2). Mix well and cook the mixture, covered, for 10 minutes. Add the zucchini, tomatoes, sausage, garlic and the reserved cooking liquid from the mussels. Cover pan and cook over low heat for 1 hour and 10 minutes. Add the rice and saffron (step 3) and boiling water to cover. Cook covered, over low heat for 10 minutes. Add the peas, artichoke hearts, shelled mussels and a few olives, and continue cooking for 10 minutes. Add reserved mussels, heat through and serve immediately. Serves 6–8.

Rice à la Grècque

Heat 2 tablespoons butter in a flameproof earthenware casserole with a cover. Add 1 onion, chopped finely, and cook without browning. Add 1 clove of garlic, peeled and crushed, 4 lettuce leaves, shredded, 2 tablespoons dried mushrooms, softened in lukewarm water, squeezed dry and sliced, 2–3 tomatoes, peeled and chopped, 4 oz sausage, peeled and chopped, or sausage meat, 1½ cups rice, 4 cups hot stock, salt and pepper. Cover the casserole and bake in a hot oven (400°F) for 20–25 minutes. When cooked, add 1 tablespoon melted butter, ¾ cup cooked peas, 1 diced red pepper and 3 tablespoons raisins, cooked in a little butter. Mix gently and serve.

Risotto Novara

Ingredients: *1 ½ cups rice · ¾ cup dried red or kidney beans, soaked in cold water for 12 hours · ¾ lb cabbage · 2 celery stalks · 1 carrot · 3 tomatoes · 1 ¾ oz bacon rind, scalded in boiling water and cut up · 8 cups water · 1 stock cube, if desired · salt · 1 salami, or 1 sausage · 2 ¼ oz bacon · 1 slice onion · 1 tablespoon butter · ½ glass red wine · pepper*

Clean the cabbage and cut into pieces, slice the celery and carrot, chop the tomatoes (step 1), and put all the vegetables in a large pan with the drained beans, bacon rind, water, stock cube, if using, and salt. Cover pan and cook over low heat for about 2 hours. Chop the salami or sausage, bacon, and onion (step 2), and sauté in the butter in another pan. Add the rice and cook the mixture for a few minutes. Add the wine and let evaporate. Continue cooking the rice, adding the vegetables and stock gradually as required, stirring occasionally (step 3), until rice is *al dente*. Add pepper to taste. Transfer to a warm serving platter, let stand for a few minutes and serve.

Rice Valencienne

Sauté 6 tablespoons onion, finely chopped, in 1 tablespoon butter until golden. Add 2 cloves of garlic, peeled and crushed, and a generous pinch saffron. Add $\frac{3}{4}$ cup rice, stirring with a wooden spatula. Add $2\frac{1}{2}$ cups chicken stock or water and $\frac{3}{4}$ cup peas. Bring to a boil, cover and bake in a moderate oven (350°F) for 15–18 minutes. Separate the rice grains with a fork and gently mix in 1 tablespoon butter. Transfer to a warm serving platter and serve immediately.

Rice with Sausage and Celery

Sauté $\frac{1}{2}$ onion, chopped, in 1 tablespoon butter. Add 4 oz sausage, peeled and chopped, or sausage meat, and $\frac{3}{4}$ cup celery stalks, finely chopped. Cook for a few minutes. Add 2 teaspoons tomato sauce, thinned with a little hot water, and cook the mixture over low heat for about 40 minutes. Add $1\frac{1}{2}$ cups rice and continue cooking, adding 6 cups stock gradually, as required, stirring occasionally, until the rice is *al dente*. Blend in 1 tablespoon butter and a few tablespoons grated Parmesan cheese. Transfer to a warm serving platter and serve immediately.

Rice with Squash

Blanch $1\frac{1}{2}$ lb large summer squash in boiling salted water for 10 minutes. Drain well, then cut in half lengthwise and remove the seeds. Cut across each half into 1-inch thick slices.

Dip $\frac{3}{4}$ lb ripe tomatoes in boiling water, drain and remove the skins. Halve the tomatoes. Heat 3 tablespoons olive oil in a flameproof casserole and fry 2 large onions, peeled and sliced, until golden. Stir in $\frac{1}{2}$ cup long-grain rice and cook, stirring, for 2 minutes. Add $1\frac{1}{4}$ cups water, the tomatoes, squash and salt and pepper to taste and bring to a boil. Cover and simmer for 15–20 minutes or until the rice is *al dente*. Sprinkle with parsley before serving.

Risotto Chartreuse

Ingredients: for the risotto, 1¼ cups rice ·
2 cups shrimps · 1 leek, 1 sliced onion,
1 celery stalk, 1 small carrot and parsley, all
chopped together · 1 clove of garlic, peeled and
quartered · 2½ tablespoons butter · 2 tablespoons
oil · salt · pepper · 6 cups fish stock

For the fish: 4–6 perch fillets · flour ·
1 slice onion · 2 tablespoons butter ·
½ glass dry white wine · 1 cup canned peeled
tomatoes, coarsely chopped · salt · pepper

Cook the shrimps in boiling salted water until
tender. Drain, reserving the cooking liquid.
Shell and devein, reserving 8–10 in their shells
for decoration, and cut in small pieces (step 1).
Pound the shells in a mortar (step 2), return to
reserved liquid and cook for 10–15 minutes.

Strain and reserve liquid. Sauté the vegetables
and garlic in 2 tablespoons butter and the oil.
Add the reserved liquid, salt and pepper and
cook gently for 10 minutes. Discard garlic. Add
the rice, cook for a few minutes and add the
shrimps, reserving about 2 tablespoons. Pour
in the fish stock gradually, stirring occasionally, and cook until rice is *al dente*.

Sauté the onion in the butter, and discard.
Lightly flour the fish fillets, add to pan and
sauté lightly without drying. Add the wine,
and let evaporate. Add the tomatoes, reserved
shrimps, salt and pepper. Cover pan and cook
mixture for about 15 minutes. Remove rice
from heat, add remaining butter and pile rice
onto a warm serving platter. Place the fish
fillets around the risotto, garnish with reserved
shrimps and pour tomato sauce over (step 3).

118

Rice alla Pilota

Cook 2 sausages, peeled and chopped, or about
½ lb sausage meat, chopped, in 2 tablespoons
butter over low heat for about 1 hour. Bring
a deep pan of lightly salted water to a boil, and
using a sheet of paper rolled into a cone, pour
in 1½ cups rice slowly so that the rice forms a
cone in the middle of the pan. With a ladle
remove water until water remaining in pan
just covers the point of the cone. Bring mixture
to a boil, cook for a few minutes and remove
pan from heat. Add the sausage mixture,
1½ tablespoons grated Parmesan cheese, a
pinch of cinnamon and mix gently. Cover the
rice with a folded cloth and cover pan. Wrap
pan in a towel and let stand for 20–25 minutes.
Add salt if necessary and serve immediately.

Chicken Biriani

Cut up a 3-lb chicken and put into a saucepan
with 3 cups water. Add 1 garlic clove, a 1-inch
piece of ginger root, finely chopped, 2 fresh green
chili peppers, seeded and sliced, 1 green pepper,
seeded and sliced, a cinnamon stick and salt and
pepper. Cover and simmer until the chicken is
tender. Drain the chicken, reserving the stock,
and cool. Strain the stock.

Melt 2 tablespoons butter in a saucepan and
stir in 1 cup rice, 4 cardamom pods, lightly
crushed, 4 cloves, 1 tablespoon each turmeric,
ground coriander and cumin and ½ teaspoon
cayenne. Fry, stirring, for 3 minutes. Add 2½
cups of the reserved stock and simmer for 15
minutes or until the rice is *al dente*.

Meanwhile, remove the chicken meat from
the carcass and cut into neat pieces. Add the
chicken to the rice mixture and cook for a
further 5 minutes to heat through.

119

Risotto with Shellfish

Ingredients: *1 ½ cups rice · 1 lb mussels · 1 lb clams · ¾ cup shrimps or scampi · 1 tablespoon oil · celery, carrot and onion, all chopped together · 3 tablespoons butter · 1 small glass brandy · 1 cup dry white wine · salt · pepper · 1 slice onion, chopped · 5 cups stock*

Wash and scrub the mussels and clams thoroughly. Cook in the oil over high heat until the shells have opened (step 1), drain, reserving the cooking liquid, and shell. Shell and devein the shrimps or scampi. Sauté the chopped vegetables in 2 tablespoons butter and the brandy, add the wine and let reduce by half. Add the shrimps or scampi, mussels, clams (step 2), salt, pepper and a little of the reserved cooking liquid from the mussels and clams, strained through a sieve. Cook mixture over a moderate heat for about 15 minutes, stirring occasionally.

In another pan, sauté the slice onion in the remaining butter, add the rice, and the stock gradually as required, and cook, stirring occasionally, until the rice has absorbed the cooking liquid. Place the rice on a warm serving platter ¹and pour the shellfish sauce over (step 3), arranging shellfish attractively. Serve immediately.

Risotto with Shrimps

Shell and devein 1 ½ cups shrimps or scampi, reserving shells. Sauté 1 celery stalk, 1 onion, 1 carrot, all chopped, and 1 clove of garlic, peeled, in 2 tablespoons butter for a few minutes. Discard the garlic. Add 1 cup dry white wine and the reserved shells, bring mixture to a boil and cook over low heat for 10 minutes. Add 7 cups boiling salted water, cover, and continue cooking for about 30 minutes. In another pan sauté 1 slice chopped onion in 2 ¼ tablespoons butter for a few minutes, add the shrimps or scampi, and cook for 3–4 minutes. Add 1 ½ cups rice, cook for a few minutes then add the shell stock, strained through a sieve, gradually as required. Cook, stirring occasionally, until stock is absorbed and the rice is *al dente*.

Transfer to a warm serving platter, and serve with grated Parmesan cheese in a separate dish.

Risotto Milanese

Ingredients: *1 ½ cups rice · 2 tablespoons beef marrow · 1 slice onion, chopped · 4 tablespoons butter · ½ glass dry white or red wine (optional) · saffron to taste · 6 cups hot stock · a few tablespoons grated Parmesan cheese*

Sauté the beef marrow and onion in half the butter over moderate heat (step 1), add the wine, if using, and let reduce by half. Add the rice, cook for a few minutes, add the saffron and stock gradually as required (step 2), stirring occasionally. Cook the rice over high heat until it is *al dente*, then blend in the remaining butter and the Parmesan cheese (step 3). Transfer risotto to a warm serving platter and let stand for a few minutes before serving.

Rice with Sage

Cook 1½ cups rice in 5–6 cups boiling salted water until it is *al dente*. In a pan sauté 2 cloves of garlic, peeled and crushed, and a few leaves fresh sage in 3 tablespoons butter for a few minutes. Place the rice in a warm deep serving dish; sprinkle with grated Parmesan cheese. Stir in garlic and sage mixture, mix gently and serve.

Risotto Parmigiana

Sauté 1 slice onion, chopped, in 2 tablespoons butter, add 1½ cups rice and cook for a few minutes. Add 6 cups boiling meat stock gradually as required and continue cooking the rice, stirring occasionally, until it is *al dente*. Remove the risotto from the heat, and blend in 1 tablespoon butter and a generous amount of grated Parmesan cheese.

Rice with Tomatoes and Mussels

Scald ½ lb tomatoes in boiling water, peel, and drain and chop. Wash and scrub 2 lb mussels thoroughly and cook them in 2 cups water, 6 tablespoons onion, chopped, and salt and pepper over moderate heat until the shells have opened. Remove the mussels from the pan and discard the shells. Add 1 clove of garlic, minced, the chopped tomatoes and ¾ cup rice to the pan and cook the mixture over low heat for 18–20 minutes without stirring. Add mussels, mix gently, and serve.

Arabian Risotto

Melt 2 tablespoons butter in a saucepan. Add ½ cup *cappelli d'angelo* (angel's hair) pasta, broken up, and fry, stirring, until golden. Remove from the pan and reserve. Add 3 cups chicken broth or stock to the pan and bring to a boil. Stir in 1 cup rice and simmer for 15 minutes or until the rice is *al dente*. Stir in the fried pasta, 2 tablespoons grated Parmesan cheese and salt and pepper to taste. Serve hot.

Pilaff

Ingredients: *1¼ cups rice · 3 tablespoons onion, finely chopped · 5 tablespoons butter · 3 cups hot stock*

In an ovenproof casserole cook the onion in half the butter without browning. Add the rice and stir until transparent (step 1). Add the stock and bring the mixture to a boil. Cover the casserole (step 2), and bake in a hot oven (400°F) for 15–20 minutes without stirring. Remove the rice from the oven, transfer to a warm serving dish, add the remaining butter and separate the grains with a fork (step 3). Serve immediately.

Rice à la Turque

Sauté 4 tablespoons salt pork, diced, and 1 onion, finely chopped, for a few minutes. Add 1 clove of garlic and 2 tomatoes, both peeled and chopped, and continue cooking the mixture for a few minutes. Add about 4 tablespoons chicken livers, quartered, cook for a few minutes, remove and reserve. Stir in 1 tablespoon flour, salt and cayenne pepper and pour in 1½ cups white wine. Add a pinch of thyme and 1 bay leaf, crushed, and cook the mixture over low heat for 30 minutes. Strain the mixture through a sieve, return to the heat and add ¾ cup rice. Cook the rice for 15–18 minutes until it is *al dente*. Add reserved chicken livers, mix gently, transfer to a warm serving platter, sprinkle with chopped parsley, if liked and serve immediately.

Pilaff with Sweetbreads

Wash 10 oz sweetbreads thoroughly and cook in boiling salted water for 10 minutes. Drain, cool and remove and discard tubes and membranes. Slice, flour the slices lightly and sauté in 2 tablespoons butter until golden on both sides. Sprinkle with Marsala and allow to evaporate. Add a little stock and cook over low heat for 20 minutes. Prepare a pilaff following the basic recipe above, place on a warm serving platter in a dome. Pour the sweetbreads and their sauce on top and sprinkle with finely chopped parsley. Serve immediately.

Risotto with Peas

Ingredients: *1¼ cups rice · 4½ cups fresh peas or 1¼ cups canned or frozen peas · 2 tablespoons bacon, diced · 1 slice onion and 1 sprig parsley, both chopped · 2¼ tablespoons butter · 2 tablespoons oil · 6 cups hot stock · grated Parmesan cheese · salt · pepper*

Shell the peas (step 1), if using fresh peas. Sauté the bacon, onion and parsley in half the butter and the oil for a few minutes (step 2), add the peas and cook the mixture for 1 minute. Add the rice (step 3), and cook until transparent. Add the stock gradually as required, and continue cooking the rice, stirring occasionally, until it is *al dente*. Blend in the remaining butter and Parmesan cheese, sprinkle with salt and pepper, transfer to a warm serving platter and serve immediately.

Risotto with Mushrooms

Sauté 1 slice onion, chopped, in 2 tablespoons butter for a few minutes, add 1½ cups fresh mushrooms, wiped, trimmed and sliced (or 3 tablespoons dried mushrooms, softened in lukewarm water for 30 minutes, squeezed dry and sliced), and cook the mixture for a few minutes. Add 1½ cups rice and ½ glass dry white wine and let evaporate. Add 6 cups hot stock gradually as required and continue cooking the mixture, stirring occasionally, until the rice is *al dente*. Remove the risotto from the heat, stir in 1 tablespoon butter and grated Parmesan cheese, transfer the mixture to a warm serving platter and allow to stand for 1 minute. Sprinkle with grated Parmesan cheese to taste, and serve immediately.

Risotto with Spinach

Clean, wash and cook $1\frac{1}{4}$ cups spinach in boiling salted water until tender, and drain. Sauté $\frac{1}{2}$ clove of garlic, peeled, and parsley, both chopped, in 1 tablespoon butter for a few minutes, add the spinach and $1\frac{1}{2}$ cups rice, mixing well. Add 6 cups hot stock gradually as required, and continue cooking, stirring occasionally, for about 15 minutes or until the rice is *al dente*. Blend in 1 tablespoon butter and a generous amount grated Parmesan cheese, transfer to a warm serving platter and serve immediately.

Indonesian Apple Rice

Cook $1\frac{1}{4}$ cups rice in boiling salted water until *al dente*. Meanwhile, heat 2 tablespoons oil in another saucepan and add 2 apples, cored and chopped, and 1 onion, peeled and chopped. Fry until transparent. Stir in 3 tablespoons raisins, 2 tablespoons sliced almonds, $\frac{1}{2}$ cup mushrooms, sliced, $\frac{1}{3}$ cup ripe olives and $\frac{1}{3}$ cup stuffed green olives. Cook for a few minutes, then add 2 teaspoons brown sugar, 1 tablespoon curry powder and a pinch of salt. Mix well and cook for a further 3–4 minutes.

Drain the rice, if necessary, and add to the curried mixture. Combine thoroughly. Serve hot, garnished with apple slices.

Cantonese Rice

Soak 6 dried Chinese mushrooms in warm water for 30 minutes. Drain and chop, discarding the stalks. Heat 3 tablespoons oil in a frying pan and add the mushrooms and 2 small onions, peeled and cut into thin wedges, $\frac{1}{2}$ lb slab bacon, diced, and $\frac{1}{2}$ lb (1 cup) cooked pork or chicken, finely shredded. Stir-fry for 3–4 minutes. Add 3 cups cooked rice and stir-fry for a further 1 minute. Stir in $\frac{1}{3}$ cup shelled cooked shrimp, 1 tablespoon chopped chives, $\frac{1}{4}$ teaspoon cayenne and salt to taste. Stir-fry for 3 minutes.

Lightly beat 2 eggs with 1 tablespoon cold water and seasoning. Cook in another pan to make a thin omelet. Roll up the omelet and shred finely. Use to garnish the rice.

Risotto with Asparagus Tips

Ingredients: *1 ½ cups rice · 2 lb asparagus ·
4 tablespoons butter · 6–6 ½ cups hot stock ·
1 slice onion, chopped · parsley, minced ·
grated Parmesan cheese to taste*

Scrape and wash the asparagus, halve them,
and reserve the tips (step 1). Cut half remaining
asparagus sticks into small pieces. In a pan
melt 2 tablespoons butter, add the asparagus
pieces and cook for a few minutes. Add the
rice (step 2), continue cooking, stirring
occasionally, and adding a little stock as

required, until rice is *al dente.* In another pan
melt 1 tablespoon butter, add the chopped
onion and cook for a few minutes. Add the
asparagus tips and cook, adding a little stock
occasionally, until asparagus is tender. Sprinkle
with chopped parsley. Remove risotto from
heat, stir in remaining butter and some grated
Parmesan cheese and transfer to a warm
serving platter, arranging in a dome shape.
Place the asparagus tips vertically around the
risotto (step 3), and serve immediately.

128

Genoese Risotto

Sauté ½ onion, chopped, in 2 tablespoons butter until golden, add 6 oz fresh sausage, peeled and sliced, or sausage meat, 1 cup fresh peas and the tender part of 1 artichoke, finely sliced. Cook for a few minutes. Add 2 tablespoons dried mushrooms, softened in lukewarm water, squeezed dry and sliced, ½ cup canned peeled tomatoes, a little hot stock, salt and pepper. Bring the mixture to a boil, covered, and cook for about 20 minutes. Boil 1½ cups rice in salted water for 8 minutes, drain and add to the sauce. Blend in 2 tablespoons grated Parmesan cheese and 3 cups hot stock and pour the mixture into an oiled mold or casserole. Bake in a hot oven (400°F) for 15 minutes. Sprinkle with blended breadcrumbs and Parmesan cheese, and return to oven until crusty and golden.

Rice Pompadour

In a flameproof casserole sauté 2 small onions, chopped, in 1 tablespoon butter for a few minutes, add 1 clove of garlic, peeled and crushed, 6 tablespoons mushrooms, finely sliced, and cook for a few minutes. Add ¾ cup rice, salt, pepper and 2½ cups hot water, cover and bring to a boil. Bake in a hot oven (400°F) for 15–18 minutes. Stir in ¾ cup chicken meat, diced, ½ cup heavy cream and ¾ tablespoon butter. Garnish with green olives.

Lentil Risotto

Wash and pick over 1 cup dried lentils. Soak in cold water overnight, and drain. Melt ½ cup butter in a large saucepan and add 1 onion, peeled and finely chopped. Fry until transparent. Stir in the lentils and add enough water to cover. Bring to a boil, then cover and simmer for 1 hour.

Add 1½ cups rice and 1 quart broth or stock. Cover again and simmer for a further 15 minutes or until the rice is *al dente*. Stir in ½ cup grated Parmesan cheese and salt and pepper to taste.

Country Timbale

Ingredients: for the sauce: *2 tablespoons dried mushrooms softened in lukewarm water, squeezed dry and sliced · 1 clove of garlic, peeled · 1 tablespoon butter · 1 small glass brandy · stock*

For the meatballs: *6 oz ground beef · 3 tablespoons chopped ham · 1 handful white bread, soaked in milk and squeezed dry · 1 egg yolk · 2 tablespoons grated Parmesan cheese · salt · grated nutmeg · flour · butter*

For the risotto: *1 ½ cups rice · 1 slice onion, chopped · 2 tablespoons butter · 6 cups hot stock · 2 eggs · grated Parmesan cheese, to taste · breadcrumbs · ¾ cup fresh ricotta cheese, sliced · melted butter*

Sauté the mushrooms and the garlic in the butter for a few minutes. Discard the garlic, sprinkle mushrooms with brandy and let it evaporate. Add a little stock and continue cooking until sauce has thickened.

Prepare the meatballs: in a bowl mix the ground beef with the ham, bread, egg yolk, Parmesan cheese, salt and grated nutmeg. Using the fingers, make walnut-sized balls, flour lightly and cook in butter until evenly golden.

Prepare the risotto: sauté the onion in the butter for a few minutes, add the rice and cook until transparent. Add 4 cups stock and cook the rice, stirring occasionally, adding the remaining stock gradually as required until rice is *al dente*. Remove from the heat, blend in the eggs, 4 tablespoons Parmesan cheese (steps 1 and 2), and spread rice out on an oiled cookie sheet to cool without further cooking.

Butter a high-sided mold and dust it lightly with breadcrumbs. Line the bottom and sides with risotto, reserving a little. Fill the mold with alternate layers of meatballs, mushroom sauce, ricotta cheese (step 3), Parmesan cheese to taste and butter curls. Cover with the reserved risotto, sprinkle with breadcrumbs and add a little melted butter. Bake the timbale in a hot oven (400°F) for about ½ hour. Unmold on a warm serving platter.

131

Pasta

Spaghetti with Eggplant

Ingredients: $\frac{3}{4}$ *lb spaghetti · 1 clove of garlic,
peeled · 1 slice onion · oil · 1 tablespoon butter ·
2 cups canned peeled tomatoes · salt · pepper · a
few basil leaves · 4 eggplants · grated Parmesan
cheese*

To garnish: *sprig of fresh basil (optional)*

Sauté the garlic and onion in oil and the butter,
discard garlic and add the tomatoes (step 1).
Add salt and pepper to taste and cook over
low heat for $1\frac{1}{2}$ hours. Add basil leaves. Slice
the eggplants and fry quickly in boiling oil
(step 2). Pour the tomato sauce on the
spaghetti, cooked in boiling salted water until

132

it is *al dente* and drained, sprinkle with grated Parmesan cheese and garnish with the egg-plant slices (step 3). Mix well, top with sprig of fresh basil leaf, if liked. Serve immediately.

Spaghetti alla Romana

Sauté 1–2 cloves of garlic, peeled and thinly sliced, and 1 piece of hot pepper in 2½ table-spoons butter for a few minutes, add 2 anchovies, desalted and mashed, and let soften. Add ¾ lb fresh tomatoes, peeled, seeded and coarsely chopped, 1 tablespoon capers, washed under cold running water, and ½ cup pitted black olives. Cook the sauce over low heat for 8–10 minutes and pour on ¾ lb spaghetti, cooked in boiling salted water until it is *al dente* and drained. Mix well and serve.

Spaghetti with Peas

Sauté 1 onion, thinly sliced, in 3½ tablespoons butter for a few minutes, add 1 cup canned peeled tomatoes and cook the mixture for 10 minutes. Add a few lettuce leaves, chopped, and cook for a further 15 minutes. Add ½ cup canned peas, salt and pepper to taste and continue cooking the sauce for 8–10 minutes. Mix the sauce with ¾ lb spaghetti, cooked in boiling salted water until *al dente* and drained.

Three-Flavored Spaghetti

Sauté 1 tablespoon dried mushrooms, soaked in lukewarm water, squeezed dry and sliced, or ¾ cup fresh mushrooms, thinly sliced, in 2 tablespoons butter for a few minutes. Add 2 oz ham, cut into thin strips, 4 tablespoons fresh peas and a little stock, and cook the sauce over low heat for ½ hour. Mix the sauce with ¾ lb spaghetti, cooked in boiling, salted water until it is *al dente* and drained, and serve with grated Parmesan cheese.

Spaghetti with Shellfish

Ingredients: $\frac{3}{4}$ lb spaghetti · 1 lb mussels ·
2 tablespoons butter · 1$\frac{1}{4}$ cups shrimps ·
2 cloves of garlic, peeled · 1 tablespoon dried
mushrooms, soaked in lukewarm water,
squeezed dry and sliced · 2 tablespoons tomato
paste · 4 tablespoons tuna fish in olive oil ·
salt · pepper · 2 tablespoons chopped parsley

Wash and scrub the mussels (step 1) and cook
them, covered, over high heat with 1 tablespoon butter until all the shells have opened.
Drain, reserving the liquid, and shell. Strain
the cooking liquid through a fine sieve, bring
to a boil, add the shrimps and cook for about
5 minutes. Drain the shrimps, reserving the
liquid, shell and devein them and add them to

the cooked mussels. In another pan, sauté the
cloves of garlic in the remaining butter for a
few minutes and discard. Add the mushrooms
and cook for a few minutes. Add the tomato
paste and the mussel and shrimp cooking
liquid, gradually, and cook the sauce over
low heat until it has thickened. Add the tuna
fish, reserved mussels and shrimps, salt to
taste and a generous amount of freshly ground
pepper (step 2). Cook the sauce until all the
ingredients are heated through. Cook the
spaghetti in boiling salted water until it is *al
dente*, drain, mix with the sauce (step 3) and
mix in some chopped parsley. Transfer to a
serving platter and sprinkle with parsley.

Spaghetti with Oil and Garlic

In a small pan cook 4 tablespoons oil, 1–2 cloves of garlic, peeled and crushed, and a generous amount freshly ground pepper over very low heat. Remove pan from heat as soon as the garlic starts to brown and pour the sauce on $\frac{3}{4}$ lb spaghetti, cooked in boiling salted water until it is *al dente* and drained. Add a generous amount of chopped parsley.

Spaghetti with Clams

Wash and scrub 2 lb clams thoroughly. Cook them in 1 tablespoon oil, covered, over high heat until all the shells have opened, without allowing oil to boil. Drain, reserving the liquid, and discard shells. Sauté 1 clove of garlic, peeled, in 3 tablespoons butter for a few minutes, add a generous amount chopped parsley, 1 cup canned peeled tomatoes, worked through a sieve, and pepper to taste, and cook the mixture for about 5 minutes. Add the reserved liquid and continue cooking the sauce until it has thickened. Remove and discard the garlic, add the clams and cook the sauce for 1 minute. Pour the sauce on $\frac{3}{4}$ lb spaghetti, cooked in boiling salted water until it is *al dente* and drained. Transfer to a warm serving platter, and serve immediately.

Spaghetti with Chicken Sauce

Heat 2 tablespoons butter with 2 tablespoons oil in a saucepan and add 2 thick slices of bacon, diced, and $\frac{3}{4}$ lb boned chicken breasts, cut into strips. Fry until browned. Dip 1 lb tomatoes in boiling water, then drain and remove the skins. Chop the tomatoes and add to the pan with 1 garlic clove, crushed, 2 tablespoons tomato paste, $\frac{1}{2}$ teaspoon sugar and salt and pepper to taste. Add $\frac{3}{4}$ cup dry white wine, cover and simmer for 20 minutes. Pour the sauce on $\frac{3}{4}$ lb spaghetti, cooked in boiling salted water until it is *al dente* and drained. Toss together well, then transfer to a warm serving dish.

Spaghetti with Artichoke Sauce

Ingredients: *¾ lb spaghetti · 2–3 artichokes · juice of 1 lemon · 1 slice onion, chopped · 4 tablespoons oil · 1½ cups canned peeled tomatoes · salt · pepper*

To garnish: *chopped parsley*

Wash the artichokes, discard the hard outer leaves and trim the spiky ends. Halve them, discard the chokes, slice horizontally (step 1), and soak the slices in water with lemon juice to prevent discoloration. Sauté the onion in the oil for a few minutes, add the drained artichokes and cook the mixture over low heat for a few minutes. Add the tomatoes, drained and chopped, salt and pepper to taste and cook the sauce over low heat (step 2) for 35–40 minutes. Pour the sauce on the spaghetti, cooked in boiling salted water until it is *al dente* and drained, sprinkle with parsley (step 3) and serve immediately.

136

Macaroni with Gravy

Cook ¾ lb macaroni in boiling salted water until it is just *al dente*; drain. Place a layer of macaroni in a buttered baking dish, cover with gravy from a roast, sprinkle with grated Parmesan cheese and continue in this manner until all ingredients are used up. Add butter and bake the mixture in a hot oven (400°F) until golden.

Macaroni with Zucchini Sauce

In 2 tablespoons butter cook ¾ lb small zucchini, sliced, over low heat without letting them brown. Remove the zucchini from the heat and mix in 2 eggs, beaten with 2 tablespoons milk, 4 tablespoons grated Parmesan cheese, salt and pepper to taste. Mix the sauce with ¾ lb macaroni, cooked in boiling salted water until it is *al dente* and drained. Mix well and serve immediately.

Macaroni with Ricotta Cheese

Cook ¾ lb macaroni in boiling salted water until it is *al dente*. In a deep serving dish mix ⅔ cup ricotta cheese with ½ teaspoon cinnamon and 1 tablespoon butter and thin the mixture with a few tablespoons cooking water from the pasta. Drain the macaroni, add to cheese mixture, season with salt and pepper to taste, and serve.

Spaghetti Printanière

Cook ¾ lb spaghetti in boiling salted water until it is *al dente*; drain. Chop ½ lb fresh tomatoes coarsely and slice 1 fresh mozzarella cheese thinly. Pour the mixture on the spaghetti, add a generous amount of fresh basil leaves, salt and freshly ground pepper to taste and serve immediately.

Macaroni with Mushrooms

Ingredients: *¾ lb macaroni ·*
1 cup fresh mushrooms or 2 tablespoons dried
mushrooms, softened in lukewarm water,
drained and sliced · 2¼ tablespoons butter ·
½ glass brandy · stock ·
3–4 triangles processed cheese cut in pieces ·
3 tablespoons grated Parmesan cheese ·
1 glass milk · salt · pepper ·

Clean, trim and finely slice the fresh mushrooms,
if using (step 1). Sauté mushrooms in ¾
tablespoon butter for a few minutes, add the
brandy (step 2) and let it evaporate. Add 1½
tablespoons stock and cook the mixture over
low heat for 25 minutes. Cook the macaroni
in boiling salted water until it is *al dente*. Heat

the remaining butter in a large pan, add the
processed cheese, Parmesan cheese and milk
(step 3), and cook the mixture until it is creamy.
Add the mushroom mixture, salt and pepper
to taste and continue cooking the mixture,
stirring constantly, until it is well blended.
Add the drained macaroni, mix gently and
transfer to a warm serving platter. Serve
immediately.

Macaroni Marinara

Slice $\frac{1}{2}$ cup green olives, pitted, in thin strips. In a pan heat $3\frac{1}{2}$ tablespoons butter, add 1 clove of garlic, peeled, and sauté for a few minutes. Discard garlic. Add 2 anchovy fillets, desalted, and parsley, chopped, and cook the mixture over low heat for a few minutes. Add the olives and $1\frac{1}{4}$ cups canned peeled tomatoes and cook the sauce for about 10 minutes. Cook $\frac{3}{4}$ lb macaroni in boiling salted water until it is *al dente*, drain and add to the sauce. Sprinkle with freshly ground pepper to taste, transfer to a warm serving platter and serve.

Macaroni with Meatballs

Mix 6 oz ground beef with 1 handful white bread, soaked in milk and squeezed dry, 1 egg yolk, 2 tablespoons grated Parmesan cheese, salt and grated nutmeg. Using the fingers, make walnut-sized balls, roll in flour and cook in boiling oil until evenly golden on all sides. In a saucepan heat 1 tablespoon butter with 1 tablespoon olive oil, add a little onion, chopped, $1\frac{1}{2}$ cups canned peeled tomatoes, salt and pepper to taste. Cook the sauce for about 20 minutes, add the meatballs and continue cooking the mixture for a few minutes. Cook $\frac{3}{4}$ lb macaroni in boiling salted water until it is *al dente*, drain thoroughly and mix the macaroni gently with the sauce. Sprinkle with grated Parmesan cheese, transfer to a warm serving platter and serve immediately.

Macaroni Nests

Cook $\frac{1}{4}$ lb long macaroni in boiling salted water until it is *al dente*. Drain and rinse in cold water. Starting in the center of the bottom, line the bottom and sides of 4 greased ramekins with the macaroni. Dice $\frac{1}{4}$ lb cooked ham and divide between the ramekins. Break an egg into the center of each and season with salt and pepper. Sprinkle with shredded cheese and chopped parsley. Cover the ramekins with foil, place in a bain-marie and cook in a hot oven (425°F) for 20 minutes. Unmold to serve.

Gratinéed Macaroni

Ingredients: *¾ lb short macaroni · ½ onion ·
3 tablespoons butter · 6 oz ground beef ·
2 bay leaves · 1 cup canned peeled tomatoes ·
salt · pepper · stock ·
2 tablespoons grated Parmesan cheese*

*For the béchamel sauce: 1 tablespoon butter ·
1 tablespoon flour · 1 cup milk · salt ·
grated nutmeg · 1 egg, beaten ·
2 tablespoons grated Parmesan cheese*

Chop the onion (step 1) and sauté in butter
until golden. Add the beef and bay leaves
(step 2) and cook for a few minutes. Add the
tomatoes, salt and pepper to taste, and cook
for about 1 hour, adding a little stock
occasionally. Remove the sauce from heat
and add the grated Parmesan cheese. Cook
the macaroni in boiling salted water until it is
al dente, drain and blend with the sauce. Pour
into a buttered ovenproof dish. Make a
béchamel sauce with the butter, flour, milk,
salt and grated nutmeg, remove from the heat,
stir in the beaten egg and the grated Parmesan
cheese. Pour over the macaroni (step 3) and
bake in a moderate oven (350°F) for 40–45
minutes or until top is golden and crisp. Serve
immediately.

Baked Macaroni with Cauliflower

Sauté 1 small onion, chopped, in 2 tablespoons
butter until golden, add 6 oz ground beef and
cook for a few minutes. Add a few tablespoons
tomato sauce, thinned with a little water, salt
and pepper to taste, and cook for about 15
minutes. Cut 1 cauliflower into small flowerets
and parboil in boiling salted water. Remove
and reserve flowerets. Add ¾ lb short macaroni
to the cooking water and cook until *al dente*.
Drain and mix gently with ½ the sauce and
2 tablespoons grated Parmesan cheese. Sauté
the flowerets in 3 tablespoons butter until
golden. Butter an ovenproof dish, dust with
breadcrumbs and fill with alternate layers of
macaroni, cauliflower, sauce, and grated
Parmesan cheese to taste. Bake in a hot oven
(400°F) for 15 minutes or until top is golden
and crisp. Serve immediately in the cooking
dish.

Noodles Bolognese

Ingredients: for the pasta, *2 cups presifted flour · 4 eggs · ⅔ cup spinach, cooked and chopped (optional)*

For the sauce: *2 tablespoons bacon, chopped · 2 tablespoons butter · 1 celery stalk, 1 carrot and ½ onion, all chopped together · 6 oz ground beef · a few dried mushrooms, soaked in lukewarm water, squeezed dry and sliced (optional) · ½ glass white or red wine · salt · pepper · grated nutmeg · 2 tablespoons tomato paste · 1½ cups stock or water · 1 glass milk (optional)*

Prepare the pasta: sift the flour on a lightly floured board, make a well in the center and break in the eggs (step 1). Add the spinach if green noodles are required. Work flour and eggs together with a round-bladed knife (step 2) until a smooth dough is formed. Roll out, not too finely (step 3). Let dough dry for a few minutes then fold over to form a 4-inch wide strip and cut into ¼-inch strips. Pick up 5–6 strips at one time, shake out gently and let dry on the board (step 4).

Prepare the sauce: in a pan sauté the bacon in the butter for a few minutes, add the chopped vegetables and cook until they start to brown. Add the beef and mushrooms (if using), and

Curried Noodles

cook for a few minutes. Stir in the wine, add salt, pepper and nutmeg to taste, and cook the sauce until wine has evaporated. Add the tomato paste, thinned with ¼ cup stock or water, and cook, covered, over very low heat for about 2 hours, adding a little more stock or water occasionally. Add the milk (if using) gradually and continue cooking for 1 hour. Pour the sauce on the noodles, cooked in boiling salted water until they are *al dente* and drained. Mix well and serve immediately.

Sauté 1 medium onion, finely chopped, in 3½ tablespoons butter without browning. Add 2 teaspoons curry powder, salt, and 4 tablespoons ham, chopped, and cook the mixture for a few minutes. Pour the seasonings on ¾ lb noodles, cooked in boiling salted water until *al dente* and drained. Mix well and serve immediately. Serve grated Parmesan cheese separately.

Green Noodles with Cheese

Ingredients: *¾ lb green noodles ·
¼ cup Emmenthal · ¼ cup Gouda or other
Dutch cheese · ¼ cup Parmesan · ¼ cup
mozzarella · 4 tablespoons butter, melted ·
salt · pepper · grated Parmesan*

Dice all the cheeses (step 1), and melt the butter.
Cook the pasta in boiling salted water until it
is *al dente*, drain and put on a warm serving
platter. Stir in the diced cheese (step 2), pepper
to taste and half the butter. Mix quickly (step
3), add the remaining butter, sprinkle with
grated Parmesan and serve immediately.

Golden Noodles

Cook ¾ lb noodles in boiling salted water until
they are *al dente*; drain. In a bowl beat 3 eggs
with 1 glass milk, 3½ tablespoons grated
Parmesan cheese and 3½ tablespoons butter,
melted. Add 3 triangles of processed cheese,
diced, 3 oz ham, diced, salt and pepper to taste
and the pasta. Transfer the mixture to a
buttered baking dish, sprinkle with 1 tablespoon grated Parmesan cheese and add butter
curls. Bake in a hot oven (400°F) for 25 minutes.

Baked Noodles with Artichokes

In a saucepan cook 1 tablespoon butter with 1½ tablespoons flour and stir in 1½ cups stock until the mixture is smooth. Add 1 onion, stuck with 1 clove, 1 celery stalk and 1 small carrot, both sliced, 1 bay leaf, pepper to taste and a pinch of thyme. Simmer the mixture slowly for 25–30 minutes. In a large pan heat 1 tablespoon butter and add 8–10 artichoke hearts, cut into thin strips, in one layer only. Add salt and pepper to taste and cook the artichokes over low heat, adding a little stock if necessary. Remove the sauce from the heat and, using a wooden spoon, stir in ½ cup cream. Strain the sauce through a sieve into another pan and stir in 2 eggs yolks, one at a time, and 4 triangles of processed cheese, melted in 2 tablespoons milk. Put ¾ lb green noodles in boiling salted water, return to a boil and drain. Pour the pasta in a bowl and mix in 1 tablespoon butter and ¾ of the white sauce. Arrange 3 layers of pasta and 2 layers of cooked artichokes in a buttered baking dish. Pour in the remaining white sauce, sprinkle with grated Parmesan cheese and bake in a hot oven (400°F) until the top is golden.

Crusty Noodle Shapes

Cook ¾ lb egg noodles in boiling salted water until *al dente*. Drain well and place in a bowl. Add 2 cups mornay sauce (see p. 85) and mix well. Press into a roasting pan to ½ inch thickness and leave to cool.

Cut the noodle mixture into diamonds or other shapes. Dip in beaten egg, then coat in dried bread crumbs. Deep fry in hot oil until golden brown. Drain and serve hot.

'Straw-and-Hay' with Cream and Ham

Ingredients: *6 oz each of green and white pasta ('straw-and-hay')* · *3 tablespoons butter* · *1 cup cream* · *4 tablespoons grated Parmesan cheese* · *salt* · *grated nutmeg* · *3 oz ham, diced*

Straw-and-hay consists of equal measures of pasta prepared with spinach (green) and pasta prepared with egg (white). It resembles thin noodles (step 1). Cook the pasta in boiling salted water until it is *al dente*. In a large pan cook the butter, cream, Parmesan cheese, salt, grated nutmeg to taste and diced ham over moderate heat, stirring constantly, until the mixture has the consistency of a thick cream (step 2). Drain the pasta, add to the pan and mix gently but thoroughly (step 3). Transfer to a warm serving platter, and serve immediately.

Gratinéed Straw-and-Hay

Cook ¾ lb straw-and-hay, if fresh, or 10 oz if dried, in boiling salted water until it is *al dente*; drain. Sauté 1 slice onion, chopped, in 1 tablespoon butter and 1 tablespoon oil until transparent. Add 3 oz ham, diced, salt and pepper to taste and cook for a few minutes. Add ¾ cup canned peeled tomatoes, worked through a sieve, and cook for a further 15 minutes. In a separate pan, cook ½ cup peas in boiling salted water until they are tender and add them to the sauce. Butter an ovenproof casserole, put a layer of pasta in the bottom, add half the sauce and cover with a few slices of Emmenthal cheese. Add the remaining pasta, the remaining sauce, a few more slices of Emmenthal cheese and dot with butter curls. Bake in a hot oven (400°F) for 15 minutes or until the top is golden brown and crisp. Serve immediately.

Straw-and-Hay Nests

Cook 10 oz straw-and-hay in boiling salted water until it is *al dente*, drain and transfer to a deep dish. Mix in 1 tablespoon grated Parmesan cheese, 2 tablespoons ham, chopped, and 3 eggs, beaten with salt and pepper. Pour on a buttered platter and let it cool. Divide the pasta into 12 equal parts and twirl each part on a fork to form a nest. Sprinkle the nests with flour and flatten them slightly with the palm of the hand. Pick up the nests with a slotted spatula and sauté them in 4 tablespoons butter until golden on both sides. Serve immediately with a tomato sauce in a sauce-boat.

147

Pasta Shells with Cream Cheese and Ham

Ingredients: $\frac{3}{4}$ *lb pasta shells ·*
2 tablespoons butter at room temperature ·
$\frac{1}{2}$ cup ricotta cheese · $\frac{1}{2}$ cup cream cheese ·
$\frac{1}{4}$ cup ham or tongue · salt

In a bowl beat the butter, add the cheeses and
salt to taste and beat the mixture until it is
light and foamy (step 1). Cut the ham or
tongue into thin strips (step 2) and add it to
the cheese mixture. Cook the pasta shells in
boiling salted water until they are *al dente,*
drain and mix gently in a warm serving
platter with the cheese mixture (step 3).
Serve very hot.

Shells with Basil

In a small pan cook 2 tablespoons butter,
1 stock cube and a few tablespoons water
over moderate heat for a few minutes. Add
3 triangles processed cheese and continue
cooking the mixture, stirring constantly, until
the cheeses have melted. Stir in 1 generous
tablespoon fresh basil, chopped, and pour the
sauce onto $\frac{3}{4}$ lb pasta shells, cooked in boiling
salted water until they are *al dente* and
drained. Serve immediately on a warm serving
platter.

Stuffed Shells

Cook 10 oz giant pasta shells in boiling salted water with 1 tablespoon oil until they are *al dente* and drain on a cloth. Prepare a béchamel sauce with 2 tablespoons butter, $\frac{1}{4}$ cup sifted flour, 2 cups milk, salt and grated nutmeg to taste. Add $\frac{1}{2}$ cup fontina or Gruyère cheese diced, and cook the sauce until the cheese is melted. Blend in 2 egg yolks and fill the shells with the mixture. Place the shells, filled side up, in a buttered ovenproof dish. Add a little melted butter, sprinkle with grated Parmesan cheese and bake in a hot oven (400°F) for 20 minutes or until golden. Serve immediately.

Shells Niçoise

Scald 3 tomatoes in boiling water, drain and peel. Halve them and drain again. In a pan heat 3 tablespoons oil, add 1 onion, chopped, 1 clove of garlic, peeled and crushed, the tomatoes, 1 cup water, a pinch of thyme and basil, chopped and 1 bay leaf. Cook over moderate heat for 20 minutes. Cook $\frac{1}{2}$ lb pasta shells in boiling salted water until they are *al dente*; drain. Stir in 2 tablespoons butter and cover with the sauce. Transfer to a warm serving platter, sprinkle with a little grated Gruyère cheese and serve immediately.

Pasta Shells with Lamb and Tomato Sauce

Dip 1 lb tomatoes in boiling water, then drain and remove the skins. Chop the tomatoes. Heat 2 tablespoons oil in a saucepan and add 4 bacon slices, chopped. Fry for 5 minutes, then add 1 large onion, peeled and chopped, and 1 garlic clove, crushed. Fry until transparent. Add $\frac{3}{4}$ lb ($1\frac{1}{2}$ cups) ground lamb and fry till browned. Stir in $1\frac{1}{4}$ cups red wine, the tomatoes and salt and pepper to taste. Cover and simmer for 40 minutes. Pour the sauce on $\frac{3}{4}$ lb pasta shells, cooked in boiling salted water until *al dente* and drained. Serve immediately.

Orecchiette with Turnip Leaves

Ingredients: *1 ½ cups sifted flour ·
¾ cup semolina · salt · lukewarm water ·
¾ lb turnip leaves · olive oil · black pepper*

Work the flour and semolina with enough salted lukewarm water to make a fairly solid dough, like bread dough. Cover to prevent drying. Using a little dough at a time, form rolls 1 inch in diameter and 15 inches in length (step 1). Slice the rolls (step 2) and, using the round edge of a knife, pull out one edge of each slice on the board, forming little ears (*orecchiette*) by shaping the slices with the thumb. Cook the orecchiette in boiling salted water, add the turnip leaves and continue cooking until the orecchiette are *al dente*. Drain the mixture (step 3) and add olive oil and freshly ground black pepper to taste. Transfer to a warm serving platter and serve immediately.

Orecchiette with Meat Sauce

Pound 4 slices stewing beef for a few minutes. Put a few strips of bacon and pecorino or Parmesan cheese on each slice. Sprinkle with garlic and parsley, chopped. Roll up the slices and tie them with heavy thread. In a frying pan heat a little oil, add a little onion, chopped, and sauté for a few minutes. Add the beef rolls and sauté until evenly golden. Add ½ glass red or dry white wine and let it evaporate. Add a little stock and 1½ cups canned peeled tomatoes, worked through a sieve, and continue cooking the rolls over low heat until the sauce has thickened. Cook ¾ lb orecchiette in boiling salted water until they are *al dente*, drain and mix gently with the meat sauce. Transfer to a warm serving platter and serve the orecchiette immediately. Serve the rolls separately.

Apulian Orecchiette

Cook 2 lb fresh tomatoes, peeled, seeded and drained, ½ onion, sliced, 2 cloves of garlic, peeled and crushed, a few basil leaves and salt to taste, covered, for 30 minutes. In another pan sauté a little onion, sliced, 2 cloves of garlic and 2 bay leaves in 4 tablespoons oil for a few minutes. Discard the bay leaves. Add

1¼ lb beef or veal in one piece and cook until evenly golden. Add ½ glass red wine and the tomato mixture, worked through a sieve, and cook, covered, over low heat for 1½ hours, adding a little stock if necessary. Remove the meat, cut 1 slice, chop and add to the sauce.

Cook ¾ lb orecchiette in boiling salted water until they are *al dente*, drain and mix gently with the meat sauce and a little grated pecorino cheese. Transfer to a warm serving platter and serve immediately. Serve the meat separately.

Creamy Tortellini

Ingredients: for the pasta, *2 cups presifted flour · 4 eggs · 2 tablespoons water*

For the filling: *3 oz pork, chopped · 2 oz turkey or chicken breast, chopped · 2 tablespoons butter · 3 oz Italian prosciutto · 3 oz mortadella · 1¾ oz beef marrow · 1 egg · salt · grated nutmeg*

For the sauce: *3½ tablespoons butter · 1 cup cream · 6 tablespoons grated Parmesan cheese · salt · grated nutmeg*

Prepare the dough: sift the flour on a board, make a well in the center, break in the eggs and add the water. Work ingredients together until smooth, cover and let stand.

Meanwhile, prepare the filling: cook the pork and turkey or chicken meat in the butter, chop finely together with the prosciutto, mortadella and beef marrow, and work mixture through a sieve. Blend in the egg and salt, and nutmeg to taste. Roll out dough into a thin sheet and cut into 2½-inch squares (step 1). Put a little filling in the center of each square and fold squares over so as to form triangles, pressing edges firmly together. Twist each triangle around one finger, pressing the 2 lower corners firmly one on top of the other (step 2). Gather dough trimmings together, roll out into a thin sheet and repeat process until all dough and filling is used up. Cook the tortellini in boiling salted water until *al dente*.

Prepare the sauce: in a large pan heat the butter, cream, Parmesan cheese and salt and grated nutmeg to taste, over a moderate heat, stirring constantly. Drain the pasta, add to the pan (step 3) and cook until sauce has thickened. Serve immediately on a warm platter.

Tortellini Parma Style

Halve a 3-lb pumpkin and discard the seeds. Cook in the oven until tender, and peel. In a bowl mash the pulp with 5½ tablespoons crushed macaroons, ½ cup grated Parmesan cheese, 1 or 2 eggs, the grated peel of ½ lemon, and salt to taste.

Prepare a dough as for above recipe, using 2 cups presifted flour, 2 eggs, and 6 tablespoons water. Roll out dough into a thin sheet and put walnut-sized mounds of the filling on half the dough. Fold dough over and pat it down so that no air is trapped. Cut filled dough in rectangles, pressing the edges together and pressing the 2 opposite corners one on top of the other. Cook in boiling salted water and drain. Toss in melted butter and grated Parmesan cheese and serve immediately.

153

Thin Tortellini with Cheese

Ingredients: for the pasta, *2⅓ cups presifted flour · 3 eggs · 8 tablespoons water*

For the filling: *1⅓ cups ricotta or other white cheese, sieved · 6 tablespoons grated Parmesan cheese · 2 eggs · parsley, chopped · salt · grated nutmeg*

To finish: *5 tablespoons butter, melted · 4 tablespoons grated Parmesan cheese*

Prepare the filling: in a bowl mix the cheeses, eggs, parsley and salt and nutmeg to taste.

Prepare the pasta: sift the flour on a board, make a well in center, break in the eggs and add the water. Work ingredients together until dough is smooth, roll out into a thin sheet and cut into circles with a pasta or cookie cutter (step 1). Put a little filling on each circle (step 2), fold over, pressing the edges together, and press the corners together to form tortellini (step 3). Cook the tortellini in boiling salted water for a few minutes and remove them with a slotted spoon as they rise to the surface. Toss in the melted butter and Parmesan cheese and serve immediately. Serves 5–6.

154

Tortellini with Cream and Mushrooms

In a bowl blend $\frac{3}{4}$ cup ricotta cheese, 5 tablespoons capon breast or pork, finely chopped and cooked in butter, 3 tablespoons grated Parmesan cheese, 1 egg plus 1 egg yolk, a little grated lemon rind, salt, pepper and grated nutmeg. Prepare the dough with $1\frac{1}{2}$ cups flour, 3 eggs and water as above. Roll out thinly and cut into 3-inch squares. Put a little filling on each square and fold over to form triangles. Twist each triangle around one finger, pressing the 2 lower corners firmly together.

Cook $3\frac{1}{2}$ tablespoons dried mushrooms, soaked in lukewarm water and squeezed dry, in 1 tablespoon butter for a few minutes. Sprinkle with $\frac{1}{2}$ glass brandy and flame. Add $\frac{1}{4}$ cup stock and cook gently for 25 minutes.

Cook the tortellini in boiling salted water until *al dente*. In a large pan heat $2\frac{1}{2}$ tablespoons butter, add 1 cup cream, 6 tablespoons grated Parmesan cheese, salt and grated nutmeg to taste and the mushroom mixture, and cook for a few minutes, stirring constantly. Drain pasta, add to pan, heat through and serve.

Tortellini in Tomato Sauce

Heat 2 tablespoons oil in a saucepan, add 1 large onion, peeled and finely chopped, and fry until transparent. Add $\frac{1}{2}$ lb (1 cup) ground beef and fry until browned and crumbly. Add 1 garlic clove, crushed, a 16-oz can of tomatoes, 1 tablespoon tomato paste, $\frac{3}{4}$ cup red wine, $\frac{1}{2}$ teaspoon dried oregano and salt and pepper to taste. Bring to a boil, then simmer for 20 minutes.

Pour the sauce on $\frac{3}{4}$ lb tortellini, cooked in boiling salted water until *al dente* and drained. Toss together lightly, then serve immediately, sprinkled with grated Parmesan cheese.

155

Vol-au-vent with Tortellini

Ingredients: *a 10-inch round vol-au-vent ·
1 lb fresh tortellini (see p.97) · 1 slice onion ·
2 tablespoons butter · 1 cup canned peeled
tomatoes, worked through a sieve · stock ·
½ cup cream · 3½ tablespoons grated Parmesan
cheese · grated nutmeg*

Sauté the onion in ½ the butter and discard.
Add tomatoes and some stock and cook for
½ hour. Boil the tortellini in salted water and
drain. In a casserole heat remaining butter, add
the tomato sauce, cream, Parmesan cheese,
nutmeg and tortellini (steps 1 and 2). Reheat
gently. Heat the vol-au-vent in a hot oven
(400°F) for a few minutes, fill with the tortellini
(step 3), add the pastry cover and serve immediately.

Tortellini Timbale

Prepare a dough with 1½ cups presifted flour,
⅔ cup butter, 1 egg, 6 tablespoons milk and
salt, and let stand.

Cook 6 tablespoons beef or veal marrow in
boiling water for 3 minutes, drain and dice.
Melt 1 tablespoon butter, add 2 tablespoons
dried mushrooms softened in lukewarm water,
squeezed dry and coarsely chopped, the
marrow and 2 tablespoons Marsala and cook
the mixture for a few minutes. Add ½ cup
stock and continue cooking over low heat for
25 minutes, adding a little more stock if
necessary.

Prepare a béchamel sauce with 1½ tablespoons butter, 1 tablespoon flour, ⅓ cup milk,
and salt and grated nutmeg to taste. Parboil
2 cups tortellini in boiling salted water, drain
and toss in 1 tablespoon butter, 1 cup cream
and a few tablespoons grated Parmesan cheese.
Roll out ⅔ of prepared dough into a 20-inch
circle and use to line a 12-inch pie pan,
buttered and sprinkled with breadcrumbs. Add
½ the tortellini, ½ the marrow sauce mixed
with the béchamel sauce, and sprinkle with
grated Parmesan cheese. Repeat the procedure
with remaining ingredients and cover with
remaining dough, rolled out into a circle. Press
edges together firmly and prick the surface
with a fork. Brush with egg yolk and bake in a
hot oven (400°F) for 35–40 minutes. Let
stand for a few minutes before unmolding.

Ravioli

Ingredients: for the pasta, 2¼ cups sifted flour ·
4 eggs · 6 tablespoons water

For the filling: *10 oz beef · 1 tablespoon bacon ·
2¼ oz pork fillet ·
2 tablespoons butter or margarine ·
onion, celery, carrot, all chopped together ·
salt · pepper · ½ glass dry white wine ·
½ lb Savoy cabbage · 2¼ oz mortadella ·
1 handful white bread soaked in milk and
squeezed dry · milk · 1 egg
grated Parmesan cheese · grated nutmeg*

For the sauce: *meat sauce or gravy from a
roast or braised meat ·
grated Parmesan cheese for sprinkling*

For the filling: 1 day before serving, put
the beef, barded with the bacon, in a pan with
the pork, butter or margarine, onion, celery
and carrot, and sauté over moderate heat,
turning the meat occasionally, until all the
ingredients are golden. Add salt and pepper
to taste and the white wine, and cook the
mixture, covered, over very low heat for 2
hours. Remove the meat from the pan and
reserve. Add the cabbage, cooked in boiling
salted water for 10 minutes, to the pan and
sauté for a few minutes. Work the cabbage,
meats and mortadella through the medium
blade of a food chopper. Add the white bread,
egg, grated Parmesan cheese, salt, pepper and
grated nutmeg to taste, and blend well.

Make a dough of the flour, eggs and water
(see p.142), and roll out thinly. Shape the
filling into small balls and set them about
2 inches apart on the dough (step 1). Fold the
dough over (step 2) and cut with a ravioli or
cookie cutter (step 3) or with a small glass.
Seal the edges. Cook the ravioli in boiling
salted water until it is *al dente*, drain, and put
on a warm serving platter. Cover with meat
sauce or gravy and sprinkle with grated
Parmesan cheese. Serves 5–6.

Genoese Ravioli

Boil $\frac{1}{2}$ cup each of endives and spinach in salted water for 5 minutes and drain. Dice 6 oz veal, $2\frac{1}{2}$ oz pork, 3 oz sweetbreads, scalded and peeled, and sauté in 2 tablespoons butter for a few minutes. Add a piece of brain, scalded and peeled, and 1 oz beef marrow and cook for a few minutes. Chop with marjoram and pound in a mortar. Add $1\frac{3}{4}$ oz sausage meat, a little bread, soaked in milk and squeezed dry, grated Parmesan cheese and salt, and mix well. Prepare the dough and proceed as left.

Mushroom Ravioli

Melt 2 tablespoons butter in a saucepan. Add 1 lb mushrooms, finely chopped, and 1 onion, peeled and finely chopped, and cook for about 10 minutes or until the onion is softened and any liquid from the mushrooms has evaporated. Season with salt and pepper and cool. Prepare dough and proceed as left. Toss the cooked ravioli in melted butter.

159

Gratinéed Cannelloni

Ingredients: for the dough, *2 cups sifted flour ·*
4 eggs · 3 tablespoons water

For the filling: *2 tablespoons butter ·*
1 slice onion, chopped ·
3 tablespoons ham, chopped · ¾ lb beef, diced ·
½ bay leaf · 1 tablespoon flour · stock · salt ·
pepper · grated nutmeg · 1 egg ·
1 handful white bread, soaked in milk and
squeezed dry · Parmesan cheese ·
tomato or béchamel sauce · butter ·
grated Parmesan cheese

Prepare the dough (see p.142) and let stand.
Roll out thinly and cut into 4 or more 5-inch
by 4-inch rectangles. Cook these, a few at a
time, in boiling salted water until tender, drain
(step 1), and place on a damp cloth. In a pan
heat the butter, add the onion and ham and
cook for a few minutes. Add the beef and the
bay leaf and cook for a further few minutes.
Stir in the flour, add a little stock, salt, pepper
and grated nutmeg to taste. Cook the mixture
over low heat for 45 minutes, discard the
bay leaf. Work mixture through the medium

blade of a food chopper, add the egg, the bread and grated Parmesan cheese and work mixture until well blended. Put a little filling on each rectangle and roll up (step 2). Place the cannelloni side by side in a buttered ovenproof dish. Cover with tomato sauce (step 3) or with a rather thin béchamel sauce, dot with butter and sprinkle with grated Parmesan cheese. Gratiné the cannelloni in a hot oven (400°F) until golden. Serve immediately.

Cannelloni Maison

Prepare 12 little crêpes: in a bowl mix 2 eggs with 10 tablespoons sifted flour and 1 pinch salt, add 1 cup milk or water and 1 tablespoon melted butter gradually. Beat the batter with a wire whip until smooth. Heat a 7-inch frying pan and add a little oil. Pour in 2 tablespoons batter and quickly tilt and rotate the pan so that the batter coats the bottom thinly and evenly. Cook the crêpe on both sides until golden. Continue until all the batter is used. Prepare a béchamel sauce with 2 tablespoons butter or margarine, $\frac{1}{4}$ cup sifted flour, 2 cups milk, salt, pepper and grated nutmeg to taste. Remove from heat and stir in $2\frac{1}{2}$ tablespoons grated Gruyère cheese. Pour a little béchamel sauce onto each crêpe, add $\frac{1}{2}$ slice ham to each and roll up crêpes. Place side by side in a buttered ovenproof dish, add 1 cup heavy cream and sprinkle with grated Parmesan cheese. Bake in a hot oven (400°F) for 15 minutes and serve immediately. Cannelloni may also be filled with meat or vegetables.

Cannelloni with Tuna Fish

Prepare dough rectangles as left. Drain oil from a 7-oz can of tuna fish into a frying pan and heat. Add 2 onions, peeled and chopped, and fry until golden. Add 1 garlic clove, crushed, 3 tablespoons capers and the tuna fish and cook for 5 minutes. Remove from the heat and stir in 1 cup soft bread crumbs, 1 tablespoon lemon juice, 2 tablespoons chopped parsley and 1 egg. Season with salt and pepper. Use to fill the cannelloni and proceed as above.

161

Baked Lasagne

Ingredients: for the pasta, 2½ *cups sifted flour ·*
4 eggs · 1 lb spinach

For the sauce: *½ cup butter or margarine ·*
1 carrot, 1 celery stalk, 1 onion, all chopped
together · 6 oz ground beef · salt · pepper ·
grated nutmeg · 1 cup milk · tomato sauce

For the béchamel sauce:
2 tablespoons butter or margarine ·
2 tablespoons flour · 2 cups milk · salt ·
grated nutmeg · grated Parmesan cheese

Heat half the butter or margarine, add the
onion, celery and carrot, and cook until golden.
Add the beef, salt, pepper and nutmeg to taste
and cook the mixture for 20 minutes. Add the
tomato sauce, thinned with a little hot water,
cover the pan and simmer until the tomato
sauce is well blended. Add the milk and cook,
covered, over low heat for 1 hour.

Meanwhile prepare the dough (see p.142)
with the flour, eggs and spinach, cooked in
boiling salted water, drained well and worked
through a sieve. Roll out the dough in a very
thin sheet and cut into 3½-inch squares
(step 1). Make the béchamel sauce with the
butter or margarine, flour, milk, salt and
grated nutmeg to taste, remove from the heat
and stir in 2–3 tablespoons grated Parmesan
cheese. Cook the lasagne, a few at a time, in
boiling salted water with 1 tablespoon butter
or margarine so that the squares do not stick,
for a few minutes (step 2), wash under cold
running water, drain and dry on a clean cloth.
Grease a baking dish with butter or margarine,
add a layer of lasagne, cover with a little
béchamel sauce, a little meat sauce (step 3),
grated Parmesan cheese and curls of butter or
margarine. Continue until all the ingredients
are used. Bake in a hot oven (400°F) for
30–40 minutes until top is golden. Serves 5–6.

Lasagne 16th Century Style

Prepare and cook the dough as left using $1\frac{1}{2}$ cups sifted flour and 3 eggs.

Wash and pat dry $\frac{3}{4}$ lb perch or sole fillets, dip them in egg beaten with salt, then in breadcrumbs and sauté them lightly. Prepare a béchamel sauce with 2 tablespoons butter, 2 tablespoons flour, 2 cups milk, salt and grated nutmeg, remove from heat and stir in 2 tablespoons grated Gruyère cheese. Grease a baking dish, add a layer of lasagne, cover with béchamel sauce and add a few fish fillets. Continue in this manner until all the ingredients are used. Add curls of butter and bake the lasagne in a moderate oven (350°F) for about 30 minutes or until the top is golden.

Lasagne con Pesto

Prepare and cook the dough as left. Put 2 peeled garlic cloves in a mortar with 4 tablespoons chopped fresh basil. Pound with a pestle, gradually adding 4 tablespoons olive oil and $\frac{1}{4}$ cup grated Parmesan cheese. Add salt to taste. Layer the lasagne, basil mixture and additional grated Parmesan cheese in a greased baking dish and dot the top with butter. Bake in a moderate oven (350°F) for about 20 minutes.

163

Macaroni and Pigeon Pie

Ingredients: *10 oz short macaroni ·
2 tablespoons butter · grated Parmesan cheese ·
12 oz shortcrust pastry, homemade or frozen*

For the sauce: *1 tablespoon butter ·
1 slice onion, chopped · 1 tablespoon dried
mushrooms soaked in lukewarm water, squeezed
dry and sliced · 2 pigeons or other small birds,
cleaned and cut in pieces · 3 tablespoons Italian
prosciutto, chopped · salt · pepper · 1 small
glass Marsala or dry white wine · stock*

For the béchamel sauce: *1 tablespoon butter ·
2 tablespoons flour · 1 cup milk · salt ·
pepper · grated nutmeg*

Prepare the sauce by heating the butter
in a pan, add the onion, mushrooms, pigeon
pieces, prosciutto, salt and pepper to taste,
and sauté the mixture until all ingredients
are golden. Add the Marsala or white wine
and let evaporate. Add a little stock and cook
gently, covered, for 35–40 minutes.

Meanwhile, cut the macaroni into 4-inch
pieces, cook in boiling salted water until *al
dente* and drain. When the pigeon sauce is
cooked, remove the pigeon pieces, bone and
reserve. Mix the sauce gently with the
macaroni, 2 tablespoons butter and grated
Parmesan cheese. Divide the dough into 2
pieces, one slightly larger than the other, and
roll each out thinly. Butter a 12-inch pie pan
and line with the smaller piece of dough (step 1).
Add $\frac{2}{3}$ of the macaroni mixture, the reserved
pigeon pieces (step 2), cover with the
remaining macaroni and add the béchamel
sauce. Sprinkle with Parmesan cheese and
cover with the second piece of dough, pressing
edges together. Cut shapes from any remaining
dough to decorate top of pie. Brush with the
beaten egg (step 3), prick surface with a fork
and bake in a moderate oven (350°F) for 1
hour, or until golden. Let stand for about
3–4 minutes before unmolding on a warm
serving platter. Serve grated Parmesan cheese
separately. Serves 6.

Macaroni with Tuna

Melt 2 tablespoons butter in a large saucepan, add 1 onion, peeled and chopped, and fry until golden. Add ¾ cup chicken stock and seasoning and bring to a boil. Simmer for 5 minutes.

Divide a medium cauliflower into florets and cook in boiling salted water for 4 minutes. Remove with a slotted spoon and reserve. Add ½ lb short macaroni to the boiling water and cook until *al dente*. Drain well.

Melt ¼ cup butter in a frying pan, add the cauliflower and fry until golden. Stir in 6 roughly chopped anchovy fillets and ½ cup soft bread crumbs and fry until the bread crumbs are crisp. Remove from the heat.

Add the macaroni to the stock mixture with a 7-oz can of tuna fish, drained and flaked, 2 tablespoons grated Parmesan cheese and seasoning. Heat through gently, stirring frequently. Pour the mixture into a flameproof dish and scatter the cauliflower mixture on top. Sprinkle with another 2 tablespoons of grated Parmesan cheese and broil until the top is golden brown. Serve immediately.

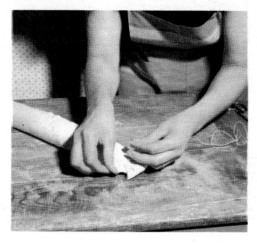

Spinach Roll

Ingredients: for the pasta,
*1 ½ cups presifted flour · 2 eggs ·
4 tablespoons lukewarm water · salt*

For the filling: *2 cups spinach · salt ·
¾ cup ricotta cheese ·
¾ cup grated Parmesan cheese · 2 eggs ·
grated nutmeg*

To finish: *tomato sauce ·
grated Parmesan cheese or 4 tablespoons butter
clarified*

Sift the flour on a board, make a well in the center and add the eggs, water and salt. Work ingredients together until well blended, form the dough into a ball, wrap in wax paper and let stand for about ½ hour.

Meanwhile, prepare the filling: clean and wash the spinach and cook without water, with a little salt. Drain thoroughly and work through a sieve with the ricotta cheese. In a bowl blend this mixture with the Parmesan cheese, eggs, salt and grated nutmeg to taste. Roll out the dough in a thin rectangle, cover with the spinach mixture (step 1) and roll up (step 2). Roll in a clean cloth (step 3) and tie both ends with string (step 4). Cook in

166

simmering salted water for about 1 hour, transfer to a warm serving platter and serve, sliced, with tomato sauce and grated Parmesan cheese or clarified butter poured over the spinach roll.

Cheese Strudel

Sift $1\frac{1}{4}$ cups flour on a board, make a well in the center and add 1 egg and 5 tablespoons water. Blend ingredients thoroughly, form the dough into a ball, wrap in wax paper and let stand for $\frac{1}{2}$ hour. Meanwhile, in a bowl beat 3 eggs for a few minutes, add 4 tablespoons soft butter, 6 tablespoons breadcrumbs, 1 cup milk, salt and grated nutmeg to taste, and blend well. Roll out the dough thinly on a floured cloth, cover with the egg mixture and sprinkle evenly with 4 tablespoons grated Parmesan cheese. Lifting one edge of the cloth, roll up the strudel, sealing the edges with a little milk or water, and roll it round into the form of a snail. Tie the four corners of the cloth together and cook the strudel in boiling salted water for 45 minutes. Remove the cloth, cut the strudel in quarters and serve with 4 tablespoons clarified butter and grated Parmesan cheese to taste.

167

Gnocchi à la Parisienne

Ingredients: for the gnocchi, *2 cups milk ·
4 ½ tablespoons butter · salt · grated nutmeg ·
1 ⅓ cups presifted flour · 5–6 eggs ·
5 ½ tablespoons grated Parmesan cheese*

For the mornay sauce: *2 tablespoons butter ·
2 tablespoons flour · 2 cups milk · salt ·
grated nutmeg · 1 egg yolk · 3 slices Emmenthal
cheese, chopped, or 5 tablespoons grated
Gruyère cheese*

To finish: *1 tablespoon butter, melted ·
4 tablespoons grated Parmesan cheese*

Prepare the pasta: in a large pan bring the
milk, butter and salt and grated nutmeg to
taste to a boil, pour the sifted flour in all at once
and cook mixture, stirring constantly, until it
leaves the sides of the pan (step 1). Remove
pan from heat and let cool slightly. Add the
eggs, one at a time, and the Parmesan cheese,
beating vigorously; allow to cool.

Prepare the mornay sauce with the butter,
flour, milk and salt and grated nutmeg to
taste, and remove from heat. Stir in the egg
yolk, cheese and remaining butter. Using a
pastry bag fitted with a large round tube, pipe
the dough out, cutting it off in 1-inch lengths
with a knife dipped in hot water (step 2), to
fall into a large pan of boiling salted water.
Remove the gnocchi with a slotted spoon as
they rise to the surface, and drain. Pour a thin
layer of mornay sauce into an ovenproof dish,
add the gnocchi, cover with remaining sauce
(step 3), and sprinkle with melted butter and
grated Parmesan cheese. Cook in a hot oven
(400°F) for about 15 minutes or until golden.

Spinach Gnocchi

Wash and cook 1½ lb fresh spinach without water. Drain and work through a food chopper into a bowl. Add 1¼ cups ricotta or other white cheese, 2 eggs plus 2 egg yolks, ¾ cup sifted flour, a generous handful of grated Parmesan cheese and salt and grated nutmeg.

Stir well. Shape mixture into small balls and sprinkle with flour. Drop into boiling salted water and remove with a slotted spoon as they rise to the surface. Put on individual plates and sprinkle with grated Parmesan cheese to taste. Heat 4 tablespoons butter with 1 clove of garlic, peeled, cook until golden, discard garlic and pour sauce over gnocchi.

Potato Gnocchi

Ingredients: for the gnocchi, *2 lb potatoes* ·
1½ cups flour · *1 egg* · *salt*

For the sauce: *1 tablespoon butter* ·
1 tablespoon oil · *1 slice onion, chopped* ·
*6 oz pork sausage, peeled and chopped, or
sausage meat* · *1 bay leaf* · *1½ cups canned
peeled tomatoes, worked through a sieve* · *salt* ·
pepper · *stock* · *grated Parmesan cheese*

Cook the potatoes in boiling salted water until
tender, peel and work through a potato ricer
(step 1). Add the flour, egg, and salt to taste,

onion for a few minutes, add the sausage or
sausage meat and cook for a few minutes. Add
the bay leaf, tomatoes and salt and pepper
to taste, and cook for ½ hour, adding a little
stock if necessary. Discard bay leaf, pour
sauce over gnocchi on a serving platter and
sprinkle with grated Parmesan cheese.
and work mixture until well blended. Shape
into finger-sized cylinders, cut into thick slices
(step 2) and press against a cheese grater
(step 3). Sprinkle with flour, drop into boiling
water and remove as they rise to the surface.

Prepare the sauce: cook the butter, oil and

Sicilian Gnocchi

Slice 10 oz stale bread and let soak in 2 cups hot milk for about $1\frac{1}{2}$ hours. Drain, squeeze dry if necessary, and mash with a fork. In a bowl beat 2 eggs, add the bread, $\frac{1}{3}$ cup Italian prosciutto or smoked bacon, diced, 2 tablespoons grated Parmesan cheese, 3 tablespoons flour, and salt and a little chopped parsley to taste, and stir mixture until well blended. With fingers dipped in water, shape mixture into small eggs. Sift $\frac{3}{4}$ cup flour on a board and roll the gnocchi in the flour until well coated. Drop into boiling salted water and remove with a slotted spoon as they rise to the surface. Transfer to a warm serving platter and serve immediately tossed in melted butter and grated Parmesan cheese.

Potato Gnocchi with Cheese

Prepare the gnocchi as for the basic recipe left and cook in boiling salted water. Drain. Dice $\frac{3}{4}$ cup fontina, Bel Paese or Gruyère cheese. Put the gnocchi on individual plates, add a generous handful of diced cheese and sprinkle with grated Parmesan cheese. Heat 2 tablespoons butter with 1 clove of garlic, peeled, until golden; discard garlic and pour butter over gnocchi. Serve very hot.

Gnocchi Roll

Work 1 lb boiled potatoes through a potato ricer. Blend in 1 egg, $\frac{3}{4}$ cup sifted flour and a little salt and work mixture until smooth. Place dough on a lightly floured cloth and roll it out $\frac{1}{2}$ inch thick. Cover the dough with $\frac{3}{4}$ cup fontina or Bel Paese cheese, sliced; roll up, wrap in the cloth and tie securely at both ends. Cook in boiling salted water for 25 minutes. Serve in slices with melted butter and grated Parmesan cheese, or with tomato sauce.

171

Gnocchi alla Romana

Ingredients: for the gnocchi, *4 tablespoons butter · salt · grated nutmeg · ½ lb semolina · 2 tablespoons grated Parmesan cheese · 2–3 egg yolks, mixed with a little milk*

To finish: *2 tablespoons butter, melted · 6 tablespoons grated Parmesan cheese*

Bring the milk, butter, and salt and grated nutmeg to taste, to a boil, and gradually pour in the semolina (step 1), stirring constantly. Cook over moderate heat for 15–20 minutes, stirring constantly. Remove pan from heat and stir in the Parmesan cheese and egg yolks. Pour mixture onto a marble slab or cookie sheet sprinkled with water, flatten to the thickness of a finger with a spatula dipped in water and let cool. Using a small cookie cutter or glass, cut mixture into circles (step 2), place circles in layers (step 3) in a buttered oven-proof dish, covering each layer with melted butter and Parmesan cheese. Bake in a hot oven (400°F) for about ½ hour or until golden on top.

Quick Gnocchi

Bring 1 cup water and 1 teaspoon salt to a boil, add 1 cup cold milk and pour the liquid into a bowl containing 1 envelope potato flakes. Let stand for 1 minute and blend until smooth. Add 1 tablespoon flour, 2 eggs, lightly beaten, 5 tablespoons grated Parmesan cheese and a little grated nutmeg, and work the mixture until smooth. With wet fingers, form into egg shapes and flatten them. Butter an ovenproof dish, sprinkle the bottom and sides with breadcrumbs, place a layer of gnocchi in the bottom, cover with 1 tablespoon butter, melted, and sprinkle with grated Parmesan cheese. Add another layer of gnocchi, melted butter and Parmesan cheese, and bake in a hot oven (400°F) for $\frac{1}{2}$ hour or until golden.

Gnocchi with Prunes

Prepare potato gnocchi as for the basic recipe above. Soak dried prunes in lukewarm water until tender, pit them and fill with a little sugar. Shape the potato dough into fairly large balls, putting a prepared prune in the middle of each. Cook the gnocchi in boiling salted water as above, and drain. Toss in breadcrumbs sautéed in butter, sugar and cinnamon.

Gnocchi Mornay

Prepare semolina gnocchi as left and layer circles in a buttered ovenproof dish. Melt $\frac{1}{4}$ cup butter in a saucepan and stir in $\frac{1}{4}$ cup flour. Cook for 1 minute, then gradually stir in 2 cups hot milk. Bring to a boil, stirring, and simmer until thickened. Add $\frac{1}{2}$ cup each grated Swiss and Parmesan cheeses and stir until melted. Stir in 2 tablespoons heavy cream and season with salt and pepper. Pour sauce on gnocchi and bake as left.

173

Polenta

Polenta with Gorgonzola

Sauté ½ onion in butter; add ¾ cup Gorgonzola cheese, crumbled, and a little milk. Cook until cheese is melted. In an ovenproof dish, make layers of polenta and cheese sauce, and top with butter curls. Bake in a hot oven (400°F).

Plain Polenta

Ingredients: *3 ¼ quarts water, or ¼ water,*
¼ milk · 1 handful of rock salt ·
4 cups corn meal

Bring the water and salt to a boil in a pan.
Gradually pour in the corn meal (step 1),
stirring constantly and always in the same
direction (step 2) until the mixture binds
together. Turn the polenta out onto a wooden
board or block (step 3) and slice with a string
or a wooden knife.

Polenta can also be poured into variously
shaped individual molds.

If little time is available, polenta can also be
made in a pressure cooker. Serves 8.

Polenta is very good served with jugged
hare or rabbit.

Polenta with Cheese

Prepare the polenta following the basic recipe
above, with 1 small handful of rock salt and
3 cups corn meal. Cook for 45–50 minutes,
stirring constantly. Stir in 1 ¼ cups fontina or
Gruyère cheese and 5 ½ tablespoons butter,
both diced, and cook for 5–10 minutes, or
until well blended. Transfer to a warm serving
platter and cover with 4 tablespoons butter,
melted. Serve immediately. Serves 6–8.

Polenta with Mushrooms

In a small pan sauté 1 clove of garlic in 1 tablespoon butter until golden, discard garlic and
add 2 tablespoons dried mushrooms soaked in
lukewarm water, squeezed dry and sliced, or
1 cup fresh mushrooms, coarsely chopped or
sliced. Cook for about 20 minutes, adding a
little stock if necessary.

Prepare a béchamel sauce, using 2 ½ tablespoons butter, 2 tablespoons flour, 2 cups milk,
and grated nutmeg to taste. Remove from heat
and add 2 tablespoons grated Parmesan cheese,
and salt and pepper to taste. Mix ¾ of the sauce
with the mushrooms and blend well. Butter
an ovenproof dish and fill with alternate layers
of thin slices of mozzarella and grated
Parmesan cheese, about 1 lb thinly sliced cold
polenta and the mushroom béchamel. Finish
with a layer of plain béchamel sauce, a few
tablespoons grated Parmesan cheese and
butter curls. Bake in a moderate oven (350°F)
for 45 minutes or until golden on top.

175

Grandmother's Polenta

Ingredients: for the polenta, $3\frac{1}{2}$ pints water · rock salt · 2 cups fine grain corn meal · 4 tablespoons butter

For the stuffing: 2 cups sweetbreads, skinned and diced · flour · 1 slice onion, chopped · 4 tablespoons butter · $\frac{1}{2}$ glass Marsala · stock · 2 cups fresh mushrooms, sliced, or 2 tablespoons dried mushrooms, soaked in lukewarm water, squeezed dry and sliced · salt · pepper

To finish: $\frac{1}{2}$ cup Italian prosciutto, thinly sliced · 1 egg, beaten · $3\frac{1}{2}$ tablespoons grated Parmesan cheese · butter curls

Prepare the polenta (see p.175): bring the water to a boil in a large pan, gradually pour in the corn meal, stirring constantly, and cook the mixture over high heat for about 45–50 minutes, stirring constantly with a wooden spoon to prevent lumps forming. Add the butter during last minutes of cooking and pour the polenta into a buttered high-sided mold. Leave to cool.

Meanwhile, prepare the filling: sprinkle the sweetbreads with flour and sauté them with the onion in almost all the butter for a few minutes (step 1). Add the Marsala, let it reduce, add a little stock and cook for about 20 minutes. Add the mushrooms and a little more stock and cook until thick. Season with salt and pepper to taste.

Unmold the polenta and turn it upside down, and with a knife make a circular incision around the middle, leaving a 1-inch border.

Slice the middle part thinly, without cutting all the way through to the bottom, and remove slices carefully (step 2), leaving a polenta shell. Brush the mold with remaining butter and line with prosciutto slices; brush with the beaten egg. Return polenta shell to mold and fill with layers of sweetbread sauce, polenta slices, grated Parmesan cheese (step 3) and butter curls. Finish with polenta slices and prosciutto slices. Bake in a hot oven (400°F) for 35–40 minutes and unmold onto a warm serving platter. Serves 4–6.

Soufflés

Spinach and Carrot Mold

Ingredients: for the spinach mold, *1 lb spinach · 1 egg · 1 tablespoon butter · 1 tablespoon flour · ⅓ cup milk · salt · grated nutmeg · ½ teaspoon potato starch · 1 tablespoon grated Parmesan cheese*

For the carrot mold: *½ lb carrots · 1 tablespoon butter · 1 tablespoon flour · ⅓ cup milk · 1 tablespoon grated Parmesan cheese · salt · grated nutmeg · 2 eggs*

Cook the spinach in boiling salted water for a few minutes, work through a sieve (step 1), leave to cool, then mix in the egg yolk, reserving the white. Make a béchamel sauce with the butter, flour, milk and salt and grated nutmeg to taste, and blend into the spinach, together with the potato starch and Parmesan cheese.

Cook the carrots in boiling salted water until tender, work through a sieve (step 2), then sauté in butter for a few minutes. Add the flour, stirring constantly, then the milk a little at a time off the heat. Cook over low heat for 10 minutes. Remove from heat, stir in the Parmesan cheese, and salt and grated nutmeg to taste, and leave to cool. Add 2 egg yolks, reserving the whites, and beat the mixture for 10 minutes.

Add 2 egg whites, beaten until stiff, to carrot mixture and 1 egg white, also beaten until stiff, to spinach mixture. Butter a high-sided ovenproof mold and carefully pour in the spinach mixture and the carrot mixture, without mixing the two (step 3). Bake in a bain-marie in a moderate oven (350°F) for about 1 hour. Unmold and serve immediately.

Other vegetables, such as cauliflower, may also be used in this manner to make vegetable molds.

179

Cheese Soufflé

Ingredients: *4 tablespoons butter ·
6 tablespoons flour · 2 cups boiling milk ·
2 tablespoons grated Parmesan cheese ·
6 tablespoons grated Gruyère cheese · salt ·
4 eggs*

Heat the butter in a pan, add the flour and
cook for a few minutes. Add the milk and cook,
stirring constantly, for 5 minutes. Remove
from heat, add cheeses and salt (step 1). Beat
the egg yolks until foamy and add gradually.
Whip the egg whites until stiff, then fold in
gently (step 2). Pour into a soufflé dish, buttered
and lightly sprinkled with flour (step 3) and
bake in a hot oven (400°F) for 20 minutes or
until risen and golden. Serve immediately.

Asparagus Soufflé

Cook the tender parts of 1 lb asparagus in
boiling salted water for a few minutes, drain
and place in a buttered soufflé dish. Heat 1 cup
milk with 3 slices onion and ½ bay leaf; strain.
In a pan heat 3 tablespoons butter, add 3 tablespoons flour and cook for a few minutes. Add
the milk all at once and cook, stirring constantly, for about 5 minutes. Remove from
heat and stir in 3 egg yolks, beaten with salt,
pepper and paprika to taste, and 3 tablespoons
grated Parmesan cheese. Leave to cool and
fold in 3 egg whites, whipped until stiff. Pour
mixture on the asparagus and bake in a hot
oven (400°F) for about 20 minutes or until
risen and golden on top. Serve immediately.

Fish Soufflé

Melt 2 tablespoons butter in a pan, add 3 table-spoons flour and cook for a few minutes. Add 1 cup boiling milk all at once and cook, stirring constantly, for about 5 minutes. Remove from heat and stir in salt and pepper to taste, 5 tablespoons grated Gruyère cheese, 3 egg yolks, one at a time, and 6 tablespoons cold white fish, freshly cooked and shredded. Fold in 3 egg whites, beaten until stiff, and pour mixture into a buttered soufflé dish. Bake in a hot oven (400°F) for 20 minutes, or until risen and golden on top. Serve immediately.

Brussels Sprouts Soufflé

Cook 1 lb Brussels sprouts and $\frac{1}{2}$ lb potatoes, peeled, in boiling salted water for 20 minutes, or until tender, then work through a sieve or food chopper. Add 3 egg yolks, 4 tablespoons butter and salt and pepper to taste, and beat the mixture until smooth. Fold in 3 egg whites, beaten until stiff, and pour mixture into a soufflé dish. Sprinkle with grated Gruyère cheese and bake in a hot oven (350°F) for 20 minutes or until risen and golden on top. Serve the soufflé immediately. Serves 6.

Sweet Potato Soufflé

Peel 1 lb yams or sweet potatoes and cut into $\frac{1}{2}$-inch cubes. Put into a saucepan with 1 cup milk and a little salt. Bring to a boil, cover and simmer for 20 minutes or until tender. Drain, reserving the milk. Mash the yam or sweet potato.

Melt $\frac{1}{4}$ cup butter in a clean pan and stir in 2 tablespoons flour. Cook for 1 minute, then stir in the reserved milk, made up to $1\frac{1}{4}$ cups with more milk if necessary. Simmer until thickened, then cool slightly.

Separate 4 eggs and beat the yolks into the sauce with the yam or sweet potato purée, 1 cup shredded cheese, a pinch of cayenne and a little salt. Beat the egg whites until stiff and fold in. Pour into a greased soufflé dish and bake in a moderately hot oven (375°F) for 30 minutes. Serve immediately.

Cream Soups

Cream of Artichoke Soup

Ingredients: *4 large artichokes · lemon juice ·*
3 tablespoons butter · ¼ cup flour ·
1 ¾ cups milk · salt · grated nutmeg ·
3 cups stock

To finish: *parsley, finely chopped ·*
bread croûtons, toasted or sautéed in butter
until golden on all sides · grated cheese

Clean the artichokes, halve them, discard the
chokes and let stand in water with lemon juice
to prevent discoloration. Cut in quarters and
sauté over low heat in 1 tablespoon butter for
10–15 minutes (step 1). Prepare a béchamel
sauce with the butter, flour, milk and salt and
grated nutmeg to taste. Work the artichokes
through a food chopper or sieve (step 2), add
to the béchamel sauce and return pan to heat
for 10 minutes. Add the stock and bring
mixture to a boil. Add a generous amount of
parsley. Serve with croûtons (step 3) and
grated cheese.

Cream of Lentil Soup

Put ¾ cup dried lentils in cold water to cover
with 1 clove of garlic, 1 carrot and 1 onion,
all peeled, and a bouquet garni. Bring to a boil,
skim off the scum and cook for about 1½ hours.
Remove and discard vegetables and bouquet
garni and work lentils and their liquid through
a food chopper or sieve. Prepare croûtons as
for above recipe. Stir 1 tablespoon butter and
½ cup cream into the sieved lentils, reheat
gently and serve immediately. Serve the
croûtons separately.

Cream of Carrot Soup
(Potage Crécy)

Put ½ lb carrots, peeled, 3½ tablespoons rice,
1 onion, peeled, 1 bouquet garni, 1 leek,
cleaned, and 1 quart water in a pan. Bring to
a boil and cook over low heat for about 45
minutes. Remove and discard the bouquet
garni and work the mixture through a food
chopper or sieve. Prepare bread croûtons to
taste. Stir 1 tablespoon butter and ½ cup
cream into the sieved vegetables, reheat gently
and serve immediately. Serve the croûtons
separately.

Cream of Mushroom Soup

Ingredients: *1 ¼ cups fresh mushrooms or 2 tablespoons dried mushrooms, soaked in lukewarm water, squeezed dry and sliced · 3 ½ tablespoons butter · 3 cups stock · ¼ cup flour · 1 ¾ cups milk · salt · grated nutmeg*

To finish: *parsley, chopped · croûtons*

Clean and trim fresh mushrooms (if using) and slice them finely (step 1). Heat 1 tablespoon butter in a small pan, add the mushrooms and sauté for a few minutes. Add ¼ cup stock and cook, covered, over very low heat for about 15 minutes. Prepare a béchamel sauce with remaining butter, the flour, milk and salt and grated nutmeg to taste (step 2). Work mushrooms through a food chopper (step 3), add them to the béchamel sauce and cook over moderate heat for 10 minutes. Add remaining stock, bring to a boil and stir in the parsley. Serve with croûtons separately.

Cream of Pea Soup

Cover 1¼ cups dried split peas with cold water and let stand for 1 hour. Drain, put in a pan with cold water to cover and a little salt and bring to a boil. Skim the scum from the surface, cover pan and cook over low heat for about ½ hour.

In another pan cook ½ onion, finely chopped, in 2 tablespoons butter until golden, add 1 carrot, peeled, the green part of 2 leeks, cleaned, a few chopped lettuce or spinach leaves and ¼ bay leaf and cook for a few minutes. Add the peas and their cooking water and cook, covered, over low heat for about 1 hour. Work through a food chopper or sieve and return to the heat and reheat gently. Add salt to taste, 2 tablespoons butter and a few tablespoons cream, if desired. Serve with 3½ tablespoons diced ham, croûtons and a generous amount of grated Parmesan cheese.

Cream of Tomato Soup

Cook 1½ lb tomatoes, peeled and chopped, 1 medium onion, sliced, ½ teaspoon sugar and a pinch of salt for ½ hour. Work the mixture through a food chopper or sieve and keep warm. In another pan heat 4 tablespoons butter, add 4 tablespoons flour and cook, stirring constantly, until well blended. Stir in 1 quart cold milk and a pinch of salt and cook over low heat for about 20 minutes. Put a pinch of sodium bicarbonate in a soup tureen, pour in the tomato mixture and stir in the hot milk mixture. Mix well and serve with croûtons.

Brussels Sprouts Soup

Wash and trim 2 cups Brussels sprouts and cook in boiling salted water with ½ bay leaf, ½ onion, thinly sliced, ¼ clove of garlic and a few parsley sprigs until tender. Drain and work through a food chopper. Add salt, pepper and grated nutmeg to taste, and 1 quart stock, and bring to a boil. Serve with croûtons.

Potage Santé (Vichyssoise)

Ingredients: *2–3 leeks, depending on size ·
3 tablespoons butter · 1 lb potatoes, peeled and
quartered · water · salt · hot milk ·
3½ oz sorrel leaves, chopped and cooked in
1 tablespoon butter · 1–2 egg yolks ·
a few tablespoons cream · ½ teaspoon chervil*

To finish: *croûtons*

Slice the white parts of the leeks finely and cook
in 1 tablespoon of the butter for a few minutes
(step 1). Add the potatoes, 6 cups water and a
little salt to taste, and cook until potatoes are
tender. Work mixture through a food chopper
or sieve (step 2), and thin the soup if necessary, with a little water and hot milk. Add the
sorrel leaves and pour soup into a tureen
(step 3). Stir in the egg yolks, mixed with the
cream, the remaining butter and the chervil.
Serve with fried or toasted croûtons in a
separate dish.

Cream of Vegetable Soup

Clean and trim 1 small Savoy cabbage, slice finely, cover with boiling water and leave to stand. Finely slice 2 carrots, 2 potatoes, 1 turnip and the white part of 2 leeks, and cook over moderate heat in 1 tablespoon butter for a few minutes. Add 6 cups boiling stock and cook over low heat for 1 hour. Drain the cabbage and add to the mixture with 1 clove of garlic, peeled and crushed, and cook for 25 minutes. Work through a food chopper or sieve and add enough hot stock to obtain 1 quart liquid. Reheat. Put 1–2 slices fried bread in each plate and pour the soup over.

Potage Dubarry

In a pan, cook 1 cauliflower, 1 onion, and 1 bay leaf in boiling salted water until cauliflower is tender.

Prepare a roux: in a small pan heat 3 tablespoons butter, add 3 tablespoons flour and cook mixture, stirring constantly, adding a few tablespoons cooking water from the cauliflower, until well blended and golden. Work the cauliflower and its cooking liquid through a food chopper or sieve, return to heat and stir in the roux, 2 egg yolks and $\frac{1}{2}$ cup cream, without letting the mixture boil. Serve the soup immediately with crusty bread served separately.

Cream of Watercress Soup

Cook $\frac{3}{4}$ lb potatoes, peeled, and 1 bunch watercress, washed and trimmed, in boiling salted water for $\frac{1}{2}$ hour. Work through a food chopper or sieve and add 2 tablespoons butter and $\frac{1}{2}$ cup cream. Reheat gently and serve the soup immediately with croûtons in a separate dish.

187

Thick Soups

Zucchini and Tomato Soup

Ingredients: *4 zucchini · 1 or more tomatoes, depending on size · 1 tablespoon butter · 1 clove of garlic, peeled · 5 cups stock · ½ cup rice*

To finish: *grated Parmesan cheese*

Melt the butter in a large pan, add the garlic, cook for a few minutes then discard. Dice the zucchini (step 1) and sauté until golden (step 2). Chop the tomato and add to mixture. Cook for a few minutes, add the stock (step 3) and bring to a boil. Stir in the rice and cook until *al dente*. Serve with grated Parmesan cheese.

Pistou

Wash 2 leeks, dry them and slice finely. Dip 4 tomatoes in boiling water and peel. Wash and peel 6 oz potatoes and dice them. Put the leeks, 2 chopped tomatoes, the potatoes, ¾ cup green beans and ½ cup kidney beans in a large pan with 2 quarts water. Add salt and pepper to taste and cook for 15 minutes. Add 3 oz vermicelli and cook for 15 minutes. Chop 3 cloves of garlic, the remaining 2 tomatoes and a generous amount of basil very finely, and stir in 4 tablespoons olive oil and 3½ tablespoons grated Gruyère cheese. Put garlic mixture in the bottom of a soup tureen and pour in soup.

Leek and Rice Soup

Heat 2 tablespoons butter in a pan, add ¾ lb leeks, washed, dried and thinly sliced, and cook for a few minutes. Add 1 teaspoon tomato paste and 6 cups stock and cook for about 20 minutes. Add ¾ cup rice and cook until rice is *al dente*. Add parsley, finely chopped, and serve with grated Parmesan cheese.

Greek Vegetable Soup

Bring about 5 cups chicken stock to a boil, add about ¾ cup rice and cook until rice is *al dente*. In a soup tureen beat 2 egg yolks with the juice of 1 or 2 lemons and add ½ cup warm stock, stirring constantly. Add the rice and stock and serve immediately.

Minestrone Milanese

Ingredients: *1 oz smoked bacon ·*
4 tablespoons olive oil · parsley, chopped ·
sage · 1 clove of garlic, peeled and finely
chopped · 1 onion, finely chopped ·
a few celery stalks · 2 carrots · 1 leek ·
1 tomato · 4 potatoes · fresh basil leaves,
chopped · ¾ cup fresh beans, or dried beans
soaked overnight in cold water and drained ·
2 stock cubes · salt · pepper · ½ small Savoy
cabbage, separated into leaves · 4 oz rice or
vermicelli

To finish: *grated Parmesan cheese*

Chop and sauté the bacon, discarding liquid
fat. In a large pan cook the oil, parsley to
taste, sage, and the garlic and onion for a few
minutes. Add the bacon, celery, carrots and
leek, all finely sliced (step 1), the tomato,
chopped, 2 potatoes, diced, and 2 whole
potatoes (step 2), the basil and the beans (step
3). Cook for a few minutes, stirring constantly,
add 10 cups hot, not boiling, water, the stock
cubes, and salt and pepper to taste, and bring
to a boil. Cook, covered, over low heat for
1¾ hours. Add the cabbage leaves and continue cooking for 45 minutes (in winter, cook
cabbage for only 20 minutes). Add the rice
20 minutes before the end of the cooking time,
or the vermicelli 8 minutes before the end of
the cooking time, and serve with a generous
amount of grated Parmesan cheese served
separately.

Minestrone Genovese

Wash and chop 2 oz carrots, 3 oz zucchini,
10 oz potatoes and 5 oz Savoy cabbage. Place
in a large pan with 1 tablespoon dried mushrooms, soaked in lukewarm water and squeezed
dry, ¾ cup fresh peas, 6 tablespoons dried
beans, soaked overnight in cold water and
drained, about 10 cups water, 1 tablespoon
butter, salt and pepper to taste and 2 stock
cubes. Cook for about 2 hours, then work
through a food chopper or sieve. Return to
heat and bring to a boil. Add 3 oz fine
vermicelli.

Five minutes before serving the soup, blend
in a chopped mixture of parsley, basil and
garlic to taste, ½ tablespoon butter and 1½
tablespoons grated Parmesan cheese, all
pounded together in a mortar.

Bean and Noodle Soup

Ingredients: *¾ cup dried red or kidney beans, soaked in cold water for 12 hours and drained · 3½ tablespoons bacon fat, 1 celery stalk, 1 small onion, 1 clove of garlic, parsley, basil, 6 tablespoons canned peeled tomatoes, all chopped · 2 quarts cold water · 2 stock cubes · salt · pepper · 1 tablespoon oil · ¾ cup short noodles or macaroni*

Put the beans in a large pan (step 1), with the bacon fat, celery, onion, garlic, parsley, basil, tomatoes, and the water. Bring the mixture to a boil, add the stock cubes, salt and pepper to taste, and cook, covered, over low heat for about 1½ hours. Work ½ the beans through a sieve (step 2), and return to the pan. Raise the heat, add the noodles (step 3), and cook until noodles are *al dente*. Remove soup from the heat and let stand for a few minutes. Stir in the oil and serve immediately.

Potée Savoyarde

In a saucepan sauté 6 tablespoons chopped salt pork, for a few minutes, add 2 leeks and 1 onion, both sliced, and sauté for a few minutes. Add 1 celery stalk and $1\frac{1}{4}$ cups potatoes, peeled and sliced, and 1 quart water and bring the mixture to a boil. Cook over medium heat for 30 minutes then stir in 2 cups milk. Bring to a boil and cook over high heat for a few minutes, adding salt and pepper to taste. Grate 3 oz Gruyère cheese, sprinkle on slices of crusty bread, and toast in the oven until golden. Serve with the soup.

Pumpkin Rice Soup

Heat $\frac{1}{4}$ cup butter in a saucepan. Add 1 large onion, peeled and finely chopped, 1 celery stick, finely chopped, 1 large carrot, scraped and finely chopped, and $\frac{1}{4}$ cup diced slab bacon. Fry for 5 minutes, stirring occasionally. Remove the seeds from $1\frac{1}{2}$ lb pumpkin and cut into chunks, leaving the skin on. Add to the pan and fry, stirring, for a further 5 minutes. Add $1\frac{1}{2}$ quarts chicken stock, 1 garlic clove, crushed, and salt and pepper to taste and simmer for 10 minutes.

Add 1 cup rice and simmer for a further 15 minutes or until the rice is *al dente*. Stir in 3 tablespoons grated Parmesan cheese and serve immediately.

Vegetable and Bread Soup

Wash and pick over 1 cup dried lentils, then soak in cold water overnight. Drain and place in a saucepan with $1\frac{1}{2}$ quarts water. Bring to a boil and simmer for 45 minutes.

Meanwhile, shell 1 lb each fresh fava or lima beans and peas.

Sieve or purée the lentils and their cooking liquor and return to the pan. Add the beans and peas, $\frac{1}{2}$ cup diced slab bacon, 6 cups shredded cabbage, 4 cups shredded spinach and seasoning. Return to a boil and simmer for 25 minutes. Line soup bowls with thin slices of brown bread and pour in the soup. Serve immediately.

Onion Soup

Ingredients: *6 oz onions, thinly sliced ·*
2 tablespoons butter · 2 level tablespoons flour ·
5 cups stock · salt · pepper · thin slices of bread ·
5 tablespoons grated Gruyère cheese

Sauté the onions in the butter for a moment,
sprinkle them with the flour (step 1) and, as
soon as they start to brown, stir in the stock.
Add salt and pepper to taste and cook for about
20 minutes. Place thin slices of bread in the
bottom of a soup tureen, sprinkle with grated
Gruyère cheese (step 2) and pour the soup
over (step 3). Let stand for 10 minutes before
serving, or sprinkle with more Gruyère cheese
and put in a hot oven (400°F) until golden
and crusty on top.

Lentil Soup

Soak 2 cups dried lentils in lukewarm water
for 12 hours, drain and put in a pan with
cold water to cover. Cook, covered, for 2–3
hours, then work through a food chopper or
sieve. In a small pan, heat 2 tablespoons
butter, add a mixture of onion, celery, garlic
and sage leaves, all chopped, and sauté for a
few minutes. Stir the mixture into the lentils,
add 2 stock cubes, salt and pepper to taste,
and return the soup to the heat. Bring to a
boil, remove from heat and serve with slices
of bread fried in butter and a generous amount
of grated Parmesan cheese.

194

Spinach Soup

Clean and wash $1\frac{1}{2}$ lb fresh spinach, cook without water and chop coarsely. Sauté quickly in 1 tablespoon butter and leave to cool. In a bowl beat 2 eggs with 2 tablespoons grated Parmesan cheese, and salt and grated nutmeg to taste, and stir into the spinach. Pour spinach into 5 cups boiling stock, return to heat and bring to a boil. Place 2 toasted bread slices in each plate, add soup and a generous amount of grated Parmesan cheese and serve immediately.

Auvergne Soup

In a large pan put 2 quarts water, 4 carrots and 2 turnips, both sliced, one 2-lb cabbage, quartered, and 1 clove of garlic, peeled and crushed. Bring to a boil and simmer for about 10 minutes. Add 4 small potatoes, peeled and sliced, salt and pepper to taste, and cook for 10 minutes. Fry 4 tablespoons diced lean bacon in a skillet, drain and add to the soup. Simmer for 5 minutes. Place a slice of French bread in each plate and pour the soup over them. Serves 6–8.

Spicy Bortsch

Put 1 carrot and 1 lb parsnips, all peeled and chopped, in a saucepan with 4 tomatoes, chopped, 1 onion spiked with 9 cloves, 1 lb beef bones, cracked, and 1 lb beef for stew, diced. Add 1 teaspoon sugar, 6 black peppercorns, 1 bay leaf, 5 cups cold water and $\frac{1}{2}$ teaspoon salt and bring to a boil. Cover and simmer for 2 hours or until the beef is tender.

Remove the bones, onion and bay leaf. Add $1\frac{1}{2}$ lb raw beets, peeled and coarsely shredded, and $1\frac{1}{2}$ cups chopped red or green cabbage, and simmer, uncovered, for a further 12–15 minutes. Serve hot.

Broths and Consommés

Meat Consommé

Ingredients: *¾ lb stewing beef · ¾ lb stewing veal · 1 beef bone · 1 veal knuckle · chicken neck and bones, if desired · 3½ quarts water · salt · 3 peppercorns · 1 carrot, peeled · 1 onion, peeled and stuck with 1 clove · 1 bouquet garni of parsley and celery*

To clarify: *1 egg white*

Put the meats, bone and knuckle, and chicken neck and bones, if using, in a large pan with the water, salt and peppercorns, and bring very slowly to a boil, skimming the scum as it forms on the surface (step 1). Add the vegetables and bouquet garni (steps 2 and 3), and bring to a boil. Cook, covered, over low heat for 3 hours. Strain through a sieve, reserving the meats for other uses, and discard fat from surface, if soup is to be served immediately. (The broth can be left to stand until cold, and fat can then be removed from surface.)

To clarify: put 1 quart cold broth in a pan with 1 egg white and bring to a boil, beating constantly with a wire whisk. Simmer, covered, over very low heat for ½ hour and strain through a sieve covered with a cloth.

Chicken Consommé

Prepare a small chicken for cooking, slicing and reserving the heart and liver. If possible, brown it in the oven in a little butter. Place in a large pan with the reserved heart and liver, 3 quarts water, and salt to taste. Bring slowly to a boil, skimming the scum as it forms on surface. Add 1 carrot, peeled, 1 leek, cleaned, and 1 small onion, quartered, and bring to a boil. Cook the chicken, covered, over low heat for 1½–2 hours. Remove and discard vegetables and strain broth through a sieve covered with a cloth soaked in water and wrung dry. Serve very hot, preferably in small bowls or cups.

Classic Consommé

Ingredients: *2 quarts warm broth, prepared with beef, chicken and vegetables · ½ lb lean beef · 1 small carrot and 1 leek, both thinly sliced · 1 egg white*

Clean the meat, removing all fat, and chop it. In a pan beat the meat and carrot, leek and egg white with a wire whisk (step 1). Beating constantly, add the broth a little at a time (step 2). Bring the mixture slowly to a boil, stirring constantly, and cook, covered, over very low heat for about 1 hour. Strain through a fine cloth, soaked in lukewarm water and wrung dry (step 3), then bring to a boil. The consommé should be perfectly clear. Serve in small bowls or cups.

Consommé Fantasia

Beat 3 eggs with a little salt until light and foamy, and stir in a generous handful of fresh spinach, chopped, 1 tablespoon Italian prosciutto, chopped, and 2 tablespoons grated Parmesan cheese. Cook the mixture on both sides as you would a frittata and cut it into thin strips. Divide the strips equally between 4 bowls or cups and pour in boiling consommé. Serve immediately.

Chicken Consommé with Marsala

Prepare chicken broth, leave to cool and remove the fat from the surface. Return to the heat, stir in 1 egg white and bring to a boil, beating constantly with a wire whisk. Strain the consommé through 2 or 3 fine cloths or through cheesecloth. Return to the heat, stir in 1 glass dry Marsala for each quart of consommé, and bring to a boil. Serve immediately in small bowls or cups.

Calabrian Consommé

Ingredients: *¾ cup ricotta or other white cheese · 4 tablespoons grated Parmesan cheese · 2 eggs, separated · salt · pepper · grated nutmeg · 1 quart boiling consommé*

Work the ricotta through a sieve into a bowl and stir in half the Parmesan cheese, the egg yolks, salt, pepper and grated nutmeg to taste. Beat egg whites until stiff and, with a metal spoon, fold into mixture (step 1). Butter an ovenproof rectangular mold and line it with buttered wax paper. Pour the mixture into the mold (step 2), and cook in a bain-marie in a moderate oven (350°F) until set and golden on top. Remove the mold from the oven and leave to cool. Remove the wax paper carefully and cut the cheese mixture into small cubes (step 3). Put the cubes into individual soup plates, pour in boiling consommé and serve immediately with the remaining grated Parmesan cheese.

200

Cold Jellied Consommé

Cook 1 lb tomatoes, peeled and quartered, and 1 celery stalk in 3 quarts consommé for 1 hour. Work the consommé through a sieve lined with a thin cloth and leave to cool. Refrigerate until lightly set, putting very thin sheets of paper on the surface to remove the fat rising to the surface. Serve the consommé in individual bowls or cups with a small sprig of parsley and a thin slice of lemon in each. Serves 12.

Consommé Celestine

In a bowl blend 2 eggs with 10 tablespoons flour and ½ teaspoon salt. Stir in 1 cup milk, a little at a time, ½ tablespoon butter, lightly melted, and 1·tablespoon parsley, chopped. Beat the batter with a wire whisk until smooth. Heat 2 tablespoons butter in a small skillet, pour in about 1 tablespoon batter and quickly tilt and rotate the pan so that the bottom is thinly and evenly coated. Cook the crêpe until the bottom is golden, flip it over and finish cooking. Continue in this manner until all the batter is used. Roll up the crêpes and slice thinly. Pour boiling consommé over the strips and serve immediately with grated Parmesan cheese.

Chicken, Lemon and Egg Drop Soup

Place a 1 lb shank of veal in a saucepan and pour on 7 cups water. Bring to a boil, then cover and simmer for 1 hour. Meanwhile, cut up a 3-lb stewing chicken. Add to the pan with the giblets, the grated rind of 1 lemon, 2 onions, each spiked with a clove, and salt and pepper to taste. Cover again and simmer for 1 hour or until the chicken is tender.

Remove the chicken and strain the stock into a clean pan. Remove the chicken meat from the bones and chop into small pieces. Add to the stock with the juice of 1 lemon. Bring back to a boil. Beat 2 eggs together lightly. Pour the soup into a tureen and drizzle the beaten egg in a thin stream, stirring constantly. Serve immediately.

Cock-a-Leekie Soup

Ingredients: *one 2-lb lean chicken ·
the white parts of 6 leeks, thinly sliced ·
2 quarts veal stock · 1 small carrot ·
1 small onion, peeled · 1 celery stalk · salt ·
2 tablespoons butter*

To serve: *16 prunes, cooked and pitted
(optional)*

Put the chicken and stock in a pan and bring
to a boil. Skim the scum as it forms on the
surface, add the carrot, onion, celery, and salt
to taste, and cook, covered, over low heat for
about $1\frac{1}{2}$ hours. Put chicken on a chopping
board, remove and discard skin and bones and
cut flesh into thin strips (step 1). Cook the
leeks in the butter and a little salt (step 2).
Remove fat from chicken broth and strain
through a sieve. Return the chicken and leeks
to the broth (step 3), and serve very hot.
Prunes are traditionally served separately.
Serves 4–6.

202

Mulligatawny Soup

Sauté one 2-lb chicken, cut into pieces, in 1 tablespoon butter until golden on all sides. Add 1 green apple, 1 green pepper and 1 carrot, all chopped, and cook for a few minutes. Sprinkle with 1 tablespoon flour, mixed with $\frac{1}{2}$ tablespoon curry powder, and stir in 3 quarts hot water, a little at a time, $\frac{1}{2}$ tablespoon parsley, chopped, 1 clove, 1 pinch of pepper and $\frac{1}{2}$ tablespoon each of salt and sugar. Cover pan and cook over low heat for $1\frac{1}{2}$ hours. Half an hour before the end of the cooking time, add $\frac{1}{2}$ cup tomatoes, worked through a food chopper or sieve, and continue cooking the mixture until chicken is tender. Remove the chicken from pan, discard skin and bones and cube the flesh. Strain the broth through a sieve and return the broth and chicken to the heat for a few minutes. Serve immediately in warm soup dishes, with boiled rice, in a separate platter.

Tregaron Broth

Heat 2 tablespoons butter in a large saucepan. Add 1 lb slab bacon, cut into 1-inch pieces, and 1 lb beef shank, cut into chunks. Fry for 5 minutes. Add 1 large leek, sliced, 1 lb potatoes, peeled and chopped, $\frac{1}{2}$ lb carrots, peeled and chopped, $\frac{1}{2}$ lb parsnips, peeled and chopped, and 1 small rutabaga, peeled and chopped. Fry for 5 minutes longer.

Add $1\frac{1}{2}$ quarts water and bring to a boil. Stir in 1 small head white cabbage, shredded, $\frac{1}{3}$ cup fine or medium oatmeal and salt and pepper to taste. Cover and simmer for 45 minutes. Taste and adjust the seasoning before serving.

203

Gnocchetti in Broth

Ingredients: *1 tablespoon butter, at room temperature · 3½ tablespoons grated Parmesan cheese · 2 eggs, separated · salt · grated nutmeg · 3 oz semolina · 5 cups broth*

In a bowl beat the butter with the Parmesan cheese. Add the egg yolks, beating constantly, and salt and nutmeg to taste. Beat the egg white with a wire whisk until stiff (step 1) and fold into mixture with a metal spoon. Add the semolina (step 2). Bring the broth to a boil, drop in the semolina mixture, a teaspoon at a time (step 3), and cook for about 15 minutes. Serve immediately.

Liver Gnocchetti for Consommés and Broths

Chop 6 oz veal liver very finely or work it through the finest blade of a food chopper. In a skillet sauté 1 slice onion and a little parsley, both finely chopped, in 2 tablespoons butter for a few minutes. Add the liver and 2 oz white bread, soaked in milk and squeezed dry, and cook the mixture over moderate heat for a few minutes, stirring constantly. Let stand until cool, stir in 2 eggs, 4 tablespoons breadcrumbs, a little grated nutmeg, and salt to taste, and let stand for ½ hour.

With floured fingers, form walnut-sized balls and cook them in about 5 cups broth for 20 minutes. Serve immediately in warm soup dishes.

Chicken Gnocchetti for Consommés and Broths

Cook 4 oz potatoes in boiling salted water until tender, drain, peel and put them through a potato ricer or work them through a sieve. Stir in ½ chicken breast, cooked until tender in a little water and finely chopped, 2 tablespoons grated Parmesan cheese, 2 egg yolks, 2 tablespoons flour, salt and grated nutmeg to taste, and mix well. On a floured board form the mixture into small finger shapes and cut them into thick slices. Cook the gnocchetti in 5 cups boiling broth for 6–8 minutes. Serve immediately in warm soup dishes, with grated Parmesan cheese.

Passatelli in Bouillon

Ingredients: *4 tablespoons breadcrumbs ·
2 eggs · 2 tablespoons grated Parmesan cheese ·
1 tablespoon flour · ¾ oz beef marrow · salt ·
pepper · nutmeg · 5 cups boiling broth*

To serve: *grated Parmesan cheese*

In a bowl blend the breadcrumbs together with
the eggs, Parmesan cheese, flour, beef marrow,
and salt, pepper and grated nutmeg to taste,
until mixture is smooth (step 1). Work the paste
carefully through a passatelli machine (step 2),
a food chopper, using the blade with the
largest holes, or a potato ricer. As the passatelli
form, scrape them with the blade of a knife into
the boiling broth (step 3). Cook gently over
low heat for 5 minutes, pour into warm soup
dishes and serve with grated Parmesan cheese
in a separate dish.

206

Gnocchetti Bolognese

Melt 2 tablespoons butter over low heat without letting it brown; leave to cool. Stir in $3\frac{1}{2}$ tablespoons flour, 1 egg, 3 tablespoons grated Parmesan cheese, salt and grated nutmeg to taste, and spread the mixture on a plate. Bring 5 cups broth to a boil and, using 2 teaspoons dipped occasionally in the boiling broth, drop mixture by spoonfuls into the broth. Cook over moderate heat for 3–4 minutes, and serve with grated Parmesan cheese.

Soup in a Bag

In a bowl beat 3 eggs and stir in 6 tablespoons flour, 5 tablespoons grated Parmesan cheese, 4 tablespoons butter, melted, salt to taste and a little grated nutmeg. With floured fingers, shape mixture into a ball and place in the middle of a damp cloth or in a cotton bag, tying firmly with string. Put the bag in 6 cups boiling broth and cook for 40 minutes. Remove bag from broth and let cool. Remove mixture from bag, cut into slices and then into cubes. Return cubes to broth and cook for 8 minutes. Serve with grated Parmesan cheese.

Stracciatella

Bring 5 cups broth to a boil. In a bowl beat 4 eggs with 2 tablespoons breadcrumbs, 4 tablespoons grated Parmesan cheese, a little parsley, chopped, salt and grated nutmeg to taste. Add 2 tablespoons water or cold broth, pour the mixture into boiling broth and cook over moderate heat for 3–4 minutes, stirring constantly with a wire whisk. Serve with grated Parmesan cheese.

207

Profiteroles for Consommé

Ingredients: *¼ cup water · ½ tablespoon butter · 3 tablespoons flour · 1 egg*

In a small pan bring the water, butter and a pinch of salt to a boil, remove the pan from the heat and pour the flour in all at once. Stir the mixture until well blended, then return to the heat for 3–4 minutes, stirring constantly. Leave to cool, stir in the egg (step 1), and beat vigorously until the dough is light. Using a pastry bag fitted with a large tube (step 2), pipe the dough into walnut-sized balls on a slightly damp cookie sheet (step 3), leaving some space between each ball. Cook the profiteroles in a hot oven (400°F) for about 15 minutes or until they are puffed and golden. Do not open the oven door during the cooking time. Serve with boiling consommé in a separate dish.

Julienne for Consommé

Clean and wash 1 onion, 1 carrot, 1 leek, 1 celery stalk or other vegetables to taste and cut them into thin strips. Cook in 1 tablespoon butter for a few minutes, add a little salt and some broth and cook, covered, over low heat until they are *al dente*. Drain the vegetables, put them in a soup tureen or in individual bowls or cups, pour in boiling consommé and serve the soup with grated Parmesan cheese in a separate dish.

Royale for Consommé

Beat 2 eggs vigorously and slowly stir in 1 cup chicken broth, 1 tablespoon asparagus purée, 1 tablespoon pea purée, salt and pepper to taste. Pour the mixture in a buttered bowl and cook in a bain-marie or in the top of a double boiler for 20–25 minutes or until set. Remove from the heat and leave to cool. Cut the royale into cubes or other shapes to taste. Pour boiling consommé over the cubes and serve the soup immediately.

Successful Sauces

Not for nothing is the sauce cook at the top of the hierarchy in a big kitchen. A sauce can be the making of a tasty dish, or can ruin it; making a good sauce is a basic skill for any lover of cooking and offers scope for the highest flights of imagination.

A sauce is a seasoning; it draws out the flavor of other foods, emphasizes it and subtly blends with it. In some cases, the sauce makes the food more digestible; in all cases it should make a good food even better. Never allow the sauce to swamp the food; a couple of tablespoons per person will be enough to moisten and flavor the food without drowning it.

There are no short-cuts to successful sauce making. It is absolutely essential to measure the ingredients exactly, for it is the proportion of fat to flour to liquid that dictates the final consistency.

Flavorings for sauces are a combination of tradition and imagination. For a beginner it is best to follow tradition until you have learnt through taste which herbs and spices go best with which foods. The secret is never to overseason and to use the very best ingredients. If your sauce calls for stock, it should be rich, home-made stock, full of goodness. The slow cooking of different bones or vegetable cuts with water and seasonings will give your sauces flavors that stock cubes cannot give. Of course cubes are handy to have in an emergency, but if you use them all the time you will never know how delightfully different sauces can be.

Flour sauces

The basis of flour sauces is a roux, a mixture of flour cooked in fat. The proportions are very important, as is the way in which you cook the roux. If you cook it for just a moment or two so that it does not change color, you will have a white sauce; if you cook it till it is a pale straw color, the sauce will be creamy looking; if you cook the roux to a creamy coffee color, you will have a brown sauce (gravy is made from a brown roux and the fat from meat). Always cook the roux over a low heat and with the brown one, stir from time to time to make sure it does not burn.

Never try to blend a boiling liquid with the roux. Take the pan from the heat so that the roux stops cooking. If you are using hot stock or milk let it cool a little then blend it in a little at a time. If you keep a small sauce whisk especially for this blending it will be easier still. Return the pan to the heat and cook for the required length of time, stirring constantly. This way you should get perfect results every time.

No-flour sauces

There are many sauces which are not based on flour. Apple sauce to serve with pork is a sweet antidote to the richness of the meat; mint sauce to serve with lamb has a slightly acid herby flavour to bring out all the sweetness of the young meat. Savory butters flavored various ways are the simplest of sauces – formed into pats and placed cold on top of grilled steaks or chops, the butter melts into the meat.

Another basic is mayonnaise which many people do not bother to make because bought varieties are so readily available. There is a great deal of difference though between the commercial product and the one you make yourself. As with so much of cooking, once you know how to do it, it is easy. A good home-made mayonnaise is rich and creamy-textured, full of the flavor of egg yolks and oil, lightly acidulated with just enough vinegar or lemon juice to complement the cold or hot food it will be served with, from hors d'oeuvres to main courses. The basic sauce can also be varied to bring out the best of different foods.

The secret of mayonnaise lies in having everything at room temperature. If you keep your eggs in the refrigerator, take out the number you want an hour before and place them with the oil and the mixing bowl so that when you start, all will be at the same temperature. The oil you choose, traditionally olive, a lighter corn or sunflower oil, will give your mayonnaise its individual flavor. When you start to mix add the oil to the seasoned egg yolks very, very gradually, just a drop at a time at first, while you whisk all the time with the other hand. You may find it helps to wedge the bowl with a cloth to stop it moving so you have both hands free to work. After you have added about half the oil, you can add it a little more quickly – but your patience is the secret. Rush it and the mayonnaise will curdle; in which case start again, with a fresh egg yolk in another bowl and very, very gradually beat in the curdled mixture. Mayonnaise can also be made in blenders, but follow the manufacturer's instructions carefully.

Marinades can· become sauces, so they should be mentioned here too. Meat marinades tend to be based on an acid solution of wine or vinegar, spices and/or aromatic herbs and vegetables. A marinade can be used as part of the cooking liquid, giving the finished dish a deep, rich flavor. However, if the meat being marinated has a strong flavor, such as game can have, it is best to throw away the marinade after the steeping period is completed, as it may give the finished dish too gamy a taste if used for basting.

Fresh pork, whether roasted, grilled or sautéed, will be more tender and will develop a full flavor if it is marinated before cooking. You can use a dry marinade of salt, ground sage or thyme, allspice and ground bay leaf; or a liquid one of oil, either lemon juice or wine, such as a dry white wine or a dry white vermouth, and vinegar with herbs which compliment the pork, such as tarragon, sage, basil, juniper berries, thyme, and aromatic vegetables like carrots, onions and celery. Chops and steaks will require a minimum of 2 hours; although 6–12 hours is better. Loin roasts need a minimum of 6 hours, but 24 is recommended. A leg or shoulder should be steeped for at least 2 days. If the meat is to be set in the refrigerator during marination you will need to increase the minimum time by a third.

Beef for braising or cooking *en daube* is much improved by steeping in a marinade of red wine, aromatic herbs and vegetables for a minimum of six hours. However, if you are in a hurry you can omit the marination period and tip the marinade ingredients over the meat after browning; this will help to enrich and tenderize the meat. A leg of mutton soaked in a marinade based on a full-bodied red wine such as Beaujolais, Burgundy or Macon, will, when roasted, have a gamy flavor of venison. The rather insipid taste of veal can be developed and made more robust by a marinade which includes brandy, Madeira, aromatic herbs and vegetables.

The flavor of fish, particularly grilled fish, whether whole, filleted or in steaks, can be enhanced if it is marinated before cooking. Oily fish such as mackerel and fresh tuna needs an acid marinade to sharpen the rich flavor; and fish with rather a dull color or coarse texture will be much improved by using a honey, paprika or tomato-flavored marinade. Barbecued fish particularly needs to be well marinated before cooking as well as basted with the sauce during the cooking to develop the flavor and keep the delicate flesh moist. Fish only requires to be steeped in a marinade for 1–2 hours. If you are going to use the marinade for basting during cooking it may need to be strained first to remove any pieces of flavoring, such as a bay leaf, which could burn during grilling and spoil the food.

A basic marinade for grilled fish, sufficient for 4 steaks or 4 fillets, consists of 2 tbsp (30 ml) oil (olive oil is best) 2 teasp (10 ml) lemon juice, ¼ teasp (1·75 ml) salt and a pinch of pepper. To give more zest to this marinade add a tablespoon of anisette; or a teaspoon of Worcestershire sauce; or a tablespoon of clear honey and half a teaspoon of paprika; or half a grated onion, a tablespoon chopped parsley and a teaspoon paprika.

Very simple mixtures such as a French dressing seasoned with fresh or dried herbs, vinaigrette or Ravigote sauce make delicious short-term marinades for vegetables, such as mushrooms, which are to be served as an hors d'oeuvre or a salad.

Bastes

Bastes are not strictly speaking sauces, they are liquids which are poured over or brushed on grills or roasts during cooking to keep the food moist and tender as well as adding flavor and zest. Bastes may be pan drippings, seasoned butters, seasoned vinegar or wine and oil, or a special sauce. Bastes are perhaps the essence of good barbecue cooking and all barbecue sauces, which are bastes, are based on oil or melted butter or margarine, with the addition of fairly strong seasonings such as ketchups, Worcestershire sauce, soy sauce, mustard, vinegar, herbs, spices and garlic. Salt tends to be omitted from meat bastes as it draws out the succulent juices and toughens the meat. Bastes can be prepared well in advance, closely covered to prevent their pungent flavors penetrating other foods, and stored in the refrigerator; this allows time for the flavors to develop and for dried herbs to release their volatiles.

The delight of bastes is that you can use your own creative flair to make a recipe to suit the occasion and the food.

A basic barbecue grill baste for brushing over sausages, hamburgers, chops, steaks or chicken pieces before cooking is a blend of 1 tbsp (15 ml) prepared mustard, ½ teasp (2·5 ml) pepper, 1 tbsp (15 ml) soft brown sugar, 2 tbsp (30 ml) wine vinegar or lemon juice, 3 tbsp (45 ml) tomato ketchup. To this basic mixture can be added chopped, fresh or dried herbs and a crushed garlic clove. For a more exotic mix try a wine baste consisting of equal quantities of olive oil and wine – use either red or white wine, sherry or vermouth – seasoned with a little chopped marjoram or thyme or rosemary, a crushed garlic clove and a bay leaf, and allow it to infuse in a cool place for several hours.

A simple baste for fish, such as cod, haddock or mackerel, is a blend of 2 oz (50 g) melted butter, 1 tbsp (15 ml) lemon juice, 1 teasp (5 ml) mild mustard, pepper and salt and finely chopped parsley or dill weed. This is also good for pouring over hot cooked vegetables, particularly cabbage or celery.

Sauces for eggs and fish

You will find a range of different recipes for sauces on pages 82 to 99 but it is worth remembering the major sauces from which others are made. Béchamel, for example, so often served with eggs and fish, is the base for Aurore sauce, Maître d'hôtel sauce, caper sauce, curry sauce, mornay sauce, cream sauce, Soubise sauce and white wine sauce. Béchamel can be made in bulk and frozen in 225 ml (½ pt) portions, and the flavorings added later.

Hollandaise is an essential standby if you like fish – from the basic you can make Béarnaise sauce, as well as mustard, tomato and Maltese. Because like mayonnaise it has a tendency to curdle, hollandaise does not freeze but it will store for two weeks in a refrigerator if well covered; freezing is not really necessary. Velouté sauce, from which Parisian, Suprême and Chaud-froid are made, is another handy sauce for eggs and fish. It is creamy colored and can be made up with different flavored stocks. To freeze it in bulk (225 ml/½ pt portions), make the roux and stir in the stock. Leave to cool then freeze. Add the flavorings when you recook the sauce as you need it.

Italian green sauce and green pepper sauce are unusual but excellent with eggs and fish. Why not try them? They can only enlarge your reputation as a distinctive and imaginative cook.

Introduction to Eggs and Fish

After meat, eggs and fish are the main sources of protein in our diet; eggs are a remarkably cheap way to ensure good and healthy eating. They are incredibly versatile and may be served at any meal of the day, from breakfast on to supper, and may be appetizer, starter, main dish, dessert, sauce or part of a soup. They are nourishing and satisfying, they add volume and flavor to cakes and batters and nothing can really replace them as a binding agent in meat loaves and croquettes. Eggs are one of the most essential aids to good cooking in the kitchen, with them a meal can be prepared, completed or extended.

Fish are more notable for the variety available than for the different uses to which they may be put. Though fish (especially smoked) is sometimes served at breakfast, it is usually a main meal dish. For very formal dinners, it can even have a course on its own. Few fish are farmed and their flesh therefore presents the gourmet with a wider variety of flavors than meat. Both sea and freshwater fish offer all shades of texture and flavor, to be plainly grilled and baked or richly dressed in delicate sauces. Shellfish which range from lobster and oysters through crab and scallops to the tiniest shrimps, are always a gastronomic treat and feature among the luxury dishes of the world.

Eggs

Eggs are very versatile, they contain large proportions of protein and fats, calcium, iron, the most vital amino acids and many vitamins. They are also very easy to digest, which is why they feature so largely in invalid diets. While it would be unwise to try and live entirely on eggs, they can well replace meat at two or three family meals a week, and you need never be at a loss to feed unexpected guests if you keep a stock of fresh eggs in the refrigerator.

When cooking eggs always be sure they are fresh. Be particularly careful if you keep them in the refrigerator, since the cold almost always prevents you smelling a bad one. To test an egg, place it, whole, in a jug of cold salted water; if it is very fresh it will sink and the staler it is the higher it will float in the water. It is a wise precaution, when mixing several eggs for an omelet or a cake, to break each egg separately into a cup before adding it to other eggs or other ingredients — if one egg then turns out to be bad it will not have spoilt the rest.

Poached Eggs

To poach an egg, first break it into a cup. Use a shallow, wide pan such as a skillet, fill it with boiling water and add a little vinegar to help prevent the white separating from the yolk. Keep the water simmering very gently and slide each egg into the pan from the cup. Poach for about $3\frac{1}{2}$–$4\frac{1}{2}$ minutes until set. Lift egg out with a draining spoon and let all the water drain away before serving it.

Soft-boiled (soft-cooked) Eggs

There are two ways of boiling eggs and no two cooks will agree on which is the best. Either place the egg in a pan of cold water, bring it slowly to a boil and simmer steadily for 2–3 minutes depending how soft you like your eggs; or bring the pan of water to a boil and add the egg when it boils, allow the water to return to a boil and boil gently for 4–5 minutes from that time. If using the second method it is important that the egg should be at room temperature before it is put into the pan of boiling water, or it will crack. If the shell does crack, a little vinegar added to the water will prevent the white running out.

Eggs unfortunately turn an aluminum pan black, so it is best to use an enamel or non-stick pan, or to keep a small pan specially for eggs. If you have to use one of your best aluminum pans, a little vinegar in the water will help to prevent discoloration.

Hard-boiled (hard-cooked) Eggs

For hard-boiled eggs, always put the eggs into boiling water. Allow 10–12 minutes steady boiling, but take care not to leave them any longer or the yolks will start to turn black and the whites will toughen. When the cooking time is up, drain off the hot water and pour cold water into the pan, so the eggs are cool enough to handle.

Fried Eggs

Fried eggs need careful cooking if they are not to be greasy and tough. If the fat is too hot the whites will certainly be tough, so place the pan of shallow fat over a moderate heat. Break each egg into a cup and slide it into the fat. Baste the eggs with the fat so that they cook evenly and, when set, lift them out carefully with a draining spoon or fish slice and drain the fat away thoroughly before serving them.

Omelets

An omelet can be a meal in itself, so it is important to learn to make a good, basic omelet. Once that is mastered, there is no end to the variety of fillings that can be added. The first requirement is for a good omelet pan. This should be made of cast iron or thick aluminum — nothing else will give such good, even heat distribution to the whole of the pan. Non-stick pans are ideal for omelets, but if you use an ordinary surfaced pan you can still get perfect results if you keep the pan for omelets only. An iron or aluminum pan will have to be seasoned and is best never washed — in that way it builds up a good, smooth surface to which your omelet will never stick. If you keep the pan for omelets only you can wipe it clean after use with a damp cloth or paper towel dipped in salt. Obviously if you use it for other foods which might stick, the pan will have to be washed. The pan should also be small, not more than 7–8 inches in diameter, otherwise the eggs will spread out into a thin layer and the omelet will be dry.

For one person, use 2–3 eggs. Break them into a bowl and beat them well with a fork. Add about a tablespoon of water, and season with a little salt and pepper. Then put the empty pan on the heat and let it get hot before adding butter (if you put the butter into the cold pan, it will be burnt before the pan is hot enough for your omelet). Use very little butter, just enough to coat the base and sides of the pan all over but without leaving a pool of butter in the middle. Pour in the beaten egg mixture, let it set for a moment then stir it gently round with a spatula or the flat of a fork. As the omelet cooks, lift the edge and let the raw egg run underneath, into contact with the hot pan; as it cooks through the center of the omelet will bubble up. Do not overcook it or it will be dry and rubbery, but when just cooked fold one side over the other carefully, using a spatula, and slide it out on to a hot plate. Don't try to keep omelets hot in the oven or they will go rubbery — serve them straight away. If serving two people, it is better to make one large omelet and divide it rather than two separate ones.

Fish

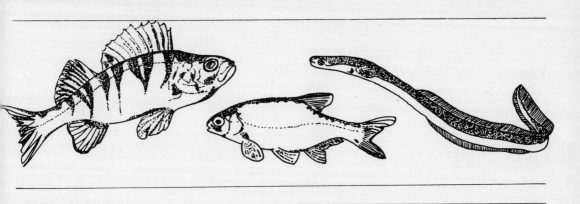

Bass

The name bass covers a large family of sea and fresh-water fish. If there is no fisherman in your family, to bring home fresh bass, substitute salmon trout in recipes calling for bass.

Carp

These live to a very great age and may weigh 40 lb or more. Carp are fresh-water fish, very popular in continental Europe and in Jewish communities all over the world. Though carp steaks or small carp may be fried or stewed like any other fish, it is traditional to bake a carp whole, with a stuffing to help it keep its shape. Carp often require soaking for a long time in fresh clean water to remove a slightly muddy flavor.

Cod

An excellent, meaty fish suitable for all methods of cooking. A good cod may weigh many pounds, so the flesh is often sold in steaks or fillets (including smoked fillets), but a small fish can be baked whole to give a very tasty dish.
Salt Cod is a Mediterranean favorite and if this is not readily available, where a recipe calls for salt cod, fresh cod may be used instead, though the flavor of the finished dish will be affected.

Crab

Crabs, like lobsters, are frequently sold ready killed and dressed; they are boiled in the same way as lobsters. When choosing a crab, pick a medium sized one rather than a very big one, or one that is heavy for its size. An average crab about 6 inches across should weigh 2½–3 lb.

Cuttlefish

A type of squid, usually cut into pieces, fried and served with a rich garlic-flavored sauce.

Eel

There are many types of eel, from the small silvery fresh-water eel, which is sweet and delicate in flavor, to the great conger eel which has meat like a tough steak. Large eels need long, slow cooking, but all are suitable for pies and soups. The smaller varieties may be fried, poached, broiled and jellied. Smoked eel is a delicacy usually served as an appetizer, either alone or as part of a mixed hors d'oeuvre.

Frog

A frog is an amphibian rather than a fish, but frogs' legs are generally treated as fish rather than meat. Only the hind legs are used, these being the fleshiest. They are either boiled and served with a sauce or fried in butter. Frogs' legs are generally served as an appetizer or entrée rather than as a main course.

Hake

Another meaty, white fish, hake is suitable for baking, frying, steaming and stewing. Its bones can be removed more easily than those of most other fish, which makes it particularly suitable for children.

Halibut

Halibut is a large flat fish, suitable for cooking by all methods. A halibut may be very large indeed (up to 200 lb) and is therefore sold in small portions. Its flavor is good and delicate if the fish is very fresh; if it

Cooking and Serving Fish

has been kept on ice it may need the help of a good sauce. To savor the very best halibut, buy 'chicken halibut' – a very young fish weighing not more than 3 lb.

Herring

This succulent fish, smaller and slightly less strongly flavored than mackerel, should be eaten very fresh, either broiled or fried, and is also good soused in a vinegar liquor.

Herring are available salted or pickled, kippered or smoked, and as herring pâté.

Lobster

One of the largest shellfish, lobster is highly prized in all parts of the world. As with all shellfish, lobster should be eaten as fresh as possible and should preferably be bought alive; most fishdealers will, however, supply them ready cooked. A lobster is usually killed by boiling; it may be immersed in cold water and brought gradually to a boil or it may be plunged straight into boiling water. After preparation in this way the lobster may be dressed and served cold, or it may be cooked again for serving as a hot dish. If you are serving lobster hot, and can buy a live one, it is in fact preferable to kill the lobster by piercing the nerve at the top of the spinal cord with a sharp knife, so that the flesh has to be cooked only once. For a hot dish it may be sautéed, broiled or baked.

Mackerel

An excellent, oily fleshed fish that must be eaten very fresh. If it is at all stale (indicated by a limp body) the flesh is indigestible and can be poisonous. Mackerel are excellent broiled or baked, particularly if served with a sharp sauce such as a mustard sauce. Like herring, mackerel are excellent soused in vinegar.

Mussel

These bivalve molluscs, found all over the seashores of Europe and the USA, should be still alive when you buy them, with their shells tightly closed. To prepare them for cooking, wash them in several bowls of fresh water and scrub the shells thoroughly. If there are any open shells, tap them sharply with the brush; discard any that do not respond by closing immediately as these are probably dead. The easiest way to cook a small quantity of mussels is in their own steam in a tightly covered pan; when cooked the shells open and the 'beard' can be removed and discarded. They also make excellent stews and soups.

Perch

A small fresh-water fish, best boiled, fried or stewed. In certain areas of Europe it is a very fine fish indeed. Perch is rarely sold in a fishdealer's store, so if you cannot find a supply substitute rainbow trout.

Pike

The pike is a coarse fleshed fish. A big pike may be 30 lb or more, but the best for eating weigh between 3 lb and 7 lb. It may be baked, fried or stewed, but may be rather dry if broiled.

Red Mullet

This is a prime fish for broiling, frying and baking. It is usually cooked whole, with the head and tail still on. Though it is normally cleaned of its intestines, the liver is left inside as a delicacy.

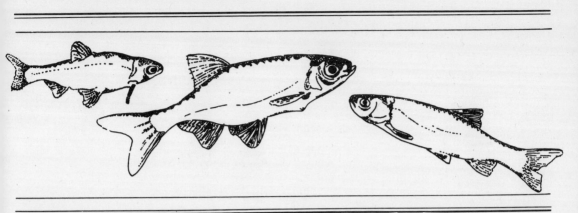

Salmon

Salmon is regarded as a prize fish in all parts of Europe and North America. It is an oily fleshed fish, but without the coarseness of tuna, and its flavor is excellent. It may be boiled, poached, broiled, baked, fried or stewed and served with a variety of sauces. Although the salmon lives for the most part in the sea, it is caught when it comes up the rivers to spawn, and is therefore a seasonal fish, at its best in Britain from February to August. The best salmon are said to come from Norway, Scotland and Canada. For a big celebration, a salmon is often poached whole and served cold with mayonnaise.

Smoked salmon is also a delicacy, served as an hors d'oeuvre.

Sardine

This is the young of the pilchard, in the herring family. Neither the sardine nor the pilchard keep well and are therefore rarely seen fresh away from coastal areas. Both are very common in cans, in a simple dressing of olive oil or in a rich tomato sauce. Where a recipe calls for fresh sardines, small herrings or mackerel may be substituted.

Scallops

These are bivalve molluscs, usually 3–6 inches across. They are generally sold ready opened and their shells are used as dishes. Scallops are a delicacy and can be cooked many ways, including baked, fried, broiled or poached. The most popular recipes are for poached scallops, served with a rich sauce and often gratiné.

Scampi

These are the best and the largest of all prawns. Scampi is their Italian name, the Dublin Bay prawn being the same species. As an appetizer, scampi are frequently served deep fried in a crisp batter, accompanied by tartare sauce, but there are many other ways of cooking them. The flavor is full enough to go well with a rich sauce such as Tartare, or a spicy sauce such as curry, or they may be part of a mixed seafood dish such as paella.

Shrimps

These tasty, small shellfish are often served with other fish, in a sauce or garnish, or in a salad. They are generally bought cooked and may be served cold or added to hot dishes.

Snails

Snails are not fish, but since they are not truly meat either they are usually grouped with fish. Not all snails are edible, and for culinary purposes, they are generally imported from France. They may be fried, or more popularly boiled, sautéed and served with a rich sauce flavored with garlic or red wine.

Sole

The term sole is used for many types of flat fish, the best of which is the Dover sole. The lemon sole, Torbay sole, witch and megrim are all sold as sole, but are inferior varieties. They may nevertheless be cooked by the same methods. A fillet of poached, broiled or lightly sautéed sole is an excellent entrée for a four course meal, and two fillets make a good main dish. Although sole may be cooked by any method, its flavor is delicate and could easily be spoiled by deep frying in batter, or by too spicy a sauce. Ideally sole is served plain with a wedge of lemon, or lightly coated with a delicately flavored sauce. When buying sole, choose if possible those without roes as the flavor will be more delicate.

Squid

An ink-fish which is cut into pieces, fried and served with a sauce made from the black liquid from the fish's pouch, flavored with herbs and garlic.

215

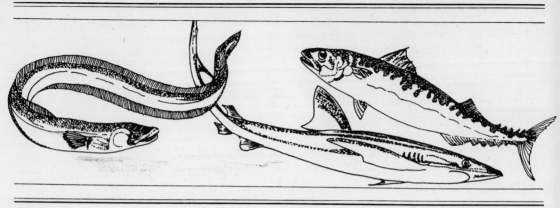

Trout

There are many varieties of trout. Some are entirely
fresh-water fish, spending their whole lives in their
parent river; some spend most of their adult life in
lakes, returning to the rivers only to spawn – these
are the rainbow trout; the salmon trout lives exactly
like the salmon, spending its adult life in the sea and
returning to the rivers to spawn. The salmon trout is
pink fleshed like the salmon, and is often substituted
for salmon; the flesh is, however, not quite so fine and
the fish do not grow so large. Of fresh-water trout, the
rainbow is the finest for eating. Large river trout are
cooked as salmon, but the smaller fish are generally
cooked whole, broiled, fried, smoked or poached.

Tuna

Tuna is another fish largely sold in cans. It is a coarse
fleshed, oily fish, usually cut into steaks. Cod can be
substituted in most recipes for tuna. The canned fish
is extremely useful in the preparation of hors d'oeuvres
and savories.

Whiting

The flavor of a whiting often needs the help of a good
sauce, but the flesh is light and easily digested. It is an
excellent fish to add to a stew of mixed fish, such as
bouillabaisse, since it will give body to the dish without
fighting with the flavor of other more choice fish.

Filleting and Skinning Fish

Filleting and skinning are usually done by a fishdealer
but you may have to do your own at some time. The
essential tool is a sharp, thin bladed knife; a clean
piece of muslin helps you grip if the skin is very slippery.

First clean the fish thoroughly. Rinse it in cold
water and scrape off the scales with the back of a
knife, working from the tail to the head. Next slit the
skin on the underside from just below the head, along
the belly to the tail. Scrape out the intestine and any
dark skin inside the cavity and wash the, fish
thoroughly again under cold running water.

If the fish are small you may wish to cook them
whole. In this case the heads are usually left on and
the tails trimmed into a deep 'V' shape to neaten
them. If you prefer you may of course cut off the head
and tail – this helps the fish lie flat in the pan.

To Fillet Round Fish

Run a sharp knife alongside the backbone, insert the
point at the head end and work the fish away from
the bone, moving the knife towards the tail with a
sawing motion. Keep a firm hold on the head with the

other hand. Then repeat on the other side of the back
bone. Turn the fish over and remove the fillets
from the underside, discarding the head and the bone.
Lay the fillets skin side down on a board, lift the tail
of each and slip the knife between the flesh and the
skin. Hold the tail skin firmly and cut the skin carefully away from the flesh, keeping it in a single piece.

To Fillet Flat Fish

The action is similar to that with round fish but work
the knife away from the backbone towards the side
fins, moving gradually down to the tail until the fillet
is detached. To remove the skin, cut off the fins with
scissors and slip your thumb between the skin and the
flesh. Then hold the skin firmly and work it away
from the flesh with a knife.

Large fish, such as cod, are often cut into steaks
rather than fillets. Clean and scale the fish as usual
and, using a strong knife, cut down through the
whole fish, bone as well. Steaks may be anything
from $\frac{3}{4}$ inch to 2 inches thick, depending how they
are to be cooked.

Egg and Fish Recipes

Poached Eggs in Mornay Sauce

Ingredients: *4 eggs · 4 round croûtons, toasted and buttered · 1 cup fresh mushrooms, sliced and cooked in butter and brandy · ½ cup mornay sauce (see p.85) · grated Parmesan cheese · a few asparagus tips*

To finish: *4 whole button mushrooms · grated Parmesan cheese · tomatoes*

Poach the eggs, place each on a croûton (step 1) and put in an ovenproof dish. Add the mushrooms to the mornay sauce and cover each egg with the mixture (step 2). Sprinkle with grated Parmesan cheese (step 3) and gratiné in a hot oven (400°F) until golden. Put the asparagus tips in a hot serving dish, arrange the eggs on top, place a mushroom cap on each and sprinkle with grated Parmesan cheese.

Garnish the dish with whole skinned tomatoes and serve with a hot tomato sauce.

Poached Eggs in Fish Stock

Prepare 2 cups stock with fish leftovers or fish pieces, celery, carrot, $\frac{1}{2}$ bay leaf, onion and 1 stock cube. Strain through a fine wet cloth. In the same pan melt $\frac{3}{4}$ tablespoon butter or margarine, stir in about 1 tablespoon flour, then pour in stock. Add salt and pepper, bring to a boil, stirring with a whisk, and simmer for 10 minutes. Cut 4 slices of bread into 8 triangles and brown lightly in oil. Place 2 bread triangles on each plate, add 1 poached egg, and pour over the boiling fish stock.

Eggs Letizia

Brown 1 small onion, chopped, in butter. Add $\frac{3}{4}$ cup rice, 1 teaspoon curry powder, and let stand 2 minutes. Pour in gradually 3 cups boiling stock (preferably chicken stock), and cook for about 20 minutes, stirring occasionally. Meanwhile, poach 4 eggs. Melt $\frac{1}{2}$ tablespoon butter in a pan, stir in 1 tablespoon flour and 1 teaspoon curry powder and cook for 1 minute. Remove from the heat, gradually stir in 1 cup chicken stock, return to heat and cook for about 10 minutes. On a warm serving platter or individual plates, arrange the cooked rice in 4 heaps, making a hollow in each one. Place 1 egg in each hollow and pour over hot sauce. Garnish with parsley.

Eggs with Brussels Sprouts

Clean 2 cups Brussels sprouts and cook for 5 minutes in boiling salted water; drain. Put sprouts into fresh boiling salted water and cook for another 15–20 minutes, or until tender. Drain thoroughly and mix with 1 tablespoon butter. (This way of cooking sprouts makes them more digestible. Frozen sprouts can be used if liked.) Arrange sprouts in a crown in a buttered ovenproof dish, break 4–6 eggs in center of dish, add salt and pepper to taste, sprinkle with grated Parmesan cheese and dot with melted butter. Place the dish in a moderate oven (350°F) and cook for a few minutes until eggs are set.

Poached Eggs Breton

Ingredients: *4 eggs · 4 artichoke hearts, boiled · butter · 1 slice cooked ham (about 4 oz) · 2 tablespoons grated Parmesan cheese*

To garnish: *1 hard-boiled egg · parsley sprigs*

Poach 4 eggs. Cook the artichoke hearts in butter for a moment (step 1). Cut the ham into 4 and place a piece on each artichoke heart (step 2). Put the eggs on the ham (step 3), sprinkle with Parmesan cheese and pour over piping hot melted butter. Garnish the serving platter with quartered hard-boiled eggs and parsley sprigs.

Poached Eggs in Mushroom Caps

Dip 4 large mushroom caps in a mixture of beaten egg and breadcrumbs. Brown and cook slowly in butter, add salt to taste and arrange them, inverted, on a hot serving dish. Poach 4 eggs and place 1 in each mushroom cap. Serve immediately accompanied by a sauce prepared as follows: in a pan cook very slowly $\frac{1}{2}$ cup dry white wine with 1 shallot, finely chopped, until wine is reduced by half. Add 2 tablespoons reduced stock, 1 tablespoon butter, pepper and $\frac{1}{2}$ teaspoon lemon juice. Remove from heat and add a little chopped parsley.

Poached Eggs on Croûtons

Dip 4 slices of bread in milk beaten with egg and a little salt. Fry lightly in butter or margarine. Put on individual plates, and place a poached egg on each one. Serve tomato sauce separately.

Eggs Marinalla

Melt in a pan 2 tablespoons butter and cook until golden, add 3 tablespoons thinned tomato sauce and enough stock to obtain a smooth sauce. Break 4 eggs one by one and slide them into the pan. Add salt and pepper to taste, cover and cook slowly for about 5 minutes. Serve the eggs with the sauce on slices of toast. Sprinkle with grated Parmesan cheese.

Poached and Fried Eggs

Prepare a batter: beat 1 egg yolk and 1 tablespoon butter or margarine in a bowl. Add $\frac{1}{4}$ cup flour, 1 pinch salt and 2 tablespoons dry white wine. Let stand for about 1 hour. Just before using the batter beat 1 egg white until stiff and fold it carefully into the bowl. Poach 4 eggs, dip them in the batter, then fry singly in hot deep oil. Drain, and serve hot garnished with parsley.

Poached Eggs on Bread Rolls

Halve 2 bread rolls and toast in the oven. Place on each half 1 slice ham, fried in butter, 1 poached egg, and 2 tablespoons hot Hollandaise (see p.86) or mornay sauce (see p.85).

221

Poached Eggs with Mushroom Sauce

Ingredients: *4 eggs · 2½ tablespoons butter or margarine · 1–2 cloves of garlic, peeled · 2 tablespoons dried mushrooms soaked in lukewarm water, squeezed dry and sliced, or 1¼ cups fresh mushrooms, sliced · 2 cups canned peeled tomatoes, roughly chopped · ½ bay leaf · salt, or 1 stock cube · pepper · 4 slices bread · chopped parsley*

Heat the butter or margarine, add 1 clove of garlic, and cook until golden-brown. Remove garlic, put in the mushrooms and sauté for 2–3 minutes. Add the tomatoes, the bay leaf, the salt, or stock cube to taste, and the pepper. Let the sauce simmer for 45 minutes, adding a few spoonfuls water if it becomes too thick. Poach the eggs (step 1), drain and trim them (step 2) and place on slices of bread toasted in the oven (step 3). If liked, the bread may be rubbed with a clove of garlic. Pour the sauce around the bread slices, sprinkle with chopped parsley, and serve immediately.

222

Poached Eggs Allegria

Melt 1 tablespoon butter with 2 tablespoons flour, pour in 1 cup water, add salt, pepper or paprika to taste, and simmer for 5 minutes. Remove the sauce from the heat, mix in 2 egg yolks and the juice of ½ lemon, and keep warm in a double boiler, stirring occasionally. In a lightly oiled frying pan brown on both sides. Toast in oven 4 slices of bread and place on a platter or on individual plates. Put on each bread slice 1 slice ham, 1 slice tomato and 1 poached egg. Season with salt and pepper to taste, and pour the hot sauce over the top.

Poached Eggs Burgundy Style

In a covered pan boil for 30 minutes, or until the wine is reduced by half, 2 cups red wine (preferably Burgundy type), onion, chopped, 1 clove of garlic, peeled and crushed, parsley to taste, 1 sprig of thyme and 1 bay leaf. Poach 4 eggs and place each egg on 1 fried croûton. Strain the sauce through a sieve. Add 2 egg yolks, 2 tablespoons butter, salt and pepper to taste, and blend thoroughly. Reheat the sauce gently, pour over the eggs and serve.

Oeufs Parmentier

Peel 1½ lb waxy potatoes and grate coarsely into a bowl of cold water. Drain well, tip onto a cloth and squeeze dry.

Heat ¼ cup butter and 2 tablespoons oil in a large frying pan. Divide the grated potato into 4 and put into the pan in piles, flattening the center of each with the back of a spoon. Fry gently until crisp and golden on each side. Arrange hollow-side up on a serving dish and keep hot.

Poach 4 large eggs as left, drain and trim. Place an egg in the hollow of each potato cake. Mix 4 tablespoons heavy cream with 2 teaspoons chopped chives and salt and pepper to taste and spoon over the eggs. Garnish with tomato wedges and watercress and serve immediately.

223

Poached Eggs in Aspic

Ingredients: *4 poached eggs · 2 cups commercial or homemade aspic (see p.104) · 4 tablespoons butter or margarine at room temperature · ½ cup tuna fish in olive oil · 1 tablespoon capers · 2 anchovy fillets, desalted · canned pimiento*

Pour a little aspic, cool but still liquid, into 4 individual molds to form a ½-inch layer (step 1). When it is almost set, place in the center of each mold 1 cold poached egg (step 2). Whip the butter or margarine until foamy, mixing in the tuna fish, capers (reserving 4 for decoration) and anchovies, all worked through a sieve. Pipe the mixture in a border around the eggs, using a pastry bag fitted with a star nozzle (step 3). Decorate each with a small piece canned pimiento and top with reserved capers. Pour the remaining liquid aspic carefully into the molds, and let stand in the refrigerator until completely set.

Poached Eggs with Mayonnaise

Poach 4 eggs and trim carefully. Arrange on a serving platter 4 round slices cooked ham, and place 1 egg on each slice. Cover completely with mayonnaise (commercial or homemade), and garnish with strips of black olives and canned pimiento. Arrange lettuce leaves around the edges of the platter.

Poached Eggs with Liver Pâté

Poach 4 eggs and trim carefully. Put them on a plate and cover with aspic mayonnaise (see p.99). Let stand until completely set. Place a layer of liver pâté or liver sausage at the bottom of 4 individual molds, and put in each 1 prepared egg. Pour over enough aspic, cool but still liquid, to fill the molds, and let stand in the refrigerator until completely set. Garnish the edges with small triangles or strips of liver pâté or sausage, kept in the refrigerator until hard enough to slice, or whip the pâté or sausage until it is foamy. Use a pastry bag fitted with a star nozzle. Garnish the center with grated black truffle or pitted olives.

224

Egg and Prosciutto Rolls in Aspic

Ingredients: *8 eggs · 8 slices lean prosciutto ·
½ cup gherkins · a few tablespoons mayonnaise ·
4 cups commercial or homemade aspic (see
p.104)*

To garnish: *a few black olives · 1 slice lemon
(optional)*

Poach the eggs. Remove from the water with a
slotted spoon (step 1), put them on a napkin
and trim with a knife (step 2). When cold,
place each egg on 1 slice prosciutto lightly
spread with mayonnaise. Add a few thin slices
gherkin, reserving 8 gherkins for decoration,
and fold the prosciutto to make a roll (step 3).
Arrange the rolls on a platter and pour over the
cool but still liquid aspic. Put the platter in the
refrigerator for a few hours, and, before
serving, garnish with the reserved gherkins
cut into fan shapes, pitted olives, and lemon.

Poached Eggs in Shells

Poach 4 eggs. Put 1 tablespoon aspic mayonnaise (see p.99) in each of 4 scallop shells or
small dishes. Pour some more aspic mayonnaise
over the eggs. When set, put 1 egg in each shell
and put chopped cooked ham or tongue, and
gherkins, around the egg, or cut the ham or
tongue and gherkins into small circles with a
round cutter and arrange them alternately
round the egg. Place ½ black olive in the center
of each egg. Keep cool until serving.

Poached Eggs with Olives

Poach 8 eggs until quite firm. Let cool on a
serving platter. Cover with a fairly stiff mayonnaise (see p.98) and spread over it a generous
amount of green olives, pitted and finely chopped.
Garnish the edge of the platter with desalted
anchovy fillets rolled around pieces of canned
red pimiento.

Poached Eggs in Green Sauce

Prepare the green sauce in the following manner: clean, wash and chop finely 1 tablespoon parsley, and put it in a bowl. Add 1 tablespoon white bread (without crust) soaked in vinegar, squeezed dry, and worked through a sieve. Add 4 mashed, desalted anchovy fillets, 1 teaspoon capers, chopped, $\frac{1}{2}$ clove of garlic, crushed (optional), a little salt and enough oil and vinegar to obtain a smooth paste. Blend thoroughly. If a creamier sauce is preferred, put all the ingredients in a blender. Poach 8 eggs (allowing 2 per person). Place on a serving platter and pour the sauce over.

Eggs with Aurora Sauce

Fry 8 small rounds or squares of bread in butter until golden on both sides. Drain and arrange on a serving dish. Keep hot. Poach 8 eggs and place on the bread. Spoon over 2 cups aurora sauce (see p. 84) and sprinkle with sieved hard-cooked egg yolk. Serve immediately.

227

Oeufs à la Coque

Bring salted water to a boil (salting the water will usually prevent the cracking of the egg shell), slide in 4 eggs carefully with a spoon (step 1), and count 3 minutes from the moment the water starts boiling again. Remove the eggs, put them in egg cups (step 2), and cut off the tops (step 3).

Eggs in a Cup

Soft boil 2 eggs per person, as above. Break them on the edge of a heated cup, take the eggs out of the shells with a spoon, and drop them into the cup. Add salt and pepper to taste, and eat with buttered toast.

Oyster Eggs

Use only the freshest eggs. Break 1 raw egg and separate the yolk from the white. Put the yolk in a tablespoon, season with a pinch of salt, a generous measure of pepper, and a few drops of lemon juice. Eat it immediately – swallowing it whole if possible. This is the simplest way of eating an egg, and also the most digestible. It is recommended for convalescent or anaemic people. The taste is most pleasant, faintly re-calling that of an oyster.

Soft-boiled Eggs on Toast

Toast slices of bread (2 per person), butter them and break 1 soft-boiled egg (see above) on each slice of bread. Season generously with salt and pepper.

Eggs with Russian Salad

Place on a serving platter a layer of Russian salad (a mixture of carrots, turnips, potatoes, French beans, peas: see p.44). Make 4 hollows and put in each hollow 1 egg, cooked for 6 minutes as above. Cover with mayonnaise (see p.98). Garnish with capers and keep cool.

229

Eggs in Tomato Aspic

Ingredients: *4 eggs · 1 tablespoon tomato sauce · 1 cup aspic, commercial or homemade · 3 tablespoons butter or margarine · ½ teaspoon anchovy paste · 4 anchovy fillets, desalted · 4 capers · 1 hard-boiled egg, quartered*

Mix the tomato sauce into the cool but liquid aspic (see p.104), and let stand until almost set. Put the eggs in salted cold water, bring to a boil, and cook for 6 minutes. Put the eggs in cold water for a few minutes, then shell. Melt the butter or margarine over medium heat with the anchovy paste, and dip the eggs into this mixture (step 1). Pour into 4 individual molds a ½-inch layer of aspic, let stand until completely set, and place 1 egg in each mold (step 2). Cover with the remaining aspic (step 3), and let stand in the refrigerator until aspic is completely set. Unmold on a serving platter, top each with an anchovy fillet rolled around a caper and garnish platter with hard-boiled egg quarters.

Eggs on Artichoke Hearts

Cook 4 artichoke hearts in boiling salted water. (If using canned or frozen artichokes cook according to package directions.) Season the inside with oil, lemon and salt and pepper to taste. Cook 4 eggs for 6 minutes as above, shell, and allow to cool. Place 1 egg in each artichoke heart. Cover with mayonnaise, or aspic mayonnaise, if liked (see p.99). Garnish with parsley sprigs or pickled vegetables to taste.

Eggs in a Crown

Cook 6 eggs for 6 minutes as above, shell, and allow to cool. Pour into a crown-shaped mold a layer of cool but still liquid aspic, well seasoned with salt, pepper and lemon juice. When it begins to set put in the eggs and put the mold in the refrigerator until cold. Cover the eggs with aspic and return to the refrigerator until completely set. Unmold the crown onto a serving platter, and place in the center lettuce cooked in boiling salted water, drained and mixed with mayonnaise, or diced boiled potatoes tossed in mayonnaise. Add 1 tablespoon grated horseradish to the mayonnaise if a sharper taste is desired. The dish can be garnished with lettuce leaves tossed in an oil and vinegar dressing.

Eggs Ciao Ciao

Cook 4 eggs for 6 minutes as above, and shell. Flake 8 oz canned crab meat, and mix it with 2–3 tablespoons mayonnaise (see p.98). Cut off the bottom of each egg so that it stands upright. Place 1 egg in the center of each individual plate and cover with mayonnaise or aspic mayonnaise. When completely set, arrange around the egg a border of the crab meat mixture. Garnish each egg with parsley sprigs and a piece of canned red pimiento. Keep cool until serving.

Eggs Mimosa

Ingredients: *4 hard-boiled eggs, shelled · 2½ tablespoons butter, at room temperature · 1 cup tomato sauce · salt · pepper · 1 cup béchamel sauce (see p.84)*

To garnish: *2 hard-boiled egg yolks · chopped parsley*

Halve the hard-boiled eggs lengthwise. Remove the yolks carefully with a teaspoon, mash with a fork and mix with the butter, 3 tablespoons of the tomato sauce and salt and pepper to taste (step 1). Fill the egg whites with the mixture, and place in a buttered ovenproof dish. Cover with a lid or foil and heat through in a moderate oven (350°F) for 10–15 minutes. Meanwhile, blend together the béchamel sauce and the remaining tomato sauce, both piping hot (step 2). Pour the sauce over the eggs (step 3), sprinkle with the hard-boiled egg yolks worked through a sieve and the chopped parsley, and serve immediately.

Egg Rolls with Eggplant

Prepare a flaky pastry with 1 cup flour, ½ cup butter or margarine, 2 tablespoons cold water and 1 pinch salt, wrap in wax paper and let stand in the refrigerator for ½ hour. Or use frozen flaky pastry. Roll out very thinly and use it to line the bottom and sides of an 8-inch pie pan. Prick the dough with a fork and bake in a hot oven (425°F) for 20–25 minutes. Meanwhile prepare 4 hard-boiled eggs, shell and cut each into 4 pieces. Work through a sieve 1½ cups canned peeled tomatoes until a purée is formed. Heat until golden brown 1 tablespoon butter with 1 slice onion. Remove the onion. Add the tomato purée and cook for a few minutes on high heat with a few basil leaves and 1 pinch salt. Peel and slice lengthwise 3 eggplants, to make 16 slices. Fry a few at a time in a little hot oil until golden, taking care they do not become dry, then drain on absorbent paper. Cover each slice with 1 tea-

spoon of the tomato sauce, and put on it 1 slice hard-boiled egg. Fold each eggplant slice to form a roll, and arrange them in a ring inside the pastry crust. Sprinkle generously with grated Parmesan cheese or cover with 3 slices Emmenthal cheese. Pour the remaining tomato sauce over and put in a hot oven (450°F) for 10–15 minutes, or until the cheese is melted.

Hard-boiled Eggs with Curry

Halve 4 shelled hard-boiled eggs lengthwise. Remove yolks carefully with a teaspoon and mash them with a fork together with 3 tablespoons mayonnaise, $\frac{1}{2}$ tablespoon curry powder, $\frac{1}{2}$ tablespoon chopped onion, $\frac{1}{2}$ tablespoon chopped parsley, and salt and pepper to taste. Fill the egg whites with the mixture and keep in the refrigerator for a few hours. Place the eggs in a buttered ovenproof dish and cover with 2 cups béchamel sauce (see p.84). Put the dish in a moderate oven (350°F) to gratiné for about $\frac{1}{2}$ hour.

Eggs and Spinach Gratiné

Boil 4 eggs for 10 minutes, dip them in cold water, shell and slice. Clean and wash 3 cups fresh spinach. Sauté in butter 1 slice onion until golden, remove onion, add $1\frac{1}{4}$ cups canned tomatoes, chopped, the spinach, and 1 pinch salt. Simmer, stirring occasionally, until the liquid has reduced. Arrange the spinach, hard-boiled egg slices, and grated Parmesan cheese to taste, in layers in a buttered ovenproof dish. Top with grated Parmesan cheese and dot with butter. Put in a hot oven (425°F) for a few minutes to gratiné.

Scotch Eggs

Ingredients: 4 hard-boiled eggs, shelled · ¾ lb
sausages or sausage meat · chopped basil and
parsley · 1 egg · 1 tablespoon water ·
breadcrumbs · oil for frying

To garnish: sprigs of parsley

Roll the hard-boiled eggs in flour (step 1). Peel
the sausages, if using sausages, or crumble the
sausage meat, and blend in the chopped basil
and parsley to taste. Divide the meat into
4 and completely cover each egg (step 2).
Roll them again in flour, then in the egg beaten
with the water, and finally in breadcrumbs.
Let stand 15 minutes, then fry them in hot deep
fat (step 3), preferably using a deep fat bath.
Drain and serve them hot, whole or halved,
garnished with parsley sprigs and with tomato
sauce served in a separate dish, or green
salad.

Egg Croquettes

Keep 6 hard-boiled eggs in their shells in cold water. Melt in a pan $2\frac{1}{2}$ tablespoons butter or margarine, add 4 tablespoons flour, and, stirring constantly, 1 cup milk all at once. Add salt, pepper and grated nutmeg to taste. Let simmer for 8–10 minutes, then cool thoroughly. Shell the hard-boiled eggs, dice them and add to the sauce with 4 oz salami, diced, and 1 tablespoon grated Parmesan cheese. Mix well and shape with the hands into croquettes. Roll them in beaten egg then in breadcrumbs, let stand $\frac{1}{2}$ hour, then fry them, a few at a time, in hot deep oil until golden brown and crisp. Drain the croquettes and serve hot. Serves 6.

Fried Stuffed Eggs

Halve 4 shelled hard-boiled eggs lengthwise, remove the yolks carefully with a teaspoon and mash them with a fork. Mix in a pan 2 tablespoons melted butter and 1 teaspoon anchovy paste. Add 1 cup fresh mushrooms, chopped, or 1 tablespoon dried mushrooms, soaked in lukewarm water, squeezed dry and chopped, a little onion to taste, and cook, stirring, for 2 minutes. Add 2–3 tablespoons light cream, 1 teaspoon chopped parsley and 1 pinch pepper. Mix with the mashed egg yolks, fill the egg whites with the mixture, and put egg halves back together. Dip them in a beaten egg, then roll in breadcrumbs. Put in the refrigerator for 1 hour (they can be prepared the day before), then fry, a few at a time, in hot deep oil until golden. Drain and serve with tomato sauce, if liked.

Stuffed Eggs Lidia

Ingredients: *6 hard-boiled eggs, shelled · 1 tablespoon anchovy paste · mayonnaise, commercially prepared or homemade (see p.98) · Worcestershire · chopped parsley · 2–3 tomatoes · paprika*

To garnish: *parsley sprigs · 1 hard-boiled egg (optional)*

Halve the hard-boiled eggs lengthwise. Remove the yolks carefully with a teaspoon (step 1) and work them through a sieve (step 2). Mix them with the anchovy paste, a little mayonnaise, and a few drops Worcestershire, to form a rather stiff paste. Shape into small nut-size balls, and roll in the chopped parsley. Put a layer of mayonnaise in each egg white, and put in the prepared balls. Place the eggs on raw tomato slices, and sprinkle with paprika before serving. Garnish the platter with parsley sprigs and put a whole hard-boiled egg in the center for decoration, if liked.

Mushroom Eggs

Put on the bottom of a serving platter a layer of mayonnaise mixed with chopped parsley, or thin strips of chicory tossed in oil, vinegar, salt and pepper to taste. Cut off the bottoms of 4 hard-boiled eggs, shelled, and set them upright on the platter. Top them with halves of tomatoes, slightly hollowed, and dot with mayonnaise. Garnish the edge of the platter with slices of hard-boiled egg, alternating with halves of stuffed olive.

Marinated Eggs

Cook slowly for a few minutes 1 tablespoon sugar, 1 teaspoon salt, 1 celery stalk, chopped, 1 cup vinegar and 8 tablespoons water. Strain and cool the liquid. Put 6 hard-boiled eggs, shelled, in a tureen and pour the marinade over them, adding $\frac{1}{2}$ clove of garlic, crushed. Cover and let stand in the refrigerator for 3 days before serving. Drain the eggs, and serve sliced.

236

Eggs Stuffed with Prosciutto

Ingredients: *4 hard-boiled eggs · 4 oz prosciutto or cooked ham, chopped · 1 tablespoon chopped capers · 1 teaspoon mustard · 1 tablespoon butter or margarine · 1 tablespoon mayonnaise · salt*

To garnish: *capers · shrimps · anchovy fillets, desalted · mayonnaise*

Shell the hard-boiled eggs (step 1), remove the yolks carefully with a teaspoon, and work them through a sieve (step 2). Blend in the chopped prosciutto (or cooked ham) and capers, the mustard, butter or margarine, mayonnaise, and salt to taste. Fill the egg whites with the mixture, using a pastry bag (step 3). Garnish some eggs with capers, some with whole shrimps, and some with anchovy fillets rolled around dots of mayonnaise, on top of the eggs. Keep cool until serving.

Eggs Stuffed with Anchovy

Halve 4 shelled hard-boiled eggs lengthwise. Remove the yolk carefully with a teaspoon and work them through a sieve together with 2 tablespoons butter or margarine at room temperature and 2–3 desalted anchovy fillets, or 1 teaspoon anchovy paste. Mix well, adding enough mayonnaise to obtain a soft smooth mixture. Fill the egg whites with the mixture, using a pastry bag. Garnish each egg with 1 anchovy fillet, desalted and rolled around a dot of mayonnaise, if liked.

238

Eggs Stuffed with Shrimps

Halve 4 shelled hard-boiled eggs lengthwise. Remove the yolks carefully with a teaspoon, mash them with a fork, and mix with a few shrimps, finely chopped, and tomato ketchup. Fill the egg whites with the mixture, garnish with mayonnaise and 1 shelled shrimp. Refrigerate, and serve on lettuce leaves.

Eggs Stuffed with Olives

Halve 4 shelled hard-boiled eggs lengthwise. Remove yolks, mash and mix with 4 oz chopped ham, a few green olives, chopped, and mayonnaise to bind mixture. Fill the egg whites with the mixture.

Egg and Parsley Mayonnaise

Shell and slice 8 hard-cooked eggs. Arrange half the egg slices in a shallow serving dish and sprinkle over 2 scallions, finely chopped, and 2 tablespoons chopped parsley. Mix together $\frac{3}{4}$ cup mayonnaise (see p. 98) and $\frac{3}{4}$ cup sour cream. Season to taste with salt and pepper. Spoon $\frac{3}{4}$ of this mixture over the eggs. Arrange the remaining egg slices on top and spoon or pipe the remaining mayonnaise mixture over them. Chill for 1 hour. Just before serving, sprinkle with a little more chopped parsley.

Eggs with Yogurt and Mint Dressing

Lightly beat together 1 cup plain yogurt, 2 tablespoons lemon juice, 1 garlic clove, crushed, 1 tablespoon chopped fresh mint and $\frac{1}{2}$ teaspoon salt. Pour into a large serving dish or individual serving dishes.

Halve 8 shelled hard-cooked eggs lengthwise and place, cut sides down, in the yogurt dressing. Melt $\frac{1}{4}$ cup butter, stir in 1 teaspoon paprika and pour over the eggs. Cool completely before serving.

239

Spanish Fried Eggs

Ingredients: *4 eggs · ½ cup oil · 2 onions · butter · 2 peppers · garlic · 2 tomatoes · salt · sugar*

Fry the eggs in the oil (step 1) and arrange them in a circle on a round platter. Slice 1 onion into rings, fry in butter (step 2) and place it in the center. Place around the eggs a piperade (step 3) prepared in advance in the following manner: cook 1 chopped onion in oil until golden brown, add the seeded peppers, chopped garlic, and tomatoes, peeled, seeded and crushed. Season with salt and sugar and cook slowly. Serve immediately.

Fried Eggs with Emmenthal Cheese

Melt some butter or margarine in a pan, or in individual ovenproof dishes. Break eggs into the pan, sprinkle with grated Emmenthal cheese and salt and pepper to taste. Cover and cook on moderate heat until eggs are cooked. Gratiné in a hot oven before serving.

240

Italian Fried Eggs

Fry eggs in oil, and arrange them in a circle on a warm round serving dish, alternating with slices of prosciutto fried in butter. Pour tomato sauce in the center of the dish, and serve piping hot.

Fried Eggs with Eggplants

Fry thick eggplant slices in oil, and arrange them in a circle on a warm serving platter. Place a fried egg on each eggplant slice and pour tomato sauce in the center. Sprinkle with chopped garlic, parsley and basil to taste.

Fried Eggs Boulangère

In a large frying pan cook 1 clove of garlic, peeled, in butter until golden. Remove garlic, add 4 slices of bread, diced, without crusts. Cook slowly, stirring, until golden. Break 4 eggs into the pan, lower the heat and cook very slowly until the eggs are set. Season with salt and pepper to taste, remove the eggs carefully, making sure there is some bread with each egg.

Portuguese Fried Eggs

Dip 4 tomatoes in boiling water, peel and seed. Crush them and sauté in a pan with 2½ tablespoons butter and 1 onion, finely chopped. Fry 4 eggs, arrange on 4 slices toast, and surround with the tomatoes, seasoned with salt and pepper to taste and sprinkled with chopped parsley.

Fried Stuffed Eggs

Halve 4 shelled hard-boiled eggs lengthwise, remove the yolks carefully with a teaspoon and mash with a fork together with 1 tablespoon Gorgonzola or other blue cheese. Add 2 celery stalks, finely chopped, 1 small green pepper, seeded and finely chopped, and salt and pepper to taste. Fill the egg whites with the mixture and reassemble them. Dip the eggs twice in beaten egg, then roll in breadcrumbs. Fry in hot deep oil until golden, drain and serve with tomato sauce.

Eggs and Bacon

Ingredients for each serving: *2 eggs · ½ tablespoon butter or margarine · 1–2 rashers bacon · salt · pepper*

Melt the butter or margarine in a pan or an ovenproof dish, brown the bacon slices on a high heat (step 1), drain and reserve. Break the eggs into the pan, lower the heat and cook for a few minutes until set (step 2). Add salt to taste, depending on the saltiness of the bacon, pepper, and the fried bacon (step 3). Serve immediately.

Fried Eggs Bercy

Fry 4 eggs, season with salt and pepper to taste. Serve immediately with small sausages or small frankfurters, broiled separately for a few minutes, and tomato sauce served in a separate dish.

Swiss Eggs

Melt 1 tablespoon butter or margarine in a pan. Break in 4 eggs, season with salt and pepper to taste, and cook briefly on low heat. Place on each egg ½ slice Emmenthal cheese, and pour 4–5 tablespoons light cream over. Cover and keep on very moderate heat until the cheese begins to melt. Serves 2.

Egg Cutlets

Put a layer of breadcrumbs on a large shallow dish, and break 6–8 whole eggs carefully on them, taking care to keep the eggs separate. Cover with more breadcrumbs and let stand for 1 hour. With a slotted spoon transfer 1 egg at a time to a frying pan, letting the excess breadcrumbs fall, and cook until golden on both sides in butter or margarine. Drain on absorbent paper, and serve immediately with tomato sauce.

Eggs Harlequin

Dice 2 potatoes, 2 carrots and 2 zucchini, chop $\frac{1}{2}$ onion, quarter 2 tomatoes, peeled and seeded and shell 1 cup peas, or use frozen vegetables. Melt 2 tablespoons butter or margarine in a pan, add the vegetables and cook slowly, adding a little stock occasionally if necessary. When the vegetables are cooked, mix in chopped parsley and basil to taste, and, using a wooden spoon, make 4 hollows in the mixture, or 1 large hollow in the center. Break in 4 eggs, season with salt and pepper to taste, and cook on moderate heat until the eggs are set.

Eggs Daisy

Melt a little butter in a pan, add 1 slice onion and sauté for a few minutes. Remove the onion, add 4 chicken livers, and cook them for a few minutes. Sprinkle with Marsala and salt to taste. In a separate pan sauté 4 tablespoons cooked or canned green peas in butter. On each plate place 2 eggs fried in butter or oil according to taste and garnish with 1 chicken liver and 1 tablespoon peas. Serve piping hot.

Fried Eggs with Onions

Slice 2 large onions and sauté until golden. Make 4 hollows in the onions, break 1 egg in each, season to taste, and cook until the eggs are set. Serve immediately.

Scrambled Eggs with Shrimps

Ingredients: *6 eggs · 1 cup cooked shelled shrimps · 2 tablespoons butter · 1 cup milk · salt · pepper · chopped parsley · round slices of bread, toasted and buttered*

To garnish: *sprig of parsley (optional)*

Chop the shrimps, reserving 6 whole ones for the garnish. Melt the butter, add the milk, salt and pepper to taste, and chopped shrimps, and heat through. Beat the eggs, without making them too foamy, pour them into the milk (step 1) and cook on low heat, stirring constantly with a wooden spoon (step 2). When soft and smooth, add the chopped parsley to taste, and pour the mixture on the buttered toast (step 3). Garnish with the reserved whole shrimps, and a sprig of parsley, if liked. Transfer to a warm serving platter and serve immediately.

Scrambled Eggs with Cheese

Separate 4 eggs, reserve the yolks and beat the whites until they are stiff. Put in a flameproof pan ½ lb grated Swiss cheese, and dot it with 2 tablespoons butter. Pour in 1 cup dry white wine, add ½ teaspoon chopped parsley, and salt, pepper and grated nutmeg to taste. Put the pan on low heat and stir constantly until the cheese is melted. Turn the heat down to very low and add the egg yolks one at a time, beating the mixture constantly. Add the egg whites and continue cooking, stirring constantly, until the eggs are set. Serve on buttered toast, or toast spread with a mixture of butter and anchovy paste. Serve immediately.

Scrambled Eggs with Ham

Melt 2 tablespoons butter, and add 6 oz cooked ham, diced. After a few minutes, pour in 6 eggs beaten with salt and pepper to taste, and cook on low heat, stirring constantly with a wooden spoon, until the eggs are about set. Add 1 teaspoon finely chopped parsley, and serve piping hot.

Eggs Marta

Melt 1 tablespoon butter or margarine in a frying pan, add 4 eggs beaten with salt and pepper to taste, and 2 oz grated Swiss cheese. As soon as the eggs are set, place them on a warm serving dish, spread a few tablespoons tomato sauce over them, and sprinkle with chopped basil and parsley to taste. Serve immediately. The eggs could also be served in puff pastry *vol-au-vent* cases.

Tartlets Primavera

Ingredients: *6 eggs · 1 lb asparagus tips ·
4 tablespoons butter · 12 tartlets, bought or
homemade with 8 oz rich shortcrust or flaky
pastry · salt · pepper*

Cut off the asparagus tips (step 1), cook them in
salted boiling water until tender, then sauté
them in ½ the butter. Cook the tartlets in a hot
oven (400°F) for 15–20 minutes until golden;
if using bought tartlets heat them through.
Melt the remaining butter in a pan, add the
eggs, beaten with salt and pepper to taste, and
cook, stirring constantly, until they begin to
set (step 2). Fill each tartlet with the egg
mixture (step 3), garnish with asparagus tips
and serve piping hot.

Eggs with Peas

Cook 1 cup green peas in boiling salted water
for a few minutes and drain, or use canned peas.
Finish cooking peas in 1 tablespoon butter with
2 oz cooked ham cut into strips. Ten minutes
before serving, melt 1 tablespoon butter in a
pan, then stir in 1 tablespoon flour and 2–3
tablespoons milk. Cook for 2–3 minutes, stirring constantly, and add 3–4 eggs, beaten with
salt and grated nutmeg to taste. Do not allow
mixture to boil. When creamy, remove from
heat. Arrange the peas on a warm serving
platter, cover with the egg mixture, and serve
immediately with bread croûtons fried in butter.

Scrambled Eggs with Tomato Sauce

Beat 6 eggs lightly, add a few drops cold water, and season. Melt $2\frac{1}{2}$ tablespoons butter in a pan, pour in eggs, and cook gently until creamy, stirring constantly. Remove from heat; add 1 tablespoon soft butter. Serve with tomato sauce, parsley and basil.

Scrambled Eggs with Cream

Fry 4 slices of bread in 4 tablespoons butter or margarine and keep warm. In another pan, melt 1 tablespoon butter and pour in 6 eggs beaten with $\frac{1}{4}$ cup milk or light cream, 4 tablespoons grated Parmesan cheese, and salt, pepper and grated nutmeg to taste. Cook on very low heat, stirring constantly, until set. Spread on the fried bread, and serve.

Scrambled Eggs with Cod

Shred $\frac{1}{2}$ lb fresh cod and sauté in $2\frac{1}{2}$ tablespoons butter. Add 1 cup milk, a little chopped onion, chopped parsley to taste, and $\frac{1}{2}$ bay leaf. Cook for 8–10 minutes, stirring occasionally, then add 4–5 eggs, lightly beaten with pepper (but no salt). Continue cooking until the eggs are creamy, and serve immediately.

Scrambled Eggs with Lettuce

Melt $\frac{1}{4}$ cup butter in a frying pan. Add 1 onion, peeled and finely chopped, and cook until transparent. Stir in 1 small head Boston lettuce, shredded, 1 cup frozen peas and 1 tablespoon chopped parsley. Cook, stirring, for 5 minutes.

Lightly beat 4 eggs and add salt and pepper to taste. Pour into the pan and cook gently, stirring, until creamy. Serve immediately.

Eggs en Cocotte with Spinach

Ingredients: *4 eggs · 2 tablespoons butter · 4 tablespoons spinach, cooked and roughly chopped · 4 tablespoons light cream · salt · pepper*

Butter 4 individual soufflé or ramekin dishes (step 1) and put 1 tablespoon spinach in each (step 2). Break 1 egg into each dish and pour in 1 tablespoon cream (step 3). Dot with butter and sprinkle with salt and pepper to taste. Place the dishes in a baking dish half full of hot water, and bake in a very hot oven (450°F) for 8–10 minutes, or until the whites of the eggs are set.

Farmhouse Eggs en Cocotte

Melt in a pan 2½ tablespoons butter, stir in 2 tablespoons flour, cook for 1–2 minutes, remove from heat, then stir in 2 cups boiling milk. Cook for 2 minutes, stirring constantly, add salt to taste and ½ cup grated Parmesan or Swiss cheese. Cook until the cheese is melted. Pour the mixture into 8 buttered individual soufflé or ramekin dishes. Break 1 egg into each, sprinkle with salt and pepper to taste, place the dishes in a baking dish half full of hot water, and bake in a hot oven (450°F) for 8–10 minutes, or until the whites of the eggs are set.

Eggs en Cocotte with Cheese

Butter 8 individual soufflé or ramekin dishes. Break 1 egg into each, season with salt and pepper to taste, and cover with a little light cream. Place a thin slice of Emmenthal cheese over each egg, and add another tablespoon cream. Cook as above.

Eggs en Cocotte with Mushrooms

In each buttered dish put 1 tablespoon chopped cooked mushrooms, add 1 egg, 1 tablespoon light cream, dot with butter, and sprinkle with salt and pepper to taste. Cook as above.

Egg and Ham Molds

Coat the bottom and sides of 8 buttered dariole molds with ¾ cup finely chopped cooked ham. Break an egg into each mold and sprinkle with a little salt. Bake as left, and unmold to serve.

Eggs en Cocotte with Bacon

In the bottom of each buttered dish place 1 slice smoked bacon. Add 1 egg, season with salt and pepper to taste, and cook as left.

Tyrolean Eggs

Ingredients: *2 hard-boiled eggs, quartered ·
butter · 1 large can tomatoes, drained · anchovy
paste · parsley · breadcrumbs · salt · pepper ·
3 eggs · 1 cup light cream*

Butter generously an ovenproof dish, and place
a layer of tomatoes on the bottom (step 1).
Beat a few tablespoons butter until foamy, with
anchovy paste to taste, spread over the
tomatoes and sprinkle with chopped parsley
to taste. Arrange the hard-boiled egg quarters
on top, then sprinkle with breadcrumbs
seasoned with salt and pepper to taste (step 2).
Beat the eggs together with the cream and a
little salt and pepper, pour the mixture over
the eggs (step 3) and bake in a hot oven
(425°F) for about ½ hour, until the eggs are
well set in the cream. Serve piping hot in the
baking dish.

Eggs Gratiné

Boil 4 eggs for 10 minutes, dip them in cold
water, shell, and slice. Prepare a béchamel
sauce with 2½ tablespoons butter, 4 tablespoons flour, 2 cups milk, and salt, pepper
and grated nutmeg to taste (see p.84). When
cooked, blend in 1 tablespoon grated Parmesan
cheese. In a buttered ovenproof dish, arrange a
layer of white bread (without crusts) crumbled
and mixed with grated Parmesan cheese to
taste. Top with a layer of hard-boiled egg
slices, then a layer of cooked ham, chopped
(about ½ lb), and finally a layer of béchamel
sauce. Repeat, finishing with crumbled bread.
Sprinkle with grated Parmesan cheese, and dot
with butter. Bake in a hot oven (425°F) for
about 10–15 minutes, or until a golden crust
has formed on top.

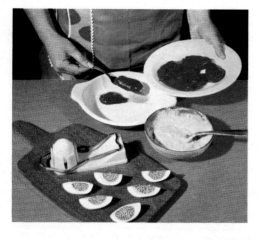

Eggs Françoise

Boil 4 eggs for 10 minutes, shell, and halve. In a pan, melt 1 tablespoon butter, add 2 oz salt pork, soaked in cold water for 1 hour, drained and cut into strips, 1 slice onion, and 1 clove of garlic, finely chopped, and cook until golden. Add 1 cup water, $\frac{1}{2}$ cup dry white wine, 3 tablespoons tomato sauce, 1 bay leaf, and salt and pepper to taste. Cook for 10 minutes, then add 1 tablespoon butter blended with 1 tablespoon flour, and let the sauce reduce slowly. Cook 1 cup tagliatelle in boiling salted water until *al dente*. Drain, and put into a buttered ovenproof dish. Arrange the hard-boiled eggs in the center of the dish. Pour the sauce over and sprinkle with 3 tablespoons grated Parmesan cheese. Dot with butter and put in a hot oven (425°F) for a few minutes to gratiné.

Baked Eggs in Potatoes

Scrub and dry 4 large baking potatoes and push a metal skewer lengthwise through each. Bake in a hot oven (400°F) for 1-1$\frac{1}{4}$ hours or until tender. Pull out the skewers, then cut a slice lengthwise from the top of each potato. Scoop out the flesh leaving a shell about $\frac{1}{2}$ inch thick. Mash the scooped-out flesh with $\frac{1}{4}$ cup butter and seasoning. Mix in $\frac{1}{2}$ cup shredded cheese. Press the mixture back into the potato shells, leaving a hollow in the centers large enough for an egg. Break an egg into each hollow. Spoon over a little heavy cream. Bake in a very hot oven (450°F) for 8–10 minutes or until the eggs are set. Serve hot, sprinkled with chopped chives.

Frittata with Mozzarella Cheese

Ingredients: for the frittata, *6 eggs · 2 tablespoons flour · 2 tablespoons milk · salt · 2½ tablespoons butter*

To garnish: *1 mozzarella cheese, sliced · 1 cup thick tomato sauce · black olives · oregano (optional) · anchovy fillets, desalted (optional)*

Beat the eggs, add the flour and milk (step 1), and the salt to taste. Cook the mixture on both sides in the butter (step 2) until set. Arrange mozzarella cheese slices over the frittata, pour tomato sauce between the slices (step 3), and decorate with a few black olives. Sprinkle with oregano, if liked. Anchovy fillets can also be added at this stage. Cover, and cook on low heat until the cheese has melted. Serve hot.

Omelet Poulard

Separate 8–10 eggs. Beat the yolks and add salt and pepper to taste. Beat the whites separately until stiff. Heat 4 tablespoons butter in a pan, pour in the yolks and stir when they begin to set. Mix in about ½ cup light cream, and fold in the whites. Shake the pan quickly over high heat. Fold the omelet and flip it into a long platter. Serve immediately.

Spanish Frittata

Broil 2 peppers, remove skins and seeds. Dip 2 tomatoes in boiling water, peel, halve, and squeeze them to remove the seeds. Crush the peppers and tomatoes together. Beat 8 eggs. Heat 2½ tablespoons butter or olive oil in a pan. Put in the peppers and tomatoes, and salt, pepper and chopped garlic to taste. Add the eggs and stir until they are set. Serve immediately.

Portuguese Omelet

Dip 3 tomatoes in boiling water, peel, halve, squeeze to remove the seeds, and crush them. Beat 8 eggs. Heat 2½ tablespoons butter in a pan, add the tomatoes and 1 clove of garlic, chopped. Add salt and pepper to taste. Cook for a few minutes, then pour in the eggs. Stir until the eggs are set, fold the omelet, and serve immediately on a long warm platter.

Zucchini Frittata

Ingredients: *5 eggs · 2 tablespoons butter · 1 tablespoon oil · 1 small onion, finely chopped · ¾ lb zucchini, washed, dried and sliced · salt · pepper · 3 ripe tomatoes, peeled, seeded and crushed*

Heat the butter and oil in a pan, add the onion and cook until golden brown. Add the zucchini (step 1), the salt and pepper to taste, and the tomatoes. Cook until the zucchini are almost tender. Beat the eggs with a pinch of salt. Pour them over the zucchini (step 2), and mix together. When the frittata is golden-brown on 1 side, turn it over and cook on the other side on moderate heat (step 3).

Asparagus Frittata

Beat 6 eggs with 1 tablespoon flour, 2 tablespoons grated Parmesan cheese, 2 tablespoons milk and salt and pepper to taste. Melt 2½ tablespoons butter in a pan, add the egg mixture and cook on both sides until set. Cover with asparagus tips cooked in boiling salted water, and 1 cup ricotta, or cottage cheese. Cook on low heat for a moment to melt the cheese, then serve immediately.

Omelet Argenteuil

Cook 1 lb asparagus in boiling salted water. Cut off the tips — 1½ inches long. Beat 8 eggs, add salt and pepper to taste, and 3½ fl oz light cream. Heat 2 tablespoons butter in a frying pan, pour in the eggs when the butter is very hot. Stir, and add the asparagus tips. Roll the omelet, and serve immediately on a long warm platter.

Old-Fashioned Omelet

Dice ½ lb lean bacon. Cook it for 5 minutes in boiling water, drain. Fry in butter until lightly golden 20 small croûtons (½-inch bread squares). Beat 8 eggs, and season with salt and pepper to taste. Sauté the bacon and croûtons in 2 tablespoons butter in a frying pan. Add the eggs. Serve the omelet immediately, without folding.

Tomato frittata

Cook on high heat with a little salt 10 oz tomatoes, peeled, seeded, and chopped. Beat 6–8 eggs, add grated Parmesan cheese, basil, parsley, salt and pepper to taste. Add tomatoes when their liquid has boiled away. Heat 2 tablespoons butter, pour in egg and tomato mixture, and cook frittata on both sides until golden.

Potato Frittata

Cook 1 lb potatoes, diced, in 2 tablespoons butter until golden. Season and cook until tender, drain. Beat 6 eggs, add the potatoes and grated Parmesan cheese, pour mixture back into pan. Cook for 5 minutes, turn it over, and cook on other side for another 5 minutes; add more butter if necessary. Serve immediately, piping hot.

Rolled Ham Omelet

Ingredients: for the omelet, *6 eggs · 1 tablespoon flour · 1 tablespoon grated Parmesan cheese · 2 tablespoons milk · salt · 2 tablespoons butter*

For the stuffing: *2½ tablespoons butter at room temperature · 1 tablespoon prepared mustard · a few pickled gherkins, chopped · 4 oz cooked ham, sliced*

To garnish: *radishes, tomatoes, green salad*

Blend together the eggs, flour, Parmesan cheese, milk, and salt to taste (step 1). Heat the butter in a pan, pour in the egg mixture and cook the omelet on both sides. Remove from the pan and let cool. Mix in a bowl the butter, mustard and gherkins (step 2), beat until creamy, and spread over the omelet. Place the ham slices over the mixture (step 3), roll the omelet, and keep in the refrigerator for a few hours. Slice it, arrange the slices on a serving platter, and garnish with radishes, quartered tomatoes or green salad, according to taste.

Omelet Chasseur

Cook 1 onion, finely chopped, in 1 tablespoon butter in a heavy pan until golden-brown. Add 1 crushed clove of garlic, then stir in 2 tablespoons flour. Cook for 1–2 minutes. Remove from heat, stir in 1 teaspoon tomato paste, about ½ cup dry white wine, 1 sprig thyme and ½ bay leaf. Return to heat, bring to a boil and simmer. Meanwhile, sauté in a pan 4 chicken livers, quartered, and ½ cup mushrooms, sliced. Add them to the sauce and season with salt and pepper to taste. Beat 8 eggs, heat 2½ tablespoons butter in the pan, pour in the eggs and cook the omelet over high heat. Fold, slide onto a warm serving platter, slice it in the middle, and stuff with the mushroom and chicken liver mixture. Pour any remaining sauce around it, and serve immediately.

Rolled Frittata

Blend together 5–6 eggs, 1 tablespoon flour, 2 tablespoons milk, and salt to taste. Heat 2 tablespoons butter in a pan, pour in the egg mixture, cook on both sides and let cool. Work through a sieve $\frac{1}{2}$ cup canned tuna fish, drained, and 4 anchovy fillets, desalted. Beat this mixture in a bowl with $2\frac{1}{2}$ tablespoons butter, softened, until foamy. Add lemon juice. Spread mixture over the frittata, roll, wrap in wax paper and refrigerate before serving.

Fried Eggs Massena

Cook 4 artichokes for 30 minutes, or until tender, in boiling salted water, to which the juice of 1 lemon or 1 tablespoon wine vinegar has been added. Remove the leaves and the tough part in the center. Sauté the artichoke hearts quickly in butter, and 6 oz mushrooms, sliced. Place the sliced mushrooms over the artichoke hearts, fry 4 eggs and place on top. Serve immediately.

Stuffed Crêpes Bolognese

Ingredients: for the crêpes, *3 eggs · ¾ cup flour · salt · 1 cup milk · 4 tablespoons butter*

For the stuffing: *Bolognese sauce (see p.88) · 12 thin slices Emmenthal cheese*

To garnish: *½ tomato (optional)*

Mix the eggs with the flour and 1 pinch salt in a bowl. Add the milk, gradually, and 1 table-spoon butter, melted. Whip the mixture thoroughly. Heat a 6-inch frying pan on high heat, and, using a small amount of batter at a time (see p.260), make 12 small crêpes (step 1). Place 1 at the bottom of a buttered round oven-proof dish, slightly larger in size than the crêpes. Cover with Bolognese sauce, and put 1 slice Emmenthal cheese over the sauce (step 2). Repeat these layers (step 3) until all ingredients are used up, ending with a crêpe. Dot with remaining butter and bake in a hot oven (425°F) for 10 minutes or until crêpes are heated through and cheese has melted. If liked, garnish with ½ tomato, grilled or fried.

Stuffed Crêpes with Spinach

Prepare 12 small crêpes as above. Cook 1¼ lb spinach in a little boiling salted water, wash, drain and chop, then mix with ½ cup grated Parmesan cheese. Place a layer of spinach and 1 desalted anchovy fillet on each crêpe. Roll the crêpes and arrange them in a buttered ovenproof dish. Sprinkle with grated Parmesan cheese and put in a hot oven (425°F) for a few minutes to gratiné.

Crêpe Mold

Discard the outer leaves of 3 artichokes, and cut artichokes in small pieces with 1 carrot, 1 celery stalk and 1 tablespoon dried mushrooms, soaked in lukewarm water and squeezed dry. Melt 4 tablespoons butter in a pan, add a little onion, chopped, and cook until golden. Add the vegetables, together with 2 cups green peas, shelled. Cook for 2 minutes, sprinkle

with $\frac{1}{2}$ tablespoon flour, cook for a further 2–3 minutes, stirring, then add 2 tablespoons tomato sauce, diluted with stock. (The liquid should cover the vegetables.) Season with salt and pepper to taste, cover and let simmer for $1\frac{1}{2}$ hours until the sauce has reduced. Prepare 12 small crêpes (see p.260) and let cool. Butter an ovenproof dish, about 8 inches wide and 2 inches high, and line the bottom and sides with crêpes. Fill the dish with layers of crêpes and vegetable mixture, ending with a crêpe. Cook in a bain-marie in a moderately hot oven (375°F), or in the top of a double boiler, for $1\frac{1}{4}$ hours. Remove from the heat, leave to stand for 10 minutes, then unmold onto a warm serving platter.

Crêpes Suzette

Ingredients: for the crêpes, *2 eggs · ¾ cup flour · ¼ teaspoon salt · 1 cup milk or water · 1 tablespoon butter, melted · 1 tablespoon Cointreau or Curaçao according to taste · ½ tablespoon sugar · grated peel of ½ orange*

For the sauce: *¼ cup butter at room temperature · ½ cup sugar · the zest of 1 orange · 4 tablespoons Cointreau or Curaçao*

For frying: *2½ tablespoons butter*

Mix the eggs with the flour and salt in a bowl. Add the milk or water gradually, and the butter. Whip the mixture thoroughly, add the Cointreau or Curaçao, sugar and grated orange peel. Wrap the butter for frying in a piece of cheesecloth. Heat a 6-inch frying pan on high heat, and quickly wipe the wrapped butter over the bottom. Pour 2 tablespoons of the crêpe mixture into the hot pan, and move it so that the bottom of the pan is spread with a very thin layer of batter (step 1). Turn the crêpe over

when the edges become slightly golden and dry, and continue cooking on reduced heat, moving the pan occasionally. Repeat the operation until all the crêpe mixture has been used (about 12 crêpes). Prepare the sauce by beating together the butter, sugar, orange or tangerine zest, orange juice, and Cointreau or Curaçao. Spread a thin layer of sauce over each crêpe. Fold crêpes in flour (step 2), arrange on a warm platter, sprinkle with sugar, pour over the hot Cointreau, and flame while serving (step 3).

Apricot Crêpes

Mix 2 eggs with $\frac{3}{4}$ cup flour, 2 tablespoons sugar and a pinch of salt in a bowl. Add $\frac{3}{4}$ cup milk and 4 tablespoons water gradually to make a smooth batter. Stir in a few drops of vanilla. Make the crêpes as left, spreading each with apricot jam and rolling it up as it is cooked. Just before serving, dredge with confectioners' sugar or sprinkle with chopped or ground nuts.

Fruity Crêpes

Mix 2 eggs with $\frac{3}{4}$ cup flour, 2 tablespoons sugar and a pinch of salt in a bowl. Add $\frac{1}{2}$ cup milk and 4 tablespoons cider or white wine gradually to make a smooth batter. Stir in the grated rind of 1 orange and a few drops of vanilla. Rub 6 sugar cubes over the rind of another 2 oranges until they have absorbed the zest (oil). Crush the sugar lumps and mix with 1 teaspoon ground cinnamon. Peel and chop the oranges and mix with 4 apples, peeled, cored and diced. Heat an 8-inch frying pan and oil lightly, then pour in $\frac{1}{8}$ of the batter. Move the pan to spread out the batter evenly, then cook until the base bubbles and is firm. Spoon over $\frac{1}{8}$ of the fruit and cinnamon mixtures. Place the pan under a hot broiler and cook until the filling is bubbling. Fold the crêpe and lift out onto a serving dish. Keep hot while you make 7 more crêpes in the same way. Serve with whipped cream.

Flamed Omelet

Ingredients: *6 eggs · salt · 1 tablespoon butter · 1 pot of jam (flavor according to taste)*

To garnish: *¼ cup confectioners' sugar · 4 slices canned pineapple, halved · 8 glacé or maraschino cherries · 1 small glass rum*

Beat the eggs with a pinch of salt (step 1). Melt the butter in a heavy frying pan and pour into the beaten eggs. Reheat the pan thoroughly, pour in the eggs, and cook them on high heat (step 2), stirring with a fork or a wooden spoon, until they are completely set. Turn the omelet over, and finish cooking. When the edges are golden, spread the omelet with the jam (step 3), roll it with the help of a spoon, and slide it into a warm oval serving platter. Sprinkle generously with the sugar and, with a red hot skewer, draw a diamond pattern over the surface if desired. Arrange the pineapple slices around the omelet, and place a candied cherry on each. Bring the rum to a boil, ignite it, and pour it over the omelet. Serve immediately.

Frittata with Apples

Beat together 4 eggs, 1 tablespoon flour, 1 glass milk, and a pinch of salt. Melt 1 tablespoon butter in a large frying pan, pour into the eggs, mixing quickly, and add 1–2 apples, peeled and sliced very thinly. Pour the egg and apple mixture into the hot, buttered pan and cook the frittata slowly on one side; add 1 tablespoon butter, then cook frittata on the other side. Cook for another 15 minutes, shaking the pan from time to time. Sprinkle with sugar according to taste and serve immediately.

Orange Omelet Soufflé

Beat 6 egg yolks with 1 cup sugar until the mixture is thick, stir in the peel of 2 oranges, cut into thin strips, and fold in 8 egg whites, beaten until very stiff. Pile the mixture onto an oval metal platter, buttered and sprinkled with sugar, shaping into a 'mound' with a spatula. Bake the omelet in a moderate oven (350 F) for 20–25 minutes. A few minutes before taking it from the oven, glaze the top by sprinkling it with confectioners sugar.

Apple Soufflé Omelet

Peel, core and roughly chop 1½ lb tart apples and place in a saucepan with 2 tablespoons water and 2 tablespoons butter. Cover and cook gently for 15 minutes. Remove from the heat and add 6 tablespoons sugar and a few drops of vanilla. Beat until smooth and leave to cool.

Separate 2 eggs and put the yolks in a bowl with 2 whole eggs. Add 4 tablespoon sugar and beat until light and frothy. Stir in ½ cup milk and ½ teaspoon vanilla. Beat the egg whites until stiff and fold in. Melt 2 tablespoons butter in a frying pan and pour in ½ the egg mixture. Cook gently until the base is set and golden brown, then place the pan under a hot broiler and cook until the top is set. Spread over half the apple filling and fold the omelet in half. Slide onto a serving dish and keep hot while you prepare the second omelet in the same way. Dredge the omelets with confectioners' sugar and serve flamed with brandy.

Sea Fish

Fresh Herring au Vert

Ingredients: *1½ lb fresh small herring or mackerel · 2½ tablespoons butter · garlic and parsley, chopped · 2 anchovy fillets, desalted and mashed · ¼ cup dry white wine · salt*

To garnish: lemon

Remove the head and main bone from the fish (step 1) without opening them, wash and dry with absorbent paper. Melt the butter in a pan, add the chopped garlic and parsley to taste, cook for 1–2 minutes then remove from heat and add the mashed anchovy fillets (step 2). Continue cooking on low heat, then add the white wine and a small pinch of salt. After a few minutes arrange the fish in the pan (step 3) and cook for about 10 minutes. Serve hot with the sauce. Garnish with lemon slices.

Neapolitan Herring

Prepare $1\frac{1}{2}$ lb small herring or mackerel as left. Sauté chopped garlic and parsley to taste in $\frac{1}{4}$ cup oil. Add $1\frac{1}{4}$ cups canned tomatoes, chopped, cover with stock and simmer for a few minutes. Arrange 2 cups potatoes, thinly sliced, in a buttered dish, cover with the prepared fish and spread over the tomato sauce. Cover and cook slowly for about 30 minutes or until potatoes are tender. If there is too much sauce, reduce on high heat for a few minutes.

Herring with Tomato Sauce

Sauté 1 clove of garlic, soaked in a little milk and mashed, in 1 tablespoon butter, add 1 cup canned tomatoes, chopped, and cook for about 20 minutes. Meanwhile prepare $1\frac{1}{2}$ lb small herring or mackerel as left and sauté them in $\frac{1}{4}$ cup oil for about 10 minutes. Sprinkle with a little salt. Pour the sauce into a warm serving platter, put in the cooked fish, sprinkle with chopped basil and parsley to taste, and serve immediately.

Herring in Batter

Prepare a batter by blending $1\frac{1}{4}$ cups flour, 1 egg, salt and $\frac{3}{4}$ cup beer. Add a little water and let stand for 1–2 hours. Clean, wash and dry $1\frac{1}{2}$ lb small herring or mackerel, and sprinkle with salt. Whip 2 egg whites, and fold into the batter. Roll fish in batter and fry in hot deep fat. Remove, and cut off heads and tails. Serve with tartare sauce or tomato sauce.

Rolled Herring with Capers

Remove heads and bones from $1\frac{1}{2}$ lb small herring or mackerel, and cut each into 2 fillets. Place a few capers on each and roll up. Sauté chopped garlic to taste in $\frac{1}{4}$ cup oil, arrange the fillets in the pan and cook slowly for 10 minutes. Season, add $\frac{1}{4}$ cup parsley, chopped, and $\frac{1}{2}$ cup dry white wine. Increase heat and cook until the sauce has reduced.

Gratin of Sardines

Ingredients: *2 lb fresh sardines, or small herring or mackerel · 2½ tablespoons breadcrumbs · 2 cloves of garlic, chopped · chopped parsley · salt · pepper · juice of 1 lemon · 2½ tablespoons butter · 2 eggs · ½ cup milk*

To garnish: *parsley*

Open fish, remove heads and bones (step 1), wash and dry. Arrange half the fish side by side in a buttered ovenproof dish (step 2). Mix together the breadcrumbs, garlic and parsley, and salt and pepper to taste, and spread half over the fish (step 3). Sprinkle with lemon juice and dot with half the butter. Arrange another layer of fish over this, and cover with the remaining breadcrumb mixture. Pour over the eggs beaten with the milk, melt the remaining butter and pour over the top. Bake in a moderate oven (350°F) for 30 minutes or until golden. Serve in cooking dish, garnished with parsley.

Sardine Croquettes

Clean, wash and dry 1 lb sardines, small herring or mackerel, and cut into small pieces after removing the heads and bones. Mix 1 egg in a bowl with 1 tablespoon pine nuts, 1 tablespoon raisins, 2 tablespoons breadcrumbs, 2 tablespoons grated Parmesan or Swiss cheese, 1 tablespoon chopped parsley, and salt and pepper to taste. Add the fish and mix well. Shape into croquettes about 2½ inches long on a floured board. Roll in flour, then sauté. Serve with green (p.97) or tomato sauce (see p.88).

Portuguese Sardines

Clean, wash and dry 1 lb sardines, small herring or mackerel, and remove the heads and bones. Mash ½ lb cod with 2 egg yolks, and salt, pepper and basil to taste. Add 1 tablespoons fine breadcrumbs. Stuff the fish with this mixture. Cook ½ cup onion, chopped, in butter until transparent. Add 2 cups tomatoes, peeled, seeded and chopped, 1 pinch basil, 1 tablespoon chopped parsley, 2 cloves of garlic, crushed, and salt and pepper to taste, and cook slowly until a thick sauce has formed. Roll fish in flour and cook in ½ cup oil and ½ cup butter until golden. Pour the sauce into a warm dish, arrange fish over and serve.

Grilled Swordfish

Ingredients: *4 slices swordfish (6–8 oz each, about 1 inch thick) · salt · pepper · 2¼ tablespoons butter kneaded with anchovy paste or chopped mixed herbs to taste*

To serve: *melted butter · chervil · rosemary · basil · juice of 1 lemon*

To garnish: *green beans · canned peeled tomatoes*

Season the fish slices with salt and pepper, cover with the butter (step 1), and cook on a buttered grill (step 2) for 5–6 minutes on each side (step 3). Serve with melted butter mixed with chopped chervil, rosemary, basil and lemon juice in a separate dish. Garnish the serving platter with sliced green beans and tomatoes.

Spanish Swordfish

Put ½ cup oil in an earthenware dish with ½ cup onion, finely chopped, 2 cloves of garlic, crushed, ½ cup green and red peppers, seeded and sliced, and 2 cups tomatoes, peeled, seeded and chopped. Cook slowly for 20 minutes, then add 1½ lb swordfish in 1 piece. Season with salt and pepper to taste, and add 1 twig thyme and 1 bay leaf. Cook the fish for 5 minutes on each side. Serve in the cooking dish.

Swordfish with Capers

Take 4 slices swordfish (about $1\frac{1}{2}$ lb). Cook in $\frac{1}{4}$ cup oil until golden on both sides. Sprinkle with salt. Add 2 tablespoons tomato sauce, thinned in a little hot water, and 2 tablespoons capers. Cook slowly for about 30 minutes, and serve with the reduced cooking juices.

Halibut in Tomato Sauce

Melt 2 tablespoons butter in a frying pan, add 1 onion, peeled and chopped, and fry until golden. Dip 2 tomatoes in boiling water, then drain and remove the skins. Chop the tomatoes and add to the pan. Cook for a further 5 minutes. Pour the mixture into a baking dish and place 4 halibut steaks on top. Pour in $\frac{3}{4}$ cup each dry white wine or cider and water and season. Cover and cook in a hot oven (425°F) for 20–30 minutes.

Transfer the halibut steaks to a serving dish and keep hot. Pour the cooking liquid into a saucepan. Dissolve 1 teaspoon cornstarch in a little water and add to the pan. Simmer, stirring, until thickened. Stir in 2 tablespoons light cream and 1 tablespoon chopped parsley. Pour the sauce over the fish and serve.

Halibut with Creamy Shrimp

Season 4 halibut steaks (6 oz each) and place in a frying pan. Pour over $\frac{3}{4}$ cup milk and dot with 2 tablespoons butter. Cover and poach gently for 10–15 minutes.

Drain the fish, reserving the cooking liquid, and keep hot. Melt 2 tablespoons butter in a saucepan, stir in 2 tablespoons flour and cook for 1 minute. Gradually stir in the reserved cooking liquid and 4 tablespoons dry white wine and bring to a boil, stirring. Simmer until thickened. Remove from the heat and stir in $\frac{3}{4}$ cup light cream, $\frac{2}{3}$ cup shelled cooked shrimp, 1 teaspoon lemon juice and 1 tablespoon chopped fresh fennel. Heat through gently, then season. Spoon over the fish and serve immediately.

269

Sicilian Stuffed Swordfish

Ingredients: *4 large, flattened slices swordfish ·
4 tablespoons· breadcrumbs · 4 tablespoons
grated Parmesan cheese · 1 tablespoon chopped
capers · a few pieces tomato · salt · pepper ·
butter · 2 cups tomato sauce*

To garnish: *capers · parsley sprigs*

Mix together the breadcrumbs, Parmesan,
chopped capers and tomato, add salt and
pepper to taste, and enough melted butter to
obtain a smooth paste (step 1). Spread over the
4 fish slices. Roll them (step 2), tie them with
string (step 3), and cook for about ½ hour in the
tomato sauce, turning them over carefully half
way through the cooking. Transfer to a warm
serving platter and garnish with capers and
parsley sprigs.

Salmon Bellevue

Put 1 quart dry white wine in a fish poacher or kettle with 2 quarts water, 2 carrots, sliced, 2 onions, sliced, a few cloves, 1 bouquet garni, made with 2–3 sprigs of parsley, 1 sprig of thyme, 1 bay leaf, 1–2 cloves of garlic, a handful of rock salt and 6 whole peppercorns. Bring to a boil, skim the scum, and cook for 45 minutes. Scale, clean and wash a whole salmon (6–8 lb). Trim off gills and fins, and trim the tail. Place it in the court bouillon and simmer slowly for 25–30 minutes. Turn off the heat and cool in the court bouillon. Remove the salmon from the liquid when cool, discard the skin and place the fish on a folded white napkin on a large platter. Cover the fish with cool liquid aspic (see p.104) and allow to set.

Prepare 16 hard-boiled eggs. Halve them lengthwise, remove the yolks and mash them together with mayonnaise to make a stiff cream. Fill the egg whites with this mixture, using a pastry bag fitted with a star nozzle. Cut off the tops of 10 tomatoes, remove seeds and pulp and fill with a macédoine mixed with mayonnaise (see p.9). To prepare the macédoine: cook until tender 1 lb carrots, diced, with 2 cups green peas, shelled, and 2½ tablespoons turnips, diced, in boiling salted water; drain. Cook until tender 10 artichoke hearts in boiling salted water with a little vinegar; drain. Place small shrimps dipped in mayonnaise on top of artichoke hearts. Arrange everything around the salmon on the platter with lettuce leaves and lemon slices. Serve with tartare sauce (see p.99) in a separate dish.

Stuffed Salmon Slices

Ingredients: *2 slices fresh salmon, or other similar fish such as halibut, ¾ inch thick and about 10 oz each · 1 slice chopped onion · 1 tablespoon chopped parsley · butter or margarine · 1 generous handful of bread, soaked in milk and squeezed dry · 1 cup finely sliced mushrooms · salt · pepper · 1 cup light cream*

To serve: *chopped parsley · boiled potatoes*

Fry the onion and parsley lightly in 2½ tablespoons butter or margarine on low heat. Mix in a bowl with the bread, mushrooms, and salt and pepper to taste (step 1). Butter generously an ovenproof dish, put in one salmon slice, and spread the mushroom mixture over it (step 2). Cover with the second salmon slice, pour over the cream, previously heated (step 3), dot with butter, and sprinkle with salt and pepper. Cook in a moderate (350°F) oven for about ½ hour, basting occasionally with the cooking juices. Transfer to a warm serving platter, sprinkle with chopped parsley and serve with boiled potatoes.

Salmon Brochettes

Arrange on oiled skewers 1½ lb fresh salmon, or swordfish, or halibut cut into pieces, alternating with mushroom caps, halved tomatoes, slices of onion and green pepper. Sprinkle with salt and pepper, and pour over 1 cup olive oil and ½ cup dry white wine. Let stand for 3½ hours. Broil, turning occasionally and basting with the marinade. (This is a perfect dish to prepare over charcoal.)

Salmon Cutlets Pojarski

Mash 1¼ lb cooked salmon (leftovers from a poached salmon are ideal) and mix it with ¾ cup breadcrumbs. Add ½ cup milk, and salt and pepper to taste. Stirring continuously, blend in 4 egg yolks one by one. Let stand for 15 minutes, then shape into cutlets. Dip them in 2 eggs beaten with a few drops oil, 1 pinch each of salt and pepper, and roll in fine white breadcrumbs. Brown in butter; serve with tartare sauce (see p.99) in a separate dish.

273

Hake Provençal

Ingredients: *4 slices hake (about 6 oz each) ·
1 cup mushrooms · 2½ tablespoons butter ·
salt · pepper · ½ onion, finely chopped · ½ clove
of garlic, crushed · 1 tablespoon chopped
parsley · 1¼ cups canned peeled tomatoes,
chopped · ½ cup dry white wine*

Clean the mushrooms, slice them (step 1) and
sauté in 1 tablespoon butter; reserve. Arrange
the hake slices, sprinkled with salt and pepper,
in a generously buttered ovenproof dish (step 2).
Sprinkle with the onion, garlic and parsley
(step 3), add the tomatoes, the cooked mushrooms and the wine. Cover, bring to a boil,
then lower the heat and cook for about 15
minutes or until the fish is tender. If the sauce
is too liquid, reduce it on high heat. Transfer
to a warm serving platter and serve immediately.

Hake au Gratin

Clean, wash and dry thoroughly 2 lb hake.
Place in each fish 1 clove of garlic, peeled, and
a few leaves of rosemary. Leave to stand for
½ hour in 6 tablespoons oil, seasoned with salt
and pepper to taste and a few sprigs rosemary.
Drain, reserving the oil, and roll in breadcrumbs,
then arrange in a buttered ovenproof dish.
Pour the reserved oil over and cook in a hot
oven (425°F) for about 20 minutes or until the
fish is tender and golden. Baste occasionally
with the cooking juices. Serve immediately.

Breaded Hake à l'Anglaise

Make an incision along the back of 4 hake,
about 5 oz each, then, taking hold of the tail
remove it, together with the main bone, and
cut off the head. Flatten the fish with a knife,
and dip into 2 eggs beaten with salt and pepper
to taste, and ½ cup oil. Roll the fish in 2½ tablespoons breadcrumbs mixed with 1 tablespoon
flour. Fry in a pan in a mixture of half oil, half
butter until tender and golden. Arrange fish
on a warm platter with parsley and serve.

Fillets of Sole Meunière

Ingredients: *2 soles (1–1¼ lb each) or 1½ lb sole fillets, fresh or frozen · flour · salt · pepper · ¼ cup butter · juice of 2 lemons · parsley, chopped*

To garnish: *lemon slices*

Remove and discard the heads from the soles, and skin them (step 1). Wash and drain. Make an incision along the center bone of each sole (step 2) and detach the 4 fillets carefully with a knife (step 3). Roll the fillets lightly in flour seasoned with salt and pepper, and cook slowly in a pan in 4 tablespoons of the butter until they are golden on all sides. Arrange them on a warm serving platter, sprinkle with the lemon juice, and the chopped parsley to taste. Melt the remaining butter in the pan, cook until lightly golden, then pour evenly over the sole. Serve immediately, garnished with lemon slices.

Sole Bonne Femme

Arrange 8 sole fillets, prepared as left, in a buttered ovenproof dish. Sprinkle over $\frac{1}{2}$ cup shallots and $\frac{1}{2}$ cup mushrooms, finely chopped, season with salt and pepper to taste, and add 1 cup dry white wine and a little fish stock. Cover with buttered wax paper or foil and bake in a moderate oven (350°F) for 15–20 minutes. Strain the cooking juices, thicken over heat with a little beurre manié (equal quantities of butter and flour kneaded together), remove from the heat, and blend in 2 egg yolks. Pour the sauce back over the sole, and return to the oven for a few minutes to gratiné.

Fillets of Sole Florentine

Clean and wash $2\frac{1}{2}$ cups spinach, and cook until tender in a little boiling salted water, drain, and keep warm. Melt $2\frac{1}{2}$ tablespoons butter in a pan, stir in 2 tablespoons flour, and cook for 1–2 minutes. Remove from heat and stir in 1 cup boiling milk, and salt, pepper and grated nutmeg to taste. Simmer for 10 minutes, stirring with a wire whisk or wooden spoon. Remove from heat and stir in $\frac{1}{2}$ cup light cream and $2\frac{1}{2}$ tablespoons Gruyère cheese, grated. Roll 8 sole fillets, prepared as left, in flour seasoned with salt and pepper, and cook them slowly in 4 tablespoons butter until golden on all sides. Put the spinach in a buttered oven-proof dish, and arrange the sole fillets over the spinach. Blend 2 egg yolks into the sauce, and pour it over the fillets. Sprinkle with grated Gruyère cheese, and put in a hot oven (425°F) for a few minutes to gratiné.

Fish Scabecia Style

Clean, wash and dry $1\frac{1}{2}$ lb sole fillets, or sardines, or other fish according to taste, roll in flour and fry in oil a few at a time. Arrange in a bowl. In the remaining oil (add more if necessary) cook until golden 1 onion, sliced, and 2–3 cloves of garlic, crushed. Remove from the heat, add 4 bay leaves, 1 twig of thyme, vinegar and salt and pepper to taste. Pour immediately over the fried fish, and let stand in the refrigerator for at least 2 days.

Fritto Misto Mare

Ingredients: *8 small sole fillets · 1 cup shrimps · ¾ lb small frying fish (sprats, whitebait, sardines) · ½ lb cuttlefish · oil · flour · salt*

To garnish: *lemon quarters · parsley (optional)*

Clean and wash the fish and prepare for cooking (step 1). Cut the cuttlefish into small pieces (step 2) and fry gently in oil until tender (this may take 20 minutes to 1 hour). Dry all the fish well and roll in flour. Fry the fish in very hot deep oil (step 3) until golden. Drain on absorbent paper, sprinkle with salt, and serve piping hot with lemon quarters, and fried parsley, if liked.

Salt Cod Beignets

Soak, wash and dry 1½ lb salt cod fillets (see p.284) and cut into small pieces. To prepare the batter: beat in a bowl 1 egg yolk with 1 tablespoon melted butter, add 1 cup flour, sifted, 1 pinch salt, and 1 cup beer. Mix without beating. Let the mixture stand for 1 hour, then fold in 1 egg white, whipped until stiff. Dip the fish pieces into the batter and fry in very hot deep oil until golden and crusty. Drain, and serve immediately, garnished with lemon quarters.

Sole Dugléré

Prepare 8 sole fillets (see p.276) and place in a buttered ovenproof dish. Surround them with ½ cup onions, finely chopped, 2 cups tomatoes, peeled, seeded and chopped, and chopped parsley to taste. Add ½ cup dry white wine, and season with salt and pepper to taste. Cover with wax paper or foil, and poach in a moderate oven (350°F) for 15–20 minutes. Remove the sole, and keep warm on a serving platter. Reduce the cooking juices over high heat on top of the stove, then remove from heat and add ½ cup light cream and the juice of ½ lemon. Pour over the sole and serve immediately.

278

Cod Provençal

Ingredients: *2 lb cod fillets · salt · pepper ·
flour · 2 tablespoons grated Parmesan cheese ·
grated nutmeg · 1 small onion, chopped · 1 clove
of garlic, chopped · ¼ cup oil · 6 anchovy fillets,
soaked in a little milk and mashed · 1 teaspoon
chopped parsley · ½ cup dry white wine · 3 cups
hot milk · 1 tablespoon butter*

To serve: *polenta or mashed potatoes*

Clean and skin cod and cut in large pieces.
Sprinkle with salt and pepper and roll in flour
(step 1). Arrange in 1 layer in an ovenproof

dish and sprinkle with the Parmesan cheese
mixed with a pinch of nutmeg. In a pan, sauté
the onion and garlic lightly in oil, then add the
anchovy fillets, parsley and white wine.
Reduce on low heat, then pour in the hot milk
(step 2), stirring thoroughly, and add the
butter in small pieces. Pour over the fish
(step 3), bring to a boil, cover, and cook in a
slow oven (250°F) for 2 hours. After cooking,
the cooking juices should be almost completely
absorbed. Serve with piping hot polenta or
mashed potato.

Cod Casserole

Clean and skin 2 lb cod fillet, and cut into pieces. Place in a casserole with 3 onions, sliced, 2 cups canned peeled tomatoes, chopped, ½ cup oil and a little water. Cover and cook gently for 2 hours. Serve with polenta or mashed potato.

Cod Niçoise

Prepare 1½ lb cod fillet as above, and sauté in a casserole with ½ cup onion, chopped, 2 cloves of garlic, chopped, and 1 cup olive oil. Add 1½ cups tomatoes, peeled, seeded and crushed, chopped parsley, 1 bay leaf, and salt and pepper. Cook briefly, then add 3 cups potatoes, quartered. Cover with boiling water and cook for about 1 hour. Add ½ cup pitted black olives.

Ligurian Cod

Sauté 1 clove of garlic, crushed, and 1 teaspoon chopped parsley lightly in ½ cup oil. Add 4 anchovy fillets, desalted and mashed, ½ cup pitted green olives, 2½ tablespoons pine nuts, lightly sautéed in butter, and a few capers. After a few minutes, add 2 lb cod fillets, cleaned, skinned and cut into pieces. Season to taste, cover, and cook gently for 1½ hours, adding 1 cup dry white wine gradually during cooking.

Flemish Cod

Cut 2 lb cod fillets into 2-inch pieces and place in a buttered baking dish. Cover the fish with 3 onions, peeled and thinly sliced, and 2 lemons, peeled and thinly sliced. Sprinkle over 1 tablespoon each chopped parsley and fresh dill, a little fish seasoning and salt and pepper to taste. Pour on ¾ cup dry white wine and sprinkle 6 tablespoons soft bread crumbs on top. Dot with ¼ cup butter. Bake in a hot oven (425°F) for 25 minutes. Serve immediately.

Spiced Cod

Ingredients: *1 ½ lb fresh cod, cut into 4 slices ·
1 small onion, chopped · 1 teaspoon chopped
parsley · ½ cup oil · salt · 1 tablespoon flour ·
1 bay leaf · ground cinnamon · ¼ cup dry white
wine*

To garnish: *parsley sprigs*

Sauté the chopped onion and parsley lightly in
the oil. Add the slices of cod and cook on both
sides until golden (step 1). Sprinkle with salt.
After about 15 minutes, add the flour blended
with a little water, the bay leaf (step 2), and a
pinch of cinnamon, and continue cooking a
further 15 minutes. Before removing from the
heat, add the white wine (step 3), and reduce.
Transfer to a warm serving platter and garnish
with parsley sprigs.

282

Cod with Olives

Soak $1\frac{1}{2}$ lb fresh cod in cold water for $\frac{1}{2}$ hour. Dry it, and place in an ovenproof dish with $2\frac{1}{2}$ tablespoons melted butter. Sprinkle the fish with breadcrumbs, place over it 2 tomatoes, sliced, 4 tablespoons pitted green olives, finely chopped, 1 tablespoon capers, and salt and pepper to taste. Add $\frac{1}{4}$ cup oil, and bake in a moderate oven (350°F) for about 30 minutes. This dish can also be cooked on top of oven.

Cod with Tomatoes

Roll 4 slices fresh cod, seasoned with salt and pepper, and cook until golden in $\frac{1}{4}$ cup oil. In a separate pan, sauté $\frac{1}{2}$ onion, chopped, in $\frac{1}{4}$ cup oil. Add 1 teaspoon chopped parsley, then $\frac{1}{2}$ cup dry white wine, and reduce. Add 3 anchovy fillets, desalted, and $1\frac{1}{2}$ cups canned peeled tomatoes. Cook for 15 minutes, then add the fish slices. Cook for about a further 15 minutes and serve immediately.

Broiled Cod with Tartare Sauce

Season 4 slices fresh cod (about $1\frac{1}{2}$ lb) with salt and pepper. Roll in flour, brush with oil, and place under a hot broiler. Turn them over when they are well broiled on one side. Prepare a tartare sauce with mayonnaise, chopped onion, parsley, tarragon, chervil, chives, gherkins and capers (see p.99). Serve the fish on a warm serving platter, with the tartare sauce in a separate dish.

Broiled Cod with Bacon

Brush 4 large cod fillets with oil and season with salt and pepper. Cook under a hot broiler for about 15 minutes, turning them over halfway through the cooking time. Meanwhile, broil or fry $\frac{1}{4}$ lb bacon slices. Arrange the fish and bacon on warmed serving plates and pour over $\frac{1}{4}$ cup melted butter and 2 tablespoons lemon juice. Serve immediately, garnished with lemon wedges and parsley sprigs.

283

Neapolitan Salt Cod

Ingredients: *1½ lb salt cod fillets, soaked overnight in 2 changes of cold water · flour · oil · 2–3 large onions, sliced · 2 cups canned tomatoes, chopped · salt · pepper*

Wash the cod under cold running water and dry. Cut into large pieces (step 1), roll in flour, and fry in plenty of hot oil until cooked (step 2), and keep warm. Brown the onions lightly in a few tablespoons oil. Add the tomatoes, season with salt and pepper to taste, and cook slowly until a rich sauce has formed. Ten minutes before removing the pan from the heat, add the fried pieces of cod (step 3) and heat through. Transfer to a warm serving platter and coat the fish with the sauce. Serve immediately.

Salt Cod Provençal

Prepare and cut into pieces 1½ lb salt cod fillets as above. Roll in flour and fry in ¼ cup oil until cooked, drain and keep warm. In the same pan, add a little more oil and brown 2 cloves of garlic, crushed. Remove the garlic, add 2 cups canned tomatoes worked through a sieve, 1 tablespoon capers, ¾ cup pitted black olives and 1 pinch oregano. Cook for 10 minutes. Add the pieces of cod to the sauce and heat through. Serve immediately.

Salt Cod Croquettes

Bake 1½ cups potatoes in their jackets in the oven, halve, and remove the insides. Poach 1½ lb salt cod fillets (prepared as above) in water to cover for a few minutes – do not allow to boil. Drain and mash with ½ cup onion, finely chopped, 2 eggs, salt and pepper to taste, and the potato. Shape the croquettes on a floured board, roll in an egg beaten with a little oil and salt, and fry until golden in medium-hot oil. Serve with a tomato sauce, if liked.

Salt Cod with Aïoli Mayonnaise

Soak, wash and dry 1½ lb salt cod fillets as left. Cut into 4 pieces and poach in water to cover for 15–20 minutes. Do not allow to boil. In a separate pan, cook 1 small cauliflower, cut into flowerets, 1½ cups carrots, peeled, and 2 cups potatoes, unpeeled, in boiling salted water until just tender. Meanwhile, make the aïoli (garlic) mayonnaise: in a mortar, crush 6 cloves of garlic, peeled, add 1 pinch salt, white pepper to taste and a dash of vinegar. Mix in 1 egg yolk and pour in very slowly 1 cup olive oil, stirring constantly, until thick. Drain the cod and vegetables and serve with the aïoli.

Salt Cod in Brandade

Soak 1½ lb salt cod fillets overnight in 2 changes of water. Wash under cold running water, dry, and poach until tender. Mash in a mortar with 1¼ cups potatoes, boiled and drained, and a few drops oil and milk, until creamy. Add pepper and check the seasoning before adding salt.

Grilled Sea Bass

Ingredients: *1 sea bass, or salmon trout, about*
2 lb · salt · pepper · olive oil · 2½ tablespoons
butter, melted · juice of ½ lemon · 2 tablespoons
chopped rosemary and parsley

To garnish: *lettuce leaves · lemon slices ·*
parsley · canned red pimiento (optional)

Clean the sea bass or salmon trout and remove
the central bone (step 1). Wash and dry,
sprinkle with salt and pepper (step 2) and dip
in oil. Place in a double grill or under the
broiler, and cook slowly, turning frequently,
and basting with the butter mixed with the
lemon juice and the chopped herbs (step 3).
Transfer to a warm serving platter and garnish
with lettuce leaves, lemon slices and parsley.
Stuff the eye with a little parsley and a small
slice of canned red pimiento, if liked. Serve
immediately.

Sea Bass with Tomato Sauce

Clean, wash and dry a 2-lb sea bass or salmon
trout as left. Heat 2 tablespoons oil in a pan, put
in the fish and brown lightly for a moment.
Add ¼ cup dry white wine, ¼ cup water, 1 twig
thyme, 1 bay leaf, and salt and pepper to taste.
Cook for 35–40 minutes, basting the fish
occasionally with the cooking juices. Meanwhile, in a separate pan sauté 1 small onion,
finely chopped, in 1 tablespoon oil until golden.
Add 2 cups canned peeled tomatoes worked
through a sieve, and salt and pepper to taste,
and cook slowly for ½ hour. Remove the fish
from the pan, drain, and place on a warm
serving platter. Reduce the cooking juices on
high heat after removing the thyme and bay
leaf, add the tomato sauce and 1 tablespoon
chopped parsley, mix well and pour over the
fish. Serve immediately.

Sea Bass Forestière

Prepare a 2-lb sea bass or salmon trout as left, flatten it and remove the head. Place 1 cup fresh mushrooms mixed with 1 tablespoon chopped parsley at the bottom of an ovenproof dish. Put in the fish and sprinkle with salt. Add ½ cup dry white wine and ½ cup fish stock, prepared with the head and bones of the fish and thickened with ½ teaspoon flour. Bring to a boil on top of the stove, then cover the dish with wax paper or foil and bake in a moderate oven (350°F) for 20–25 minutes or until the fish is tender. Remove the foil and continue cooking for another 5 minutes. Lift out the fish and keep warm on a serving platter. Mix 2 tablespoons butter gradually into the cooking juices, and heat through. Pour the sauce and mushrooms over the fish, and serve immediately.

Salmon Trout au Gratin

Clean, wash and dry a 2-lb salmon trout (see left). Season it inside with salt, pepper and lemon juice to taste. Place the fish in a buttered ovenproof dish and spread over it ½ cup onion, chopped, ½ cup shallots, chopped, 1 tablespoon chopped parsley, ½ cup mushrooms, sliced, then add 1 cup dry white wine, 2½ tablespoons butter in small pieces, and 1 tablespoon breadcrumbs. Cover the dish and bake in a moderate oven (350°F) for 35–40 minutes. Serve immediately.

Porgy with Mushrooms

Thinly slice ½ lb button mushrooms and scatter most over the bottom of a greased baking dish. Sprinkle over 1 onion, peeled and finely chopped. Place a 2-lb porgy or other whole fish, cleaned as left, on top. Season with salt and pepper and pour on 1 cup water. Scatter over the remaining mushrooms, 1 tablespoon chopped parsley and ½ teaspoon dried thyme. Pour over ¼ cup melted butter. Cover and bake in a hot oven (400°F) for 40 minutes, basting the fish occasionally with the juices in the dish. Remove the cover for the last 10 minutes. Serve hot, garnished with lemon wedges.

Red Mullet en Papillote

Ingredients: *4 red mullet or red snapper* *(½—¾ lb each) · 1 cup mushrooms, sliced · butter · 2 tablespoons tomato paste · ½ cup stock or dry white wine · chopped parsley · salt · pepper · oil · ¼ lb cooked ham, cut into strips*

To serve: *tomatoes · parsley*

Scale and clean the fish and remove the gills. Make a few deep slits in the sides with a knife (step 1), and dry. Cook the mushrooms in butter, add the tomato paste and the stock or white wine, and parsley, salt and pepper to taste, and continue cooking slowly. Cut out 4 ovals of wax paper or aluminum foil, each one large enough to enclose a fish (step 2), and oil generously on one side. Place on each sheet some of the mushroom sauce and 1 fish, and over the fish a few strips of cooked ham. Fold the papillotes, twisting the ends so that they are sealed and juices will not escape (step 3). Arrange them in a buttered ovenproof dish and bake in a moderate oven (350°F) for about 15 minutes. To serve, unwrap the fish carefully and arrange on warm serving plates garnished with whole baked tomatoes and parsley.

288

Red Mullet Provençal

Scale and dry 4 red mullet (about $\frac{1}{2}$ lb–$\frac{3}{4}$ lb each). Remove the gills. Sprinkle with salt and pepper and roll them lightly in flour. Cook in a little oil on moderate heat until golden brown on all sides. Remove carefully from pan with a spatula and keep warm on a serving platter. Heat $\frac{1}{4}$ cup oil in a pan, add 1 slice of onion, chopped, and 1 clove of garlic, peeled, and cook until golden. Remove the garlic, add a pinch of crumbled thyme and 1 bay leaf, $1\frac{1}{4}$ cups peeled tomatoes, and salt and pepper to taste. Cook for a further 10 minutes, then pour the sauce over the fish. Sprinkle with chopped parsley and serve.

Stuffed Red Mullet

Prepare 4 red mullet as above and remove the center bone. Prepare a stuffing with 4 tablespoons breadcrumbs, chopped rosemary, 1 clove of garlic, chopped, salt, pepper and chopped rosemary to taste, and a few tablespoons oil. Mix well together. Put a portion of this mixture inside each fish. Heat plenty of oil in a frying pan with 1 clove of garlic, peeled. Remove the garlic, add the red mullet to the pan and cook on high heat until golden brown on all sides (about 15 minutes each side). Serve piping hot with lemon quarters.

Braised Monkfish

Sprinkle a 2-lb piece of monkfish with seasoned flour. Melt $\frac{1}{4}$ cup butter in a flameproof casserole, add the fish and brown on all sides. Remove from the pot and reserve. Add $\frac{1}{2}$ lb onions and 1 carrot, all peeled and thinly sliced, to the casserole and fry until golden. Stir in a garlic clove, crushed, and $1\frac{1}{2}$ cups chopped tomatoes. Return the fish to the casserole with a bouquet garni and 1 cup dry white wine or fish stock. Cover and simmer for about 30 minutes. Discard the bouquet garni before serving.

Eel with Peas

Ingredients: *2 lb eel · ½ onion, chopped · 1 clove of garlic, crushed · 3 tablespoons oil · salt · pepper · 1 cup white wine · 1 tablespoon tomato sauce · 1 tablespoon hot water · 6 cups fresh green peas, shelled, or 4 cups canned peas · chopped parsley*

To serve: *polenta or mashed potatoes*

To skin the eel, make an incision around the body just under the head. Holding head with a cloth, pull skin off from top to tail at one stroke (step 1). Clean the eel and cut into 2-inch sections, discarding the head. Brown the onion and garlic in the oil in a pan, then add the eel slices, and salt and pepper to taste (step 2). When the eel slices are golden brown, and the liquid has evaporated, add the white wine, tomato sauce, water and peas (step 3). Continue cooking for 20–30 minutes or until eel is tender; add more water if fish becomes dry. (If using canned peas, add near end of cooking time.) Transfer to a warm serving platter, sprinkle with chopped parsley and serve with piping hot polenta or mashed potato.

290

Eel with Herbs

Prepare and slice 2 lb eel as left. Cook on high heat for 5 minutes in $2\frac{1}{2}$ tablespoons butter with 1 tablespoon chopped celery and 1 tablespoon chopped onion, stirring occasionally. Add 2 cups dry white wine. 1 pinch thyme, 1 bay leaf, crumbled, salt and pepper to taste, a handful each of sorrel leaves, spinach leaves and watercress, all washed and finely chopped, 1 pinch tarragon, and 1 tablespoon each of chopped parsley and chervil. Add a few leaves of sage and mint, wrapped in a piece of muslin. Cook on high heat, stirring with a spatula, for 10–15 minutes or until the eel is tender. Remove from the heat. Take out the sage and mint bag, and stir into the sauce 3 egg yolks, beaten. Add 1 teaspoon lemon juice. Arrange the eel slices in a platter, and pour the sauce over. This dish is equally delicious hot or cold.

Stewed Eel en Matelote

Prepare and slice 2 lb eel as left. Put the slices in a pan with $\frac{1}{2}$ cup onions, sliced, and $\frac{1}{2}$ cup mushrooms, sliced, 1 bouquet garni, 3 cloves of garlic, crushed, salt and pepper to taste, and $1\frac{1}{2}$ cups dry white wine. Bring to a boil and, after a few seconds, add $\frac{1}{2}$ cup brandy. Cook slowly for 20–30 minutes or until the eel is tender. Remove the eel slices and keep warm on a serving platter. Continue cooking the sauce on high heat until reduced by half. Remove from the heat, stir in 1 tablespoon butter, pour sauce over the eel, and serve.

Eel Brochette

Prepare $1\frac{1}{2}$ lb eel as left and cut into 1-inch slices. Rub the eel with the cut sides of a clove of garlic. Toast 4 thick slices of bread and cut each slice into 4. Thread the bread squares and eel slices alternately onto skewers, with bay leaves and fresh sage leaves in between. Brush with oil and lemon juice and season. Cook under a hot broiler for about 25 minutes, turning frequently.

291

Fish Stew with Red Wine

Ingredients: *3 lb mixed fish (halibut, cod, flounder, mackerel, bass, red snapper, shrimps mussels, scallops, squid cut into rings) · 1 celery stalk, chopped · 1 carrot, sliced · 1 onion, sliced · 2 cloves of garlic, crushed · ½ cup oil · 1 slice red pepper · parsley, chopped · 1 cup red wine · 2 cups canned peeled tomatoes · salt · pepper*

To serve: *French bread · garlic*

Clean, wash and dry the fish, cutting the larger fish into pieces and leaving the smaller ones whole (step 1). Boil in salted water the heads, bones, tails and skins of the fish, together with the celery carrot and onion. Cook the garlic lightly in the oil, then add the red pepper and parsley to taste (step 2). Add the wine, let it reduce, then add the tomatoes. Strain the stock and add it gradually to the sauce. Cook for 10 minutes, add the squid and continue cooking for 15 minutes. Transfer to a large flameproof pan — preferably earthenware — taste for seasoning and add the remaining fish, scallops, shrimps and mussels last (step 3). Cover and cook for 20–30 minutes, adding more stock if necessary. (Many connoisseurs believe the dish is best if left to stand for a few hours and re-heated on low heat before serving.) Just before serving, toast slices of French bread, rub them with garlic, arrange them in each individual plate, and spread the fish, seafood, and sauce over them.

Mediterranean Bouillabaisse

Prepare for cooking 5 lb mixed fish (whiting, red mullet, halibut, perch, cod, hake, conger eel, mackerel, bass, lobster, crab). Cut the larger fish into pieces and leave the smaller ones whole. Put the fish (except for the tender varieties like red mullet) into a large pan, together with ¾ cup onion, sliced, 2–3 cloves of garlic, crushed, 2 tomatoes, peeled and cut into pieces, 1 bay leaf, and parsley, saffron, salt and fennel to taste. Cover with water, bring to a boil and cook for 15 minutes. Add the remaining fish and cook very slowly for a further 7–8 minutes. Serve piping hot with slices of dry bread. Serve in a separate dish a mayonnaise (see p.98).

293

Fresh-Water Fish

Carp in Tomato Sauce

Ingredients: *1 carp (about 2½ lb) · 1 slice onion finely chopped · ½ cup oil · a few leaves sage · salt · pepper · ground cinnamon · 1¼ cups tomatoes, peeled (fresh or canned)*

Scale the carp (step 1), clean, wash, salt, and let stand between 2 plates for about 2 hours. Cook the onion until golden in the oil in a fish poacher or kettle. Put in the carp (step 2), and brown on both sides. Add the sage leaves, salt and pepper to taste, and a pinch of cinnamon and continue cooking for about 15 minutes, adding a few spoonfuls of hot water from time to time. Add the tomatoes (step 3), and continue cooking for another 20 minutes. The sauce must be thick. Transfer the carp to a warm serving platter and surround with the sauce.

294

Perch Fillets with Olives

Float ¼ cup oil in a pan, then add chopped parsley to taste. Add to the pan 1¼ lb perch, sliced, or rainbow trout, sliced, and sauté lightly on moderate heat. Sprinkle with salt and pepper to taste and add ¼ cup dry white wine. Let it reduce by half, then add ½ cup pitted green olives. Continue cooking for a few minutes, adding a few spoonfuls hot water or stock if necessary.

Golden Perch Fillets

Cover 8 perch fillets or rainbow trout in a marinade of oil, lemon juice, salt, pepper and chopped onion. Let stand for about 1 hour, turning them over occasionally. Remove them from the marinade, dry carefully, roll in flour, beaten egg and breadcrumbs. Brown them in ½ cup very hot oil, and arrange on a warm serving platter. Add ¼ cup oil and a few sage leaves to the pan, and cook on high heat. Pour over the fillets and serve with lemon quarters.

Baked Perch with Herbs

Clean and scale 4 whole perch, each weighing about 1 lb. Sprinkle inside and out with salt and pepper, and put a bay leaf, fresh sage leaf, sprig of fresh rosemary and a pat of butter inside each fish. Place the fish in a greased baking dish and sprinkle over chopped parsley, lemon juice and olive oil. Cover tightly and bake in a hot oven (425°F) for 20 minutes. Serve hot, garnished with fresh herbs and lemon slices.

Spiced Carp in Red Wine

Prepare a carp as left, then cut into thick slices. Place the slices in a fish kettle or flameproof casserole with ¾ cup fish stock, 1 cup red wine, 2 tablespoons oil, ½ teaspoon confectioners' sugar, ½ lemon, sliced, 2 cloves and ½ teaspoon ground cinnamon. Bring to a boil and simmer gently for 15 minutes.

Lift the fish onto a serving dish and keep hot. Strain the cooking liquid and reserve. Melt ¼ cup butter in a saucepan, stir in 2 tablespoons flour and cook for 1 minute. Gradually add the cooking liquid and bring to a boil, stirring. Simmer until thickened. Serve this sauce with the carp.

Stuffed Pike

Ingredients: *1 large pike (about 3 lb) · 1 egg · 1 handful breadcrumbs · ½ cup grated Parmesan or Gruyère cheese · chopped parsley · garlic, crushed · salt · pepper · ½ cup oil · a few sage leaves · 1 bay leaf*

To serve: *macédoine of vegetables or polenta*

Clean the pike and remove the center bone (step 1), wash and dry. Mix in a bowl the egg, breadcrumbs, Parmesan or Gruyère cheese, parsley, garlic, and salt and pepper to taste. Stuff the pike (step 2) with mixture, sew with string (step 3), and put it in an ovenproof dish, with the oil, sage and bay leaves. Cover, and cook in a moderately hot oven (350°F) for 40–50 minutes, basting occasionally with the cooking juices. Transfer to a warm serving platter, and surround with a buttered macédoine of vegetables or with polenta.

Baked Pike with White Wine Sauce

Prepare 1 large pike (about 3 lb) as left. Cut slits under the skin of the fish, and insert small strips of bacon. Put in a buttered ovenproof dish, cover and cook in a moderately hot oven (375°F) for 25 minutes. Remove the fish and keep warm on a serving platter. Pour 1½ cups dry white wine into the baking dish, and mix with the cooking juices. Add 2½ tablespoons butter, simmer for 5 minutes, then pour over the fish.

Pike Fricassée

Prepare 1 large pike (about 3 lb) as left, and cut into pieces. Put in a pan with ¼ cup oil, ¾ cup mushrooms, chopped, and a bouquet garni of parsley, thyme and 1 bay leaf. Sprinkle the fish with 1 teaspoon flour, and salt and pepper, then add 3 tablespoons stock and ½ cup dry white wine. Cook on fairly high heat until fish is tender, stirring carefully from time to time. Take out the fish and keep warm on a serving platter. Remove the bouquet garni, and blend into the sauce 1 egg yolk, beaten with a little lemon juice. Let thicken without boiling, then pour over the fish.

Pike Médaillons

Prepare 1 large pike (about 3 lb) as above, and cut into slices 1½ inches thick, removing the bones. Dip the slices in egg beaten with a little salt, then roll in breadcrumbs. Heat plenty of oil in a pan and brown the fish on all sides. Transfer to a warm serving platter, garnish with parsley, and serve with tomato sauce (see p.88) in a separate dish.

297

Trout in Aspic

Ingredients: *1 trout (about 3 lb)*

For the court bouillon: *4 quarts water · ½ cup white (distilled) vinegar · 1 medium-sized onion, sliced · 1 carrot, sliced · 1 slice of lemon · 2–3 sprigs parsley · ½ bay leaf · a few crushed peppercorns · 1 handful of rock salt*

For the aspic: *5 oz whiting or flounder, chopped · 2 egg whites · 1 leek, finely chopped · a few parsley sprigs · 6 sheets isinglass, soaked in tepid water and squeezed*

To garnish: *radishes · gherkins · black olives*

To prepare the court bouillon: put the water in a large pan with the vinegar, onion, carrot, lemon, parsley, ½ bay leaf, peppercorns and salt. Bring to a boil, then simmer gently for ¾ hour. Strain the liquid and let cool. Scale, clean and wash trout. Place it on grid of a fish kettle, cover it with 3 quarts cold court bouillon, and poach it for 10 minutes at a temperature just below boiling. Turn off heat and let cool in court bouillon; drain and reserve. Strain liquid through a wet cloth.

To prepare the aspic: add the whiting or flounder to 1 quart of the strained cooking liquid, blend in the egg whites, leek and parsley

sprigs. Bring to a boil, and add the isinglass. Skim the scum, and cook on very low heat for about $\frac{1}{2}$ hour, stirring occasionally. Do not allow to boil. Strain through a fine wet cloth. Or use jellied fish stock (see p.104). Pour a thin layer into a long, narrow serving platter. Put in the refrigerator to set. Meanwhile, let the remaining aspic cool, without getting too hard. Carefully remove the center skin of the trout, leaving the tail and head whole (step 1). When the aspic in the serving platter is set, place the trout on top (step 2), and garnish the skinned part with slices of radish, gherkin, and olive (step 3). Pour over a few spoonfuls of aspic. Garnish the platter with more gherkin and radish slices.

Trout with Almonds

Clean 4 trout (8–10 oz each), sprinkle with salt and pepper, and roll in flour. Brown them on both sides in a mixture of half butter, half oil. Add 1 small glass brandy, bring to a boil and flame. Reduce the heat to low and add salt and pepper to taste, and $\frac{1}{2}$ cup light cream. Heat through gently, without letting the cream boil. Serve the trout with the cooking juices and sprinkle with $\frac{1}{2}$ cup almonds, sliced and toasted.

Welsh Trout

Cream together $\frac{1}{2}$ cup butter, 2 tablespoons chopped parsley and 2 teaspoons each chopped fresh sage, rosemary and thyme. Season with salt and pepper. Clean 4 trout (about $\frac{1}{2}$ lb each) and spread the insides with the herb butter. Wrap each trout in 2 bacon slices. Place the trout in a greased baking dish and bake in a moderate oven (350°F) for 25 minutes. Serve garnished with sprigs of parsley.

Shellfish

Lobster Bellevue

Ingredients: *1 live lobster (about 2½ lb)*

For the court bouillon: *1 tablespoon butter ·
1 carrot, sliced · 2 onions, sliced · 1 quart dry
white wine · 1 quart water · 1 bouquet garni of
parsley, thyme and bay leaf · salt · peppercorns*

To garnish: *6 artichoke hearts, fresh, frozen or
canned · 2 cups Russian salad, commercially
prepared or homemade (see p.44) · 4 hard-boiled
eggs · mayonnaise, commercially prepared
or homemade · 1¼ cups rice · lettuce leaves ·
aspic (optional) · truffles (optional) · radish roses*

To prepare the court bouillon: heat the butter
in a large pan, add the carrot and onions and
cook until golden. Add the wine, water,
bouquet garni, and salt and peppercorns to
taste. Bring to a boil, then put in the live
lobster. Cook for 20–25 minutes, then leave to
cool in the cooking liquid. Meanwhile, cook
fresh artichoke hearts in boiling salted water,
drain, allow to cool, then fill with the Russian
salad. Halve the hard-boiled eggs, remove the
yolks carefully with a spoon, work them
through a sieve, and mix with mayonnaise to
make a stiff cream. Fill the eggs with this
mixture, using a pastry bag fitted with a star
nozzle. Cook the rice in boiling salted water
until it is *al dente*, drain, and place at one end
of an oval serving platter, making a hollow in
the center. Cover with lettuce leaves. Remove
the lobster, put it on its back on a towel, and
cut it lengthwise with scissors from head to
tail (step 1). Take the flesh out carefully in one
piece, then cut into regular slices (step 2).
Arrange lobster shell on the platter, the head
resting on the rice and lettuce. Cover with
lobster slices, garnished with little liquid aspic
(step 3) and truffles cut into star shapes, if
liked. Place artichoke hearts and eggs round
lobster and garnish with lettuce and radish
roses.

301

Brochettes of Scampi

Ingredients: *24 scampi tails (langoustines) ·
3 zucchini · 16 mushroom caps · butter or oil*

For the marinade: *a few spoonfuls olive oil ·
1 clove of garlic, crushed · 1 bay leaf, crumbled ·
salt · pepper · lemon juice*

To garnish: *lemon slices or wedges · green
salad leaves*

Shell the raw scampi tails (step 1), slice the
zucchini (step 2), clean the mushroom caps,
and put everything into a bowl. Mix all the
marinade ingredients together, pour into the
bowl, and let stand for 1 hour. Drain the
scampi, zucchini and mushrooms (reserving
the marinade), and arrange them on oiled
metal skewers (step 3). Spread a shallow baking
dish with butter or oil and put in the brochettes.
Cook in a hot oven (425°F) for about 15
minutes, basting occasionally with the reserved
marinade. Transfer the brochettes to a warm
serving platter and garnish the edges of the
platter with lemon slices or wedges and
green salad leaves.

Serve with mixed salad, dressed according
to taste, in a separate dish.

Algerian Shrimps

Blend together 3 cloves of garlic and $\frac{1}{4}$ cup
parsley, chopped. Heat 1 cup oil. When very
hot, put in 32 large shrimps and sauté, adding
salt and cayenne pepper. Add the garlic and
parsley, cook for a further 2 minutes and serve
immediately.

Shrimps with Mayonnaise

Put 2 quarts water in a large pan with 1 celery
stalk, chopped, 1 onion, sliced, 2 bay leaves,
1 twig of thyme, and parsley and salt to taste.
Boil for a few minutes, put in the tails of about
$2\frac{1}{2}$ lb shrimps, and poach for 5 minutes. Drain,
and leave to cool. Shell them, brush with oil
and lemon juice, and let stand for a few hours.
Serve with mayonnaise (see p.98), and garnish
with salad and hard-boiled eggs.

Mussels au Gratin

Ingredients: *3 lb mussels · ¼ cup dry white wine · 1 slice of onion, finely chopped · freshly ground pepper · vinegar · chopped parsley · 2 cloves of garlic, chopped · breadcrumbs · salt · pepper · 3 tablespoons oil mixed with 1 tablespoon vinegar or lemon juice*

Scrape the mussels (step 1), wash in running water, discarding any that are open, and put in a large pan together with the white wine, onion, pepper, and a few drops vinegar. Cover and cook on high heat, shaking the pan from time to time, until the mussels are all opened (discard any that do not open). Drain them and discard the empty halves of the shells, keeping those where the mussel is attached. Arrange the mussels in an ovenproof dish (step 2), and cover each with a mixture of parsley, garlic, breadcrumbs, and salt and pepper to taste (step 3). Pour the oil and vinegar over, and put the dish in a hot oven (425°F) for a few minutes to gratiné. Serve immediately.

Stuffed Mussels

Prepare 3 lb mussels as left, heat them in a frying pan until they are all opened (discard any that do not open). Meanwhile, prepare the stuffing: mix 3 oz mortadella, chopped finely, with 3 oz sausage meat, and a handful of the white part of bread, soaked and squeezed dry, 1 tablespoon chopped parsley, 1 clove of garlic, chopped, and salt and pepper to taste. When the mixture is smooth, stuff mussels, close them and tie them with string. Cook in a large pan 2 cups tomatoes, peeled, seeded, and crushed, a few basil leaves, a little chopped onion, a few spoonfuls oil and a pinch of salt. Then put in the mussels and cook for another 30 minutes. Remove mussels from sauce, discard string, then return mussels to sauce to reheat. Serve piping hot.

Mussel Soup

Prepare 5 lb mussels as left. Heat them in a frying pan until they are all open (discard any that do not open). Add a few spoonfuls hot water, and cook for about 15 minutes. Meanwhile, cook 1–2 cloves of garlic, peeled, in $\frac{1}{2}$ cup oil until golden; remove the garlic and add a generous measure of chopped parsley and basil. Pour over the mussels, adding more hot water if necessary, and boil for a few minutes. Arrange in individual dishes slices of bread fried in butter, pour over the mussels and their sauce, and serve immediately.

Mussels Marinière

Put 1 cup dry white wine in a pan with 1 twig thyme and 1 small bay leaf. Add 3 lb mussels (prepared as left). Cover and cook on high heat until mussels are all opened (discard any that do not open). Take out the mussels and keep warm on a serving platter. Make a roux with $2\frac{1}{2}$ tablespoons of butter, 2 tablespoons flour, and the cooking juices from the mussels. Pour over the mussels, and sprinkle them with a mixture of finely chopped parsley to taste and $\frac{1}{4}$ cup shallots, finely chopped, or finely chopped garlic to taste.

Assorted Dishes

Algerian Octopus

Ingredients: *1 octopus (about 2½ lb) · ¼ cup oil · 2–3 cloves of garlic, crushed · 1 red pepper, seeded and chopped · 2 cups tomatoes, peeled and sliced · chopped parsley · salt*

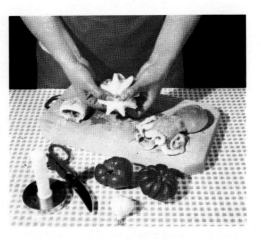

Skin and clean the octopus, remove the eyes, mouth and pouch (step 1), and pound or beat thoroughly to tenderize it (step 2). Wash well and put in a high, narrow pan (preferably earthenware) with the oil, garlic, red pepper, tomatoes, and chopped parsley and salt to taste. Cover the pan, using a sheet of thick paper or foil under the cover to seal it (step 3), and cook slowly for about 2 hours. Serve hot or cold.

Valencian Octopus

Prepare 1 octopus (about 2½ lb) as above. Simmer it, covered, for 2 hours in salted water with 1 twig of thyme. Meanwhile, cook ¾ cup onion, finely chopped, in ½ cup oil until transparent. Add 3 cloves of garlic, chopped, 1 cup rice, 1 cup green peas, shelled, and a little saffron. When the octopus is cooked, slice it and add to the vegetable mixture.

Greek Octopus

Prepare 1 octopus (about 2½ lb) as above. Cut into large pieces. Put into an earthenware pan with 1 onion, sliced, 1 clove of garlic, crushed, 1 clove, salt to taste and a few tablespoons of cold water. Cover, and seal the pan by putting a paste, made by mixing of flour and water together, around the edges of the lid. Cook in a moderate oven (350°F) for about 2 hours. Remove the paste from the lid, and serve in the cooking pan. This dish is also excellent cold.

Genoese Octopus

Prepare 2½ lb small octopus as above. Cut into strips. Sauté lightly in ½ cup oil, ¾ cup onions, chopped, 3 cloves of garlic, crushed, ¼ cup mushrooms, sliced, 3 tablespoons tomato paste, ½ cup pitted black olives, and thyme, rosemary, salt and pepper to taste. Add the octopus. Cover and cook slowly for about 1 hour, adding stock if necessary. Remove the octopus, and keep warm on a serving platter. Reduce the sauce, pour it over the octopus, and serve with croûtons fried in oil.

Italian Stuffed Squid

Ingredients: *4 squid or cuttlefish (about 1½ lb) ·
¾ cup ricotta, or cottage cheese · 1cup spinach ·
2 eggs · 1 tablespoon grated Parmesan cheese ·
garlic to taste · chopped parsley · 1 celery stalk,
1 carrot and 1 onion, all chopped together ·
¼ cup oil · 1 tablespoon tomato paste · salt ·
pepper*

To garnish: *parsley sprigs*

To serve: *mashed potatoes*

Skin the squid, cut off the head, remove the
internal cuttlebones and discard (step 1). Wash
them without opening, and dry. Clean and
wash the spinach, cook it in a little boiling salt
water until tender, then squeeze dry. Work it
through a sieve together with the ricotta, or
cottage cheese (step 2), then mix in a bowl
with the eggs, Parmesan cheese, and garlic
and chopped parsley to taste. Stuff the squids
with this mixture (step 3), and sew them with
string. Sauté the celery, carrots and onion
mixture lightly in the oil. Add the tomato
paste diluted in a little water, and salt and
pepper to taste. After a few minutes add the
stuffed squids, and cook slowly for about 1
hour or until tender. Transfer squid to a warm
serving platter, surrounded with the sauce, and
garnish the platter with parsley sprigs and
serve with mashed potatoes.

Livornese Squid

Skin 4 squid or cuttlefish (about 1½ lb). Remove
and discard the heads, internal cuttlebones,
and the pouches containing a black, ink-like
fluid. Cut them into pieces, wash and dry.
Clean and wash 2½ cups spinach. Cook for a
few minutes without water, and squeeze
well. Sauté lightly 1 onion, chopped, in ½
cup oil with 1 tablespoon chopped parsley and
1 clove of garlic, peeled. Add the squid. Dilute
1 tablespoon tomato paste with a little stock,
pour it over the squid, adding more stock if dry.
After 15 minutes, remove the garlic and add
the spinach. Cover and cook very slowly for
about 1 hour, or until the squid are tender.
The sauce must be thoroughly reduced.

Snails Bourguignon

Ingredients: *48 large snails · rock salt ·
vinegar · flour · dry white wine · 1 carrot and 1
onion sliced together · 1 shallot, chopped ·
garlic to taste, peeled · 1 bouquet garni ·
peppercorns*

For the stuffing: *2 cups butter, softened ·
1 tablespoon shallot or onion, finely chopped
4 cloves of garlic, crushed · 2 tablespoons
chopped parsley · 1 teaspoon salt · 1 pinch each
pepper and spices*

To garnish: *parsley sprigs*

You can now buy canned snails, already
cleaned and prepared, accompanied by clean
empty shells, and ready to cook. If, however,
you choose to use fresh snails, there must be
lengthy preparations. First, the snails must be
left to disgorge for 2–3 days in a container
where they can get enough air, but from which
they cannot escape. If the snails are bought
live in a shop, this has usually been done. Dip
the snails in plenty of cold water and stir well
to rid the shells of the diaphragm and particles
of earth. Put the washed snails in a pan containing rock salt, vinegar, and a little flour.
Let them disgorge for 2–3 hours, shaking the
pan occasionally. Wash once more in running
water. Put the snails in a large pan, cover with
cold water, and bring to a boil on low heat.
Skim the scum, and boil on high heat for 8
minutes. Lift the snails out, drain and put in
cold water for a moment. Put them back in a

pan, and cover with equal parts of water and white wine. Add rock salt ($\frac{1}{2}$ tablespoon for 1 quart of liquid), the carrots and onions, shallot, bouquet garni, and garlic cloves, and peppercorns to taste. Bring to a boil on a moderate heat, and continue cooking for 2–3$\frac{1}{2}$ hours, according to the size of the snails. When cooked put them in a sieve to drain. Remove snails from shells (step 1), and remove the black part at the end of the helix. Wash the shells thoroughly in warm water, and dry in the oven.

To make the stuffing, blend together the butter, chopped shallots or onion, crushed garlic, parsley, salt, pepper and spices (step 2). Put some of this mixture at the bottom of each empty shell (step 3), put in the snail, and seal the shell with more of the mixture, pressing it down firmly. Arrange the shells, open side up, on special snail dishes (*escargotières*), or on ovenproof dishes filled with a layer of rock salt, and bake in a hot oven (425°F) for 5 minutes. Garnish with parsley sprigs before serving.

Snails in Tomato Wine Sauce

Heat 6 tablespoons olive oil in a frying pan. Add 1 onion, peeled and finely chopped, 1 garlic clove, crushed, 1 cup sliced button mushrooms, and 1 tablespoon chopped fresh basil (or 2 teaspoons dried basil). Cook for 5 minutes, then add a 16-oz can of tomatoes. Break them up with a spoon and season with salt and pepper. Simmer gently for 30 minutes, stirring occasionally. Add 1 cup dry white wine and a 16-oz can of snails, drained. Cook for a further 10 minutes, then serve immediately.

Fried Frogs' Legs

Ingredients: *1½ lb frogs' legs · ½ cup dry white wine · 1 clove of garlic, crushed · 1 tablespoon chopped parsley · salt · pepper · grated nutmeg · flour · 1 egg · 2 tablespoons milk · oil for frying*

To garnish: *lemon slices · parsley sprigs*

Skin the frogs' legs and cut off the fingers. Wash, and let stand for 1–2 hours in a marinade prepared with the white wine, garlic, parsley, and salt, pepper and nutmeg to taste (step 1). Drain them, and dry carefully. Roll them in flour, then dip in the egg, beaten with the milk and a pinch of salt (step 2). Fry, a few at a time, for about 5 minutes, in very hot oil (step 3). Take out when golden and crisp, put on a warm serving platter, sprinkle with salt, and serve with lemon slices and parsley sprigs.

Frogs' Legs Provençal

Dip 24 large frogs' legs, prepared as above, in milk. Drain and roll in 1 tablespoon flour. Put 2½ tablespoons butter and ¼ cup oil in a frying pan and heat until smoke begins to rise. Add the frogs' legs and sauté quickly on high heat. Sprinkle with salt and pepper, and 4 chopped cloves of garlic and chopped parsley.

Frogs' Legs Meunière

Roll in flour 24 large frogs' legs, prepared as above. Sprinkle with salt and pepper. Sauté them quickly in ½ cup oil, then keep warm on a serving platter. Put 2½ tablespoons butter into a pan. Sprinkle the frogs' legs with parsley and lemon juice and pour the butter over.

Frogs' Legs Orly

Prepare 24 frogs' legs, as above. Make a batter with 1½ cups flour, ½ cup beer, 2 egg yolks, 1 tablespoon oil and a pinch of salt. Let it stand for 1 hour. Whip the 2 egg whites until stiff, and fold into the batter. Dip the frogs' legs into the batter, and sprinkle with salt. Put some oil in a frying pan, and add the frogs' legs when boiling. Take them out when they are golden and crisp and serve immediately with a tomato sauce (see p.88) in a separate dish.

312

Introduction to Meat, Poultry and Game

Meat is our highest quality protein food. All varieties, whether farmed or wild, four-footed or winged, are important sources of nutrition – and of gastronomic pleasure. The killing, dressing, buying and cooking of meats of all kinds are among the most skilful arts concerned with food, for the flavor and texture of meat is always different and is very largely dependent on the way the beast or bird is treated before it reaches the table. Fortunately, few home cooks now need to know how to kill and dress meat, how to butcher it or how long to hang it – this is knowledge special to the butchery trade.

It is, however, important to be able to buy well, and for this reason it is best to go regularly to one tradesman who will get to know you and who will be pleased to advise you. Supermarket meat is often cheaper than that offered at a butcher's shop, but unless the supermarket has its own meat department with butchers actually behind the counter, you will not have the advantage of specialist knowledge.

Buying well does not necessarily mean buying expensively; cheaper cuts can taste excellent if cooked in the style that suits them. The secret of success is knowing exactly what you have bought and the best way to cook it. With the help of this comprehensive range of recipes, you will be able to serve your family and guests with some of the finest meals they have ever tasted.

Beef

How to cook cuts of beef

Steaks (other than for pan frying or broiling)

Sirloin tip	Broil or stew
Flank	Broil or braise
Chuck (blade) rump	Stew or braise
Round shoulder arm	Stew

Roasts

Rib fillet (tenderloin)	Roast
Rump	Roast, pot roast or braise
Sirloin tip	Roast or braise
Shoulder arm chuck (blade)	Pot roast or braise
Round	Braise
Flank	Broil or braise
Brisket	Simmer or braise
Short ribs short plate shank: oxtail; neck	Simmer or stew
Heel of round	Stew or braise
Cross cut foreshank hind shank	Simmer
English cut	Stew

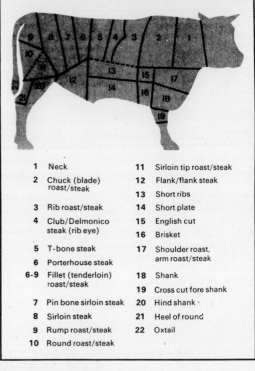

1	Neck	11	Sirloin tip roast/steak
2	Chuck (blade) roast/steak	12	Flank/flank steak
		13	Short ribs
3	Rib roast/steak	14	Short plate
4	Club/Delmonico steak (rib eye)	15	English cut
		16	Brisket
5	T-bone steak	17	Shoulder roast, arm roast/steak
6	Porterhouse steak		
6-9	Fillet (tenderloin) roast/steak	18	Shank
		19	Cross cut fore shank
7	Pin bone sirloin steak	20	Hind shank
8	Sirloin steak	21	Heel of round
9	Rump roast/steak	22	Oxtail
10	Round roast/steak		

Roasting times for beef

On the bone	
375°F	15 minutes per lb, plus 15 minutes (rare)
375°F	20 minutes per lb, plus 20 minutes (medium)
375°F	25 minutes per lb (medium—well done)
Boned and rolled	
375°F	20 minutes per lb, plus 20 minutes (rare)
375°F	25 minutes per lb, plus 25 minutes (medium)
375°F	30 minutes per lb (medium—well done)

Roasting beef

Beef is very rich in protein, whether you choose one of the best roasting cuts or a more economical piece of shin for stewing.

It is traditional to serve roast beef slightly underdone but this is only suitable for the best, most tender cuts and of course not everyone likes it that way. Roasting is done in a hot oven at 190°C/375°F/gas 5 in an open pan. The high temperature sears the meat quickly and seals in the juices, giving an excellent flavor. If you are not very confident about the quality of your roast, cook it more slowly at a less high oven temperature as this will ensure that the meat will not harden during cooking.

If, in order to keep your oven clean, you wish to cover the joint with a lid, roasting bag or foil, this will help keep the meat moist and succulent but it will not have quite the same traditional roast flavor. If roasting covered, uncover the joint for the last 30 minutes of cooking time to brown the outside.

A brief guide as to which cuts to stew, braise or boil is given above.

A meat thermometer tells you even more accurately when your roast is cooked to your taste. The thermometer is inserted into the thickest part of the roast, taking care that it does not touch the bone. Using a meat thermometer you can even cook a frozen roast with confidence; simply start to cook the roast and insert the thermometer when it is sufficiently thawed. The temperature registered on the thermometer is the internal temperature of the meat so there can be no doubt that when the thermometer shows the required temperature, the meat is cooked. The following is a guide to using a thermometer to cook beef:

140°F – rare   160°F – medium
170°F – well done   180°F – very well done

Beef steaks

Steaks are cut from the sirloin, rump and adjacent cuts. They can be broiled or fried, the cooking time being the same for either method.

Rump steak has the best flavor but may not be quite as tender as other cuts unless it is really prime beef, well hung; it is normally cut about 1 inch thick.

Sirloin steak (also known as entrecôte) is cut from the top part of the sirloin. This is cut $\frac{3}{4}$–1 inch thick.

T-bone steak is a slice cut right across the sirloin, including the bone. This is normally cut $1\frac{1}{2}$–2 inches thick and will weigh about $1\frac{1}{2}$ lb. One side of the T-bone the meat is very tender, the other not quite so good.

Minute steak is a thin slice of sirloin steak, cut about $\frac{1}{4}$ inch thick. It should be cooked very quickly (hence the name) so that it does not dry out.

Fillet steak is usually the most expensive per lb to buy and the most tender to eat. The fillet is a small portion which lies under the sirloin and is cut in slices 1–$1\frac{1}{2}$ inches thick. There is no fat on fillet steak.

Cooking times for steaks

Rump	6–7 minutes	Rare
	8–10 minutes	Medium
	15 minutes	Well done
Sirloin	5 minutes	Rare
	6–7 minutes	Medium
	9–10 minutes	Well done
T-bone	7–8 minutes	Rare
	8–10 minutes	Medium
	13–15 minutes	Well done
Minute	1–$1\frac{1}{2}$ minutes	Rare
	2–3 minutes	Medium
	It dries out if cooked too well	
Fillet and Tournedos	6 minutes	Rare
	7–8 minutes	Medium
	9–10 minutes	Well done
Chateaubriand	16–20 minutes	Rare/medium
Porterhouse	7–8 minutes	Rare
	8–10 minutes	Medium
	13–15 minutes	Well done

Tournedos is a small round cut from the center of the fillet, the same thickness as a fillet steak, but with the edges trimmed off.

Chateaubriand is a piece 3–4 inches thick cut from the heart of the fillet. It is cooked in the piece and sliced downwards for serving.

Porterhouse steak is cut from the wing rib, without bone. It is cut $1\frac{1}{2}$–2 inches thick.

Veal

Cooking and serving veal

Veal is butchered into the same cuts as lamb, though the leg is known as fillet.

Because a veal animal is so young there is virtually no fat in the meat so it takes careful cooking to prevent drying and shrivelling up. Roast on the bone at 375°F for 25 minutes per lb, plus 25 minutes; off the bone, rolled, roast at the same temperature for 30 minutes per lb, plus 30 minutes. A temperature of 175°F on the meat thermometer shows that the joint is cooked.

Apart from roasting, the most popular ways of serving veal are in pies, often accompanied by ham for extra flavor, as scallops and many variations on the traditional fried scallop, coated in egg and breadcrumbs, known as a Wiener Schnitzel.

How to cook cuts of veal

Shoulder/blade roast	Pot roast
blade steak	Braise or simmer
Rib roast	Roast
chop	Pan fry or stew
Loin chops	Pan fry or stew
Sirloin roast	Roast or pot roast
steak	Pan fry or stew
Leg (round) roast	Roast or pot roast
cutlets	Pan fry or stew
noisettes	Pan fry or braise
scallops	Pan fry
Breast	Roast or pot roast
Neck	Simmer
Foreshank	Simmer or stew

Lamb

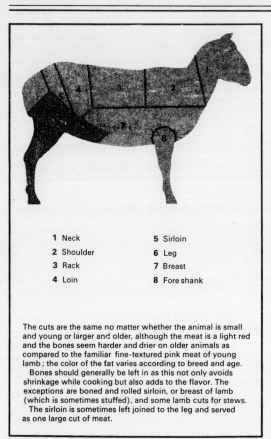

1 Neck   5 Sirloin
2 Shoulder   6 Leg
3 Rack   7 Breast
4 Loin   8 Fore shank

The cuts are the same no matter whether the animal is small and young or larger and older, although the meat is a light red and the bones seem harder and drier on older animals as compared to the familiar fine-textured pink meat of young lamb; the color of the fat varies according to breed and age.
    Bones should generally be left in as this not only avoids shrinkage while cooking but also adds to the flavor. The exceptions are boned and rolled sirloin, or breast of lamb (which is sometimes stuffed), and some lamb cuts for stews.
    The sirloin is sometimes left joined to the leg and served as one large cut of meat.

Cooking and serving lamb

The leg and loin are the meatiest roasts on a lamb (a saddle is the loin from both sides of the animal, still joined) and both roast well. A very small joint, but with choice, tender meat, is the rack of ribs; this can also be cut into small cutlets for entrées. It is the rack of lamb that is used for a traditional crown roast of lamb and for a *carré* (see p. 367). The shoulder is slightly fattier than the leg or loin, but the meat is sweet, moist and tasty and many people prefer this joint. Scrag end of neck and breast of lamb both have a lot of bone and fat. Scrag makes excellent stews, but the fat should be skimmed off the cooked dish before it is served; the dish will be more pleasant if the bones are removed. Breast of lamb is usually boned and rolled before cooking, otherwise it is an unwieldy joint; occasionally it is stuffed and roasted.
    Lamb is usually served well done, though the

How to cook cuts of lamb

Shoulder	Roast or pot roast
chops	Pan fry, broil or stew
Rack or rib roast	Roast or broil
(best end of neck)	
Loin	Roast, pot roast or braise
chops	Pan fry or broil
Sirloin	Roast or pot roast
chops	Pan fry, broil or stew
Leg	Roast or pot roast
Breast	Roast, pot roast or braise
Neck	Simmer or stew
Foreshank	Simmer, braise or stew

Roasting times for lamb (to give a well done roast)

On the bone	
425°F	20 minutes per lb, plus 20 minutes
350°F	27 minutes per lb, plus 27 minutes
Boned and rolled	
425°F	25 minutes per lb, plus 25 minutes
350°F	35 minutes per lb, plus 25 minutes

Broiling times for lamb

Cutlets and noisettes	7–8 minutes
Loin chops	10–12 minutes (more if very large)

French prefer it underdone. A reading of 175°F on a meat thermometer indicates a well cooked roast.
    Cuts most used for broiling are the cutlets from the rack of ribs and chops from the loin. Chunks of boneless meat from the leg or shoulder are threaded on to barbecue skewers to make kebabs, and sometimes a slice is cut from the end of the leg for broiling. Rib rack cutlets may be boned and tied into a neat circle with string to make 'noisettes'.

Pork

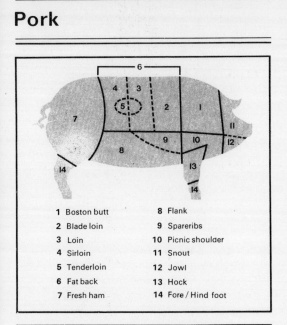

1 Boston butt	8 Flank
2 Blade loin	9 Spareribs
3 Loin	10 Picnic shoulder
4 Sirloin	11 Snout
5 Tenderloin	12 Jowl
6 Fat back	13 Hock
7 Fresh ham	14 Fore / Hind foot

How to cook cuts of pork

Loin	Roast or pot roast
Sirloin	Roast, pot roast or braise
Fresh ham (leg)	Roast or pot roast
Spareribs	Roast or broil
Boston butt; blade loin; tenderloin; picnic shoulder	Pot roast or braise
Fat back; flank; jowl	Pan fry
Loin/sirloin chops	Pan fry or stew
Snout	Simmer
Hock	Simmer or braise
Fore foot	Boil, then broil or braise

Cooking and serving pork

All pork should be well cooked. The leg and loin are the best cuts to roast, giving the best flavor; picnic shoulder is a good roast, but has less flavor. When the leg and loin are roasted, the skin is left on and served as 'crackling'. It is well scored, rubbed with oil and salt and when cooked becomes crisp and tasty; for serving, the crackling is removed from the joint first, the meat is carved and the crackling then divided up. Ask the butcher to chine the loin, (take out the bone) to make carving easier.

Roast pork on the bone at 375°F for 25 minutes per lb, plus 25 minutes.

If the joint is boned and rolled, roast at 375°F for 30–35 minutes per lb, plus 35 minutes. A reading of 185°F on the meat thermometer indicates a moist but well cooked joint.

Pork is a very rich meat and to counteract this richness a sweet sauce such as apple or gooseberry is usually served with it. A boned and rolled joint is often stuffed with a savory stuffing.

Loin chops are the best for broiling, and these should be well trimmed of surplus fat. Be careful to cook the chops for 12–15 minutes, until well cooked through.

To stew, braise or boil meat

To stew meat. For a brown stew first brown the meat, then take it out and add a little flour before nearly covering with hot stock; for white stew blanch the meat (not brown) and thicken liquid towards end of cooking. Liquid should simmer, not boil. Cook at 325°F, or simmer on top of cooker for up to 2 hours, according to recipe.

For braising use a smaller quantity of liquid so that meat cooks more in the steam.

For boiling, do not brown meat but place in boiling water for 5 minutes, then simmer until tender (20–25 minutes per lb plus 20 minutes), skimming often.

Variety Meats

Many variety meats, if cooked quickly, would be coarse in texture and flavor. But skilled preparation and long, slow cooking can produce dishes that are a true gastronomic delight and turn sweetbreads and kidneys, for instance, into delicacies of the table.

Variety meats should always be eaten very fresh. They should not be hung and should preferably be eaten on the day they are bought. They may be kept for 1–2 days in the refrigerator but should be well covered to prevent the smell contaminating other foods, and should be checked carefully before cooking; if in any doubt about the freshness, do not use them.

Most of these meats are nutritionally very good. Like all meats they are a source of protein; liver, particularly, is rich in iron and vitamins; kidney is also a good source of iron. Certain variety meats, chiefly the feet and stomach (tripe, pigs' trotters, cow heel, calves' feet), are very rich in gelatin. The feet are useful additions to stocks and casseroles to give a good, rich gravy. They may also be cooked as a meal in their own right but this is less common these days, as we seem to have lost the taste for gelatinous meats.

Preparation of variety meats

Liver

The livers of calves, oxen, pigs and sheep, as well as those of poultry and game, are all used. Calves' liver is the best, being very tender and delicate in flavor. It may be lightly broiled or fried. Lamb's liver is also good though a little stronger in flavor; this may also be broiled or fried and is good in casseroles. Pig's liver is generally used only for pâté. It has a strong flavor and a soft texture which many people do not like. Ox liver is usually the cheapest, being also the most coarse. It is too tough for frying or broiling, and should be casseroled or stewed; the flavor is quite strong.

Kidney

This is often used as a flavoring ingredient in a rich stew or pie. For this purpose ox kidney is ideal as the flavor is good and, the texture being a little coarse, it needs long, slow cooking to make it tender. Calves' kidney is more tender and more delicate in flavor than ox kidney, but is also used in stews; it is rarely tender enough to cook quickly. Lamb's kidney is very tender and broils well — this is a popular ingredient in a mixed grill. Pig's kidney will also broil, though it is not quite so tender.

Heart

The heart is usually stuffed and then either braised or roasted. Whichever animal the heart is from, slow cooking is to be recommended, though of course a lamb's heart will be more tender than an ox heart. Ox heart is sometimes sold sliced for including in stews and pies.

Tongue

Ox tongue is extremely popular served cold. The tongue is usually salted, then it is boiled gently with flavoring vegetables and pressed until cold. Calves' tongues may also be served like this. Lambs' tongues, however, are usually served hot, in a casserole. All tongues need a certain amount of extra preparation; they need soaking before cooking, trimming carefully and skinning.

Sweetbreads

A real luxury food, sweetbreads have a very delicate flavor and texture. Ox and calves' sweetbreads need slow, gentle cooking in a casserole to make them tender, but lambs' sweetbreads are tender enough to be fried or sautéed. Before cooking sweetbreads, soak them in cold water for 3–4 hours, then drain and put them into a pan. Cover with fresh cold water and a little lemon juice, bring to a boil and blanch them for 5 minutes. Drain them well, press to remove all surplus moisture and trim them to remove all the stringy tissue attached. They are then ready for cooking according to the recipe chosen.

Brains

Only calves' and lambs' brains are normally eaten, calves' being considered the best. Poached brains on toast is a very simple and popular dish, perhaps with a sauce, or brains may be stewed or casseroled.

Tripe

There are two types of tripe, known as 'blanket' and 'honeycomb', taken from the first and second stomachs of a beef animal respectively. There is no difference in the way they are cooked, or in the flavor, it is only the texture that is different. Tripe has to be cleaned very thoroughly and this is usually done by the butcher; he cleans it and partly cooks it before offering it for sale. Even so, tripe must be cooked for a long time to break down the strong cells and make the meat tender. Properly cooked and flavored, tripe makes a delicious dish.

Spleen

Ox spleen is sometimes used in casseroles.

Poultry

Poultry is the general term used for all birds reared in the barnyard for eating purposes.

Chicken and turkey are white-fleshed birds with little natural fat; they are suitable for broiling, roasting, frying or casseroling. Duck and goose are darker-fleshed and have a thick covering of fat under the skin. These are best roasted or pot roasted so as to keep the skin crisp; as much of the fat as possible is drained off during cooking and a sharp sauce served with the meat to counteract the richness.

When selecting a bird for roasting, watch the following points. The flesh should be firm, the legs soft and free from scales. The wings and the tip of the breast bone should be pliable (in birds less than a year old the tip of the breast bone will still be cartilage; if it has hardened into bone this denotes an older bird). There should be a small amount of fat on the back, and a good fleshy breast; too much fat should be avoided. The skin and shanks may be white or yellow according to breed but either way they should be a good even color, with no signs of bruising. Some birds even have blue shanks but these are rarely offered for sale by a poulterer because they look unattractive; if you are offered one privately, however, the flesh will taste just as good.

Do not forget when you buy a chicken ready dressed by the poulterer to ask for the giblets and preferably also the neck and feet. The liver is a delicacy that can be prepared in many tasty ways, while the kidney, heart, gizzard, neck, feet and wing tips will make an excellent broth for soup and other dishes. If the neck and feet are not available, the rest of the giblets will make tasty broth but it will not have the jellying quality supplied by the feet.

Trussing

Most birds need to be trussed if cooked whole, to keep them in good shape. The simplest way to truss is using skewers and string.

For a chicken, a not very large skewer is inserted right through the body just below the thigh bone; for a larger bird 2 skewers will be necessary, one on either side. Next turn the bird over on to is breast; pass the string under the protruding ends of the skewers, catching in the wing tips, and cross it over the back. Turn the bird over and tie the ends of the string round the tail, holding the drumsticks in place.

A more complicated way to truss, but much firmer and really the better method, is using a trussing needle threaded with fine string. The needle is inserted close to the second joint of one wing; it is pushed right through the body and brought out in the corresponding place on the other side. It is then re-inserted, this time into the first joint of the wing, through the flesh at the back of the body and catching in the wing tips and neck skin, to come out in the first joint of the wing on the other side. The ends of the string are tied in a bow. Then the needle is re-threaded to secure the legs; it is inserted through the gristle beside the parson's nose and the legs and tail are tied firmly together.

Always remember to remove the trussing string before serving up the bird.

Types of Chicken

Poussin
This term means a very young chicken weighing not more than 1–2 lb. A really small one will serve only 1 person, a larger one will serve 2. Poussins should be roasted, broiled or pot roasted.

Spring chicken
Also known as broilers, these birds weigh between 2–3½ lb, and will serve 3–4 people. These are suitable for roasting or pot roasting, sautés and casseroles. Most frozen chickens are broilers.

Roaster
These are chickens weighing from about 3½–5½ lb. weight and therefore make excellent, tender meat for roasting while serving more people than a spring chicken. As well as roasting they may of course be boiled or pot roasted.

Boiler
Chickens of over 1 year old are more suitable for boiling, as the flesh will be less tender and more fatty. A boiler may weigh anything from about 4–6 lb.

Capon
As adult male birds do not normally make good eating, so young cocks not required for breeding are castrated and fattened specially for the table. The result is a much larger bird than a chicken – up to 8 lb – and excellent, tender meat for roasting.

Turkey

A good, fully grown turkey may weigh up to 30 or 40 lb, but many small breeds are produced which may be put on sale at 10–12 lb. As with chicken, the hen bird is the more tender, with less bone in proportion to flesh; they are best eaten at 7–9 months old. When choosing a turkey, look for good, white flesh, a broad, plump breast and a short neck.

Duck

The term duck may refer to all sorts of swimming bird (see also Game), but when considering it as a form of poultry we are generally referring to the mallard, bred specially for the table; these birds will usually have done little swimming, and that will all have been in fresh water, and they will have been provided with food. The food a bird eats has a considerable effect on the flavor of its flesh and there is therefore a world of difference between the domesticated duck and the wild duck which has to grab what food it can.

When buying duck, look for a good, broad, meaty breast. There is a large proportion of bone to flesh on any duck and a 4-lb bird (dressed weight) will serve only 4 people.

There is plenty of fat on a duck so you will not need to add any to the roasting tin, as you would for chicken. The bird should be turned every 20 minutes or so during cooking, to ensure that the whole of the skin becomes crisp. Many people like to prick the skin during cooking so that the fat escapes and can be poured away; this takes some of the richness from the meat.

Goose

Geese very quickly run to fat and become tough. It is therefore very important when choosing one for the table to pick a young bird. This should still have a little down on its legs, and the legs should be soft and pliable.

The liver of the goose is of course much prized as the chief ingredient in pâté de foie gras. Although true foie gras is obtained only from force-fed geese an ordinary goose liver will still make good pâté.

A goose is cooked in much the same way as duck and is usually stuffed with a savory stuffing of sage and onion, to counteract the richness of the flesh.

The size of a goose depends on the breed; 6–10 lb is usual, but the larger breeds may reach up to 20–24 lb after fattening.

Game

The term game covers all wild birds and animals hunted and killed for food. Here most game is protected from hunters by law during the breeding season and when the animals are young and very small; the exceptions to this are rabbit, hare and pigeon on which there is no restriction. Also sold with game, and cooked in similar ways, are the rabbits bred for the table and squabs, which are specially reared pigeons. Many birds eaten as game in other parts of the world are completely protected here.

Game falls into three groups. First are the small birds; these are not drawn before eating, but roasted or broiled, entrails and all, when very fresh – 'when the gun is smoking' is the traditional expression. Since they are only generally obtainable frozen or canned, this rule no longer carries any practical meaning.

The larger birds are perhaps the most important group of game, providing the most highly prized meats. This group includes many varieties of wild duck, pheasant, partridge and pigeon or squab. These are hung for several days to make the meat more tender and digestible. The joy of these birds, by contrast with poultry, is the variation in flavor which is produced by the food the bird has habitually eaten. For instance, a wild duck may be a sea bird and taste noticeably fishy, or it may be a fresh water bird and have taken amongst its food considerable amounts of plant and insect life. Although these are termed 'large' birds, they are not large by comparison with poultry.

The largest will usually serve only 4 people.

The last group of game consists of animals: hare, rabbit and deer (known in culinary terms as venison). Neither hare nor rabbit are protected. These meats have to be well hung to render them tender and tasty, and venison in particular is usually marinated as well before cooking.

Game seasons

The actual dates of the close seasons (when hunting is prohibited) are changed from time to time, to take into account changes in the habits of the animals and birds, how prolifically they are breeding and climatic trends.

Game sold at any other time of the year is invariably frozen. Wild rabbits are at their best in the winter, hare from late summer to spring.

Pheasant

Only the young birds are good for eating, and the huntsman detects the age of the bird by the shape of its wing tip – in young birds this is short and rounded and in older birds it becomes gradually more pointed and elongated. The hen is generally better than the cock, more tender and fatter.

Pheasant is hung by the neck undrawn and unplucked for anything from 3–10 days, depending on the weather and the condition of the bird after shooting and transportation. If the bird was carelessly shot, receiving a number of wounds, or if it was bruised at all in transportation, it should not be hung as long as one in perfect condition. If the bird is plucked and drawn before hanging, the flavor is nothing like as good.

A pheasant will serve 4 people.

Partridge

Young birds are best for roasting, and this means birds in their first year. These are again distinguished by their wings, the first flight feathers being pointed instead of rounded as in the older birds. Partridges of 1–2 years old are still good to eat but should be braised or casseroled rather than roasted as they will not be so tender.

Partridges can be hung as for pheasants, though the usual time is only 3–6 days.

A partridge is a small bird, serving only 1–2 people.

Wild duck

There are innumerable varieties of wild duck, from the large mallard which serves 4–5 people, to the tiny teal which will just about serve 1 person. Widgeon is generally one of the most popular. It tends to keep away from the sea, preferring to feed on short, sweet grass, which gives it a more delicate flavor than many ducks.

Squab

A young pigeon or squab has very delicate flesh that is excellent roasted. An older one will make a good casserole or tasty pie. Unlike other game birds, pigeons are plucked before hanging. When they are drawn, the liver is left inside to give added flavor to the meat.

Hare and rabbit

Hare and rabbit are hung by the feet and drawn after hanging. The blood of the hare is collected for thickening the sauce with which it is served. When young, either of these animals may be roasted, but they are more commonly casseroled or 'jugged' as the flesh may be rather dry.

Meat, Poultry and Game Recipes

Beef

Steak Tartare

Ingredients: *1¼ lb raw fillet steak or rump, minced · salt · freshly ground pepper · parsley · 4 egg yolks · 4 tablespoons chopped onion · 4 tablespoons capers · 4 teaspoons mustard · oil · lemon · Worcestershire*

Divide the raw beef into 4 portions (step 1), season with salt and pepper to taste. Chop the parsley (step 2) and sprinkle it over the meat. Make a hollow in each meat portion, and put 1 raw egg yolk in each (step 3). Arrange on the edge of each plate 1 tablespoon chopped onion, 1 tablespoon capers and 1 teaspoon mustard. Serve oil, lemon and Worcestershire separately.

Hamburgers

Mix in a bowl 1¼ lb ground beef, 1 finely chopped onion, and salt and pepper to taste. Shape the mixture into a ball, and beat it repeatedly against the bottom of the bowl. Divide into 4, shape into patties, roll in flour and cook in a frying pan on high heat in 2 tablespoons butter or oil. Cook on both sides, lower the heat, and continue cooking more slowly until done according to taste. Serve the hamburgers, covered with fried onion rings and spread with tomato ketchup, in buns.

Hamburgers with Barbecue Sauce

Mix in a bowl 1 lb 2 oz ground beef, 4 tablespoons crushed cornflakes (optional), 2 tablespoons grated onion, and salt and pepper to taste. Work the mixture as above and divide into 4 patties. Brown on both sides in ¼ cup butter or oil, and remove them from the pan. Add to the cooking juices 1 onion and 1 celery stalk, both sliced, 1 green pepper, deseeded and cut into strips, 4 teaspoons mustard, ¼ cup stock and salt and pepper to taste. Cook for 10 minutes, then add the hamburgers and continue cooking on low heat for ½ hour. Serve with the reduced sauce.

Steak alla Pizzaiola

Ingredients: *4 tender beef steaks ·
¼ cup butter or 4 tablespoons oil · salt ·
pepper · 2 cloves of garlic, peeled ·
1¼ cups canned peeled tomatoes, roughly
chopped · 1 generous pinch oregano*

To garnish: *parsley*

Brown the steaks on both sides in the butter
or oil on high heat (step 1) and continue
cooking according to taste. Remove them,
place on a warm serving platter, and season
with salt and pepper to taste. Cook the cloves
of garlic in the juices remaining in the pan
until golden, remove them, add the tomatoes
(step 2), salt and pepper to taste, and oregano.
Continue cooking for 8–10 minutes, put the
steaks back into the pan (step 3), re-heat
quickly, and serve, coated with some of the
sauce, on the hot serving platter. Garnish with
parsley and serve with remaining sauce.

Steak à la Bismark

Brown on both sides, on high heat, 4 slices fillet steak (each about 6 oz) in $\frac{1}{4}$ cup butter or oil. Continue cooking according to taste. Season with salt and pepper to taste, arrange them on a hot serving platter, and keep warm. Place on each steak 1 egg, fried in $\frac{1}{4}$ cup butter. Add a few spoonfuls stock to the cooking juices of the meat, mix well, boil rapidly for a few seconds, then pour over the steaks. Serve immediately.

Steak Chasseur

Brown 4 tender steaks on both sides in $\frac{1}{4}$ cup butter or oil on high heat, and continue cooking according to taste. Remove the steaks and put them on a warm platter. In the cooking juices remaining in the pan, cook 1 slice onion, chopped, and 1 cup mushrooms, cleaned, trimmed and sliced, until golden. Stir in 1 glass dry white wine, $\frac{1}{4}$ cup stock and 1 tablespoon tomato paste. Continue cooking on low heat for 10—15 minutes, then return steaks to the pan to reheat, and add chopped parsley.

Steak Lyonnaise

In 1 tablespoon butter cook until transparent, but not browned, 2 large onions very thinly sliced. Remove and reserve. Brown 4 steaks (4—6 oz each) on both sides in 2 tablespoons butter or oil on high heat. Continue cooking according to taste. Season with salt and pepper to taste halfway through the cooking. Remove the steaks from the pan and place on a warm serving platter. Add $\frac{1}{2}$ glass dry white wine to the cooking juices, boil for 2 minutes, add the onions, and, as soon as they are hot, pour over the steaks.

Tournedos Renata

Ingredients: *4 slices fillet of beef, 1¼ inches thick · 1 cup butter · 2 lb mushrooms · 1 clove of garlic, peeled · salt · pepper · 1 small glass brandy · 1 cup light cream · thyme · marjoram · 4 slices lemon · 1 tablespoon chopped parsley*

Cut out 4 pats of butter — ¼ inch thick — with a small round cutter (step 1), and keep them in the freezer or ice box. Trim the stems of the mushrooms, wash and dry, and slice them. Brown the garlic in the butter then remove it, add the mushrooms and sauté them quickly. Add salt and pepper to taste, pour in the brandy, and flame it. Add half the cream, cover, lower the heat and cook slowly for about ½ hour. In the last few minutes add the rest of the cream, and prepare the tournedos. In a separate pan, cook them quickly in 2 tablespoons browned butter, adding pepper, thyme, marjoram and salt to taste. Put the mushrooms in a warm oval serving platter, arrange the tournedos in the center (step 2), and place over each 1 lemon slice and 1 pat of butter sprinkled with chopped parsley (step 3). Serve immediately.

Tournedos Rossini

Brown in 1 tablespoon butter 1 carrot and 1 small onion, both roughly chopped. Mix in 1 teaspoon flour, add ½ cup stock, ½ glass dry white wine, 1 bouquet garni made of parsley, thyme and bay leaf, and salt and pepper to taste. Cook very slowly for 25 minutes, then strain through a sieve. Fry 4 large bread croûtons in 2 tablespoons butter and keep warm on a serving platter. Cook in 2 tablespoons browned butter, on high heat, 4 tournedos for 2–3 minutes on each side. Season with salt and pepper to taste. Arrange them on the croûtons, and place on each 1 slice liver pâté and 1 slice truffle. (Where truffles are not easy to obtain, a flat mushroom may be substituted.) Dissolve the cooking juices in the pan with 1 small glass Madeira, and mix with the sauce. Pour some of the sauce over the tournedos, and serve immediately with the rest of the sauce separately.

Broiled Piquant Steak

Mix in a bowl 6 oz Gorgonzola or Roquefort cheese together with 3–4 tablespoons oil, 1 mashed clove of garlic and 1 tablespoon brandy or whisky. Broil over charcoal, or under the broiler 2 ribs of beef, each 1¼–1½ lb. Spread the cheese mixture over them and serve when cheese melts.

Steak with Mustard Sauce

Brush with oil 4 ribs of beef or veal slices, and cook on a hot grill, over a dripping pan, or in an iron skillet. When they are cooked to taste, remove them and keep them warm. If the cooking has been done on a grill gather the cooking juices, discarding excess fat, and put them in a pan. Add 1 tablespoon strong mustard, ½ glass dry white wine, let it reduce on high heat, then add 1 cup light cream, lowering the heat until sauce has thickened. Do not let boil. Add 1 small glass brandy, and put back the meat to re-heat it. Serve on a warm platter together with the mustard sauce served separately.

Fondue Bourguignonne

Cut 1 lb fillet of beef into 1-inch cubes (step 1),
removing any fat and gristle. Put in a small
pan — the classic pans for this dish are usually
made of copper — a generous measure of oil,
1 pinch of thyme or 1 bay leaf (optional) and
bring slowly to a boil. Place the pan over a
portable burner in the center of the table so
that it continues to boil.

Each guest spears a cube of meat with a
long fork, dips it into the hot oil until cooked
to taste, transfers it to his own plate and dips
it into one of several sauces which accompany
the dish. The sauces (see the following sug-

gestions) should be prepared beforehand (steps
2 and 3).

Garlic Sauce
Crush in a mortar 1 head of garlic (about 1 oz).
Mix with 1 raw egg yolk and 1 pinch salt in a
bowl. Stirring constantly with a wooden
spoon, pour in gradually 1 cup oil and the
juice of 1 lemon, as for mayonnaise. If the
sauce is too thick, dilute with a few drops hot
water. If, on the contrary, the sauce does not
stiffen, or curdles, beat a fresh egg yolk in a
separate bowl and add the sauce to it gradually —
again as for mayonnaise (see p.98).

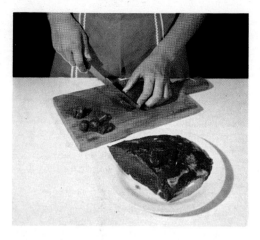

Andalusian Sauce

Roast 1 pepper in the oven or over a flame, peel and sauté it in a skillet in a little oil with a pinch of salt, let cool, deseed it, and cut into thin strips. In a bowl, mix the strips with 1 cup mayonnaise, diluted with $\frac{1}{4}$ cup homemade tomato sauce, sieved, reduced and cooled.

Caper Sauce

Mix into 1 cup mayonnaise a handful of capers, and some gherkins, finely chopped.

Rémoulade Sauce

In a bowl, mix 1 cup mayonnaise with 4 gherkins and 1 tablespoon capers, finely chopped, $\frac{1}{4}$ teaspoon anchovy paste or $\frac{1}{2}$ teaspoon mustard, 1 teaspoon chervil, 1 teaspoon chopped parsley, 1 teaspoon chopped shallot, and 1 pinch cayenne pepper. Add salt if necessary.

Mustard Sauce

In a bowl mix 6 tablespoons mayonnaise with 2 tablespoons French mustard, and 2 chopped scallions or 1 tablespoon chives.

Kishaili Sauce

In a bowl, mix $\frac{2}{3}$ cup fresh ricotta or cottage cheese with celery salt and pepper to taste, and enough oil and vinegar to obtain a smooth paste. Add 1 bunch radishes, washed, trimmed and sliced thinly, and let stand 48 hours.

Aurore Sauce

In a bowl mix 1 cup mayonnaise with 1 teaspoon paprika, 2 tablespoons tomato ketchup, 1 tablespoon ground pine nuts, 1 tablespoon capers chopped with 1 slice onion and some parsley, 1 tablespoon brandy, and salt.

329

Fillet of Beef Stuffed with Mushrooms

Ingredients: *1 whole piece of fillet of beef, preferably the middle part (about 2 lb)* · *1 cup dry white wine* · *½ cup butter or oil* · *1 small glass brandy* · *1 bay leaf* · *1 pinch thyme (optional)* · *salt* · *1 medium-sized onion, thinly sliced* · *10 oz fresh mushrooms, or 1½ tablespoons dried mushrooms, soaked in water, squeezed dry and sliced*

To garnish: *mushrooms* · *parsley*

Put the beef in a bowl, add the white wine, and leave to marinate overnight. Melt in a pan half the butter, add the brandy, bay leaf, thyme, and salt to taste. Add the onion and cook slowly until golden. Add the mushrooms and continue cooking. Meanwhile, drain the beef, reserving the marinade, and make an incision along the narrow side with a sharp knife (step 1). Stuff with the mushrooms (step 2), seal the two ends with 2 pieces of

meat from the inside of the fillet, and tie the meat with string to keep the stuffing inside (step 3). Brown the fillet on all sides over high heat in the remaining butter or oil, baste it with some wine from the marinade, cover the pan, lower the heat, and continue cooking for about 40 minutes — or less, according to taste. Alternatively the fillet may be cooked in the oven. Baste with the cooking juices from time to time. Serve the steak sliced, with the cooking juices, and garnish with whole mushrooms sautéed in butter, and parsley.

Fillet of Beef with Olives

Put one 2-lb piece of fillet of beef in a baking pan with $\frac{1}{4}$ cup butter or oil. Place in a moderate oven (350°F), and cook for 25–30 minutes, basting occasionally with dry white wine and stock. Brown in a separate pan $\frac{1}{4}$ cup butter mixed with 2 tablespoons flour, add the cooking juices of the meat, and continue cooking for 8–10 minutes, adding more wine and stock if necessary, until the sauce is smooth and creamy. Add about 1 cup pitted green olives, pepper, a little salt, and, when the mixture is hot, some chopped parsley. When the fillet is cooked, slice it and arrange on a warm serving platter with the sauce.

Fillet of Beef with Parsley

Mix a few tablespoons olive oil with chopped parsley and freshly ground pepper. Put into the mixture 1 whole piece of fillet of beef ($1\frac{1}{2}$–2 lb) and let stand for 24 hours, turning occasionally. Then put everything in a flame-proof casserole, and cook on high heat for 20–25 minutes, or more according to taste. Halfway through the cooking time season with salt and pepper to taste, and add more chopped parsley. Add a few spoonfuls stock if the meat becomes too dry.

Slice the meat and serve immediately on a warm serving platter, covered with the cooking juices.

331

Roast Beef

Ingredients: *2 lb roast of beef (sirloin, rump, fillet or rib)* · *¼ cup melted butter* ·
1 carrot and 1 onion, peeled and cut in quarters ·
salt · *pepper*

To garnish: *tiny whole potatoes, boiled*

Tie the meat with string (step 1), brush it with half the butter (step 2) and place on a rack in a roasting pan with the carrot and onion. Put it in a very hot oven (450°F) and cook for 25–30 minutes, turning it and basting occasionally with the remaining butter (step 3). (Do not puncture the meat during cooking; use 2 spoons to turn it over.) Sprinkle it with salt and pepper halfway through the cooking. To check whether the meat is done, prick it with a fork: a drop of pink juice should escape. When cooked, remove beef from the pan, untie, and let stand. Pour off excess fat from the pan, discard carrot and onion, then add a few tablespoons stock to the pan to detach the glazed cooking juices, and bring to a boil. Slice the beef, arrange on a warm serving platter, and pour the gravy over, or, if preferred, serve it separately in a sauce boat. Garnish the platter with tiny whole boiled potatoes if liked.

Roast beef can also be cooked in a pan on top of the stove: tie the meat with a sprig of rosemary, and put it in the pan with 3–4 tablespoons oil. Brown on high heat on all sides, cover the pan, lower the heat, and continue cooking slowly for 15–20 minutes, sprinkling the meat with salt and pepper halfway through the cooking. When cooked, remove the meat, let stand, then slice it, and serve as above.

Roast Beef in Salt

Put at the bottom of a high and narrow pan 2 lb rock salt. Place in the center a 2-lb roast of beef and put another 4 lb rock salt around and over the meat, covering it completely. Cover the pan and put in a hot oven (375–400°F) for about ¾ hour. Overturn the pan on a sheet of thick paper and crack the salt crust with a hammer. Remove all the salt from the meat with a brush, and serve the meat hot or cold. The salt can be used again. Serves 6–8.

Roast Beef Croquettes

Chop 1 lb rare roast beef and 7 oz Italian prosciutto. Mix with chopped parsley and salt and pepper to taste. Form croquettes with the mixture, roll them in flour, brown them on all sides over high heat and cook them for a few minutes in $1\frac{1}{2}$ tablespoons butter or margarine.

Leftover Beef Stew

Fry 2 large onions, sliced, in drippings until golden. Add $\frac{3}{4}$ lb carrots, sliced, and 2 cups chopped roast beef. Fry for 5 minutes, then add 1 cup beef stock, 1 tablespoon vinegar and seasoning. Cover and simmer for 20 minutes.

Beef Braised in Wine

Ingredients: *1 rump roast (2 lb)* · *4 oz salt pork* · *¼ cup butter* · *1 slice onion* · *flour* · *salt*

For the marinade: *1 pint Barolo or other Burgundy-type wine* · *1 stalk celery* · *1 medium sized onion and 1 carrot, both sliced* · *1 clove of garlic, peeled and crushed* · *rosemary* · *1 bay leaf* · *3 peppercorns*

To garnish: *tiny whole potatoes, boiled* · *butter* · *parsley*

Lard the beef with half the salt pork (step 1), tie it with string, pour the prepared marinade over (step 2) and leave overnight. Chop the remaining salt pork, brown it in butter together with the onion. Drain the meat (reserving the marinade), dry it, roll in flour, add to the pan and brown on all sides over high heat (step 3). Add the reserved marinade, salt, cover, lower the heat and cook very slowly for about 3 hours. When cooked, remove the meat from the pan and let stand. Strain the sauce, boiling to reduce if too thin. Slice the meat and arrange on a warm serving platter with some of the sauce poured over. Serve the remaining sauce separately, and garnish the platter with tiny whole potatoes, tossed in butter and sprinkled with parsley.

Braised Beef

Lard a 2-lb rump roast with strips of salt pork, chopped garlic (optional), and chopped parsley mixed with pepper and mixed herbs. Tie the meat with string, brown it on all sides over high heat in 1 tablespoon butter and 2 tablespoons oil. Sprinkle with salt and pepper. Add chopped celery, carrot and onion, 1 bouquet garni made of parsley, thyme and 1 bay leaf, and 1 small onion stuck with 1 clove. Pour in 1 cup good red wine, and 2 tablespoons brandy (optional). Cover the pan with wax paper or aluminum foil, lower heat, and cook very slowly for about 3 hours (or $1\frac{1}{4}$ hours in a pressure cooker), turning the meat over with 2 spoons occasionally. After 2 hours, strain the cooking juices, put them back into the pan, and thicken them with a little beurre manié (equal parts of butter and flour, blended together). When the cooking is done, remove the meat from the sauce and let stand 5–10 minutes, slice, and arrange on a warm serving platter with the sauce poured over it. Serves 6.

Beef with Oranges

Score the fat on a 2-lb roast of rolled sirloin tip or rib, then rub all over with salt, pepper and dried thyme. Heat oil in a roasting pan and brown the beef on all sides. Add the juice of 2 oranges. Roast in a hot oven (425°F) for 50–55 minutes, basting occasionally. Place the beef on a platter and surround with orange slices. Leave to rest for 10 minutes.

Meanwhile, pour the cooking liquid into a saucepan and add $\frac{3}{4}$ cup hot beef stock. Simmer for a few minutes. Dissolve 2 tablespoons cornstarch in a little water and add to the pan. Cook, stirring, until thickened. Stir in $\frac{1}{2}$ cup light cream, the grated rind of 1 orange and seasoning.

Flame the beef with 1 tablespoon each Grand Marnier and brandy, and serve with the sauce.

Grandmother's Meat Loaf

Ingredients: *1½ lb top rump of beef · 1 thick slice mortadella (6 oz) · ¾ lb frozen chopped spinach, thawed according to package instructions (or fresh spinach, cooked and worked through a sieve) · 4 tablespoons butter or oil · 1 cup ricotta or cottage cheese · 1 egg yolk · 2 tablespoons grated Parmesan cheese · salt · pepper · nutmeg · 1 small glass Marsala or ½ glass dry white wine · stock*

To garnish: *carrots*

Dry the spinach over moderate heat with 1 tablespoon butter. When it has cooled, add the ricotta or cottage cheese, the egg yolk, Parmesan cheese, and salt, pepper and nutmeg to taste (step 1). Pound the meat well, put the mortadella slice on top, cover with the spinach mixture (step 2), roll up, and sew it (step 3). Brown the loaf on all sides over high heat in ¼ cup butter or oil, add the Marsala or wine and let it reduce. Sprinkle the meat with salt, and add ¼ cup stock. Cover, lower the heat and cook slowly for about 2 hours, adding more stock if the meat becomes dry. Remove the loaf from the pan, let stand for

5–10 minutes, then slice, and arrange on a warm serving platter with the reduced cooking juices. Garnish with diced carrots. This dish is also very good when served cold – perhaps with aspic.

Meat Loaf with Frittata

Pound 1½ lb top rump of beef in the slice. Prepare a frittata (a flat, Italian-style omelet) in the following way: beat 2 eggs with 1 tablespoon chopped parsley, 2 tablespoons grated Parmesan cheese, 2 tablespoons milk, and salt and pepper to taste, and cook the mixture on both sides in 1½ tablespoons butter or margarine, then let it cool. Place on the beef 1 or 2 slices cooked ham (each ¼ inch thick), the frittata, and a few slices Emmenthal cheese. Roll up the meat, tie with string, and brown on all sides over high heat in ¼ cup butter. Add 1 small glass brandy or grappa, and flame it, or add ½ glass dry white wine and allow to reduce. Season with salt and pepper to taste, add ¼ cup stock, cover, lower the heat and cook slowly for about 2 hours, adding more stock if the meat becomes dry. Remove the loaf from the pan, let stand for 5–10 minutes, then slice it and arrange on a warm serving platter with the reduced cooking juices. Veal may equally well be used for this recipe as beef.

Bobotie

Soak 1 cup soft bread crumbs in 5 tablespoons milk. Melt ¼ cup butter in a frying pan and fry 3 onions, peeled and finely chopped, until transparent. Stir in 2 teaspoons curry powder and 12 split almonds and fry for 1 minute. Add 3 tablespoons lemon juice, 2 teaspoons sugar, ⅓ cup chopped dried apricots, ⅓ cup raisins and salt to taste and cook for 3 minutes.

Meanwhile, squeeze the bread crumbs dry and mix with 2 lb ground beef. Add the fried mixture and combine well. Bind with 1 egg. Press into a greased baking dish and press 2 bay leaves into the top. Beat 1 egg with 5 tablespoons milk and pour over the meat mixture. Bake in a moderately hot oven (375°F) for 45 minutes. Serve hot.

Ground Meat Loaf

Ingredients: *1¼ lb ground beef ·
4 oz mortadella · 2 eggs · 1 handful white
bread, soaked in milk and squeezed dry ·
¼ lb boiled potatoes (optional) ·
2 tablespoons grated Parmesan cheese ·
parsley · salt · pepper · nutmeg · flour ·
4 tablespoons butter or margarine ·
2 tablespoons Marsala or dry white wine ·
¼ cup hot stock · 3 hard-boiled eggs, shelled ·
3 carrots, blanched*

To garnish: *petits pois*

Mix in a bowl the ground beef, chopped
mortadella, eggs, bread, and the potatoes (if
using) worked through a sieve, Parmesan
cheese, chopped parsley, and salt, pepper and
nutmeg to taste (step 1). Make a ball of the

mixture and pound it repeatedly against the
bottom of the bowl. Flatten the mixture on a
board, place the hard-boiled eggs and carrots
in the center (step 2), and roll up, shaping it
into a loaf. Roll it in flour (step 3), and brown
on all sides on high heat in butter or margarine.
Season with salt, sprinkle with Marsala or
wine and when it has reduced, add the hot
stock. Cover, lower the heat, and cook slowly
for about 1 hour, adding more stock if the loaf
becomes dry. Remove the loaf from the pan, let
stand for 5–10 minutes, then slice it and
arrange on a warm serving platter with some
of the reduced cooking juices. Garnish with
petits pois and serve cooking juices separately.

Meat Loaf Clementina

Mix in a bowl 1¼ lb ground beef, ¼ cup chopped mortadella, ¼ cup grated Parmesan cheese, 1 egg, and salt, pepper and nutmeg to taste. Shape the mixture into a ball, and beat it repeatedly against the bottom of the bowl, then spread it about ½ inch thick on a piece of cloth. Put over the meat one ½-inch thick slice cooked ham, cut into strips, and 2 hard-boiled eggs. Roll the meat, wrap it in the cloth and tie at both ends. Boil in a generous amount salted water for about 2 hours, topping up with more hot water as it evaporates. Prepare a sauce in the following way: cook in a few spoonfuls hot oil in a pan ¼ cup mashed anchovy fillets until well blended, without allowing them to brown. Add 1 tablespoon chopped capers and some chopped parsley, and continue cooking slowly for a few minutes. Remove the sauce from heat and add the juice of 1 lemon. Remove the loaf from the pan, let stand for 5–10 minutes, then slice it and arrange on a warm serving platter, with the sauce poured over. Serve with mashed potato or green vegetables.

Beef and Horseradish Loaf

Mix 2 cups soft bread crumbs with ¾ cup boiling beef stock. Add 1 lb ground beef, 1 large onion, peeled and finely chopped, 1 tablespoon grated horseradish, 3 eggs, 2 tablespoons sweet sherry and seasoning. Mix well, then press into a greased baking dish. Bake in a moderate oven (350°F) for 45 minutes. Serve hot.

Veal

Rolled Veal with Frankfurters

Ingredients: *1½ lb veal in the slice ·
4 frankfurters · ¼ cup butter or oil ·
½ glass dry white wine · salt · ½ cup hot stock*

Pound the meat slice (step 1), place the frankfurters over it lengthwise (step 2), roll and tie
it with string (step 3). Brown on all sides over
high heat in the butter or oil, add the white
wine, and, when the wine has reduced,
sprinkle the meat with salt, add the hot stock,
cover, lower the heat, and cook slowly for 1½
hours. If there is too much juice, reduce it on
high heat during the last minutes of cooking.
Remove the roll from the pan and let stand
5–10 minutes. Slice it, arrange on a warm
serving platter and pour the cooking juices
over. The dish can also be served cold, in aspic,
if desired. Beef can be used instead of veal.

Veal Loaf Cesira

Chop ½ lb veal, mix it with 1 egg, 2 tablespoons
grated Parmesan cheese, and salt and grated
nutmeg to taste. Quarter 2 hard-boiled eggs
and cut 3 oz cooked ham and 3 oz mortadella
into strips. Pound 1½ lb veal in the slice,
spread over it a layer of the chopped meat
mixture, then a layer of hard-boiled eggs, ham
and mortadella strips, and continue until all
the ingredients have been used. Roll the meat,
tie with string, and brown on all sides over
high heat in ¼ cup butter. Cover, lower the
heat and cook for 1½ hours, adding stock
occasionally. When cooked, lift out the loaf,
add to the pan 2 tablespoons beurre manié
(1 tablespoon butter blended with 1 tablespoon
flour), the juice of 1 lemon and more stock if
necessary. Cook for a few minutes, then return
loaf to the pan and reheat. Transfer to a warm
serving platter, slice, and serve with the juices
poured over. Serves 4–6.

341

Stuffed Breast of Veal Home Style

Ingredients: *2 lb breast of veal, boned ·
1 celery stalk · 1 onion, peeled and quartered ·
1 carrot, peeled and quartered · ½ bay leaf ·
salt*

For the stuffing: *1 slice onion · ¼ cup butter ·
4 oz lean veal · 4 oz veal brains ·
4 oz sweetbreads · 1¾ oz marrow, scalded,
skinned and cut into pieces · 1 small carrot,
sliced · ¾ cup shelled green peas or canned peas ·
3 tablespoons grated Parmesan cheese ·
1 pinch marjoram (with a little garlic if
desired) · 1 tablespoon pistachio nuts · salt ·
pepper · grated nutmeg · 6 eggs*

To garnish: *lettuce · tomatoes*

Have the butcher make a pocket in the breast
of veal. Prepare the stuffing: sauté the onion
in the butter (it can then be removed, according to taste), the veal, cut into thin slices, the
brains, the sweetbreads, chopped, and the
marrow. Add the carrot and cook slowly for
20–30 minutes. Add ⅓ of the green peas,
cooked in boiling salted water, and divide the
mixture into 2 parts. Work 1 part through a
sieve, and chop the other part. Put both in a
bowl, add the remaining green peas (step 1),
the Parmesan cheese, marjoram, the pistachio
nuts, scalded and peeled, and salt, pepper and
nutmeg to taste. Beat the eggs, blend them
into the mixture, and pour it – it will be fairly
liquid – into the pocket cut in the breast of

veal (step 2), taking care that it does not fill more than $\frac{2}{3}$ of it. Sew it up with string (step 3) and wrap it in a wet piece of cloth. Tie well. Put in a pan, cover with cold water, add the celery, onion, carrot, bay leaf, and salt to taste, and bring slowly to a boil, pricking it occasionally with a trussing needle so that it does not burst as it swells. Continue cooking for about 2 hours, remove it from the stock, and put it on a plate with a weighted plate on top of it. Serve sliced, hot or cold, garnished with lettuce leaves and tomato slices. Serves 8. Any leftovers can be rolled in beaten egg and breadcrumbs, sautéed in butter and served with lemon quarters. Or they may be rolled in beaten egg and breadcrumbs, heated for a few minutes and served with green peas and homemade tomato sauce.

Roast Veal with Prunes

Pit $\frac{1}{2}$ lb plump prunes and soak in 5 tablespoons brandy overnight.

Melt 2 tablespoons butter in a flameproof casserole, add $\frac{1}{2}$ lb Canadian bacon slices, halved, and fry until golden brown. Remove the bacon and reserve. Coat a $2\frac{1}{2}$-lb rolled boned leg of veal with seasoned flour, then add to the casserole and brown on all sides. Add $\frac{3}{4}$ cup light stock and bring to a boil. Cover tightly and cook in a hot oven (400°F) for 1 hour.

Drain the prunes, reserving the brandy. Warm the brandy, pour over the veal and set alight. When the flames have died down, add the prunes and bacon to the casserole. Cover and cook in the oven for a further 30–40 minutes. Serve hot.

Roast Veal Sirloin

Ingredients: *2 lb veal sirloin ·
2 oz diced salt pork · chopped rosemary mixed
with salt and pepper · 1 tablespoon oil ·
¼ cup butter or margarine · salt · pepper ·
dry white wine (optional)*

To garnish: *green beans, sliced*

Make lengthwise incisions in the meat (step 1),
roll the salt pork in the rosemary mixture
(step 2), and insert in the meat (step 3). Tie
the meat with string, brush it with the oil, and
place it on a rack in a roasting pan, with the
butter or margarine, in small pieces. Put the
pan into a moderate oven (350°F) and roast
the meat for 1½–1¾ hours. When the meat is
brown, sprinkle with salt and pepper, and
dry white wine according to taste. Turn it
over occasionally during the cooking, basting
it with its own juices. When the meat is
cooked, remove from pan, let stand for 5–10
minutes, then slice it and arrange on a warm
serving platter.

344

Roast Veal in Piquant Sauce

Lard 2 lb veal sirloin with 2 cloves of garlic, peeled and sliced, and 4 anchovy fillets, desalted. (Shoulder of veal, boned, rolled and tied, may also be used for this recipe.) Put the meat in a bowl with 1 cup dry white wine and let stand for 24 hours, turning it over occasionally. Drain the meat, reserving the wine, brush with oil, place it on a rack in a roasting pan, and cook it for 1½ hours in a moderate oven (350°F). Baste frequently with the reserved wine. When the cooking is done, remove the meat, cover, and keep warm. Add to the pan 1 tablespoon flour mixed with a little cold water, stir with a wooden spoon to incorporate all the cooking juices, and continue cooking for a few minutes. Add ½ cup light cream, 1 tablespoon washed and dried capers (whole if small, chopped if large), and heat the cream without boiling. Slice the meat and arrange on a warm serving platter. Serve the sauce separately. Serves 4–6.

Veal Pot Roast with Kidneys

Have the butcher bone 2 lb shoulder of veal. Halve 1 veal kidney lengthwise, let it stand in water and lemon juice for 1 hour, drain, and remove the membrane and skin. Put the 2 kidney pieces inside the roast, in place of the bone. Tie the meat with string, brush with oil, and put in a pan with ¼ cup butter or margarine in small pieces, and a sprig of rosemary. Brown it on all sides over high heat, pour over 1 small glass of brandy, and flame it. Cover, lower the heat, and cook on moderate heat for about 2 hours, adding a little stock occasionally if the meat becomes dry. Sprinkle with salt and pepper halfway through the cooking. When the cooking is completed, remove the meat from the pan, let stand for 5–10 minutes, then slice it and arrange on a warm serving platter with the reduced cooking juices poured over.

Mexican Paupiettes

Ingredients: *1 ¼ lb veal cut into 8 small scallops · 3 oz pork loin · 3 oz prosciutto · ½ clove of garlic (optional) · ¼ cup white bread, soaked in milk and squeezed dry · 1 egg yolk · grated lemon peel · 1 ½ tablespoons grated Parmesan cheese · salt · pepper · grated nutmeg · sage leaves · 4 tablespoons butter or margarine · flour · stock*

To serve: *mashed potato*

Trim and pound the veal scallops (they should be about 3 by 5 inches). Mince until very fine the pork loin, the prosciutto, the garlic (if using), and the bread. Mix in the egg yolk, grated lemon peel, Parmesan cheese, and salt, pepper and nutmeg to taste. Blend the mixture thoroughly, then spread over the meat slices with a knife (step 1). Roll them up tightly, and stick them 2 by 2 on toothpicks, with 1 sage leaf between (step 2). Melt the butter or margarine in a pan, put in the paupiettes lightly coated with flour, and brown them on all sides over high heat. Add some stock (step 3), cover, lower the heat, and cook slowly for about ¾ hour, or until the paupiettes are cooked and the juice is reduced. Serve on a bed of mashed potato.

346

Italian Paupiettes

Trim 8 small veal scallops (about $1\frac{1}{4}$ lb), and pound well. Chop 4 oz lean prosciutto and mix it with 4 mashed and desalted anchovy fillets. Add 1 egg yolk, 3 tablespoons grated Parmesan cheese, and some grated white truffle (optional). Shape the mixture into 8 balls and put one in the center of each meat slice. Roll the slices, tie with string, and brown them on all sides over high heat in $\frac{1}{4}$ cup butter or margarine. Cover, lower the heat, and cook slowly for about 45 minutes. If you want to have a sauce add some stock during the cooking and let it reduce.

Florentine Paupiettes

Pound 8 small veal scallops (about $1\frac{1}{4}$ lb). Trim the edges and chop the trimmings together with 4 oz pork loin, a handful of spinach, celery, carrot and parsley. Cook the mixture in 2 tablespoons butter. Allow to cool, and mix with 1 egg, grated Parmesan cheese, and salt and grated nutmeg to taste. Spread the mixture over the meat slices, roll them, tie with string, and brown on all sides over high heat in $\frac{1}{4}$ cup butter or margarine with a little chopped onion. Sprinkle with salt, add 1 tablespoon tomato sauce diluted with a little water or stock, cover, lower the heat and cook slowly for about $\frac{3}{4}$ hour.

You could use beef instead of pork for the stuffing, in which case cook a little longer.

Poached Veal Puffs

Beat 3 cups hot mashed potato with 4 tablespoons flour, $\frac{1}{4}$ cup butter and 4 tablespoons grated Parmesan cheese. Season with salt and pepper. Cool, then chill until firm. Meanwhile, mix $1\frac{1}{2}$ cups ground cooked veal with 4 oz ($\frac{1}{2}$ cup) cream cheese, a few drops of hot pepper sauce and seasoning.

Divide the potato mixture into 12 portions. Shape into balls with floured hands. Make a hole in the center of each, fill with the veal mixture and seal again. Poach in boiling salted water for about 10 minutes. Drain and arrange in a serving dish. Pour over $\frac{3}{4}$ cup warmed light cream, sprinkle with paprika and serve immediately.

Veal Scallops with Ham

Ingredients: *4 veal scallops (about 1 lb)* ·
4 slices cooked ham · *4 slices Emmenthal*
cheese · *4 small canned artichokes* ·
¼ cup butter or margarine · *salt* ·
1 cup dry white wine · *1 cup hot stock*

To garnish: *artichoke hearts* · *peas* · *carrots*

Trim the veal slices, and pound well (step 1).
Cover ½ of each slice with 1 slice of ham and 1
of cheese (step 2), and 1 artichoke cut into
thin slices. Fold the meat and seal the three
open sides with toothpicks (step 3). Brown the
scallops on all sides over high heat in butter
or margarine. Sprinkle with salt. Add the
wine, let it reduce, then add the stock. Cover,
lower the heat, and cook slowly for 15–20
minutes. Serve garnished with artichoke
hearts and a macedoine of peas and carrots.

Veal Scallops with Frankfurter and Cheese Stuffing

Trim 8 small veal scallops and pound them.
Put on 4 of them ½ slice Emmenthal cheese,
½ frankfurter (sliced lengthwise) and 1 teaspoon mustard. Cover them with the remaining
scallops, and press the edges together to seal
them. Dip them in egg beaten with a little salt
and breadcrumbs. Let them stand for ½ hour,
then brown on all sides over high heat in 4
tablespoons butter or margarine. Cover, lower
the heat, and cook slowly until golden.

Veal Scallops with Prosciutto Stuffing

Trim 8 small scallops of veal (about 1 lb) and pound well. Put on each scallop 1 slice prosciutto and 1 sage leaf, sprinkle with lemon juice, season with salt and pepper, then fold it. Close with toothpicks. Cook until golden and cooked through on high heat in oil mixed with butter, or in a moderate oven, as above. Thin slices of fillet of beef can also be used for this recipe.

Cutlets with Cheese Stuffing

Make an incision along the side of 4 veal or pork cutlets, without cutting all the way through. Insert 1 slice Emmenthal cheese and 2 sage leaves. Press the edges of the incision together to seal. Brown the cutlets on both sides over high heat in 4 tablespoons butter or margarine with 2 sage leaves. Season with salt and pepper to taste, cover, lower the heat, and cook for 20–25 minutes.

Veal Cutlets in Ginger Sauce

Mix together 2 onions, peeled and chopped, 2 tablespoons oil, 2 tablespoons lemon juice, $\frac{1}{2}$ teaspoon dried thyme, 1 teaspoon ground ginger and seasoning in a bowl. Add 8 small veal cutlets (about 1 lb) and turn to coat them. Leave to marinate for 30 minutes.

Drain the veal, reserving the marinade, and pat dry. Coat the cutlets with flour. Heat 2 tablespoons butter with 2 tablespoons oil in a frying pan, add the cutlets and brown on both sides. Remove the veal from the pan as it is browned.

Strain the reserved marinade into the pan and add 1 cup light stock and 1 tablespoon tomato paste. Stir well. Add $\frac{1}{4}$ cup cooked tongue, $\frac{1}{4}$ cup cooked ham and $\frac{1}{4}$ cup button mushrooms, all cut into fine strips. Return the cutlets to the pan and cook gently for 10 minutes.

Saltimbocca
Roman Style

Ingredients: *8 small veal scallops (about 1¼ lb) · salt · pepper · 8 slices prosciutto (both the lean and the fat) · flour · ¼ cup butter or margarine · 8 sage leaves · dry white wine*

To garnish: tiny whole potatoes, boiled · butter · parsley

Trim the veal scallops, and pound, making them all roughly the same size. Season with salt and pepper (step 1), and put on each 1 sage leaf. Cover with 1 slice prosciutto (step 2) and fasten with a toothpick (step 3). Dip them lightly in flour. Melt half the butter or margarine in a pan, add the meat slices side by side, increase the heat, and brown on both sides. Continue cooking for a few minutes, until golden and cooked through. Put on a warm serving platter and remove the toothpicks. Add the wine to the cooking juices, and let it reduce on high heat, stirring with a wooden spoon, until it has almost evaporated. Add the remaining butter or margarine, and pour over the saltimbocca. Serve immediately, garnished with tiny whole potatoes tossed in butter and sprinkled with chopped parsley.

Veal Scallops in Piquant Sauce

Trim 8 small veal scallops (about 1¼ lb), pound, and dip in flour. Brown on all sides over high heat in 4 tablespoons butter or margarine. Sprinkle with salt and arrange the scallops on a warm serving platter. Prepare a sauce with 8 anchovy fillets, desalted and mashed with 1 tablespoon capers, chopped parsley, and a little oil and vinegar. Pour the sauce over the scallops.

Sautéed Veal Scallops

Trim 8 small veal scallops (about 1¼ lb) and pound well. Dip them in flour, and brown on all sides over high heat, in 4 tablespoons butter or margarine. Season with salt and pepper to taste, add ¼ cup stock, lower the heat and continue cooking for about 15 minutes. Arrange the meat on a serving platter and keep warm. Remove the pan from the heat, add 2 egg yolks and the juice of 1 lemon, stir well and pour over the meat.

351

Veal Scallops Viennese Style

Ingredients: *4 large veal scallops (about 1 lb) ·
salt · pepper · flour · 1 egg · breadcrumbs ·
4 tablespoons butter or margarine ·
4 lemon slices · 2 olives · 4 anchovy fillets ·
1 tablespoon capers*

To garnish: *hard-boiled eggs · parsley*

Trim the veal and pound well, season with salt
and pepper to taste, dip lightly in flour, then in
beaten egg (step 1), and in breadcrumbs,
pressing well to make them adhere. Brown the
scallops, a few minutes on each side, over
high heat, in butter or margarine (step 2).
Arrange them on a warm serving platter,
putting in the center of each 1 peeled lemon
slice, 1 anchovy fillet, desalted, rolled around
$\frac{1}{2}$ pitted olive, and a few capers (step 3).
Garnish the edges of the platter with hard-
boiled egg slices and sprigs of parsley and serve
immediately.

Veal Cutlets Bolognese Style

Trim the bone off 4 veal cutlets, pound them lightly, season with salt and pepper to taste, dip in flour, then in beaten egg, and finally in breadcrumbs, pressing well to make them adhere. Let them stand for $\frac{1}{2}$ hour, then brown on all sides over high heat in 4 tablespoons butter or margarine. Arrange them in a roasting pan, put on each 1 slice prosciutto, sprinkle with grated Parmesan cheese, dot with butter and put in a very hot oven (475°F) for 2 minutes. Transfer to a warm serving platter, add a few tablespoons of gravy from a roast, or meat extract diluted in hot water, to the cooking juices, and pour over the cutlets.

Cutlets Valdostana Style are also made in this way but fontina (or Gruyère) cheese slices are used instead of Parmesan cheese.

Veal Cutlets with Sweetbread Stuffing

To prepare the stuffing lightly sauté 4 oz sweetbreads and 4 oz veal in 2 tablespoons butter mixed with chopped parsley and onion. Chop these ingredients and mash them in a mortar (or work them through a sieve) with 1 handful white bread, soaked in stock and squeezed dry. Add 1–2 eggs, 2 tablespoons grated Parmesan cheese, salt and pepper to taste, and mix well. The proportions can be adjusted according to the size of the cutlets. Pound 4 veal cutlets (with bone), season with salt and pepper to taste, and spread the stuffing on both sides of each cutlet.

Dip in beaten egg and in breadcrumbs, and fry in hot oil, or, if preferred, in oil and butter until cooked through. Drain well and serve immediately, garnished with parsley and with lemon quarters.

353

Veal Pie with Marrow and Chicken Livers

Ingredients: *6 veal scallops (about 1¼ lb),
trimmed and well pounded · ¼ lb beef marrow ·
4 oz chicken livers · ½ glass brandy
¼ lb sliced cooked ham · 1 slice mortadella
(4 oz) · 2 egg yolks · ½ cup grated Parmesan
cheese · 1 cup light cream · salt · pepper ·
grated nutmeg · butter or margarine ·
4–6 slices prosciutto*

To garnish: *green peas*

Scald the marrow in boiling water for a few
minutes (step 1). Slice it, and slice the chicken
livers. Sauté both in 1 tablespoon butter for a
few minutes, add the brandy, flame it, remove
from the heat and let cool. Add the chopped
ham and mortadella, the egg yolks, Parmesan

cheese, enough cream to obtain a soft mixture,
and salt, pepper and nutmeg to taste. Grease
a 7 × 3-inch mold with butter or margarine,
and line it with prosciutto slices (step 2).
Put 2 veal scallops at the bottom of the mold,
spread ½ the stuffing over (step 3), repeat the
layers, finishing with a layer of meat (i.e.
3 layers of meat and 2 of stuffing). Put over
the whole the remaining slices of prosciutto.
Bake in a moderate oven (350°F) for about
1 hour. If, during the cooking, the prosciutto
becomes too dry, cover with aluminum foil.
Let the pie stand for 5 minutes before turning
out onto a warm serving platter. Strain the
cooking juices, reduce on high heat if necessary,
and serve separately. Garnish the dish with
buttered green peas. Serves 4–6.

Meat Pie Ligurian Style

Prepare a mushroom sauce as follows: soak 1 tablespoon dried mushrooms in lukewarm water, squeeze dry, chop roughly, and put in a pan with 1 clove of garlic, peeled, 1 glass oil, 1 tablespoon chopped capers, and chopped parsley to taste. Let the mixture simmer for a few minutes, then take from the heat, remove the garlic, and let cool. Using in all $1\frac{1}{2}$ lb sliced veal or beef, put a layer of meat (about $\frac{1}{2}$ lb) at the bottom of a high, narrow buttered pan. Cover with a layer of mushroom sauce, then a layer of thin slices of salt pork. Repeat the layers, ending with a layer of veal or beef. Put over it a weighted plate or cover. Cook slowly for about $1\frac{1}{4}$ hours.

Czech Veal with Caraway Seeds

Cut 2 lb boneless veal into 1-inch cubes. Heat 4 tablespoons oil in a flameproof casserole, add the veal cubes and brown on all sides. Mix together 1 tablespoon white wine or cider vinegar, 2 teaspoons paprika, $1\frac{1}{4}$ cups buttermilk and $\frac{1}{2}$ teaspoon salt and pour on the veal. Add 1 tablespoon lightly crushed caraway seeds. Cover and cook for 20 minutes.

Peel, core and thickly slice 1 large tart apple. Add to the casserole with 2 teaspoons sugar. Cook uncovered for 20 minutes.

Dissolve 1 tablespoon cornstarch in a little cold water and add to the casserole. Cook, stirring, until the liquid is thickened. Serve hot.

Veal and Sage Casserole

Cut $1\frac{1}{2}$ lb boned shoulder of veal into $1\frac{1}{2}$-inch cubes. Heat $\frac{1}{4}$ cup butter and 2 tablespoons oil in a flameproof casserole. Add the veal cubes and brown on all sides. Add 1 large onion, peeled and chopped, a crushed garlic clove, 2 sprigs of fresh sage and seasoning. Fry, stirring, for 3 minutes. Sieve an 8-oz can of tomatoes with its juice and add to the casserole with 2 cups light stock. Bring to a boil, then cover and simmer for 1 hour.

Peel and quarter $1\frac{1}{2}$ lb waxy potatoes. Add to the casserole and simmer for a further 20 minutes. Discard the sage and sprinkle with chopped fresh sage before serving.

355

Ossobuco

Ingredients: *four 2-inch thick slices (about 2 lb) of veal shank (ossobuco) · 4 tablespoons butter or margarine · flour · ½ glass dry white wine · 1 celery stalk, 1 small carrot, ½ onion, 2 desalted anchovy fillets, all chopped · salt · pepper · 1¼ cups canned peeled tomatoes, chopped · stock · garlic, parsley and the zest of ½ lemon, all chopped*

To serve: *mashed potato or risotto*

Melt the butter or margarine in a pan, and immediately put in the floured veal slices (step 1). Brown them on all sides over high heat, add the dry white wine and let it reduce. Add the chopped celery, carrot, onion and anchovy fillets, and salt and pepper to taste. Cook until golden and add the tomatoes (step 2). Cover, lower the heat, and cook slowly for about 1¼ hours, adding stock occasionally to obtain a fairly thick juice. A few minutes before completing the cooking, add the chopped garlic, parsley and lemon zest to taste (step 3). Transfer to a warm serving platter and serve with mashed potatoes, or with a risotto.

Ossobuco with Mushrooms

Roll 4 slices of veal shank (about 2 lb) in flour mixed with salt and pepper. Brown them on all sides over high heat in $\frac{1}{4}$ cup butter or margarine. Add $\frac{1}{2}$ glass dry white wine, let it reduce, then add chopped onion, carrot, garlic, parsley and grated lemon zest to taste, and 1 tablespoon dried mushrooms, soaked in lukewarm water and squeezed dry. Add 2 tablespoons tomato sauce and $\frac{1}{2}$ cup stock. Cover, lower the heat, and cook slowly for about 1 hour.

Ossobuco with Green Peas

Brown 4 floured slices of veal shank (about 2 lb) on all sides over high heat, in 4 tablespoons butter or margarine with 1 chopped onion. Sprinkle with salt. Add $\frac{1}{2}$ glass dry white wine, let it reduce, then add $\frac{3}{4}$ cup canned peeled tomatoes, chopped, or some tomato sauce, a few ladles stock, and $1\frac{1}{4}$ lb fresh or frozen peas. Cover, lower the heat, and cook slowly for about 1 hour. Halfway through the cooking, add $\frac{1}{2}$ cup hot water if the juice is too thick.

Sweet and Sour Veal

Cut 2 lb boneless veal into cubes. Place in a saucepan with 1 carrot, peeled and halved, 1 celery stick, chopped, 1 tablespoon chopped parsley, 2 bay leaves and seasoning. Just cover with water. Bring to a boil, then cover and simmer for $1\frac{1}{2}$ hours.

Drain the veal, reserving the cooking liquid. Strain the cooking liquid and set aside 2 cups for the sauce.

Melt $\frac{1}{4}$ cup butter in a clean saucepan. Stir in 2 tablespoons flour and cook for 1 minute, then gradually stir in the cooking liquid. Simmer, stirring, until thickened. Add 1 thin-skinned lemon, thinly sliced, $\frac{1}{3}$ cup raisins, 1 teaspoon sugar and 2 tablespoons dry white wine. Stir in the veal and simmer for 15 minutes, stirring occasionally.

357

Pork

Roast Pork

Ingredients: *2 lb pork loin, boned and rolled · 2 cloves of garlic · rosemary · 2–3 cloves · salt · freshly ground pepper · olive oil*

To garnish: *tiny whole potatoes*

Lard the meat with halved or quartered cloves of garlic (step 1), rosemary and cloves. Tie it with string, season with salt and pepper to taste (step 2), brush with oil, and put it into an oiled roasting pan. Place in a hot oven (400°F) and roast for at least $1\frac{1}{2}$ hours, or until the meat is cooked through and the juices are no longer pink, turning it over occasionally with 2 spoons and basting with the cooking juices. Untie it (step 3), let stand 5–10 minutes, and slice. Arrange the slices on a warm serving platter, garnished with tiny whole potatoes, boiled, tossed in butter and sprinkled with chopped parsley, and other vegetables according to taste. The dish is equally good when served cold. Serves 6.

Roast Pork with Orange Sauce

Tie 2 lb boned pork loin with string (see p.332). Season with salt and pepper to taste. Place in a buttered roasting pan with 1 slice onion and 1 celery stalk, cut into thin slices, 1 peeled orange in sections, 1 glass orange juice, and 1 tablespoon vinegar or 2 tablespoons dry white wine. Put the pan into a hot oven (400°F) and cook for at least $1\frac{1}{2}$ hours, until the meat is cooked through, turning it and basting occasionally with the cooking juices. Remove meat from the pan, let stand 5–10 minutes, then slice it and place on a warm serving platter. Serve cooking juices separately.

Pork Loin with Piquant Sauce

Roll in flour 1 piece pork loin (about 2 lb). Melt in a pan $2\frac{1}{2}$ tablespoons butter or margarine with chopped onion and capers to taste. Add the meat, brown on all sides over high heat, cover, lower the heat and cook very slowly for at least $1\frac{1}{2}$ hours, until the meat is cooked through, turning and adding stock occasionally. Add salt halfway through the cooking. When cooked, remove meat from the pan, let stand 5–10 minutes, then slice and arrange on a warm serving platter with the cooking juices and the juice of 1 lemon poured over. Sprinkle with capers. Serves 4–6.

Pork Baked with Cheese

Melt $\frac{1}{4}$ cup butter in a large flameproof casserole. Add a 3-lb boned and rolled pork top loin and brown on all sides. Add $\frac{1}{2}$ cup each carrots and onions, all peeled and chopped, and cook for 5 minutes. Add a bouquet garni and seasoning. Cover and cook very gently for $1\frac{1}{4}$–$1\frac{1}{2}$ hours, turning the pork occasionally.

Remove the pork and cool. Sieve the cooking liquid (discard the bouquet garni) into a saucepan.

Make deep cuts in the pork, not cutting all the way through, about $\frac{1}{4}$ inch apart. Place a slice of Cheddar or Swiss cheese in each cut. Season and put the pork in a baking dish. Bake in a hot oven (400°F) for 15 minutes. Meanwhile, add $\frac{1}{2}$ cup each dry white wine and water to the sieved cooking liquid and boil for 5 minutes. Serve this sauce with the pork.

Crown Roast of Pork

Ingredients: *One 9-rib piece of pork* (carré)

For the stuffing: *8 oz prosciutto or mortadella, chopped · 1 egg · 1 handful white bread, soaked in milk and squeezed dry · a few tablespoons Parmesan cheese · 1 tablespoon French mustard and 1 teaspoon Worcestershire (optional) · chopped parsley · salt · pepper · oil*

To garnish: *tomatoes*

Prepare the *carré* by stripping the meat from the upper part of the bones, and making incisions in the meat between the lower pieces of bone (step 1), or ask the butcher to prepare it. Remove a little meat from the inside and chop it. Shape the ribs into a crown and tie it with string (step 2). Prepare the stuffing in the following manner: mix the chopped pork with the prosciutto, egg, bread, Parmesan cheese, mustard, Worcestershire (if using), parsley, and salt and pepper to taste. Put the mixture, thoroughly blended, inside the crown, and place in an oiled roasting pan. Brush it with oil (step 3) and cap the bone ends with aluminum foil. Place in a hot oven (400°F) and cook for at least 1½ hours, until the meat is cooked through, basting occasionally with the cooking juices. The crown may be filled, if liked, with small potatoes, fried in butter. Garnish with paper frills and tomatoes. Serves 6.

Roast Pork with Prunes

Soak 12 prunes in cold water overnight. Drain. Take 1½ lb pork tenderloin – or any other boneless cut suitable for roasting – and make a deep incision lengthwise into it. Insert the pitted prunes with a wooden spoon handle. Brown the meat on all sides over high heat in 1 tablespoon butter or margarine, season with salt to taste, add ¼ cup stock, cover, lower the heat, and cook for about 1 hour, turning and basting occasionally with the cooking juices, adding more stock if the meat becomes too dry.

The cooking can also be done in the oven at 350°F. Halfway through the cooking add 4 apples, peeled and cored, with a pat of butter in the center.

Spare Ribs Stew

Ingredients: *1¼ lb spare ribs · 4 oz pork rind ·
1 pig's foot · 1 onion · 2 oz salt pork ·
1 tablespoon butter · 3 celery stalks ·
2–3 carrots · 3 tablespoons tomato sauce ·
salt · pepper · 3 or 4 lb cabbage ·
¾ lb sausages*

Scrape and scorch the rind and the pig's foot. Halve the foot lengthwise, and cook in boiling water for ½ hour, skimming most of the fat. Drain and cut into pieces. Chop the onion and salt pork, and brown in butter. Add the foot, rind, and spare ribs also cut into pieces (step 1). When browned, add the celery and carrots, roughly chopped (step 2), the tomato sauce diluted in a little hot water, and salt and pepper to taste. After a few minutes add enough water to cover. Cover the pan, and cook slowly for 2½–3 hours. Separate the cabbage leaves, wash, and put in a pan of boiling water. Drain after 10 minutes. Half an hour before the cooking is complete, add the cabbage (step 3), and the sausage cut into pieces. The cooking juices must be thoroughly reduced before the dish is served.

Sauerkraut with Frankfurters

Wash thoroughly 3 lb sauerkraut, drain and squeeze to remove all water. Put in a pan with plenty of water $\frac{1}{2}$ lb smoked bacon, $\frac{1}{2}$ calf's foot and 6 oz pork rind. Bring to a boil, then drain. Line the bottom of a pan with the pork rind, put in half the sauerkraut, the bacon, $\frac{1}{2}$ lb smoked pork shoulder, the calf's foot, 6 frankfurters, 1 garlic sausage, 1 carrot, 1 small onion stuck with 1 clove, 10 juniper berries, 1 bouquet garni, made of parsley, thyme and 1 bay leaf, salt, $2\frac{1}{2}$ tablespoons butter or margarine, and the remaining sauerkraut. Add 1 cup dry white wine, and enough water to cover. Seal the pan with a double sheet of wax paper or aluminum foil, and cook very slowly for about $2\frac{1}{2}$ hours. After $\frac{1}{2}$ hour remove the sausage and the frankfurters and keep on one side, and after $1\frac{1}{2}$ hours, remove the pork shoulder and the bacon. Add $\frac{3}{4}$ lb peeled potatoes, and continue cooking for $\frac{1}{2}$ hour. Put back everything to reheat for 10 minutes. By the end of the cooking, the liquid must be almost completely absorbed. The calf's foot is used only to give consistency to the stock and is not served with the sauerkraut, but it can be boned, cut into strips, and served separately, seasoned with oil, vinegar, and raw onion slices, if liked. Serves 4–6.

Frankfurter Kabobs

Cut 8 frankfurters into 3 pieces. Blanch 24 pearl onions in boiling water for 5 minutes, then drain and peel. Thread the onions and frankfurter pieces alternately onto greased skewers. Mix 6 tablespoons oil with $1\frac{1}{2}$ tablespoons coarse-grain mustard. Brush over the kabobs and cook under a hot broiler for about 10 minutes, turning occasionally and brushing with the mustard mixture.

Stuffed Pig's Foot with Lentils

Ingredients: *1 pig's foot (about 2 lb) ·
1 lb lentils · 2 oz salt pork · ¾ lb sausage meat ·
2 celery stalks · 1 carrot, peeled ·
2 onions, peeled · 1 tablespoon butter or
margarine · stock · tomato sauce (optional) ·
salt · pepper*

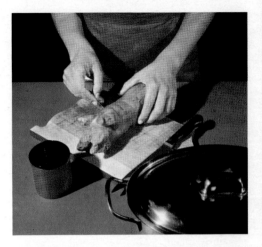

Soak the pig's foot and the lentils separately
in cold water for 24 hours. Remove the pig's
foot from the water (reserving the water),
prick with a trussing needle (step 1), or a
fork, and make small incisions near the nails
(step 2). Wrap it in a cloth (step 3), and tie
with string. Put it in a pan with the reserved
soaking water and bring to a boil. Lower the
heat and cook slowly for 3½ hours. Soak the
salt pork in cold water for 1 hour. Remove the
pig's foot from the heat and let it stand in the
cooking liquid for 30 minutes. Remove from
pan, bone carefully and stuff with the
sausage meat. Tie with string, return to pan
and cook until tender together with 1 celery
stalk, the carrot and 1 onion. Drain the
lentils. In the butter or margarine sauté the
salt pork and remaining onion and celery,
chopped together. Add the lentils with a little
stock and tomato sauce, if using. Cover and
cook slowly until all the liquid is absorbed.
Serve the stuffed pig's foot sliced with the
lentils and with cabbage.

Rolled Garlic Sausage

Pound thoroughly 1¼ lb beef or veal in the
slice. Cover it with a layer of spinach — fresh
or frozen — lightly sautéed in butter with a
little garlic. Place a skinned ¾-lb garlic sausage
in the center, roll the meat lengthwise and
tie it with string. Brown the meat on all sides
over high heat in 1½ tablespoons butter,
add ½ glass dry white wine, let it reduce,
season with salt to taste, and add ¼ cup stock.
Cover, lower the heat and cook for 2 hours,
adding more stock if the meat becomes dry.
Let the roll stand for 10 minutes, slice and
serve with the reduced cooking juices.

Sausage Hotpot

Sauté a little chopped onion in 1 tablespoon butter or margarine. Add 8 sausages (skinned or not, according to taste) and brown them. Add 2 tablespoons tomato paste diluted in a little hot water, or $\frac{3}{4}$ cup peeled tomatoes worked through a sieve and 1 bay leaf. Cover, and cook slowly for about $\frac{1}{2}$ hour. Serve with mashed potato or polenta.

Frankfurter Fritters

Make a batter from 1 cup flour, $1\frac{1}{2}$ teaspoons salt, 1 egg, 1 tablespoon oil and $\frac{3}{4}$ cup beer. Beat 2 egg whites until stiff and fold in. Cut 16 frankfurters in half, coat in seasoned flour and dip in the batter. Fry in hot oil until crisp and golden. Drain and serve immediately.

Lamb

Stuffed Shoulder of Lamb

Ingredients: *1 shoulder of lamb (about 2 lb) ·
4 oz salt pork (soaked in cold water for 1 hour
and drained), or prosciutto ·
a generous measure of fresh rosemary,
parsley and a few celery leaves ·
1 clove of garlic, peeled (optional) · salt ·
pepper · ¼ cup butter or margarine ·
½ glass dry white wine · stock*

To garnish: *macedoine of mixed vegetables*

Chop the salt pork or prosciutto together with
the rosemary, parsley, celery and garlic (if
using). Season with salt and pepper to taste.
Bone the shoulder of lamb (step 1), or ask
your butcher to do it for you. Pound it until as
flat as possible, and cover the inside with the
chopped mixture (step 2), roll it and tie with
string (step 3). Brown it on all sides over high
heat in the butter or margarine, and sprinkle
with salt. Add the white wine, let it reduce,
then add ¼ cup stock. Cover, lower the heat,
and cook for about 1½ hours until tender, adding more stock if the meat becomes dry.
Remove from the pan, let stand for 10 minutes, then remove string and slice the meat.
Arrange on a warm serving platter with the
cooking juices. Garnish with a macedoine of
mixed vegetables.

Carré d'Agneau

Have the butcher prepare a *carré* of lamb with
best end of neck cutlets, cutting through the
base of each cutlet without completely separating them. Brown over high heat in ¼ cup
butter or margarine on top of the stove, then
put it in a wide buttered ovenproof dish.
Season with salt and pepper to taste, and put
the *carré* in a hot oven (400°F). Cook for at
least 1 hour until the meat is tender, turning it
once. Prepare a mixture of parsley, mint and
garlic, chopped, breadcrumbs, and salt and
pepper to taste. Spread it over the fatty parts of
the lamb, pressing to make it adhere. Pour over
melted butter and gratiné.

Roast Lamb

Ingredients: *1 leg of lamb (about 3 lb) ·
¼ cup butter or margarine · garlic, rosemary
and parsley · a few tablespoons breadcrumbs ·
salt · pepper*

In an ovenproof casserole brown the leg of
lamb in ¾ of the butter or margarine on all
sides over high heat. Season with salt and
pepper to taste and add the remaining butter
or margarine. Put it in a hot oven (400°F) and
cook for about 1 hour 20 minutes or until
tender (step 1). Chop the garlic, rosemary and
parsley, and mix with the breadcrumbs (step
2). Spread the mixture over the meat (step 3),
and continue cooking for 5–10 minutes, in
the top of the oven, until a golden crust has
formed.

Braised Lamb

Cut into pieces 3 lb lamb meat (neck, shoulder
etc.). Roll the pieces in flour, and brown them
on all sides over high heat in ¼ cup butter or
margarine. Add ½ glass dry white wine, let it
reduce, then add 1 crushed clove of garlic,
1 large onion and 1 carrot cut into slices, 1
clove and 1 bouquet garni made of parsley,
thyme and 1 bay leaf. After 2 minutes add
2 tablespoons tomato paste diluted in 1 cup
water. Season with salt and pepper to taste,
cover, lower the heat and cook slowly for
about 1 hour or until the meat is tender.
Remove the bouquet garni and the garlic
before serving.

Lamb Paupiettes

Mince 1 lb boned lamb shoulder. Mix it with
1–2 handfuls white bread soaked in milk and
squeezed dry, 2–3 tablespoons grated Parmesan or Gruyère cheese, 1 egg, and salt and
pepper to taste. Blend well, shape into a ball
and beat repeatedly against the bottom of the
bowl. Make 4 flat paupiettes – or 8 smaller
ones – and roll them in flour. Brown them on
all sides over high heat in 1 tablespoon butter
or margarine and cook for about 30 minutes,
turning them once. Serve a tomato sauce
separately.

369

Variety Meats

Sweetbreads with Mushrooms

Ingredients: *1¼ lb veal sweetbreads ·
lemon juice or vinegar · pinch of salt · flour ·
1 lb fresh mushrooms · 2½ tablespoons butter ·
½ small glass brandy · ¼ cup stock · ¼ cup
heavy cream*

*To finish: 1 egg yolk · juice of ½ lemon ·
chopped parsley · whole button mushrooms
(optional)*

Soak the sweetbreads in cold salted water for
3 hours with a little lemon juice or vinegar.
Rinse them, put them in a pan, and cover with
cold water. Add salt and more lemon juice
or vinegar. Bring to a boil and cook for 5
minutes, skimming occasionally. Take out the
sweetbreads, drain, and rinse again in fresh
cold water. Remove the fat, skin and ducts,
and let the sweetbreads cool. Slice them
(step 1), roll lightly in flour, and brown them
on all sides over high heat in the butter. Add
the brandy and flame it. Add the mushrooms
cut into thin slices (step 2), and, after a
moment, add the stock. Lower the heat and

cook slowly for 25 minutes. Add the cream, let it thicken on very low heat, then turn off the heat. Add the egg yolk beaten with the lemon juice (step 3), and serve as soon as it has blended with the other ingredients. Sprinkle with chopped parsley, garnish with sprigs of parsley and serve with whole button mushrooms, if liked.

Paupiettes of Brains

Soak 1 lb calf's brains in cold salted water, with the juice of $\frac{1}{2}$ lemon for 2–3 hours. Drain. Cover the brains in stock or water, and simmer for 10–15 minutes until firm, then take them out, drain, and rinse under cold running water. Remove the skins. Dry the brains and let cool. Chop finely and mix with 2 beaten eggs, 2 tablespoons grated Parmesan cheese, and chopped parsley, salt, pepper and grated nutmeg to taste.

Brown the mixture, 1 spoonful at a time, on all sides in melted butter. Serve on a warm platter garnished with parsley sprigs and lemon quarters.

Beef Marrow Paupiettes

Soak 1 lb beef marrow in cold water for 1 hour, drain, and cook in boiling water for 10 minutes. Season with salt towards the end of the cooking. Drain, rinse under cold running water, remove the skins, dry and let cool. Sauté in butter and cut carefully into 3-inch pieces.

Place each piece on 1 slice ham with 2 white truffle slices, and roll the ham. Tie each paupiette with string. Dip in beaten egg and breadcrumbs, and brown them on all sides in golden butter.

Sweetbread Kabobs

Cut 1 lb prepared sweetbreads in half. Cut 4 thick bacon slices into 1-inch pieces. Thread the bacon and sweetbreads alternately onto greased skewers. Mix together 6 tablespoons oil, 1 tablespoon lemon juice and seasoning in a shallow dish. Add the kabobs and marinate for 1 hour, turning occasionally. Cook under a hot broiler, turning and brushing with the marinade frequently, for 15–20 minutes.

Stuffed Veal Heart

Ingredients: *1 veal heart (about 2 lb) ·*
¼ cup butter or margarine · 1 onion, sliced ·
10 oz carrots, sliced · 1 bouquet garni, made
of parsley, celery, sage and 1 bay leaf ·
½ glass dry white wine

For the stuffing: *4 oz pork loin, chopped,*
or sausage meat · ½ onion · 1 clove of garlic ·
parsley · 1 egg · 2 tablespoons grated
Parmesan cheese · salt · pepper

To prepare the stuffing: mix the chopped pork
loin or sausage meat with the ½ onion, garlic
and parsley, all chopped, the egg, the grated
Parmesan cheese, and salt and pepper to
taste (step 1). Trim the heart with scissors,
cutting the wall dividing the interior. Soak in
salted water for 1 hour, and dry. Put in the
prepared stuffing (step 2), and sew up the
opening with string (step 3). Brown in the
butter or margarine. Add the sliced onion and
carrot, bouquet garni, wine, and salt and
pepper to taste. Cover, and cook on moderate
heat for 1½ hours, or until tender. Serve the
sliced heart with the cooking juices.

Veal Kidneys Bolognese Style

Skin 4 veal kidneys, slice them lengthwise
and remove the core. Soak them for 1 hour
in water mixed with a little vinegar. Drain,
dry, and cut into slices. Brown in 2 tablespoons
butter or margarine some parsley and onion,
finely chopped, add the kidney slices and let
them brown. Add salt and pepper to taste,
1½ tablespoons vinegar, a few tablespoons stock
to cover, and continue cooking for a further
10 minutes, until kidneys are tender. Serve
immediately.

Veal Kidneys with Capers

Prepare and slice 4 veal kidneys, as above.
Roll the slices in flour, season with salt and
pepper to taste, and brown then on high heat
in 2 tablespoons butter or margarine. Add 1
glass dry white wine, let it reduce, and add
1 tablespoon capers, chopped if large, whole
if small. Mix well, continue cooking for 10 or
more minutes until kidneys are tender. Serve
immediately, sprinkled with chopped parsley,
if liked.

372

Calves' Liver with Onions

Ingredients: *1¼ lb calves' liver, thinly sliced ·
2 large onions · 4 tablespoons butter · salt ·
pepper · flour*

To serve: *lemon quarters*

Cut the onions into thin slices (step 1). Cook
them very slowly in half the butter until
golden-brown. Season with salt and pepper to
taste. Roll the liver slices lightly in flour
(step 2). Brown them quickly in the remaining
butter in a separate pan, and continue cooking
for just a few minutes. Remove from the heat,
sprinkle with salt, place on a warm serving
platter, arrange the onions around them, and
serve immediately with lemon quarters. Calves'
Liver Venetian Style is prepared in a slightly
different way: the onions should be cut into
somewhat thicker slices and browned in oil
on high heat. The liver, cut into small slices
or strips, should be put in the same pan as the
onions. After 2 or 3 minutes, season with salt
and pepper and serve with lemon quarters.

Braised Calves' Liver with Sage

Lard $1\frac{1}{4}$ lb calves' liver with 4 oz finely diced salt pork (soaked in cold water for 1 hour and drained). Brown lightly, in a high, narrow pan, $\frac{1}{4}$ cup butter or margarine together with 15 sage leaves, add the liver and sauté it quickly on all sides. Sprinkle with salt, and cover with stock. Cover, and cook slowly for about 2 hours. Ten minutes before the cooking is completed, add 1 glass milk, and reduce the juices on high heat. Serve the sliced liver with the cooking juices strained through a sieve, accompanied by mashed potatoes.

Calves' Liver with Red Wine

Cut into thin slices $1\frac{1}{4}$ lb calves' liver. Roll the slices in flour, and brown them quickly in 2 tablespoons butter. Add 1 tablespoon grated onion, cook for 1–2 minutes but do not brown, add 1 glass good red wine, and boil for a few minutes. Blend in a knob of butter, season with salt to taste, then remove the liver slices and arrange them on a warm serving platter. Pour over the cooking juice, and sprinkle with chopped parsley.

Liver Soufflé

Cut $\frac{3}{4}$ lb calf or lamb liver into thin slices. Melt $\frac{1}{4}$ cup butter in a frying pan, add the liver and fry for 2–3 minutes on each side. Sprinkle over 3 tablespoons warmed brandy and set alight. When the flames have died down, purée the mixture in a blender. Mix the purée with 2 cups béchamel sauce (see p. 84).

Separate 2 eggs and beat the yolks into the liver mixture. Beat the whites and fold in. Pour into a greased 8-inch soufflé dish. Bake in a hot oven (400°F) for 25 minutes. Serve immediately.

Calves' Tongue with Olives

Ingredients: *2 calves' tongues, about 2 lb ·
chopped onion, garlic and parsley ·
4 tablespoons butter or margarine ·
about 1 cup medium-sized green olives ·
stock · salt · pepper*

Bring the tongues to a boil in water, rinse
under cold running water and drain. Simmer
in enough water to cover for 1½–2 hours until
tender, then skin (step 1) and slice. Melt the
butter, and sauté on low heat the chopped
onion, garlic and parsley, together with the
olives, pitted or whole according to taste
(step 2). Add the tongue slices (step 3) and 1½
tablespoons stock and continue cooking until
the tongue is well heated and has absorbed
much of the flavor of the other ingredients.

Transfer to a warm serving platter and
serve the tongue with the cooking juices,
surrounded by the olives.

Calves' Tongue with Scallions

Bring 2 calves' tongues (about 1¾ lb) to a
boil in salted water, rinse under cold running
water and drain. Simmer in enough water to
cover for 1½–2 hours until tender. Skin them,
dry, and roll lightly in flour. Sauté 1 sliced
onion in ¼ cup butter. Add the tongue and
brown it. Add ½ glass dry white wine, let it
reduce, add ½ lb peeled tomatoes or 1 tablespoon tomato paste diluted in a little stock.
Add ½ cup hot stock, cover, and continue
cooking for 15 minutes. Meanwhile, soak 1 lb
scallions in boiling water. Peel them, put
them in the pan, and continue cooking until
the tongue has absorbed the flavor of the
cooking juices. Slice the tongue and serve with
the reduced cooking juices, garnished with the
scallions.

Braised Beef Tongue

Cook 1 beef tongue (about 5 lb) in salted boiling water for $\frac{1}{2}$ hour. Drain and skin. Roll strips of bacon or salt pork (soaked in cold water for 1 hour and drained) in a mixture of chopped garlic, parsley, salt and pepper to taste. Lard the tongue with them. Roll the tongue lightly in flour. Brown in a large shallow pan $\frac{1}{4}$ cup butter or margarine. Add the tongue, 2 onions and 2 carrots, thinly sliced. Skim the fat, then add 1 cup dry white wine, and let it reduce by half. Add $\frac{1}{2}$ cup stock, 1 bouquet garni made of parsley, thyme, celery and 1 bay leaf, and salt and pepper to taste. Cover, and continue cooking very slowly for $2\frac{1}{2}$–3 hours until very tender, adding more stock as necessary – the juices must be thick and not fatty. Serve the tongue with the cooking juices poured over, strained if liked. Serves 8–10.

Braised Oxtail

Heat 2 tablespoons oil in a flameproof casserole. Add 2 lb oxtail, chopped, and fry until well browned on all sides. Pour off the fat into a frying pan. Add $\frac{3}{4}$ cup dry white wine and 3 tablespoons brandy to the oxtail. Season, cover and cook in a cool oven (300°F) for $2\frac{1}{2}$ hours.

Heat the fat in the frying pan. Add $\frac{1}{2}$ cup diced slab bacon, $\frac{1}{4}$ lb peeled pearl onions, 3 carrots, peeled and sliced, and 2 small turnips, peeled and sliced. Fry until softened. Add the bacon and vegetables to the oxtail with a crushed garlic clove, a handful of celery leaves and salt and pepper to taste. Mix well, then cover and cook for a further 1 hour. Skim off as much fat as possible before serving.

Braised Tripe with Spanish Beans

Ingredients: *2 lb honeycomb tripe · milk ·
salt · ½ lb dry white Spanish beans ·
¾ cup butter · 1 oz salt pork, soaked in cold
water for 1 hour and drained · chopped celery,
carrot, onion, garlic and sage, to taste ·
½ glass dry white wine · 1¼ cups canned
peeled tomatoes, sieved · 1 bay leaf · pepper ·
mixed herbs · stock · grated Parmesan cheese
(optional)*

Soak the beans in cold water for at least 12
hours. Put them in cold water without salt,
bring to a boil, and cook until tender. Cook the
tripe in a mixture of milk and water to cover
and a pinch of salt for 1 hour. Drain. Cut into
strips (step 1). Brown the butter together with
the salt pork and chopped vegetables (step 2).
Add the tripe and, after 1–2 minutes, the
white wine. Let it reduce, add the tomatoes,
the bay leaf, and salt, pepper and mixed herbs
to taste, and cook for about 1½ hours, adding
stock occasionally if the tripe becomes dry.
Fifteen minutes before the end of the cooking,
add the drained beans (step 3). Before serving
the tripe, together with the reduced juices, add
grated Parmesan cheese, if desired.

Tripe Creole

Cook 2 lb tripe as left, and cut into strips. Brown ¼ cup butter or margarine together with 1 large chopped onion. Add 1 oz chopped salt pork, soaked in water for 1 hour and drained, 1 clove of garlic, chopped, 1 bay leaf, and, after a few minutes, ¾ lb tomatoes, peeled and chopped, 2 green peppers, cut into strips, the tripe, and a little salt and pepper to taste.

Cover and cook slowly for about 1¼ hours, adding stock if the tripe becomes dry.

Braised Tripe with Potatoes

Cook 2 lb tripe as left and cut into strips. Brown in 4 tablespoons butter or margarine a chopped mixture of garlic, onion, carrot and rosemary to taste, and 2 green olives. Add the tripe and, after a few minutes, 2–3 tablespoons tomato paste diluted in a little stock, or ¾ cup canned peeled tomatoes passed through a sieve, and a pinch of grated nutmeg. Cover, and cook on very low heat for ¾ hour. Add 1¼ lb potatoes, cut into pieces, a little stock, and cook for a further 30–45 minutes.

Tripe with Garlic and Parsley

Peel and chop 1 large onion and carrot. Place in a saucepan with 2 chopped celery sticks, 6 black peppercorns, 1 bay leaf, 1½ quarts cold water and 1 tablespoon lemon juice. Bring to a boil, then half cover and simmer for 30 minutes.

Strain the liquid and return to the pan. Cut 1½ lb partly cooked tripe into pieces, add to the pan and bring back to a boil. Skim off any scum, then cover and simmer for 1½–2 hours or until tender.

Drain the tripe and cut into strips about ½ inch wide. Coat with seasoned flour. Heat ¼ cup butter and 4 tablespoons oil in a frying pan, add the tripe and fry until golden brown on all sides. Sprinkle over 2–3 chopped garlic cloves and lots of chopped parsley, season and serve immediately.

379

Poultry

Boiled Stuffed Capon

Ingredients: *1 capon (about 5 lb) ·
1 celery stalk · 1 leek · 1 potato ·
¼ lb small onions, peeled and halved · 1 carrot ·
stock*

*For the stuffing: ¼ cup butter or margarine ·
the capon's liver, finely chopped ·
2 oz boned pork loin, finely chopped ·
2 oz prosciutto, finely chopped · 2 oz sweetbreads
or brains (see p.370), optional · 1 handful white
bread, soaked in milk
and squeezed dry · parsley or truffles ·
2 egg yolks · grated Parmesan cheese · salt ·
pepper · grated nutmeg*

Wash and dry the capon (step 1). If you like, remove the bones from inside the breast, taking care not to spoil the shape of the bird. Peel the vegetables and cut into pieces if large.

Prepare the stuffing: sauté lightly in the butter or margarine the capon's liver, pork loin, prosciutto, and the sweetbreads or brains, if using. Add the bread and parsley. (If truffles are used, cut them into thin slices and add them later to the chopped mixture.) Put the mixture in a bowl with the egg yolks, grated Parmesan cheese, and salt, pepper and nutmeg to taste, and blend thoroughly. Stuff the capon with the mixture, sew it with string (steps 2 and 3), wrap it in a clean napkin or cloth, and tie at both ends. Put it in a pan, cover with

stock and bring slowly to a boil. Skim the scum, add the vegetables and continue cooking slowly for about 2 hours, or until the capon is tender. Remove it from the pan, take it out of the cloth, and let stand 10 minutes. Remove string, transfer meat to a warm serving platter, and surround with the vegetables from the cooking juices. Serve with a variety of sharp sauces, according to taste. If liked, the capon can be carved before serving and reshaped on the serving platter. The stuffed capon can also be roasted in a moderate oven (375°F) for 2 hours, instead of being boiled. Serves 6–8.

Capon with Chicken Livers and Mushrooms

Wash and dry a 5-lb capon. Clean $\frac{3}{4}$ lb mushrooms, chop them, and sauté for a few minutes in 1 tablespoon butter, together with 3 sliced chicken livers. Season with salt and pepper to taste, add 2 tablespoons hot brandy, bring to the boil and flame. Remove from the heat after a few minutes, and mix with 1 handful white bread, previously soaked in milk and squeezed dry, 1 egg yolk, grated Parmesan cheese and chopped parsley to taste. Stuff the capon with the mixture and proceed as above.

Portuguese-style Capon

Season a 5-lb capon inside and out and put in a deep pot. Pour over 2 cups dry white wine. Cover and marinate for a few hours in the refrigerator.

Cook the capon's heart in boiling water for 10 minutes. Add the liver and cook for a further 10 minutes. Drain and chop finely.

Melt $\frac{1}{2}$ cup butter in a frying pan. Add 2 onions, peeled and finely chopped, and fry until golden. Remove from the heat and add $\frac{1}{4}$ teaspoon each nutmeg and cinnamon, $\frac{1}{2}$ cup finely chopped green olives, 2 chopped hard-cooked eggs, $\frac{1}{2}$ cup soft bread crumbs, 6 tablespoons milk, 1 teaspoon vinegar, the chopped heart and liver and seasoning. Combine well, then use to stuff the capon. Place the capon in a greased roasting pan and pour in the marinating wine. Roast in a hot oven (400°F) for $1\frac{1}{2}$-2 hours, basting occasionally. When cooked, reduce the wine by boiling rapidly and serve as a sauce with the capon.

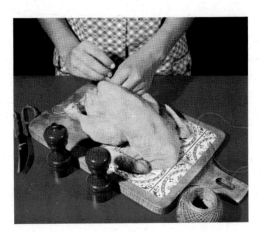

381

Chicken Cooked in Clay

Ingredients: *1 chicken (about 3 lb) ·
a finely chopped mixture of juniper berries,
sage, 1 bay leaf, thyme and peppercorns · salt ·
4 oz salt pork (soaked in cold water for 1 hour,
drained and sliced) or prosciutto slices*

Wash and dry the chicken, put inside it 1
teaspoon of the chopped mixture and salt
(step 1), and tie it with string. Brush it with the
remaining mixture, then cover with the salt
pork or prosciutto slices. Wrap in aluminum
foil, sealing it well. Soak the clay and work it
thoroughly. Spread clay in a layer not less than
½ inch thick, and cover the wrapped bird on
all sides with the clay (step 2). Put in a very
hot oven (475°F) until the clay begins to
crack. Break the clay (step 3), remove the bird,
and open the wrapping when you serve. The
chicken can also be cooked in the aluminum
foil, without the clay, in a hot oven (400°F) for
1−1½ hours or until tender.

Chicken with Lentils

Soak in cold water for 12 hours 1 lb lentils. Drain, put in cold water, and cook for 2 hours together with 1 clove of garlic, 1 celery stalk and salt. Meanwhile prepare for cooking a 3-lb chicken. Put inside it 1 bay leaf and salt and pepper to taste. Put on the bottom of a casserole 4 tablespoons butter or margarine in small pieces, some celery, carrot and onion, roughly chopped, some chopped ham fat, and $\frac{1}{2}$ clove of garlic, peeled. Put in the chicken and brown very slowly. Sprinkle with plenty of salt and pepper. Add $\frac{1}{2}$ glass dry white wine, let it reduce, then add a few ladles stock. Cover and continue cooking slowly for $1\frac{1}{2}$ hours or until tender. Lift out the bird and keep it warm. Drain the lentils, sauté them for a few minutes in the chicken's cooking juices, and serve them with the carved bird.

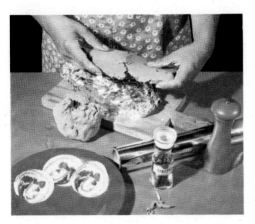

Roast Chicken

Wash and dry a 3-lb chicken. Chop sage, rosemary and garlic, and season it with plenty of salt and pepper. Put 1 tablespoon of the mixture inside the chicken and roast in a hot oven (400°F) for about $1\frac{1}{2}$ hours.

Roast Ginger Chicken

Mix together 1 tart apple, peeled, cored and grated, a 1-inch piece of ginger root, grated or finely chopped, $\frac{2}{3}$ cup cooked rice, $\frac{1}{2}$ cup plain yogurt, $\frac{1}{4}$ cup softened butter and seasoning. Use to stuff a 3-lb chicken. Place the chicken in a roasting pan and dot with 2 tablespoons butter. Roast in a hot oven (400°F) for 1 hour, turning and basting from time to time. Serve with gravy made with the pan juices.

Chicken Breasts with Cheese Cream

Ingredients: *4 chicken breasts (about 1 lb) ·*
flour · salt · pepper · 2 tablespoons butter or
margarine · dry white wine or brandy · stock

For the Cheese Cream: *4 oz cream cheese ·*
1 tablespoon butter · 1 tablespoon milk ·
pepper · truffles or black olives (optional) · peas

Pound lightly the chicken breasts, season with
salt and pepper to taste, flour them lightly, and
cook them in the butter or margarine on both
sides, on high heat, until golden (step 1). Add
the white wine or brandy (if using brandy,
bring it to a boil and flame it), let it reduce,
then add immediately a few tablespoons stock
and stir to combine all the cooking juices.
Cover and cook slowly for 30–35 minutes.

To prepare the cheese cream, put in a pan
the cheese (step 2), butter, milk, and pepper to
taste and blend over low heat until creamy.
Spread it over the chicken breasts (step 3), and
put them under the broiler to brown for a few
seconds. Transfer to a warm serving platter
and garnish with a few sliced truffles or pitted
black olives, if liked, and serve with peas.

Chicken Breasts with Brandy

Melt $\frac{1}{4}$ cup butter in a skillet. Put in, side by
side, 4 chicken breasts (about 1 lb), lightly
pounded and floured. Season with salt and
pepper to taste Brown them quickly on both
sides, on high heat, then cover, lower the heat,
and cook slowly for 30–35 minutes. When
cooked, arrange them on a warm serving
platter, covered with the cooking juices. Heat
1 small glass brandy, flame it, pour over the
chicken breasts, and serve immediately.

Chicken Cooked in Terracotta

Ingredients: *1 chicken (about 3 lb) ·
8 juniper berries · 1 teaspoon peppercorns ·
leaves of 1 twig rosemary · leaves of 1 twig
sage · salt · 4 oz sliced prosciutto, or salt pork
soaked in water for 1 hour and drained, or
streaky bacon · ¼ cup butter or margarine in
small pieces*

To garnish: *twigs of rosemary*

Clean (step 1), wash and dry the chicken.
Crush the juniper berries and peppercorns in a
mortar and chop them together with the rosemary and sage leaves. Put 1 teaspoon of the
mixture inside the chicken with a pinch of salt
(step 2). Arrange the prosciutto, salt pork or
bacon slices around the chicken on aluminum

foil. Dot with butter or margarine, and spread
the remaining herb mixture over the chicken.
Sprinkle liberally with salt and close the
aluminum foil (step 3). Put the wrapped
chicken in an earthenware dish, cover, and
cook in a hot oven (400°F) for about 2 hours.
Remove the dish from the oven, taking care
not to break it by putting it on a cold surface.
Remove the chicken, take off the aluminum
foil and transfer to a warm serving platter.
Arrange paper frills on the legs and garnish
with twigs of rosemary. Guinea fowl may also
be prepared in this way.

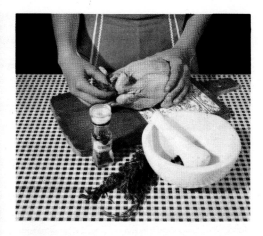

Chicken with Parsley

Wash and dry a 2½-lb chicken. Put in a pan the chicken neck, leg and wing tips, and gizzard, together with 1 celery stalk, 1 carrot, peeled and chopped, 1 onion, peeled and sliced, and salt and pepper to taste. Cover with water and simmer 1−2 hours. Strain. Sauté the liver in ½ tablespoon butter or margarine, then chop it with a generous handful parsley, and mix with 1 teaspoon grated lemon peel, ¼ cup butter, and salt and pepper to taste. Put the mixture inside the chicken, sew the opening and tie the bird with string. Sprinkle liberally with salt and pepper, and brown it on all sides over high heat in 1 tablespoon butter. Add ¼ cup of the hot stock, cover, lower the heat, and cook very slowly for about 1 hour or until tender, adding more stock if the chicken becomes dry. Remove the chicken from the pan, take off the string, and keep warm. If the sauce is too thin, let it reduce on high heat. Add ½ cup light cream, and let the sauce thicken, without boiling, on moderate heat. Carve the chicken, arrange on a warm serving platter and garnish with parsley sprigs. Serve the sauce in a separate dish.

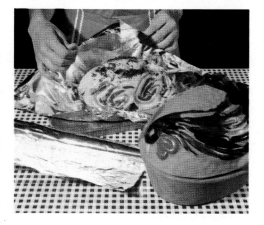

Tunisian Chicken

Season a 3-lb chicken inside and out. Chop the giblets and mix with ½ cup drained canned whole kernel corn, 1 cup diced Cheddar cheese, 1 egg and 1 tablespoon soft bread crumbs. Mash 1 hard-cooked egg and add to the corn mixture with seasoning. Use to stuff the chicken.

Dip 4 tomatoes in boiling water, then drain and remove the skins. Quarter the tomatoes and place in a flameproof casserole with 3 carrots, peeled, 3 potatoes, peeled and chopped, 1 celery stick, 1 parsley sprig and 5 cups water. Bring to a boil, then add the chicken with 2 tablespoons butter. Cover and simmer for 1½ hours.

Remove the chicken and set aside. Sieve the cooking liquid and return to the casserole. Reheat and serve this as a soup before the chicken. Heat 2 tablespoons butter and 4 tablespoons oil in a frying pan and brown the chicken on all sides before serving.

Stuffed Roast Chicken

Ingredients: *1 chicken (about 3½ lb) · 1
slice cooked ham (about 4 oz) · 1 slice tongue
(about 4 oz) · 1 tablespoon pistachio nuts ·
¼ cup butter or margarine · 1 small glass brandy*

For the stuffing: *½ lb stewing veal ·
4 oz pork loin · 4 oz sausage meat · 2 eggs ·
¼ cup grated Parmesan cheese · 1 handful white
bread soaked in milk and squeezed dry · salt ·
pepper · mixed herbs*

To garnish: *artichoke hearts · green peas ·
carrots · radish roses (optional)*

Wash and dry the chicken, cut off the tips of
the wings and legs. Put it on a carving board,
breast side down, cut the skin with scissors
from the neck to the tail (step 1), and remove
the bones, except for the leg bones. Spread it
on the board leaving the skin intact.

Prepare the stuffing: chop the veal and the
pork loin, and mix in a bowl with the sausage
meat, eggs, grated Parmesan cheese, white
bread, and salt, pepper and mixed herbs to
taste. Blend thoroughly. Cut the ham and
tongue into strips. Put ½ the stuffing in the
center of the chicken (step 2), sprinkle with ½
the pistachio nuts, and arrange a layer of ½
the ham and tongue strips on top. Cover it with
the remainder of the stuffing, and end with a

layer of remaining pistachio nuts, ham and
tongue. Fold the skin of the chicken over the
stuffing, tuck the neck skin inside, and sew
carefully together with string (step 3). Tie the
chicken with string. Melt the butter or margarine in a roasting pan, put in the chicken,
sewed side down, and brown in a moderate
oven (350°F). Bring the brandy to a boil in a
pan, and flame it. Pour it quickly over the
chicken, sprinkle with salt, and cook slowly for
$1\frac{1}{2}$–2 hours until tender, basting occasionally
with the cooking juices. When cooked, remove
from pan, let stand for 10 minutes, then untie
and slice it. Arrange on a warm serving platter
with paper frills on the legs. Garnish with artichoke hearts sautéed in butter and stuffed with
green peas and carrots, and radish roses, if
liked. Serve with potatoes mashed in butter
and eggs and seasoned with salt, black pepper
and grated nutmeg. This dish may also be
served cold.

Chicken with Garlic

In a large pan with a tight-fitting lid, mix $\frac{1}{2}$ glass
olive oil, 4 celery stalks, chopped, and chopped
parsley and salt to taste. Add 4 chicken pieces
to the pan, stir, and add 40 unpeeled cloves of
garlic and $1\frac{1}{2}$ glasses brandy. Cover the pan
and seal it with a paste made of flour and water.
Put it in a moderate oven (350°F) for about
$1\frac{1}{2}$ hours. Remove garlic before serving.

Stuffed Chicken Breasts

Pound lightly 4 chicken breasts (about 1 lb),
and put in the center of each a stuffing prepared
in the following manner: mix 3 oz cottage or
ricotta cheese with 1 egg yolk, 1 teaspoon
chopped parsley, 1 teaspoon grated lemon peel,
and salt and pepper to taste. Roll the meat and
tie with string. Flour lightly and brown on all
sides over high heat in 2 tablespoons butter or
margarine. Season with salt and pepper to
taste. Add 1 small glass brandy, heated, bring
to a boil, flame it, let it reduce, then add $\frac{1}{4}$ cup
hot stock. Cover, lower the heat, and cook
slowly for about 30–35 minutes.

Turkey Stuffed with Chestnuts

Ingredients: *1 turkey (about 7½ lb) ·*
2 slices salt pork soaked in water for 1 hour
and drained, or streaky bacon · ¼ cup butter ·
salt · pepper · ½ glass dry white wine · stock

For the stuffing: 1¼ lb roasted chestnuts,
peeled · ¼ cup butter · ½ lb prunes, soaked
according to package directions, and pitted ·
2 large apples · ½ lb sausage meat

To garnish: chestnuts · watercress

Wash and dry the turkey. Prepare the stuffing:
sauté the chestnuts in the butter (step 1) for
10–15 minutes, together with the prunes,
the apples, peeled and cored, and the sausage
meat, stirring occasionally. Put it inside the
turkey (step 2) and sew up the opening with
string. Cover the breast with the salt pork or
bacon slices (step 3) and tie the bird. Put it in
a flameproof casserole with the butter in small
pieces, and brown on all sides over high heat.
Sprinkle liberally with salt and pepper, add the
wine, let it reduce, and add ¼ cup stock. Cover,
lower the heat, and cook for about 2 hours, or
until turkey is tender, basting occasionally
with the cooking juices and adding stock if the
meat becomes too dry. Remove the cover for
the last 10 minutes and finish cooking on high
heat. Remove turkey from pan, transfer to a
warm serving platter, and let stand 10 minutes
before untying and carving. Garnish with
whole cooked chestnuts and watercress, and
decorate turkey legs with paper frills. The
turkey can also be roasted in a moderate oven
(350°F) for 2 hours. Serves 6–8.

Braised Turkey

Cut into pieces 2½ lb turkey meat. Brown it in
¼ cup butter or margarine together with 2 oz
diced salt pork, soaked in cold water for 1 hour
and drained. Add a mixture of chopped celery,
carrot, onion and garlic. Add 1 tablespoon
dried mushrooms, soaked in lukewarm water,
squeezed dry and mashed with 1 tablespoon
flour. Blend well, and, after a few minutes, add
¾ lb tomatoes, peeled and chopped, ¼ cup
stock, 1 bay leaf, and salt and pepper to taste.
Cover, and cook slowly for about 1 hour, adding more stock if necessary.

Roast Goose

Ingredients: *1 goose (about 7¼ lb) ·
¼ cup butter or margarine · sage · rosemary ·
salt · pepper · ½ glass dry white wine*

To garnish: *tiny whole potatoes, boiled ·
parsley sprigs*

Wash and dry the goose. Put inside it 1 tablespoon butter or margarine mixed with chopped
rosemary and sage, and salt to taste (step 1).
Tie with string and sprinkle the outside liberally with salt and pepper (step 2). Dot the
goose with the remaining butter or margarine,
place it in a roasting pan with more chopped
rosemary and sage to taste in a hot oven
(475°F). When brown, baste it with white wine
(step 3), lower the heat to moderate (375°F),
and continue cooking for about 2 hours,
pricking occasionally with a fork to let the fat
escape. When the goose is cooked, remove from
the pan and let stand 10 minutes. Remove
string, transfer to a warm serving platter,
arrange paper frills on legs and garnish with
tiny whole potatoes and parsley sprigs. (Half a
goose can be roasted in the same way: place
it in a lightly buttered roasting pan with the
skin above so that it can be pricked occasionally.) Serves 6–8.

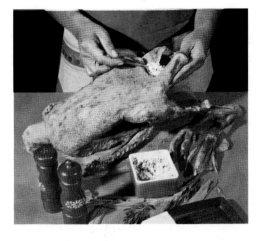

Stuffed Goose Neck

Detach the skin from the neck, turning it inside out without breaking it, wash, dry, and tie with string at one end. Soak the liver from the goose in tepid water for 1 hour, then drain and chop it. Sauté it in a little butter or margarine, together with the chopped goose heart, without letting them brown. Chop ½ lb raw pork loin. Mix liver, heart and pork with 4 oz sausage meat, 1 handful white bread, soaked in milk and squeezed dry, 1 slice of onion (optional), chopped parsley to taste, 2 tablespoons brandy, and plenty of salt and pepper. Stuff the mixture into the neck skin, leaving a little space to provide for swelling during the cooking, and tie the other end. Roll it with the hand to make it regular, and prick it all over with a fine needle. Put it in cold stock, and cook it for about 1 hour. Slice it, and serve it hot with buttered spinach or mashed potatoes. Or you may serve it cold, possibly with aspic and a green salad.

An alternative way of cooking this dish is to brown the goose neck in goose fat and then braise it slowly with chopped celery, carrot, garlic, 1 bay leaf, and stock for about 1 hour.

Goose with Fennel

Melt 2 tablespoons butter in a flameproof casserole, add an 8-lb goose, cut up, and brown on all sides. Add ½ lb carrots, peeled and chopped, 3 fennel bulbs, quartered, and 1 crushed garlic clove and cook for 5 minutes. Sprinkle over 3 tablespoons flour and cook, stirring, for 2 minutes, then gradually add 5 cups stock. Bring to a boil, stirring. Add 4 bay leaves, 1 teaspoon dried thyme and seasoning and simmer gently for 1 hour.

Peel and chop 1 lb potatoes. Add to the casserole with ½ lb peeled pearl onions and simmer for a further 30 minutes. Just before serving stir in 1 tablespoon chopped parsley.

Duck with Orange

Ingredients: *1 wild duck (about 4 lb) · salt ·
pepper · butter or margarine ·
1 glass dry white wine · 4—5 oranges ·
½ cup reduced stock · ½ lemon ·
2 tablespoons brandy · 1 tablespoon sugar ·
1 tablespoon vinegar*

Wash and dry the duck, and tie with string,
the legs turned backwards. Sprinkle liberally
with salt and pepper, and brush with melted
butter or margarine. Brown on all sides over
high heat in a buttered pan (step 1), cover,
lower the heat and cook for about 45 minutes
or until the duck is tender. Baste occasionally
with a little white wine. When cooked, take out
and keep warm. Cut into thin strips the rind
of 2 oranges (step 2), boil them for a few
minutes, drain and refresh in cold running
water. Discard excess fat from the cooking
juices, mix in the stock gradually, add the
juice of 2—3 oranges and the ½ lemon (step 3),
the brandy, and a caramel made by dissolving the sugar in the vinegar, then boiling
it vigorously with the boiled orange rind. Continue cooking the sauce on low heat for 8—10
minutes until reduced. Remove string from
duck, and transfer to a warm serving platter.
Pour the sauce over, arranging strips of orange
rind decoratively over the breast. Garnish
platter with segments from remaining orange,
after removing the skin, pith and membrane.
Decorate the duck's legs with paper frills.

Rolled Duck
with Grand Marnier

Wash and dry a 4-lb duck. Cut it along the back and bone it, being careful not to split the skin. Cover the inside of the flesh with prosciutto slices and very thin slices of orange, from which the skin, pith and membranes have been removed. Roll the duck and tie with string, like a roast. Brown on all sides over high heat in $\frac{1}{4}$ cup butter or margarine, cover, lower the heat, and cook for about $1\frac{1}{4}$ hours, or until tender. When cooked, take the duck out and keep warm. Discard the excess fat from the cooking juices. Put in another pan $\frac{1}{4}$ cup sugar and 1 tablespoon white vinegar. Heat slowly until sugar dissolves, bring to a boil, and when the sugar begins to caramelize add the juice of 1–2 oranges, 4 tablespoons Grand Marnier, and the grated peel of $\frac{1}{2}$ orange. Continue cooking for 3–4 minutes, then add the cooking juices from the duck, and the rind of 1 orange cut into thin strips, boiled in water for 5 minutes and drained. Remove the string from the duck, slice it, and arrange on a warm serving platter. Pour the sauce over the duck.

Normandy Duck

Place a few sprigs of tarragon inside a 4-lb duck. Prick the skin all over with a fork. Melt $\frac{1}{4}$ cup butter in a large flameproof casserole. Add the duck and brown on all sides. Pour over 2 tablespoons warmed Calvados or brandy and set alight. When the flames have died down, season the duck, cover and simmer for 45 minutes. Turn the duck over halfway through the cooking.

Peel and core 4 Granny Smith apples and cut into thick slices. Melt 2 tablespoons butter in a frying pan and fry the apple slices until golden brown.

Place the duck on a serving dish and surround with the apple slices. Keep hot. Skim the fat from the cooking juices in the casserole, then add $\frac{3}{4}$ cup dry white wine. Reduce by boiling fast for a few minutes. Stir in 1 cup light cream and a little chopped fresh tarragon. Serve this sauce with the duck.

Game

Stuffed Boned Rabbit

Ingredients: *1 rabbit (about 4 lb) ·
a generous measure rosemary and sage · salt ·
pepper · 6 oz prosciutto (sliced), or salt pork
(soaked in cold water for 1 hour, drained and
sliced) · 1 clove of garlic, peeled ·
¼ cup butter · 2 tablespoons oil ·
2 glasses dry white wine · stock*

To garnish: *macedoine of vegetables*

Wash and dry the rabbit. Place it on its back
on a cutting board with the neck towards
you, and make a cut lengthwise along the
breast and belly (step 1). Using a very sharp
knife carefully remove all the bones (step 2),
so as to obtain 1 large piece of meat. Mix the
rosemary and sage with salt and pepper to
taste, spread ½ the mixture over the meat,
arrange a layer of prosciutto or salt pork slices
over it, and top with the remainder of the herb
mixture. Roll the meat (step 3), tie it with
string as for any roast meat. Sauté the garlic

in the oil and butter until golden, add the meat and brown on all sides over high heat. Remove the garlic. Stir in the white wine, let it reduce, then add salt to taste and $\frac{1}{4}$ cup stock. Lower the heat and cook slowly for $1\frac{1}{4}$ hours. When cooked, remove the roll from the pan, let stand 10 minutes, then remove the string, slice the meat and arrange on a warm serving platter with the reduced cooking juices poured over. Garnish the platter with a macedoine of vegetables, if liked. The rabbit can also be cooked in a moderate oven (350°F) for $1\frac{1}{2}$–2 hours, basting the meat occasionally with the cooking juices. Serves 6–8.

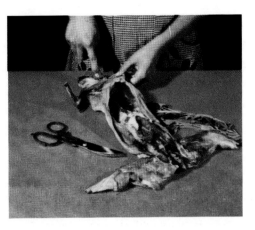

Rabbit with Curry Sauce

Wash and dry 1 rabbit (about $2\frac{1}{2}$ lb). Cut into serving pieces, roll in flour, and brown on all sides over high heat in 2 tablespoons butter. In another pan, sauté until golden 1 clove of garlic, peeled, in 4 tablespoons butter. Remove the garlic, add 1 medium-sized green apple, cored and roughly chopped, 1 medium-sized onion, finely chopped, and $\frac{1}{2}$ teaspoon curry powder – or more, according to taste. Cook slowly until the onion is tender, then add 2 tablespoons flour, and salt to taste. Stir constantly, and, after 2 minutes, add 2 cups hot stock. Add the pieces of rabbit, cover, lower the heat and cook slowly for 40–45 minutes or until tender. Serve with the cooking juices poured over, and boiled rice or pilaff in a separate dish, if liked.

Rabbit with Tarragon Cream

Heat 4 tablespoons oil in a flameproof casserole, add 2 lb rabbit pieces and fry until browned on all sides. Remove the rabbit and reserve. Pour off the oil. Melt $\frac{1}{4}$ cup butter in the casserole, add 3 large onions, peeled and thickly sliced, and fry until golden. Add 2 tablespoons flour and cook until golden, then gradually stir in $\frac{1}{2}$ cup dry white wine and 1 cup chicken stock. Bring to a boil, stirring. Return the rabbit to the casserole. Cover and simmer for about $1\frac{1}{4}$ hours.

Add $\frac{1}{2}$ cup light cream, 1 tablespoon chopped fresh tarragon and seasoning. Heat through gently and serve.

Jugged Hare

Ingredients: *1 hare (about 7½ lb) with the blood · 2 tablespoons white wine · 4 oz calves' liver, sliced · 2 oz pork fat · 1 onion, chopped · ¼ cup butter or margarine, or a few tablespoons oil · flour*

For the marinade: 6 cups good, Burgundy-type red wine · 1 celery stalk · 1 carrot, sliced · 2 onions, chopped · 1 small bunch parsley · 1 clove of garlic, crushed · 1 bay leaf · a few leaves thyme, marjoram, sage, rosemary · a few juniper berries · 3–4 peppercorns · 3 cloves · 1 small stick cinnamon · 1 pinch mixed herbs and rock salt

Wash and dry the hare. Keep the blood in a bowl, mixed with the white wine to prevent coagulation, until blending it with the sauce at the last moment. Cut the hare into serving pieces (step 1), and put them in a bowl together with the liver, heart and lung, and the calves' liver, and pour over the marinade (step 2). Let stand for 24 hours, stirring occasionally. The next day, brown in a casserole the butter, margarine or oil, pork fat and chopped onion. Drain the pieces of hare (reserving the marinade), dry them, roll lightly in flour, and put them in the casserole. Brown the meat on all sides over high heat, add all the marinade (except the livers), bring to a boil, then cover, lower the heat, and cook for about 2 hours, adding the livers after 1½

hours. If the sauce is too thick, add some stock or hot water. A few minutes before serving take out the pieces of hare, and strain the cooking juices through a sieve (step 3). Return the sauce to the casserole, stir in the blood, add the meat, and as soon as it is hot serve with croûtons fried in butter or a polenta. Serves 10.

Braised Hare

Wash and dry 1 hare (about 7½ lb). Cut into serving pieces and rub generously with salt and pepper. Put in a bowl together with ½ cup brandy, 2 tablespoons oil, 1 chopped bay leaf, and ½ onion, finely chopped. Marinate for 2 hours, turning the pieces over occasionally. Chop the hare's liver, place in a bowl and cover with 1 cup good red wine. Brown in a casserole 1 tablespoon butter, ½ chopped onion, and 2 oz salt pork, soaked in cold water for 1 hour, drained and chopped. Add the pieces of hare and the marinade (reserving the liver), passed through a sieve, cover, and cook very slowly for about 1 hour, adding stock if necessary. Add the chopped liver and 1 lb sliced mushrooms, and continue cooking for 1 hour, or less if the hare is tender. Transfer hare to a warm serving platter, thicken the sauce if necessary with a little beurre manié (equal quantities of butter and flour kneaded together), and pour over the hare.

Serve with bread croûtons fried in butter or a polenta. Serves 10.

Rabbit with Prunes

Put a 3-lb rabbit, cut up, into a shallow dish. Add 1 small onion, peeled and sliced, a bay leaf and 1 cup dry white wine. Leave to marinate overnight.

Drain the rabbit pieces and place in a casserole. Strain over the marinade. Add 3 carrots, peeled and chopped. Cut ½ lb fresh pork sides into strips. Pit ¾ cup plump prunes and stuff with some of the pork strips. Add to the casserole with the rest of the pork strips, 1 cup hot chicken stock, 2 tablespoons currant jelly and seasoning. Cover and cook in a moderate oven (325°F) for 1½ hours.

Pheasant on Croûtons

Ingredients: *1 pheasant, preferably a hen bird, (about 2½ lb) · 1 bay leaf · 2 juniper berries · 2 slices prosciutto, salt pork or bacon · ¼ cup butter or margarine · salt · pepper · 1 twig rosemary (optional) · ½ glass dry white wine · 1½ tablespoons stock · bread croûtons fried in butter*

Wash and dry the pheasant. Chop the bay leaf and juniper berries together with 2 prosciutto, salt pork or bacon slices and ½ tablespoon butter or margarine. Add salt and pepper to taste. Shape into a ball and place inside the bird (step 1). Sew the opening with string, cover the breast with the remaining prosciutto, salt pork or bacon slices, and tie the bird with string. Brush with melted butter, sprinkle liberally with salt and pepper, put it in pan with the rosemary, if using, and brown on all sides over high heat. Pour over the wine (step 2), return to heat, let it reduce, and add the stock. Cover, and cook slowly for about 45–50 minutes or until tender, basting occasionally with the cooking juices. The cooking can also be done in a moderate oven (350°F). Arrange the croûtons on a warm serving platter, place the pheasant (whole or carved, according to taste) over the croûtons, and pour over the cooking juices before serving (step 3). Decorate with paper frills.

Pheasant Magyar Style

Wash and dry a 2½-lb pheasant. Chop 1 bay leaf, 1 clove, 1 clove of garlic, peeled, 1 tablespoon parsley and 1 lemon slice (peeled and without pips). Put the mixture, with salt and pepper to taste, inside the bird, and sew up with string. Cover the breast with a thin slice of fresh pork fat, tie the bird with string, and sprinkle it with Hungarian Tokay wine, or a similar sweet white wine. Sprinkle liberally with salt and pepper, and put it in a casserole with a few slices of onion and mushrooms, then add 1 glass of the wine previously used and 1 glass stock. Put the casserole in a moderate oven (350°F) for 45–50 minutes, basting from time to time with the cooking juices. Drain the pheasant, remove string, cut the bird into serving pieces, and keep it on a warm serving platter. Strain the sauce, removing the excess fat, reduce it on high heat if necessary, stir in 2 tablespoons redcurrant jelly, if liked, and pour over bird.

Broiled Grouse with Marsala Sauce

Clean 2 grouse, then cut each in half along the breastbone with poultry shears. Rub each piece with oil and sprinkle with salt. Cook under a hot broiler for about 10 minutes, turning once.

Meanwhile, melt ¼ cup butter in a saucepan. Add ¼ cup chopped Canadian bacon, and 1 small onion, peeled and chopped, and fry for 5 minutes. Stir in 1 tablespoon flour and cook for 2 minutes, then gradually stir in ½ cup stock and 4 tablespoons Marsala. Bring to a boil, stirring. Add a bay leaf, seasoning and the juices from the broiler pan. Cook for 20 minutes, stirring occasionally.

Sieve the sauce (discard the bay leaf) and reheat. Place the grouse pieces on slices of toast or fried bread and pour over the sauce.

Partridge with Grapes

Ingredients: *2 plump partridges, or 4 smaller ones · 2 (or 4) slices pork fat · butter · salt · pepper · 1 small glass brandy or ½ glass dry white wine · ¼ lb white grapes · stock · 4 bread croûtons fried in butter*

Wash and dry the partridges. Cover the breasts with 1 slice pork fat, and tie them with string, keeping the legs parallel with the bodies (step 1). Brush generously with melted butter, sprinkle with salt and pepper, and cook in a roasting pan in a hot oven (400°F) for about ½ hour, basting from time to time with the cooking juices. Drain them and keep warm. Pour out the fat from the pan, leaving the sediments, and add the brandy or white wine. Dissolve the sediments on low heat, stirring with a wooden spoon. Peel the grapes, remove the pips, and put the grapes in the pan with the partridges (step 2). After a few minutes, add a few tablespoons stock and 1 tablespoon butter. Reduce the juice over high heat, strain it to separate the grapes, and keep it warm. Garnish the serving platter with the fried croûtons, put in the partridges, after removing string and the grapes (step 3) and serve with the cooking juices in a separate dish.

Partridge Polish Style

Wash and dry 2 partridges. Sauté for a few minutes in a skillet the partridges' livers with 1 tablespoon butter or margarine, 1 chopped scallion, 1 tablespoon chopped parsley, ½ bay leaf, salt and pepper to taste. Remove the bay leaf, and pass the other ingredients through a sieve. Put a little of the mixture inside each bird, and sew up with string. Cover the breasts with slices of salt pork, soaked in cold water for 1 hour and drained, or bacon, according to taste, and tie the birds with string. Put them in a casserole with 1½ tablespoons stock. Put the casserole in a moderate oven (350°F), and cook for ½ hour, basting from time to time with the cooking juices. You may also cook them on top of the stove, browning them first in butter, and adding stock gradually as required. Take partridges from casserole, remove string and cut the partridges in half. Arrange them on a warm serving platter, pour over the cooking juices and sprinkle with 1 tablespoon breadcrumbs lightly browned in butter. Garnish with lemon quarters and parsley.

403

Stuffed Roast Pigeons

Ingredients: *2 large pigeons · 4 slices salt pork, soaked in cold water for 1 hour and drained, or streaky bacon · 1 tablespoon butter · ½ glass brandy · salt · 1 bay leaf · stock*

For the stuffing: *1 tablespoon butter · livers from the pigeons, minced · 2 oz prosciutto, diced · ½ glass brandy · 1 handful white bread, soaked in milk and squeezed dry · 1 egg yolk · 2 tablespoons grated Parmesan cheese · chopped parsley · salt · pepper*

To serve: *carrots in white sauce*

Wash and dry the pigeons, cutting off the feet (step 1). Prepare the stuffing: sauté lightly in 1 tablespoon butter the minced livers and prosciutto. Add ½ glass brandy, bring to a boil, flame it, and remove from the heat. Mix the livers and prosciutto with the bread, egg yolk, grated Parmesan cheese, and parsley, salt and pepper to taste. Stuff the pigeons with the mixture and sew the openings with string. Place 2 slices salt pork or bacon on the breast of each bird (step 2), tie them with string, and brown on all sides over high heat in the remaining butter. Pour over the remaining brandy (step 3), bring to a boil, flame it, sprinkle with salt, add the bay leaf, cover, lower the heat, and cook for about 1 hour until tender, adding stock if the meat becomes dry. If the pigeons are small, allow 1 per person and double the quantity of stuffing ingredients. When cooked, remove the string, transfer to a warm serving platter and serve surrounded by carrots in a white sauce.

Pigeons with Mushrooms

Wash and dry 2 large pigeons (or 4 small ones). Tie them with string, sprinkle with salt and pepper. Brown them in 1 tablespoon butter, add 1 small glass brandy, bring to a boil, and flame it. Cover, lower the heat, and cook slowly for about ½ hour. Take the birds from the pan, remove string and keep warm. Put in the pan 1 tablespoon chopped onion, ½ lb sliced mushrooms, 6 oz tomatoes, peeled and chopped, 1 bay leaf, and salt and pepper to taste. Cook for 10—15 minutes, put the pigeons back into the pan, and when they are hot, serve them covered with the sauce. Garnish with whole button mushrooms, if liked.

Pigeons with Saffron

Quarter 3 pigeons and coat with seasoned flour. Heat ¼ cup butter and 1 tablespoon oil in a flameproof casserole, add the pigeon pieces and brown on all sides. Meanwhile, pound 6 saffron strands in a small bowl. Add 2 tablespoons warm water and leave to soak for 10 minutes.

Add the saffron liquid to the casserole with 3 tablespoons lemon juice. Cover and cook gently for 20 minutes. Transfer the pigeon pieces to a serving dish and keep hot. Add 1 small onion, peeled and finely chopped, to the cooking liquid in the casserole and simmer for 3 minutes. Stir in 2 tablespoons chopped parsley, spoon over the pigeons and serve immediately.

Squabs with Truffles

Ingredients: 4 young squabs · salt · pepper · truffles · 4 slices prosciutto, or lean salt pork soaked in cold water for 1 hour and drained · 4 tablespoons butter or margarine · ½ glass brandy · a few tablespoons stock or water

To garnish: parsley sprigs

Wash and dry the squabs, sprinkle with salt and pepper, and put inside each thin slices of truffle (step 1). Wrap them in prosciutto or salt pork slices, tie them with string (step 2), and brown in butter or margarine. Pour over the brandy, bring to a boil, flame, and add the water or stock, and cook for 25–35 minutes or until tender. Remove from the pan, untie, arrange them on piped mashed potatoes or risotto, and keep warm. Add chopped truffle to the cooking juices (step 3), heat slowly for a few minutes, stirring well. Pour over the squabs, garnish with parsley sprigs and serve immediately.

Squabs en Brochette

Wash and dry 4 young squabs. Put them on oiled wooden or metal skewers, alternating each one with a piece of pork fat (blanched for 5 minutes in boiling water) and a piece of mushroom. Place the skewers in a buttered roasting pan, season with salt and pepper to taste, and pour over melted butter. Cook in a very hot oven (450°F) for 10 minutes. Take out the pan, sprinkle the birds with crumbs of white bread and baste them with the cooking juices. Put the pan back into the oven, and continue cooking for another 5–6 minutes. Remove the skewers, and arrange the birds on a warm serving platter. Pour into the pan 1 small glass brandy, bring to a boil, flame, and reduce the juices. Pour over the birds and serve immediately.

Squabs with Juniper Berries

Wash and dry 4 young squabs. Put inside each bird salt and pepper to taste, 1 small piece butter, and 3 crushed juniper berries. Wrap each bird in 1 slice pork fat, tie with string, and put in a buttered skillet. Brown on all sides over high heat, lower the heat, and cook for 15–20 minutes. Arrange on bread croûtons on a warm serving platter. Dissolve the cooking sediments with a little stock and pour over the birds.

Squabs with Mushrooms

Wash and dry 4 squabs. Put a sprig of rosemary, 2 sage leaves and a slice of bacon into each. Place the squabs in a roasting pan and spread with butter. Roast in a very hot oven (450°F) for 15 minutes or until browned.

Meanwhile, blanch pearl onions in boiling water for 5 minutes, then drain and peel. Melt $\frac{1}{4}$ cup butter in a flameproof casserole, add the onions and $\frac{1}{2}$ cup chopped slab bacon, and fry until golden. Add 2 cups thickly sliced mushrooms and cook for a further 2 minutes.

Remove the squabs from the roasting pan and place on top of the vegetables in the casserole. Pour over $\frac{1}{2}$ cup dry white wine and season. Cover the casserole and cook in a hot oven (400°F) for 15–20 minutes.

407

Assorted Meat Dishes

Italian Pot-au-feu

Ingredients: *3 quarts water · 1 tablespoon rock salt · 2 lb stewing beef in the slice · 1 carrot, peeled and sliced · 1 onion, peeled and sliced · 1 celery stalk · 1 clove of garlic, crushed · 1 small tomato, quartered (optional) · 1¼ lb stewing veal in the slice · 1 calves' foot · a few potatoes (optional)*

Bring the water and rock salt to a boil, add the beef (step 1), and skim the scum (step 2). For a richer stock, put the meat in cold rather than boiling water. Add the vegetables and continue cooking for 3 hours. Add the veal and the calves' foot halfway through the cooking (step 3). Add the potatoes, if liked. ½ hour before the cooking is completed. Remove meats from pan, slice, and arrange on a warm serving platter. Pour over 1½ tablespoons of the boiling stock. Serve with the vegetables and various sauces to taste, such as ketchup, mustard, green sauce and pickles. You may also add other meats, such as ½ chicken or capon, or garlic sausage cooked separately for 1 hour. Serves 7–8.

Boiled Meat with Tuna Sauce

Cut ¾ lb boiled meat (veal or beef) into thin slices, and arrange them on a shallow platter. Prepare a mayonnaise with 1 egg yolk, ¾ cup oil, the juice of 1 lemon, and salt and pepper to taste. Mix it with 6 oz tuna fish in oil, 2 anchovy fillets, desalted, and a few capers — all worked through a sieve. Dilute the sauce with a few tablespoons cold stock. Pour it over the meat, and garnish with slices of lemon and red peppers.

Boiled Beef au Gratin

Cut into thin slices, or chop roughly, ¾ lb boiled beef. Put it in a buttered ovenproof dish. Cover with tomato sauce, seasoned with chopped onions and mixed with chopped parsley and basil. Add a layer of mashed potato, and sprinkle with breadcrumbs and grated Gruyère cheese in equal proportions. Dot with butter. Put the dish in a hot oven (400°F) for 15–20 minutes, or until a golden crust has formed. Serve immediately in the same dish.

Mixed Meat Casserole

Cut up ½ a 3-lb chicken. Cut 1 lb each boned lamb, lean pork and chuck steak into 2-inch cubes. Arrange the meats and chicken in a casserole and top with ½ lb shelled raw shrimp, ½ lb spinach and a 16-oz can of tomatoes, drained. Sprinkle with 1 tablespoon oil and seasoning and pour in 2 cups chicken stock or water. Cover and cook in a moderate oven (325°F) for 2 hours. Stir well before serving.

Fowl and Spinach Pudding

Ingredients: $\frac{1}{2}$ lb breast of chicken and $\frac{1}{2}$ lb breast of turkey, uncooked, or 1 lb cooked chicken and turkey meat · 2 lb fresh, or $\frac{1}{4}$ lb frozen spinach · butter or margarine · 1 slice onion · 1 tablespoon brandy · salt · pepper · grated nutmeg · mixed herbs · 4 oz white bread without crust, soaked in milk, squeezed dry and worked through a sieve · 3 egg yolks · 1 egg white · 1 cup light cream · $\frac{1}{2}$ cup grated Parmesan cheese · breadcrumbs

To garnish: *creamed carrots · parsley*

If using fresh spinach, wash and cook in salted boiling water until tender (5–10 minutes). If using frozen spinach, cook according to package instructions. Pass spinach through a vegetable mill and sauté lightly in melted butter or margarine. Cut the chicken and turkey into small pieces (step 1). Melt 1 tablespoon butter or margarine, add the onion and sauté until golden; discard the onion. Add the meat and sauté lightly. Add the brandy, bring to a boil, flame it, then add salt and pepper to taste, 1 pinch nutmeg and mixed herbs and continue cooking slowly for 10–15 minutes. Pass the meat through a meat-grinder, and mix it with the bread, eggs, spinach, cream and grated Parmesan cheese, adding more salt and mixed herbs to taste (step 2). Butter generously an ovenproof dish, 8 inches in diameter and 4 inches high, a pastry mold, or a pastry ring, and sprinkle with breadcrumbs. Pour in the prepared mixture. Insert and remove the blade of a knife to allow air to penetrate during cooking (step 3). Put in a moderate oven (350°F) and cook for about 1 hour or until the blade of a knife inserted in the pudding comes out clean. Remove from the heat and unmold. Arrange in the center of the pudding and around it creamed carrots, tossed in chopped parsley.

Veal and Cream Pudding

Brown lightly in 1 tablespoon butter or margarine 1 lb stewing veal in the slice. Season with salt to taste. Add $\frac{1}{4}$ cup stock, cover and cook slowly for 1 hour. Mince, mix with 3 eggs, 1 cup light cream, $\frac{1}{2}$ cup grated Parmesan cheese, and cook as above.

411

Fritto Misto

Ingredients: *4 oz chicken · 4 oz veal ·
4 oz pork · 2 oz butter · salt · grated nutmeg ·
2 tablespoons Marsala · 4 oz sweetbreads ·
4 oz chicken livers · 1 thick slice each of
prosciutto and mortadella · 4 oz Gruyére
cheese · hot béchamel sauce prepared with
4 tablespoons butter, ⅔ cup flour, 3 cups milk,
salt and grated nutmeg to taste, with
1 egg yolk added · 2 eggs · breadcrumbs · oil*

To garnish: *parsley sprigs · lemon wedges*

Cut the chicken, veal and pork into 1½-inch
cubes. Brown in 2 tablespoons butter, add salt
and grated nutmeg to taste and the Marsala
and continue cooking. Meanwhile, blanch the
sweetbreads and chicken livers in boiling
water. When they are cold cut them into
cubes of the same size as the meats and add
to the pan. Cut the prosciutto, mortadella and
Gruyère cheese into cubes, add them to the
pan and stir well. When meats are tender
remove all ingredients from pan and string
on small oiled wooden or metal skewers,
alternating the different ingredients. Dip the
skewers in the hot béchamel sauce, put them
on a buttered dish, and let them cool. Roll
them in beaten egg, then in breadcrumbs
(step 1), and fry them in deep hot oil. Drain
them carefully and serve on a warm platter
together with a selection of the meats and
vegetables described below. Garnish with
parsley sprigs and lemon wedges.

Fried Brains and Beef Marrow

Prepare the brains and marrow for cooking, cut them into pieces, roll them in flour, then in beaten egg and breadcrumbs, and fry in butter. You may also dip them in batter, made of water, flour, grated cheese and egg, and fry them in hot oil.

Chicken Croquettes

Chop 1 lb cooked chicken together with 2 oz prosciutto or salami. Prepare a béchamel sauce with 2 tablespoons butter, 4 tablespoons flour, $\frac{3}{4}$ cup milk, salt and nutmeg. Remove the béchamel sauce from the heat, add the chicken and prosciutto or salami, 2 tablespoons grated Parmesan cheese, chopped parsley and 1 egg yolk. Pour the mixture on a buttered board and spread it to obtain a 1-inch layer. Let it cool, cut into pieces, and make into croquette shapes $2\frac{1}{2}$ inches long and $\frac{1}{2}$ inch in diameter. Roll them in flour, then in beaten egg and breadcrumbs (step 3), and brown and cook them in deep hot oil. Take them out with a slotted spoon, and drain them on paper towels as above. Serve with lemon quarters.

Corned Beef Patties

Soak 4 tablespoons soft bread crumbs in 3 tablespoons milk. Squeeze the bread crumbs dry, then mix with 1 lb mashed corned beef, 1 egg, 2 tablespoons grated Parmesan cheese and the grated rind of $\frac{1}{2}$ lemon. Shape the mixture into patties with floured hands. Dip the patties into beaten egg, then coat with dried bread crumbs. Heat $\frac{1}{4}$ cup butter and 1 tablespoon oil in a large frying pan. Add the patties and brown on both sides. Drain and serve hot, garnished with lemon wedges and parsley sprigs.

413

Brochettes Home Style

Ingredients: *10 oz veal · 10 oz calves' liver · 4 oz salt pork in the slice, soaked in cold water for 1 hour and drained · 1 red pepper and 1 green or yellow pepper (fresh or canned) · sage leaves · ¼ cup butter or margarine · salt · pepper · ½ glass dry white wine · stock*

To garnish: *lemon slices · salad (optional)*

Cut the meat, liver, salt pork and peppers in equal pieces. String them with the sage leaves on oiled wooden or metal skewers, alternating the ingredients (step 2). Brown on all sides over high heat in the butter or margarine (step 3). Season with salt and pepper to taste, add the white wine, let it reduce, add the stock, lower the heat and cook slowly or until meats are tender. Serve with the reduced cooking juices. The cooking can also be done under the broiler. Garnish with slices of lemon and salad, if liked.

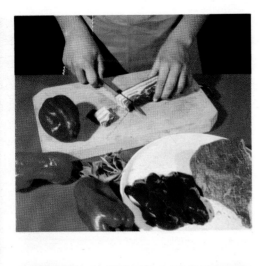

Veal en Brochette

Cut 1½ lb veal into 1-inch cubes. Marinate them for 1½ hours in a mixture of oil, lemon juice and salt. String on oiled wooden or metal skewers, alternating with sage leaves and diced salt pork, soaked in cold water for 1 hour and drained. Cook on charcoal or under the broiler until meat is tender, turning and basting from time to time with the marinade.

Shish Kebab

Cut 1¼ lb lamb (leg is the most suitable cut for this) into 2-inch cubes. Let them stand for 1½ hours in a marinade prepared in the following manner: mix together 2 tablespoons oil, the juice of 1 lemon, 1 tablespoon chilli powder (or 1 pinch paprika), 1 tablespoon finely chopped onion, 1 mashed clove of garlic, 1 pinch ginger, 1 pinch salt and 1 teaspoon curry powder. Drain lamb and discard marinade. String the pieces of lamb on long oiled wooden or metal skewers, alternating with pieces of onion, peppers, mushroom caps and halves of tomatoes. Cook over charcoal or under the broiler until lamb is tender, turning and brushing with butter or oil.

Chinese Brochettes

Cut 1½ lb pork (loin, fillet or leg are the most suitable cuts) into 1½-inch cubes. Let them stand for 3 hours in a marinade prepared as follows: mix together 2 tablespoons soy sauce (or Worcestershire), 2 tablespoons dry Marsala, ½ teaspoon sugar and ½ clove of garlic, peeled. Drain pork, reserving the marinade. String the pieces of pork on oiled metal skewers and cook very slowly over charcoal or under the broiler until tender and cooked through, turning and brushing from time to time with the marinade.

Mixed Grill

Ingredients: *4 lamb cutlets · 2 veal kidneys · 4 slices calves' liver · 2 sausages · $\frac{1}{2}$ chicken · butter or oil · $\frac{1}{2}$ cup boiling stock · 2 tablespoons oil · 1 tablespoon tomato ketchup · $\frac{1}{2}$ teaspoon Worcestershire · $\frac{1}{2}$ clove of garlic and 1 scallion, both chopped · salt · pepper*

To make the lamb cutlets tastier let them stand for 2—3 hours in a marinade prepared with 9 tablespoons oil, 3 tablespoons vinegar, 1 crushed clove of garlic, 4 chopped mint leaves and salt and pepper to taste. Halve the kidneys, remove the core, slice the liver (step 1), and brush with butter or oil and put on a hot grill. Cook for 2—3 minutes on each side. Cook the sausages but do not brush them with fat.

Meanwhile, bring to a boil the stock mixed with 2 tablespoons oil, the tomato ketchup, Worcestershire, garlic and scallion mixture, and salt and pepper to taste, and continue cooking on very low heat for 6—8 minutes. Brush the chicken with the sauce and put it on the hot grill with the skin uppermost (step 2). Cook for 30—35 minutes, turning and brushing with the sauce occasionally. Drain the cutlets, reserving the marinade, and put them on the grill. Cook for 12—15 minutes, turning them and brushing with the marinade.

Kebabs Eastern Style

Prepare a marinade with 1 cup pineapple juice, $\frac{1}{2}$ mashed clove of garlic, and $1\frac{1}{2}$ tablespoons soy sauce (or Worcestershire). Cut $1\frac{1}{4}$ lb lamb into 2-inch cubes, and let stand in the marinade for $2\frac{1}{2}$ hours. String them on small, oiled metal skewers, alternating with pineapple pieces (step 3) and broil.

Nuts

Nuts are considered fruits but they are rich in protein and fats and are therefore excellent in a vegetarian diet. In an ordinary diet they can be used in different ways, as appetisers, in main meals, with vegetables and desserts and on their own after dessert.

Almond
The kernel of the almond is a flat, oval, white nut. It has a mild flavor. Sweet almonds are widely used in cooking (especially Chinese style) as well as in cakes and confectionery. When dried and salted they are served with cocktails. Bitter almonds have to be used very carefully as large quantities may be poisonous. Native to Europe and the United States.

Brazil
Brazil kernels grow in tightly-packed clusters of 20 to 30, forming a large round fruit. Each kernel is enclosed in a very hard wedge-shaped shell. It is a delicious, smooth, oily nut which can be used in some savory dishes, in confectionery and eaten as a dessert nut.

Cashew
This curved, juicy nut from a tropical tree, has a very high fat content. Use the kernel fried in butter in a savory dish, or salted as a cocktail snack.

Chestnut
The best chestnuts for culinary use come from Italy and France. The kernel is large and floury in texture when cooked and has a sweet, delicate flavor (they are not eaten raw). The nuts are widely used as a flavoring for stuffings, in stews and desserts. Marrons glacés are candied chestnuts.

Coconut
Fruit of the tropical coconut palm. The outer fibrous husk is removed leaving a fleshy sphere filled with coconut milk. Shredded, dried coconut is used to complement many savory dishes in Indonesia but in Europe it is mainly used in baking and confectionery.

Hazelnut (Filbert, Cobnut)
Native to Europe and widely grown in the United States, hazelnuts are mainly eaten as a dessert nut or used in baking and confectionery. The kernel is small, round, brittle and sweet.

Hickory
A nut used in confectionery.

Pecan
A species of hickory, this is a smooth, oblong, thin-shelled nut. It has a flavor very similar to a walnut.

Peanut
The kernels come in pairs in a pod-shaped husk easily broken with the fingers. Raw peanuts can be used in cooking, in biscuits and confectionery. Peanuts are most commonly eaten roasted and salted as a cocktail savory. They have a high oil content and are used for cooking oil and for peanut butter.

Pine Nut
A thin, sweetish nut from the big pine cones found around the Mediterranean, it is much used in Italian and Middle East cookery to add flavor to meat, vegetables and rice. They can also be used in sauces, salads and biscuits.

Pistachio
Oblong, green-coloured kernel used as a flavoring in baking and confectionery. Native to Europe and the Middle East.

Walnut
Grown all over Europe and the United States, walnuts rarely ripen sufficiently in England to be eaten as dessert and the green nuts are pickled instead. When ripe, the kernel is brown and naturally falls into two halves. Halved, chopped and ground walnuts can be used in similar ways to almonds in savory and sweet dishes.

Introduction to Vegetables and Cheese

One of the marks of a good cook is the way in which basic ingredients are used to produce varied, interesting and nutritive menus. Vegetables with their very valuable vitamins have a major part to play. In this book you will find many ways of using ones that are both familiar and strange, so that your family and guests can eat well at all times of the year. With modern methods of packaging and transport you are rarely tied to purely local, seasonal produce, but even with foreign supplies becoming more readily available everywhere, there are times when what you can buy is limited by price. The serving suggestions here, some economical, others more extravagant, should spark the imagination even in the depths of winter. In this part of the book, cheese is used as a basic ingredient (for more information about cheeses, and which to serve after a meal see page 422). Cooked cheese dishes can make a super lunch or supper dish to offer to your most discerning guests. Rich in protein, cheese can quite successfully replace meat in a main course.

Glossary of Vegetables

Vegetables play an extremely important part in our diet. In fact our whole body structure can be said to depend to a large extent on vegetable foodstuffs as our meat and dairy foods come from animals which feed almost entirely on vegetation.

Vegetables supply almost all the minerals and vitamins we need. While it is easy enough to keep alive on protein foods alone, it is virtually impossible to keep healthy, either physically or mentally without those essential minerals and vitamins. On the other hand, it is equally possible to keep fit and mentally alert on a totally vegetarian diet in which protein is supplied through nuts, cheese and eggs.

Cooking vegetables

Many vegetables are at their best eaten uncooked, when they are crisp and fresh. Those that have to be cooked to make them digestible should never be overcooked; too much cooking not only renders them unpalatable and unappetising, but also completely destroys the delicate vitamin and mineral content.

Green vegetables such as cabbage and Brussels sprouts, seed vegetables such as peas and beans, need no more than perhaps half an inch of water in the bottom of the pan and will then cook in the steam created by that and their own moisture. Do not try and keep greens hot after cooking – that too has a detrimental effect on their nutritional value. Tubers which have to be covered with water to prevent discoloration (such as potatoes, Jerusalem artichokes and others), should be barely covered and cooked until just tender – not until they start to break up in the water.

Do remember to save the water you have cooked vegetables in. It can be used as stock or as the base of a soup. Even saved potato water can be used, cold from the refrigerator, to make pastry (do not add extra salt to the mix though, as the water will be salted).

Artichoke

A form of thistle that has been carefully cultivated and improved over hundreds of years until it is now considered a table delicacy. It is the flower part of the artichoke that is eaten, both for its fleshy petals and the heart or fond which is tender and has a special taste.

It is the very small and tender artichoke that can be eaten raw as a crudité. If it is not available do not substitute a raw large one for these do need to be boiled before being served cold with a vinaigrette dressing as a starter. Alternatively, the petals of the cooked artichoke may be pulled apart and mixed into a salad. The cooked artichoke hearts may be served as an accompaniment to meat or fish, or included in other dishes as you will find in the recipe section.

Jerusalem artichoke

Small and irregularly-shaped tuber that has no relation to the globe artichoke except a faint similarity in flavor. It is best scrubbed and cooked in its skin, and the skin rubbed off before serving.

Asparagus

Spear-shaped vegetable with a hard woody stalk, up to 8 or 9 inches long depending on the variety, and a tender tip. In some varieties the stalk is virtually inedible, in others it may be quite tender. For cooking, the spears are tied in bundles and the ends all cut to the same length; the bundle should then be stood upright in a tall pan of boiling salted water, with the spears immersed and the tips above the water. This way it is possible to cook it until the hard stalks are tender, without over-cooking the soft tips.

Asparagus is often served as an appetizer, in which case it is eaten with the fingers and dipped in melted butter or a sauce. It is equally good hot or cold, as an accompanying vegetable or in a salad.

Avocado

Pear-shaped fruit with a large seed, listed here as it is generally used in hors d'oeuvres and salads. The skin is thick, dark green and of a coarse texture unsuitable for eating. The flesh is smooth and almost white but faintly tinged with green.

Serve half an avocado per person, with vinaigrette dressing or stuffed with shrimps, or cut into slices for a salad.

Beans (Fresh and Dried)

Strictly speaking a bean is the kidney-shaped edible seed that comes from an inedible pod. However, there are many vegetables also known as beans in which the pod is edible. The more common varieties are listed below.

French Beans (Haricots Verts) are topped and tailed before cooking and eating whole. The seeds may be extracted and either dried, or canned, as **Kidney** beans **(Flageolets)**.

String, Green or **Snap Beans** Similar to French beans but coarser. Top and tail, slice and remove strings before cooking.

Broad Beans Large and green. The pod is only edible when very young and freshly picked.

Butter Beans and **Small White Haricots** are large seeds from an inedible pod.

Lentil Seed vegetable usually dried for use in wintertime. Dried lentils are usually light orange in colour and a rather flat shape.

Lima Beans These seeds from an inedible pod come fresh or dried. After soaking, the dried ones cook in about the same time as the fresh.

Beans *continued*

Soybeans, Red Kidney Beans and a variety of **White (Haricot) Beans** including **Great Northern**, navy, and **Pea Beans** are all dried legumes that need soaking according to the package directions before slow simmering.

Bean Sprouts are the newly germinated shoots from bean seeds, usually **Mung**, or **Soya**, beans. The Chinese eat them fresh and they are sometimes obtainable fresh in the West but normally sold canned.

Beet

Thick, fleshy root vegetable, generally deep purple in color. Most commonly eaten as a salad vegetable (cooked and cold) but also hot as an accompaniment to hot dishes. Borsch, a beet soup, is a national dish of Poland and Russia. Other varieties of beet are cultivated for sugar production and for cattle food.

Broccoli

Similar to cauliflower, but with a green or purple flower. Some varieties have a large, single flower head like cauliflower; other sprouting varieties carry a number of smaller flower heads on a longer stem. Generally served hot with meat or fish.

Brussels Sprouts

Very small, compact cabbage with leaves that curl closely over each other to form a tight ball. The smaller and more freshly picked, the better they taste. Serve hot as an accompaniment to meat dishes.

Cabbage

Vegetable with a large leaf that may be eaten cooked or fresh. The leaves should be separated and washed very thoroughly before use, or if the leaves grow too closely to be separated, shred the whole cabbage finely to wash it. Cabbage should be cooked in a minimum of boiling salted water for the least possible time required to render it just tender, otherwise the entire vitamin content will be destroyed. The most common cabbage varieties are green-leaved, but white and red cabbages are also available. Cabbage is also a good vegetable for pickling.

Cardoon

Member of the thistle family and related to the artichoke. The root and the ribs of the inner leaves are the only parts tender enough to eat.

Carrot

Long, tapering root vegetable, most commonly orange-colored. When young, carrots may be eaten fresh as a salad vegetable; as they get older they require cooking to make them digestible. The goodness in a carrot lies almost entirely in and immediately under the skin, which should therefore not be removed for cooking. Instead, scrub the carrots with a hard vegetable brush. If the skin is very unsightly, remove after cooking.

Cauliflower

Variety of cabbage cultivated for its large white flowers. It has very little green leaf, and this is cut almost entirely away before cooking. First soak cauliflower in cold salted water to make sure that any grubs are soaked out, then slit the base of the hard stem, to allow the heat to penetrate more easily, and steam or lightly boil until flower is just tender.

A sauce or melted butter is often served with cauliflower, or it may be lightly cooked and allowed to cool before breaking into flowerets for a salad.

Celeriac (Turnip-rooted Celery)

Variety of celery, the stem base being eaten rather than the stalks. The very tough skin has to be removed but the flesh has a delicate flavor.

Celery

It is the stalks of celery that are eaten and these are 'blanched' by banking up with earth as they grow, or kept in the dark by other means, so that even the fully-grown stalks are white and tender. Young celery is best eaten fresh, when it gets older it needs cooking but is one of the few vegetables that is best not cooked by boiling — but by braising in a well flavored stock. Celery also makes excellent soup and is a good flavoring ingredient for stews.

Chickpea

The seeds, or peas, of the chickpea are used fresh and dried, mostly in soups and stews.

Chicory

Another plant that is blanched while growing, like celery, so that its leaves are silvery white at the base and yellow at the tips. This has a bitter but refreshing flavor. The leaves can be pulled off and dressed for serving as a salad, or the whole chicory can be braised and served as an accompaniment.

Cucumber

Long, thin vegetable with a watery flesh that is pleasantly refreshing when eaten fresh as a salad vegetable. The skin contains a substance that aids digestion, and the vegetable is therefore best prepared by washing and slicing with the skin on, rather than by peeling. There is little food value in cucumber.

Eggplant

Elongated, gourd-like vegetable with a deep purple skin. It may be baked, broiled, braised or fried, or stuffed with a spicy meat mixture.

Endive, Curly (or Chicory)

Crisp, fresh flavored salad vegetable the shape of a lettuce. The leaves are small, sharply toothed and curled, and have a more pronounced flavor than lettuce. The heart is sometimes blanched while growing to keep it white and tender.

Fennel
The roots of this plant are treated much as celeriac, the stems as celery. The seeds are used as herbs.

Leek
One of the onion family, but more delicately flavored than most other varieties. Leeks grow as tall, closely packed leaves and are blanched like curly endive while growing so that the lower part remains white and tender. Delicious served with meat dishes or as a flavoring ingredient in soups and stews.

Lentil (see Beans)

Lettuce
The green leaves, which may be round, flat, pointed or curved according to variety, should be broken off – not cut by a steel knife – then washed and dried for salad; they can then be left to 'crisp' in the refrigerator. Lettuce may be cooked.

Lima (see Beans)

Mushroom
Edible fungi of many varieties, both wild and cultivated. Fungi have no real food value but since the flavor of many varieties is excellent, they are widely used to accompany other foods and to flavor sauces. In the USA and Britain we rarely use more than one or two well known varieties. In Europe they are gathered in the wild and there is much greater knowledge of which types are poisonous and which are not. Very young, fresh mushrooms are good eaten fresh, with a light, oil dressing; larger ones may be broiled, sautéed, baked or used to flavor soups and stews. Large, fleshy mushrooms are good coated in egg and breadcrumbs and fried.

Olive
Mediterranean fruit eaten as a savory relish as well as in cooked dishes. Oil for culinary use is extracted from the ripe (black) olive.

Onion
No cook can get far without onions in her kitchen. Their properties as flavoring vegetables are unique, blending with almost any meat, fish or other vegetable. Soups and stews are almost invariably flavored with onion and they may also be used alone, boiled, baked, fried or braised. Fully-grown onion bulbs keep well after pulling and are a staple winter vegetable. The first bulbs are used whole in cooking (button onions) and are favorites for pickling.
Scallions are used as a salad vegetable.

Pea
Generally, only the seeds of the pea are eaten, though a few varieties have edible pods as well, such as the Sugar pea (Mange-tout). Peas are a favorite vegetable in many parts of the world and respond well to differ-ent methods of preserving, notably freezing. When freshly picked, young garden peas are excellent to eat uncooked, although they tend to be indigestible and are therefore usually cooked and served hot, or cooled for a salad.

Pepper
A hollow vegetable, either round or oblong in shape. All types, whether green, red or yellow, are good as salad ingredients, though they are more digestible if blanched first, and may also be baked and stuffed, fried or included in stews.

Potato
Potatoes contain plenty of food value, though this is mostly in, or next to, the skins. Therefore, unless very old and dirty, potatoes are best cooked in their skins, and peeled after cooking. The skins of new potatoes are pleasant to eat, while the jackets of crisply baked old potatoes are excellent. Potatoes may be served plain boiled, boiled and creamed with butter and milk, steamed, baked, sautéed or fried.

If included in soups and stews no other thickening agent is required. Young, waxy potatoes are good cooked, cooled and dressed with mayonnaise for a salad. Potatoes are one of the world's staple foods.

Pumpkin
Large, fleshy, slightly sweet vegetable good in soups, and as an accompanying vegetable. Pumpkin pie is the traditional American dessert for Thanksgiving Day.

Radish
Small, crisp root vegetable with white flesh and red skin. Radishes are best pulled young and served fresh with salads; they are not so good cooked.

Salsify
Basically a root vegetable though the young spring leaves can be eaten in salads. The long, thin and white roots have a delicate flavor when boiled.

Scallion (see Onion)

Spinach
Green, large-leafed vegetable with a pronounced and distinctive flavor. Spinach leaves contain a high proportion of water and, after thorough washing, they need no extra water for cooking. Only very fresh leaves should be used; when the leaves wilt their flavor is spoiled too. Well washed and dried, spinach can be eaten raw.

Sweet Potato
Tuber similar in appearance to a large potato, but the flesh is tender, sweet and slightly perfumed. It may be boiled and mashed, roasted or fried.

Tomato

A fruit that is normally treated as a vegetable, the tomato is round, fleshy and usually red. A good tomato is at its best eaten fresh as a salad vegetable. Some varieties lose their flavor if cooked; others are good halved and broiled or sautéed, or stuffed with a spicy meat mixture. Peeled tomatoes add flavor to a casserole dish. Use concentrated purée (paste) as a flavoring ingredient for savory dishes.

Truffle

Fragrant tuber that grows wild and is found only in certain regions. The truffles of the Périgord district of France are said to be the best. Truffles are rarely eaten alone, but are used to flavor and scent other foods. Foie gras, which doesn't smell particularly good alone, is frequently scented with truffles; they are also added to egg and chicken dishes.

Turnip

Root vegetable, larger than the potato and either long and tapering, or round. The flesh is white and slightly sweet. Turnips are excellent in stews and with rich foods such as duck or goose, they are good roasted in the pan round a cut of meat, or boiled and mashed with butter. The leaves can also be eaten when fresh.

Zucchini

Small variety of edible gourd. Zucchini are generally 5–8 inches long and about 1¼ inches in diameter. The flesh is creamy white and the skin, which is not removed for cooking, is green. Slice and sauté in butter, or steam them, and flavor with herbs. Zucchini have little flavor of their own and are therefore not particularly good plain boiled. Zucchini may also be stuffed with a spicy meat mixture, as for tomatoes or eggplant.

Cheeses of the World

Cheese is one of the few foodstuffs that still remain intensely regional. Not that cheeses are not widely distributed, both nationally and internationally, but they still retain regional names and characteristics that are often difficult or even impossible to imitate in other parts of the world.

Cheddar is an exception. The 'Cheddaring' process happens to lend itself well to mechanization and good Cheddar-type cheese is produced as far from its English place of origin – Somerset – as New York, Wisconsin and Canada. At the other extreme are cheeses like French Roquefort, made from the milk of sheep grazed on limestone pastures and matured in the limestone caverns of the Roquefort region. No one has yet succeeded in making an imitation of Roquefort anywhere else in the world. The soil on which the sheep graze, the method of cheese production and the local conditions in which it is matured all have a marked effect on the finished food.

Listed here are some of the most important cheeses of the world, with brief descriptions of their characteristics.

British Cheeses

Blue Dorset Hard cheese made from skimmed milk. It is white with a blue vein and has a rather strong flavor.

Caerphilly Crumbly, whole milk cheese that does not mature well. It is white, mild-flavored and best eaten fresh, not cooked.

Cheddar Hard, yellow, whole milk cheese, smooth-textured and varying in flavor from mild to quite strong. Farmhouse Cheddar is still considered the best and is usually slightly harder than bulk-produced varieties.

Cheshire A hard cheese. Some types are red and mild-flavored; if these are allowed to ripen until blue veining appears the flavor becomes very rich. A white Cheshire cheese has a moderate flavor.

Derby Hard, close-textured, white cheese. If eaten young it is mild, but develops a stronger flavor with age. Sage Derby has sage leaves added to produce a green cheese.

Double Gloucester Hard, orange-colored cheese with a rather crumbly texture. The rich flavor is similar to that of mature Cheddar.

Lancashire Fairly hard cheese but crumbly when cut. Its mild flavor strengthens as the cheese matures.

Leicester Hard, orange-red colored cheese with a mild, slightly sweet flavor.

Stilton Semi-hard cheese made from rich milk with extra cream added. It is white with a blue veining caused by mold inoculated into the cheese (the same strain of mold as that used in Roquefort). Stilton is made in rounds about 12–14 inches across and 9–10 inches deep; the crust is dull and wrinkled but should not be cracked as this allows the cheese to dry out.

A milder, white Stilton is also available. Neither variety is suitable for cooking.

Wensleydale Another double cream cheese (i.e. made from rich milk with extra cream added). It is a mild, flaky cheese, white, and eaten young.

French Cheeses

Brie Soft farmhouse cheese made from whole milk. It is inoculated with a mold to give it its characteristic flavor and slightly reddish crust. The cheese itself is creamy-colored, soft, mild and rich; it is made in large flat rounds and sold in wedges. It does not keep, nor does it cook particularly well.

Camembert This is also a farmhouse cheese made from cow's milk and inoculated with mold. It is made in smaller, thicker rounds than Brie; it has the same reddish crust, although the taste is stronger and the texture slightly firmer. It should not look chalky inside, or have too strong a smell.

Demi-Sel Soft cream cheese, sold in square, foil-wrapped packs.

Fromage a la Creme Soft, fresh cream cheese.

Petit Suisse (Petit Gervais) Very mild, unsalted cream cheese sold in small, cylindrical packs. Petits Suisses are often used in sweet dishes with fruit, or served plain with sugar.

Pommel Unsalted double cream cheese, not unlike Petit Suisse.

Pont-l'Evêque Soft cheese that is salted repeatedly during maturing. Like Camembert, it should be eaten while it is still soft and not overripe. Made in small squares.

Port-Salut Semi-hard round cheese, creamy yellow in color and with a mild flavor. It should be eaten while still slightly soft.

Roquefort Made from ewe's milk layered with a culture of molded breadcrumbs. It is made only in the lambing season and only in the Roquefort district. The end result is a whitish, curd-like cheese, mottled with blue veins. The taste is sharp.

Swiss Cheeses

Emmenthal Also made in Italy and Austria, this hard, smooth-textured cheese has large 'eyes' or holes caused by the rapid fermentation of the curd. The color is a pale yellow, the flavor distinctive. Emmenthal cooks extremely well and is often used in conjunction with Parmesan to give the combination of a creamy texture and sharp flavor to a dish.

Gruyère Also made in the USA and France where it has large holes resembling Swiss Emmenthal, and in Italy. Although similar to Emmenthal, the 'eyes' are much smaller. The flavor is distinguishable if you have the two side by side, that of Gruyère being sharper.

Italian Cheeses

Bel Paese Rich, creamy cheese with a mild flavor.

Dolcelatte Very mild, creamier form of Gorgonzola.

Gorgonzola Semi-hard, blue-veined cheese with a sharp flavor.

Mozzarella Semi-soft cheese with a mild flavor that is excellent for cooking.

Parmesan The most famous of Italian cheeses, and the hardest of all. It is a pale straw color and is full of tiny pin-prick holes. As its flavor is very strong and characteristic, even when grated very finely, it is often used to add flavor to cooked dishes.
(**Pecorino** can be substituted for Parmesan.)

Ricotta Soft cheese with a mild flavor not unlike creamed cottage cheese, often used for savory and sweet fillings.

Dutch Cheeses

Edam Firm, smooth cheese with a mild flavor. The cheeses are made in a ball shape, deep yellow inside, and with a bright red skin on the outside. It cooks quite well.

Gouda This is both creamier and tastier than Edam, though a cut portion of Gouda might look much the same. The whole cheeses are larger and have a yellow skin. Some smaller cheeses are made for export.

Scandinavian Cheeses

Danish Blue White, crumbly cheese with blue veining produced by the introduction of a mold. The flavor is sharp and rather salty.

Havarti (Danish). Smooth, light yellow cheese with lots of large and small holes. Full-flavored. Sold in a foil package.

Jarlsberg The Scandinavian answer to the high price of Swiss cheeses. Jarlsberg resembles Gruyère and Emmenthal in flavor, though it is slightly milder; the texture is a little softer and there are large and small holes in the cheese.

Mycella (Danish). Mild cheese, pale yellow in color, with green veining.

Mysöst (Norwegian). Hard, dark brown goats' milk cheese. The flavor is slightly sweet but so strong that it is always eaten in very thin slivers.

Samso (Danish). A firm cheese with even-sized holes. The flavor is mild, sweet and slightly nut-like.

Vegetables Preserved and Fresh

Once you have mastered the art of preserving, you can serve your chutneys, vinegars and preserves with cold meats, roasts, cheese and savories all year round. Not only will the flavors be different and more delicious than commercially made preserves, but you will have kept more of the nutritional value.

Herb Vinegar

These are delicious for flavoring salads and for adding to dressings and sauces. Very few varieties are widely available in food stores, but at home you can experiment with all your favorite herbs. The recipes given in our section on herb vinegars use basil, mint, tarragon, rosemary, cloves and bay, along with various spices, but many variations are possible. Use good quality wine vinegars and pick the herbs just before the plants flower for this is when the leaves have the finest flavor. In some cases you can use dried herbs but the results will always be much better with fresh ones.

To make flavored vinegar you must steep the herbs in vinegar for days or weeks and then strain the mixture before use.While the herbs are being steeped, keep them in the dark. To do this you can either use an opaque jar such as an earthenware one, or dark glass; or you can wrap each jar in paper to exclude the light. A dark cupboard will also do so long as it is not being constantly opened. Once strained, the vinegar is best put into small bottles so that it is handy to use. If the flavor is too strong, you can dilute it with more vinegar before rebottling.

Pickled Vegetables

When pickling vegetables be sure always to select the best quality produce. It is worthless to try to preserve damaged food or that which is past its best; all vegetables should be firm and healthy, clean and dry. If the vegetables have to be washed or wiped, be sure always to dry them thoroughly before starting the preserving process.

For vegetables that have to be soaked in brine, use the best quality rock salt rather than free running table salt. The additives in table salt, which are what keep it fine grained and free running, while not harmful in any way do not give the best brine for pickling. Rock salt can be bought in crystal form or in blocks, which should be ground by rubbing on a grater or by cutting the block in half and rubbing the two halves together.

Again, the best quality vinegar should be used. Cheap brands may not contain sufficient acetic acid to preserve the vegetables. Wine vinegar has a delicate flavor that will not mask that of the vegetables, and white malt distilled vinegar can also be used quite successfully.

Chutney

Fresh, good quality vegetables, the best vinegar and careful mixing of spices will put you well on the way towards making a good chutney. The remainder of the story is in the cooking. Chutneys need to be cooked until all the ingredients are broken down and well blended and the liquid is evaporated to leave a thick purée. A heavy, wide preserving pan and slow, steady simmering, sometimes for several hours, are what will help you achieve good results. Stir the chutney from time to time as it cooks, to make sure it is not sticking to the bottom of the pan, and cook it slowly and carefully until it is the correct consistency. Like all pickles, it will then need a little time in the jar before it is sufficiently matured to make good eating.

General Rules

Pickling must always be carried out under the right conditions, to keep the food wholesome and safe to eat. Here are the important points to remember.

Vinegar is a highly corrosive liquid and will quickly eat into many metals, forming poisonous substances. Aluminum and stainless steel will resist corrosion from vinegar for the limited period a chutney might be in the pan; our recipes recommend an earthenware or enameled pan, but never use chipped enameled pans as the vinegar will quickly reach the steel or iron beneath. True pickle jar lids are coated with a special vinegar resistant substance, and only this type of screwtop should be used. If not available, use corks for narrow necked bottles or several thicknesses of wax paper tied firmly in place with string, for wide necked jars. Alternatively, you may be able to obtain a special parchment called 'pickling skin' which is slightly less porous than paper, and very useful if you do a lot of preserving.

Any type of jar can be used for chutney and most households have a stock of empty jam jars. However, these are not always suitable for vegetable pickles. For these you need really wide necked jars so that you can put in the whole vegetables or slices without breaking them. Special pickle jars can be bought; these are usually square, which makes storage more convenient.

All jars should be thoroughly washed and sterilized with boiling water before use. Never pour boiling chutney or vinegar into a cold jar as it will crack. Warm the jar first under the hot tap or in a low oven.

Vegetable, Salad and Preserving Recipes

Stuffed Artichokes

Ingredients: *8 medium-sized artichokes ·
juice of 1 lemon · 1 cup stock ·
2 tablespoons oil*

For the stuffing: *4 oz tongue or cooked ham,
diced · 4 oz mozzarella or Gruyère cheese,
diced · 4 tablespoons fresh white breadcrumbs,
fried in butter · 4 tablespoons grated Parmesan
cheese · 1 egg yolk · chopped parsley · salt ·
pepper · oil*

To garnish: *sprigs of watercress (optional)*

Remove the stems of the artichokes and the
outer leaves, and cut off the tips of the
remaining leaves. Put in water mixed with the
lemon juice (step 1). Prepare the stuffing:
mix the diced meat and cheese in a bowl with
the breadcrumbs, Parmesan, egg yolk, and
parsley, salt and pepper to taste, and enough
oil to obtain a smooth paste. Drain the artichokes well, and either remove the chokes, or
spread the leaves out carefully with the fingers.
Put the prepared stuffing into the centers of the
artichokes piling it up in the middle (step 2).
Press back into shape around the stuffing. Put
the artichokes in an ovenproof casserole
(step 3). Add the stock and the oil, cover, and
cook slowly in a moderate oven (350°F) for
about 1 hour, basting from time to time with
the cooking juices. To gratiné the artichokes,
uncover the casserole for the last few minutes
of cooking. Serve on a warm serving platter,
garnished with watercress, if liked.

Artichokes Argenteuil

Prepare and soak 8 medium-sized artichokes as for Stuffed Artichokes. Boil them in salted water for 25 minutes, then drain, cool and remove all the leaves and the choke from the center. Prepare and cook 1 lb asparagus (see p.432), and drain well. Meanwhile, prepare a béchamel sauce (see p.84) and add 2 tablespoons grated Gruyère cheese. Check for seasoning and add salt and pepper if necessary. Fill the artichoke hearts with the asparagus tips. Cover with the béchamel sauce and sprinkle with 1 tablespoon grated Gruyère cheese. Gratiné in a hot oven (400°F) for a few minutes and serve immediately in the cooking dish.

Artichokes alla Giudea

Prepare 8 medium-sized artichokes as left, and put them in water mixed with the juice of 1 lemon. Drain well, and spread out the leaves with the fingers. Sprinkle with salt and pepper. Put about $2\frac{1}{2}$ inches oil in a flameproof earthenware casserole or deep frying pan. Heat the oil – but do not let it smoke – and put in the artichokes upside down (the oil should come halfway up the artichokes). Cook on moderate heat, turning them over once after a few minutes, then turning more frequently for about 20 minutes. Return artichokes to original position, squeeze them delicately, and continue cooking on higher heat until they are well browned and crisp. Drain, and serve piping hot with lemon quarters.

Fried Artichokes

Discard the hard outer leaves of 4 artichokes, quarter them, and let stand for a few minutes in water and lemon juice. Drain them, dry, cover in beaten egg, then in breadcrumbs and fry them in hot oil until golden.

Artichokes Clamart

Ingredients: *8 medium-sized artichokes ·
juice of 1½ lemons · 2 tablespoons flour ·
1 teaspoon salt · 4 tablespoons butter or
margarine · 8 tablespoons fresh or frozen green
peas · 4 tablespoons tomato paste, or canned
peeled tomatoes, sieved · 2 oz cooked ham,
diced · 4 oz mozzarella cheese, diced*

Prepare the artichokes as for Stuffed Artichokes
(see p.426) and put in water mixed with the
juice of 1 lemon. Drain well and either
remove the choke or spread the leaves out
carefully with the fingers. Mix the flour with a
little cold water, add 1 quart cold water, pass
through a fine sieve into a pan, add the
remaining lemon juice, the salt, 2 tablespoons
butter or margarine and the prepared artichokes and cook until artichokes are *al dente*
(at least 25 minutes). Drain well, sauté lightly
in ¼ of the butter or margarine (step 1), remove
from heat and keep warm. Put the peas in a
pan of boiling salted water, and cook gently
until tender. Drain well, then sauté in remaining butter or margarine. Add the tomato paste
or canned tomatoes, and continue cooking for
5 minutes. Add the ham and continue cooking
for a further 5 minutes to reduce the sauce.
Remove from the heat, add the mozzarella
cheese (step 2), and spread the mixture in and
around the artichoke hearts (step 3). Cover,
and keep on low heat for a few minutes.

Artichokes Barigoule

Prepare and soak 8 medium-sized artichokes
as above, and cook for 10 minutes in 2 inches
of boiling salted water. Drain well. Remove the
choke from the center. Chop finely 4 oz onion,
4 oz carrots, 6 oz mushrooms, 6 oz lean salt
pork (previously soaked in cold water for 1
hour), and cook gently in 4 tablespoons
butter. Add 2 tablespoons tomato paste and
2 crushed cloves of garlic. Continue cooking for
a few more minutes, and season with salt and
pepper to taste. Fill the artichokes with the
mixture, wrap them in thin slices of pork fat,
tie them with string, and put them in an
ovenproof dish. Pour over 1 cup dry white
wine, and cook in a moderate oven (350°F)
for 1 hour, basting often. Remove the strings
and pork fat, arrange the artichokes on a
platter and pour over the cooking juices.

Artichoke Soufflé

Ingredients: *1 lb fresh artichokes · lemon juice · 2½ tablespoons butter · 4 tablespoons flour · 1 cup milk · 1 tablespoon grated Parmesan cheese · salt · nutmeg · 3 eggs · breadcrumbs*

Wash the artichokes, and cook in boiling salted water mixed with a little lemon juice for about 40 minutes. Drain, and work through a food mill (step 1), or sieve. Sauté for 5 minutes in the butter, add the flour, stirring constantly, and finally the milk, little by little (step 2). Continue cooking for about 15 minutes, remove from the heat, and blend in the Parmesan cheese, salt and nutmeg to taste. Pour into a bowl, let cool, then add the eggs, well beaten. Mix thoroughly for 10 minutes (step 3). Butter a soufflé dish (or a round mold) about 7 inches in diameter and 2½ inches deep, sprinkle it with breadcrumbs and pour in the artichoke mixture. Cook in a bain-marie in a moderate oven (350°F) for about 30 minutes until set. Unmold on a warm serving platter and serve immediately. If a golden crust is desired, put in a hot oven (425°F) for a few minutes before serving, and serve in the cooking dish. This soufflé is good eaten with meatballs in tomato sauce, which can be spooned around it on the serving platter.

430

Carrot Soufflé

Clean, wash, and cook 1 lb carrots for about 20 minutes in boiling salted water until tender. Drain, and work through a food mill or sieve. Sauté for 5 minutes in $2\frac{1}{2}$ tablespoons butter, then add 4 tablespoons flour, stirring constantly, and finally, little by little, 1 cup milk. Continue cooking for about 15 minutes. Remove from the heat, and blend in 1 tablespoon grated Parmesan cheese, salt and grated nutmeg to taste. Pour into a bowl and let cool. Add 3 whole eggs, well beaten, and mix thoroughly for 10 minutes. Butter a·soufflé dish (or a round mold) about 7 inches in diameter and $2\frac{1}{2}$ inches deep, sprinkle it with breadcrumbs, and pour in the carrot mixture. Cook in bain-marie in a moderate oven (350°F) for about 30 minutes until set, and unmold on a warm serving platter and serve immediately. The soufflé can be served in the cooking dish, after putting it in a hot oven (425°F) for a few minutes, so that a golden crust forms on the surface.

Chicory Soufflé

Melt $\frac{1}{4}$ cup butter in a frying pan. Add 2 tablespoons each finely chopped onion and bacon and fry until the onion is transparent. Drain the mixture in a sieve, then mix with 4 tablespoons diced cooked potato.

Melt another $\frac{1}{4}$ cup butter in a saucepan. Stir in 2 tablespoons flour and cook for 1 minute, then gradually stir in 1 cup milk. Bring to a boil, stirring, and simmer until thickened. Cool slightly. Separate 6 eggs and beat the yolks into the sauce. Mix in the vegetable mixture, 6 tablespoons chopped chicory and seasoning. Beat the egg whites until stiff and fold in. Pour into a greased 6-inch soufflé dish. Bake in a moderately hot oven (375°F) for 25–30 minutes. Serve immediately.

431

Asparagus au Gratin

Ingredients: *5 lb asparagus · salt · pepper ·*
½ cup butter · 1 glass dry white wine ·
4 oz cooked ham, cut into strips · 2
tablespoons grated Parmesan cheese

Trim the bottom off each stalk of asparagus to
make them all the same length, scrape the
white part, wash well and tie the stalks
together in small bundles. Cook for 15–20
minutes until tender in plenty of boiling salted
water, with the green tops out of the water,
and the pan partly covered. Drain and arrange
in an ovenproof dish (step 1). Sprinkle with
salt and pepper, add ¾ of the melted butter,
the wine (step 2), ham and Parmesan (step 3).
Dot with remaining butter. Put the asparagus
in a hot oven (400°F) to gratiné for about
10 minutes.

Asparagus Vinaigrette

Prepare and boil the asparagus as above, place
on a serving platter, sprinkle with chopped
parsley and serve with a vinaigrette dressing
(3 parts oil to 1 part vinegar or lemon juice,
salt and pepper to taste).

Asparagus with Eggs

Prepare and boil 5 lb asparagus as above. Leave
to dry on a napkin (they can be served either
hot or cold) then arrange on a serving platter
with the tips toward the center of the platter.
Mash 4 hard-boiled eggs with a fork, and mix
them with plenty of vinaigrette dressing (see
above). Pour over the tips of the asparagus.

Asparagus with Mousseline Sauce

Prepare and boil 5 lb asparagus as above.
Meanwhile, make the mousseline sauce: dilute
3 egg yolks in a little water in a small saucepan,
over very low heat. Beat gently with a wire
whip, gradually adding 1 cup butter in small
pieces, and from time to time 1 teaspoon cold
water to make the sauce lighter. When all the
butter has been absorbed, remove the sauce
from the heat, add 1 tablespoon lemon juice,
salt and white pepper to taste, and whip in 3
tablespoons heavy cream. Drain the asparagus
and serve with the mousseline sauce.

432

433

String Beans
with Tomato Sauce

Ingredients: *2 lb string beans · 1¼ lb tomatoes, preferably Italian plum type · 1 slice onion, chopped · 2 cloves of garlic · 2 sage leaves · ¼ cup butter or margarine · salt · pepper · stock*

To garnish: *fresh sage leaves (optional)*

Remove strings and tips of the beans, and wash in cold water. Cook, uncovered, in boiling salted water until tender (step 1); drain. Dip the tomatoes in boiling water, skin, seed and chop them. Brown the onion, garlic and sage leaves lightly in the butter or margarine (step 2). Remove them and discard. Add the string beans, sauté lightly, then add the tomatoes (step 3). Season with salt and pepper to taste, and continue cooking slowly for about 30 minutes, adding hot stock from time to time if necessary. Serve immediately, garnishing serving platter with fresh sage leaves, if liked.

String Beans Lyonnaise

Prepare and cook 2 lb string beans until tender, as left; drain. In a pan, brown lightly $\frac{1}{4}$ cup butter or margarine and $\frac{1}{2}$ lb onions, thinly sliced. Add the drained string beans, season with salt to taste and heat through.

String Beans with Poulette Sauce

Prepare and cook 2 lb string beans until tender, as left; drain. Melt in a pan 4 tablespoons butter or margarine, stir in 1 tablespoon flour, cook for 1–2 minutes, remove from the heat and add 1 cup boiling milk, stirring constantly, 2 egg yolks, and salt and pepper and chopped parsley to taste. Return to the heat, add the beans, mix well, cook until sauce is thick and beans are heated through and well coated.

Spanish String Beans

Prepare 2 lb string beans for cooking as left. In a pan, brown $\frac{1}{4}$ cup butter or margarine with 1 onion, 1 green pepper and 1 garlic clove, all chopped. Add $\frac{3}{4}$ cup canned peeled tomatoes worked through a sieve, or a few tablespoons tomato paste diluted in water. Continue cooking for a few minutes, then add the string beans, 6 oz prosciutto or cooked ham cut into strips or diced, and salt and pepper to taste. Cover, and cook slowly until beans are tender, adding stock from time to time if necessary. Transfer to a warm serving platter and garnish the edges of the platter with hard-boiled egg wedges decorated with tiny strips of black olive.

String Beans with Almonds

Prepare and cook 2 lb string beans until tender, as left. Meanwhile, roast 2 oz almonds, peeled, in the oven. When the beans are cooked, melt 4 tablespoons butter or margarine in a pan, add the drained beans, the almonds, and salt and pepper to taste. Sauté over high heat. Sprinkle with lemon juice.

435

Beet Salad with Onions

Ingredients: *2 medium-sized beets, cooked ·*
2 medium-sized onions · marjoram ·
¼ clove of garlic, chopped

For the vinaigrette dressing: *oil · vinegar ·*
salt · pepper · mustard (optional)

Peel the beets and the onions, cut the beets
into thin slices and the onions into rings
(steps 1 and 2). Toss in a generous amount of
vinaigrette dressing (see p.501), and arrange
decoratively in a salad bowl with a pinch of
marjoram and the garlic (step 3). Alternatively,
this salad can be made with cooked onions —
bake them, unpeeled, in a moderately hot
oven (375°F) for 1½ hours then use as raw
onion above. omitting marjoram and garlic.

Sour Beets

Peel and cut into very thin slices 2 medium-
sized cooked beets. Put in a flameproof dish,
and sprinkle with salt and pepper. Add ½ pint
sour cream, or heavy cream seasoned a few
hours before with lemon juice. Put the dish in a
hot oven (400°F), or on top of the stove on
moderate heat, until the cream begins to boil
and thicken. Serve immediately.

Sweet-and-Sour Beets

Peel and dice 2 medium-sized cooked beets.
Sauté lightly in melted butter. Add 1 teaspoon
sugar and 2 tablespoons vinegar. Continue
cooking for a few minutes. Serve immediately.

Beets à l'Anglaise

Blanch 4 small cooked beets in boiling water
for a few minutes. Drain and peel. Cut into
thick slices and serve with fresh butter.

Stuffed Beets

Peel and halve lengthwise 4 or more small
cooked beets, and remove part of the flesh in
the center. Fill with Russian, chicken or fish
salad mixed with mayonnaise (commercially
prepared or homemade). Arrange the beets on a
serving platter and garnish with lettuce leaves
tossed in vinaigrette dressing. Keep in a
refrigerator or cool place before serving.

Glazed Beets

Peel and slice 2 medium-sized cooked beets. Put in a buttered ovenproof dish alternating layers of beets, béchamel sauce (see p.84) and 1 tablespoon sugar, and continue to cook for a few more minutes, shaking the pan from time to time to ensure that beets are evenly glazed. Serve immediately.

Beets au Gratin

Peel and slice 2 medium-sized cooked beets. Put in a buttered ovenproof dish alternating layers of beets, béchamel sauce (see p.33) and grated Parmesan cheese. Finish with a layer of béchamel and Parmesan, and dot with butter. Put in moderate oven (350°F) for 15–20 minutes, or until golden.

437

Broccoli Niçoise

Ingredients: *2–3 lb broccoli · oil · 1 onion, thinly sliced · 4 oz black olives, pitted and sliced · 8 anchovy fillets, desalted by soaking in a little milk · 3 oz Gruyère cheese, grated · salt · pepper · 1 cup good red wine, preferably Burgundy type*

Wash the broccoli and cut into flowerets (step 1). Put $\frac{1}{4}$ of the broccoli in a flameproof casserole (preferably earthenware) with 1 tablespoon oil, $\frac{1}{2}$ the onion, a few slices of olive, and a few pieces of anchovy. Add another layer of broccoli to the casserole and sprinkle generously with $\frac{1}{2}$ the grated cheese (step 2). Add another tablespoon oil and salt and pepper to taste. Repeat layers once more, then pour over the wine (step 3). Cover, and cook very slowly on top of the stove or in a moderate oven (350°F) for 1 hour, or until the broccoli is tender and has absorbed most of the cooking juices. Serve in the cooking dish.

Golden Broccoli

Wash 2 lb broccoli and cut into flowerets. Cover with boiling salted water and cook gently until *al dente*. Drain, rinse in cold water, put on a paper napkin to dry, then roll in flour, and dip in egg beaten with a little salt and pepper. Fry a few at a time in very hot deep oil until golden. Lift out of the oil with a slotted spoon, drain on a paper napkin, and serve on a warm serving platter garnished with parsley and lemon quarters.

Broccoli Pudding

Wash 3 lb broccoli and cut into flowerets. Peel and slice 1 lb potatoes and 1 large onion. Peel 1 lb tomatoes and chop roughly. Put a few tablespoons olive oil in the bottom of a flameproof dish (preferably earthenware) and add onion, potatoes, broccoli and tomatoes in layers, ending with a layer of tomatoes. Spoon oil over top of vegetables, sprinkle with salt and pepper. Add 1 glass water, cover, and cook slowly on top of stove or in a moderate oven (350°F) for about 1 hour, or until vegetables are tender. Shake the dish from time to time during cooking. Serve immediately in the cooking dish.

Broccoli with Ham

Wash 2 lb broccoli and divide into spears. Cook in boiling salted water until *al dente*. Drain, place in a serving dish and keep hot.

Heat $\frac{1}{4}$ cup butter in a frying pan, add 2 onions, peeled and chopped, and fry until transparent. Stir in 1 cup diced cooked ham and pepper and grated nutmeg to taste. Heat through, stirring, then pile on top of the broccoli. Serve immediately.

Brussels Sprouts
with Bacon

Ingredients: *2 lb fresh or frozen Brussels sprouts · juice of ½ lemon · 4 slices smoked bacon, rind and bones removed · 2 tablespoons butter or margarine · salt · pepper · 1 teaspoon chopped parsley*

Prepare the Brussels sprouts for cooking, putting them at once in cold water mixed with the lemon juice. Cook them in plenty of boiling salted water for about 20 minutes until they are *al dente*. Drain (step 1). Cut the bacon into strips (step 2). Brown the butter or margarine in a skillet, add the bacon and, when the bacon is crisp, add the sprouts (step 3). Season with salt and pepper to taste, and cook slowly until sprouts are heated through and coated in the cooking fat. Transfer to a warm serving platter, sprinkle with chopped parsley and serve immediately.

Brussels Sprouts with Chestnuts

Peel 1 lb chestnuts, put in cold salted water with 1 bay leaf, bring to a boil and cook for about $\frac{3}{4}$ hour. Meanwhile, prepare and cook 2 lb fresh or frozen Brussels sprouts as left. In a pan melt 4 tablespoons butter or margarine, add the cooked chestnuts and sprouts, both well drained, and cook and serve as left.

Sautéed Brussels Sprouts

Prepare for cooking 2 lb fresh or frozen Brussels sprouts as left. Cook in plenty of boiling salted water, with 1 onion, sliced, 1 bay leaf and 2 cloves for about 20 minutes until they are *al dente*. Drain the sprouts (discarding onion, bay leaf and cloves), brown them lightly in $\frac{1}{4}$ cup butter or margarine, and serve immediately.

Fried Brussels Sprouts

Prepare for cooking $1\frac{1}{2}$ lb fresh or frozen Brussels sprouts as left. Cook in plenty of boiling salted water for 10 minutes. Drain, roll in flour, then in egg beaten with salt, and then in breadcrumbs. Fry in hot deep oil until golden, lift them out with a slotted spoon, and drain them. Serve with lemon wedges.

Creamed Brussels Sprouts

Prepare and cook 2 lb fresh or frozen Brussels sprouts as left. Drain and sauté lightly in $\frac{1}{4}$ cup butter or margarine, melted. Add 1 cup light cream, 2–3 tablespoons grated Parmesan cheese, salt and grated nutmeg to taste. Cook on moderate heat, stirring constantly with a wooden spoon, until the sauce has thickened.

441

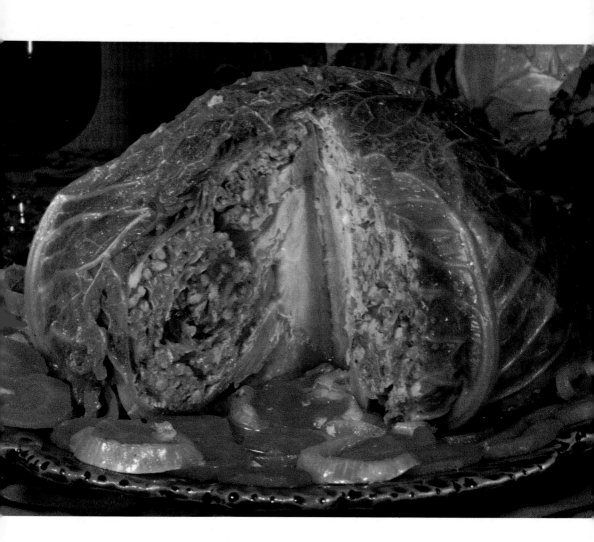

Stuffed Cabbage

Ingredients: *1 large green cabbage · 4 quarts boiling water · ¼ cup butter · 1 tablespoon olive oil · 2 carrots, peeled and thinly sliced · 2 onions, peeled and thinly sliced · 1 bay leaf · ¼ cup hot stock*

For the stuffing: *½ onion, chopped · 2 tablespoons chopped parsley · 2 tablespoons butter or margarine · 1 lb ground beef or veal · 4 oz ground pork loin · 4 oz rice · 1 egg, lightly beaten · 1 teaspoon Worcestershire (optional) · salt · pepper · 1 pinch mixed herbs · 8 tablespoons hot stock*

Discard the outer leaves of the cabbage, and wash the cabbage under cold running water. Put in a large pan, add the boiling water, let stand for 5 minutes, then drain. Prepare the stuffing: brown the onion and parsley lightly in the butter or margarine. Put the mixture in a bowl, add the meat, rice, egg, Worcestershire (if using), salt and pepper to taste, herbs and the hot stock. Mix well. Trim the bottom part of the cabbage so that it will stand upright. On a wooden board arrange crosswise 2 lengths of string, stand the cabbage upright over the string and spread out the leaves (step 1). Insert the prepared stuffing between the leaves (step 2). Close the leaves, and tie the cabbage with the string (step 3). In a large casserole, melt the butter with the oil, and arrange the carrots and onions in the bottom. Stand the cabbage in the casserole, add the stock and the bay leaf, cover, and cook over moderate heat for about 2 hours until cabbage is tender and cooked through, adding more stock if necessary. When cooked, place the cabbage on a warm serving platter, remove the string, and garnish with the carrots and onions. Serves 6.

Braised Cabbage

Slice $1\frac{1}{2}$ lb carrots and $\frac{1}{2}$ lb onions. Crush 3 cloves of garlic. Peel and seed 1 tomato. Cut into strips 6 oz fresh pork rind. Melt in a large, heavy pan $\frac{1}{4}$ cup lard, add the carrots, onions, garlic, tomato, and pork rind. Brown quickly. Meanwhile, blanch 1 medium-sized white cabbage, by plunging into boiling salted water for 1 minute then draining and refreshing under cold running water. (If green cabbage is used, blanching is not necessary.) Put the cabbage in the pan with 1 cup dry white wine and 1 bouquet garni. Season with salt and pepper to taste, add a little water, and bring to a boil. Cover the pan and put in a low oven (300°F) for about 2 hours until the cabbage is tender.

Dutch Baked Cabbage

Discard the outer leaves of a large head of white cabbage and cut out the core. Stand the cabbage upright in a saucepan, pour over 1 cup each hot stock and water and add a bay leaf, garlic clove and onion spiked with 2 cloves. Season with salt and pepper. Bring to a boil, then cover and simmer for 10 minutes. Lift out the cabbage and cut into wedges. Place the wedges in a greased baking dish. Strain the cooking liquid and reserve 1 cup. Melt $\frac{1}{4}$ cup butter in a saucepan. Add 2 tablespoons flour and 1 teaspoon curry powder and cook for 1 minute, then gradually stir in the reserved cooking liquid. Bring to a boil, stirring, and simmer until thickened. Stir in 1 cup light cream, and adjust the seasoning. Pour the sauce on the cabbage and sprinkle with 2 tablespoons ground hazelnuts. Bake in a hot oven (425°F) for 15 minutes.

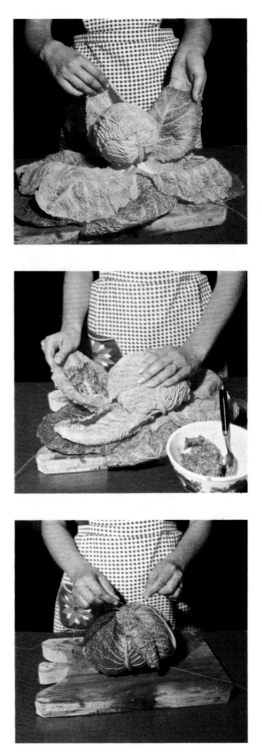

443

Creamed Carrots

Ingredients: *2 lb carrots · 1 cup hot water ·
salt · 2 tablespoons butter or margarine ·
2 egg yolks · ½ cup light cream ·
1 tablespoon chopped parsley*

To garnish: *sprigs of parsley*

Scrape and wash the carrots; leave them
whole if they are young and small, or slice
them if they are large. Place in a pan, add the
hot water (step 1), a pinch of salt, and ½ the

butter or margarine (step 2), and cook,
covered, for about ½ hour, or until tender.
Stir from time to time, and take care that the
cooking liquid is not completely absorbed.
When the carrots are tender, remove from the
heat, add the egg yolks mixed with the cream,
remaining butter or margarine (melted) and
the chopped parsley (step 3). Return to heat
and continue cooking very gently until the
cream has thickened – do not let it boil. Serve
immediately garnished with sprigs of parsley.

Carrots Vichy

Prepare 2 lb carrots as left. Put in a pan with 1 quart water, 4 tablespoons butter or margarine, a pinch of salt and 3 lumps sugar. Boil, uncovered, until all the water has evaporated and the butter begins to fry. Sprinkle with chopped parsley and serve.

Sautéed Carrots

Prepare 2 lb carrots as left and put in cold salted water to cover. Bring to a boil and continue cooking for about ½ hour or until tender. Drain, leave to cool slightly, then cut into thin slices. Sauté in ¼ cup butter or margarine. Season with salt to taste, sprinkle with vinegar, boil to evaporate, and serve.

Glazed Carrots

Prepare 2 lb carrots as left. Put in a pan, cover with cold water, cover the pan, and cook until they are tender, or the water is absorbed. Add 1 pinch salt, ¼ cup butter or margarine, 2 tablespoons honey or sugar, and continue cooking, uncovered, stirring from time to time, until the carrots are golden. (If liked, sprinkle with 1 teaspoon vinegar.)

Purée Crécy

Scrape and wash 1½ lb carrots. Put in cold water and bring to a boil. After 15 minutes, add ½ lb potatoes, peeled. When carrots and potatoes are tender, drain, and pass through a fine sieve. Add ½ cup butter or margarine and ½ cup light cream. Mix well, check the seasoning, and serve with roasts.

Carrots in Batter

Scrape and wash 1 lb carrots, then cut them in half crosswise. Place 2 tablespoons butter and 1 cup water in a saucepan and bring to a boil. Add the carrots and ¼ teaspoon salt and simmer for 20 minutes. Meanwhile, make a batter from 1 cup flour, ¼ teaspoon salt, ½ cup milk and 2 eggs. Drain the carrots and pat dry. Coat with flour, then dip in the batter. Fry in deep fat for 3 minutes or until golden. Drain and serve hot.

Cauliflower Gourmet

Ingredients: *1 medium-sized cauliflower ·
salt · 1 slice lemon · 1 slice bread · 6 eggs ·
5 slices Emmenthal cheese · grated Parmesan
cheese · ½ cup butter or margarine, melted*

Remove the large outer leaves of the cauliflower and trim the stalk (step 1). Wash
thoroughly. Cook in boiling salted water,
together with the lemon and bread (to
eliminate the cooking smell) until *al dente*
(about 15 minutes) and drain. Meanwhile,
prepare 3 frittatas (flat, Italian-style omelets,
cooked on both sides), each using 2 eggs and
about 6 inches in diameter, according to the
size of the cauliflower. Arrange the 3 frittatas
on an ovenproof serving platter one on top
of the other, with 2½ slices of Emmenthal
between the first and second frittata and
between the second and third (step 2). Place
the cauliflower on top, sprinkle with grated
Parmesan, pour the butter or margarine over
(step 3), and put in a hot oven (425°F) for
about 10 minutes to gratiné.

Cauliflower au Gratin

Remove the hard outer leaves of a medium-sized cauliflower, keeping the more tender ones, trim the stalk and wash thoroughly. Cook until *al dente* as left. Drain, leave until lukewarm, then divide into flowerets and leave to dry on a clean napkin. Prepare a béchamel sauce (see p.84). Add 1 tablespoon grated Parmesan cheese. Arrange the cauliflower flowerets in a buttered ovenproof dish, pour the béchamel sauce over, sprinkle with a mixture of equal quantities of grated Parmesan cheese and breadcrumbs, pour over melted butter and gratiné as above.

Paupiettes of Cauliflower and Ham

Prepare and cook 1 medium-sized cauliflower as left. Drain, leave until lukewarm then divide into flowerets, and leave to dry on a clean napkin. Wrap each floweret in a small slice of cooked ham or prosciutto, securing with a toothpick or skewer if necessary. Dip in beaten egg and roll in breadcrumbs. Let stand in a refrigerator or cool place for ½ hour, then brown and cook in golden butter or hot oil. Drain well (remove toothpick or skewer if used) and serve piping hot. You can also deep fry the flowerets, after dipping them in batter (see Cardoon Fritters, p.449)

Cauliflower with Piquant Sauce

Prepare and cook 1 medium-sized cauliflower as left. Meanwhile, prepare the piquant sauce: brown ½ cup butter lightly in a small pan, remove from the heat, blend in 8 anchovy fillets, desalted by soaking in cold milk, and mashed, return to heat, add ½ tablespoon chopped parsley and mix well. When the cauliflower is *al dente*, drain and arrange on a warm serving platter, pour the sauce over, sprinkle with the juice of ½ lemon, and serve immediately.

447

Cardoon au Gratin

Ingredients: *1 large cardoon · 1 lemon ·
2 tablespoons flour · 1 quart cold water ·
salt · 3 tablespoons butter or margarine ·
grated Parmesan cheese · 2 glasses milk; or
1 glass milk and 1 glass light cream · pepper*

Remove the coarse ribs of the cardoon, split
and cut stalks into 2-inch pieces. Remove the
tough part of the core and slice it. Rub with $\frac{1}{2}$
the lemon (step 1). Cook the cardoon pieces
in the flour, water, juice of remaining $\frac{1}{2}$ lemon,
1 teaspoon salt and $\frac{1}{2}$ the butter or margarine
(step 2), on a very low heat for about $1-1\frac{1}{2}$
hours, stirring often. Drain well, arrange in
layers in a buttered ovenproof dish, alternating
with grated Parmesan cheese (step 3). Add the
milk, or milk and cream, sprinkle with grated
Parmesan, and salt and pepper to taste and
dot with remaining butter or margarine.
Put in a moderate oven (350°F) for $\frac{1}{2}$ hour, or
until golden and all the cooking liquid has
evaporated. Serve hot in the cooking dish.

Cardoon Bolognese

Prepare 1 large cardoon as left and cook it in the water and flour mixture until tender. Meanwhile, prepare a Bolognese or tomato sauce (see p.88). Drain cardoon, dry well, and dip in egg beaten with a little salt, then in flour. Fry in very hot deep oil. Arrange in a buttered ovenproof dish layers of cardoon, Bolognese sauce, grated Parmesan cheese and pieces of butter, ending with a layer of cheese and butter. Put in a hot oven (425°F) for 20–25 minutes, or until a golden crust forms on the surface.

Cardoon Fritters

Prepare a batter: mix 1 whole egg and 2 egg yolks with $\frac{3}{4}$ cup flour, 1 cup beer and 1 tablespoon oil. Season with salt and pepper to taste, and let stand for 2 hours. Meanwhile, prepare 1 large cardoon as above and put in water mixed with lemon juice. Cook for about $1\frac{1}{2}$ hours in boiling salted water. Add 2 egg whites whipped until stiff to the batter and chopped parsley to taste. Dip the cardoon sticks into the batter and fry them in deep hot oil until golden. Drain on absorbent paper.

Cardoon with Hollandaise Sauce

Prepare and cook a $2\frac{1}{2}$-lb cardoon until tender, as left; drain well. Arrange on a platter, and serve with Hollandaise sauce (see p.86).

Celery in Yogurt Sauce

Prepare and cook 2 lb celery until tender, as left. Drain well, reserving 1 cup of the cooking liquid. Melt 1 tablespoon butter in a saucepan, stir in 1 tablespoon flour and cook for 1 minute. Gradually stir in the reserved cooking liquid. Bring to a boil, stirring, and simmer until thickened. Stir in $\frac{1}{2}$ cup each plain yogurt and sour cream and season with grated nutmeg, salt and pepper. Heat through, then pour this sauce over the celery and serve.

449

Braised Celery Hearts

Ingredients: *2–3 white celery hearts ·*
1 onion, sliced · 1 small carrot, sliced ·
¼ cup beef marrow, sliced · ¼ bay leaf · stock ·
1 tablespoon butter · 1 tablespoon flour · salt ·
pepper

Trim off all leaves and coarse stalks from the
celery (step 1). Wash and halve if small.
Blanch for 5 minutes in boiling salted water
and drain. Place a layer of sliced onion and
carrot at the bottom of a flameproof casserole,
put in the celery hearts (step 2), the marrow,
the bay leaf, and cover with stock. Bring to a
boil on top of the stove, then cover the
casserole and put in a moderate oven (350°F)
for 1 hour, or until celery is tender. Drain the
celery and put it in a buttered ovenproof dish.
Reduce the cooking juices left in the casserole
to 8–10 tablespoons, remove the bay leaf,
add the butter mixed with the flour, season
with salt and pepper to taste, and, as soon as
the sauce has thickened, pour it over the
celery (step 3). Put in a hot oven (425°F) for a
few minutes to gratiné.

Celeriac à la Française

Peel 2 large celeriac, dice them and put in cold
water mixed with a little lemon juice. Drain,
dry and sauté for 5 minutes in 1 tablespoon
butter or margarine. Cover with stock, cover
the pan and cook until celeriac is tender and
the juices have reduced. Blend in 1 hard-boiled
egg yolk, worked through a sieve, 1 teaspoon
chopped capers, and, little by little, 1 tablespoon butter mixed with 1 tablespoon flour.
Stir carefully so that all the ingredients are
thoroughly blended, and keep over low heat
until a thick sauce is obtained. Check seasoning
and pour onto a warm serving platter.

Purée of Celeriac and Potato

Peel and quarter 1 large celeriac and ¾ lb
potatoes. Put in cold salted water, bring to a
boil, and cook for about 20 minutes or until
tender. Drain, work through a food mill or
sieve (or purée in a blender). Put back over
low heat, stirring constantly with a wooden
spoon, season with salt and pepper to taste, add
½ cup butter and ½ cup cream. Serve in a warm
vegetable dish, garnished with croûtons.

Eggplants Anna

Ingredients: *4–8 round eggplants, according to size · cloves of garlic, thinly sliced · 3 oz pecorino or Gruyère cheese, thinly sliced · basil leaves · salt*

For the tomato sauce: 1 slice onion, chopped · ½ cup olive oil · 1¼ lb fresh ripe tomatoes, peeled, seeded and quartered · 2 basil leaves · salt · pepper

Remove and discard the stems of the eggplants, wash and dry. Make 3–4 lengthwise incisions in each eggplant (step 1). Insert into each incision 1 slice each of garlic and cheese, and 2 basil leaves rolled in salt (step 2). To make the sauce: brown the onion in the oil, add the tomatoes, basil, and salt and pepper to taste. Bring to a boil, add the eggplants (step 3), cover and cook slowly for about 1 hour, adding stock if necessary. Transfer eggplants to a serving platter and spoon sauce over.

Eggplants with Cheese

Peel 4–8 eggplants, according to size, slice them lengthwise, sprinkle with salt, leave for $\frac{1}{2}$ hour, then pass under cold running water, drain and dry. Brown on both sides, a few at a time, in hot oil; drain. Arrange the slices in a buttered ovenproof dish, alternating layers of eggplant with slices of Emmenthal cheese, a few basil leaves (optional), and freshly ground pepper to taste. Finish with a layer of eggplant, and sprinkle with breadcrumbs and melted butter. Put in a moderate oven (350°F), and cook for 25–30 minutes, or until the eggplant is tender and the cheese has melted. Serve in the cooking dish. For an even richer dish, put a few tablespoons béchamel sauce between each layer of eggplant and cheese.

Fried Eggplants

Prepare 4–8 eggplants for cooking as for Eggplants with Cheese, roll in flour, and fry on both sides, a few at a time, in hot oil. Drain and serve immediately.

Eggplants à la Turque

Prepare 4–8 eggplants for cooking as for Eggplants with Cheese, but do not peel them. Roll in flour, and fry on both sides, a few at a time, in hot oil. Drain, sprinkle with salt, and keep warm in a serving platter. Sauté lightly 2 oz onion, chopped, in a little of the oil in which the eggplants have been fried. Add 3 cloves of garlic, crushed, 3 tomatoes, peeled and chopped, 1 bay leaf, and salt, pepper, and thyme to taste. Cook slowly for 35 minutes. Add a pinch of cayenne pepper, stir, and pour over the eggplants. Serve hot or cold.

Sicilian Eggplants

Ingredients: *4–8 eggplants, according to size ·
oil · ¼ cup grated Parmesan cheese · basil
leaves, finely chopped · 1 mozzarella cheese,
sliced · 2 tablespoons breadcrumbs*

For the tomato sauce: *1½ lb ripe Italian
tomatoes, peeled, seeded and chopped, or canned
peeled tomatoes, chopped · 1 slice onion,
chopped · 1 clove of garlic, crushed ·
2 tablespoons oil · 3 basil leaves   salt · pepper*

Prepare the tomato sauce: brown the onion
and garlic lightly in the oil. Add the tomatoes,
basil leaves, salt and pepper to taste, and cook
for 30–35 minutes. Work through a sieve.
Peel the eggplants, slice them lengthwise, and
let stand for ½ hour in cold salted water. Drain,
dry thoroughly, and brown on both sides, a
few at a time, in hot oil (step 1). Drain, arrange
a layer of half the eggplants in a greased
ovenproof dish, sprinkle with half the grated
Parmesan cheese, basil leaves to taste, and a
layer of half the mozzarella cheese. Cover with
half the tomato sauce (step 2). Repeat these
layers with remaining ingredients (step 3) and
top with breadcrumbs. Cook in a hot oven
(400°F) for ½ hour. Serve hot or cold.

454

Eggplants Turinois

Prepare 4–8 eggplants for cooking as for Eggplants with Cheese (p.453). Cut 4 cooked
ham slices and 8 Emmenthal cheese slices to
the same size as the eggplant slices. Put 1 slice
ham and 1 slice cheese between 2 slices eggplant, pressing firmly to make them adhere.
Roll in flour, dip in 2 eggs beaten with 3
tablespoons milk and a little salt, and fry
immediately on both sides, a few at a time, in
hot oil. Lift with a slotted spoon, put on paper
napkins, and serve piping hot, with a tomato
sauce in a separate dish.

Stuffed Eggplants

Halve 4–8 eggplants (according to size)
lengthwise. Make criss-cross incisions into the
flesh. Sprinkle with salt. Fry, cut side down, in
hot oil. Lift with a slotted spoon, remove most
of the flesh with a teaspoon (reserving skins),
chop it and mix with 10 oz lean salt pork
(previously soaked in cold water for 1 hour),
2 oz onion, 2 cloves of garlic, parsley to taste,
all finely chopped, and 2 tablespoons breadcrumbs and 1 tablespoon tomato paste.
Blend well, season with salt and pepper to
taste, and stuff the eggplant skins with this
mixture. Brush with olive oil, put in a
generously buttered ovenproof dish and bake
in a hot oven (400°F) for about $\frac{1}{2}$ hour.

Eggplants Provencal

Prepare 4–8 eggplants for cooking as for
Eggplants with Cheese (p.453). Roll in flour, and
fry on both sides, a few at a time, in hot
oil with a mixture (to taste) of garlic and
parsley, chopped; drain. Season with salt and
pepper to taste and serve immediately.

Fennel au Gratin

Ingredients: *4–8 fennel, according to size*
¼ cup butter or margarine · 2 tablespoons
grated Parmesan cheese

For the béchamel sauce: *¼ cup butter or*
margarine · 3 tablespoons flour · 1 pint milk ·
salt · grated nutmeg · 1 tablespoon grated
Parmesan cheese, 1 egg yolk, and 2 oz cooked
ham, cut into strips or diced (optional)

Clean and quarter the fennel (step 1) and
parboil it. Drain, and sauté in half the butter
or margarine. Prepare the béchamel sauce:
melt the butter or margarine in a pan, stir in
the flour, cook for 1–2 minutes, remove from

the heat and add the cold milk gradually,
stirring constantly. Return to the heat and
cook for 10 minutes. Remove from the heat,
add salt and grated nutmeg to taste, the
Parmesan cheese, egg yolk, and ham if using.
In a buttered ovenproof dish, arrange the
fennel and béchamel sauce in layers (step 2),
the fennel with its curved part uppermost.
Finish with a light layer of béchamel sauce
(step 3), sprinkle with grated Parmesan
cheese, dot with remaining butter or margarine, and put in a hot oven (425°F) for
20–25 minutes, or until a golden crust has
formed on the top. Serve immediately in the
cooking dish.

Lima Beans with Salt Pork

Prepare for cooking 2 lb fresh Lima beans —
or use frozen beans. In a pan, brown $\frac{1}{4}$ cup
lard together with 6 oz salt pork (previously
soaked in cold water and cut into slices) and
1 slice of onion, chopped. Add the beans, $\frac{1}{4}$ cup
stock, salt and pepper to taste and cook over
high heat for about 35 minutes or until
tender. Serve piping hot in a warm vegetable
dish.

Greek Lima Beans

Prepare for cooking 2 lb fresh Lima beans —
or use frozen beans. In a pan, brown 1 onion,
chopped, with 4 tablespoons oil. Add 1 fennel,
cut into strips, sauté for a few minutes, then
add the Lima beans. Add $\frac{1}{4}$ cup stock, season
with salt to taste and cook slowly for about
35 minutes until all the liquid is absorbed and

Sicilian Lima Beans

Shell $\frac{3}{4}$ lb each fresh lima beans and peas. Heat 2
tablespoons oil in a saucepan, add 1 small onion,
peeled and chopped, and fry until transparent.
Add the beans, peas, 4 tablespoons water or
stock, a pinch of grated nutmeg and seasoning.
Bring to a boil, then cover and simmer for 30
minutes.

Drain 4 canned artichoke hearts and cut each
into 8. Add to the pan and continue cooking for
10 minutes. Stir in 2 tablespoons coarsely chopped fresh mint and cook for 5 minutes longer.
Cool slightly before serving.

To serve the dish cold, add $\frac{1}{2}$ teaspoon sugar
and 2 teaspoons vinegar with the mint. Chill for
15 minutes before serving.

Jerusalem Artichoke Fritters

Ingredients: *1½ lb Jerusalem artichokes*

For the batter: *4 tablespoons flour · salt · 3 tablespoons dry white wine · 1 tablespoon butter or margarine, melted · 1 or 2 egg whites*

To garnish: *sprigs of parsley*

Prepare the batter: in a bowl, sieve the flour and the salt, and stir in the white wine and the butter or margarine. Let stand for 1 hour.

Meanwhile, scrape the Jerusalem artichokes, wash them, and cook for about 15 minutes in boiling salted water until tender. Drain, let cool, then cut into ¼-inch slices (step 1). Whip the egg whites until stiff then fold into the batter. Dip the artichokes, a few at a time, into the batter (step 2), and fry them in hot oil (step 3). Lift them out with a slotted spoon when golden, drain on absorbent paper, and serve immediately in a warm vegetable dish garnished with sprigs of parsley.

Jerusalem Artichokes Provençal

Scrape, wash and slice $1\frac{1}{2}$ lb Jerusalem artichokes. Heat $\frac{1}{2}$ cup olive oil in a skillet. Add the Jerusalem artichokes and sauté until tender. Season with salt and pepper to taste. A few minutes before serving, add a persillade of chopped parsley and 4 cloves of garlic and mix well.

Purée of Jerusalem Artichokes

Scrape and wash $1\frac{1}{2}$ lb Jerusalem artichokes. Cook in boiling salted water, together with $\frac{1}{2}$ lb potatoes, peeled and washed, for about 15 minutes until both are tender. Drain well and work through a food mill or sieve (or purée in a blender). Put the purée over the heat, and let it dry, stirring constantly. Add $\frac{1}{2}$ cup butter, season with salt to taste, and add 1 cup light cream. Stir. Serve in a warm vegetable dish, garnished with croûtons fried in butter.

Barquettes of Cucumber

Halve two large cucumbers lengthwise, then cut each piece in half across. Carefully remove the seeds and flesh with a teaspoon without damaging the shell. Dice the flesh. Put in a pan with $\frac{1}{4}$ cup butter, paprika and salt to taste. Cover with water, and cook until all the water has evaporated. Add 1 cup light cream. Stir well.

Meanwhile blanch the barquettes in boiling salted water. Drain, fill with the diced flesh, and serve immediately.

Creamed Cucumbers

Pare 2 cucumbers – about $1\frac{1}{2}$ lb – in the shape of large olives. Put in a pan with $\frac{1}{4}$ cup butter and a pinch of salt, and cover with water. Cook uncovered until all the water has evaporated. Add 1 cup light cream, continue cooking for a few more minutes, and serve immediately.

Leeks with Prosciutto

Ingredients: *2 lb large leeks · $\frac{1}{4}$ cup sliced prosciutto or cooked ham · grated Parmesan cheese · $\frac{1}{2}$ cup butter or margarine, melted · salt · pepper*

Remove and discard the green part of the leeks (step 1), peel off the thin skin of the white part, and pare the bottoms. Wash thoroughly and cook in boiling salted water for 15–20 minutes until tender. Drain, leave to dry on a napkin, then wrap 2–3 leeks – according to size – in a slice of prosciutto (step 2). Arrange in a buttered ovenproof dish, sprinkle with grated Parmesan cheese, salt and pepper to taste, brush with melted butter or margarine (step 3), and put in a moderate oven (350°F) to gratiné. Serve in the cooking dish.

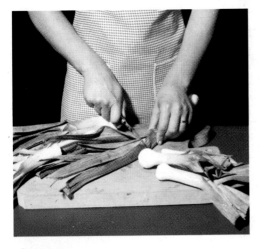

Braised Leeks

Prepare 2 lb leeks as for Leeks with Prosciutto left. Dry thoroughly. Arrange in a buttered ovenproof dish. Cover with a mixture of finely chopped celery, carrot and onion to taste. Add 1 bay leaf, sprinkle with salt and pepper, and cover with stock. Cover the dish, and cook in a moderate oven (350°F) for 40–45 minutes, or until the leeks are tender and all the cooking liquid has been absorbed. Serve the dish as it is or add 2 whole eggs beaten with $\frac{1}{2}$ cup milk and a pinch of salt and return to the oven for a few minutes.

Leeks Vinaigrette

Prepare 2 lb leeks as for Leeks with Prosciutto left, taking care to cut all the leeks to the same size. Poach in salted water for about 25–30 minutes until tender, but not too soft. Drain, cool, and serve coated in vinaigrette dressing (see p.501) as an hors d'oeuvre.

Leeks au Gratin

Prepare 2 lb leeks as left and cook in boiling salted water for 15–20 minutes until tender. Drain, and cut into short pieces. Meanwhile, prepare a mornay sauce in the following manner: in a pan, melt $2\frac{1}{2}$ tablespoons butter, stir in 4 tablespoons flour, cook for 2 minutes, remove from the heat, and add gradually 2 cups cold milk, stirring constantly. Return to the heat, bring to a boil and let simmer for 10 minutes. Remove from the heat, add 1 egg yolk, $\frac{2}{3}$ cup grated Parmesan cheese, salt and grated nutmeg to taste. Stir well. In an ovenproof dish, arrange the leeks in a layer, pour the sauce over them, sprinkle with breadcrumbs, dot with butter, and put in a moderate oven (350°F) to gratiné. Serve in the cooking dish.

461

Stuffed Lettuce Heads

Ingredients: *4 lettuce heads · $\frac{1}{4}$ cup black olives, pitted and cut into thin strips · $\frac{1}{4}$ cup anchovy fillets, desalted by soaking in a little milk and cut into pieces · 2 tablespoons capers · 4 tomatoes (preferably Italian plum type), peeled, seeded and sliced · $\frac{1}{4}$ cup pecorino or mozzarella cheese (optional), diced · 1 tablespoon butter or margarine · 4 tablespoons oil · salt*

Remove and discard the outer leaves of the lettuce heads, and wash the lettuce thoroughly under cold running water. Blanch in salted water then place upside down to drain on a cloth. When quite dry, insert the olives, anchovies, capers, and cheese if using, between the leaves of the lettuce heads (step 1). Melt the butter or margarine in a pan, remove from the heat and put in the lettuce heads (step 2). Pour over each 1 tablespoon oil (step 3), sprinkle with salt, cover, and cook for 20–25 minutes over low heat. Transfer to a serving platter and add fresh tomato.

Braised Lettuce Heads

Prepare, blanch and drain 4 lettuce heads as left. Tie neatly together with string, and place over lettuce 1 onion, sliced, 1 carrot, sliced, 1 celery stalk, sliced, and 1 clove of garlic, crushed. Dot with $\frac{1}{4}$ cup butter and add 1 bouquet garni. Sprinkle with salt, cover with water, and cook until tender, about 25 minutes.

Braised Belgian Endives

With a sharp knife, cut off the hard core from 8 endives. Remove and discard the yellow outer leaves, and wash the endives thoroughly. Blanch in salted water, then drain and place in an ovenproof dish over a layer of 2 oz onions, sliced, and 1 carrot, sliced. Dot with $\frac{1}{4}$ cup butter, add 1 bouquet garni, and salt and pepper to taste. Add a little water – not enough to cover the Belgian endives completely – and cook on top of the stove or in a moderate oven (350°F) for 40–50 minutes.

Belgian Endives au Gratin

Prepare, blanch and drain 8 endives as above. Put in an ovenproof dish, dot with $\frac{1}{4}$ cup butter and pour a little water around the endives. Cook on top of the stove or in a moderate oven (375°F) for 40–50 minutes or until tender. Meanwhile, prepare a béchamel sauce with $\frac{1}{4}$ cup butter, 1 tablespoon flour, and 1 cup milk. Add 4 tablespoons grated Gruyère cheese, and salt and grated nutmeg to taste. Pour over endives, sprinkle with grated Gruyère cheese, and gratiné.

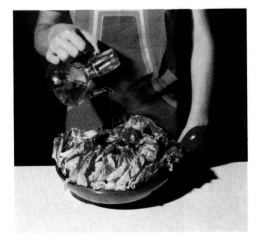

Deep-fried Endive

Blanch 4 heads of Belgian endive in boiling salted water, with 2 tablespoons lemon juice added, for 10 minutes. Drain and pat dry. Lightly beat 1 large egg with seasoning. Dip the endive heads in the egg, then coat with dried bread crumbs. Fry in deep fat for 2–3 minutes or until golden brown. Drain and serve hot.

463

Mushroom Caps
on Vine Leaves

Ingredients: *4–8 large mushroom caps,
according to size · 4–8 vine leaves · a few
tablespoons olive oil · salt · pepper · parsley,
garlic and oregano to taste, all chopped together*

Clean the mushrooms with a wet cloth (step 1).
Make 2–3 incisions in the center of each cap
(step 2). Brush the inside of an ovenproof
dish with oil, place the vine leaves at the
bottom, put in the mushroom caps (step 3),
pour oil over them, sprinkle with salt and
pepper to taste, and spread with the parsley,
garlic and oregano mixture. Put in a hot oven
(425°F), and cook for about 20 minutes.

Stuffed Mushrooms

Remove the stems of 8 large mushrooms.
Clean the caps with a wet cloth. Wash the
stems, chop them together with 3 cloves of
garlic, 4 oz lean salt pork (previously soaked
in cold water), and some parsley to taste.
Add 1 tablespoon breadcrumbs, and season
with salt and pepper to taste. Stuff the mushroom caps with this mixture. Brush with olive
oil and beaten egg, and cook in the oven for
10–12 minutes until mushrooms are tender.
Serve with lemon wedges and parsley sprigs.

Creamed Mushrooms

Clean 1 lb mushrooms with a wet cloth. Trim the stems. Sauté lightly in $\frac{1}{4}$ cup butter. Add $\frac{1}{2}$ glass port, Madeira or Marsala. Cook over low heat until the wine has almost completely reduced. Add 1 cup light cream. Season with salt and pepper to taste, cover and cook very slowly for 15–20 minutes, or until mushrooms are tender and sauce is reduced.

Mushrooms Bordelaise

Clean 1 lb mushrooms with a wet cloth. Remove the stems and chop them together with 4 shallots and 1 clove of garlic. Cut the mushroom caps into large pieces. In a skillet, heat $\frac{1}{3}$ cup olive oil. Add the mushroom caps, then the chopped stems and the shallots. Season with salt and pepper to taste. When all the mushroom liquid has evaporated, sprinkle with chopped parsley and serve.

Mushroom Pie

Prepare and bake 'blind' pastry in a 10-inch pie pan (see p.486). Meanwhile, clean and slice $1\frac{1}{4}$ lb fresh mushrooms. Brown lightly $\frac{1}{2}$ onion in 2 tablespoons butter or margarine. Remove the onion, put in the mushrooms and sauté lightly. Add 1 small glass flamed brandy (optional) and, after a few minutes, salt and pepper to taste, 1 glass light cream and a few tablespoons béchamel sauce (see p.84). Continue cooking on very low heat for 10 minutes. When the pastry is cooked, remove the paper and beans, fill with the mushroom mixture, sprinkle with grated Parmesan cheese and dot with butter. Return to the oven for 5 minutes to gratiné. Serve immediately, piping hot.

Stuffed Onions

Ingredients: *4 large onions · 1 celery stalk, finely chopped · 1 clove of garlic, crushed · 2 sage leaves, finely chopped · 4 tablespoons breadcrumbs · 4 tablespoons grated Parmesan cheese · 1 tablespoon chopped parsley · salt · pepper · 2 tablespoons butter or margarine*

Peel the onions and parboil them. Drain, cut the tops off, and scoop out the centers, leaving about ½ inch around the sides (step 1). Chop the scooped-out onion finely (step 2), and sauté lightly over low heat for 6–7 minutes with the celery, garlic and sage. Add the breadcrumbs, continue cooking for 2 minutes, remove from the heat, and mix in the grated Parmesan cheese, parsley, and salt and pepper to taste. Melt ½ the butter or margarine with a little salt and pepper in an ovenproof dish, put in the onions, and fill with the stuffing (step 3). Dot each onion with the remaining butter. Cook in a hot oven (425°F) for 30–35 minutes until tender, basting from time to time with the cooking juices. Garnish with sprigs of parsley and tomato wedges before serving. (If liked, chopped leftover meat or sausage meat can be used in the stuffing.) Stuffed onions can be served cold as well as hot, in which case they should be cooked in oil rather than butter.

466

Glazed Scallions

To garnish meat dishes: peel carefully about 30 small scallions. Put them in a pan, cover with salted water, add 1 tablespoon butter and 1 teaspoon sugar. Cook slowly, uncovered. When all the water has been absorbed, the onions are cooked. Continue cooking until caramelized, shaking the pan from time to time.

Fried Onions

To garnish meat dishes: peel and slice onions, separate into rings and dip in flour seasoned with salt. Deep fry in very hot oil (380°F).

Purée Soubise

Peel 1 lb onions. Cover with salted water, and cook together with $\frac{1}{2}$ cup rice. When both onions and rice are cooked, drain, and work through a fine sieve. Season with salt and pepper to taste. Add $\frac{1}{4}$ cup butter and $\frac{1}{2}$ cup heavy cream. Mix well. Serve with croûtons fried in butter.

Onions with White Wine

Peel and thinly slice 2 lb onions and separate the slices into rings. Melt $\frac{1}{4}$ cup butter in a saucepan and fry the onions until pale golden, stirring frequently. Add $\frac{1}{2}$ teaspoon sugar, 1 tablespoon flour and seasoning and fry, stirring, for 2 minutes. Gradually stir in 1 cup dry white wine and bring to a boil, still stirring. Add a crushed garlic clove, a sprig of thyme and 1 tablespoon lemon juice. Cover and simmer for about 15 minutes.

Discard the thyme and sprinkle with chopped parsley before serving.

Green Peas with Lettuce

Ingredients: *4 lettuce heads · 2 cups green peas (shelled) · ½ cup small new onions, sliced · ½ cup butter or margarine · salt · 3 tablespoons hot stock · chopped parsley · pepper*

Remove and discard the large outer leaves of the lettuce heads, wash the lettuce thoroughly under running water, and drain. In a large pan, melt ½ the butter or margarine over low heat. Add the peas, the onions (step 1), and the lettuce heads (step 2). Season with salt to taste, add the stock, cover, and cook slowly for 15–20 minutes. Add parsley and pepper to taste (step 3) and remaining butter or margarine and cook until juice is reduced.

Green Peas à la Française

Chop $\frac{1}{2}$ lettuce head, washed and drained as above. Put 2 cups green peas in a pan, add 3 tablespoons butter or margarine, 1 tablespoon flour, 4 oz onions, sliced and the chopped lettuce. Stir with a wooden spoon, add 3 tablespoons sugar, $\frac{1}{2}$ teaspoon salt, and cover with water. Boil over high heat, uncovered, for 15–20 minutes, until peas are tender and water has been absorbed.

Flemish Green Peas

Scrape and dice 10 oz carrots. Put in a pan, cover with water, season with salt to taste, add $\frac{1}{4}$ cup butter or margarine and 1 teaspoon sugar. Cook, uncovered, until all the liquid has been absorbed. Meanwhile, in another pan, cook 2 cups green peas in boiling salted water – uncovered – for 15–20 minutes or until tender. Drain, and mix with the carrots. Add $\frac{1}{4}$ cup butter or margarine, sprinkle with chopped parsley to taste, stir well and serve.

Green Peas with Salt Pork

Dice 6 oz lean salt pork (previously soaked in cold water for $\frac{1}{2}$ hour). Chop finely $\frac{1}{4}$ cup onion (or use $\frac{1}{2}$ cup small onions, whole). Cook 2 cups green peas in boiling salted water with a twig of thyme. Brown the onion and the salt pork in 1 tablespoon butter or margarine. Cook for a few minutes, then add to the peas. Blend $\frac{1}{4}$ cup butter or margarine with 1 tablespoon flour. Add to the peas, and continue cooking until they are tender. Sprinkle with chopped chervil to taste before serving.

Stuffed Sweet Peppers

Ingredients: *4 large peppers (preferably red or yellow)*

For the stuffing: 1 large eggplant · 2 celery stalks · 1 small green pepper · 4 oz tuna fish packed in oil · 2 anchovy fillets, desalted by soaking in a little milk · ½ cup oil · 1 clove of garlic · ½ cup green olives · 1¼ cups capers · 1 tablespoon tomato paste · stock · little salt

Wash the large peppers, cut off tops and remove the seeds and white pith (step 1). Blanch in boiling salted water for 5 minutes then rinse under cold running water; drain well. Prepare the stuffing: peel and dice the eggplant, cut the celery into pieces, remove seeds and pith from the green pepper, and cut into strips (step 2), drain the tuna fish and the anchovy fillets, and chop. In ½ the oil, brown the garlic, then remove and discard it. Add the eggplant, celery, pitted olives and capers, then the tomato paste and a little stock. Season with a little salt, cover, and cook slowly, adding a little more stock occasionally, until vegetables are tender. Remove from the heat and add the vinegar. Stuff the peppers with this mixture (step 3), and place them in a skillet with the remainder of the oil and a little water. Cook in a moderate oven (350°F) for about ½ hour, or until peppers are tender.

Peperonata

Wash 2 lb red and yellow sweet peppers, halve, remove seeds and pith and cut into wedges. Dip 1¼ lb ripe tomatoes (preferably Italian plum type) in boiling water, peel, and cut into pieces and remove seeds. In a pan, put ½ cup oil, the peppers, the tomatoes, 1 medium-sized onion, sliced, and a few basil leaves. Cover, and cook over low heat for about 1½ hours. Halfway through the cooking, season with salt to taste. If necessary, add a few spoonfuls of water, or, if there is too much liquid, uncover the pan and reduce over high heat. Serve hot, as an accompaniment to meats (particularly boiled meats) or cold as an hors d'oeuvre.

Duchesse Potatoes

Ingredients: *2½ lb potatoes · ¼ cup butter or margarine · 1 whole egg and 3 egg yolks, lightly beaten together · salt · pepper*

To gratiné: *1 egg, beaten with a little salt*

Peel the potatoes, cut them into pieces and put in a pan. Cover with cold salted water, bring to a boil and simmer until tender, taking care they do not break; drain, put back over the heat, shaking the pan, until the potatoes are dry. Work through a sieve, potato ricer or presse-purée (step 1). Add the butter or margarine (step 2), eggs, and salt and pepper to taste. Beat the mixture until fluffy, and put it in a pastry bag fitted with a large rose nozzle. Pipe small mounds on a buttered cookie sheet (step 3). Brush with beaten egg and gratiné.

If liked, small nests can be piped and filled with vegetables to taste – for example, green peas with ham, etc. Begin by piping the center, then form flat spirals until the required width is obtained. Pipe layers round the edge (step 4).

Potato Croquettes

Prepare, cook and sieve 2½ lb potatoes as above. Put over very low heat, add 2 egg yolks, salt and grated nutmeg to taste, beat well, remove from the heat, and leave to cool. If liked, add 2 tablespoons grated Parmesan cheese. Shape into croquettes on a floured board, dip into 1 egg white, lightly beaten, then roll in breadcrumbs. Let stand for a while, then fry in hot deep oil. Lift out with a slotted spoon and drain on absorbent paper.

Mashed Potatoes

Prepare, cook and sieve 2½ lb potatoes as above. Add 4 tablespoons butter or margarine, and, beating constantly, 1 cup milk, and salt and grated nutmeg to taste. When the mixture is fluffy and smooth, put in a pan over low heat and reheat, stirring constantly.

Potatoes Chantilly

Prepare, cook and sieve 2½ lb potatoes as above. Mix with ½ cup light cream whipped until stiff with salt and pepper to taste, put in a buttered ovenproof dish, sprinkle with grated Gruyère cheese, and gratiné.

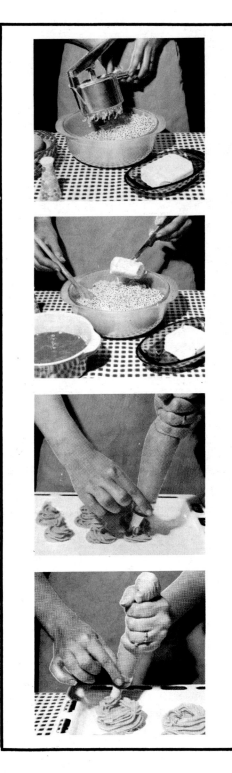

472

473

Fried Potatoes

Peel 2 lb potatoes, preferably mature potatoes, squaring off the ends and sides. Cut into slices $\frac{1}{4}$ inch thick, then into matchsticks $\frac{1}{4}$ inch wide. Soak in cold water until cooking time. Drain, dry thoroughly in a cloth, and put in appropriate frying basket. Cover with the other part of the basket, and plunge into hot deep oil (step 1). When the potatoes are crisp and golden, lift basket out, unmold carefully on absorbent paper, sprinkle with salt and serve immediately. (Creamed or buttered vegetables can also be cooked in the basket in this way.)

Potatoes Pont-Neuf

Peel 2 lb mature potatoes, squaring off the ends and sides. Cut into $\frac{1}{2}$-inch thick slices, then into sticks 2 inches or more in length. Soak in cold water until cooking time, drain, dry thoroughly in a cloth, and put, a few at a time, in about 2 quarts hot deep oil for 8–10 minutes until golden, shaking the pan from time to time. Between each batch of potatoes, reheat the oil to very hot. Drain the potatoes on absorbent paper, sprinkle with salt and serve.

Puffed Potatoes

Peel 2 lb mature potatoes, wipe them with a cloth, but do not wash them, and cut them into slices $\frac{1}{4}$ inch thick. Then proceed as for Potatoes Pont-Neuf, cooking the potatoes until lightly colored in hot oil (350°F), lifting out with a slotted spoon and draining them on absorbent paper, then heating the oil to a higher temperature (400°F), and cooking them again, until they swell up and are golden brown. Lift out with a slotted spoon, drain on absorbent paper, sprinkle with salt and serve.

Potatoes Chasseur

Wash and parboil 2 lb potatoes. Drain, peel, let cool and cut into pieces. Brown 4 tablespoons oil with 1 clove of garlic, peeled. Remove garlic, add the potatoes, and when golden add $\frac{1}{2}$ glass dry white wine. Let evaporate, add 1 lb canned peeled tomatoes, 1 bay leaf, and salt and pepper. Cover, and cook slowly until potatoes are tender. Remove bay leaf.

Potato Chips

Peel 2 lb mature potatoes, cut into very thin ($\frac{1}{8}$ inch) slices (step 2), and put in cold water until cooking time. Drain, dry thoroughly in a cloth, and cook in hot deep oil until golden and crisp, shaking the pan from time to time. Lift out with a slotted spoon, put on absorbent paper, sprinkle with salt, and serve straight away.

Potato Gaufrettes

Prepare and cook 2 lb potatoes as for Potato Chips above, cutting potatoes very thinly with a mandoline (step 2).

Straw Potatoes

Proceed as for Potatoes Pont-Neuf, cutting potatoes $\frac{1}{8}$ inch thick. Cook in a frying basket, if available (step 3).

475

Stuffed Potatoes au Gratin

Ingredients: *8 large oval potatoes*

For the stuffing: *¼ cup butter or margarine ·
1 tablespoon flour · 1 pint milk · salt ·
grated nutmeg · ¼ cup grated Parmesan cheese
or cream cheese · 4 oz cooked ham, diced ·
boiled green peas (optional) · 1 egg yolk*

To garnish: *watercress*

Peel the potatoes and halve them lengthwise.
Remove some of the pulp from the center with a
sharp knife (step 1). Trim the bottoms so they
can stand upright. Put in cold salted water,
bring to a boil and cook for 5 minutes, lift out
with a slotted spoon, drain, and let cool on
absorbent paper. Meanwhile, prepare a béchamel sauce: melt the butter or margarine in a
pan, stir in the flour, cook 1–2 minutes,
remove from the heat and add the cold milk
gradually, stirring constantly. Return to the
heat and cook for 10 minutes. Remove from
the heat, add salt and grated nutmeg to taste,
the cheese, ham, peas (if using) and, finally, the
egg yolk. Blend well, and fill the potatoes with
this mixture (step 2). Arrange in a buttered
ovenproof dish (step 3), and bake in a moderate
oven (350°F) for 30–40 minutes until potatoes
are tender. Garnish with watercress.

476

Potatoes Lyonnaise

Peel 2 lb potatoes, wash, cover with cold salted water, bring to a boil and simmer until tender. Drain, let cool and slice. Meanwhile, blanch 1 large onion, thinly sliced, for a few minutes in boiling water, drain, and dry in a cloth. Sauté lightly in 1 tablespoon butter, and continue cooking slowly. In a large skillet, brown $\frac{1}{4}$ cup butter or margarine, add the potatoes and, when they are golden, add the onion slices. Season with salt and pepper to taste, continue cooking for a few minutes over high heat, sprinkle with chopped parsley, and serve.

Potatoes Anna

Peel 2 lb potatoes. Cut into very thin, regular slices. Sauté in $\frac{1}{4}$ cup butter in a skillet, taking care they do not stick together. Butter generously a pastry mold or round ovenproof dish. Sprinkle the potato slices with salt, and arrange in the mold in a spiral pattern. When the bottom of the mold is covered, dot with butter, and continue layering the potatoes, buttering every other layer. Cover, and cook in a hot oven (400°F) for 45 minutes. Unmold.

Potato Pancakes

Peel $1\frac{1}{2}$ lb waxy potatoes and grate coarsely into a bowl of cold water. Drain and squeeze dry in a cloth, then put into a dry bowl. Add 2 eggs, 1 tablespoon flour and seasoning and mix well.

Heat a little oil in a frying pan and add $\frac{1}{4}$ of the potato mixture. Flatten into a pancake with the back of a pancake turner and fry for about 5 minutes or until the edges are golden. Turn and brown the other side. Remove from the pan and keep hot while cooking 3 more pancakes in the same way. Serve hot.

Glazed Sweet Potatoes

Ingredients: *2 lb medium-sized sweet potatoes ·*
1 cup clear honey · cinnamon powder or grated
lemon peel · ¼ cup butter or margarine

Wash the sweet potatoes well, cover with cold
salted water, bring to a boil and simmer for
about ½ hour until they are *al dente*. Drain, let
cool, peel and cut in ¼-inch slices (step 1).
Arrange the slices in a generously buttered
ovenproof dish (step 2). Pour the honey over
(step 3), sprinkle with cinnamon or lemon
peel to taste, dot with butter or margarine,
and bake in a moderate oven (350°F) for
about ½ hour, basting from time to time with
the cooking juices. Serve in the cooking dish
at the end of a meal, or as an accompaniment
to ham, roast pork, or roast turkey.

Sweet Potato Croquettes

Prepare and cook until *al dente* 2 lb sweet
potatoes, as above. Drain, let cool, peel, mash
and work through a sieve. In a pan, melt ¼ cup
butter or margarine on low heat, add the
sweet potatoes, and cook for a few minutes.
Remove from the heat, add salt and grated
nutmeg to taste, 1 whole egg, and 1 egg yolk.
Blend well, then pour the mixture onto a
floured board. Shape into croquettes, dip them
into 1 egg white, lightly beaten, then roll in
breadcrumbs. Let stand for a while, then fry
in hot deep oil until golden. Lift out with a
slotted spoon and drain on absorbent paper.

Fried Sweet Potatoes

Prepare and cook until *al dente* 2 lb sweet
potatoes as above. Drain, let cool, peel and
slice. Fry in hot deep oil. Lift out with a
slotted spoon and drain on absorbent paper.

Sweet Potatoes with Rum

Prepare, cook and sieve 2 lb sweet potatoes as
for Sweet Potato Croquettes above. Place in a
bowl, blend in ¼ cup butter, softened, 4–5
tablespoons light cream, 4 tablespoons rum,
and salt and pepper to taste. Pile the mixture
into a buttered ovenproof dish, pour a few
spoonfuls melted butter over, and cook in a
very hot oven (450°F) until a golden crust
has formed on top.

478

479

Breaded Pumpkin

Ingredients: *2 lb pumpkin · 1 egg · salt · breadcrumbs · 4 tablespoons butter or margarine · pepper · sliced Emmenthal cheese*

To garnish: *sprigs of parsley*

Remove the rind from the pumpkin, the seeds and filaments. Cut into ¾-inch thick slices (step 1). Dip in the egg, beaten with a pinch of salt, then roll in breadcrumbs (step 2). Let stand in a cool place for ½ hour. Brown lightiy on both sides in the butter or margarine, and continue cooking without letting the slices overlap, until pumpkin is tender. Season with salt and pepper to taste. Cut the cheese into small circles if liked, and place on each pumpkin slice on a flameproof serving platter (step 3). Cover, and keep over low heat until the cheese has melted, or put in a hot oven (425°F) for a few minutes. Garnish the edges of the platter with sprigs of parsley and serve immediately.

Creamed Pumpkin

Prepare 2 lb pumpkin as left. Cut into pieces, and cook in a little boiling salted water for 12–15 minutes until tender. Drain, and mash with a fork. Put back over the heat with $\frac{1}{4}$ cup butter or margarine, and, stirring constantly, let dry completely. Remove from heat and let cool. Meanwhile, in a bowl, mix 2 tablespoons flour and 4 tablespoons light cream (or milk). Add 3 eggs, and whip until fluffy. Add $\frac{1}{4}$ cup grated Parmesan cheese, and salt and grated nutmeg to taste, and blend into the mashed pumpkin. Pour the mixture into an ovenproof dish, and cook in a moderate oven (350°F) for 25–30 minutes. Serve immediately in the cooking dish.

Pumpkin au Gratin

Prepare and cook 2 lb pumpkin as for Creamed Pumpkin above. Drain, slice, and arrange the slices in a buttered ovenproof dish. Sprinkle with pepper, a generous amount of grated Parmesan cheese, and $\frac{1}{4}$ cup melted butter. Put in a moderate oven (350°F), and bake for about 50 minutes. Serve in the same dish. If the pumpkin gets too dry while cooking, add a few tablespoons milk or cream.

Greek Pumpkin

Remove the seeds and filaments from 2 lb pumpkin. Cut into chunks, leaving the rind on. Heat 3 tablespoons olive oil in a saucepan, add 2 onions, peeled and each cut into 8 wedges, and fry until transparent. Stir in a 16-oz can of tomatoes, $\frac{1}{4}$ teaspoon ground cumin and the pumpkin, then add 1 cup water, 1 tablespoon chopped parsley and seasoning. Bring to a boil, cover and simmer for 25–35 minutes or until the pumpkin is tender. Serve hot.

Spinach Gourmet

Ingredients: $1\frac{1}{2}$ lb spinach · 1 handful white
bread soaked in milk and squeezed · 2 oz tuna
fish packed in oil, drained · 2 anchovy fillets,
desalted by soaking in a little milk · 2 whole
eggs · 4 tablespoons grated Parmesan cheese ·
about 4 tablespoons breadcrumbs · salt ·
pepper

To garnish: mayonnaise · lemon slices ·
pieces of sweet red pepper

Clean and wash the spinach, removing hard
stems and damaged leaves. Drain and cook for
10 minutes without water. Squeeze and put

through a food mill or sieve (or purée in a
blender) together with the bread (step 1).
Mix with the chopped tuna fish and anchovy
fillets, the eggs, Parmesan cheese, breadcrumbs,
and salt and pepper to taste. Shape the mixture
into a long roll, wrap it in a wet gauze or
cheesecloth (step 2), and tie at both ends.
Place in a flameproof casserole (step 3), cover
with cold salted water, bring to a boil, and
simmer gently for about 45 minutes. Drain,
let stand for 15 minutes, then remove the
gauze. Serve cold, the slices garnished with
mayonnaise, and the dish decorated with half
slices of lemon topped with pieces of red pepper.

This dish and the following dishes may be
made with frozen spinach. Use 1 lb frozen
spinach and follow directions on package.

Spinach Croquettes

Clean, cook and purée 1½ lb spinach as left. Sauté lightly in butter over moderate heat. Prepare a béchamel sauce with 2½ tablespoons butter or margarine, 4 tablespoons flour, 1 cup milk, and salt, pepper and grated nutmeg to taste. When the sauce is lukewarm, add the spinach mixed with 2 whole eggs and ½ cup grated Gruyère cheese. Cook the mixture, one tablespoon at a time, in hot deep oil. Lift out the croquettes with a slotted spoon, drain them on absorbent paper, and serve immediately, piping hot.

Creamed Spinach

Prepare 1½ lb spinach for cooking as left. Cook uncovered in boiling salted water for 5 minutes until tender. Drain, press to remove moisture, and work through a food mill or sieve (or purée in a blender). Prepare a sauce in the following way: melt in a pan 2½ tablespoons butter, stir in 1 tablespoon flour, cook for 2 minutes, then add spinach and 1 cup light cream, stirring constantly. Season with salt and grated nutmeg to taste. Serve immediately.

Spinach à l'Anglaise

Prepare 1½ lb spinach, cook, drain and purée as for Creamed Spinach above. Put in a pan with 4 tablespoons butter. When the butter is golden-brown lift out the spinach with a fork. Serve immediately in a warm vegetable dish, with ½ cup heavy cream poured around, and croûtons fried in butter.

Sautéed Salsify

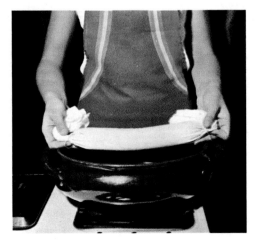

Scrape 2 lb white salsify. Cut into pieces, and put immediately in water mixed with lemon juice. Cook for about 40 minutes in boiling salted water until tender. Drain, and sauté in ¼ cup butter or margarine, with 2 cloves of garlic. Remove the garlic, season and serve.

Baked Tomatoes Stuffed with Rice

Ingredients: *8 large round, ripe tomatoes ·*
8 tablespoons rice · 1 clove of garlic ·
parsley or mint to taste · 4 tablespoons butter
or margarine · salt · pepper · a few tablespoons
tomato paste · stock

To garnish: *8 mint leaves*

Wash the tomatoes and slice off the top of
each (step 1). Remove the pulp with a teaspoon (step 2), seed, squeeze, and reserve,
together with the caps. Crush the garlic with
the parsley or mint. Mix in a bowl with the
rice, 1 tablespoon melted butter, 2 tablespoons
tomato pulp, salt and pepper to taste. Put a
little melted butter or margarine and salt and
pepper in each hollowed tomato and on the
inside of each cap. Arrange the tomatoes in a
generously buttered ovenproof dish. Fill them
with the prepared rice mixture (step 3). Cover
with the caps, pour around the tomato paste
diluted with stock, and bake in a moderate
oven (350°F) for 30–35 minutes. Serve in the
cooking dish, garnishing with mint leaves.

Stuffed Tomatoes

Wash 8 large round, ripe tomatoes and slice off the top of each. Remove the pulp carefully with a teaspoon, and reserve. Season the insides with salt, and keep them upside down on a plate so that the water runs out. In a bowl, mix 1 generous handful of bread, soaked in milk and squeezed, with $\frac{1}{2}$ lb chopped cooked meat to taste, chopped parsley and onion to taste, 1 egg yolk, a few spoonfuls grated Parmesan cheese, salt and pepper to taste, and enough reserved tomato pulp to obtain a smooth mixture. Dry the tomatoes, stuff with the meat mixture and arrange in a buttered ovenproof dish. Sprinkle with breadcrumbs, dot with butter, and cook in a moderate oven (350°F) for 30–35 minutes until a golden crust has formed on the tops of the tomatoes. Serve in the cooking dish.

Tomatoes au Gratin

Wash and halve 4 tomatoes. Remove the pulp with a teaspoon as above and reserve. Season the insides with salt, and keep upside down on a plate. In a skillet, brown 8 tablespoons breadcrumbs in 6 tablespoons hot oil. Remove from the heat, add anchovy paste to taste (or anchovy fillets desalted in a little milk, drained and mashed) diluted in a little oil, the reserved tomato pulp, chopped parsley, salt and pepper to taste. Dry the tomatoes, stuff with this mixture, and put them in a buttered ovenproof dish. Brush with a little oil, and cook in a moderate oven (350°F) for 30–35 minutes, until a golden crust has formed on the tops of the tomatoes. Serve in the cooking dish.

Tomato Pie

Ingredients: for the pastry, $\frac{3}{4}$ *cup flour · salt ·*
4 tablespoons butter or margarine ·
3 tablespoons cold water

For the filling: *1$\frac{1}{4}$ lb tomatoes, (preferably*
Italian plum type)· 1 onion, chopped ·
1 clove of garlic, crushed · 1 bouquet garni
made of parsley, basil and 1 bay leaf · salt ·
pepper

For the mornay sauce: *1 tablespoon butter or*
margarine · 1 tablespoon flour · 1 glass milk ·
salt · pepper · 2 oz grated Gruyère cheese

To garnish: *sprig of basil or parsley (optional)*

Prepare the dough: sift the flour with a pinch of
salt onto a working surface or pastry board.
Add the butter or margarine, cut into pieces,
and work into the flour with the fingers until
the mixture resembles fine breadcrumbs. Add
the water gradually until a firm dough is
formed, knead and roll dough into a ball,
wrap in wax paper and let stand in a cool
place or refrigerator for $\frac{1}{2}$ hour. Meanwhile,
dip the tomatoes in boiling water, peel them,
seed them, and cut them into pieces (step 1).
Put in a pan together with the onion, garlic,
bouquet garni, and salt and pepper to taste.
Cook uncovered for $\frac{3}{4}$ hour or until mixture
becomes a thickish purée. Meanwhile, flatten
out the dough with a rolling pin to a thickness

486

of $\frac{1}{4}$ inch and use to line the bottom and sides of a pie pan (about 10-inch diameter). Prick the bottom of the dough with a fork, cover with wax paper or aluminum foil, and put dry beans or rice over the paper so that the dough will not swell. Bake 'blind' in a hot oven (425°F) for 25–30 minutes. Meanwhile, prepare mornay sauce: melt the butter or margarine on moderate heat, stir in the flour, cook for 1–2 minutes, remove from the heat and add the cold milk gradually, stirring constantly. Return to heat and cook for 10 minutes, stirring occasionally. Remove from the heat, add salt and pepper to taste, and the cheese. When the pastry is cooked, remove the paper and beans, spread the tomato purée over (step 2), and pipe the mornay sauce over the tomato in an attractive pattern (step 3). (Alternatively the mornay sauce can simply be spooned over.) Put the pie back into the hot oven for 5–8 minutes, or until golden. Serve hot, garnished with a sprig of basil or parsley if liked.

Tomato Quiche

Make a pastry from 2 cups flour, $\frac{1}{2}$ teaspoon salt, 4 tablespoons sour cream and $\frac{1}{2}$ cup butter. Chill for 30 minutes.

Roll out the dough and use to line a 12-inch quiche pan. Cover the bottom with 5 thinly sliced tomatoes, then arrange 6 oz cheese, thinly sliced, on top. Cover the cheese with 8 thin slices of French bread. Lightly beat $\frac{1}{2}$ cup each heavy and sour creams together with 4 eggs, $\frac{1}{2}$ teaspoon paprika, a pinch of grated nutmeg and seasoning. Pour into the pastry case and dot the top with 2 tablespoons butter. Bake in a hot oven (400°F) for 30–40 minutes or until firm and golden. Serve hot.

Stuffed Turnips

Ingredients: *4 large turnips (or 8 small ones) ·
½ cup Emmenthal cheese, sliced · 4 oz
prosciutto, sliced · grated Parmesan cheese ·
4 tablespoons butter or margarine, melted*

Peel the turnips, wash them, and cook until
al dente (about 15 minutes) in boiling salted
water. Drain, cool, and slice them horizontally
(step 1). Put them back into shape alternating
layers of turnip, cheese and prosciutto (step 2),
and place in a buttered ovenproof dish (step 3).
Sprinkle with grated Parmesan cheese, brush
with melted butter or margarine and put in a
moderate oven (350°F) for 20–25 minutes,
or until the turnips are cooked and lightly
golden. You can also cover the turnips with
béchamel sauce before putting them in the
oven. Serve in the cooking dish.

Turnips au Gratin

Peel and wash 1 lb turnips. Cook for 15–20 minutes in boiling salted water until tender. Drain, cool, and slice. Brown in 1 tablespoon butter or margarine. Put in an ovenproof dish in layers, covering each layer of turnips with a few tablespoons béchamel sauce (3 tablespoons butter, 3 tablespoons flour, 2 cups milk, salt and grated nutmeg to taste) and grated Gruyère cheese to taste. End with a layer of béchamel sauce, sprinkle with breadcrumbs, dot with butter, and put in a hot oven (400°F) for 10–15 minutes to gratiné.

Glazed Turnips

Wash 1½ lb young white turnips and pare in the shape of large olives. Brown in butter, adding a pinch of salt and 1 teaspoon sugar. Add beef stock to cover half the turnips, cover the pan and continue cooking on very low heat until all the juice has evaporated. Add more butter to taste and serve.

Turnips with Garlic and Cheese

Peel and wash thoroughly 4 lb turnips. Sauté lightly in a frying pan 2 cloves of garlic, crushed, in ½ cup oil. Add the turnips, salt and pepper to taste, cover and cook slowly for about ¾ hour, adding a few tablespoons water if turnips become dry. Sprinkle with grated Parmesan cheese before serving.

Purée Freneuse

Peel and wash 1½ lb turnips. Cut into quarters, and cook in boiling salted water for 15–20 minutes, together with ¾ lb potatoes, peeled and quartered. Drain, work through a food mill or sieve (or purée in a blender), put back over the heat, stirring constantly with a wooden spoon. Add ½ cup butter and ½ cup light cream, season with salt and pepper to taste, and serve in a warm vegetable dish garnished with croûtons fried in butter.

Marinated Zucchini

Ingredients: $1\frac{1}{2}$ lb zucchini · oil for frying

For the marinade: $\frac{1}{2}$ onion · 3–4 cloves of garlic · sage leaves · 1 cup vinegar · 1 pinch salt

Wash the zucchini, dry and slice lengthwise. Fry the slices a few at a time in oil (step 1). Lift them out with a spatula and drain on absorbent paper. Arrange on a platter. Fry the onion and garlic, both finely chopped, in hot oil. Add the sage, the vinegar (step 2) and the salt. Boil for a few minutes, pour over the zucchini (step 3), cover, and let marinate for at least 24 hours. Serve cold.

Stuffed Zucchini

Wash and dry 8 small zucchini or 4 large ones. Halve lengthwise. Remove most of the flesh carefully with a teaspoon, without damaging the shell, and reserve. Parboil the shells in boiling salted water to cover. Meanwhile, chop the reserved flesh, and mix with $\frac{1}{2}$ lb chopped cooked meat. (Leftovers are ideal, especially lamb.) Cook the mixture in 4 tablespoons butter or margarine for 15 minutes, then add $\frac{1}{2}$ cup breadcrumbs, and continue cooking for a few more minutes. Remove from the heat, add $\frac{1}{4}$ cup grated Parmesan cheese, 1–2 whole eggs, and salt and pepper to taste. Blend well. Drain the zucchini shells, put in a buttered ovenproof dish, fill with prepared stuffing, sprinkle with grated Parmesan cheese, dot with butter, and bake in a moderate oven (350°F) for 25–30 minutes. Serve as soon as a golden crust has formed on the surface.

Zucchini with Green Sauce

Wash and dry 1½ lb zucchini. Cut into slices (crosswise or lengthwise) and fry, a few at a time, in hot oil. Take out with a slotted spoon and drain on absorbent paper. Prepare a green sauce: chop a generous handful of parsley with 1 clove of garlic and 4 anchovy fillets (previously desalted by soaking in a little milk). Blend in enough oil and vinegar to obtain a smooth, fluid mixture. Season with salt and pepper to taste. Arrange the zucchini in layers in a dish, alternating with layers of green sauce and ending with the latter. Let stand for a few hours before serving.

Zucchini with White Wine

Wash and dry 1½ lb zucchini. Cut lengthwise in 4, then cut into squares. In a skillet cook until golden 1 chopped scallion in ¼ cup butter or margarine. Add the zucchini and cook over high heat for 10 minutes. Add ½ cup dry white wine and salt and pepper to taste, cover, lower the heat, and continue cooking, stirring occasionally, until the zucchini are very tender and the cooking juices have reduced. Toward the end of the cooking, raise the heat again to make the zucchini crisp. Just before serving, stir in ¼ cup diced prosciutto or cooked ham and 1 tablespoon fresh butter or margarine, and sprinkle with grated Parmesan cheese to taste.

Fried Zucchini

Cut zucchini lengthwise in thin slices, dry them, roll them in flour, then in egg and breadcrumbs, and fry in deep hot oil. Other vegetables can also be prepared in this manner.

Neapolitan Ratatouille

Ingredients: *2 large onions · 3 eggplants ·
1 lb ripe tomatoes (preferably Italian plum
type) · 4 zucchini · 4 green peppers · ½ lb
fresh, frozen or canned artichoke hearts,
quartered · ½ cup oil · 1 or 2 cloves of garlic,
peeled · 1 bouquet garni made of parsley,
1 bay leaf and 1 twig of thyme · salt · pepper*

Peel and slice the onions, cut the eggplants,
tomatoes and zucchini into pieces (step 1), and
the green peppers into strips, having removed
tops, pith and seeds. In a pan (preferably
earthenware) put the oil and the onions, and
cook until tender, but not browned. Add the
eggplants, zucchini, peppers, tomatoes, the
garlic cloves, the bouquet garni, and salt and
pepper to taste (step 2). Cover, and cook very
slowly for about 1 hour, stirring gently from
time to time. If toward the end of the cooking
there is too much liquid, raise the heat and
remove the cover. A few minutes before
the end of the cooking, add the artichoke
hearts (step 3). Take out the garlic cloves and
bouquet garni. Serve hot or cold.

Artichokes and Potatoes Country Style

Remove the outer leaves and the stems of 4 artichokes, quarter them and put in water mixed with lemon juice. Peel and quarter 3–4 medium-sized potatoes. Sauté in ½ cup oil 1 chopped scallion and 1 clove of garlic. Remove garlic, add the drained artichokes and the potatoes, and brown. Add 1 cup canned peeled tomatoes cut into pieces, a few basil leaves, and salt and pepper to taste. Cover, and cook slowly for 40–50 minutes, adding stock if necessary.

Ratatouille Niçoise

Peel, seed and cut into pieces 4 large tomatoes. Put in a pan with 2 tablespoons olive oil, 2 twigs fresh thyme (or ½ teaspoon dried thyme), and a few basil leaves (or 1 teaspoon dried basil), 1 bay leaf and 2 teaspoons salt. Let simmer. Meanwhile, peel and slice 2 large onions (preferably Spanish), and sauté them in oil, in a skillet, together with 1 clove of garlic, crushed. Add to the pan in which the tomatoes are simmering, and cover. Wash 2 green peppers, cut off tops, discard seeds and pith and slice flesh. Sauté in oil in the skillet and add to the pan. Cook in the same way 1 large eggplant, cut into ¼-inch slices but not peeled, and put it in turn into the pan. Let the ratatouille simmer for about ½ hour. If there is too much liquid after that time, remove the cover and cook a little longer. Check the seasoning. Add freshly ground pepper and serve. The ratatouille is equally good served cold, and keeps well in the refrigerator.

Mixed Vegetables Irma

Peel 3 potatoes, 3 tomatoes and 3 onions. Wash 3 peppers, preferably red or yellow, cut off tops and discard seeds and pith. Chop, together with 3 zucchini. Put in a pan with olive oil, salt and pepper to taste. Cover and cook over very low heat for 3 hours, adding a little water if necessary.

Spanish Chickpeas

Ingredients: $1\frac{1}{4}$ *lb chickpeas* · $\frac{1}{2}$ *tablespoon sodium bicarbonate* · *salt* · *1 slice bread* · *2 tablespoons oil* · *1 tablespoon butter or margarine* · *1 medium-sized onion, chopped* · $\frac{3}{4}$ *cup canned peeled tomatoes, roughly chopped* · *1 clove of garlic* · *1 hard-boiled egg* · *pepper*

Let the chickpeas stand in plenty of cold water (step 1) for 24 hours. Drain, sprinkle with sodium bicarbonate, mix well and leave for 15 minutes. Rinse under cold running water. Put in a casserole, add 2 quarts cold water, bring to a boil and cook on moderate heat

for about 2 hours until tender, seasoning with salt to taste towards the end of the cooking. In another casserole, fry the bread until crisp in the oil and butter, remove and reserve. Add the onion, cook until golden, then add the tomatoes. After a few minutes, add the drained chickpeas and a few tablespoons of their cooking liquid. In a mortar crush the clove of garlic with the fried bread and the yolk of the hard-boiled egg (step 2). Add 1–2 tablespoons water to make a smooth mixture, then add to the chickpeas, together with the chopped white of the egg (step 3). Cover, and cook for $\frac{1}{2}$ hour, seasoning with salt and pepper.

494

Chickpea Salad

Prepare 1 lb chickpeas for cooking as left. Put in a pan with 1½ quarts cold water, bring to a boil, and cook on moderate heat for about 2 hours until tender. In a bowl put 1 clove of garlic, crushed, 1 onion, chopped, 1 tomato and 1 green pepper, chopped. Add the drained chickpeas. Season with oil, vinegar, salt and freshly ground pepper to taste, and mix well.

Chickpeas with Pork

Prepare 1¼ lb chickpeas for cooking as left. In a large pan brown ¼ cup butter or margarine lightly with 2 oz salt pork, previously soaked in cold water and chopped, and 1 onion, chopped. Add 2 quarts cold water and the chickpeas. Bring to a boil, add 1 quart stock, 1 carrot, peeled and chopped, 2–3 celery stalks, cut into strips, 3 sage leaves and 3 lb assorted pork meat (spare ribs, rind, pig's foot or ear). Season with salt and pepper to taste, and cook over moderate heat for about 2 hours or until chickpeas and pork are tender. Serve the chickpeas with the meat and the broth.

Chickpea Purée

Prepare and cook 1 lb chickpeas as left. Peel ½ lb potatoes and cook in boiling water. Drain the chickpeas (reserving a little of the cooking liquid) and potatoes and work through a sieve. In a mortar, crush 2 cloves of garlic with 2 egg yolks, and blend in 1 cup olive oil. Add, a little at a time, to the chickpea and potato purée, beating constantly until a smooth mixture is obtained, and adding from time to time a spoonful of the reserved juices. Add salt and pepper to taste. Sprinkle with chopped chervil, basil, onion, garlic, parsley and capers. Serve with toast.

Haricots with Ham

Ingredients: ¾ lb dried haricot beans · 1 ham bone · salt · 4 oz pork rind · ½ clove of garlic, crushed · a little onion and parsley, chopped together · 1½ tablespoons oil · 1 cup canned peeled tomatoes, worked through a sieve · pepper

Soak the beans in cold water overnight. Drain, put in plenty of cold water together with the ham bone and salt, cover, bring to a boil and cook about 1 hour, until the beans are tender. Meanwhile, scorch the pork rind, scald in boiling water, cut into pieces, put in a pan, cover with cold water, and cook very slowly until tender. When both the beans and the pork rind are cooked, in a large pan brown the garlic, onion and parsley in the oil. Add the tomatoes (step 1), and season with salt and pepper to taste. Cook for 15 minutes. Drain the beans (reserving the cooking juices) and the pork rind, and add to the tomato mixture with the meat from the ham bone, cut into strips (step 2). Continue cooking over low heat for another 20 minutes, adding a few spoonfuls of the reserved cooking juices from the beans if the mixture becomes too thick (step 3).

Haricots Bretonne

Cook 1 lb fresh haricots in lightly salted boiling water until tender, together with 1 onion stuck with 2 cloves. Meanwhile, in a pan, cook 8 shallots, finely chopped, in ½ cup butter until transparent, add 4 tomatoes, peeled and crushed, and season with salt and pepper to taste. When the beans are cooked, drain (discarding onion) and add to tomato mixture. Sprinkle with chopped parsley before serving.

Boston Baked Beans

In a high and narrow earthenware pot, soak 1¼ lb dried kidney beans in cold water overnight. Drain, and cover again with cold water. Cover the pot, put it over moderate heat, and cook slowly for 1 hour. Drain, reserving the cooking water. Put 6 oz salt pork in the piece (previously soaked in cold water) at the bottom of the pot, add the beans, add 10 oz salt pork (soaked and chopped) and push it into the beans. Mix ½ cup molasses with an equal amount of the reserved cooking water from the beans, ½ cup mustard powder, 1 pinch paprika, and 1 teaspoon chopped onion. Pour into the pot. Cover, and cook for 6 hours in a slow oven (250°F). Every hour add a little more of the reserved cooking water from the beans, and stir lightly with a wooden spoon. Remove the cover from the pot for the last hour of cooking so that a golden crust forms on top.

Haricots Panachés

Cook ½ lb fresh haricots in lightly salted boiling water until tender. (Dried haricot beans can be used, in which case, soak them overnight in cold water, then cook them in plenty of salted water for about 1 hour, until they are tender). In a separate pan, cook ½ lb string beans, uncovered, in salted boiling water until tender. When beans are cooked, drain, mix together and sauté lightly in ½ cup butter or margarine. Season with salt and pepper to taste. Sprinkle with chopped parsley and serve immediately, piping hot.

497

Lentils with Pork

Ingredients: *1 ½ cups dried lentils · 2 oz pork fat, chopped · a mixture (to taste) of onion, celery, carrot, parsley, all chopped · ¼ cup butter or margarine · ½ lb canned peeled tomatoes or 1—2 tablespoons tomato paste · salt · pepper · stock*

To serve: *sausages, or duck or pork paupiettes (optional)*

Soak the lentils in cold water overnight. Drain (step 1). In a casserole (preferably earthenware) brown the pork fat and the chopped vegetable mixture in the butter or margarine. Add the lentils (step 2), cook for a few minutes then add the tomatoes (step 3) or tomato paste, and salt and pepper to taste. Cover, and cook very slowly for about 1½ hours, adding hot stock from time to time, until the lentils are tender and the juice is thoroughly reduced. Serve with sausages, duck, or (as in the picture above) pork paupiettes.

498

Lentils Bordelaise

Soak 1½ cups dried lentils in cold water overnight. Drain, put in cold water, bring to a boil, skim the scum, add 1 whole onion, peeled and stuck with 2 cloves, 2 tomatoes, peeled, and 1 bouquet garni. Cover, lower the heat and cook slowly for 1 hour. Add 1 cup white wine, 2 cloves of garlic, chopped, and ½ cup butter. Season with salt to taste. Cook for a further 30 minutes, then season with pepper to taste. When lentils are tender, discard onion and bouquet garni, sprinkle with chopped parsley to taste and serve.

Lentil Salad

Soak 1½ cups dried lentils and drain as above. Put in an earthenware pot with lots of water and a generous pinch of salt. Bring to a boil, skim off the scum, cook slowly for about 1½ hours until lentils are tender. Rinse under cold running water, drain, and let cool. Toss in vinaigrette dressing (see p.501) and finely chopped garlic and parsley to taste. Let stand for a while in a cool place or refrigerator before serving.

Lentil Meatballs

Put ½ cup dried lentils into a saucepan, cover with water and bring to a boil. Cover and simmer for 15 minutes. Meanwhile, mix 1 lb ground beef with 1 small onion, peeled and chopped, 2 fresh green chili peppers, seeded and chopped, 1 teaspoon ground cumin and seasoning. Drain the lentils and add to the beef mixture. Combine thoroughly. Shape the mixture into balls about 1½ inches in diameter using floured hands. Heat 4 tablespoons oil in a frying pan, add the meatballs and fry for about 10 minutes, turning frequently, until crisp and brown. Drain and serve hot.

Mixed Salad

Ingredients: *1 small cauliflower · 6 oz string beans · 2 hard-boiled eggs · 6 oz cooked white chicken meat, cut into strips · 4 oz Emmenthal cheese, cut into strips · 2 tomatoes, sliced · mustard powder · vinaigrette dressing (see opposite) · chopped parsley and basil*

Cook the cauliflower and string beans separately in boiling salted water until *al dente*; drain. Break the cauliflower into flowerets. Separate the whites from the yolks of the hard-boiled eggs, and cut the whites into strips. Put the cauliflower, string beans, chicken, cheese, tomatoes and egg whites in a salad bowl. Mash the egg yolks and blend with mustard powder and vinaigrette dressing to taste. Pour over the salad and toss lightly. Sprinkle with chopped parsley and basil to taste. Serves 6.

Country Salad

Mix chicory, celery cut into strips, and beets, cooked and sliced, and toss in vinaigrette dressing (see right).

Artichoke and Celery Salad

Cut raw artichoke hearts and celery stalks into thin strips. Let stand for a while in cold water and lemon juice. Drain, dry well, and toss in vinaigrette dressing (see right).

Dried Bean Salad

Mix canned or cooked kidney or Lima beans with onion and parsley, chopped. Toss in vinaigrette dressing (see right).

String Bean Salad

Mix string beans, cooked, with 1 teaspoon chopped onion and 1 teaspoon chopped parsley. Toss in vinaigrette dressing (see right).

Tomato Salad

Cut 1 large onion into thin slices. If a mild taste of onion is preferred, soak it in cold water for a little while. Arrange the onion slices at the bottom of a salad bowl. Cover with tomatoes, sliced, sprinkle with chopped parsley, basil, celery and scallion to taste, pour over vinaigrette dressing (see right) and let stand in refrigerator before serving.

Belgian Endive and Beet Salad

Trim endives, and halve them lengthwise. Add beets, cooked and sliced. Toss in vinaigrette dressing (see right) flavored with mustard powder to taste.

Vinaigrette Dressing

Ingredients: *1 tablespoon vinegar · salt and freshly ground pepper to taste · 3 tablespoons oil*

Put the salt, pepper and vinegar in a bowl. Blend well, add the oil and beat lightly with a fork. The quantity can be altered as necessary, as long as the proportions — 1 part vinegar, 3 parts oil — are the same. To make a large amount, put the ingredients in a screwtop jar or bottle, and shake well. Vinaigrette dressing will keep in the refrigerator for 3–4 days. There are many variations of this basic salad dressing (see the following suggestions).

Garlic dressing (for any salad): let 2 cloves of garlic, peeled, stand in the vinegar for 2–3 days before use.

Tarragon dressing (for any salad): keep a few tarragon twigs in the vinegar bottle.

Mushroom dressing (for green salads): add 4 oz raw mushrooms cut into very thin slices.

Roquefort or Gorgonzola cheese dressing (for green salads): add 2 tablespoons Roquefort or Gorgonzola cheese, mashed with a fork.

Mustard and anchovy dressing (for potato and cauliflower salads): add 1 teaspoon French mustard powder and 1 teaspoon anchovy paste.

Oil and Lemon Dressing

Proceed exactly as for vinaigrette dressing, but replace the vinegar by lemon juice — in the same proportions. Other ingredients may be added to taste (see the following suggestions).

Caper dressing (for green and fish salads): add 1 teaspoon chopped capers and ½ clove of garlic, mashed.

Lobster roe dressing (for fish salads): add the roe of a cooked lobster, mashed with a fork, ½ tablespoon chopped parsley, and a few drops Worcestershire.

Curry dressing (for green salads): add 1 teaspoon curry powder, and 1 teaspoon chopped shallots or scallions.

Chef's Salad

Ingredients: *1 clove of garlic, peeled ·*
1 lettuce head, washed, drained, dried and
broken into pieces · 2 tomatoes, quartered ·
1 small bunch radishes, sliced · 1 green pepper,
cut into strips · 4 oz each cooked ham and
chicken, cut into thin strips · ½ cucumber,
sliced · 2–3 hard-boiled eggs, quartered ·
2 oz Gruyère cheese, cut into strips ·
2 celery stalks, chopped

For the dressing: 8–9 tablespoons oil ·
¼ teaspoon Worcestershire · 2–3 tablespoons
vinegar · 1 clove of garlic, halved · salt · pepper

Prepare the dressing: put all the ingredients
in a screwtop jar with salt and pepper to taste.
Close the jar and shake it well (step 1). Rub
the inside of the salad bowl with the whole
clove of garlic (step 2). Put all the prepared
salad ingredients in the bowl and pour in
prepared dressing, (step 3) removing the halved
garlic cloves. Toss lightly just before serving.

502

Caesar's Salad

Rub the inside of the salad bowl with a halved clove of garlic. Put in 1–2 lettuce heads – according to size – washed, drained, dried, and broken into pieces. Mix 5–6 tablespoons olive oil in a screwtop jar as above with the juice of 1 lemon, ½ teaspoon mustard powder, salt and pepper to taste. Just before serving, pour the dressing over the salad, add 2 egg yolks, lightly beaten, and mix thoroughly but carefully. Fry lightly over low heat 2 slices of bread, diced, in a little oil with 1 clove of garlic, crushed. Add to the salad, mix quickly – the bread should remain crisp – and serve immediately. If a more highly seasoned salad is preferred, add anchovy fillets, desalted by soaking in a little milk and cut into pieces, and Worcestershire.

Chicory Salad with Salt Pork

Clean, wash, drain, dry and break into pieces 1 lb chicory. Put in a salad bowl. Sauté 4 oz salt pork (previously soaked in cold water) or bacon, diced, in 1 tablespoon oil until golden. Drain and add to the chicory with 2 hard-boiled eggs, chopped. Pour the fat remaining in the sauté pan over the salad, add vinegar to taste, toss lightly and serve immediately. In France this salad is made with dandelion leaves.

Swiss Salad

Peel ¾ lb boiled new potatoes and slice into a bowl. Peel, core and slice an apple and add to the bowl with 2 tablespoons white wine vinegar, 4 tablespoons oil, 1 teaspoon prepared mustard and seasoning. Toss gently together.

Line a salad bowl with lettuce leaves and arrange the potato mixture in the center. Scatter 6 oz Swiss cheese, cut into matchsticks, around the edge and cover with 4 sliced hard-cooked eggs. Sprinkle with 2 teaspoons chopped chives and 1 teaspoon paprika and serve immediately.

Piedmontese Salad

Ingredients: $\frac{1}{4}$ *lb boiled artichoke hearts ·*
$\frac{1}{4}$ *lb boiled asparagus tips · 6 oz mushroom*
caps · 1 white truffle · lettuce leaves

For the dressing: *salt · pepper ·*
2 tablespoons lemon juice · 4 tablespoons oil

Slice the artichoke hearts (step 1), and cut the
asparagus tips into small pieces. Cut the mushroom caps into very thin slices. Arrange in
small separate piles in a serving platter.
Garnish the edges of the platter with lettuce
leaves (step 2). Scrape, wash and dry the
truffle, and slice very thinly over the other
vegetables (step 3). Prepare the dressing,
mixing first the salt and pepper in the lemon
juice, then adding the oil. Serve the dressing
separately.

Truffles in Mushroom Caps

Clean 8 mushroom caps, and cook them for 3—4
minutes in boiling salted water with a little
lemon juice and 1 tablespoon butter, or use
them raw, if they are fresh. Scrape, wash and
dry 1 medium-sized white truffle. Slice it very
thinly, and sprinkle with oil, lemon juice and
freshly ground pepper. Divide truffle between
mushroom caps. Arrange on a serving platter
garnished with parsley and wedges of lemon.

Truffles Baked in Ashes

Scrape, wash and dry 4 black truffles. Soak them in brandy for 2 hours. Put 4 slices of pâté de foie gras over 4 slices of salt pork (previously soaked in cold water for $\frac{1}{2}$ hour), each large enough to enclose 1 truffle. Put 1 truffle over each. Roll piecrust dough into squares big enough to enclose salt pork, foie gras and truffle. Wrap truffles, sealing pastry edges with water and wrap in a triple thickness of wax paper. Put under ashes covered with hot coals for at least 30 minutes. If ashes are not available, cook them in a moderate oven (350°F) for 30 minutes.

Truffles in White Wine

Scrape, wash and dry 4 small black truffles. Put in a pan with 1 glass dry white wine, a pinch of salt, and a little freshly ground pepper. Cover the pan so it is airtight, and cook over high heat for about 10 minutes, or until the wine has completely evaporated.

Tunisian Mixed Salad

Dice $1\frac{1}{2}$ lb cooked waxy potatoes and $\frac{1}{2}$ lb cooked carrots. Drain 3 canned artichoke hearts and cut into 4. Place the potatoes, carrots and artichoke hearts in a serving dish and add $1\frac{1}{2}$ cups cooked peas, 2 tablespoons capers, 12 pitted ripe olives and 12 pitted green olives. Whisk 4 tablespoons olive oil with 2 tablespoons lemon juice, 1 tablespoon chopped parsley, $\frac{1}{4}$ teaspoon ground coriander and seasoning. Pour this dressing over the salad and toss lightly. Chill for 30 minutes before serving.

Cooked Vegetable Salad

Ingredients: *1 small cauliflower · 1 lb carrots ·
5 artichokes · ½ lb Brussels sprouts · ½ lb fresh,
frozen or canned green peas, shelled ·
mayonnaise, commercially prepared or
homemade, mixed with chopped parsley and
diluted with lemon juice to taste*

*For the dressing: 1 celery stalk · 2 oz onion,
chopped · oil · vinegar · salt · pepper*

Cook the vegetables separately in boiling
salted water until *al dente*. Break the cauliflower
into flowerets. Cut the carrots into strips (step
1). Discard the outer leaves from the artichokes
and quarter them. Combine all the dressing
ingredients together and pour over the vegetables in separate dishes (step 2). Let stand for
at least 1 hour. Place lettuce leaves on a
large round serving platter. Put the peas in the
middle, and arrange all the vegetables around,
varying the colors as much as possible (step
3). Serve the mayonnaise separately. Serves 6.

Cauliflower Salad

Remove the outer leaves of 1 medium-sized cauliflower and trim the stalk. Wash, and cook in boiling salted water with a slice of lemon and a slice of bread for about 15 minutes until *al dente*. Pass under cold running water, drain, and break into flowerets. Put in a salad bowl with 2 tablespoons capers, 6 anchovy fillets, desalted by soaking in a little milk and cut into pieces, ¼ cup black olives. pitted and sliced. In a bowl, blend 3 tablespoons oil, 3 tablespoons vinegar (the proportions can be changed according to taste), a few basil leaves and salt and pepper to taste. Pour over the cauliflower, toss lightly, and let stand in a cool place or refrigerator for at least ½ hour before serving.

Potato Salad

Boil, drain and peel 2 lb potatoes. Slice, and put in a salad bowl with just enough cold stock to moisten. Slice 1 onion into very thin rings and add to the bowl. Let stand in a cool place or refrigerator for ½ hour. Pour over vinaigrette dressing (see p.501) before serving, and sprinkle with chopped parsley to taste. Garnish with hard-boiled egg slices, decorated with rolled anchovy fillets (desalted by soaking in a little milk), and tomato quarters.

Sweet and Sour Corn Salad

Drain an 8-oz can whole kernel corn and place in a bowl. Add 2 tablespoons wine vinegar, 3 tablespoons oil and seasoning and mix well. Cover and chill. Meanwhile, peel and dice 1 lb boiled potatoes. Slice ½ lb tomatoes. Drain an 8-oz can pineapple chunks, reserving 2 tablespoons of the syrup. Peel and slice 2 bananas. Place the potatoes, tomatoes, pineapple and banana in a bowl. Mix together the reserved pineapple syrup, 5 tablespoons lemon juice, 1 tablespoon French mustard, ½ cup sour cream, 2 tablespoons milk, 1 teaspoon paprika and seasoning. Add this dressing to the potato mixture and toss gently. Chill for 30 minutes.

Line a salad bowl with lettuce leaves. Spoon the potato mixture around the edge and pile the corn mixture in the center.

507

Aspic Aurora

Ingredients: *1 tablespoon powdered gelatin ·
1¼ lb tomatoes, chopped · 1 small onion,
chopped · 1 celery stalk, chopped · 1 clove ·
1 bouquet garni made of parsley, thyme and
1 bay leaf · ½ teaspoon sugar · salt · pepper ·
juice of ½ lemon · hard-boiled eggs · pitted
black olives · tomatoes · gherkins · carrots,
green peas and cauliflower flowerets, all cooked*

To garnish: *olives · lemon · parsley*

Soak the gelatin in a little cold water in a
heatproof bowl. Meanwhile, put the tomatoes
in a pan with the onion, celery, clove, bouquet
garni, sugar, salt and pepper to taste, and a
little water. Cook very slowly for about ½ hour,
then work through a vegetable mill or sieve,
and add enough water to obtain 2 cups of
sauce. Return to the heat, bring to a boil and
remove from the heat immediately. Strain the
sauce through a cloth into a measuring jug

and, if there is less than 2 cups, add a little hot water. Stand the bowl containing the gelatin in a pan of hot water and allow to dissolve over low heat. Mix it with the tomato sauce (step 1), and add the lemon juice. Pour a $\frac{1}{4}$-inch layer of this tomato aspic into the bottom of a large round mold, and put the mold in the refrigerator. As soon as it has set, arrange carefully over the aspic slices of egg, olive, tomato, gherkin, carrot and a few green peas and cauliflower flowerets (step 2). Pour over another thin layer of aspic (step 3), and let it set in the refrigerator. Repeat these layers until all the ingredients have been used, finishing with a layer of aspic. Keep in the refrigerator until serving time. To unmold: turn the mold over on a large serving platter, and cover it with a cloth soaked in boiling water and squeezed; or, plunge the mold in hot water for a few seconds. When the aspic has dropped onto the platter, return to the refrigerator for a few minutes. Garnish with whole olives, slices of lemon and parsley sprigs.

Aspic à la Russe

Peel 6 oz carrots and 6 oz turnips and cut into strips. Cover with boiling salted water and cook until tender. Meanwhile, cover 9 oz each of fresh or frozen green peas and beans with boiling salted water, add 1 tomato to the pan together with 1 onion stuck with 1 clove, and 1 bouquet garni, and cook until peas and beans are tender. Drain vegetables and reserve both cooking liquids. Put reserved cooking liquids into a clean pan and continue boiling, with the bouquet garni and 1 celery stalk, until reduced. Soak 1 tablespoon powdered gelatin in cold water. Strain the vegetable stock through a cloth once it has reduced to 2 cups. Check the seasoning. Stir the soaked gelatin into the stock and stir to dissolve. Put a layer of this vegetable aspic at the bottom of a large round mold, and let it set in the refrigerator. Proceed as for the above recipe, placing layers of vegetables and vegetable aspic alternately in the mold. Unmold as above.

Preserves

Spiced Herb Vinegar

Ingredients: *1 quart red wine vinegar · ¼ cup fresh rosemary · ¼ cup fresh mint leaves · 10 fresh sage leaves · 2 small bay leaves · 2–3 cloves of garlic, peeled · 2 teaspoons salt · ¼ oz each of cinnamon sticks, whole cloves, peppercorns and mustard seeds*

In an earthenware jar, put all the dry ingredients (step 1). Pour in the vinegar (step 2), then cover the jar with a triple thickness of wax paper and tie securely. Keep in a cool place for at least 15 days, rotating the jar gently every day. Strain the vinegar first through a sieve, then through a paper filter or wet gauze or cheesecloth. Remove the garlic. Pour the vinegar into small sterilized bottles, which will be easier for everyday use, and seal them with corks (or use screwtop jars).

Garlic Vinegar

In a mortar, preferably of marble, mash 4 cloves of garlic with a wooden pestle. Add 1 cup red wine vinegar, and stir for a few minutes. Pour into a 1-quart jar, add 3 more cups vinegar, and stir again. Close the jar tightly and keep in a cool dark place for 2–3 days, before straining and bottling the vinegar as above.

Basil Vinegar

Bring to a boil in an earthenware or enamel pan 1 quart red wine vinegar. Add 1 generous handful of fresh basil leaves, cleaned with a cloth but not washed, and turn off the heat immediately. (If fresh basil is not available, use 3 tablespoons dried basil.) Cover the pan tightly and let stand for at least 48 hours, before straining and bottling the vinegar as above.

Mint Vinegar

Proceed as for Basil Vinegar above, but using 2 generous handfuls of fresh mint leaves to 1 quart white wine vinegar. Strain the bottle and leave to stand for a few weeks before using the vinegar.

Tarragon Vinegar

Bottle about ¼ cup fresh twigs of tarragon in 1 quart red wine vinegar. Seal and let stand for about 48 hours before using the vinegar: there is no need to strain it. You may do the same, in the same proportions, with white wine vinegar.

Pickled String Beans

Ingredients: $2\frac{1}{2}$ lb young fresh string beans · water · rock salt · white vinegar · $\frac{1}{4}$ oz each of cinnamon, whole cloves, mace and peppercorns to each quart of vinegar

Wash the string beans, and put them in a bowl. Bring to a boil enough water to cover the beans with 3 tablespoons rock salt to each quart of water. Let cool, and pour over the beans. Let stand for 24 hours. Meanwhile, in an earthenware or enamel pan bring to a boil enough white vinegar to cover the beans, with $\frac{1}{4}$ oz of each of the spices to each quart, cover, turn off the heat, and leave to infuse for 2–3 hours. Strain through a gauze or cheesecloth. Drain the beans, rinse under cold running water and drain again. Dry thorough-

ly. Arrange in sterilized jars (step 1) and pour over the cold vinegar to cover (step 2). Seal the jars, and let stand in a cool dark place at constant temperature, wrapping jars in a cloth to protect from sunlight if necessary (step 3), for at least 2 months before using.

Pickled Onions

Ingredients: *2½ lb small white pickling onions · 1 quart white vinegar · 1 clove of garlic, peeled · 2 whole cloves · 8 peppercorns · 2 bay leaves · 1 cinnamon stick · fresh thyme (optional) · 1 tablespoon rock salt · oil*

Dip the onions in boiling water, cool and peel. Put the garlic, cloves, peppercorns, bay leaves, cinnamon, thyme (if using) and salt in a small muslin bag. Put it with the vinegar in a large earthenware or enamel pan, and bring to a boil. Add the onions, continue boiling for 5 minutes, then drain the onions, reserving the vinegar and discarding the bag. Pack the onions tightly in sterilized jars. Bring the vinegar again to a boil, remove from heat, let cool, and pour over onions to cover. Add 1 bay leaf to each jar, and a layer of oil. Seal and keep as above for 2–3 weeks before using.

Pickled Hot Peppers

Clean with a wet cloth 4 lb hot green peppers, and remove the stems. Place in a very low oven for a few hours to dry out completely. Pack them fairly tightly in warm sterilized earthenware jars, cover with boiling vinegar, add 1 handful rock salt to each jar, and seal with cork or stopper. After 30 days, drain off the vinegar, cover with fresh vinegar, and add a few cloves of garlic, peeled and blanched. Keep as Pickled Onions.

Pickled Gherkins

Put 4 lb gherkins – about 2 inches long – in a napkin with 4 tablespoons rock salt and shake well, holding the napkin by its corners. Rub them one by one with a cloth or a soft brush. Arrange them in an earthenware or enamel bowl, mix with 1 lb rock salt and let stand for 6–7 hours to make them lose their water. Remove and dry one by one. Put in sterilized glass jars together with 4 cloves of garlic, peeled and blanched, and 3 hot red peppers. Cover with vinegar, and seal the jars. Keep as above, changing the vinegar after 1 month.

Preserved Mixed Vegetables

Ingredients: *1 cauliflower · 4 carrots · 4 celery stalks · 2 green peppers · ½ lb red and yellow peppers · ¼ cup olives · 1 quart white vinegar · 1 cup olive oil · ¼ cup sugar · 2 teaspoons salt · ½ teaspoon pepper · 1 teaspoon oregano*

Detach the cauliflower flowerets and slice, scrape the carrots and cut into sticks, cut the celery into pieces, discard the tops, seeds and white pith from the peppers and cut flesh into strips; leave the olives whole. In a large earthenware or enamel pan, put all the vegetables — washed and thoroughly dried — the vinegar, oil, sugar, salt, pepper and oregano (steps 1 and 2). Bring to a boil, stirring from time to time, cover, and cook slowly for 5 minutes. Turn off the heat, leave to cool, then put the vegetables together with the cooking liquid in sterilized jars (step 3). Seal, and let stand in a cool dark place at constant temperature for at least 2 months before using.

Pickled Mushrooms

Put 3 blades of mace and $\frac{1}{2}$ oz peppercorns in a muslin bag and put in an earthenware or enamel pan together with 1 quart vinegar. Bring to a boil, cover, turn off the heat, and leave to infuse for 2–3 hours. Strain. Peel and trim fresh mushrooms, put in a pan, sprinkle lightly with salt, and cook gently until juice flows. Continue cooking until juice has evaporated. Cover with the spiced vinegar and simmer for 2–3 minutes. Let cool. Pour into sterilized jars, seal, and keep as left.

Pickled Eggplants

Remove stems and green parts of medium-sized eggplants. Slice them lengthwise, without peeling, and put in an earthenware or enamel pan. Cover with water, add a generous amount of salt, and let stand for 24 hours. Meanwhile, bring to a boil enough vinegar to cover the eggplants with 1 oz each of garlic, basil or mint leaves, parsley and peppercorns in a muslin bag. Cover, turn off heat, and leave for 2–3 hours. Strain. Drain the eggplants, rinse, drain again, and dry well. Pack in sterilized jars with the cold vinegar, seal, and keep as left.

Pickled Sweet Peppers

Remove tops from 7 lb yellow and red sweet peppers and cut peppers into wedges: 6 wedges to each pepper. Discard the seeds and white pith. Wipe with a wet cloth. Put in an earthenware or enamel pan together with 1 quart white vinegar, 1 cup olive oil, and 1 tablespoon salt. Bring to a boil, and cook for 3 minutes. Remove from the heat, let cool, and put the peppers with the cooking liquid in sterilized jars. Seal, and keep as left.

Chow Chow

Ingredients: *2 quarts water · ¾ cup rock salt ·
1 cup each of quartered green tomatoes, small
cucumbers, whole or halved, chopped gherkins,
whole small white pickling onions, chopped
celery, string beans, cut into pieces, cauliflower
flowerets, cut into pieces, chopped green
peppers · 3 cups white wine vinegar · ½ cup
sugar · 2 tablespoons flour · ½ teaspoon
turmeric · 2 tablespoons mustard powder*

Boil the water with the salt. Let stand until cold
and pour over the prepared vegetables. Let
stand for at least 12 hours. Drain, rinse the
vegetables under running water, and drain
again. Put in an earthenware or enamel pan,
add the vinegar, and bring slowly to a boil.
Meanwhile, in a bowl, mix the sugar with the
flour, the turmeric, the mustard, and enough
vinegar from the pan to obtain a smooth
paste (step 1). Add to the vegetables (step 2),
and continue cooking over moderate heat for
5–6 minutes, stirring constantly. Pour immediately into 1-pint warm sterilized jars, filling
them up to the top (step 3). Seal, and keep in a
cool dark place at constant temperature.

Prune Chutney

Pit and slice in four 3½ lb prunes. Peel 1¼ lb apples, remove the cores, and chop finely. Chop 10 oz onions. Mix in a bowl with 1 lb small grapes. In an earthenware or enamel pan, bring to a boil 1 quart white vinegar, with 1 lb sugar, 1 teaspoon powdered cloves, 1 teaspoon powdered cinnamon, 1 teaspoon ground ginger, 1 teaspoon mixed spice, and 2 tablespoons salt. Add the fruit and the onion, and cook very slowly, stirring from time to time, until a well blended, thick mixture is obtained. Pour the chutney immediately into 3 warm sterilized 1-pint jars. Seal, and keep in a cool dark place at constant temperature. If a sharper taste is desired, add chili powder. The chutney can be used immediately.

Pickled Walnuts

Select 50 fresh (green) walnuts and prick them with a needle to make sure they are not hard. Boil enough water to cover walnuts with 1 tablespoon rock salt for each quart water. Pour over the walnuts. Let stand for 10 days, changing the salted water every 3 days. After that time, drain the nuts, dry them with a cloth, and prick them repeatedly with a large needle. In a bowl, mix 3 tablespoons fresh root ginger, or ground ginger, 2 tablespoons peppercorns, 2 tablespoons mixed spice, 1 tablespoon whole cloves, 1 tablespoon mustard seeds, and ½ tablespoon grated nutmeg. Put the walnuts in warm sterilized jars, alternating with layers of spices, and fill the jars with cider vinegar boiled for 4–5 minutes. Seal and keep as above for at least 2 months.

Sweet-and-Sour Olives

Wash, drain and dry 2 cups green or black olives. Put the olives in ½- or 1-pint warm sterilized jars. In an earthenware or enamel pan, put ¼ cup sugar, 4 tablespoons rock salt, 4 tablespoons mustard seeds, 1 quart white vinegar, and 1 cup water. Bring to a boil, and cook for 4 minutes. Pour immediately over the olives, and seal the jars. Keep as above for at least 15 days before using.

517

Grapes in Brandy

Ingredients: *3–4 lb white grapes · 1 cinnamon stick · 1 quart brandy · ¾ cup sugar · 6–8 cloves · 1 pinch of ground coriander (optional)*

Using a pair of scissors, cut each grape from the bunch, leaving a small piece of stem to each grape (step 1), and dry gently. Put in an airtight glass jar with the cinnamon stick. In a bowl beat the brandy with the sugar, cloves, and coriander if using until the sugar has completely melted. Pour the mixture into the jar (step 2), close hermetically and let stand in a cool place for at least 2 months.

Macedoine of Fruit in Brandy

Make this recipe during the strawberry season, using other seasonal fruit. Using a 2½-quart glass jar make a layer of strawberries and raspberries, cleaned but not washed, add an equal weight of sugar and enough brandy to cover. Add a layer of cherries, wiped with a cloth, an equal weight of sugar and enough brandy to cover, and seal the jar hermetically. When you can obtain ripe apricots, clean and pit them and add them to the jar, pit side down, with an equal weight of sugar and enough brandy to cover. Do the same with plums and peaches, pears, peeled and diced, and grapes, prepared as above, as the different fruit come into season. Always add an equal weight of sugar and enough brandy to cover (step 3). Seal the jar hermetically and let stand for at least 2 months. Before serving, mix the fruit gently with a wooden spoon.

Prunes in Brandy

Put prunes in a glass jar and add sugar, 1 cinnamon stick, a few cloves and enough brandy to cover. Seal the jar hermetically and let stand for at least 2 months. Dried apricots may be prepared in the same way.

Raisins in Cognac

Put raisins in a glass jar and add enough Cognac to cover. Add 1 cinnamon stick and a few cloves, seal the jar hermetically and let stand for at least 2 months.

Cherries in Brandy

Cover a tray with a cloth, put Bing cherries on top and let stand for at least 24 hours. Trim the stems and wipe the cherries gently. Put the cherries in a large glass jar with 1 tablespoon sugar (optional), 4 cloves and 1 cinnamon stick; cover with brandy. Seal jar hermetically.

Kumquats in Brandy

Wipe kumquats with a soft cloth and put them in a 2-cup glass jar. In a pan dissolve 2 tablespoons sugar in 2–3 tablespoons water, then boil until the syrup is thickened, and let cool. Pour it into the jar and add enough brandy to cover. Seal the jar hermetically.

Pear Jam

Ingredients: *2 lb pears · 3 cups sugar · the juice of ½ lemon*

Peel the pears (step 1), discard the seeds, and cube the fruit. Put in a bowl, add the sugar and lemon juice and let macerate for 2 hours. Pour the fruit into a large pan, preferably of untinned copper, and cook over moderate heat for 15–20 minutes, stirring occasionally and removing the scum as it forms on the surface (step 2). To test if done, drop a little jam on a dry plate: if it does not run when the plate is tilted, the jam is ready. Spoon it immediately into hot sterilized jars (step 3), and set on a damp towel so that the jars do not break. Seal the jars immediately with slightly damp cellophane and a rubber band or string, or with cellophane and stopper or lid.

Strawberry Jam

Hull and clean (do not wash) 2 lb strawberries. Put them in an enamel pan, cover with 4 cups sugar and let stand for 3 hours. Bring the mixture to a boil, cook for 8 minutes, add ½ cup lemon juice and continue cooking the mixture for 2 minutes. Remove from the heat, skim the scum from the surface, spoon into hot sterilized jars, and seal as above.

Grape Jelly

In a large enamel pan put a layer of firm ripe white or black grapes and mash with a fork. Repeat the process, using 8 lb grapes in all. Add 4 apples, unpeeled and cubed, and water to cover if juice does not cover fruit. Bring the mixture slowly to a boil and cook until the apples are tender. Pour the fruit into a damp cheesecloth held over a bowl, tie the four corners of the cheesecloth and let stand until all the fruit juice has dripped through. The juice should be clear and very perfumed. If more juice is needed, return the fruit to the pan, add water to cover, mix well and bring to a boil. Boil the mixture for 15 minutes and repeat the draining process. Measure the juice, reheat and add 4 tablespoons sugar for each cup liquid.

Cook the liquid, stirring constantly so as to melt the sugar, until it will fall in sheets from a metal spoon. Pour immediately into hot sterilized jars and seal the jars as above.

Introduction to Desserts

The culmination of most meals is the dessert course. By the time we reach this we are way beyond the realms of what is necessary for nutrition, and into the most delightful creations a cook can make. Fruits and gâteaux, ices and cakes, hot and cold soufflés, parfaits and bombes – these are the treasures of a cook's repertoire and can show off the ultimate in her skills.

The art in a dessert is to balance it perfectly against the courses that have gone before and within the dessert dish itself to balance the sweet flavoring with the most pleasing effect to the eye. For many of the decorative dishes in this book, practice will be necessary before you can produce perfection. In almost all cases beginners will be able to capture the flavor, but only those with practice or a very steady hand will master the intricacies of decorating a traditional gâteau or producing a perfect hot soufflé. But do not be deterred – persevere and become your own master chef.

For further pleasure you may wish to venture into the realms of homemade candies and the fine domestic arts of preserving. Whether you choose to make nougat or to preserve peaches in brandy, there is something here for you. There is also something for the host in the section on mixing cocktails to serve before dinner – plus information about liqueurs with which to bring the meal to a happy end.

Guide to Pastrymaking

Making cakes and pastries is not difficult but requires just that amount of care and attention to detail that will divide the creative cooks from those who are not. Skill with dough and skill with decorating can quickly be acquired by those with the inclination to learn.

Pastry

When making pastry, always work in cool conditions. If you have other cooking to do, make the pastry first, before the kitchen becomes too warm and steamy. If your hands are warm, hold them under cold running water before you start to work; be sure all your ingredients are cool (butter must not be either too firm or warm). Use iced water for mixing, and work on a cool surface – laminated or steel, or marble slab.

Try to work quickly and deftly, avoiding too much handling of the dough. If you have added too much water, the dough will be soft and sticky and hard to handle; it will shrink in the baking and become hard and tough to eat. If you haven't used enough water, the dough will crack as you roll it and be dry to eat.

Do not use too much extra flour (usually all-purpose) when rolling out, and apply even pressure. Pastries with a lot of fat and little water can take a lot more working than shortcrust, but keep your hands cool.

When the pastry is made, chill it in the refrigerator for 30 minutes to 1 hour before baking. The chilling will relax it and prevent it shrinking away from the sides of the dish during baking. Finally, always put pastry into a preheated oven (usually a high heat) to 'set' it and enable you to time the cooking accurately.

Cakes

The success of home-baked cakes depends for both flavor and texture on the preparation – the choice of ingredients and the way they are mixed. Flour, for instance, should always be sifted to aerate as well as

remove any small lumps. Sift the salt at the same time to distribute it evenly.

Fats play an important role and while butter will give the best flavor, hard block margarine may be substituted. Do not use soft tub-type margarine unless the recipe specifies it – it needs different treatment.

Sugar types have an immediate effect on a cake mixture. For a creamed cake, superfine is easier to combine than granulated, but both can be used. Brown sugars are used when color, moistness and rich flavor are needed, for example in gingerbread and rich fruit cakes, but not in plain sponges.

Eggs raise a cake and they also add flavor and protein. Do not use them straight from a refrigerator. Take them out an hour before you make the cake so they will be at room temperature.

Yeast mixtures

Yeast is a living organism and requires food and warmth to grow. In baking, yeast feeds on the sugar and the warmth it is given during proving (the rising process) enables the cells to multiply. The high heat of baking then kills the yeast so that it does not continue to grow. Cold on the other hand only suspends the activity of the cells, so yeast dough can be kept in a refrigerator for a short period, or frozen successfully for longer.

Fresh yeast should be stored only for a few days in a refrigerator – it comes in a block like a very soft cheese. Dried yeast, in granules, or brewer's yeast will keep almost indefinitely. If using dried, do not add it directly to the other ingredients. Let it start work first by creaming it with sugar and adding a little lukewarm liquid (neither warm nor cool to the touch) so that a froth forms. It must be distributed well through the mixture which is why kneading is a very important stage to obtain dough that is smooth and elastic.

Glossary of Fruit

Fruit is perhaps the most perfect of desserts, ranging from the familiar to the exotic. Most fruit is good eaten fully ripe and freshly picked, when it will be sweet and juicy. Some fruits, however, such as currants and gooseberries, are very astringent to eat unless cooked, when they are delicious, especially in pies and tarts or puddings.

Almost all fruits can be used in some way to give a refreshing and digestible end to a good meal and may be more or less richly dressed according to taste and to the occasion.

Apple
This fruit is more common in the United States and Britain than anywhere else in the world. It is probably true to say that the apple is England's best and most common native fruit.

Dessert apples are sweet and aromatic and the best are firm fleshed. The most common dessert varieties are Cox's Orange Pippin, James Grieve, Worcester Pearmain, Blenheim Orange and Laxton's Superb; there are hundreds of other good varieties but some do not keep well and are not often seen in the shops. Dessert apples do not normally cook well; they tend to lose flavor and become insipid, some also become tough and rubbery in texture.

Cooking apples, particularly Bramley Seedling, Newton Wonder and Lane's Prince Albert, are sharp flavored, keep well and cook to a juicy, sweet pulp. Eaten raw, cooking apples may seem hard, acid and indigestible, but raw dessert apples are excellent eaten with cheese, nuts or dates. Cooked apples are a traditional ingredient for pies and tarts.

Apricot
Small, golden fleshed fruit with a velvety bloom on the golden skin. Apricots have a single pit which is removed before cooking. They are native to places with temperate climates such as California, Australia, South Africa and some southern parts of Europe. Although they may be eaten fresh, the flavor of apricots is improved by cooking.

Dried apricots are also excellent.

Banana
Tropical fruit, much exported to colder countries. This long fruit with its white, firm flesh, ripening towards brown, encased in a thick, bright yellow skin, has a high sugar and carbohydrate content when fully ripe and is easily digested, making it a good food for children and invalids.

Unripe bananas are, however, extremely indigestible, while overripe ones quickly become bad and unsafe to eat. Bananas are best eaten fresh but can be fried or cooked to form a soft, slightly sweet background for other foods.

Barberry
Black or dark blue berry generally used for sauces and for flavoring drinks, ices and sherbets.

Bilberry (Whortleberry, Blaeberry)
Small black berry with a pleasant flavor, used mainly for jams and jellies, pies and tarts. Common in the USA and Britain.

Blackberry
The fruit of the bramble, which grows very freely in the woods and hedges of Britain and is also cultivated, both in Britain and the USA. With a high proportion of seed to flesh, it is often used with apples which provide bulk without destroying the deliciously sweet but sharp flavor of the blackberry. This fruit is commonly used for jams and jellies, and in pies and tarts. It is rarely found to be a satisfactory commercial fruit since it does not store or travel well.

Blackcurrant
Very small, fleshy fruit, more suited to cooking in pies than to eating fresh. The blackcurrant has a high pectin content which makes it an ideal choice for jam. This fruit is much more popular in Europe than the USA, although it grows equally well in the States.

Blueberry
Principally an American fruit with similar characteristics to the bilberry. Blueberry is also the name given to several edible Australian fruits.

Bullace
Small, very sour wild plum with a light green skin, good for use in jams and jellies.

Cape Gooseberry
Round, yellow berry native to tropical America and South Africa. It may be eaten fresh as a dessert, but is more commonly canned or made into jam.

Cherry
Small pit fruit varying in color from black, through various shades of red to white with only a faint blush of red. There are hundreds of varieties, some good as dessert fruit, others best for cooking or preserving. Popular throughout the USA and Europe.

Citron
Citrus fruit shaped like a large lemon. The thick green rind is often candied, and is more commonly used than the flesh.

Clementine
Seedless citrus fruit related to the tangerine.

Crab Apple
Small pip fruit with a yellow and orange skin. It is native to the East but is now widely grown in the USA and Europe. The fruit is very bitter and is rarely eaten uncooked, but it makes good jelly.

Cranberry
Small, red berry with a very sharp flavor, chiefly used for sauces, tarts and preserves. It is more commonly used in the USA although it grows widely all over Europe.

Currant (see also Blackcurrant, Redcurrant)
Small seedless grape, of the variety known as Corinth grape, dried either by the sun or artificially.

Custard Apple
Name given to several varieties of tropical fruit, including the pawpaw.

Damascene
Small, round variety of damson, but without such good flavor.

Damson
Small, black plum mostly cooked in tarts, pies and preserves. It has an excellent, tart flavor.

Date
The fruit of the date palm tree, cultivated in North Africa and Western Asia. Soft and juicy, dates are always exported boxed or packaged rather than loose.

Fig
Chiefly a Mediterranean fruit but also well established in California and the Gulf States. The shape may be round or oblong, according to variety, the color of the skin dark purple or green, the flesh red or white. Where the fruit is native it is widely eaten fresh but it travels best if dried first and is therefore better known in this form.

Gooseberry
Large berry, either green, red or black, native to Europe. The flavor is very acid and gooseberries are therefore best cooked and make an excellent purée.

Grape
The fruit of the vine, widely used for wine but also first class as a dessert fruit. Grapes do not cook well, but in the USA grape jelly is popular. Grapes are cultivated in all the warmer parts of the USA and Europe.

Grapefruit
Large, round citrus fruit with a thick yellow skin. The flesh is sharp, sweet and refreshing. The fresh sections are excellent in fruit salads and halves are popular for breakfast or as a simple starter to a three-course meal. Halves can be served hot with a caramelized top.

Lemon
Smallish, oblong citrus fruit with a yellow skin. The flesh is rarely used in desserts but the pared or grated rind and the juice are used as flavorings.

Lime
Another small citrus fruit, looking much like a green lemon. Again its juice and rind are much used as flavorings in all branches of cooking.

Litchi
Small Chinese fruit with a shell that is removed before eating. The flesh is white and sweet.

Loganberry
Hybrid raspberry, slightly larger and more acid in flavor. Excellent as a dessert fruit and for tarts and preserves.

Mango
Seed fruit native to Malaya and the West Indies, used more in chutneys or salads than sweet dishes.

524

Glossary of Fruit

Medlar
European plum-sized fruit, eaten fresh if very ripe but it is more usually made into jelly.

Melon
Sweet pulpy fruit with a hard rind, varying in size from 4–5 inches diameter for the cantaloup or ogen to 12–18 inches diameter for the water melon. Some are round, others oblong, with skin varying from yellow, through light green to very dark green. Flesh colors may be pink, pale green or orangey tones. Melon is never cooked but may be served fresh as a dessert or hors d'oeuvre.

Mulberry
Large deep purple berry, more usually cooked as compote or in pies and tarts than eaten fresh.

Nectarine
Small, smooth skinned variety of peach, grown under glass in Britain.

Orange
Citrus fruit cultivated in many warmer parts of the world. Sweet oranges make excellent dessert fruit and the juice is popular as a breakfast drink. Bitter varieties are used for preserves and confectionery.

Peach
Universally popular as a dessert fruit, the peach is a pit fruit with a yellowy flesh and a thin, bloomed skin. There are many, many varieties which all vary slightly in flavor; the best are good raw, but all may be cooked and used for preserves.

Pear
This fruit, with a pale green or golden skin, has a characteristic shape — wide at the flower end and tapering to the stalk end. There are thousands of varieties, some sweeter, some more acid. Like apples, pears may be divided into dessert fruit and cooking fruit. The best known varieties are Conference, Williams and Doyenne du Comice.

Pineapple
Large, fleshy, tropical fruit whose flesh varies in color from pale to deep yellow. The skin is thick and spined and the fruit is sold with its long, spiky leaves still attached. When fully ripened before picking, it is very sweet indeed; when ripened off the plant it retains a characteristic acidity.

Plum
Pit fruit widely grown in the USA and Europe. The fruit varies in color according to variety, from yellow and green to red and dark purple. Plums are eaten fresh and cooked.

Pomegranate
Eastern fruit with a hard, reddish skin, filled with large seeds. The juice is used as a flavoring.

Prune
Dried plum, of selected varieties.

Quince
Golden fruit, round or pear shaped, and too astringent to eat fresh. It makes excellent preserves, particularly jelly and fruit cheese.

Raisin
Dried white grape, used widely in cakes, puddings, preserves.

Raspberry
Small, red, many seeded berry native to the USA and Europe. Best eaten fresh, but also good for jam and flavoring for drinks, ice cream and sauces.

Redcurrant
Small, red, rather acid berry generally used for jelly to serve with rich meats.

Rhubarb
Strictly a vegetable but generally served as dessert. The leaves are poisonous but the pink stalks are excellent stewed in syrup for pies or tarts.

Satsuma
Large, juicy type of tangerine, mainly from Spain.

Shaddock
Large citrus fruit, the ancestor of the grapefruit.

Sloe
Small, sour, dark purple berry used to flavor liqueurs and to make jams and jellies.

Strawberry
Soft, red fruit with an excellent flavor. Best eaten fresh, but it also makes good preserves.

Sultana
Cured and bleached fruit of a particular variety of small, seedless grape, used for a variety of cakes and puddings.

Tangerine
Small orange with a thin, loose rind and very sweet juice. North African in origin.

Preserving Fruit

When the fruits of summer are available in abundance, it makes sense to preserve them so you can use them for the rest of the year in compotes, pies and tarts and also on their own. Freezing is, of course, one way, but if you have not got a freezer, bottling will ensure a good supply for your store cupboard.

Bottling

The bottling method preserves fruit by first heating it to a temperature at which all harmful bacteria are killed. At the same time the container and the water or syrup round the fruit are also sterilized and then the container is vacuum sealed so that fresh bacteria are excluded. Provided the seal is good, the fruit should remain sound for at least a year – which is probably the longest time you will want to keep it anyway.

The acid in the fruit is one of the factors that helps to maintain sterilization after processing, and those fruits with a higher acid content will always keep better than others with a low acid content.

If when you open a bottle of fruit from store you are in any doubt about its condition it is better not to eat it.

Jars

These should be wide necked and made of thick glass to withstand heat. Buy those specially designed for the job, which will have lids capable of making an airtight seal; these may be coated metal discs edged with rubber and fixed to the jar with a screw band, or they may be glass with a separate rubber band and fixed to the jar with a strong clip.

Unless you have a very large family avoid jars of more than 2–3 lb capacity since once opened the fruit will deteriorate as quickly as fresh fruit. For soft fruits such as raspberries, blackcurrants or blackberries, use smaller jars still since the fruit packs very closely. When you are buying preserving jars they may seem expensive, but don't forget that they are a once-in-a-lifetime expenditure and if carefully handled will never need replacing. All you will need to buy each year is a fresh supply of sealing rings or metal discs, both of which are quite cheap.

Sterilizing Pan

You will also need a large sterilizing pan. If you intend bottling fruit in large quantities every year you may as well buy a special pan, which will be straight sided, have a false bottom to prevent the jars coming into direct contact with the heat and a slot in the side or lid to hold a thermometer.

Alternatively use any large pan, such as a jam pan, a fish kettle or a pressure cooker; even a metal bread or flour bin can be used. It is important that the pan be deep enough for the water in it to cover the necks of the jars. (A pressure cooker can speed up the sterilization process, so if you own one it is worth checking with the manufacturer's instructions, but the disadvantage with most pressure cookers is that they will not hold more than 2–3 jars at the same time.) If your pan does not have a false bottom, put a piece of doubled wire netting, a thick pad of newspaper or a wooden board in the bottom to keep the jars away from the heat.

Other Equipment

Other items that you will find useful, though not essential, include bottle tongs with rubber covered grips, a wooden spoon with a long handle and a thermometer. The thermometer will ensure good results by verifying that the temperature is sufficiently high – without it you will always be guessing and there is a risk that sterilization may not be complete. You will need to buy a special preserving thermometer in order to get the appropriate calibrations.

When you remove the jars from the sterilizer they may be placed directly on to a laminated surface but if this is not available have ready a wooden board, such as a bread board, or a thick pad of newspaper. If placed directly onto a cold or conductive surface the jars may crack.

Fruit for Bottling

Remember when bottling that you must be wholehearted about it. It is no good buying 10 lb of fruit in the market and then letting it stand at home for a week while you make up your mind to deal with it. Only top quality, ripe, sound fruit should be used and there must be no signs of deterioration. As soon as you have picked or bought the fruit, set to work.

Use a stainless steel knife on fruits which need cutting, remove any pits and discard any fruit that is not perfect – it may be possible to turn some of this into a pie for eating straight away, or it may be suitable for jam. Make sure that your jars are clean and rinse them out so that the insides are still wet while you work. Pack the fruit gently into the jars; pack it as closely as possible without crushing it, using the handle of a wooden spoon to push it in if necessary. Fill the jars to within $\frac{1}{2}$ inch of the top.

The liquid in the jars may be water or syrup. Syrup (made with 1–2 lb sugar to every 2 pints water) keeps the fruits a better color but, depending how you intend to use the fruit later, you may wish it not so sweet. Pour the cold water or syrup over the fruit in the jars, making sure the jars are filled right to the top. Cover the jars carefully and fix the lids in place; if using screw bands do not tighten them too far at this stage. Stand the jars in the pan on the false bottom and fill up with cold water right over the necks of the jars. Remember that any fruit in the jar above the level of the water outside will not reach the temperature required to kill bacteria. Bring the water slowly to simmering point, taking $1\frac{1}{2}$ hours to bring it to this temperature. Maintain simmering heat for 10–15 minutes for soft fruits, 30–40 minutes for plums, pears and other harder fruits.

Then lift out the jars with the bottle tongs or a thick oven cloth, place them on a heat resistant surface and allow them to cool; screw bands may now be tightened. It is during cooling that the vacuum seal is made – if you have jars with metal discs you may hear the popping sound as the disc is sucked hard down into place.

After 48 hours test the seals by removing the screw bands or clips and picking each jar up by the lid; if it stays firmly in place the seal is good, if not the fruit should either be used immediately or discarded. Replace the clips or bands, label the jars and store them in a cool, dark cupboard.

Menu Planning

Nutritional considerations are most important for all meals whether for family or guests but you should also think of the balance of flavor, texture and color. Also, when planning a meal for guests, you should choose dishes that can be made in advance and only need little last minute attention. Two to one is a good rule – a cold first course followed by an oven-cooked dish that will not spoil gives you the opportunity to have a flambé dessert; or if you need to spend more time on the middle course, have a cold first course and a dessert which can be made ahead of time.

Next in importance is the balance of textures. Many hostesses make the mistake of believing that a party is the time to produce all their favorite, richest dishes. So you are served with a lobster bisque, veal à la crème and chocolate mousse with whipped cream – so rich and creamy that few guests appreciate the whole meal. How much better to follow the lobster bisque with a light dish of grilled sole or sautéed veal cutlets, or precede the veal à la crème by something fresh and appetizing such as melon cocktail or a salad of green beans and tomatoes.

Texture is probably your best aid in planning courses that go well together. If cream, for example, or a sauce is involved in all three your palate will not be able to differentiate. Succulent fruit followed by crisp meat followed by a creamy dessert gives the contrast a good meal needs. If the first course chosen is substantial, rich and creamy, then the courses that follow should be light and offer different textures and tastes.

Pasta dishes often present difficulties for dinner party menus because they are so filling. To achieve a good balance, the Italians themselves would choose melon with a fine slice of prosciutto ham to start and fresh ripe peaches in wine to follow. If served as a first course, pasta should only be in small portions with crisp meat (for example lamb cutlets) and green vegetables or a mixed salad to follow. Finish the meal with a light ice cream, water ice or sherbert.

Calorie requirements

It is useful to understand food values when working out a menu, so that there is not a preponderence of protein or carbohydrate. The body needs proteins to build and replenish tissues; proteins are found chiefly in meat, eggs, fish, milk and dried vegetables. It needs vitamins for the skin, nervous system, eyesight and circulation, these are found chiefly in vegetables, fruit, liver, fats, eggs and dairy products. And the body needs minerals; calcium is obtained from milk, iron from liver and eggs, other minerals are present in trace amounts in most vegetables.

A balanced diet must include adequate quantities of protein, minerals and vitamins, and should also include carbohydrates which provide energy without building much body tissue. It is in this area that we tend to mostly overestimate our needs – a sedentary person does not need large amounts of bread and cereal products, sugars and chocolates, for there will be little opportunity to work off the energy.

Liqueurs

After a delicious meal, well cooked and attractively presented, what is more welcome than good coffee and liqueurs? The high spirit content of most liqueurs and the herbs that many of them contain as flavorings have a beneficial effect on a full stomach, helping the digestion and relaxing the nerves. So although we never consciously drink liqueurs for medicinal reasons, they are the ideal finish to a good meal; from feeling full and sleepy they bring you to a state of comfort and ease with nothing but pleasant memories of the meal.

Most liqueurs are based on either brandy, gin, whisky or rum. Some are based on a brandy distilled from a fruit other than grapes, others on an almost tasteless spirit made from grain or potatoes. The flavoring ingredients may be any sort of fruit, herbs, spices, nuts, seeds, roots, even leaves and flowers, and most liqueurs are heavily sweetened with sugar.

Some of the most interesting recipes for liqueurs are closely guarded secrets dating back hundreds of years. These include the popular Bénédictine and Chartreuse liqueurs – both recipes being the property of certain monasteries in the north of France and outsiders can only guess at the rich combination of herbs and fruit that makes them so delicious and fragrant.

Below are some of the most popular liqueurs, listed with their characteristics and main ingredients.

Advocaat
A thick, yellow liqueur, the texture of heavy cream. It is based on brandy and flavored with egg yolks.

Anisette
Colorless, very sweet liqueur flavored with aniseed.

Apricot Brandy
Brandy based and flavored with dried apricots. Ideally it is distilled from fresh apricots and their kernels.

Bénédictine
Made to a secret recipe by monks of the Bénédictine order at Fécamp in Normandy. It is very sweet and fragrant, and assumed to be made on a brandy base flavored with spices and herbs.

Calvados
French apple brandy, distilled from cider. The best Calvados comes from the Vallée d'Auge in Normandy.

Cassis
Brandy based liqueur flavored with blackcurrant; very popular in France where it is often diluted with dry white wine and served as a long drink.

Chartreuse
Another secret recipe, originating with French monks in a Carthusian monastery in Grenoble. Green Chartreuse has a very high alcohol content; yellow is not so strong but is much sweeter.

Cherry Brandy
The best is distilled from fresh cherries; more cherries are then soaked in the fruit brandy to add color and flavor. Cheaper brands are made on a base of neutral spirit and flavored with cherries.

Crème de Cacao
Cocoa liqueur, very sweet and entirely colorless. ('Crème' indicates a particularly sweet liqueur.)

Crème de Menthe
Very sweet liqueur flavored with fresh mint. It may be colorless or colored bright green.

Crème de Moka
Very sweet coffee liqueur.

Curaçao
Brandy or gin based, and flavored with oranges. Grand Marnier and Cointreau are brands of curaçao.

Drambuie
The only truly British liqueur. It is based on Scotch whisky and the flavoring is honey.

Himbeergeist (Crème de Framboise)
Very sweet liqueur distilled from raspberries.

Kirsch
Cherry brandy distilled from the small black cherries of Switzerland, Germany and Alsace, very popular in Europe. Widely used to macerate fruits for dessert.

Kummel
Based on a neutral but very strong spirit made from grain. It is colorless and flavored with cumin and caraway seeds.

Maraschino
Cherry liqueur, made with Marasca cherries from the Dalmatian coast of Yugoslavia.

Quetsch
Plum brandy, very full flavored and fruity.

Van der Hum
South African liqueur based on Cape Brandy. Flavored with fruits and spices, but the naartje, or South African tangerine, predominates.

Cake and Dessert Recipes

Apple Charlotte

Ingredients: *2½ lb firm apples · ¾ cup butter or margarine · 2 tablespoons potato starch · 4 tablespoons sugar · 1 teaspoon cinnamon · ¼ oz vanilla sugar · 1¼ cups apricot jam · 1½ lb white sandwich bread, or ladyfingers*

To serve: *confectioners' sugar · 1–2 glasses rum*

Peel, core and quarter the apples. Put them in a pan with 2 tablespoons of the butter and cook until puréed, stirring occasionally with a wooden spoon. Add the starch, blended with a little water, the sugar, cinnamon and vanilla sugar and continue cooking the mixture over high heat until it is a thick purée. Stir in 3 tablespoons of the apricot jam and let the mixture cool completely. Trim the crust off the bread slices, cut 6 slices into triangles and halve the other slices. Melt the remaining butter or margarine in a pan and dip the slices quickly into it. Line a high-sided buttered mold or charlotte mold with some of the bread slices, using the triangles for the bottom and overlapping the rectangles around the sides (step 1). Brush the bread slices with the remaining apricot jam, pour in the apple purée (step 2) and cover with a layer of bread slices. Cook the charlotte in a hot oven (400°F) for about 1 hour. Unmold on a warm serving platter and sprinkle with confectioners' sugar (step 3). Heat the rum, pour it on the charlotte and flame.

Zabaglione

In a bowl, using a wooden spoon, beat 4 egg yolks with 4 tablespoons sugar for about 15 minutes and stir in 1 cup Marsala, a little at a time. Cook the zabaglione, stirring constantly, over moderate heat or in a bain-marie until it thickens, without letting it boil. Remove the zabaglione and serve hot or cold or use in other recipes.

531

Liqueur Soufflé

Ingredients: *2 tablespoons butter or margarine ·
2 tablespoons flour · 1 cup milk · 1 pinch salt ·
3 tablespoons sugar · 3 tablespoons liqueur
to taste · 3 tablespoons cornstarch · 4 egg
yolks · 4 egg whites, whipped with lemon juice
and a little salt until very stiff*

Melt the butter or margarine, add the flour
and cook the mixture, stirring constantly, until
it starts to brown. Add the milk all at once,
bring the mixture to a boil and stir in the salt.
Turn off the heat, stir in the sugar, liqueur,
cornstarch and the egg yolks one at a time and
fold in the egg whites (step 1). Butter a soufflé
mold, dust with sugar (step 2), and pour in
the mixture (step 3). Bake the soufflé in a hot
oven (400°F) for 20 minutes.

Cherry Soufflé

Cook about ¾ cup pitted cherries in a syrup made by cooking 4 tablespoons sugar in 3 table-spoons water, or use 4 tablespoons thick cherry jam. Heat ½ cup milk in a pan. In a bowl blend 1 level tablespoon sugar and 1½ tablespoons cornstarch in 2 tablespoons cold milk, add this mixture to the warm milk a little at a time and cook the cream, stirring constantly, over low heat until it thickens. Remove the pan from the heat, strain the cream through a sieve and stir in 3 beaten egg yolks. Add the cooked cherries or the jam and 1 tablespoon kirsch, and fold in 3 egg whites, beaten until stiff. Pour the mixture into a buttered soufflé mold, dusted with sugar, and bake in a moderate oven (350°F) for about 30 minutes or until the soufflé is well puffed and golden. Serve immediately with vanilla sauce (see p.538).

Chestnut Soufflé

Work 1¼ cups marrons glacés through a sieve. Melt 2 tablespoons butter or margarine, add 4 tablespoons flour and 1 cup milk all at once and stir in 1 pinch salt. Cook the mixture, stirring constantly, for 8 minutes, and let cool. Blend in the puréed marrons glacés and 4 beaten egg yolks and fold in 4–5 egg whites, beaten until very stiff. Pour the mixture into a buttered soufflé mold, dusted with sugar, bake in a very hot oven (425°F) for 15 minutes, lower the heat to 400°F and continue baking for 30–35 minutes, without opening the oven. Serve immediately. Serves 4–5.

Grapefruit Soufflés

Slice the tops off 6 grapefruit. Squeeze out the juice very gently – there should be 1¼ cups. Remove the flesh and membranes from the shells and discard. Set the shells aside. Melt 6 tablespoons butter in a saucepan, stir in 3 tablespoons flour and cook for 2 minutes. Gradu-ally stir in the grapefruit juice. Bring to a boil, stirring, and simmer until thickened. Stir in 2–4 tablespoons sugar and the grated rind of 1 orange. Separate 3 eggs and beat the yolks into the grapefruit mixture. Beat the egg whites and fold in. Spoon into the grapefruit shells. Bake in a moderately hot oven (375°F) for 15–20 minutes. Serve immediately.

533

Baked Alaska

Ingredients: *1 rectangle pan di Spagna (see p.579) or sponge cake · small glass Cointreau · 4 egg whites · 4 tablespoons sugar · 2 lb vanilla ice cream*

Halve the pan di Spagna or sponge cake and place on a metal tray. Sprinkle with liqueur (step 1). Beat the egg whites with $\frac{3}{4}$ of the sugar until they form very stiff peaks. Put the very cold ice cream on the pastry (step 2), leaving a 1-inch border of pan di Spagna or sponge cake all around, and using an icing pump or a pastry bag with a large nozzle, quickly pipe out the meringue thickly, completely covering both cake and ice cream (step 3). Sprinkle with remaining sugar and bake in a very hot oven (450°F) for a few minutes or until the meringue is golden. Serves 8.

Oranges Soufflées

Using a very sharp knife, halve 4 oranges and remove the fruit very gently, keeping the orange shells intact. Reserve the fruit for another recipe and keep the orange shells in the freezing compartment of the refrigerator until very cold. Prepare a meringue by beating 3 egg whites with 4 tablespoons sugar and 1 oz vanilla sugar until very stiff. Fill the orange shells with very cold orange sherbet (see p.555) and cover the sherbet very quickly with the meringue mixture.

Bake the oranges in a very hot oven (450 F) for a few minutes or until the meringue is golden and crisp, and serve immediately on individual plates.

Apple Clafoutis

Sift ½ cup flour into a bowl, make a well in the center and add 3 eggs, 2 tablespoons sugar, 1 pinch of salt, 1 cup milk, 3 tablespoons melted butter and 1 tablespoon baking powder. Work the ingredients together quickly and thoroughly. Stir in 10 oz apples, peeled, cored and cut into very thin slices. Pour the mixture into a buttered pie pan and bake in a moderate oven (350°F) until golden-brown and the apples are cooked through.

Cherry Clafoutis

Pit 10 oz Bing cherries and macerate in a little kirsch. Sift ½ cup flour into a bowl, make a well in the center and add 3 egg yolks, 2 tablespoons sugar, 1 pinch salt, 1 cup milk, 3 tablespoons melted butter and 1 tablespoon baking powder. Work the ingredients together thoroughly and beat the mixture until it has the consistency of pancake batter. Whip 3 egg whites until stiff and fold gently into the batter. Butter a high-sided pie pan, pour in a layer of batter, add a layer of cherries, and end with a layer of batter and a layer of cherries. Bake in a moderate oven (350°F) until golden-brown and the cherries are soft.

Cherry Bread Pudding

Cut 7 slices of bread into quarters diagonally. Arrange 8 of these triangles over the bottom of a baking dish. Drain, halve and pit a 16-oz can of cherries and spread half over the bread. Cover with 8 more bread triangles, then spread over the remaining cherries. Arrange the rest of the bread triangles on top in overlapping rows. Beat 4 eggs with ½ cup sugar and stir in 2 cups milk. Scatter the grated rind of ½ lemon over the bread slices, then strain over the egg mixture. Sprinkle 1 tablespoon confectioners' sugar over the top. Bake in a moderate oven (350°F) for 15–20 minutes until the top has set. Serve hot.

Flamed Bananas

Ingredients: *4 bananas · 6 tablespoons sugar · flour · 1–2 eggs, beaten · 2 tablespoons butter or margarine · ¼ glass kirsch or Cognac*

Peel the bananas, halve lengthwise and sprinkle with sugar. Dip in flour (step 1), in the beaten egg and again in flour and sauté lightly in the butter until golden on both sides (step 2). Place the bananas on a warmed platter, with candied cherries, sprinkle with the remaining sugar (step 3) and pour the hot kirsch or Cognac over them. Flame, and then serve immediately.

Banana Delight

Peel 4 large bananas, halve lengthwise and place in a buttered ovenproof dish. Sprinkle them with 2½ tablespoons sugar, mixed with 8 tablespoons orange or lemon juice or liqueur to taste, and 1 tablespoon butter in small pieces, and cover with a ½-inch thick layer of grated coconut. Bake the bananas in a hot oven (400°F) for 10 minutes or until golden on top. Serve like this or with a vanilla or orange sauce (see p.538).

Banana Beignets

Prepare the batter: in a bowl mix $\frac{1}{2}$ cup sifted flour with 2 tablespoons sugar, 1 tablespoon melted butter or margarine, 1 pinch salt and about 4 tablespoons hot water. Add 2 tablespoons brandy or rum and 1 beaten egg yolk and let the batter stand for 1–2 hours. Peel 8 small bananas or 6 large ones, halve lengthwise and cut the halves into 2 or 3 pieces, depending on size of bananas. Fold 1 egg white, beaten until stiff, into the batter, dip the banana pieces into the mixture a few at a time and fry in hot deep oil until golden on all sides. Drain the beignets on absorbent paper, sprinkle with confectioners' sugar and serve hot or cold. Serves 4–6.

Chestnut Croquettes

Peel 2 cups chestnuts, soak in boiling water for 5 minutes and remove the inside skin with a sharp knife. Cook with 1 cup water and 2 tablespoons sugar until tender, work through a sieve and return to the heat with 2 tablespoons butter. Cook for a few minutes, remove the pan from the heat, stir in 5 egg yolks and let the mixture cool. Form the mixture into croquette shapes, roll them all in beaten egg and in fresh white breadcrumbs and fry in hot deep oil until golden on all sides. Drain on absorbent paper. Serve the croquettes with a strawberry or apricot sauce (see p.538) in a separate dish. Serves 6.

Rice Croquettes

Wash $\frac{3}{4}$ cup rice in cold running water. Put in an ovenproof dish with 3 cups milk, 2 tablespoons butter, $\frac{3}{4}$ cup sugar and a little finely grated lemon peel and cook in a moderate oven (350°F) for 20–25 minutes or until the liquid has been absorbed. Remove from the oven, fluff with a fork, stir in 5 egg yolks and 2 tablespoons raisins, softened in lukewarm water and dried, and let cool. Shape the mixture and proceed as above.

Vanilla Sauce

Ingredients: *1 cup milk · 1 cup light cream ·*
½ vanilla bean · 4 egg yolks · 4 tablespoons
sugar · ½ teaspoon flour

Heat the milk and cream with the vanilla
bean over very low heat in a bain-marie or
the top of a double boiler. In a bowl beat the
egg yolks with the sugar and flour until the
mixture is light and fluffy and stir in the hot
milk quickly (step 1). Put the mixture in a
bain-marie or in the top of a double boiler and
cook, stirring constantly, until it has thickened
(step 2). Strain the sauce through a fine sieve
and serve immediately, or let cool, stirring
occasionally to prevent a skin forming.

Apricot Sauce

Soak 1 cup dried apricots in water overnight,
drain and put in a pan with enough water to
cover. Cook over moderate heat until tender,
work through a sieve and return them to the
heat with 4 tablespoons sugar. Cook the sauce
until the sugar is melted, remove from the heat
and stir in 2 tablespoons rum, if the sauce is to
be served hot, or 2 tablespoons kirsch, if cold.
The sauce may also be prepared in the following manner: work 1 jar apricot jam through a
sieve, add 3–4 tablespoons water and 2
tablespoons sugar and heat the mixture. Add
kirsch or Cognac to taste.

Orange Sauce

In the top of a double boiler blend $\frac{1}{2}$ cup sugar with 2 tablespoons cornstarch, add 4 tablespoons boiling water and stir the mixture until it is transparent. Add 1 small piece orange peel and cook the mixture for 5–6 minutes. Remove the sauce from the heat, strain it slowly into 2 beaten egg yolks and let cool. Stir in 1 tablespoon lemon juice, 6–8 tablespoons orange juice and 1 tablespoon kirsch and refrigerate.

Coffee Sauce

Prepare vanilla sauce as left substituting 4–5 tablespoons very strong diluted instant coffee for the vanilla.

Chocolate Sauce

Melt 2 tablespoons grated chocolate with 2 tablespoons sugar and $2\frac{1}{2}$ tablespoons water in a bain-marie or in the top of a double boiler and stir the mixture into a vanilla sauce made as left.

Whipped Cream Sauce

Prepare vanilla sauce as left, halving the quantities, fold in 4 tablespoons whipped cream (step 3), and stir in liqueur to taste.

Banana Sauce

Peel 2 small ripe bananas, work through a sieve and add 4 tablespoons sugar, and 2 tablespoons kirsch. Bring the mixture to a boil over very low heat and let cool. Refrigerate and fold in whipped cream before serving.

Raspberry Sauce

Sieve $\frac{1}{2}$ lb raspberries into a saucepan. Add 2 tablespoons sugar and 3 tablespoons currant jelly. Bring to a boil, stirring. Dissolve 2 teaspoons arrowroot in a little cold water and stir into the sauce. Simmer, stirring, until the sauce thickens and clears. Allow to cool before serving.

Crème Caramel

Ingredients: *2 cups milk · ½ vanilla bean, or 1 piece lemon peel · 5 eggs · ½ cup sugar*

For the caramel: *3–4 tablespoons sugar*

Bring the milk with the vanilla bean or lemon peel to a boil, remove from the heat and discard the vanilla. In a bowl beat the eggs with the sugar and pour in the hot milk a little at a time, stirring constantly. Melt the sugar for the caramel in a deep metal mold over moderate heat, cook until it starts to turn deep golden, remove from the heat and tilt and rotate the mold until the caramel coats all sides (step 1). Strain the cream into the mold (step 2), half-covering the mold so that the steam can escape, and bake it in a bain-marie with very hot but not boiling water, on top of the stove (step 3), or, preferably, in a moderately hot oven (375 F) for 40–50 minutes until set. Remove the mold, let cool and unmold on a serving platter. Refrigerate before serving.

Custard Pots

Beat 10 eggs with 1 cup sugar until the mixture is fluffy and stir in 1 quart milk, a little at a time. Add a few drops almond or vanilla extract, or finely grated lemon or orange peel to taste. Divide the mixture equally between individual dishes and cook in a bain-marie as left until set. Serve in the dishes without unmolding.

Crème Pâtissière

In a bowl beat 4 egg yolks with 4 tablespoons sugar for about 15 minutes, add 3–4 table-spoons flour and stir in 2 cups lukewarm milk, a little at a time. Add a little lemon peel and 1 tablespoon butter or margarine and cook the cream, stirring constantly, until it thickens, without letting it boil. Remove the lemon peel before serving. Coffee or chocolate may be added to vary the flavor.

Banana Pudding

Peel 6 ripe bananas, mash with a fork and mix with 2 tablespoons rum, 1 beaten egg, $2\frac{1}{2}$ tablespoons melted butter or margarine, 1 pinch each of cinnamon and grated nutmeg and 2 tablespoons flour, sifted with 1 teaspoon baking powder. Pour the mixture in a buttered mold, sprinkled with sugar, and cook in a bain-marie on top of the stove or in the oven for about 1 hour or until set. Serve cold decorated with whipped cream and glacé cherries if liked.

Frangipane Custard

Put 2 cups milk into a saucepan with 1 vanilla bean. Bring to a boil, then remove from the heat and infuse for 10 minutes. Lightly beat 4 eggs, 4 egg yolks and $\frac{1}{2}$ cup sugar together in a heatproof bowl until frothy. Beat in 6 tablespoons flour until smooth. Place the bowl over a pan of hot water. Gradually strain in the milk, then cook gently, stirring, until the custard thickens. Cool, then fold in $\frac{3}{4}$ cup whipped cream and 1 cup crushed ratafia or macaroon cookies. Chill well.

Chocolate Meringue Cups

Ingredients: *36 small meringues, commercial or homemade (see p.593) · 9 tablespoons very strong diluted instant coffee · 1 tablespoon butter or margarine · 5 oz bitter chocolate, cut into pieces · 2 cups heavy cream · 1 heaped table-spoon confectioners' sugar*

In a small pan put the chocolate, cut into pieces, butter or margarine and coffee, and cook the mixture, stirring constantly, until the chocolate is melted (step 1). Keep the chocolate sauce warm in a bain-marie or in the top of a double boiler. Whip the cream until stiff and stir in the confectioners' sugar. Put 4 meringues in each serving dish or glass, pour in $\frac{3}{4}$ of the chocolate sauce (step 2), add 2 more meringues and cover with whipped cream. Pour the remaining chocolate sauce over (step 3). Serves 6.

Coconut Cups

Grate 1 lb fresh coconut into a bowl and stir in 1 tablespoon unsweetened cocoa powder, 2 tablespoons grated bitter chocolate and 4–5 tablespoons aniseed liqueur or other liqueur to taste. Add 2 tablespoons chocolate melted with 3 tablespoons honey in a bain-marie or in the top of a double boiler, and fold in 1 cup whipped cream. Divide between serving dishes and decorate with whipped cream.

Nutty Fruit Cups

Toast 3 oz hazelnuts in the oven for a few minutes, peel and chop. Dice 2 pineapple slices and 1 banana and macerate in maraschino. Whip $1\frac{1}{2}$ cups heavy cream until stiff, stir in 2 tablespoons confectioners' sugar, sifted with $\frac{1}{4}$ oz vanilla sugar, and gently fold in the nuts and fruit in the liqueur. Divide the mixture equally between 4 serving dishes or glasses, garnish with a few pieces pineapple and 1 cherry and refrigerate.

Romanov Cups

Wash and hull 4 cups strawberries, drain and macerate in 1 cup Grand Marnier mixed with $\frac{1}{2}$ cup sugar. Divide them between 6 serving dishes and cover with $1\frac{1}{4}$ cups heavy cream, whipped with confectioners' sugar. Serves 6.

Malaga Dessert

Put $\frac{1}{2}$ cup raisins in a saucepan with 1 tablespoon water, cover and heat until the water has been absorbed. Uncover the pan and heat until the raisins are plump and dry. Place them in a small bowl and sprinkle over 2 tablespoons rum. Leave to soak for 15 minutes. Meanwhile, toast $\frac{3}{4}$ cup sliced almonds. Beat $\frac{3}{4}$ lb cream cheese with 3 tablespoons sugar and the rum drained from the raisins until light and fluffy. Fold in the raisins and $\frac{2}{3}$ of the almonds. Divide between serving glasses and sprinkle the remaining almonds on top.

Striped Bavaroise

Ingredients: *2 packages vanilla pudding ·
1 package chocolate pudding · 1 package
strawberry pudding*

To decorate: *mixed fruit*

Prepare the puddings following package
instructions (step 1). Do not allow to set. Pour
half the vanilla pudding into a mold, moistened
with water or liqueur, and refrigerate the
mold until the mixture is set. Add the chocolate
pudding (step 2), refrigerate the mold until
set, add the remaining vanilla pudding and
refrigerate the mold until set. End with the
strawberry pudding and refrigerate the mold
for a few hours. Unmold on a serving platter
(step 3) and surround with mixed fruit.
Serves 8.

Apricot Coupe

Prepare 1 package vanilla pudding following the instructions on the package. Stir in
canned apricots to taste, drained and coarsely
chopped. Line 4 Champagne glasses or tall
glasses with sliced pan di Spagna (see p.579)
or ladyfingers, spoon in the pudding and
refrigerate until set. Before serving, decorate
each with 1 glacé cherry surrounded by piped
whipped cream.

Banana Coupe

Prepare 1 package vanilla pudding following the instructions on the package, or a crème
pâtissière (see p.541). Line 4 Champagne
or tall glasses with banana slices, macerated
in liqueur and sugar to taste, pour in the
pudding and refrigerate until set. Garnish
with whipped cream, banana slices and chopped almonds before serving.

Fruit Coupe

Prepare a crème pâtissière (see p.541), adding
grated orange peel instead of lemon peel, and
2 tablespoons curaçao or orange juice.
Macerate strawberries or raspberries in a little
curaçao and sugar. Fill 4 tall glasses with
alternate layers of crème pâtissière and prepared fruit, ending with a layer of crème
pâtissière. Top with whipped cream and fruit.

Cold Orange Soufflé

Ingredients: *8 eggs, separated · 1 cup sugar · 2 tablespoons finely grated orange peel · 1 tablespoon finely grated lemon peel · 15 tablespoons orange juice · 5 tablespoons lemon juice · 1 pinch of salt · 2 tablespoons gelatin, softened in a little lukewarm water · 2 cups heavy cream*

To decorate: *orange quarters · cherries in syrup*

In a bowl beat the egg yolks, reserving the whites, with 4 tablespoons of the sugar, the orange and lemon peel, orange and lemon juice and salt until the mixture is fluffy, stir in the gelatin and cook the mixture, stirring con-stantly, in a bain-marie of hot but not boiling water until it thickens (step 1). Remove from the bain-marie and let cool, stirring constantly. Beat the reserved egg whites until stiff, beat in the remaining sugar and fold in the heavy cream, whipped until stiff, and the cooked cream very gently. Cut a 15-inch wide strip of aluminum foil or wax paper, fold it in 3 lengthwise and tie securely with Scotch tape or string around the top edge of a large soufflé mold, to come about 2 inches above the edge (step 2). Brush the mold and foil or paper with oil, fill the mold with the mixture and refri-gerate for 3–4 hours. Remove the paper gently (step 3), decorate the top with orange quarters and cherries to taste and serve. Serves 8–10.

Vanilla Bavaroise

Soften 1 tablespoon gelatin in a little water. In a bowl beat 4 egg yolks with 4 tablespoons sugar until the mixture is fluffy and stir in 1 cup milk, heated with $\frac{1}{2}$ vanilla bean. Add the gelatin and cook the cream, stirring constantly, over very low heat until it thickens. Remove from the heat, discard the vanilla bean and let cool, stirring occasionally to avoid the formation of a skin on the surface. Beat 1 cup heavy cream until stiff and fold it into the cooked cream. Pour the cream into a wetted mold, chill for 4–5 hours, dip quickly into boiling water and unmold onto a serving platter. Surround with rosettes of whipped cream and fruit, macerated in sugar and liqueur. Serves 4–6.

Cold Chestnut Soufflé

In a bowl beat 4 eggs, 3 egg yolks and $\frac{1}{2}$ cup sugar until the mixture is very thick and light in color. Soften 2 tablespoons gelatin in 6 tablespoons rum and dissolve over hot water. Stir the gelatin mixture into the beaten eggs, add 1 cup sweetened chestnut purée and fold in 1 cup heavy cream, beaten until stiff. Prepare a soufflé mold as left, and brush the paper and the mold with oil. Pour in the mixture and refrigerate. Remove paper and decorate with whipped cream and marrons glacés. Serves 6.

Chocolate Mousse

Melt 4 (1-oz) squares semisweet chocolate in a boiler. Remove from the heat and stir in 2 tablespoons butter and the grated rind of 1 orange until smooth. Separate 4 eggs and beat the yolks into the chocolate mixture. Beat the egg whites with a pinch of salt until stiff and fold into the chocolate mixture. Pour into a serving bowl and chill for 3 hours before serving.

Melon with Macédoine of Fruit

Ingredients: *2 medium-sized melons or 4 small ones*

For the macédoine: *peaches, oranges, apples, pears, bananas, strawberries, cherries · liqueur · sugar*

Peel the fruit, discard the pits, dice (step 1), add the liqueur and sugar to taste and chill the mixture. Chill the melons until ready to use. Halve the melons, discard the seeds, remove a little of the pulp from each half with a melon ball cutter (step 2), and add the melon balls to the macédoine. Divide the macédoine equally between the melons (step 3), garnish with a strawberry or mint leaves and serve immediately.

The macédoine may be served in individual dishes if liked.

Melon with Port

Cut and reserve a small slice from the top of 1 large cantaloup melon. Using a teaspoon, remove and discard the seeds and add sugar to taste and 1–1½ cups port, Madeira or Marsala. Return the top to the melon and chill for at least 2 hours. Remove the melon from the refrigerator, remove the pulp with a spoon and serve with a little of the wine.

Melon Cups

Remove the seeds from 1 cantaloup melon and ½ watermelon and scoop out the pulp in balls with a melon ball cutter, putting each type of melon into a separate bowl. Cut canned pineapple slices into cubes and put in a separate bowl. Mix the pineapple juice with orange juice, lemon juice and sugar to taste, and divide the mixture between the three melon cups. Chill the bowls for a few hours and divide their contents equally between 4 Champagne glasses or individual serving dishes. Decorate with whipped cream.

Melon Fantasia

Peel and halve 1 melon, remove the seeds and cube the pulp. Put the melon cubes into a glass serving dish, sprinkle with a few tablespoons sugar and chill for a few hours. Sprinkle the fruit with brandy, lemon juice, raisins, softened in brandy, and chopped walnuts.

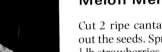

Melon Meringue

Cut 2 ripe cantaloup melons in half and scoop out the seeds. Sprinkle the flesh with sugar. Hull ½ lb strawberries or raspberries and use to fill the cavities in the melon halves. Spoon 1 tablespoon Grand Marnier over the fruit in each half, then cover and chill for at least 2 hours.

Beat 2 large egg whites until stiff. Fold in ½ cup sugar. Pipe or spoon the meringue over the melon halves, covering the berries completely. Arrange the melon halves in a roasting pan full of ice cubes, and bake in a very hot oven (475°F) for about 5 minutes or until the meringue is lightly browned. Serve immediately.

Pineapple with Fruit

Ingredients: *1 fresh pineapple with its leaves ·
1 small glass kirsch · 4 tablespoons
confectioners' sugar · ½ lb strawberries or
raspberries, fresh or frozen · the juice of
1 orange or 1 lemon · 4 tablespoons heavy
cream · ¼ oz vanilla sugar · candied peel, cut
in thin strips*

Halve the pineapple lengthwise and remove
the pulp with a sharp knife (step 1), discarding
the hard part in the middle. Dice the pulp and
macerate in the kirsch and sugar for 45 minutes. If using fresh fruit, wash quickly, halve if
necessary and macerate in a bowl with the
orange or lemon juice. Whip the cream until
stiff, stir in the vanilla sugar and chill. Mix the
strawberries or raspberries, reserving a few
for decoration, with the pineapple pulp and
divide the fruit mixture between the two
pineapple halves (step 2). Using an icing pump
or a pastry bag fitted with a large nozzle,
decorate the pineapple with the whipped
cream (step 3), add the reserved berries and
the peel, cut into thin strips, and chill before
serving.

Stuffed Peaches

Wash and dry 4 large yellow peaches, halve and discard the pit. Using a teaspoon, remove a little of the pulp from each half, forming a hollow. In a bowl, mix the chopped pulp with $2\frac{1}{2}$ oz macaroons, liqueur to taste, 1 egg yolk, 2 tablespoons sugar, 1 oz almonds, peeled and finely chopped, and 1 tablespoon butter or margarine. Fill the peach halves with the mixture, dot with butter and put on a generously buttered cookie sheet. Cook the peaches in a hot oven (400 F) for 45 minutes, transfer to a serving platter and dust with confectioners' sugar. Decorate with peeled almonds if liked.

Pears Marli

Prepare 2 cups vanilla ice cream (see p.554) and divide equally between 4 Champagne glasses or crystal cups. Stick together 8 drained canned pear halves in pairs by putting crushed marrons glacés or thick crème pâtissière (see p.541) between each pair and put 1 reassembled pear in each glass. Cover with whipped cream. Decorate with grated chocolate and cherries.

Peach Melba

Poach 4 large yellow peaches in 2 cups water and $\frac{1}{2}$ cup sugar for 15 minutes. Peel the peaches, halve, remove the pit, and chill. Put 1 large scoop vanilla ice cream in each individual dish, top with two peach halves and cover with 2 cups fruit syrup (raspberry, blackcurrant or redcurrant). Sprinkle with almonds and decorate with whipped cream.

Cherry Compote

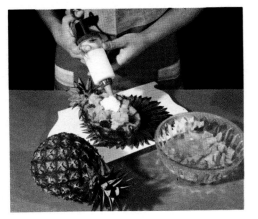

Remove the pits from $1\frac{1}{2}$ lb ripe cherries and place them in a saucepan. Add $\frac{1}{2}$ cup sugar, stir gently and leave to macerate for 2 hours.

Add a cinnamon stick, a strip of lemon rind and $\frac{3}{4}$ cup red wine to the cherries. Bring to a boil and simmer for 15 minutes or until the cherries are just tender. Cool, then discard the cinnamon stick and lemon rind. Chill before serving.

551

Savarin

Ingredients: $\frac{1}{2}$ oz dried yeast ·
8 tablespoons lukewarm milk · 1$\frac{1}{2}$ cups flour ·
4 eggs · $\frac{1}{2}$ teaspoon salt · 1 tablespoon sugar ·
$\frac{1}{2}$ cup softened butter

For the syrup: $\frac{3}{4}$ cup sugar · 2 cups water ·
10 tablespoons rum, kirsch or other liqueur ·

To finish: $\frac{3}{4}$ cup apricot jam · 2 tablespoons
sugar · $\frac{3}{4}$ cup whipped cream, lightly
sweetened · apricots in syrup · glacé cherries

Dissolve the yeast in the warm milk. Sift the flour into a bowl, make a well in the center and add the yeast mixture and the eggs, lightly beaten. Work the flour into the liquid ingredients a little at a time and lift up and beat the dough, which should be soft and a little sticky, repeatedly against the sides of the bowl (step 1). Cover the dough with a light cloth and let stand in a warm place for about 1 hour or until it has doubled in volume. Put the dough on a floured board, flatten it, sprinkle with the salt and sugar and cover with the butter. Work the dough for a few moments, lifting it and slapping

552

it against the sides of the bowl, put in a buttered savarin mold (step 2), and let stand until it has doubled in volume. Bake the savarin in a hot oven (400°F) for 10 minutes, reduce the heat to moderate (350°F) and continue cooking for about 30 minutes or until risen and golden. Remove from the oven, unmold onto a wire rack placed on a plate, and let cool. Make the syrup: dissolve the sugar slowly in the water, bring to a boil and cook over high heat for 5 minutes; remove from the heat. Stir in the rum or other liqueur, and pour the syrup on the savarin, spooning it over until all the syrup has been absorbed. Work the apricot jam through a sieve, heat with the sugar until melted and brush over the savarin (step 3). Fill the center of the savarin with lightly sweetened whipped cream and surround it with apricot halves, filled with whipped cream and topped with cherries.

Upside-down Cheesecake

Mix 3 cups finely crushed graham crackers with $\frac{1}{2}$ cup melted butter, 3 tablespoons light brown sugar and 1 teaspoon ground cinnamon. Press all but 4 tablespoons of the mixture over the bottom and sides of a greased 9-inch loose-bottomed tart pan.

Beat 12 petits suisses cheeses with 4 tablespoons light cream, 4 teaspoons flour, 6 tablespoons sugar, 1 teaspoon vanilla, the grated rind of 1 lemon and 1 tablespoon lemon juice. Separate 4 eggs and beat the yolks into the cheese mixture. Beat the whites until stiff and fold in. Pour into the crumb case and smooth the top. Press the reserved crumb mixture over the surface.

Bake in a moderate oven (350°F) for 45 minutes or until set. Leave to cool in the turned-off oven, with the door ajar. Chill for 2–3 hours, then invert onto a serving plate.

Vanilla Ice Cream

Ingredients: *4 egg yolks · ¾ cup sugar ·
1 cup heavy cream · 2 cups milk · ½ vanilla bean*

In a bowl beat the egg yolks with the sugar vigorously and stir in the cream, milk and vanilla. Pour the mixture in a pan and cook, stirring constantly, over low heat until it thickens, without letting it boil (step 1). Remove the cream from the heat, transfer to a bowl, remove the vanilla bean and let cool, stirring occasionally to avoid the formation of a skin. Pour the cream into an ice cream churn or beat vigorously and pour into a freezer or ice tray (step 2). Freeze, setting the temperature at the coldest point, until hard, turn it out into a chilled bowl and beat vigorously until foamy. Return to the freezer tray and freeze until solid.

Chocolate Ice Cream

Follow the recipe left, adding 4 oz chocolate, melted with 2 tablespoons milk in a bain-marie or in the top of a double boiler, to the beaten eggs before stirring in the cream and milk. Serve the ice cream with an ice cream scoop (step 3) in Champagne glasses with different flavored ice creams.

Coffee Ice Cream

In a small pan bring 2 cups water to a boil, stir in 2 tablespoons instant coffee powder, remove the pan from the heat, cover, let stand for 30 minutes, then strain. Beat 4 egg yolks with $\frac{3}{4}$ cup sugar vigorously, stir in 1 cup boiling milk, a little at a time, and add the coffee. Cook the mixture, stirring constantly, over moderate heat until it thickens, without letting it boil. Remove the cream from the heat and let cool, stirring occasionally to avoid the formation of a skin. Pour into an ice cream churn or into an ice tray and proceed as left.

Strawberry Ice Cream

Heat 1 cup cream, add $\frac{3}{4}$ cup sugar and stir the mixture until the sugar is melted. Let the mixture cool and add 3 cups heavy cream, $\frac{1}{4}$ oz vanilla sugar and 1 lb strawberries, washed, mashed with a fork and lightly sweetened. Pour the mixture into an ice cream churn or an ice tray and proceed as left.

Fruit Ices or Sherbets

Boil 2 cups water with $1\frac{1}{2}$ cups sugar for 5 minutes, strain the syrup through a fine cloth and let cool. Sieve $\frac{1}{2}$ lb fruit (raspberries, peaches, apricots, strawberries, oranges, lemons or bananas), stir in the juice of 1 orange and 1 lemon, a little lemon peel, and the syrup and let the mixture stand for $\frac{1}{2}$ hour. Strain the mixture through a fine cloth, pour into an ice cream churn and proceed as left.

Banana Split

Ingredients for each serving: *1 banana ·
1 scoop each of vanilla ice cream, chocolate ice
cream and strawberry ice cream · 2 tablespoons
chocolate · 2–3 tablespoons milk*

To decorate: *whipped cream ·
2 tablespoons chopped walnuts*

Peel and halve the banana lengthwise (step 1)
and place the halves along the edge of a small
oval platter. Place the ice cream scoops in the
middle (step 2) and cover with the chocolate,
melted with the milk in a bain-marie or in the
top of a double boiler (step 3). Decorate with
piped rosettes of whipped cream, sprinkle with
chopped nuts and serve immediately. To make
a richer dessert, cover the vanilla scoop with
jam, the chocolate with melted chocolate and
the strawberry with fruit syrup.

556

Ice Cream with Liqueur

Prepare 2 cups ice cream to taste (see p.554–5) and divide into 4 Champagne glasses or individual serving dishes. Add liqueur to taste. Some good combination are: vanilla ice cream with whisky, Cognac or crème de cacao; coffee ice cream with crème de menthe; peach ice cream with cherry brandy; raspberry or strawberry ice cream with kirsch.

Strawberry Sundae

Hull $\frac{3}{4}$ lb strawberries. Reserve 12 whole strawberries and sieve the remainder. Stir 2 tablespoons strawberry jam and 2 tablespoons Kirsch into the purée and stir over gentle heat until smooth. Divide between 4 serving glasses and cool.

Whip $\frac{3}{4}$ cup heavy cream with a few drops of almond extract. Add a scoop of vanilla ice cream to each glass, top with a swirl of cream and decorate with the whole strawberries. Serve immediately.

Currant Coupe

Wash and drain $\frac{1}{2}$ lb red currants. Remove the stalks. Whip 1 cup heavy cream with a few drops of vanilla. Divide the red currants between 4 serving glasses and top each with a scoop of vanilla ice cream. Sprinkle with chopped almonds and pipe a swirl of whipped cream on top. Serve immediately.

Belgian Coffee Sundae

Whip 1 cup heavy cream with 2 tablespoons milk and $\frac{1}{4}$ teaspoon vanilla until a piping consistency is reached. Chill until ready to serve.

Put a scoop of coffee ice cream in each of 4 serving glasses. Pipe the cream mixture over the ice cream in a large swirl, and decorate with candied coffee beans. Serve immediately.

Strawberry Bombe

Ingredients: *4 cups vanilla ice cream · 2 cups strawberry ice cream*

To serve: *½ lb strawberries · a few tablespoons kirsch · sugar*

Put a 3-lb bombe mold with a lid into the freezer or freezing compartment of the refrigerator until very cold, remove and line with 1 inch of vanilla ice cream (step 1). If the ice cream softens, return the mold to the freezer for a few minutes. Fill the mold with strawberry ice cream, using a spoon and patting down tightly so that there are no air pockets (step 2), and cover the top with a piece of buttered wax paper. Add the bombe lid (step 3) and seal the top by covering with a thin layer of butter. Freeze the mold for 3–4 hours. Dip the mold quickly in hot water, overturn on a serving platter. If liked, surround the bombe with strawberries, soaked in kirsch and sugar. Serve immediately. Serves 8–10.

Pineapple Bombe

Use lemon ice cream or sherbet instead of vanilla ice cream and fill the center with pineapple ice cream.

Pineapple and Orange Bombe

Use pineapple ice cream instead of vanilla ice cream and fill with orange sherbet (see p.555).

Raspberry Bombe

Use pistachio ice cream instead of vanilla ice cream and fill with raspberry sherbet (see p.555).

Hazelnut Bombe

Use orange sherbet (see p.555) instead of vanilla ice cream and fill with hazelnut ice cream.

Coffee Parfait

In a small pan bring $\frac{3}{4}$ cup sugar and 3 tablespoons water to a boil and cook over low heat for 8–10 minutes or until the mixture forms a thread from a teaspoon dipped into it. Remove from the heat, stir in 4 egg yolks beaten with 1 teaspoon water, a little at a time, and return to the heat. Cook the cream over low heat, stirring constantly, until it thickens but does not boil and stir in 2 teaspoons instant coffee diluted in 1 teaspoon warm water. Strain the cream through a sieve and put in a bowl placed into another bowl of crushed ice. Stir until cool, fold in 1 cup whipped cream and pour the mixture into a wetted mold. Cover and freeze. Unmold by dipping quickly in hot water.

Chocolate Parfait

Proceed as for Coffee Parfait but instead of the coffee stir in 2 tablespoons chocolate, melted with 2 tablespoons milk. Cool the cream, stirring constantly, over crushed ice and fold in 1 cup whipped cream. Pour the mixture into a wetted mold, close securely and freeze.

Zuccotto

Ingredients: *6 oz pan di Spagna (see p.579) or sponge cake, sliced into rectangles · liqueur to taste · 2 cups heavy cream · 3 tablespoons confectioners sugar · ½ oz gelatin, softened in a little warm water · 4 tablespoons candied peel, cut into small pieces · 4 tablespoons chocolate, cut into small pieces · 2 tablespoons cocoa*

For the chocolate syrup: *1 tablespoon butter · 1 heaped tablespoon unsweetened cocoa powder · 2¼ tablespoons water · 4 tablespoons sugar*

Make the chocolate syrup: heat the butter over low heat, add the cocoa and stir until well blended. Add the water and sugar and cook the syrup, stirring constantly, for 3–4 minutes. Dip the pan di Spagna slices in the liqueur and use them to line a 2-quart bowl (step 1) reserving some to cover. Whip the cream until stiff and fold in the sugar and gelatin gently. Divide the whipped cream into two parts and stir the chocolate syrup gently and gradually into one half (step 2). Pour the chocolate cream into the lined bowl, sprinkle with half the candied peel and chocolate pieces and pour in gently the remaining whipped cream, mixed with the remaining fruit and chocolate (step 3). Cover with pan di Spagna slices and refrigerate the zuccotto for at least 4–5 hours. Unmold and decorate to taste. Serves 6.

Iced Raspberry Mold

Soften 1 oz gelatin in a little cold water. Stir the gelatin into 2 cups boiling water, melt, stirring constantly, and let cool. Work 1 lb raspberries through a fine sieve and through a cheesecloth. Stir in the juice of 1 lemon and 1 cup sugar. Stir the gelatin mixture into the fruit syrup, pour the mixture into a high-sided round mold and refrigerate 2 or 3 hours. Unmold before serving. Strawberries, blueberries, red or black currants and cherries can also be used. Serves 6.

Magic Square

In a bowl beat 6 egg yolks with $\frac{3}{4}$ cup confectioners' sugar until the mixture is light and fluffy. Stir in $\frac{3}{4}$ lb chocolate, melted with 3 tablespoons milk in a bain-marie or in the top of a double boiler, and $\frac{3}{4}$ cup butter or margarine at room temperature, and fold in 6 egg whites, beaten until stiff. Stir the mixture until well blended and creamy. Line a 10-inch square mold with a slightly dampened cheesecloth and place a layer of ladyfingers sprinkled with rum on the bottom. Pour in half the chocolate cream, place another layer of ladyfingers on top, then add another layer of cream and end with a layer of ladyfingers, sprinkled with rum. Refrigerate the dessert for at least 12 hours, unmold onto a serving platter and remove the cheesecloth just before serving.

Decorate the sides with ladyfingers and the top with whipped cream if liked.

Lemon Meringue Pie

Ingredients: for the pastry, *1 cup flour ·
4 tablespoons butter or margarine, cut in very
small pieces · 2–3 tablespoons iced water ·
1 pinch salt*

For the filling. *¼ cup flour · 3 tablespoons
cornstarch · ¾ cup sugar · 3 cups boiling
water · 3 egg yolks · 8 tablespoons lemon
juice · peel of 1 lemon, finely grated ·
1 pinch salt · 1 tablespoon butter*

For the meringue: *3 egg whites ·
1 teaspoon lemon juice · 5 tablespoons sugar*

Make the pastry: sift the flour on a board, make
a well in the center and add the butter or
margarine, the water and salt. Work the dough
very quickly with the fingertips, form into a
ball, cover with wax paper and refrigerate for
at least 20 minutes. Roll out the dough and
use it to line a round 8-inch pie pan. Fold over
the edge all around and pinch between 2
fingers to form a scalloped border (step 1).
Prick the dough with a fork, cover with a
circle of wax paper, then with dried beans or
rice, and bake in a hot oven (400°F) for 20
minutes. Remove the beans or rice and wax
paper, bake the case for another 5 minutes,
then remove from the oven and let cool before
using.

Make the filling: in a pan sift the flour and
cornstarch and add the sugar. Mix in the boil-

ing water a little at a time and cook the mixture, stirring constantly, over low heat for 15 minutes. Beat the egg yolks lightly in a bowl, add a few tablespoons of the hot mixture to the bowl then pour into the pan. Cook the custard over low heat until it thickens, stirring constantly, remove from the heat and stir in the lemon juice and peel, salt and butter. Pour the mixture into the baked pie case (step 2), and let cool.

Meanwhile, make the meringue: beat the egg whites until stiff, add the lemon juice and 2 tablespoons of the sugar and whisk until stiff. Fold in the remaining sugar. Using a pastry bag fitted with a star nozzle, pipe the meringue onto the custard and pie crust (step 3). Sprinkle with sugar and bake in a moderate oven (350°F) for 10–15 minutes or until it is just golden. Serve cold. Serves 4–6.

Raisin Pie

In a pan mix together 3 tablespoons flour blended with 4 tablespoons cold water, $1\frac{1}{4}$ cups raisins, softened in lukewarm water and dried with a cloth, $\frac{3}{4}$ cup sugar, 1 pinch salt, $1\frac{3}{4}$ cups water, 1 level teaspoon each of finely grated lemon and orange peel, $5\frac{1}{2}$ tablespoons lemon juice and 8 tablespoons orange juice. Bring the mixture slowly to a boil and cook for 4–5 minutes or until it thickens. Let cool and pour into a 9-inch uncooked pie shell made as left, using $1\frac{1}{4}$ cups flour, $\frac{1}{4}$ cup butter or margarine, 3 tablespoons iced water and 1 pinch salt. With the leftover dough cuttings, make strips to cover the filling in a lattice pattern. Bake the pie in a hot oven (400°F) for 10 minutes, lower the heat to moderately hot (375°F) and continue baking for 30–35 minutes. Serve cold. Serves 4–6.

Cherry Torte

Ingredients: for the sandtorte pastry,
*1½ cups flour · ¾ cup butter or margarine, cut
in small pieces · 4 tablespoons sugar ·
2 egg yolks · 1 tablespoon Marsala ·
peel of 1 lemon, finely grated ·
1 pinch salt*

For the topping: *jam to taste ·
2 oz glacé cherries*

Sift the flour on a board, make a well in the center and add the butter or margarine, the sugar, egg yolks, Marsala, lemon peel and salt. Work the dough quickly, shape into a ball, cover with wax paper and refrigerate for ½ hour. Roll out ⅔ of the dough in a thin sheet and use it to line a round 9-inch buttered pie pan (step 1). With some of the remaining dough make a scalloped border all round. Spread the base of the torte with jam (step 2) and garnish with star and half moon shapes cut from the remaining dough (step 3), and with the cherries.

Bake the torte in a hot oven (400°F) for about 30 minutes until the pastry is golden. Remove from the oven and let cool. This torte is best eaten after 24 hours. Serves 6–8.

Tarte Française

Make the pastry (see p.562) using $\frac{3}{4}$ cup flour, 3 tablespoons butter, 1–2 tablespoons iced water and 1 pinch salt, and let stand for 20 minutes. Line a round 7-inch pie pan with the dough and prick it with a fork. Peel and core 1 lb apples, halve them and slice them very finely.

Place the apple slices on the dough in a circle, working from the center outwards, sprinkle with sugar and bake in a hot oven (400°F) for about 30 minutes until the pastry is golden and the apples are tender. Brush with apricot jam or other jam to taste and serve hot or cold. Serves 6.

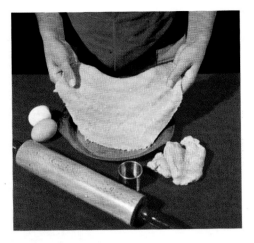

French Apple Tart

Melt 3 tablespoons butter in an 8-inch pie pan or frying pan, add 1 lb apples, peeled and finely sliced, and 2 tablespoons sugar. Sauté the mixture for a few minutes. Prepare pastry as above, using $\frac{3}{4}$ cup flour, 3 tablespoons butter and 1 pinch salt. Roll out thinly and use it to cover the apple mixture. Bake the tart in a hot oven (400°F) until the pastry is golden and the apples are tender when pierced with a skewer. Serve hot or cold.

Chocolate Walnut Tart

Make the pastry (see left), using $1\frac{1}{2}$ cups flour, $\frac{1}{2}$ cup butter, 1 tablespoon sugar and 1 egg yolk. Chill for 30 minutes. Roll out the dough and use it to line an 8-inch tart pan. Prick it with a fork and bake blind in a hot oven (400°F) for 15 minutes. Meanwhile, whip $1\frac{1}{4}$ cups heavy cream. Separate 2 eggs and add the yolks to the cream with $\frac{1}{4}$ cup sugar, 2 tablespoons cocoa powder, $\frac{1}{2}$ teaspoon cinnamon, 1 cup chopped walnuts and 2 tablespoons brandy or rum. Beat the egg whites until stiff and fold into the mixture. Pour into the pastry case and bake for a further 25 minutes or until the filling is set. Cool before serving, decorated with walnut halves.

Apple Strudel

Ingredients: for the pastry, 1¼ cups flour ·
1 egg · 1 tablespoon sugar · 1 pinch salt ·
2 tablespoons butter or margarine ·
lukewarm water

For the filling: 2 tablespoons raisins ·
2 tablespoons almonds · 1½ lb apples ·
3 tablespoons breadcrumbs ·
2½ tablespoons butter or margarine ·
grated lemon peel · a few tablespoons jam ·
4 tablespoons sugar

To finish: 2 tablespoons butter or margarine,
melted · a few tablespoons confectioners' sugar

Sift the flour on a board, make a well in the
center and add the egg, sugar, salt, the butter
or margarine, melted over very low heat with
1–2 tablespoons water, and enough lukewarm
water to obtain a fairly soft dough. Work the
dough quickly and vigorously, form into a ball,
cover with a cloth and let stand for 30 minutes.
Soak the raisins in lukewarm water for 20
minutes, drain and dry. Soak the almonds in
boiling water for a few minutes, drain, peel and
cut into thin slivers. Peel and core the apples
and slice very finely. Sauté the breadcrumbs in
half the butter or margarine until golden, then
let them stand in the pan. Put the dough on a
large floured cloth, roll out thinly with a

566

floured rolling pin and spread it gently over the back of the hands, pulling and stretching it carefully until it is paper thin and transparent (step 1). Lay it out flat on the cloth, brush with the remaining butter or margarine, melted, and cover with the apple slices, raisins, almonds, breadcrumbs and lemon peel (step 2). Dot with spoonfuls of the jam and sugar, leaving a border of dough all around. Roll up the strudel using the cloth, being careful not to touch the dough with the hands (step 3), and press the edges together so that the filling does not come out during cooking. Still holding it by the cloth, put the strudel on a buttered cookie sheet or a large buttered ovenproof pan, brush with melted butter or margarine and bake in a moderate oven (350°F) for 40–50 minutes. Remove from the oven and let stand for 10 minutes. Transfer to a serving platter and dust with confectioners' sugar. The strudel can be served hot or cold.

Apple Pie Maison

Peel, core and slice 3 apples. Put the slices in a shallow pan with 1 piece cinnamon, crushed, 2½ tablespoons raisins, softened in lukewarm water and dried, and 2 tablespoons water. Cover the pan and cook the mixture over low heat until the apples are tender, shaking the pan occasionally. On a board sift 1½ cups flour with 1 teaspoon baking powder, make a well in the center and add 7 tablespoons butter, cut into small pieces, 7 tablespoons sugar, and 1 egg yolk. Work the dough quickly, form it into a ball, cover with wax paper and refrigerate for ½ hour. Roll out the dough to a 1-inch thickness and cut into two 10-inch circles. Butter a 10-inch high-sided pie pan, line it with one circle, add the cooked apples and cover with the other circle. Cook the pie in a moderate oven (350°F) for 45 minutes or until golden.

Profiteroles

Ingredients: for the choux pastry, *1 cup water ·
½ cup butter or margarine · pinch of salt ·
¾ cup sifted flour · 4 eggs*

For the filling: *2 cups heavy cream,
whipped · 2 tablespoons sugar*

To serve: *chocolate sauce (see p.539)*

Prepare the pastry: bring the water, butter or
margarine and salt to a boil, remove the pan
from the heat and pour in the flour all at once,
stirring constantly. Return the pan to the heat,
stirring constantly, and cook for 5 minutes or
until the mixture leaves the sides of the pan.
Transfer the mixture to a bowl, let cool and add
the eggs one at a time, beating vigorously after
each addition. Beat the mixture until it forms
small bubbles and is glossy. Using an icing
pump or pastry bag fitted with a large plain
nozzle, pipe out the mixture in walnut-sized
balls onto a dampened cookie sheet, leaving a
1-inch space between the balls (step 1). Bake
the profiteroles in a hot oven (400°F) for 20
minutes, without opening the oven door, until
insides of profiteroles are empty and dry. Remove them from the oven, take off cookie sheet
and prick each one with a skewer to allow
steam to escape; let cool on a wire rack. Using
a pair of scissors, cut them open on one side
and fill with the whipped cream sweetened
with the sugar (step 2). Arrange profiteroles in
a pyramid shape on a serving platter and cover
with chocolate sauce (step 3).

Eclairs

Prepare choux pastry as for Profiteroles left. Pipe in 3-inch strips onto a dampened cookie sheet. Brush with beaten egg; bake in hot oven (400°F) for about 25 minutes or until light and golden. Remove the éclairs from the oven, take off cookie sheet and prick each one with a skewer; let cool on a wire rack then cut open on one side. Fill with crème pâtissière (see p.541), flavored with vanilla, chocolate or coffee, or with sweetened whipped cream. Prepare icing: sift $\frac{1}{2}$ cup confectioner's sugar in a bowl and add a few drops lemon juice and enough cold water to obtain a thick but spreading paste. Add a few drops flavoring to taste. Heat the icing in a bain-marie; dip éclairs quickly into icing and leave to set.

Croquembouche

Defrost frozen puff pastry and roll out into a 15-inch circle, 3 inches thick. Place the circle on dampened wax paper on a cookie sheet, and bake in a very hot oven (425°F) for 15–20 minutes or until golden and crisp. Remove from oven and allow to cool. Prepare choux pastry as for Profiteroles left, using half the quantities. Fill profiteroles with crème pâtissière (see p.541 and halve the quantities). Dissolve $\frac{3}{4}$ cup sugar slowly in 10 tablespoons water, bring to a boil and cook the mixture until it caramelizes. Remove from heat, dip the profiteroles quickly in the caramel (using cooking tongs) and set them in a pyramid shape on the pastry circle.

Choux Fritters

Prepare choux pastry as for Profiteroles left. Shape into small balls, using 2 teaspoons, scooping some paste up, then pushing it off with the second spoon. Drop the balls, a few at a time, into hot fat and deep fry for 4–5 minutes or until puffed and golden. Drain, dredge with sugar and serve hot.

Mille-Feuille

Ingredients: $1\frac{1}{2}$ *lb puff pastry (homemade or frozen)*

For the zabaglione custard: *4 egg yolks ·
4 tablespoons sugar · $\frac{3}{4}$ cup Marsala*

To finish: *confectioners' sugar*

Roll out the puff pastry very thinly between two sheets of wax paper and cut into 4 rectangles 7×13 inches (step 1). Lay the dough on dampened cookie sheets and prick with a fork (step 2) and bake in a very hot oven (425°F) for 10–15 minutes, until golden and crisp. Remove from the oven and let cool. Meanwhile, prepare the custard following the basic zabaglione recipe (see p.531), using the egg yolks, sugar and Marsala, and let cool. Put 1 rectangle of pastry on a serving platter, cover with custard, cover with another rectangle of pastry and continue in this manner ending with the last pastry rectangle (step 3). Sprinkle with confectioners' sugar before serving.

The zabaglione may be substituted by crème pâtissière (see p.541), flavored with chocolate, or by apple purée. Serves 6.

Pithiviers

Ingredients: *1 lb puff pastry (homemade or frozen)*

For the frangipane cream: *2 egg yolks · 2¼ tablespoons sugar · 2¼ tablespoons powdered almonds · 2 tablespoons flour · 1 cup milk*

Prepare the frangipane cream: mix the egg yolks with the sugar, powdered almonds and flour. Bring 1 cup milk to a boil and stir a little of it into the egg mixture. Stir the mixture for a few minutes, pour in a little more milk then pour the mixture into remaining hot milk.

Heat the cream over low heat, stirring constantly with a wire whip until it begins to boil, boil for a few minutes and let cool. Stir in a few drops almond extract. Roll out the puff pastry and cut into two 8-inch circles, reserving the remaining dough. Lay one of the circles on a dampened cookie sheet, cover with frangipane cream and then with the second circle. Roll out the remaining dough to form a slightly larger circle and use it to cover the cake, sealing the edges together. Brush the pastry with beaten egg and with a sharp knife make light incisions into the dough in a lattice pattern. Bake in a very hot oven (425°F) for about 30 minutes until golden and crisp.

Palmiers

Roll out 1 lb puff pastry to an oblong ¼-inch thick. Sprinkle with sugar. Fold in the 2 long sides to meet in the middle and sprinkle again with sugar. Fold the long sides over again to meet in the middle, to make 4 layers, and sprinkle with sugar. Cut across the folds into ½-inch thick slices. Arrange the slices on a dampened baking sheet, cut sides down, and flatten slightly. Bake in a hot oven (425°F) for 6 minutes on each side. Serve warm.

Fruit Tartlets

Ingredients: for the sandtorte pastry,
*1½ cups sifted flour · 6¼ tablespoons butter or
margarine · 4 tablespoons sugar · 2 egg yolks ·
1 tablespoon Marsala · finely grated peel of
1 lemon · 1 pinch of salt*

For the crème pâtissière: *4 egg yolks ·
3 tablespoons sugar · 3 tablespoons flour ·
2 cups lukewarm milk · lemon peel ·
1 tablespoon butter or margarine*

For the fruit filling: *bananas, sliced ·
poached cherries · large grapes · canned
pineapple slices, cubed*

To glaze: *1 cup apricot jam · 2 tablespoons
water or rum*

Prepare the sandtorte pastry (see p.564), using
the flour, butter or margarine, sugar, egg yolks.
Marsala, lemon peel and salt, roll out thinly and
cut into 4-inch circles. Line small tartlet molds
with the pastry, add a circle of wax paper to
each, cover with rice and cook the shells in a hot
oven (400°F) for 15 minutes. Remove them
from the oven, remove the wax paper and rice
and let cool. Prepare the crème pâtissière (see
p.541) using the egg yolks, sugar, flour, lemon
peel, milk and butter or margarine and let cool.
Put 1 tablespoon crème pâtissière in each shell
(step 1), and fill some shells with banana slices,
some with cherries, some with grapes and some
with pineapple cubes (step 2). Heat the jam.
work through a sieve, stir in the water or rum
and brush the fruit with the mixture (step 3).
Serve cold.

Mirlitons

Make pastry (see p.562) to line 8 tartlet molds, using ¾ cup flour, 3 tablespoons butter, 1–2 tablespoons iced water and 1 pinch salt. In a bowl mix 2 eggs with 4 tablespoons apricot jam, 4 tablespoons almonds, very finely crushed, 2 tablespoons sugar and 2 tablespoons flour. Spoon the mixture into the tartlet molds and decorate with almonds. Bake in a moderate oven (350 F) for 10–15 minutes.

Irish Apple Turnovers

Sift 2 cups flour, 2 teaspoons baking powder and ⅔ cup sugar into a bowl. Add ⅔ cup butter and rub in well. Add about 2 tablespoons cold water and bind to a smooth dough. Chill for 1 hour. Meanwhile, core 1 lb Jonathan or McIntosh apples and place on a baking sheet. Bake in a moderate oven (350°F) for 20 minutes or until tender. Peel, then mash the fruit with 1 tablespoon apricot jam and 2 tablespoons dried mixed fruit.

Roll out the dough to ⅛-inch thick and cut into rounds or squares. Spoon a little of the apple mixture into the center of each round or square and fold over into half moons or triangles. Dampen the edges and press to seal. Place on a greased baking sheet and bake in a hot oven (400°F) for 15–20 minutes. Dredge with confectioners' sugar and serve warm.

Strawberry Boats

Make pastry (see page 562) to line 10 barquette molds, using 3 cups flour, a pinch of salt, ¾ cup butter, the grated rind of 1 orange and 1 egg. Prick and bake blind in a moderately hot oven (375°F) for 25 minutes. Remove from the molds and cool. When cold, fill the pastry boats with ½ lb hulled small strawberries. Mix 1 teaspoon arrowroot with 4 tablespoons orange juice and bring to a boil, stirring until thickened. Stir in 3 tablespoons orange liqueur. Brush this glaze over the strawberries and leave to set before serving.

Sicilian Cannoli

Ingredients: for the dough, $\frac{3}{4}$ cup flour ·
1 tablespoon sugar · 2 tablespoons
confectioners' sugar · 1 tablespoon unsweetened
cocoa powder · $\frac{1}{4}$ teaspoon instant coffee
powder · 1 tablespoon butter or margarine, in
small pieces · $\frac{1}{4}$ cup dry white wine · 1 egg white

For the filling: 1 cup ricotta or cream cheese ·
$\frac{3}{4}$ cup confectioners' sugar · liqueur to taste ·
1 tablespoon candied peel, chopped · 2 oz glacé
cherries, chopped · powdered chocolate

To finish: oil for frying · confectioners' sugar

Make the dough: on a board sift the flour, sugar,
confectioners' sugar, cocoa and coffee, make a
well in the center and add the butter or
margarine and the white wine. Work the
ingredients quickly and thoroughly, shape the
dough into a ball, cover with wax paper and

let stand in the refrigerator for about 1 hour.
Meanwhile, make the filling: in a bowl blend
the cheese with the sugar and liqueur, work the
mixture through a sieve, then stir in the
candied peel and glacé cherries, reserving a
few cherries for decoration. Divide the mixture
into two parts, add the powdered chocolate to
one and chill both mixtures. Butter cannoli,
cream horn or tube molds 10 inches long by
1 inch wide. Roll out the dough thinly and
cut into 4-inch squares. Put a mold diagonally
in the center of each square (step 1), roll up
the dough around the tube and press the dough
together, brushing with a little egg white. Heat
the oil, and cook the cannoli (step 2). Drain
and let cool. Remove the molds and let the
cannoli cool. Fill half with plain cream and
half with chocolate cream (step 3), add a
cherry to each end and dust with confectioners'
sugar. Serves 6.

Baklava

Melt $\frac{1}{2}$ cup unsalted butter and brush a little over the bottom and sides of a 10×8 inch roasting pan. Layer $\frac{1}{2}$ a 1 lb packet of phyllo pastry in the pan, brushing liberally with melted butter between each sheet of pastry and folding in the edges so that the sheets will fit in the pan. Keep the rest of the pastry covered so that it will not dry out. Mix together 2 cups chopped walnuts, almonds or pistachios, 2 tablespoons sugar and $\frac{1}{2}$ teaspoon cinnamon and spread over the pastry in the pan. Cover with the remaining pastry, again brushing each sheet liberally with melted butter. Brush the top layer well with the last of the butter. Cut through the top of 2 layers of pastry with a sharp knife to divide into 4 widthwise, then cut each quarter in half diagonally to make 8 triangles. Bake in a hot oven (425°F) for 15 minutes, then reduce the heat to moderate (350°F) and bake for a further 25–30 minutes or until risen and golden.

Meanwhile, heat $\frac{1}{3}$ cup clear honey with $\frac{1}{2}$ cup water and 2 tablespoons lemon juice until melted and smooth. Cool.

Remove the baklava from the oven and pour over the honey syrup. Leave to cool in the pan. Cut along the marked lines to serve.

Sour Cream Pastries

Sift 3 cups flour into a bowl and rub in $\frac{3}{4}$ cup butter. Add 1 egg yolk and $\frac{3}{4}$ cup sour cream and mix to a soft dough. Chill for 1 hour. Roll out the dough and cut out about 40 rounds with a 2-inch cutter. Mix together $\frac{1}{2}$ lb cream cheese, $\frac{3}{4}$ cup sugar and $\frac{1}{3}$ cup raisins and put a spoonful in the center of half the dough rounds. Place the remaining rounds on top, dampen the edges and press to seal. Arrange on a baking sheet and bake in a hot oven (400°F) for 25 minutes or until golden brown.

Chocolate Cake

Ingredients: *3 eggs, separated · ¾ cup sugar ·
4 tablespoons butter or margarine, melted ·
5 tablespoons potato starch · 5 tablespoons
flour · 5 tablespoons cocoa powder ·
½ oz baking powder · ¼ oz vanilla sugar ·
½ cup milk · 1 pinch salt*

*For the icing: 2 egg whites · 1½ cups sugar ·
¼ oz vanilla sugar · 6 tablespoons water*

In a bowl beat the egg yolks, reserving the
whites, with the sugar, add the butter or margarine, the starch sifted with the flour, cocoa,
baking powder, vanilla sugar, milk and salt
and fold in the egg whites, beaten until stiff.

Pour the mixture into a deep 8 inch cake
mold, buttered and dusted with flour, and bake
in a moderate oven (350°F) for 45 minutes or
until cooked (when a skewer inserted in the
center comes out clean). Remove from the oven,
let cool and slice into 2 or 3 layers (step 1).

Make the icing: put the egg whites, sugar,
vanilla sugar and water in a bain-marie of
boiling water or in the top of a double boiler
and beat the mixture with an electric or
rotary beater for 7–8 minutes or until stiff
(step 2). Ice the top of each layer of the cake
immediately and thickly, reassemble cake,
making little peaks on the top layer with a fork
(step 3). Let the cake stand for a few hours before
serving.

Butter Icing

Sift ¾ cup confectioners' sugar with ¼ oz vanilla sugar, add 4 tablespoons butter or margarine at room temperature and 3 tablespoons milk or cream and beat the mixture until fluffy. The icing may be used as it is or may be flavored with chocolate, melted in a bain-marie or in the top of a double boiler, or with lemon or orange juice instead of milk and vanilla sugar.

Quick White Icing

In a bowl put 2 tablespoons hot milk, add 1 knob of butter and stir it until melted. Stir in ¾ cup confectioners' sugar, a little at a time, until thick enough to spread. Add a few drops of rum or vanilla extract to taste. The icing may be colored with fruit juice or commercial coloring, if desired.

Coffee Icing

Make the white icing as for the chocolate cake left, halving the quantities, and adding some very strong diluted instant coffee instead of water.

Chocolate Icing

Make a white icing as left, halving the quantities. Stir in 2 tablespoons chocolate, melted in a bain-marie or in the top of a double boiler.

Glacé Icing

Sift 2 cups confectioners' sugar into a bowl. Add 2 tablespoons hot water and beat well to make a smooth icing that will coat the spoon thickly. If necessary, add a little more hot water, a few drops at a time. The icing may be colored with food coloring and flavored with commercial flavoring or fruit juice, if desired.

Margherita

Ingredients: $\frac{1}{2}$ cup butter · 6 eggs · $\frac{3}{4}$ cup sugar · $\frac{1}{2}$ cup flour · 4 tablespoons cornstarch · 2 teaspoons baking powder (optional) · finely grated peel of 1 lemon · confectioners' sugar

Melt the butter over very low heat and let cool. Put the egg yolks (reserving the whites) and sugar in a flameproof bowl, put the bowl in a pan containing hot water and beat the mixture with a wire whip until it is light and fluffy and leaves a ribbon trail when the whip is lifted (step 1). Remove the bowl from the pan of hot water and continue beating until the mixture is cold. Mix in a little at a time the flour sifted with the cornstarch and baking powder, if using, the melted butter (discarding the liquid formed during cooling) and the lemon peel. Beat the reserved egg whites until stiff and fold them gently into the mixture (step 2). Butter a square cake pan and dust with flour. Pour in the mixture (step 3) and bake in a moderate oven (350°F) for about 40 minutes or until cooked (the top will spring back when lightly touched with the fingertip). Dust with confectioners' sugar before serving.

Italian Pandoro

In a bowl work $\frac{3}{4}$ cup butter or margarine, kept at room temperature for 10 minutes. Add 4 egg yolks, reserving the whites, one at a time and beat the mixture until light and fluffy. Stir in 7 tablespoons sugar, 1 tablespoon brandy, a pinch of salt, the juice of $\frac{1}{2}$ lemon, and, a little at a time, $\frac{3}{4}$ cup each of flour and potato starch, sifted together with $\frac{1}{4}$ oz vanilla sugar. Beat the mixture for 15 minutes and fold in the egg whites, beaten until stiff, and 1 teaspoon baking powder. Pour the mixture into a deep cake pan, lightly buttered and floured, so that it half fills the mold. Bake the cake in a hot oven (400°F) for about 40 minutes or until cooked (see above), remove from the oven and let stand for 10 minutes. Unmold onto a wire rack and dust the pandoro with confectioners' sugar before serving.

Pan di Spagna

In a bowl standing in a bain-marie or on the top of a double boiler (not touching the water), mix $\frac{1}{2}$ cup sugar with 4 eggs, the finely grated peel of 1 lemon and a pinch of salt. Beat the mixture gently with a wire whip until it begins to swell and leave a ribbon trail, remove the pan from the heat and continue beating until it thickens. Slowly add $\frac{1}{4}$ cup flour, sifted with $2\frac{1}{2}$ table-spoons potato starch, and 1 tablespoon melted butter. Pour ihto a deep 10-inch cake pan, lightly buttered and floured, and bake in a moderate oven (350°F) for 20–25 minutes.

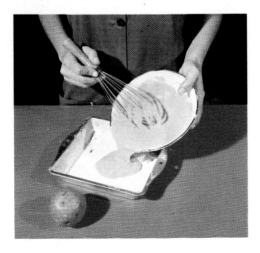

Walnut and Orange Cake

Cream $\frac{3}{4}$ cup butter with $\frac{3}{4}$ cup sugar until pale and fluffy. Beat in 3 eggs, a little at a time, then stir in the grated rind of $\frac{1}{2}$ orange. Sift 2 cups flour with $1\frac{1}{2}$ teaspoons baking powder and a pinch of salt and fold into the creamed mixture alternately with 4 tablespoons orange juice. Stir in $\frac{1}{2}$ cup chopped walnuts. Pour into a greased and lined deep 7-inch cake pan. Bake in a moderate oven (325°F) for $1\frac{1}{4}$–$1\frac{1}{2}$ hours or until a skewer inserted into the center of the cake comes out clean. Cool in the pan.

579

Rice Cake

Ingredients: $\frac{3}{4}$ cup rice · $\frac{1}{2}$ cup almonds ·
1 cup water · 3 cups milk · $\frac{3}{4}$ cup sugar ·
1 strip of lemon peel · 4 eggs · 10 macaroons,
crushed · 2 tablespoons candied peel, cut into
thin strips · butter · breadcrumbs

To serve: *raspberry syrup*

Soak the almonds in boiling water for a few
minutes, drain, peel and chop. Bring the water
and milk, 1 tablespoon sugar and the lemon
peel to a boil, add the rice and cook until it has
absorbed all the liquid (step 1). Remove the rice
from the heat, discard the lemon peel and let
the rice cool. In a bowl beat the egg yolks,
reserving the whites, with the remaining sugar,
add the chopped almonds, crushed macaroons
(reserving a few for garnish), candied peel, and
the cooked rice and fold in the egg whites,
beaten until stiff (step 2). Pour the mixture into
a 12-inch springform pan, lightly buttered and
sprinkled with breadcrumbs (step 3), and bake
in a moderate oven (350°F) for 40–45 minutes.
Unmold cake onto a wire rack and decorate
with reserved macaroons.

This cake may be served hot or cold with
raspberry syrup served separately, or with a
sauce to taste (see p.538–9).

Marble Cake

Beat $\frac{3}{4}$ cup butter together with $\frac{3}{4}$ cup sugar
until the mixture is fluffy and add 3 egg yolks,
reserving the whites, one by one. Stir in $1\frac{1}{4}$
cups flour, sifted with 1 teaspoon baking
powder, and fold in the egg whites, beaten until
stiff. Transfer one third of the mixture to a
separate bowl and stir in $\frac{3}{4}$ cup chocolate,
melted over low heat in a bain-marie or in the
top of a double boiler. Butter a round cake pan
and line with wax paper to come above the
edge. Pour in a layer of the plain mixture, a
thinner layer of the chocolate mixture and
continue alternating mixtures until all the
ingredients are used. Bake the cake in a slow
oven (300°F) for about 1 hour or until cooked
(the top will spring back when lightly touched
with the fingertip). Remove from the oven, let
stand for a few minutes then unmold onto a
wire rack and let cool. This cake is usually
covered with chocolate frosting.

581

Saint-Honoré

Ingredients: for the base, *4 tablespoons butter or margarine, melted and cooled · 6 eggs, separated · 6½ tablespoons sugar · ¾ cup flour · ¼ oz vanilla sugar · 1 teaspoon baking powder · maraschino · crème pâtissière (see p.541 and halve quantities) · 1 cup whipped cream · pan di Spagna (see p.579) · 6–8 profiteroles (see p.568) · zabaglione (see p.531)*

For the Saint-Honoré cream: *½ oz gelatin · 2 egg yolks · ½ cup sugar · 2 tablespoons flour · 1 cup milk · ¼ oz vanilla sugar · 3 egg whites · 1½ cups whipped cream · 2 teaspoons cocoa powder*

For the caramel: *3 tablespoons sugar · water*

Make the pastry base: melt the butter or margarine over moderate heat and let cool. In a bowl beat the egg yolks, reserving the whites, with the sugar for 15 minutes and add, a little at a time, the flour sifted with the vanilla sugar and baking powder. Fold the egg whites, beaten until stiff, and the melted fat gently into the mixture with a spatula. Spoon the mixture into a 12-inch cake pan, buttered and dusted with flour (step 1), and cook in a moderate oven (350 F) for 35–40 minutes.

Meanwhile, make the crème pâtissière, profiteroles (step 2), and zabaglione. Prepare the Saint-Honoré cream: soften the gelatin in cold water. Beat the egg yolks with the sugar and stir in the flour and milk. Cook the cream, stirring constantly, over very low heat until it thickens but does not boil. Stir in the gelatin, remove from the heat, add the vanilla sugar and fold in the egg whites, beaten until stiff. Let cool and fold in ⅔ of the whipped cream. Divide the mixture into two parts and stir the sifted cocoa into one half. Slice the cake into 2 or 3 layers, sprinkle them generously with maraschino liqueur and cover with crème patissière, mixed with some of the cream. Brush cake with remaining whipped cream and press pan di Spagna against it. Using a pastry bag fitted with a large nozzle, make large rosettes of plain Saint-Honoré cream on top of cake, alternating with chocolate Saint-Honoré cream. Fill profiteroles with zabaglione, dip in caramel, made by dissolving the sugar slowly in the water, then cooking until golden, and set around top of cake (step 3). Serves 6–8.

Bûche de Noël (Christmas Log)

Ingredients: for the cake, *5 eggs, separated ·
4 tablespoons sugar · ½ cup flour · ¼ oz vanilla
sugar*

To fill and top: *1 cup butter at room
temperature · 4½ tablespoons confectioners'
sugar · 2 tablespoons unsweetened cocoa
powder · 2 tablespoons diluted instant coffee ·
1 cup cream · 3 tablespoons confectioners' sugar*

Line a large cookie sheet with buttered wax
paper. Beat the egg yolks with the sugar until
the mixture is very light and fluffy, mix in the
flour a little at a time and the vanilla sugar and
fold in the egg whites, whipped until stiff.
Spread the mixture evenly on the wax paper
and bake in a moderate oven (350°F) for
12–15 minutes or until risen and golden.
Transfer immediately onto a dampened cloth,
dusted with sugar, cut off and discard the dry
edges of the cake, roll the cake up in the cloth
(step 1) and leave to cool. Meanwhile, make
the mocha cream: beat the butter with the
confectioners' sugar until light and fluffy and
stir in the cocoa and coffee. Unroll the pastry,
cover with a thin layer of mocha cream and
with a layer of cream, whipped with the con-

fectioners' sugar until stiff. Roll the cake up again (step 2), this time without the cloth. Cut off the two ends diagonally and reserve them. Cover the cake and the 2 slices with the remaining mocha cream and place the slices on the cake (to look like branches cut off from the main trunk of the tree). Using a fork, trace lines into the cream to simulate the bark of the tree (step 3). Refrigerate the cake before serving. Alternatively just fill the cake with mocha cream, which may be flavored with rum or other liqueur. Serves 4–5.

Chestnut Bûche

Peel 1 lb chestnuts, put them in lightly salted cold water and cook over low heat for about 1 hour. Drain, skin and work through a sieve or through a food chopper. In a bowl beat 2 egg yolks with 2 tablespoons sugar until the mixture is light and fluffy and stir in gently $\frac{3}{4}$ cup chocolate, melted with $\frac{1}{2}$ cup butter or margarine and 2 tablespoons water in a bain-marie or in the top of a double boiler. Stir in the chestnuts, and rum to taste, and refrigerate the mixture for about 1 hour. Form the mixture into a roll, slice off the two ends diagonally and reserve.

Make the icing: melt 4 tablespoons grated chocolate with 1 knob of butter or margarine, 1–2 tablespoons water and 1 tablespoon sugar in a bain-marie or in the top of a double boiler. Spread over the cake and the 2 slices, and place slices on cake, as above. Using a fork, trace lines in the icing to simulate the bark of the tree. Refrigerate the cake before you serve it.

Tropical Cake

Ingredients: for the cake, $\frac{1}{2}$ cup butter ·
6 eggs · $6\frac{1}{2}$ tablespoons sugar · $\frac{1}{2}$ cup flour ·
6 tablespoons cornstarch · 2 teaspoons baking
powder (optional) · finely grated peel of 1 lemon

For the filling: 6 ripe bananas · 3 oranges ·
4 single measures rum or Cognac ·
4–5 tablespoons confectioners' sugar ·
1 lb walnuts · $1\frac{1}{2}$ cups heavy cream, whipped

Make the cake following the recipe for
Margherita (see p.578). Pour into a deep cake
pan, buttered and lightly dusted with flour,
and cook in a moderate oven (350 F) for about
40 minutes or until cooked (the top will spring
back when lightly touched with the fingertip).
Remove from the oven, unmold onto a wire
rack and let cool. Meanwhile, make the filling:
peel 5 bananas, slice them and put in a bowl
with the juice of 1 orange, 2 measures rum
or Cognac and 2 tablespoons confectioners'
sugar for at least 1 hour. Shell the walnuts and
chop coarsely, reserving about 16 halves for
the decoration. Mix the juice of the remaining
oranges with the remaining rum. Slice the
cake into three layers, put the first layer on a
round serving platter and soak with some of
the orange juice and rum mixture (step 1).
Cover with $\frac{1}{3}$ of the whipped cream, add a
layer of half the drained banana slices and
sprinkle with $\frac{1}{2}$ the chopped walnuts. Repeat
these layers once more (step 2), topping them
with the third layer of cake, soaked in orange
juice and rum. Cover with whipped cream, add
rings of banana slices (step 3), and walnuts.

Candied Fruit Cake

In a bowl beat 5 egg yolks with $\frac{3}{4}$ cup sugar
until the mixture is fluffy and stir in $6\frac{1}{2}$ tablespoons peeled almonds, finely chopped, 4
tablespoons raisins, softened in lukewarm
water and dried, 4 tablespoons candied peel
and glacé cherries, cut into thin strips,
$\frac{1}{4}$ oz vanilla sugar, $\frac{1}{2}$ teaspoon baking powder,
5 oz crisp sweet biscuits, pounded finely and
6 tablespoons rum. Fold in 5 egg whites, whipped. Pour into a buttered 10-inch cake pan
and bake in a moderate oven (350 F) for about
1 hour. Unmold and slice into 3 layers. Sprinkle
each layer with rum, cover with heavy cream
and reassemble cake.

587

Iced Chestnut Cake

Ingredients: *2 lb chestnuts · 3 cups milk ·
4 tablespoons sugar · ¼ vanilla bean ·
pinch of salt · 4 tablespoons softened butter or
margarine · 2 tablespoons sweetened cocoa
powder · rum · 3 oz macaroons*

To decorate: *2 tablespoons almonds, toasted
and chopped · ½ cup whipped cream ·
marron glacé (optional)*

Peel the chestnuts (step 1), soak in boiling
water for 5 minutes and remove the skin
with a sharp knife. Bring the milk, sugar,
vanilla bean and salt to a boil, remove the
vanilla and add the chestnuts. Cook the
mixture over low heat for about 1 hour, then
work through a sieve and return to the pan.
Cook over moderate heat, stirring constantly,
until it thickens, remove from the heat and let
cool. Stir in the butter or margarine, cocoa,
and rum to taste and beat the mixture until all
the ingredients are well blended. Line a 9-inch
high-sided mold or charlotte mold with
dampened cheesecloth, pour in one third of the
mixture, add a layer of macaroons soaked in
rum (step 2), cover with another third of
chestnut mixture, then a layer of macaroons
soaked in rum, and finally the remaining
chestnut mixture. Refrigerate the cake for a few
hours, or overnight, unmold on a serving
platter and carefully remove the cheesecloth
(step 3).

Press the chopped almonds around the side
of the cake and top with whipped cream, and
the marron glacé if liked.

Mont Blanc

Prepare 2 lb chestnuts as above and put in a
pan with 1 quart hot milk and 1 vanilla bean.
Cook the mixture over low heat for about 1
hour, then remove vanilla bean and work
through a sieve. Make a syrup by dissolving
1¼ cups sugar and 1 teaspoon vanilla extract
in 9 tablespoons water, then boiling until a
teaspoon of the mixture dropped in cold water
forms a soft ball. Stir the syrup into the chestnut mixture.

Using a pastry bag fitted with a large
nozzle, pipe the mixture onto a serving platter,
shaping into a dome, and cover with stiffly
whipped cream.

589

Iced Mocha Cake

Ingredients: for the zabaglione custard,
*4 egg yolks · 4 tablespoons sugar ·
1 cup Marsala*

For the mocha cream: *1¼ cups softened
butter or margarine · ¾ cup confectioners'
sugar · ½ cup strong coffee · 3 egg yolks*

For the filling: *about ¾ lb pan di Spagna (see p.579),
or sponge cake · Marsala*

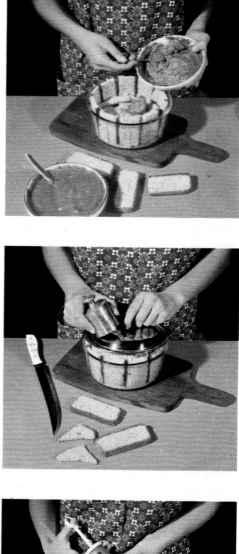

Prepare the zabaglione custard (see p.531), with
the egg yolks, sugar and Marsala and let cool.
Meanwhile make the mocha cream: beat the
butter or margarine until light and fluffy, beat
in the sugar and add the coffee drop by drop
and the egg yolks one by one. Butter a deep
9-inch round mold and line with some of the
pan di Spagna or sponge cake, cut into slices
and dipped in Marsala. Fill the mold with
alternate layers of mocha cream (step 1),
reserving a little for decoration, pan di Spagna
slices sprinkled with Marsala and zabaglione
custard. End with a layer of pan di Spagna and
cover the cake with a lid and a weight (step 2).
Refrigerate for at least 12 hours, then unmold
carefully onto a serving platter. Dust the sides
of the cake with sifted cocoa powder. Using an
icing pump or a pastry bag fitted with a star
nozzle, pipe out mocha cream rosettes on the
cake (step 3). Serves 8.

Zuppa Inglese

Prepare a crème pâtissière (see p.541) and let
cool. Stir in peeled chopped pine nuts and
almonds, and raisins softened in lukewarm
water and dried, to taste, and a few small
pieces of candied peel. Divide the cream in two
and add 1 tablespoon cocoa powder to one half.
Make a fruit syrup: work 3–4 tablespoons
apricot or peach jam through a sieve and dilute
with a little Cognac, mixing well. In an ovenproof metal dish, make alternate layers of plain
crème pâtissière, fruit syrup and cocoa crème
pâtissière, using slices of pan di Spagna,
sprinkled with liqueur to taste, between each
different layer and at the top and bottom of the
mold. Beat 4 egg whites until stiff and beat in
two tablespoons sugar. Spread or pipe the
mixture all over the cake and bake in a hot
oven (400°F) for a few minutes. Serves 6–8.

Madeleines

Ingredients: *2 eggs · 1 egg yolk ·
3 tablespoons sugar · 1 tablespoon potato
starch · ¼ cup flour · 1 tablespoon butter ·
the finely grated peel of ½ lemon ·
confectioners' sugar*
To decorate: *walnut halves (optional)*

Beat the eggs and egg yolk and the sugar with a
wire whip in a bain-marie or in the top of a
double boiler until the mixture is warm,
remove from the heat and continue beating
(step 1) until it forms a ribbon when the wire
whip is lifted. Whip in the starch and flour,
sifted together (step 2), the butter, slightly
melted and warm, and the lemon peel. Beat
the mixture until well blended, spoon into
about 12 buttered and floured madeleine
molds (step 3). If liked, place one walnut half
on each madeleine. Bake in a moderate oven
(350°F) for 10–15 minutes or until golden and
firm. Remove from the oven, unmold onto a
wire rack, let cool, and dust with confectioners'
sugar.

Small Meringues

In a bowl beat 3 egg whites until stiff and beat in ¾ cup sugar. Drop the mixture by spoonfuls on a cookie sheet, covered with wax paper, and bake the meringues in a low oven (275°F) until dry and light. Do not let them brown. Allow to cool. Makes 40 meringues.

Nut Tartlets

In a bowl beat 3 tablespoons softened butter or margarine with ¾ cup sugar until the mixture is fluffy, add 2 egg yolks, beaten with 5 table-spoons orange juice, and the finely grated rind of ½ orange and beat the mixture for a few minutes. Sift 1¼ cups flour with 3 teaspoons baking powder and 1 pinch salt, and add to the creamed mixture by spoonfuls, alternating with 4 tablespoons milk and 1 tablespoon chopped walnuts. Pour in small tartlet molds, buttered and floured, add 1 walnut half to each and bake the tarts in a moderate oven (350°F) for 15–20 minutes, or until golden. Remove from the oven, let cool and unmold onto a wire rack to cool completely. Sprinkle with con-fectioners' sugar before serving.

Yellow Tartlets

Using a wooden spoon, beat ¾ cup softened butter or margarine in a bowl for 10 minutes, add ¾ cup sugar and beat the mixture for a further 10 minutes. Add 2 eggs, one at a time, 1¼ cups sifted cornstarch and 3 tablespoons milk and stir the mixture. Divide between 6-inch tartlet molds, buttered and floured, and bake in a hot oven (400°F) for 35–40 minutes. Unmold and cool, then dust with confectioners' sugar.

Petits Fours

Ingredients: *¼ cup butter or margarine at room temperature · 3 tablespoons confectioners' sugar · ¼ oz vanilla sugar · 1 egg yolk · 1 cup sifted flour · 1 pinch salt · a few drops red food coloring or a few tablespoons unsweetened cocoa powder*

To finish: *1 egg white · 2 tablespoons water · sugar crystals*

In a bowl work the butter or margarine with the sugar, vanilla sugar and egg yolk, work in the flour and the salt until the mixture is smooth and divide into two. Add the food coloring or cocoa powder to one half (step 1). Form the dough into two balls, cover with wax paper and let stand in the refrigerator for 30 minutes. Remove the plain dough from the refrigerator, work it for a few minutes, put on a board, covered with a floured cloth, and roll out, not too thinly, into a rectangle. Roll out the colored dough in the same manner, put the plain dough on top of it (step 2), and roll up the layers together. Cover the roll in wax paper, return to the refrigerator for 1 hour and cut into slices (step 3). Place the slices on a lightly buttered cookie sheet and bake the cookies in a hot oven (400°F) for about 10 minutes. Remove from the oven, brush with the egg white mixed with the water, and sprinkle with sugar crystals. Let cool on a wire rack.

Cherry and Pine Nut Cookies

On a board sift 1 cup flour with 1 teaspoon baking powder, make a well in the center and add 3 tablespoons sugar, 2 egg yolks, ½ cup butter in small pieces and a little finely grated lemon peel. Work the ingredients together quickly, shape the dough into a ball, cover with wax paper and let stand in the refrigerator for 30 minutes. Soak 30 pine nuts in boiling water, drain and peel. Halve 15 candied cherries. Cut the dough into walnut-sized balls, make a slight hollow in the center of the balls and dip them in beaten egg white. Place on a buttered cookie sheet, cover half of them with pine nuts, the other half with cherry halves and cook in a hot oven (400°F) for about 20 minutes or until crisp and golden-brown. Remove from the oven and let cool on a wire rack. Makes 60 cookies.

Almond Cookies

In a bowl beat 4 eggs with 4 tablespoons sugar until the mixture is fluffy and stir in 1½ cups flour, sifted with a pinch each of bicarbonate of soda and cream of tartar, and 3 oz almonds, peeled and chopped. Work the ingredients together until the mixture is smooth, shape into a roll and place on a buttered cookie sheet, dusted with flour. Cook the roll in a moderate oven (350°F) for 20–30 minutes, let cool and cut into slices. Decorate each slice with peeled almonds, dipped in egg white, and return the cookies to the oven until crisp and golden-brown.

Coconut Macaroons

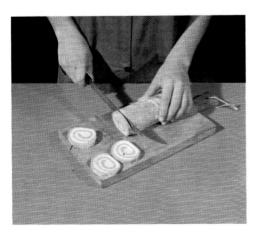

Place 1⅓ cups shredded coconut in a bowl with 1 teaspoon vanilla and ⅛ teaspoon salt. Add ¼ can of condensed milk and mix to a firm paste. Beat 2 egg whites with ½ teaspoon cream of tartar until stiff and fold into the paste. Drop in small heaps on a baking sheet lined with rice paper, leaving space for spreading. Bake in a cool oven (300°F) for 45 minutes. Leave to cool in the turned-off oven for 15 minutes.

Chocolate Truffles

Ingredients: *6 oz chocolate · 1 tablespoon rum or other liqueur to taste · 2 tablespoons hazelnuts or almonds · 3 oz langues de chats (cat's tongue) cookies*

Toast the hazelnuts in the oven and remove the skin (step 1). If using almonds, soak in boiling water for a few minutes, drain and peel. Chop the nuts. Heat the chocolate in a bain-marie or in the top of a double boiler until melted, remove from the heat and add the rum or other liqueur. Stir in the chopped nuts and cat's tongue cookies, crumbled (step 2), and mix gently. Drop the mixture by spoonfuls onto buttered wax paper (step 3), shape them into neat round balls, allow to cool and then chill the truffles for a few hours until they are hard. Makes 12 truffles.

Raisin Chocolate Truffles

Soak $\frac{3}{4}$ cup raisins in lukewarm water. Heat 6 oz chocolate in a bain-marie or in the top of a double boiler until it is melted, remove from the heat and add the drained and dried raisins and 2 tablespoons walnuts, hazelnuts or almonds, peeled and chopped. Drop the mixture by spoonfuls onto buttered wax paper, let the truffles cool, chill and serve.

Almonds Glacées

Soak 1 cup almonds in boiling water for a few minutes, drain, peel and dry in a slow oven (200°F). In a heavy pan heat slowly $\frac{3}{4}$ cup sugar and 1 pinch cream of tartar with 8 tablespoons hot water. When the mixture begins to boil, lower the heat and cook for 10–12 minutes or until the syrup starts to turn golden. Remove the pan from the heat, dip for a few minutes in cold water to stop the cooking and keep in a bain-marie. Dip the almonds in the syrup with a slotted spoon and put on a folded piece of wax paper. Let cool and harden.

Walnut Chocolate Truffles

In a pan put $\frac{1}{2}$ cup chopped walnuts, $\frac{1}{2}$ cup sugar, 2 oz chocolate, grated or cut into small pieces, and 8 tablespoons boiling water. Cook the mixture, stirring constantly, over very low heat until well blended. Remove from the heat, stir in 1 tablespoon rum and let cool. Shape the mixture into walnut-sized balls, roll in chocolate pastilles and chill and serve.

Fruits in Caramel

Put 1 cup sugar and $\frac{1}{2}$ cup water in a saucepan and add 1 tablespoon liquid glucose or honey. Bring to a boil, stirring to dissolve the sugar, and boil until the syrup turns a pale caramel color. Remove from the heat and place the pan over another pan containing hot water. Drop fruits (pitted prunes, quartered and pitted peaches, halved and pitted apricots, large white grapes, firm cherries, walnut halves, pitted dates) into the caramel and turn to coat. Lift out with a skewer and leave to set on a marble slab or baking sheet.

Stuffed Dates, Prunes and Walnuts

Ingredients: *6 oz dates · marzipan (in 3 different colors, if liked), or almond paste · 6 oz prunes · 6 oz shelled walnuts, halved*

For the syrup: *1½ cups sugar · 10–11 tablespoons water · 1 pinch cream of tartar*

Make an incision into the sides of the dates, discard the pits (step 1) and fill with a little pink marzipan (if using colored marzipans), or almond paste. Fill the prunes in the same manner, using green marzipan (step 2) and sandwich the walnut halves together, two by two, by putting a little plain marzipan between the 2 halves. Make the syrup: in a small pan cook the sugar, water and cream of tartar over moderate heat until a little of the mixture dropped in cold water forms crunchy threads. Remove the pan from the heat, dip in cold water to stop the cooking and place on a pan of hot water to keep the mixture liquid. Using a slotted spoon, toothpicks or metal skewers, dip the stuffed fruit, one at a time, into the syrup (step 3), place on an oiled wire rack and let cool.

Nougat

Soak 1½ cups almonds in boiling water for a few minutes, drain, peel and cut into thin strips or chop. In a pan heat 1½ cups sugar with a knob of butter over moderate heat, cook the mixture, stirring slowly, until the sugar is melted, and add the almonds. Cook the mixture until golden, remove from the heat and pour on a marble slab or tin, dampened with oil. Using a whole lemon, flatten the mixture quickly to a ½-inch thickness and score with a knife into squares so that it will break easily. Let cool completely. Keep in sealed jars.

Candied Orange Peel

Cut the skin of a few oranges in quarters and soak the quarters in cold water for 3 days, changing the water twice a day. Drain the quarters, cook in boiling water for 15–20 minutes, drain and cut into very thin strips discarding the white part of the skin. Weigh the strips and put them in a small pan with an equal weight of sugar and just enough water to moisten the sugar. Cook the mixture until the sugar starts to turn golden and is almost completely absorbed. The mixture should be syrup-like but not granular. Put the strips on a marble slab or a plate, separate them and let cool.

Plum Cake

Ingredients: *½ cup butter or margarine, softened · ½ cup sugar · 2 eggs · 1 egg yolk · ½ cup raisins, softened in lukewarm water, and sprinkled with flour · 2 tablespoons candied peel, sliced · 2 tablespoons rum · peel of 1 lemon, finely grated · ⅔ cup sifted flour*

In a bowl beat the butter or margarine with the sugar until the mixture is fluffy (step 1) and add the eggs and egg yolk one at a time, the raisins, candied peel, rum, lemon peel and flour and mix well. Line a plum cake mold with buttered wax paper (step 2), spoon in the mixture (step 3) and bake the cake in a very hot oven (450°F) for 5 minutes. Lower the heat to moderate (350°F) and bake the cake for a further 40 minutes or until a crust has formed on top.

Dundee Cake

Soften $\frac{3}{4}$ cup raisins in lukewarm water. Soak $\frac{3}{4}$ cup almonds in boiling water for a few minutes, drain and peel. Chop half the almonds and split the remaining ones in half. In a large bowl beat $\frac{3}{4}$ cup softened butter or margarine with $\frac{3}{4}$ cup sugar until the mixture is fluffy and add 4 eggs, one at a time, alternating with 1 cup flour sifted with 1 pinch salt. In another bowl mix the raisins, dried with a cloth, $2\frac{1}{2}$ tablespoons candied orange peel, chopped, 1 generous tablespoon flour, the chopped almonds, the finely grated peel of 1 orange, and 1 level teaspoon bicarbonate of soda blended with 1 teaspoon milk. Add this mixture to the butter and sugar mixture. Line a deep 12-inch round cake pan with buttered wax paper, spoon in the mixture and cover with the split almonds in a decorative circular pattern. Bake the cake in a moderate oven (350°F) for about 2 hours, or until cooked (a skewer inserted into the center of the cake should come out clean). Cover the almonds with aluminum foil if they brown. Remove the cake from the oven, let stand 30 minutes, then unmold. Let cool completely on a rack before slicing. Dundee cake always improves if kept before eating.

Panettone

Soften 2 tablespoons raisins in lukewarm water. In a bowl beat 2 egg yolks with 4 tablespoons sugar until the mixture is fluffy and add 4 tablespoons softened butter or margarine, and alternately, a little at a time, $1\frac{1}{4}$ cups flour sifted with 1 tablespoon baking powder, and $\frac{1}{2}$ cup milk. Stir in $\frac{1}{2}$ cup Marsala, the raisins, sprinkled with flour, 2 tablespoons candied peel, cut in thin strips, and 1 tablespoon pine nuts (optional). Fold in 2 egg whites, beaten until stiff. Butter a cake mold, dust with flour, and spoon in the mixture. Bake the cake in a moderate oven (350°F) for about 1 hour or until golden on top. Remove the cake from the oven, let stand 30 minutes, unmold, and let cool on a wire rack.

Krapfen (Jelly Doughnuts)

Ingredients: *1 oz dry yeast · 1 cup milk,
lukewarm · 2½ cups flour · 2 eggs ·
4 tablespoons butter or margarine · ¼ cup
sugar · pinch of salt · about 2 quarts frying oil ·
jelly or crème pâtissière (see p.541)*

Dissolve the yeast in ¼ of the lukewarm milk,
add ¼ of the sifted flour and work the ingredients until they form a paste. Put the paste in
lukewarm water, cover and let stand for about
15 minutes or until it rises to the surface. Sift
the remaining flour on a board, make a well in
the center and add the risen dough, the eggs,
butter or margarine, ¼ of the sugar, salt and
remaining milk. Work the ingredients together

thoroughly, put the dough in a deep narrow
dish, lined with a lightly floured cloth, cover
with another cloth and let stand in a warm
place for about 1½ hours or until it has doubled
in volume. Pound the dough for a few minutes,
divide into small balls (step 1), and flatten the
balls slightly. Let stand, covered with a light
cloth, for about 1 hour or until they have
doubled in volume. Heat the oil in a deep pan
until very hot, add the doughnuts a few at a
time and cook until golden on all sides. Drain
on absorbent paper, cut open on one side with
a pair of scissors and stuff with the jelly or
crème pâtissière. Roll them in the remaining
sugar, and serve.

Bows

Sift 1½ cups flour on a board, make a well in the center and add 1 tablespoon sugar, ½ tablespoon butter or margarine, 2–3 egg yolks, 1 pinch salt and 1 measure rum. Work the ingredients thoroughly together, roll out the dough thinly and, using a pastry wheel, cut into strips 6 × 1½ inches. Make a lengthwise incision in the middle of each strip and slip one end of the strip into it so that it comes out on the other side (step 2). Fry the bows a few at a time.

Doughnuts

In a bowl beat 3 eggs, add ¾ cup sugar, 2 tablespoons melted butter or margarine, 1 cup milk and 4 cups flour, sifted with a little salt and grated nutmeg, and work the ingredients until the dough is smooth. Roll out the dough to a ½-inch thichness on a floured board and cut into 4-inch circles with a cookie cutter or a glass. Make a 1-inch hole in the center of each doughnut with a small cookie cutter (step 3). Fry the doughnuts in deep hot oil, drain and dust with sugar.

Apple and Beer Puffs

Separate 2 eggs and mix the yolks with 6 tablespoons beer, 1 cup flour and a pinch of salt until smooth. Beat the egg whites until stiff and fold in. Peel, core and grate 1½ lb apples and fold in. Slide spoonfuls of the apple batter into deep hot fat and fry for about 5 minutes or until crisp and golden. Turn the puffs over once during cooking. Drain and roll in sugar mixed with cinnamon. Serve hot.

Potato Surprises

Mix 3 cups mashed potato with 2 tablespoons sugar, 6 tablespoons milk and 1 tablespoon melted butter. Gradually beat in 1 cup flour until smooth. Roll out the potato dough and cut into rounds. Fry in deep hot fat for about 4 minutes on each side. Drain, dredge with confectioners' sugar and serve warm.

Stuffed Plait

Ingredients: for the pastry, *6–7 tablespoons milk · 2 tablespoons sugar · 1 level teaspoon salt · 2 tablespoons butter or margarine, melted $\frac{1}{2}$ oz dry yeast or baking powder.*
2 tablespoons lukewarm water · 1 egg, beaten · 1$\frac{1}{3}$ cups flour, sifted

For the filling: *melted butter · 3–4 slices pineapple or other fruit, drained and chopped · a few tablespoons sugar · cinnamon to taste*

To finish: *1 egg yolk, beaten with a little water and sugar · candied peel and glacé cherries*

To make the pastry: heat the milk, add the sugar, salt and butter or margarine and mix until all the ingredients have dissolved together. Let the mixture cool. Mix the yeast or baking powder in the lukewarm water, stir in the milk mixture, add the beaten egg and work in the flour. Work the dough, which should be soft and not too dry, for 10 minutes, put in a buttered bowl, cover with a cloth and let stand in a warm place until it has doubled in volume. Divide the dough into three parts and roll each part into a 15×15 inch rectangle. Brush the rectangles with melted butter and cover with a little pineapple or other fruit (step 1), sugar and

604

cinnamon. Fold in half lengthwise, dampen the edges with water and pinch together securely. On a buttered cookie sheet, lightly dusted with flour, plait the filled strips (step 2). Cover and let stand until plait has doubled in volume. Brush with beaten egg, dot with peel and cherries (step 3), and bake in a moderate oven (350°F) for about 30 minutes.

Kugelhopf

Dissolve $\frac{1}{2}$ oz dry yeast or baking powder in 8 tablespoons lukewarm milk. Sift $1\frac{1}{2}$ cups flour into a large bowl, make a well in the center and add the yeast mixture, 4 eggs, lightly beaten with 4 tablespoons sugar, and a little finely grated lemon peel. Mix flour slowly into liquid ingredients and work dough. Cover and let stand until it has doubled in volume. Put on a floured board, flatten and cover with softened butter, cut into small pieces, raisins, softened in lukewarm water and dried, and almonds, peeled and chopped. Work the dough again, put it in a buttered kugelhopf mold and let stand until it has doubled in volume. Bake in a moderate oven (350°F) for about 1 hour. Unmold and dust with confectioners' sugar.

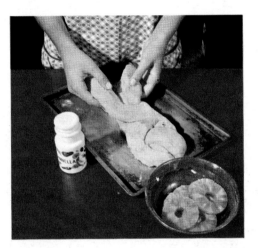

Epiphany Cake

Dissolve $\frac{1}{2}$ tablespoon dry yeast in a few drops lukewarm water in a bowl. Add 2 eggs and 1 cup sifted flour and mix the ingredients quickly and thoroughly. Heat 2 tablespoons butter in a small pan with the juice and finely grated peel of 1 orange, the juice and finely grated peel of $\frac{1}{2}$ lemon and a few drops orange flower extract. Pour the mixture drop by drop into the dough and continue working and pounding the dough until elastic. Shape the dough into a ball, cover and let stand in a warm place until it doubles in volume. Pound for a few minutes with lightly floured hands, shape into a ball, cover and let stand in a cool place until it has again doubled in volume. Put it on a floured board, work for a few minutes, make into a ball, make a hole in the middle and widen it to form a crown. Let stand until it has again doubled in volume, brush with beaten egg yolk and bake in the lowest part of a hot oven (400°F) for about 25 minutes.

Honey Snail

Ingredients: *1 tablespoon dry yeast or baking powder · $\frac{1}{2}$ cup sugar · 8 tablespoons lukewarm milk · $1\frac{1}{2}$ cups flour · 1 pinch salt · 1 oz vanilla sugar · 2 eggs · 1 teaspoon finely grated lemon peel · 3 tablespoons butter or margarine, softened*

For the topping: *2 tablespoons butter, softened · 1 tablespoon sugar · 3 tablespoons honey · 1 egg white · 2 tablespoons mixed nuts, chopped*

In a small bowl mix the yeast or baking powder and the sugar in the warm milk. Sift the flour, salt and vanilla sugar into a large bowl, make a well in the center and pour in the milk mixture, the eggs, lightly beaten, and the grated lemon peel. Work the flour slowly into the liquid ingredients, and lift the dough repeatedly. Cover the bowl with a light cloth and let the dough rise in a warm place for about 1 hour or until it has doubled in volume. Put the dough on a lightly floured board, cover with the softened butter or margarine, and work it into the dough with lightly floured hands. Form a long roll $1\frac{1}{2}$ inches thick (step 1). Butter a 12-inch pie pan and put in the roll, forming it into a spiral starting from the center (step 2). To prepare the topping: beat the butter with the sugar, honey and egg white, cover the dough with the mixture and sprinkle with the chopped nuts (step 3). Bake in a moderate oven (350°F) for 30 minutes or until risen and golden. Serve hot or cold. Serves 6.

Griddle Biscuits

On a board sift $1\frac{1}{2}$ cups flour, 3 level teaspoons baking powder, 1 level teaspoon salt and 2 tablespoons sugar. Make a well in the center, add 2 tablespoons butter or margarine, cut into small pieces, and, using the fingertips, work the flour mixture quickly into the fat. In a bowl beat 2 eggs vigorously, add 4 tablespoons milk, and mix into the dough a little at a time. Flatten the dough until $\frac{1}{2}$ inch thick and cut into $2\frac{1}{2}$-inch squares. Fold the squares to form triangles, brush with milk and sprinkle with sugar. Place on a buttered cookie sheet and bake in a moderate oven (350°F) for about 25 minutes or until risen and golden. Serve hot and buttered. Traditionally these biscuits should be cooked on a griddle – brown them on a hot, lightly greased griddle for about 10 minutes on each side.

Traditional Biscuits

On a board sift $1\frac{1}{4}$ cups flour with 4 level teaspoons baking powder. Make a well in the center and add 2 tablespoons butter or margarine, chopped in very small pieces, 1 pinch salt and $\frac{1}{2}$ cup milk. Work the flour quickly into the liquid ingredients and roll out the dough to the thickness of 1 inch. Using a cookie cutter or a small glass, cut the dough into 3-inch circles. Place on a buttered cookie sheet in a hot oven (400°F) for 12–15 minutes.•

Muffins

Sift 1 cup flour into a bowl with $2\frac{1}{2}$ teaspoons baking powder, 1 pinch salt and 2 tablespoons sugar. In another bowl beat 1 egg vigorously, add $\frac{3}{4}$ cup milk and 3 tablespoons melted butter or margarine, and pour the mixture into the center of the flour mixture. Mix quickly until the flour is moist. Pour the mixture into a buttered muffin pan, filling each mold $\frac{2}{3}$ full, and bake in a very hot oven (450°F) for 20–25 minutes until risen and golden. To make blueberry muffins, reduce the milk to 6 tablespoons and add 4 tablespoons blueberries, washed and dried. Makes 12 muffins.

Drinks

Rum Cocktail

Fill $\frac{1}{3}$ of a shaker with ice, add 1 part lemon juice, 4 parts rum (steps 1 and 2), $\frac{1}{2}$ teaspoon sugar (optional), and 2–3 dashes of grenadine. Shake vigorously and strain the drink into the glasses (step 3). This cocktail may also be prepared in a mixer and served on the rocks.

Screwdriver

Fill $\frac{1}{3}$ of a shaker with crushed ice and add 1 part orange juice and 1 part vodka. Shake vigorously and serve.

Atomic Bomb

In each glass put 1 sugar cube, a dash of Angostura, 2 parts Scotch, 1 part Aperol (optional), 1 part Cognac and the juice of $\frac{1}{4}$ orange. Do not mix. Serve with ice and a slice of orange. If prepared in a shaker, put the sugar and Angostura in each glass separately.

Brandy Cocktail

Fill $\frac{1}{2}$ a shaker with ice, add 1 part lemon juice, 2 parts curaçao, 8 parts brandy and 2 dashes of Angostura. Shake well and serve.

Dry Martini

Fill ⅓ of a mixer with ice, add 2 parts gin and 1 part dry vermouth. Mix well and pour into chilled glasses. Add a little lemon peel, 1 cube of ice and 1 green olive on a toothpick to each glass.

Alexander

After collecting all the necessary cocktail utensils together, fill ⅓ of a shaker with ice, add 1 part crème de cacao, 1 part cream and 2 parts gin or Cognac, shake well and serve immediately.

Old-fashioned

In a low glass crush 1 sugar cube with 1 teaspoon water and 1 dash Angostura. Fill ⅓ of the glass with crushed ice, add a measure of Scotch and mix well. Serve with a maraschino cherry and a twist of orange or lemon on the edge of the glass.

Whisky Sour

Fill ⅓ of a shaker with crushed ice, add 1 teaspoon sugar for each glass, 2 parts lemon juice and 8 parts bourbon. Shake vigorously and serve in chilled glasses, garnished with 1 maraschino cherry and a twist of orange or lemon on the edge of the glass.

Negroni

Fill a mixer with ⅓ ice, add 1 part Campari bitters, 1 part dry gin and 1 part red vermouth. Mix well, pour and add 1 slice of orange.

Teacher's Cocktail

In a mixer put 1 part vodka 1 part gin and 1 teaspoon dry vermouth. Mix well and pour in a glass containing ice and 1 olive.

Pernod Cocktail

Fill ¼ of a mixer with ice, add 1 part dry vermouth, 1 part sweet vermouth and 1 part Pernod. Mix well and serve in frosted glasses.

Manhattan

Fill ⅓ of a mixer with crushed ice, add 1 part sweet vermouth, 2 parts Scotch and 1 dash Angostura. Mix well and strain the cocktail into chilled glasses, each containing a maraschino cherry.

Sangria

Ingredients: *2 cups red wine · 1 cup Malaga
wine · ½ glass Cognac · 1 tablespoon sugar ·
1 pinch of cinnamon · 1 pinch of grated nutmeg ·
2 oranges · 1 lemon · 2 cups peaches, or
2 bananas*

In a large jug pour the wines and the
Cognac (step 1), add the sugar, cinnamon and
grated nutmeg. Slice the oranges and lemon
and peel and dice the peaches or bananas (step
2). Add the fruit to the wine mixture (step 3)
and let macerate for 2 hours at room temperature. Refrigerate the mixture for at least ½ day.
Serve the sangria very cold with ice cubes and
soda water. The quantities of sugar, cinnamon
and grated nutmeg may be adjusted according
to taste.

Apple Tonic

In a mixer put 2 parts cider or apple juice,
1 part tonic water and 1 part ice cold soda
water. Mix well and serve with ice cubes.

Cuba Libre

Put 1 measure white rum in each tall glass and
add ice cubes and Coca-Cola.

Gin and Tonic

Put 1 measure gin in each tall glass, add 1 slice
lemon and a few ice cubes and fill with tonic
water.

Light Drink

In a mixer put 1 measure each of gin and
bitters, the juice of ½ lemon and ½ small bottle
tonic or soda water for each person. Mix well
and serve in a tall glass with ice cubes.

Mint Julep

In each tall, chilled glass put 1 teaspoon each of
sugar and water, and 4 mint leaves. Stir with a
teaspoon until the sugar is melted. Fill the
glasses with crushed ice, add 1 measure bourbon and stir rapidly for a few minutes. Add
enough bourbon to fill the glass. Dip a fresh
mint sprig in confectioner's sugar and use to
decorate the glass. Serve with a straw.

610

Country Inn Milk

In a punch bowl pour 1 bottle good red wine, $\frac{1}{4}$ cup plum brandy and 1 dash Angostura. Mix well and serve at room temperature in punch cups. Serves 6.

This drink is particularly good with roasted chestnuts.

Tom Collins

Fill $\frac{1}{3}$ of a shaker with ice, add 1 tablespoon sugar syrup (sugar dissolved in water, then boiled), the juice of $\frac{1}{2}$ lemon and 1 measure gin for each person. Shake vigorously and serve in tall glasses. Add ice cubes and enough soda water to fill glasses.

Uncle Tom's Eggnog

Ingredients: *3 eggs, separated · 3 tablespoons sugar · 5 tablespoons bourbon · 5 tablespoons brandy · 1 tablespoon rum · 1 cup milk · 1 cup heavy cream · grated nutmeg*

Beat the egg yolks with a wire whip until they are pale yellow (step 1). Add the sugar, a little at a time, beating constantly. Stir in the bourbon, brandy and rum and refrigerate the mixture for a few hours. Just before serving, remove from the refrigerator, stir in the milk and fold in the cream and the egg whites, both whipped until stiff (step 2). Serve the eggnog in punch cups, sprinkled with grated nutmeg (step 3). Serves 10–12.

Orange Eggnog

Separate 2 eggs, reserving the whites, and beat the yolks with a wire whip until they are pale yellow. Beat in $\frac{1}{2}$ cup orange juice and $1\frac{1}{4}$ cups cold milk a little at a time. Beat the egg whites until stiff and add 4 tablespoons sugar and $\frac{1}{2}$ cup orange juice, one tablespoon at a time. Fold the egg white mixture carefully into the eggnog.

Divide the eggnog equally between 4 tall glasses and sprinkle with finely grated orange peel.

Tom-and-Jerry

Separate 4 eggs, reserving the whites, and beat the yolks with a wire whip until they are pale yellow. Add 4 teaspoons sugar, 2 teaspoons mixed spice and 4 measures white rum and continue beating the mixture thoroughly until it is creamy.

Fold in the 4 egg whites, whipped until stiff, and add 2 small glasses brandy. Pour the mixture in 4 mugs, fill with hot milk and sprinkle with grated nutmeg.

Vin Brûlé

In a pan put $2\frac{1}{2}$ tablespoons sugar, the peel of $\frac{1}{2}$ lemon, 1 piece cinnamon, 1 clove and $\frac{1}{2}$ bottle good red wine. Bring the mixture to a boil, flame the wine and strain immediately into glasses, preferably with metal glass holders, or into warm cups.

Mulled Wine

Put 2 teaspoons ground cinnamon, 1 teaspoon ground cloves, 1 teaspoon grated nutmeg, $\frac{2}{3}$ cup sugar and 2 cups water in a large saucepan. Add $\frac{1}{2}$ orange and $\frac{1}{2}$ lemon, both peeled and chopped. Bring to a boil, stirring to dissolve the sugar, then simmer gently for at least 1 hour. Strain through a cheesecloth-lined sieve and return the syrup to the pan, making up to 2 cups with additional water if necessary. Add a bottle of red wine and heat to just below boiling point. Serve hot.

Spiced Lemon Punch

Place 1 cup sugar, 2 cups water, 1 cinnamon stick, 3 cloves and the pared rind of 2 lemons in a saucepan. Bring to a boil, stirring to dissolve the sugar. Add the juice of 2 lemons, $2\frac{1}{2}$ cups red wine and $\frac{1}{2}$ cup white rum and heat through gently without boiling. Strain and serve hot. To serve the punch cold, cool, then chill thoroughly before straining.

613

Sweet-and-Sour Drink

Ingredients: *2 cups grapefruit juice ·*
3 tablespoons lemon juice · sugar ·
2 cups ginger ale · ice cubes

Blend the grapefruit and lemon juice together
in a jug (step 1) and refrigerate for a few hours.
Frost the glasses by dipping the rims in lemon
juice and then in sugar (step 2) and chilling
them. Mix the fruit juices with ginger ale and
pour into the glasses, over ice cubes and sugar.

Lemonade with Rosemary

Bring 1 quart water, $\frac{3}{4}$ cup sugar, 2 tablespoons
lemon juice and 1 teaspoon fresh rosemary
leaves to a boil and cook the mixture for 6
minutes. Strain the liquid, let cool and add 8
tablespoons lemon juice. Refrigerate the liquid
for a few hours and serve in tall glasses with 1
lemon slice and a twig of rosemary in each
glass. Serves 4–6.

Apricot and Orange Drink

In a jug mix 2 cans or bottles apricot juice with
2 cans or bottles orange juice and add the
juice of 2 lemons or of 1 grapefruit and a few
mint leaves, if desired. Refrigerate the jug for a
few hours and serve the drink over ice cubes
in frosted glasses.

Spicy Tomato Juice

In a jug mix 1 quart tomato juice with 2 teaspoons tomato ketchup, a few drops Worcestershire, the juice of $\frac{1}{2}$ lemon or more to
taste and salt and pepper. Refrigerate before
serving or serve over ice cubes.

Pink Drink

In a jug blend 1 cup tomato juice with $1\frac{1}{4}$ cups
orange juice and the juice of 1 lemon. Refrigerate for a few hours and serve over ice cubes.
Add $\frac{1}{2}$ slice orange or lemon to each glass.

Summer Drink

In a jug mix $\frac{1}{2}$ glass pineapple juice with $\frac{1}{2}$ cup grapefruit juice, the juice of 1 orange and 4 teaspoons sugar. Refrigerate the jug for a few hours and add 1 cup mineral or soda water. Serve immediately with 1 lemon or orange slice in each glass. The measurements can be adjusted to taste.

Mixed Fruit Drink

In a jug mix the juice of 4 oranges and 2 lemons, 1 can or bottle pear juice, 1 can or bottle apricot juice and 1 teaspoon raspberry syrup and refrigerate the mixture for a few hours. Mix again and pour the drink over ice cubes. Add 1 orange slice to each glass.

Iced Tea Cubes

Prepare tea to taste, add sugar and lemon juice to taste and let cool in an ice cube tray with maraschino cherries in some of the cubes, pieces of pineapple in others, mint leaves in others. Freeze the tray until solid, take out the cubes and serve in individual glasses.

Mint Tea

Put 6 teaspoons orange Pekoe tea in a teapot, add 4 cups boiling water and let stand for 10 minutes. Fill 4 tall glasses $\frac{2}{3}$ full with tea, add fresh mint leaves and pour in more tea. Serve lemon slices and sugar separately, or, add sugar while the tea is still hot, refrigerate until very cold and serve with ice cubes and lemon slices.

Iced Tea with Peaches

In a jug put 2–3 ripe peaches, peeled, pitted, cubed, sugared and mixed with lemon juice. Add strong hot tea, cool, and then refrigerate.

615

Tutti-Frutti Cream

Ingredients: *1 apple · 1 pear, or peach ·
1 banana · 1 orange · 2 apricots, fresh or
canned · 2 tablespoons sugar, or more to taste ·
1 cup milk · 3 cubes crushed ice*

Peel, pit and slice the fruit (step 1) and put in a
blender with the sugar, milk and ice (step 2).
Set the blender on high speed for 2 minutes and
pour the cream in glasses (step 3).

Pineapple Cream

In a blender put 4 slices fresh or canned pineapple, 2 peeled and sliced bananas, the juice of
2 oranges, preferably blood oranges, the juice
of 1 lemon, and a cold syrup, made by dissolving 4 tablespoons sugar in 1 cup water,
then boiling until quite thick. Set the blender
on high speed for 2 minutes then pour the
cream over crushed ice cubes in tall glasses and
decorate with pineapple slices.

616

Apple Cream

Peel, core and slice 2 apples, and peel and slice 1 banana and put them in a blender with 2 tablespoons sugar, 2 cubes crushed ice and 1 cup milk. Set the blender on high speed for 2 minutes, then pour into tall glasses.

Orange Cream

In a blender put the juice of 4 oranges and 1 lemon, the finely grated peel of $\frac{1}{2}$ orange, 1 apple, peeled, cored and sliced, 1 small glass kirsch or other liqueur to taste, 2 tablespoons sugar and 6–8 cubes crushed ice. Set the blender on high speed for 2 minutes, then pour into glasses.

Melon Cream

Peel 1 small melon, discard the seeds, slice and put in a blender. Add 3–4 tablespoons sugar, the juice of 1 lemon, 2 tablespoons liqueur to taste, 1 cup dry white wine and 3 cubes crushed ice. Blend and serve as above.

Pear Cream

Peel, core and slice 2 pears, peel and slice 1 banana and put them in a blender with 4–5 tablespoons grenadine or the juice of 1 blood orange, 1 cup milk and 2 cubes crushed ice. Blend and serve as above.

Apricot Cream

Peel and pit 4 apricots and 1 orange, and peel 1 banana. Slice the fruit and put in a blender with 1 cup milk, 2 tablespoons or more sugar to taste and 3 cubes crushed ice. Set the blender on high speed for 2 minutes and pour into glasses.

Hot Spicy Chocolate

Ingredients: *4 tablespoons unsweetened cocoa powder, sifted · 3 tablespoons sugar · 1 pinch salt · 3 tablespoons water · 6 cloves · 3 cups milk · 1 cup heavy cream · 4 cinnamon sticks*

In a pan put the cocoa, sugar, salt, water and cloves. Bring the mixture to a boil (step 1), stirring constantly, and cook for 2–3 minutes. Add the milk and ½ the cream (step 2), and heat, stirring constantly. Spoon into 4 mugs, discarding cloves (step 3), and add 1 cinnamon stick and a little whipped cream.

Hot Chocolate Chiquita

Melt 2½ tablespoons chocolate in a bain-marie or in the top of a double boiler, add 2 tablespoons sugar, a few drops vanilla extract, 2 teaspoons instant coffee powder and 4 tablespoons water and cook the mixture for a few minutes. Add 2 cups each of hot water and hot milk and heat the mixture, stirring constantly, without boiling. Serve the chocolate in mugs, topped with whipped cream and cinnamon.

French Chocolate

Melt 4 oz chocolate with 4 tablespoons water in a bain-marie or in the top of a double boiler. Remove the chocolate from the heat and beat vigorously until thickened. Stir in $\frac{1}{2}$ cup water and divide the mixture equally between 4 mugs. Add 1 quart hot milk, stirring constantly and top each mug with whipped cream and powdered cinnamon. Serve immediately.

Spanish Chocolate

Melt 2 tablespoons chocolate with 1 teaspoon butter in a bain-marie or in the top of a double boiler. Add 3 tablespoons sugar, 1 pinch grated nutmeg, 1 pinch cinnamon and $\frac{3}{4}$ cup hot black coffee a little at a time. Bring the mixture to a boil and cook for 2–3 minutes. Remove from the heat and let cool. Divide it equally between 5–6 tall glasses and fill up with cold milk.

Mexican Chocolate

Melt 2 (1-oz) squares semisweet chocolate in the top of a double boiler. Add $\frac{1}{2}$ teaspoon vanilla, 1 teaspoon ground cinnamon and 4 tablespoons heavy cream and stir until smooth. Gradually stir in 2 cups milk and heat through. Beat 2 egg yolks with 2 tablespoons sugar until foamy. Add a little of the chocolate mixture, then stir into the remaining chocolate mixture with 6 tablespoons brandy. Whisk over the heat until the mixture is hot and frothy. Serve immediately, with cinnamon sticks in each cup to use for stirring.

Iced Cocoa

Put 3 cups milk and 2 tablespoons brown sugar in a saucepan. Sprinkle 3 heaping tablespoons cocoa powder over the top and bring to a boil, stirring. Remove from the heat and cool. Place a scoop of vanilla ice cream in each of 4 glasses and pour in the cooled cocoa mixture. Decorate with whipped cream sprinkled with cocoa powder mixed with sugar.

Gourmet Coffee

Ingredients: *¾ cup chocolate · 2 tablespoons water · 1 pinch cinnamon · 4 small cups hot strong black coffee · crushed ice · sugar cubes · whipped or light cream*

Melt the chocolate in a bain-marie or in the top of a double boiler with the water. Add the cinnamon, and the hot coffee, a little at a time (step 1). Fill 4 tall glasses with crushed ice, add the chocolate mixture and more coffee if necessary, to fill the glass (step 2) and sugar to taste and serve with whipped cream on top (step 3) or light cream separately.

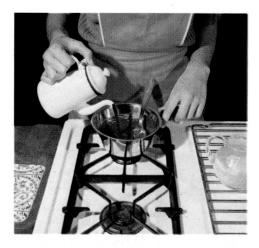

Coffee Delight

Mix 1 tablespoon instant coffee powder with 2 tablespoons hot water, add ¾ cup cold water and refrigerate the mixture until very cold. Stir in 1 cup commercially prepared or home-made coffee ice cream (see p.555), whipped until soft. Pour the mixture in tall chilled glasses, add a little whipped cream on top and serve immediately.

Sugared Coffee

Make 6 small cups of strong black coffee. In a bowl put 1 teaspoon or more sugar per person, add 4 teaspoons coffee and beat the mixture until frothy. Divide the mixture equally between 4 cups and add the hot coffee. A light froth will form on the top.

Coffee Punch

In 4 glasses, preferably with metal glass holders, put a few grains sugar, 1 small sliver orange peel, hot black coffee and brandy. Mix well.

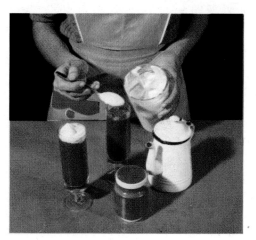

Tea Punch with Rum

In each glass put 1 teaspoon each of lemon juice and sugar, 1½ measures rum and a small sliver lemon peel. Fill with hot tea and serve.

Hot Tea with Rum

In each tall glass put equal measures of rum and strong black tea and sugar to taste. Top with hot water boiled with cloves.

Cheese

Mozzarella Cartwheels

Ingredients: *8 slices white bread · 1—2 mozzarella cheeses · 2 eggs · 2 tablespoons milk · salt · oil or pork fat · pepper*

Cut the bread slices into rounds. Put on each 1 slice mozzarella cheese (step 1). Roll in flour, dip in the egg beaten with the milk and a pinch of salt (step 2), and fry in hot oil or fat until golden (step 3). Remove from pan, drain on absorbent paper and sprinkle with pepper.

Gorgonzola Cheese Balls

Mash with a fork ½ lb gorgonzola cheese, softened with a little light cream. Add 1 tablespoon grated onion, 1 tablespoon chopped parsley and 2—3 pickled gherkins, finely chopped. Mix well and shape into balls with the hands. Roll the balls in almonds, peeled, broiled, finely chopped, and mixed with paprika to taste. Keep in the refrigerator for a few hours, and serve as an appetizer.

Fried Mozzarella

Cut 2 mozzarella cheeses into slices. Roll in flour, dip in egg beaten with a pinch each of salt and pepper, and finally roll in breadcrumbs. Dip once more in the egg, and in the breadcrumbs. Let stand in the refrigerator for ½ hour, then fry, a few slices at a time, in hot deep oil. Lift out with a slotted spoon, drain on absorbent paper, and serve piping hot, with a tomato sauce in a separate dish if liked.

Fried Cheese Balls

Whip 2 egg whites with a pinch each of salt and paprika until stiff. Blend with ¼ cup grated Parmesan cheese. Cook the mixture, 1 spoonful at a time, in hot deep oil. Lift out the balls with a slotted spoon when golden, and drain on absorbent paper. Sprinkle with paprika.

Quiche Lorraine

Ingredients: for the pastry, *¾ cup flour ·
1 pinch salt · 4 tablespoons butter ·
3 tablespoons water*

For the filling: *6 slices bacon · 8 slices
Emmenthal cheese · 4 eggs · 1 cup light
cream · grated nutmeg · salt · pepper*

To prepare the pastry, sift the flour with the
salt onto a pastry board or a table top. Put the
butter, cut into small pieces, in the center, and
gradually draw in the flour with the tips of the
fingers until the mixture resembles fine
breadcrumbs. Add the water quickly, and
knead the dough into a ball. Wrap in wax
paper, and let stand in a cool place or
refrigerator for at least 20 minutes. Then roll
out the dough with a rolling pin to a ¼-inch
thickness, and line with it a buttered shallow
tart mold, about 8–10 inches in diameter,
forming a pinched edge all around (step 1).
Prick the dough with a fork and leave to
relax. Meanwhile, fry the bacon in a skillet
until crisp, drain, and arrange on the dough.
Cover with the Emmenthal cheese (step 2). Beat
the eggs with the cream, and nutmeg, salt and
pepper to taste, and spoon over the cheese
(step 3). Put the quiche in a moderate oven
(350°F) for about 40 minutes until set and
golden.

Camembert en Surprise

Place a whole Camembert cheese in a deep
dish, and cover with dry white wine. Let stand
for 12 hours, then scrape off the surface of the
cheese, and mash the pulp together with ½
cup very fresh softened butter. Mix well and
reshape the cheese in its original form. Roll
it in almonds or hazelnuts, toasted and finely
chopped, and let stand in the refrigerator for a
few hours. Take out ½ hour before serving.
Serve at the end of a meal with hot toast.

Index

Aïoli mayonnaise 98
　with salt cod 285
Allumettes au paprika 64
Almond(s), cookies 595
　glacées 597
　with string beans 435
　with trout 299
Anchovy(ies), brochettes 69
　fillets with olives 31
　with green sauce 31
　Ligurian 15
　sauce 83
　stuffing for eggs 238
　with sweet peppers 49
Andalouse sauce 95
Andalusian sauce 329
Appetizers, allumettes au
　　paprika 64
　cheese 13
　chicken liver 62
　kaleidoscope 13
　shrimp 13
Apple, and beer puffs 603
　charlotte 531
　clafoutis 535
　frittata 263
　pie, maison 567
　rice, Indonesian 127
　soufflé omelet 263
　strudel 566
　tart, French 565
　turnovers, Irish 573
Apricot, coupe 544
　crêpes 261
　sauce 538
Arabian risotto 123
Artichoke(s), Argenteuil 427
　baked with noodles 145
　barigoule 428
　beignets 67
　canapés 35
　Clamart 428
　cream soup 183
　crudités 20
　fried 427
　frittata 78
　alla Guidea 427
　hearts 68
　　with eggs 231
　and potatoes, country style 493
　salad 21
　　with celery 501
　sauce with spaghetti 136
　soufflé 430
　stuffed 426
　stuffing for eggs 37
Asparagus, with eggs 432
　frittata 254
　au gratin 432
　with mousseline sauce 432
　risotto 128
　salad with rice 43
　soufflé 180
　vinaigrette 432
Aspic, 104
　Aurora 508
　eggs, poached in 224
　　and prosciuto rolls in 226
　mayonnaise 99
　multicolored 47
　à la Russe 509
　with shellfish 46

tomato, eggs in 230
trout in 298
Aubergine, see Eggplant
Aurore sauce 84, 329
　with eggs 227
Avocado(s), dip 11
　with prawns 11
　stuffed 11

Baby octopus with tartlets 54
Bacon, with Brussels sprouts 440
　with cod, broiled 283
　and eggs 242
　with eggs en cocotte 249
Bagna cauda 83
Baked Alaska 534
Baklava 575
Banana(s), beignets 537
　coupe 544
　delight 536
　flamed 536
　pudding 541
　sauce 539
　split 556
Barbecue sauce for hamburgers
　323
Bass, see Fish
Bavaroise, striped 544
　vanilla 547
Bean(s), dried
　Boston baked 497
　haricots, Bretonne 497
　　with ham 496
　　panachés 497
　lima, Greek style 457
　　with salt pork 457
　　Sicilian 457
　salad 501
　soup with noodles 192
　Spanish with braised tripe 378
　string,
　　with almonds 435
　　Lyonnaise 435
　　pickled 512
　　with poulette sauce 435
　　salad 501
　　Spanish 435
　　with tomato sauce 434
Béarnaise sauce 86
Béchamel sauce 66, 84
Beef 314, 323–339
　bobotie 337
　boiled, au gratin 409
　　with tuna sauce 408
　braised 335
　　in wine 334
　calves' liver, braised with
　　sage 375
　　with onions 374
　　with red wine 375
　fillet, with olives 331
　　with parsley 331
　　stuffed with mushrooms 330
　fondue Bourguignonne 328
　ground meat loaf 338
　hamburgers 323
　　with barbecue sauce 323
　marrow, with brains, fried 413
　　paupietteS 199
　　in veal pie 354
　meat loaf, Clementina 339
　　with frittata 337
　　grandmother's 336
　　with horseradish 339
　oxtail, braised 377
　roast 332
　　croquettes 333
　　with oranges 335

in salt 332
steak, à la Bismark 325
　chasseur 325
　broiled, piquant style 327
　Lyonnaise 325
　with mustard sauce 327
　alla pizzaiola 324
　tartare 323
　stew, leftover 333
　tongue, braised 377
　(calves'), with olives 376
　　with scallions 376
　tournedos, Renata 326
　　Rossini 327
Beer puffs, with apple 603
Beets, à l'Anglaise 436
　bortsch, spicy 195
　glazed 437
　au gratin 437
　salad, with Belgian endive 501
　　with onions 436
　sour 436
　stuffed 436
　sweet-and-sour 436
Beignets, artichoke 67
　banana 537
　ham 67
　salt cod 278
Biscuits, griddle 607
　traditional 607
Blini, Russian 18
Bobotie 337
Bolognese sauce 88
Bombes, various 558–559
Bordelaise sauce 92
Bortsch, spicy 195
Boston baked beans 497
Bouchées, mushroom 63
Bouillabaisse, see Fish
Bouillon, see Soups
Bows 603
Brains, see Variety Meats
Brandy, see also Drinks
　cherries in 519
　with chicken breasts 385
　grapes in 518
　kumquats in 519
　macédoine of fruit in 519
　prunes in 519
Bread, crusty mushroom 81
　soup with vegetable 193
Broccoli, golden 438
　with ham 439
　Niçoise 438
　pudding 438
Brochettes, anchovy 69
　Chinese 415
　eel 219
　home style 414
　salmon 273
　scampi 303
　squabs 407
　veal 415
Broths, see Soups
Brussels sprouts, with bacon 440
　with chestnuts 441
　creamed 441
　with eggs 219
　fried 441
　sautéed 441
　soufflé 181
　soup 185
Butters, anchovy 100
　beurre manié 100
　meunière 101
　clarified 101
　garlic 100
　green 101

horse-radish 101
icing 577
maître d'hôtel 101
paprika 101
shrimp 100

Cabbage, baked, Dutch 443
　braised 443
　stuffed 442
Caesar's salad 503
Cakes bûche de Noël 584
　candied fruit 587
　chestnut, bûche 585
　iced 589
　chocolate 576
　Christmas log 584
　coconut macaroons 595
　croquembouche 569
　Dundee 601
　Epiphany 605
　iced mocha 590
　Italian pandoro 579
　madeleines 592
　marble 580
　Margherita 578
　palmiers 571
　pan di Spagna 579
　panettone 601
　plum 600
　rice 580
　Saint-Honoré 583
　tips for success 522
　tropical 587
　walnut and orange 579
Camembert en surprise 624
Canadian herring salad 17
Canapés, caviar 18
　radish 35
　smoked eel 35
　various 34
Candied, fruit cake 587
　orange peel 599
Cannelloni, see Pasta
Cannoli, Sicilian 574
Caper(s), with rolled herring 265
　sauce 84, 329
　with swordfish 269
　with veal kidneys 372
Capon, see Poultry
Caramel, with fruit 597
Cardoon, Bolognese 449
　fritters 449
　au gratin 448
　with hollandaise sauce 449
Carp, see Fish
Carré d'agneau 367
Carrot(s), in batter 445
　cream soup 183
　creamed 444
　crudités 20
　glazed 445
　purée Crécy 445
　salad 21
　sautéed 445
　soufflé 431
　and spinach mould 179
　Vichy 445
Catering quantities 106
Cauliflower, gourmet 446
　au gratin 447
　with macaroni, baked 141
　paupiettes with ham 447
　with piquant sauce 447
　salad 507
Caviar, canapés 18
　how to serve 18
Celeriac, à la Français 451
　and fruit salad 45

and potato purée 451
rémoulade 21
Celery, crudités 20
  hearts, braised 451
  hors d'oeuvre 15
  with rice and sausage 117
  salad with artichoke 501
  stuffed 23
  with yogurt sauce 449
Charcutière sauce 93
Chasseur sauce 92
Chaud-froid sauces 95
Cheese, 422, 526
  appetizers 13
  with baked pork 359
  balls 23
    with curry 23
    fried 623
  cake, upside-down 553
  Camembert en surprise 624
  cream with chicken breasts
    385
  croque, madame 65
    monsieur 65
  with eggplants 453
  with eggs en cocotte 248
  Emmenthal with fried eggs 240
  fondue 70
  and frankfurter stuffing
    for veal 348
  fromage mystère 23
  with garlic and turnips 489
  Gorgonzola, balls 623
    mousse 22
    with polenta 174
  Gougère 69
  with green noodles 144
  Mozzarella, cartwheels 623
    fried 623
    frittata 253
    pizza 75
  with polenta 175
  with potato gnocchi 171
  quiche Lorraine 624
  Ricotta with macaroni 137
  with scrambled eggs 245
  soufflé 180
  strudel 167
  stuffing for cutlets 349
    for tomatoes 27
  and tapioca fritters 67
  with tortellini 154
  with veal scallops and ham
    348
  Welsh rarebit 64
Chef's salad 502
Cherry(ies) in brandy 519
  bread pudding 535
  clafoutis 535
  compote 551
  cookies with pine nuts 595
  soufflé 533
  torte 564
Chestnut(s) with Brussels
    sprouts 441
  bûche 585
  cake, iced 589
  croquettes 537
  Mont Blanc 589
  soufflé 533
    cold 547
  stuffing for turkey 391
Chicken, *see* **Poultry**
Chickens liver(s), *see* **Variety Meats**
Chickpea(s), with pork 495
  purée 495
  salad 495
  Spanish 494

Chicory soufflé 431
Chocolate, *see also* **Drinks**
  cake 576
  ice cream 555
  icing 577
  meringue cups 542
  mousse 547
  parfait 559
  sauce 539
  tart, with walnut 565
  truffles 596
    with raisins 597
    with walnuts 597
Choron sauce 87
choux fritters 569
Chow chow 516
Christmas log (bûche de Noël)
    584
Chutney, prune 517
Clam(s), *see* **Shellfish**
Clarified butter 101
Club sandwich 56
Cocktail, *see also* **Drinks**
  crab with grapefruit 17
  sauce 99
  shrimp 16
Coconut cups 543
  macaroons 595
Cod, *see* **Fish**
Coffee, *see also* **Drinks**
  ice cream 555
  icing 577
  parfait 559
  sauce 539
  sundae, Belgian 557
Cognac, *see also* **Drinks**
  raisins in 519
Cold sauces 96–99
Comparative measurements 632
Compote, cherry 551
Consommé, *see* **Soups**
Conversion table 632
Cooked vegetable salad 506
Cookies, almond 595
  cherry and pine nut 595
  petits fours 594
Corn, sweet and sour salad 507
Corned beef patties 413
Country, salad 501
  timbale 131
Coupe, apricot 544
  banana 544
  currant 557
  fruit 544
Crab, *see* **Shellfish**
Cream, with ham and
    'straw-and-hay' 146
    sauce 85
    with scrambled eggs 247
    sour cream pastries 575
Cream cheese, with pasta
    shells and ham 148
  with tartlets 54
Crème, caramel 540
  patissière 541
Crêpe(s), apricot 261
  fruity 261
  mold 258
  stuffed, Bolognese 258
    with spinach 258
  Suzette 260
Croissants, stuffed 64
Croque, madame 65
  monsieur 65
Croquembouche 569
Croquettes, chestnut 537
  chicken 59, 413
  egg 235

potato 472
rice 59, 537
roast beef 333
salt cod 284
sardine 267
spinach 483
sweet potato 478
Crudités 20
  Bagna cauda 83
Cucumber(s), barquettes 459
  creamed 21, 459
Currant coupe 557
Curry, with cheese balls 23
  with hard-boiled eggs 233
  sauce 84
    with rabbit 397
Custard, frangipane 541
  pots 541

Dates, stuffed 598
Demi-glace sauce 91
Desserts 521
  apple Charlotte 531
    pie, maison 567
    strudel 566
    tart, French 565
    turnovers, Irish 573
  baked Alaska 534
  baklava 575
  banana(s), beignets 537
    delight 536
    flamed 536
    pudding 541
    split 556
  bavaroise, 544, 547
  cherry bread pudding 535
    torte 564
  chocolate meringue cups
    542
  clafoutis (apple and
    cherry) 535
  coconut cups 543
  crème caramel 540
  croquembouche 569
  custard pots 541
  éclairs 569
  fruit(s), in alcohol 519
    bombes 558–559
    coupes 544
    ices/sherbets 555
  ice creams 554–555, 557
  iced raspberry mold 561
  lemon meringue pie 562
  magic square 561
  Malaga 543
  melon 548–549
  mille-feuille 570
  mirlitons 573
  Mont Blanc 589
  nutty fruit cups 543
  parfaits 559
  peach melba 551
  pears Marli 551
  pineapple with fruit 550
  Pithiviers 571
  profiteroles 568
  raisin pie 563
  Romanov cups 543
  Saint-Honoré 583
  savarin 552
  Sicilian cannoli 574
  small meringues 593
  tarts 564–565
  soufflés 532–534, 546
  stuffed peaches 551
  sweet croquettes 537
  sweet sauces 538–539
  tarte Française 565

zabaglione 531
zuccotto 560
zuppa Inglese 590
Devil sauce 93
Doughnuts 603
  jam 602
Dressings, caper 501
  curry 501
  garlic 501
  lobster roe 501
  mushroom 501
  mustard and anchovy 501
  oil and lemon 501
  Roquefort or Gorgonzola 501
  tarragon 501
  vinaigrette 501
  yogurt and mint 239
Drinks 608–621
  cocktails,
    Alexander 609
    atomic bomb 608
    brandy 608
    Cuba libre 610
    dry martini 609
    gin and tonic 610
    light 610
    Manhattan 609
    melon cream 617
    mint julep 610
    negroni 609
    old-fashioned 609
    orange cream 617
    Pernod 609
    pineapple cream 616
    rum 608
    screwdriver 608
    Teacher's 609
    Tom Collins 611
    whisky sour 609
  coffee,
    delight 621
    gourmet 621
    sugared 621
  milk,
    apple cream 617
    apricot cream 617
    French chocolate 619
    hot chocolate chiquita 618
    hot spicy chocolate 618
    iced cocoa 619
    Mexican chocolate 619
    orange eggnog 612
    pear cream 617
    Spanish chocolate 619
    Tom-and-Jerry 613
    tutti-frutti cream 616
    Uncle Tom's eggnog 612
  non-alcoholic,
    apricot and orange 614
    lemonade with rosemary
      614
    mixed fruit 615
    pink 614
    spicy tomato juice 614
    summer 615
    sweet-and-sour 614
  punches,
    apple tonic 610
    coffee 621
    country inn milk 611
    mulled wine 613
    sangria 610
    spiced lemon 613
    tea with rum 621
    vin brûlé 613
  tea,
    hot with rum 621
    iced cubes 615

iced with peaches 615
mint 615
Duck, *see* **Poultry**
Dundee cake 601

Easter torte 76
Eclairs 569
Eel, *see* **Fish**
Egg(s) 211; *see also* Omelet,
Soufflé
with asparagus 432
on artichoke hearts 231
with Aurore sauce 227
and bacon 242
baked, in potatoes 251
with Brussels sprouts 219
ciao ciao 231
en cocotte, with bacon 249
with cheese 248
farmhouse 248
with mushrooms 248
with spinach 248
croquettes 235
in a crown 231
in a cup 229
cutlets 243
daisy 243
flowers 36
Françoise 251
fried, Bercy 242
boulangère 241
with eggplants 241
with Emmenthal 240
Italian 241
Massena 257
with onions 243
Portuguese 241
Spanish 240
stuffed 235, 241
gratiné 250
hard-boiled, with curry 233
marinated 236
harlequin 243
Letizia 219
Marinalla 221
marinated 236
Marta 245
mayonnaise with parsley 239
mimosa 232
molds with ham 249
mushroom 236
nog(s), *see* **Drinks**
oeufs à la coque 229
oeufs parmentier 223
'oyster' 229
with peas 246
poached, Allegria 223
in aspic 224
on bread rolls 221
Breton 220
Burgundy style 223
on croûtons 221
with fish stock 219
and fried 221
in green sauce 227
with liver pâté 224
with mayonnaise 224
in mornay sauce 218
in mushroom caps 220
with mushroom sauce 222
with olives 226
in shells 226
and prosciutto rolls in aspic
226
in a roll 69
rolls with eggplant 232
with Russian salad 229
sandwiches, with ham 57

with sardine 57
sauces for 210
Scotch 234
Scrambled, with cheese 245
with cod 247
with cream 247
with ham 245
with lettuce 247
with shrimp 244
with tomato sauce 247
soft-boiled on toast 229
and spinach gratiné 233
spring 36
Stuffed, with anchovy 238
with artichokes 37
fried 235, 241
Lidia 236
with lobster 37
with olives 239
with prosciutto 238
with shrimp 36, 239
various 36–37
Swiss 242
tartlets primavera 246
in tomato aspic 230
Tyrolean 250
with yogurt and mint dressing
239
Eggplant(s), Anna 452
with cheese 453
with egg rolls 232
fried 453
with fried eggs 241
moussaka 72
pickled 515
Provençal 455
Sicilian 454
slices 15
with spaghetti 132
stuffed 455
Turinois 455
à la Turque 453
Emmenthal with fried eggs 240
Endive, braised 463
deep-fried 463
au gratin 463
salad with beet 501
salad with salt pork 503
Epiphany cake 605
Espagnole sauce 90

Fantasia torte 78
Fennel, crudités 20
with goose 393
au gratin 456
Figs with prosciutto 29
Fish 209, 264–299
bouillabaisse, Mediterranean
292
carp, spiced in red wine 293
in tomato sauce 294
cod, broiled with bacon 283
broiled with tartare sauce
283
casserole 281
Flemish 281
Ligurian 281
Niçoise 281
with olives 283
Provençal 280
with scrambled eggs 247
spiced 282
with tomatoes 283
eel, brochettes 291
with herbs 291
marinated 31
with peas 290
smoked, canapés 35

stewed en matelote 291
filleting and skinning 216
fillets, marinated 30
fritto misto mare 278
hake, breaded, à l'Anglaise 274
au gratin 274
Provençal 274
halibut, with creamy shrimps
269
with tomato sauce 269
herbs for 215
herring, in batter 265
fresh au vert 264
Neopolitan 265
rolled with capers 265
salad, Canadian 17
with tomato sauce 265
kipper, German 17
monkfish, braised 289
mullet (red), en papillòte 288
Provençal 289
stuffed 289
perch, baked with herbs 295
golden fillets 295
with olives 295
pike, baked with white wine
sauce 297
fricassée 297
médaillons 297
stuffed 296
porgy with mushrooms 287
salad with potato 41
salmon, Bellevue 271
brochettes 273
cutlets, Pojarski 273
slices, stuffed 273
salmon trout au gratin 287
salt cod, with aïoli mayonnaise
285
beignets 278
in brandade 285
croquettes 24
Neapoitan 284
Provençal 284
sardine(s), croquettes 267
gratin 267
Portuguese 267
sandwiches with egg 57
sauces for 210
Scabecia style 277
sea bass, broiled 286
forestière 287
with tomato sauce 286
sole, bonne femme 277
Dugléré 278
Florentine 277
meunière 276
soufflé 181
stew with red wine 292
stock, jellied 104
poached eggs with 219
swordfish, broiled 268
with capers 269
Spanish 268
stuffed, Sicilian 270
trout with almonds 299
in aspic 298
Welsh 299
tuna, with eggs 37
with macaroni 165
mayonnaise 98
mousse 33
with ravioli 161
rolls 57
with tomatoes 26
uncooked marinade for 103
Fondue, bagna cauda 83
Bourguignonne 328

Piedmontese 70
Swiss 70
in vol-au-vent 81
Foyot sauce 87
Frangipane custard 541
Frankfurter(s), fritters 365
kebabs 363
with sauerkraut 363
with veal scallops and cheese
stuffing 348
with veal roll 341
Fresh-water fish 294–299
Frittata, *see* **Omelet(s)**
Fritters, cheesy tapioca 67
frankfurter 365
Fritto misto 412
Fritto misto mare 278
Frogs' legs, fried 312
meunière 312
Orly 312
Provençal 312
Fromage mystère 23
Fruit, *see also* **Drinks**
in caramel 597
and celeriac salad 45
coupe 544
crêpes 261
glossary 523
ices 555
macédoine, in alcohol 519
with melon 548
pancakes 261
preserving 526
sherbets 555
tartlets 572
Galantine of chicken 48–9
Game 320
grouse, with Marsala sauce
401
hare, braised 399
jugged 398
partridge, with grapes 403
Polish style 403
pheasant, on croûtons 400
Magyar style 401
pigeon, and macaroni pie 164
with mushrooms 405
roast, stuffed 404
with saffron 405
rabbit, boned, stuffed 396
with curry sauce 397
with prunes 399
with tarragon cream 397
squabs, en brochette 407
with juniper berries 407
with mushrooms 407
with truffles 406
stock, jellied 104
in vol-au-vent 81
Garlic, butter 100
with chicken 389
with olives 39
sauce 328
with tripe and parsley 379
with turnips and cheese 489
Garlic sausage, rolled 364
Garnishes 107
Gelatin 104
Genevoise sauce 91
Gherkins pickled 513
Giblets, *see* **Variety Meats**
Ginger sauce, with veal 349
Glacé icing 577
Gnocchetti, Bolognese 207
in broth 205
chicken, for consommés and
broths 205

liver, for consommés and broths 205
Gnocchi, *see* Pasta
Golden rolls 66
Goose, *see* Poultry
Gorgonzola, balls 623
  mousse 22
  with polenta 174
Gougère 69
Grand Marnier, with rolled duck 395
Grandmother's meat loaf 336
  polenta 176
Grape(s), in brandy 518
  jelly 520
  with partridge 403
Grapefruit and crab cocktail 17
  soufflés 533
Green sauce, with anchovies 31
  with poached eggs 227
  with zucchini 491
Ground meat loaf 338
Grouse, *see* Game

Hake, *see* Fish
Halibut, *see* Fish
Ham, beignets 67
  with broccoli 439
  with cauliflower, paupiettes 447
  with cream and 'straw-and-hay' 146
  with haricots 496
  and horseradish rolls 29
  médaillons 50
  molds with egg 249
  mousse 33
    with tartlets 54
  omelet, rolled 256
  with pasta shells and cream cheese 148
  pie with veal and pork 52
  rolls with Russian salad 44
  sandwiches with egg 57
  with scrambled eggs 245
  with veal scallops 348
Hamburgers, *see* Beef
Hare; *see* Game
Haricots, *see* Bean(s)
Hazelnut bombe 559
Heart, *see* Variety Meats
Herbs, with baked perch 295
  with eel 291
  for egg and fish 105
  for vegetables 105
Herring, *see* Fish
Hollandaise sauce 86
  with celery 449
  mustard 87
  noisette 87
  tomato 87
Honey snail 606
Hors d'oeuvre 9–81
Horseradish, and beef loaf 339
  and ham rolls 29

Ice cream(s)
  with liqueur 557
  various 554–555
Iced, mocha cake 590
  raspberry mold 561
Icing, butter 577
  chocolate 577
  coffee 577
  glacé 577
  quick white 577
Individual pies 53
Italian, green sauce 97
  hors d'oeuvre 14

pandoro 579
pot-au-feu 408

Jam, apricot 520
  doughnuts (krapfen) 602
  pear 520
  strawberry 520
Jellied stock 104
Jerusalem artichoke(s), fritters 458
  Proençal 459
  purée 459
Julienne for consommé 208

Kebabs, eastern style 416
  frankfurter 363
  shish 415
  sweetbread 371
Kidney(s), *see* Variety Meats
Kipper(s), *see* Fish
Kishaili sauce 329
Krapfen (jam doughnuts) 602
Kugelhopf 605
Kumquats in brandy 519

Lamb 316, 366–369
  braised 369
  carré d'agneau 367
  kebabs, eastern style 416
    shish 415
  leg, roast 369
    with pasta shells and tomato sauce 149
  paupiettes 369
  shoulder, stuffed 367
Lasagne, *see* Pasta
Leeks, braised 461
  au gratin 461
  with proscuitto 460
  soup with rice 189
  stuffed 461
  vinaigrette 461
Lemon meringue pie 562
  spiced punch 613
Lentil(s), Bordelaise 499
  with chicken 383
  cream soup 183
  meat balls 499
  with pork 498
  risotto 129
  salad 499
  soup 194
  with stuffed pig's foot 364
Lettuce, braised 463
  with peas 468
  with scrambled eggs 247
  stuffed 462
Lima beans, *see* Bean(s)
Liqueur 528
  with ice cream 557
  soufflé 532
Liver, *see* Variety Meats
Lobster, *see* Shellfish

Macaroni, *see* Pasta
Madeira sauce 92
Madeleines 592
Magic square 561
Maître d'hôtel, butter 101
  sauce 84
Malaga Dessert 543
Maltese sauce 87
Marble cake 580
Margherita 578
Marinade(s), cooked 103
  quick 103
  uncooked 102, 103
Marrow, *see* Beef
Marsala sauce with grouse 401

Mayonnaise 98
  aïoli 98
  aspic 99
  Chantilly 99
  cocktail sauce 99
  egg with parsley 239
  with poached eggs 224
  with shrimp 303
  rémoulade 99, 329
  tuna 98
  tartare 99
Meat, *see also* Beef, Lamb, Pork, Veal
  assorted dishes 408–416
  balls, with lentil 499
    with macaroni 139
  casserole, mixed 409
  consommé 197
  loaf, Cesira 341
    Clementina 339
    with frittata 337
    grandmother's 336
    mince 338
  pie, Ligurian 355
Médaillons, ham 50
  pike 297
  with Russian salad 51
  tongue 51
Melon, cups 549
  fantasia 549
  with macédoine of fruit 548
  meringue 549
  with port 549
  with prosciutto 28
Menu planning 527
Meringue(s), cups with chocolate 542
Melon 549
  small 593
Mille-feuille 570
Mince, *see* Beef
Minestrone, *see* Soups
Mint sauce 97
Mirlitons 573
Mixed grill 416
Mixed vegetables Irma 493
Monkfish, *see* Fish
Mont Blanc 589
Mornay sauce 85
  with poached eggs 218
Moussaka 72
Mousse, chocolate 547
  Gorgonzola 22
  ham 33, 54
  liver 32, 54
  tuna fish 33
Mousseline sauce 87
  with asparagus 432
Mozzarella, cartwheels 623
  fried 623
  frittata 253
  pizza 75
Muffins 607
Mullet (red), *see* Fish
Mulligatawny, *see* Soups
Mushroom(s), barquettes 61
  Bordelaise 465
  bouchées 63
  with capon and chicken livers 381
  caps, with poached eggs 220
    with truffles 504
    on vine leaves 464
  cream soup 184
  creamed 465
  crusty bread 81
  with eggs, canapé 35
  with eggs en cocotte 248

with macaroni 138
  marinated 39
  with ossobucco 357
  pickled 515
  pie 465
  with pigeons 405
  with polenta 175
  with porgy 287
  ravioli 159
  risotto 126
  salad 21
  sauce 85
    with poached eggs 222
    with tomato 89
    with squabs 407
  stuffed 465
  stuffing for fillet of beef 330
  with sweetbreads 370
  with tortellini and cream 155
Mussel(s), *see* Shellfish
Mustard, hollandaise 87
  sauce 85, 329
    with steak 327

Neapolitan sauce 91
Noodles, *see* Pasta
Nougat 598
Nut(s) 417
  tartlets 593
Nutty fruit cups 543

Octopus, Algerian 307
  baby, with tartlets 54
  Genoese 307
  Greek 307
  Valencian 307
Oeufs, *see* Egg(s)
Olives, with anchovy fillets 31
  with calves' tongue 376
  with cod 283
  with fillet of beef 331
  with garlic 39
  with perch fillets 295
  with poached eggs 226
  stuffing for eggs 239
  sweet-and-sour 517
Omelet, apple soufflé 263
  Argentenil 254
  chasseur 256
  flamed 262
  frittata, with apples 263
    artichoke 78
    asparagus 254
    with meat loaf 337
    with Mozzarella cheese 253
    onion 78
    potato 255
    rolled 257
    Spanish 253
    spinach 78
    tomato 255
    zucchini 254
  ham, rolled 256
  old-fashioned 254
  Portuguese 253
  poulard 253
Onion(s), with calves' liver 374
  fried 467
  with fried eggs 243
  frittata 78
  pickled 513
  purée soubise 467
  salad with beets 436
  soup 194
  stuffed 466
  with white wine 467
Orange, with beef 335

628

bombe with pineapple 559
candied peel 599
with duck 394
omelet soufflé 263
with roast pork 359
sauce 539
soufflé 534
cold 546
and walnut cake 579
Orécchiette, *see* **Pasta**
Ossobuco 356
with green peas 357
with mushrooms 357
Oven temperature guide 632
Oxtail, *see* **Variety Meats**
Oysters 24

Paella 115
Palmiers 571
Pan di Spagna 579
Panettone 601
Parfaits, chocolate 559
coffee 559
Parisian sauce 94
Parsley, with chicken 387
with fillet of beef 331
Partridge, *see* **Game**
Pasta 108, 113
cannelloni, gratinéed 160
maison 161
with tuna fish 161
gnocchi, à la Parisienne 168
potato 170
with cheese 171
Mornay 173
with prunes 173
quick 173
roll 171
alla Romana 172
Sicilian 171
spinach 169
lasagne, baked 162
ol pesto 163
16th century style 163
macaroni, baked with
cauliflower 141
gratinéed 141
with gravy 137
Marinara 139
with meat balls 139
with mushrooms 138
nests 139
and pigeon pie 164
with Ricotta cheese 137
with tuna 165
with zucchini sauce 137
noodle(s), baked with
artichokes 145
Bolognese 142
crusty shapes 145
curried 143
golden 144
green with cheese 144
soup with beans 192
orecchette, Apulian 150
with meat sauce 150
with turnip leaves 150
ravioli 158
Genoese style 159
mushroom 159
shells, with basil 148
with cream cheese and
ham 148
with lamb and tomato
sauce 159
Niçoise 149
stuffed 149
spaghetti, anchovy sauce for 83

with artichoke sauce 136
with chicken sauce 135
with clams 135
with eggplant 132
with oil and garlic 135
with peas 133
printanière 137
alla Romana 133
Salsa Amatriciana 83
with shellfish 134
three-flavoured 133
spinach roll 166
'straw-and-hay', with cream
and ham 146
gratinéed 147
nests 147
strudel, cheese 167
tortellini, with cheese 154
with cream and mushrooms
155
creamy 152
Parma style 153
timbale 156
in tomato sauce 155
with vol-au-vent 156
Pastry-making, guide to 522
Patties, corned beef 413
Paupiettes, beef marrow 371
brains 371
cauliflower and ham 447
Florentine 347
Italian 347
lamb 369
Mexican 346
Pea(s), cream soup 185
with eel 290
with eggs 246
Flemish style 469
à la Française 469
with lettuce 468
with ossobuco 357
with risotto 126
with salt pork 469
with spaghetti 133
Peach(es) with iced tea 615
melba 551
stuffed 551
Pear, jam 520
marli 551
Pepper sauce 91
Pepper(s), broiled 15
crudités 20
green, sauce 97
hot, pickled 513
peperonata 471
salad 49
stuffed 43
sweet, with anchovies 49
pickled 515
stuffed 471
Perch, *see* **Fish**
Pesto, alla genovese 96
lasagne col 163
Petits fours 594
Pheasant, *see* **Game**
Pie(s), apple, maison 567
individual 53
lemon meringue 562
Ligurian meat 355
macaroni and pigeon 164
mushroom 465
raisin 563
tomato 486
veal, ham and pork 52
with marrow and chicken
livers 354
Piedmontese, fondue 70
salad 504

Pigeon, *see* **Game**
Pike, *see* **Fish**
Pilaff, *see* **Rice**
Pineapple, bombe 559
with orange 559
with fruit 550
Pine nut, cookies with cherries 595
Piquant sauce, with cauliflower
447
with mussels 17
with pork loin 359
with roast veal 345
with veal scallops 351
Pissaladiera 74
Pistou 189
Pithiviers 571
Pizza, with Mozzarella 75
with shellfish 75
Plum cake 600
Polenta 174–7
with cheese 175
with Gorgonzola 174
grandmother's 176
with mushrooms 175
plain 175
Pork 358–365
baked with cheese 359
with chick peas 495
Chinese brochettes 415
cutlets with cheese stuffing 349
with lentils 498
loin with piquant sauce 359
pie with veal and ham 52
roast 358
crown 361
with orange sauce 359
with prunes 361
salt, with lima beans 457
with peas 469
salad with endive 503
spare ribs stew 362
stuffed pig's foot with lentils 364
Porgy, *see* **Fish**
Port sauce 93
Potage, *see* **Soups**
Potato(es), Anna 477
and artichokes, country
style 493
baked with egg 251
with braised tripe 379
and celeriac purée 451
Chantilly 472
chasseur 475
chips 475
croquettes 472
duchesse 472
fried 474
frittata 255
gaufrettes 475
gnocchi 170
with cheese 171
Lyonnaise 477
mashed 472
and mussel salad 25
pancakes 477
Pont-Neuf 474
puffed 475
salad 507
with fish 41
straw 475
stuffed, au gratin 476
surprises 603
sweet, *see* Sweet potato(es)
with tomatoes 26
Potée Savoyarde 193
Poulette sauce with string
beans 435
Poultry 380–395

capon, boiled, stuffed 380
with chicken livers and
mushrooms 381
Portuguese-style 381
chicken, Biriani 119
breasts, with brandy 385
with cheese cream 385
stuffed 389
consomme 197
with Marsala 198
cooked in clay 382
in terracotta 386
croquettes 59, 413
galantine 48
with garlic 389
gnocchetti for consommés
and broths 205
with lentils 383
with parsley 387
roast 383
with ginger 383
stuffed 388
sauce, with spaghetti 135
soup, with lemon and egg
drop 201
Tunisian 387
duck, Normandy 395
with orange 394
rolled, with Grand Marnier
395
goose, with fennel 393
neck, stuffed 393
roast 392
turkey, braised 391
stuffed with chestnuts 391
Preserves 511–520
chow chow 516
mixed vegetables 514
various 335–336
Preserving 424
Profiteroles 568
for consommé 208
Prosciutto, and egg rolls in
aspic 226
with figs 29
with leeks 460
with melon 28
roll 29
stuffing, for egg 238
for veal scallops 349
surprise 28
Prune(s), in brandy 519
chutney 517
with gnocchi 173
with rabbit 399
with roast pork 361
with roast veal 343
stuffed 598
Pumpkin, breaded 480
creamed 481
au gratin 481
Greek 481
soup with rice 193
Purée, chickpea 495
celeriac and potato 451
Crécy (carrot and potato) 445
fréneuse (turnip and potato)
489
jerusalem artichoke 459
soubise (onion and rice) 467

Quiche Lorraine 624

Rabbit, *see* **Game**
Radish, canapés 35
crudités 20
with eggs 37
Raisin(s), in cognac 519

pie 563
truffles with chocolate 597
Raspberry, bombe 559
mold, iced 561
sauce 539
Ratatouille, Neapolitan 492
Niçoise 493
Ravioli, *see* **Pasta**
Red cabbage salad 45
Redcurrant coupe 557
Rémoulade, celeriac 21
sauce 99, 329
Rice 108, 109
cake 580
Cantonese 127
country timbale 131
croquettes 59, 537
à la Grecque 115
Indonesian with apple 127
with squash 117
paella 115
pilaff 125
with sweatbreads 125
alla pilota 119
Pompadour 129
risotto, Arabian 123
with asparagus tips 128
Chartreuse 118
Genoese 129
lentil 129
Milanese 122
with mushrooms 126
Novara 116
Parmigiana 123
with peas 126
with shrimp 120
with shellfish 120
with spinach 127
with sage 123
salad 42
with asparagus 43
Flamenco 42
with meat 42
with sausage and celery 117
soup with leek 189
soup with pumpkin 193
with tomatoes and mussels 123
à la Turque 125
Valencienne 117
Ricotta cheese with macaroni 137
Risotto, *see* **Rice**
Robert sauce 93
Romanov cups 543
Royale for consommé 208
sauce 95
Rum, *see also* **Drinks**
with sweet potatoes 478
Russian, blini 18
canapés 35
salad, wth eggs 229
with ham rolls 44
with médaillons 51
with tomatoes 26

Sage, with braised calves'
liver 375
with rice 123
Saint-Honoré 583
Salads, *see also* **Dressings**
artichoke 21
and celery 501
beets with onions 436
Caesar's 503
Canadian herring 17
carrot 21
cauliflower 507
chef's 502
chickpea 495

cooked vegetable 506
corn, sweet and sour 507
country 501
dried bean 501
endive and beets 501
endive with salt pork 503
fish and potato 41
fruity celeriac 45
lentil 499
Marly 45
Marylène 27
meat and rice 42
mixed 500
mushroom 21
Niçoise 41
pepper 49
Piedmontese 504
potato 507
and mussel 25
red cabbage 45
rice 42
and asparagus 43
flamenco 42
Russian, canapés 35
with eggs 229
with ham rolls 44
with médaillons 51
with tomatoes 26
shellfish 25
spring 41
string bean 501
Swiss 503
tomato 501
Tunisian mixed 505
Salami rolls 13
Salmon, *see* **Fish**
Salmon trout, *see* **Fish**
Salsa Amatriciana 83
Salsify, sautéed 483
Saltimbocca, *see* **Veal**
Sandwich(es), club 56
ham and egg 57
Provençal 57
sardine and egg 57
Sardine, *see* **Fish**
Sauce(s) 82–97
anchovy 83
Andalouse 95
Andalusian 329
Aurore 84, 329
Bagna cauda 83
barbecue 323
Béarnaise 86
Béchamel 66, 84
Bolognese 88
Bordelaise 92
caper 84, 329
charcutière 93
chasseur 92
chaud-froid, thin 95
white 95
choron 87
cocktail 99
cream 85
curry 84
demi-glace 92
devil 92
espagnole 90
foyot 87
garlic 328
Genevoise 91
green with anchovies 31
green pepper 97
hollandaise 86, 87
mustard 87
tomato 87
how to make successfully 209
Italian green 97

Kishaili 329
madeira 92
maître d'hôtel 84
Maltese 87
mint 97
mornay 85, 218
mousseline 87
mushroom 85
mustard 85, 329
Neapolitan 91
Parisian 94
pepper 91
pesto alla genovese 96
piquant with mussels 17
port 93
poulette 435
rémoulade 99, 329
Robert 93
royale 95
salsa amatriciana 93
soubise 85
suprême 95
sweet sauces, various 538–539
tartare with grilled cod 283
tomato 88
clam 89
fresh 89
mushroom 89
velouté 94
whipped cream 539
white wine 85
Sauerkraut with frankfurters 363
Sausage, hot pot 365
with rice and celery 117
Savarin 552
Savory butters 100–101
Savory jellies 100
Scallions, with calves' tongue 376
glazed 467
Scampi, *see* **Shellfish**
Scotch eggs 234
Sea fish 264–293
Sea urchins 24
Shellfish 300–305
clam(s), sauce with tomato 89
with spaghetti 135
crab, cocktail with grapefruit 17
lobster, Bellevue 301
stuffing for eggs 37
mussel(s) 24
barquettes 60
au gratin 304
marinière 305
in piquant sauce 17
and potato salad 25
with rice and tomatoes 123
soup 305
stuffed 305
shrimp(s), Algerian 303
appetizers 13
with avocados 11
barquettes 61
cocktail 16
with halibut 269
with mayonnaise 303
risotto 120
with scrambled eggs 244
stuffing for eggs 239
with tomatoes 26
scampi, brochettes 303
Sherbets, fruit 555
Shrimps, *see* **Shell Fish**
Sicilian cannoli 574
Smoked salmon, how to serve 18
Snails, Bourguignon 310
in tomato wine sauce 311
Sole, *see* **Fish**
Soubise sauce 85

Soufflé, artichoke 430
asparagus 180
Brussels sprout 181
carrot 431
cheese 180
cherry 533
chestnut 533
cold 547
endive 431
fish 181
grapefruit 533
liqueur 532
liver 375
orange 534
cold 546
sweet potato 181
Soups 108, 202
broths, 202–207
Cock-a-leekie 202
gnocchetti, Bolognese 207
in broth 205
chicken 205
liver 205
mulligatawny 203
passatelli in bouillon 206
soup in a bag 207
stracciatella 207
Tregarou 203
consommés 197–201
Calabrian 200
Celestine 201
chicken 197
with marsala 198
classic 198
cold jellied 201
fantasia 198
gnocchetti, chicken 205
liver 205
julienne 208
meat 197
mussel 305
profiteroles 208
royale 208
cream, 182–187
of artichoke 183
of carrot (potage Crécy) 183
of lentil 183
of mushroom 184
of pea 185
potage Crécy 183
Du Barry 187
santé 186
of tomato 185
of vegetable 187
of watercress 187
thick, 188–195
Auvergne 195
bean and noodle 192
Bortsch, spicy 195
Brussels sprout 185
chicken, lemon and egg
drop 201
Greek vegetable 189
leek and rice 189
lentil 194
minestrone, Genovese 191
Milanese 191
onion 194
pistou 189
potée savoyarde 193
pumpkin and rice 193
spinach 195
vegetable and bread 193
zucchini and tomato 189
Spaghetti, *see* **Pasta**
Spinach, à l'Anglaise 483
and carrot mold 179
creamed 483

croquettes 483
with eggs en cocotte 248
with egg gratiné 233
frittata 78
gnocchi 169
gourmet 482
pudding with poultry 411
risotto 127
roll 166
soup 195
stuffing for crêpes 258
Spring salad 41
Squabs, see **Game**
Squash with rice 117
Squid, Italian, stuffed 309
Livornese 309
Steak, see **Beef**
Stew, fish with red wine 292
leftover beef 333
spare ribs 362
Stock, jellied 104
Strawberry, boats 573
bombe 558
ice cream 555
jam 520
sundae 557
'Straw-and-hay', see **Pasta**
String beans, see **Bean(s)**
Strudel, apple 566
cheese 167
Sundae, Belgian coffee 557
strawberry 557
Supreme sauce 95
Sweetbread(s), see **Variety Meats**
Sweet doughs, doughnuts 603
griddle biscuits 607
kugelhopf 605
muffins 607
savarin 552
stuffed plait 604
traditional biscuits 607
Sweet potato(es), croquettes 478
fried 478
glazed 478
with rum 478
soufflé 181
Sweets, almonds glacés 597
candied orange peel 599
nougat 598
petits fours 594
stuffed, dates 598
prunes 598
walnuts 598
truffles 596–597
Swiss fondue 70
Swordfish, see **Fish**

Tapioca, cheesy fritters 67
Taramasalata 18
Tart, cherry 564
chocolate walnut 565
Française 565
French apple 565
Tartare sauce with grilled cod
283
Tartlets, with baby octopus 54
with cream cheese 54
fruit 572
with ham mousse 54
with liver mousse 54
mirlitons 573
nut 593
primavera 246
yellow 593
Tea, see **Drinks**
Timbale, country 131
with tortellini 156
Tomato(es), aspic, eggs in 230

baked and stuffed with rice 484
with cod 283
cream soup 185
flan 487
frittata 255
au gratin 485
Hollandaise 87
pie 486
quiche 487
with rice and mussels 123
salad 501
sauce 88, 89
with bass 286
with carp 294
with clams 89
with halibut 269
with herring 265
with lamb and pasta
shells 149
with mushrooms 89
with scrambled eggs 247
with string beans 434
with tortellini 155
soup with zucchini 189
stuffed 43, 485
with cheese 27
with potatoes 26
with prawns 26
with Russian salad 26
with salad Marylène 27
with tuna fish 26
and wine sauce with snails 311
Tongue, see **Variety Meats**
Tortellini, see **Pasta**
Tournedos, see **Beef**
Tregaron broth 203
Tripe, see **Variety Meats**
Trout, see **Fish**
Truffles, baked in ashes 505
in mushroom caps 504
with squabs 406
in white wine 505
Tuna fish, see **Fish**
Turkey, see **Poultry**
Turnip, with garlic and cheese
489
glazed 489
au gratin 489
purée fréneuse 489
stuffed 488
Turnip leaves, with orecchiette
150

Vanilla, bavaroise 547
ice cream 554
sauce 538
Variety Meats 316, 370–379
beef marrow, with brains,
fried 413
paupiettes 371
in veal pie 354
brain(s), with beef marrow,
fried 413
paupiettes 371
giblets, in vol-au-vent 80
heart (veal), stuffed 372
kidneys (veal), Bolognese 372
with capers 372
with veal pot roast 345
liver(s), (calves') braised with
sage 375
mousse 32, 54
with onions 374
with red wine 375
soufflé 375
(chicken), appetizers 62
with capon and mushrooms
381

in veal pie 354
gnocchetti for consommés and
broths 205
mousse 32
in tartlets 54
pâte with poached eggs 224
oxtail, braised 377
sweetbread(s), kebabs 371
with mushrooms 370
with pilaff 125
stuffing for veal cutlets 353
tongue (calves'), braised 377
médaillons 51
with olives 376
with scallions 376
tripe, braised, with potatoes 379
with garlic and parsley 379
with Spanish beans 378
creole 379
Veal 315, 340–357
breast, stuffed 342
en brochette 415
casserole with sage 355
cutlets, Bolognese 353
with cheese stuffing 349
with sweetbread stuffing 353
Czech with caraway seeds 355
scallops with frankfurter and
cheese stuffing 348
in ginger sauce 349
with ham 348
in piquant sauce 351
with prosciutto stuffing 349
saltimbocca Roman style 351
sautéed 351
Viennese style 352
heart, stuffed 372
kidneys, Bolognese 372
with capers 372
loaf, Cesira 341
ossobuco 356
with green peas 357
with mushrooms 357
paupiettes, Florentine 347
Italian 347
Mexican 346
pie, with ham and pork 52
with marrow and chicken
livers 354
pot roast with kidneys 345
pudding with cream 411
puffs, poached 347
roast, in piquant sauce 345
with prunes 343
sirloin 344
roll with frankfurters 341
steak with mustard sauce 327
sweet and sour 357
Vegetables 226, 426–509 see also
Salads and Artichoke, Asparagus, Beans, Beets, Broccoli,
Brussels sprouts, Cabbage,
Carrot, Cauliflower, Celeriac,
Celery, Chickpea, Chicory, Cucumber, Eggplant, Endive,
Fennel, Gherkin, Leek, Lettuce,

Mushroom, Olive, Onion, Pea,
Peppers, Potato, Pumpkin, Salsify, Scallion, Spinach, Sweet
potato, Tomato, Truffle, Turnip,
Vine leaves, Zucchini
Bagna cauda 83
cooked, salad 506
cream soup 187
Easter torte 376
Fantasia torte 78
glossary 419
à la grecque 39
Julienne for consommé 208
mixed, Irma 493
mold 179
preserving 514
soup, with bread 193
Greek 189
Velouté sauce 94
Vichyssoise 186
Vinaigrette, see **Dressings**
Vinegar, basil 511
garlic 511
mint 511
spiced herb 511
tarragon 511
Vine leaves with mushroom
caps 464
Vol-au-vent 80–1, 156

Walnut(s), and chocolate tart 565
and orange cake 579
pickled 517
stuffed 598
truffles with chocolate 597
Watercress cream soup 187
Welsh rarebit 64
Whipped cream sauce 539
Wiener schnitzel 352
Wine, see also **Drinks**
mulled 613
red, beef braised in 334
with calves' liver 375
with fish stew 292
with onions 467
with spiced carp 295
with tomato 311
white, sauce 85
with baked pike 297
with truffles 505
with zucchini 491

Yellow tartlets 593
Yogurt sauce with celery 449

Zabaglione 531
Zucchini, fried 491
frittata 254
with green sauce 491
marinated 490
sauce with macaroni 137
soup with tomato 189
stuffed 490
with white wine 491
Zucotto 560
Zuppo Inglese 590

ACKNOWLEDGMENTS

The photographs in this book were taken by
C. Mariorossi and Paola Martini.
The drawing on page 107 is by Walter Bloor
and on pages 213–216 by Francesca
Thompson. The ones on pages 107, 108, 211,
313, 418 are by Coral Mula.

COMPARATIVE MEASUREMENTS

Metric Working Equivalents

Ounce/Gram (g)	Working Equivalent
1 oz = 28·35 g	30 g
2 oz = 56·7 g	60 g
4 oz = 113·4 g	115 g
8 oz = 226·8 g	225 g
12 oz = 340·2 g	350 g
16 oz/1lb	500 g
= 453·6 g	1000 g/
2 lb = 907·2 kg	1 kilogram (kg)

Liquid Equivalents

US	British	Metric	
4½ cups, or 1 quart 2 oz	1¾ pints	1 litre	US pint = 16 fl oz = 2 cups US cup = ½ pint/8 fl oz
2 cups, or 1 pint, or 16 fl oz (generous)	¾ pint, or 15 fl oz (generous)	½ litre (demi-litre), or 425 ml	British (Imperial) pint = 20 fl oz = 560 ml British Standard cup = ½ pint/10 fl oz = 300 ml

Oven Temperatures Guide

Centigrade	Fahrenheit	Gas
250° —		
	— 475°	9
Very hot – – – – – – – – –		
	— 450°	8
225° —		
	— 425°	7
Hot – – – – – – – – – –		
	— 400°	6
200° —		
Moderate to moderately hot – – – – – –	— 375°	5
175° —	— 350°	4
Moderately slow – – – – – –	— 325°	3
150° —		
	— 300°	2
Slow – – – – – – – – – – –	— 275°	1
125° —		
	— 250°	½
Very slow – – – – – – – –		
	— 225°	¼
100° —		
	— 200°	